Social
Psychology
and
Everyday
Life

Social Psychology and Everyday Life

Edited by
Billy J. Franklin
Western Carolina University
and
Frank J. Kohout
University of Iowa

David McKay Company, Inc.
New York

SOCIAL PSYCHOLOGY AND EVERYDAY LIFE

LIBRARY OF CONGRESS CATALOG CARD NUMBER: 70–183540
MANUFACTURED IN THE UNITED STATES OF AMERICA

A Word to the Student

We have personally found social psychology to be a tremendously exciting field of study, one that is both academically challenging and socially meaningful. Unfortunately, this "flavor" of the discipline is missing from many of the textbooks and anthologies that we, as teachers, ask you to read. Good social psychology need not be staid or abstruse. We have attempted to demonstrate this conviction in this collection of readings. A number of our students consented to read these selections, along with many others, and to provide us with their candid evaluations of each in terms of clarity, interest value, implications for current concerns of students, and the necessity of statistical knowledge for understanding the selection. Many of our original choices did not withstand these evaluations. Those that comprise this volume were judged favorably by your peers on the foregoing criteria, and, in our opinion, reflect current social psychology.

While most of the readings are reports of empirical research, we have also included a number of "think pieces." Doing social psychology involves more than conducting research, albeit, research is a highly significant part of the social psychologist's work. Even in those research reports which present extensive statistical data, a mastery of statistics is not necessary for an understanding of the authors' findings and arguments. The authors of these articles have done an excellent job of presenting their findings in prose. Neither the empirical papers nor the more theoretical or speculative ones reflect a single social psychological orientation. We are of the opinion that in the introductory course you should be exposed to the diversity of perspectives that characterize the field. In subsequent courses, a concentration on a single theoretical perspective will then have more meaning; you will be better equipped to critically evaluate alternative approaches.

So much for an attempted justification for what we have done. Now a word about the structure of the book. We have organized forty-one readings into ten topical sections. These topics are those most commonly covered in current textbooks for the first course. In many instances, the decision to place a selection in one section versus another was highly arbitrary. A number of the selections could "fit" into two or more of the sections. Within each section, we have prepared introductions to each reading. Reading the introduction will not substitute for reading the article, but it should sensitize you to some of the major points dealt with by the authors. To conclude a section, we have written a brief sketch of the major emphases in that area of inquiry and have attempted to indicate how the selections in the volume relate to these emphases. If you are sufficiently stimulated by the materials in a given section to pursue the topic further, you will find assistance in *Suggestions for Further Reading.*

Contributors

Darcy Abrahams, UNIVERSITY OF MINNESOTA
Chris Argyris, HARVARD UNIVERSITY
Elliot Aronson, UNIVERSITY OF TEXAS
Vera Aronson, UNIVERSITY OF TEXAS
Kurt W. Back, DUKE UNIVERSITY
Janet H. Beavin, MENTAL RESEARCH INSTITUTE, PALO ALTO, CALIFORNIA
Leonard Berkowitz, UNIVERSITY OF WISCONSIN
James H. Bryan, NORTHWESTERN UNIVERSITY
Virginia Carpenter, WASHINGTON UNIVERSITY
M. J. Chombart de Lauwe, L'ÉCOLE DES HAUTES ÉTUDES, SORBONNE
John L. Colombotos, COLUMBIA UNIVERSITY
Vernon Cope, PORTLAND STATE UNIVERSITY
Carl J. Couch, UNIVERSITY OF IOWA
J. M. Darley, NEW YORK UNIVERSITY
Jay M. Davis, ALBERT EINSTEIN SCHOOL OF MEDICINE
Richard deCharms, WASHINGTON UNIVERSITY
Anthony N. Doob, UNIVERSITY OF TORONTO
Amerigo Farina, UNIVERSITY OF CONNECTICUT
James M. Fendrich, FLORIDA STATE UNIVERSITY
Scott C. Fraser, NEW YORK UNIVERSITY
Jonathan L. Freedman, COLUMBIA UNIVERSITY
Walter M. Gerson, UNIVERSITY OF MINNESOTA
Philip Goldberg, CONNECTICUT COLLEGE
Norman Goodman, SUNY AT STONY BROOK
Alan E. Gross, UNIVERSITY OF WISCONSIN
Irving L. Horowitz, RUTGERS UNIVERSITY
James L. Hoyt, INDIANA UNIVERSITY
James A. Inkster, COMPUTING CENTRE, UNIVERSITY OF VICTORIA
Don D. Jackson, MENTAL RESEARCH INSTITUTE, PALO ALTO, CALIFORNIA

Wendell Johnson, deceased, UNIVERSITY OF IOWA
Alan C. Kerckhoff, DUKE UNIVERSITY
Jerome Kirk, UNIVERSITY OF CALIFORNIA, IRVINE
Robert E. Knox, UNIVERSITY OF BRITISH COLUMBIA
Aharon Kuperman, OAKLAND UNIVERSITY
Bibb Latané, THE OHIO STATE UNIVERSITY
Rex A. Lucas, UNIVERSITY OF TORONTO
J. David Martin, WASHINGTON STATE UNIVERSITY
Gary T. Marx, HARVARD UNIVERSITY
Eric L. Metzner, UNIVERSITY OF ARIZONA
Louis Mezei, MICHIGAN CIVIL RIGHTS COMMISSION
Stanley Milgram, THE CITY UNIVERSITY OF NEW YORK, GRADUATE CENTER
Norman Miller, LABORATORY FOR RESEARCH IN SOCIAL RELATIONS, UNIVERSITY OF MINNESOTA
Richard J. Ofshe, UNIVERSITY OF CALIFORNIA, BERKELEY
Maurice Pinard, MCGILL UNIVERSITY
Lee Rainwater, HARVARD UNIVERSITY
H. Edward Ransford, UNIVERSITY OF SOUTHERN CALIFORNIA
Milton Rokeach, UNIVERSITY OF WATERLOO
Leon Rottmann, UNIVERSITY OF NEBRASKA
Thomas Scheff, UNIVERSITY OF CALIFORNIA, SANTA BARBARA
Edgar H. Schein, SLOAN SCHOOL OF MANAGEMENT, MASSACHUSETTS INSTITUTE OF TECHNOLOGY
Barry Schwartz, UNIVERSITY OF CHICAGO
Robert A. Scott, PRINCETON UNIVERSITY
David W. Sonenschein, UNIVERSITY OF TEXAS
Robert Sommer, UNIVERSITY OF CALIFORNIA, DAVIS
Mary Ann Test, MENDOTA STATE HOSPITAL
E. Paul Torrance, UNIVERSITY OF GEORGIA
Donald D. von Eschen, MCGILL UNIVERSITY
Nicholas von Hoffman, THE WASHINGTON POST
Elaine Walster, UNIVERSITY OF WISCONSIN
Richard H. Walters, deceased, UNIVERSITY OF WATERLOO
Paul Watzlawick, MENTAL RESEARCH INSTITUTE, PALO ALTO, CALIFORNIA
Paul R. Wilson, AUSTRALIAN NATIONAL UNIVERSITY
Louis A. Zurcher, UNIVERSITY OF TEXAS

Contents

I. *Group Structure* 1

1. *The Social Psychology of Privacy* / BARRY SCHWARTZ 3
2. *Status of Frustrator as an Inhibitor of Horn-Honking Responses* / ANTHONY N. DOOB AND ALAN E. GROSS 18
3. *The Hasher: A Study of Role Conflict* / LOUIS A. ZURCHER, DAVID A. SONENSCHEIN, AND ERIC L. METZNER 25
4. *Small Group Ecology* / ROBERT SOMMER 38

Putting It into Perspective 49

Suggestions for Further Reading 51

II. *Social Influence Processes* 53

5. *Negotiating Reality: Notes on Power in the Assessment of Responsibility* / THOMAS SCHEFF 55
6. *Some Conditions of Obedience and Disobedience to Authority* / STANLEY MILGRAM 73
7. *Compliance Without Pressure: The Foot-in-the-Door Technique* / JONATHAN L. FREEMAN AND SCOTT C. FRASER 94
8. *Bystander Intervention in Emergencies: Diffusion of Responsibility* / JOHN M. DARLEY AND BIBB LATANÉ 107
9. *Models and Helping: Naturalistic Studies in Aiding Behavior* / JAMES H. BRYAN AND MARY ANN TEST 119

Putting It into Perspective 131

Suggestions for Further Reading 133

III. *Perception: Self, Object, and Other* 135

10. *The White Negro and the Negro White* / GARY T. MARX 137
11. *The Influence of Kinship Upon Perception of an Ambiguous Stimulus* / REX A. LUCAS 149

12. *The Perceptual Distortion of Height as a Function of Ascribed Academic Status* / PAUL R. WILSON 164

13. *The "Origin-Pawn" Variable in Person Perception* / RICHARD deCHARMS, VIRGINIA CARPENTER, AND AHARON KUPERMAN 170

Putting It into Perspective 187

Suggestions for Further Reading 189

IV. *Communication* 191

14. *Some Tentative Axioms of Communication* / PAUL WATZLAWICK, JANET H. BEAVIN, AND DON D. JACKSON 193

15. *Stuttering: How The Problem Develops* / WENDELL JOHNSON 202

16. *Humor Appreciation as Social Communication* / JAY M. DAVIS AND AMERIGO FARINA 212

17. *Empathy, Communication Efficiency, and Marital Status* / NORMAN GOODMAN AND RICHARD OFSHE 219

18. *Interpersonal Communication, Group Solidarity, and Social Influence* / EDGAR H. SCHEIN 231

Putting It into Perspective 244

Suggestions for Further Reading 246

V. *Attitudes* 247

19. *Are Women Prejudiced Against Women?* / PHILIP GOLDBERG 249

20. *A Study of the Association Among Verbal Attitudes, Commitment and Overt Behavior in Different Experiment Situations* / JAMES M. FENDRICH 254

21. *Physicians and Medicare: A Before-After Study of the Effects of Legislation on Attitudes* / JOHN COLOMBOTOS 268

22. *Postdecision Dissonance at Post Time* / ROBERT E. KNOX AND JAMES A. INKSTER 292

Putting It into Perspective 300

Suggestions for Further Reading 302

VI. *Interpersonal Attraction* 305

23. *My Enemy's Enemy Is My Friend* / ELLIOT ARONSON AND VERNON COPE 307

24. *Importance of Physical Attractiveness in Dating Behavior* / ELAINE WALSTER, VERA ARONSON, DARCY ABRAHAMS, AND LEON ROTTMANN *316*

25. *Race and Shared Belief as Factors in Social Choice* / MILTON ROKEACH AND LOUIS MEZEI *330*

Putting It into Perspective *343*

Suggestions for Further Reading *344*

VII. *Aggression, Hostility, and Conflict* 347

26. *Effect of Media Violence "Justifictaion" on Aggression* / JAMES L. HOYT 349

27. *The Study of Urban Violence: Some Implications of Laboratory Studies of Frustration and Aggression* / LEONARD BERKOWITZ *357*

28. *Implications of Laboratory Studies of Aggression for the Control and Regulation of Violence* / RICHARD H. WALTERS *366*

29. *Isolation, Powerlessness, and Violence: A Study of Attitudes and Participation in the Watts Riot* / H. EDWARD RANSFORD *380*

Putting It into Perspective *395*

Suggestions for Further Reading *397*

VIII. *Socialization* 399

30. *Child Representation in Contemporary French Urban Society* / M. J. CHOMBART DE LAUWE *401*

31. *Achieving Socialization Without Sacrificing Creativity* / E. PAUL TORRANCE *416*

32. *The Socialization of the Blind in Personal Interaction* / ROBERT A. SCOTT *423*

33. *Apprenticeships in Prostitution* / JAMES H. BRYAN *432*

34. *Mass Media Socialization Behavior: Negro-White Differences* / WALTER M. GERSON *446*

Putting It into Perspective *461*

Suggestions for Further Reading *463*

IX. *Collective Behavior* 465

35. *Collective Behavior: An Examination of Some Stereotypes* / CARL J. COUCH *467*

36. Processes of Recruitment in the Sit-In Movement / MAURICE PINARD, JEROME KIRK, AND DONALD VON ESCHEN *481*

37. Sociometric Patterns in Hysterical Contagion / ALAN C. KERCKOFF, KURT W. BACK, AND NORMAN MILLER *495*

Putting It into Perspective *508*

Suggestions for Further Reading *511*

X. *Doing Social Psychology* 513

38. Some Unintended Consequences of Rigorous Research / CHRIS ARGYRIS *515*

39. Suspicion and the Experimental Confederate: A Study of Role and Credibility / J. DAVID MARTIN *533*

40. Sociological Snoopers / NICHOLAS VON HOFFMAN
Journalistic Moralizers / IRVING LOUIS HOROWITZ AND LEE RAINWATER *547*

Putting It into Perspective *558*

Suggestions for Further Reading *559*

Social
Psychology
and
Everyday
Life

CHAPTER I

Group Structure

1 Barry Schwartz, *The Social Psychology of Privacy* · 3

2 Anthony N. Doob and Alan E. Gross, *Status of Frustrator as an Inhibitor of Horn-Honking Responses* · 18

3 Louis A. Zurcher, David W. Sonenschein, and Eric L. Metzner, *The Hasher: A Study of Role Conflict* · 25

4 Robert Sommer, *Small Group Ecology* · 38

Putting It into Perspective · 49
Suggestions for Further Reading · 51

1

The Social Psychology of Privacy

BARRY SCHWARTZ

We generally consider the facilitation of interaction to be the primary function of social organization; but as Schwartz points out in the following selection, social organization also makes provision for removing oneself from interaction and public view. Such a provision serves multiple functions. First, it makes possible the termination of interaction when further contact would be irritating for all parties, and since it does so structurally, a personal interpretation of the withdrawal is made unnecessary. Second, structural provisions for withdrawal (privacy) are not equally available to all. As a scarce commodity, it reflects and reinforces status divisions. Third, privacy insulates against the knowledge of behaviors which, if made public, could jeopardize the social bond.

Both the rules and rights of privacy are often reflected in the architecture of buildings. For example, the chairman of the board of a large corporation is typically insulated from public view by means of several anterooms occupied by gatekeepers called receptionists or secretaries who selectively admit others to his presence. The physical arrangements of offices for lower level management provide significantly less insulation, whereas there may be few or no provisions for withdrawal for the rank and file members of the organization. Schwartz provides an interesting treatment of such arrangements as well as an exploration of the symbolic significance of such devices as doors, windows, walls, etc.

In concluding the selection, the author suggests that privacy also serves an ego function. Specifically, it prevents the ego from identifying itself exclusively with public roles.

Barry Schwartz, "The Social Psychology of Privacy," *American Journal of Sociology* 73 (1968): 741–52.

Patterns of coming and staying together imply counterpatterns[1] of withdrawal and disaffiliation which, as modalities of actions, are worthy of analysis in their own right. Simmel makes the identical point in his essay, "Brücke and Tür": "Usually we only perceive as bound that which we have first isolated in some way. If things are to be joined they must first be separated. Practically as well as logically it would be nonsense to speak of binding that which is not separate in its own sense. . . . Directly as well as symbolically, bodily as well as spiritually, we are continually separating our bonds and binding our separations."[2] Simmel, however, ignores the question of how separation subserves integration—of how men are bound by taking leave of one another as well as by their coming together. One sociologically relevant approach to this problem is through the analysis of privacy, which is a highly institutionalized mode of withdrawal.

The Group-Preserving Functions of Privacy

Withdrawal into privacy is often a means of making life with an unbearable (or sporadically unbearable) person possible. If the distraction and relief of privacy were not available in such a case, the relationship would have to be terminated if conflict were to be avoided. Excessive contact is the condition under which Freud's principle of ambivalence must clearly exercise itself, when intimacy is most likely to produce open hostility as well as affection.[3] Issue must therefore be taken with Homans' proposition, "Persons who interact frequently with one another tend to like one another" (providing the relationship is not obligatory).[4] The statement holds generally, but misses the essential point that there is a threshold beyond which interaction is unendurable for both parties. It is because people frequently take leave of one another that the interaction-liking proposition maintains itself.

Guarantees of privacy, that is, rules as to who may and who may not observe or reveal information about whom, must be established in any stable social system. If these assurances do not prevail—if there is normlessness with respect to privacy—every withdrawal from visibility may be accompanied by a measure of espionage, for without rules to the contrary persons are naturally given to intrude upon invisibility. "Secrecy sets barriers between men," writes Simmel, "but at the same time

---

[1] The initiation of a social contact generally entails a withdrawal from a preceding one. Therefore, men may withdraw into new social circles as well as into seclusion. In this particular sense it would be most exact to employ the term "contact-withdrawal," as opposed to a single term for engagement and another for disengagement. However, this distinction does not apply to movements into privacy.

[2] Georg Simmel, "Brücke und Tür," in *Brücke und Tür* (Stuttgart: K. F. Kochler, 1957), p. 1.

[3] Sigmund Freud, *Group Psychology and the Analysis of the Ego* (New York: Bantam Books, Inc., 1960), pp. 41–42.

[4] George C. Homans, *The Human Group* (New York: Harcourt, Brace & Co., 1950), p. 111.

offers the seductive temptations to break through the barriers." [5] Such an inclination is embodied in the spy, the Peeping Tom, the eavesdropper, and the like, who have become its symbols.

"Surveillance" is the term which is generally applied to institutionalized intrusions into privacy. And social systems are characterizable in terms of the tension that exists between surveillant and anti-surveillant modes. Much of our literature on the anti-utopia, for example, George Orwell's *1984,* which depicts the dis-eases of excessive surveillance, is directed against the former mode. But dangers of internal disorder reside in unconditional guarantees of invisibility against which many administrative arms of justice have aligned themselves. On the other hand, surveillance may itself create the disorder which it seeks to prevent. Where there are few structural provisions for privacy, social withdrawal is equivalent to "hiding." For Simmel, "This is the crudest and, externally, most radical manner of concealment." [6] Where privacy is prohibited, man can only imagine separateness as an act of stealth.[7]

Since some provisions for taking leave of one another and for removing oneself from social observation are built into every establishment, an individual withdrawal into privacy and the allowance of such a withdrawal by other parties reflects and maintains the code that both sides adhere to. Leave taking, then, contains as many ritualistic demands as the act of coming together. Durkheim, like Homans, is not altogether correct in his insistence that the periodic gatherings of the group are its main sources of unity.[8] After a certain point the presence of others becomes irritating and leave taking, which is a mutual agreement to part company, is no less a binding agent than the ritual of meeting. In both cases individual needs (for gregariousness and isolation) are expressed and fulfilled in collectively indorsed manners. The dissociation ritual presupposes (and sustains) the social relation. Rules governing privacy, then, if accepted by all parties, constitute a common bond providing for periodic suspensions of interaction.

If privacy presupposes the existence of established social relations its employment may be considered as an index of solidarity. Weak social relationships, or relationships in the formative stage, cannot endure the strain of dissociation. By contrast, members of a stable social structure feel that it is not endangered by the maintenance of interpersonal boundaries. This point is of course well reflected in the Frostian dictum, "Good fences make good neighbors."

Privacy Helps Maintain Status Divisions

It is also well known that privacy both reflects and helps to maintain the status divisions of a group. In the armed forces, for example, the non-commissioned

[5] Georg Simmel, "The Secret and the Secret Society," in Kurt Wolff, ed., *The Sociology of Georg Simmel* (New York: Free Press, 1964), p. 334.

[6] Ibid., p. 364.

[7] Ibid.

[8] Émile Durkheim, *The Elementary Forms of the Religious Life* (Glencoe, Ill.: Free Press, 1947), pp. 214–19.

officer may reside in the same building as the dormitoried enlisted man but he will maintain a separate room. The officer of higher rank will live apart from the non-commissioned, but on the same base, often in an apartment building; but officers of highest status are more likely to have private quarters away from the military establishment.

In organizational life the privacy of the upper rank is insured structurally; it is necessary to proceed through the lieutenant stratum if the top level is to be reached. In contrast, the lower rank, enjoying less control over those who may have access to it, find their privacy more easily invaded. Even in domestic life persons of the lower stratum lack "the butler" by means of whom the rich exercise tight control over their accessibility to others.

Privacy is an object of exchange. It is bought and sold in hospitals, transportation facilities, hotels, theaters, and, most conspicuously, in public restrooms where a dime will purchase a toilet, and a quarter, a toilet, sink and mirror. In some public lavatories a free toilet is provided—without a door.

Privacy has always been a luxury. Essayist Phyllis McGinley writes: "The poor might have to huddle together in cities for need's sake, and the frontiersman cling to his neighbor for the sake of protection. But in each civilization, as it advanced, those who could afford it chose the luxury of a withdrawing place. Egyptians planned vine-hung gardens, the Greeks had their porticos and seaside villas, the Romans put enclosures around their patios. . . . Privacy was considered as worth striving for as hallmarked silver or linen sheets for one's bed." [9] In this same respect Goffman comments upon the lack of front and back region differentiation in contemporary lower-class residences.[10]

The ability to invade privacy is also reflective of status. The physician's high social rank, for instance, derives perhaps not only from his technical skill but also from his authority to ignore barriers of privacy. However, this prerogative is not limited to those of high status. We must not forget the "non-person" who lacks the ability to challenge the selfhood of his superiors. Goffman cites Mrs. Frances Trollope: "I had indeed frequent opportunities of observing this habitual indifference to the presence of their slaves. They talk to them, of their condition, of their faculties, of their conduct exactly as if they were incapable of hearing. . . . A young lady displaying modesty before white gentlemen was found lacing her stays with the most perfect composure before a Negro footman." [11] In general society the assumption of the social invisibility of another is looked upon as indecency, that is, as a failure to erect a barrier of privacy between self and other under prescribed conditions.

The general rule that is deducible from all of this is that outside of the kinship group an extreme rank is conferred upon those for whom privacy shields are

---

[9] Phyllis McGinley, "A Lost Privilege," in *Province of the Heart* (New York: Viking Press, 1959), p. 56.

[10] Erving Goffman, *The Presentation of Self in Everyday Life* (Edinburgh: University of Edinburgh, 1958), p. 123.

[11] Ibid., p. 95.

voluntarily removed. The prestige afforded the physician is exaggerated in order to protect the self from the shame which ordinarily accompanies a revelation of the body to a stranger, particularly if he is of the opposite sex. Likewise, the destatusing of the servant is necessary if he is to be utilized for purposes of bathing, dressing, etc.

Persons of either high or low rank who have access to the private concerns of their clients are subject to definite obligations regarding both the manner in which secret knowledge is to be obtained and, most importantly, the way in which it is treated once it has been obtained. Explicit or implicit guarantees of confidentiality neutralize the transfer of power which would otherwise accompany the bestowal of private information. Both the possession of an extreme rank and the assurance of confidentiality thus legitimize the "need to know" and the intrusions which it makes possible.

Privacy and Deviation

Up to this point we have tried to indicate privacy's stabilizing effect upon two dimensions of social order. Withdrawal subserves horizontal order by providing a release from social relations when they have become sufficiently intense as to be irritating. Privacy is also a scarce social commodity; as such, its possession reflects and clarifies status divisions, thus dramatizing (and thereby stabilizing) the vertical order. But we must recognize that privacy also opens up opportunities for such forms of deviance as might undermine its stabilizing effects. However, privacy admits of *invisible* transgression and therefore serves to maintain intact those rules which would be subverted by the public disobedience that might occur in its absence.

Moore and Tumin, in their discussion of the function of ignorance, stated: "All social groups . . . require some quotient of ignorance to preserve esprit de corps." [12] And Goffman has made it clear that every establishment provides "involvement shields" for its members wherein "role releases" may take place, particularly deviant ones.[13] As Merton puts it:

> Resistance to full visibility of one's behavior appears, rather, to result from structural properties of group life. Some measure of leeway in conforming to role expectations is presupposed in all groups. To have to meet the strict requirements of a role at all times, without some degree of deviation, is to

---

[12] Wilbert E. Moore and Melvin M. Tumin, "Some Social Functions of Ignorance," *American Sociological Review,* 14 (December 1949): 792. See also Barney Glaser and Anselm Strauss, "Awareness Contexts and Social Interaction," *American Sociological Review,* 29 (October 1964): 669–79, in which social interaction is discussed in terms of "what each interactant in a situation knows about the identity of the other and his own identity in the eyes of the other" (p. 670). A change in "awareness context" accompanies acquisitions of knowledge, provisions of false knowledge, concealment of information, etc.

[13] The "involvement shield" and Everett C. Hughes' concept of "role release" are elaborated in Erving Goffman's *Behavior in Public Places* (New York: Free Press, 1963), pp. 38–39.

> experience insufficient allowances for individual differences in capacity and training and for situational exigencies which make strict conformity extremely difficult. This is one of the sources of what has been elsewhere noted in this book as socially patterned, or even institutionalized, evasions of institutional rules.[14]

Thus, each group has its own "band of institutionalized evasion" which expands and contracts as conditions change. Rose L. Coser, in this connection, has considered observability in terms of the social status of the observer. She indicates that persons of high rank tend to voluntarily deprive themselves of visibility by signaling their intrusion with a prior announcement.[15] The deviation band, then, is normally condoned by both the upper and lower strata.

Moore and Tumin stress the importance of preventing deviation from being known to the group as a whole.[16] No doubt, a publication of all of the sins, crimes, and errors that take place in a social unit would jeopardize its stability. The preoccupation of the press with sensational deviations from norms might be considered from this point of view. Similarly, the more one person involves himself with another on an emotional basis the more both will need private facilities to conceal nasty habits and self-defaming information from each other. If the child, for instance, became suddenly aware of all the non-public performances of his father, and if the latter were aware of all the perversions that are privately enacted by his offspring, a father-son relationship characterized by mutual admiration would be impossible. The same point is illustrated in well-adjusted marriages which depend not only upon mutually acceptable role playing but also upon the ability of both parties to conceal "indecent" performances. This presupposes a modicum of physical distance between husband and wife. Simmel, in addition, adds that a complete abandon of one's self-information to another "paralyzes the vitality of relations and lets their continuation really appear pointless." [17]

Privacy enables secret consumption. We observe, for example, the adolescent practices of smoking or drinking in their locked rooms. Similarly, "women may leave *Saturday Evening Post* on their living room table but keep a copy of *True Romance* ('something the cleaning woman must have left around') concealed in their bedroom." [18] However, some modes of secret consumption have come into the public light. The erotic "girlie magazines," for example, no longer need be employed privately by the middle-class male since the advent of the *Playboy* magazine. As some activities emerge from secrecy others go underground. Thus, the person who nowadays finds pleasure in the Bible will most likely partake of it in private rather than in a public place or conveyance. These new proprieties

---

[14] Robert K. Merton, *Social Theory and Social Structure* (New York: Free Press, 1964), p. 343.

[15] Rose L. Coser, "Insulation from Observability and Types of Social Conformity," *American Sociological Review* (February 1961): 28–39.

[16] Moore and Tumin, "Functions of Ignorance," p. 793.

[17] Simmel, "The Secret and the Secret Society," p. 329.

[18] Goffman, *The Presentation of Self*, p. 26. Needless to say, many instances of the employment of privacy for "secret production" could be given.

are perhaps specific instances of a general rule set down by Simmel, that "what is originally open becomes secret, and what was originally concealed throws off its mystery. Thus we might arrive at the paradoxical idea that, under otherwise like circumstances, human associations require a definite ratio of secrecy which merely changes its objects; letting go of one it seizes another, and in the course of this exchange it keeps its quantum unvaried." [19]

Incidentally, just as the person must employ proper language for the public situations in which he finds himself, he is required to maintain an appropriate body language as well. Differing postures must be assumed in his public encounters. But public postures do not exhaust the many positions of which the human body is capable. Anyone who has maintained a single position over a long period of time knows that the body demands consistent postural variation if it is to remain comfortable and capable of good role performance. Privacy enables the person to enact a variety of non-public postures and thus prepares him physically for public life.

It should be stressed that the absence of visibility does not guarantee privacy. The hypertrophied super-ego certainly makes impossible the use of solitude for deviant objectives. The person who is constantly in view of an internalized father, mother, or God leads a different kind of private life than those possessed by a less demanding conscience. This reveals an interesting paradox. Privacy surely provides for some measure of autonomy, of freedom from public expectation; but as Durkheim so persistently reminded us, the consequences of leaving the general normative order are moral instability and social rootlessness. (It is for this reason that secret societies compensate for the moral anarchy inherent in pure autonomy by means of ritual.) [20] Is it then possible that through privacy the ego escapes the dominion of the public order only to subordinate itself to a new authority: the super-ego? In some measure this is certainly the case, but one may also venture the suggestion that the super-ego, like the social structure whose demands it incorporates, has its own "bank of institutionalized evasion." The super-ego cannot be totally unyielding, for if every deviation of the ego called into play its punitive reaction the consequences for the self would be most severe.

Privacy and Establishments

It was earlier noted that rules or guarantees of privacy subserve horizontal and vertical order. Such rules are embodied in the physical structure of social establishments. Lindesmith and Strauss, for instance, have noted that proprieties concerning interpersonal contact and withdrawal are institutionalized in the architecture of buildings by means of a series of concentric circles. Specific regulations permit or forbid entry into the various parts of this structure, with a particular

---

[19] Simmel, "The Secret and the Secret Society," pp. 335–36.
[20] Ibid., pp. 360–61.

view to protecting the sacred "inner circle."[21] A more specific instance of the physical institutionalization of norms is found in the case of the bathroom, whose variation in size and design is limited by the requirement that body cleansing and elimination be performed privately.[22] This norm is reinforced by the architectural arrangements in which it is incorporated. The fact that the bathroom is only built for one literally guarantees that the performances which it accommodates will be solos. However, this normative-physical restriction admits of more complicated, secondary proprieties. Bossard and Boll write:

> The fact that the middle-class family rises almost together, and has few bathrooms, has resulted in a problem for it, which has been resolved by a very narrowly prescribed ritual for many of them—a bathroom ritual. They have developed set rules and regulations which define who goes first (according to who must leave the house first), how long one may stay in, what are the penalties for overtime, and under what conditions there may be a certain overlapping of personnel.[23]

The very physical arrangement of social establishments thus opens and shuts off certain possibilities for interaction and withdrawal and creates a background of

---

[21] Alfred R. Lindesmith and Anselm L. Strauss, *Social Psychology* (New York: Henry Holt & Co., 1956), p. 435. However, in an interesting statement, McGinley announces the death of the very idea of the "inner circle": "It isn't considered sporting to object to being a goldfish. On the same public plan we build our dwelling places. Where, in many a modern house, can one hide? (And every being, cat, dog, parakeet, or man, wants a hermitage now and then.) We discard partitions and put up dividers. Utility rooms take the place of parlors. Picture windows look not onto seas or mountains or even shrubberies but into the picture windows of the neighbors. Hedges come down, gardens go unwalled; and we have nearly forgotten that the inventor of that door which first shut against intrusion was as much mankind's benefactor as he who discovered fire. I suspect that, in a majority of the bungalows sprouting across the country like toadstools after a rain, the only apartment left for a citadel is the bathroom." (McGinley, "Lost Privilege," pp. 55–56.)

In contrast, Edward T. Hall observes: "Public and private buildings in Germany often have double doors for soundproofing, as do many hotel rooms. In addition, the door is taken very seriously by Germans. Those Germans who come to America feel that our doors are flimsy and light. The meanings of the open door and the closed door are quite different in the two countries. In offices, Americans keep doors open; Germans keep doors closed. In Germany, the closed door does not mean that the man behind it wants to be alone or undisturbed, or that he is doing something he doesn't want someone else to see. It's simply that Germans think that open doors are sloppy and disorderly. To close the door preserves the integrity of the room and provides a protective boundary between people. Otherwise, they get too involved with each other. One of my German subjects commented, 'If our family hadn't had doors, we would have had to change our way of life. Without doors we would have had many, many more fights. . . . When you can't talk, you retreat behind a door. . . . If there hadn't been doors, I would always have been within reach of my mother' " (*The Hidden Dimension* [Garden City: Doubleday & Co., 1966], p. 127. For a discussion of the norms regulating privacy among the English, French, Arab, and Japanese, see pp. 129–53).

[22] Alexander Kira, *The Bathroom* (New York: Bantam Books, Inc., 1967), pp. 178–84. The requirement of complete privacy for personal hygiene is only a recent phenomenon (see pp. 1–8).

[23] J. H. S. Bossard and E. S. Boll, *Ritual in Family Living* (Philadelphia: University of Pennsylvania Press, 1950), pp. 113–14 (cited by Kira, *The Bathroom*, pp. 177–78).

sometimes complex ritual in support of a foreground of necessary proprieties. Needless to say, the form taken by such ritual is always subject to modification by architectural means.

Charles Madge also urges the architect to take explicit account in his designs of the ambivalences of social life. Men, for example, are given to both withdrawal and self-display. This duality, notes Madge, requires an "intermediate area" in housing projects, such as a backyard or garden which separates the home or inner circle from the "common green." [24] But it is one thing to so divide our physical living space as to insure ourselves of interactional options; it is another to regulate the interactional patterns that the division of space imposes upon us. The latter task is most efficiently met by the door.

Doors—McGinley has referred to the door as a human event of significance equal to the discovery of fire.[25] The door must surely have had its origin among those whose sense of selfhood had already developed to the extent that they could feel the oppression of others and experience the need for protection against their presence. Continued use of the door very probably heightened that feeling of separateness to which it owed its creation. Doors, therefore, not only stimulate one's sense of self-integrity, they are required precisely because one has such a sense.

The very act of placing a barrier between oneself and others is self-defining, for withdrawal entails a separation from a role and, tacitly, from an identity imposed upon oneself by others via that role. Therefore, to waive the protection of the door is to forsake that sense of individuality which it guarantees. As Simmel points out, some measure of de-selfing is characteristic of everything social.[26]

I would like now to discuss various kinds of doors, including horizontal sliding doors (drawers) and transparent doors (windows). I shall also treat of walls, as relative impermeable interpersonal barriers, in contrast to doors, which are selectively permeable.

Doors provide boundaries between ourselves (i.e., our property, behavior, and appearance) and others. Violation of such boundaries implies a violation of selfhood. Trespassing or housebreaking, for example, is unbearable for some not only because of the property damage that might result but also because they represent proof that the self has lost control of its audience; it can no longer regulate who may and who may not have access to the property and information

---

[24] Charles Madge, "Private and Public Places," *Human Relations* 3 (1950): 187–99. F. S. Chapin (in "Some Housing Factors Related to Mental Hygiene," *Journal of Social Issues* 7 [1951]: 165) emphasizes that the need for relief from irritating public contact must be consciously and carefully met by the architect. On the other hand, Kira writes: "There are problems which cannot be resolved by architects and industrial designers alone, however; they also pose a challenge to the social scientists and to the medical and public health professions. This is an area in which the stakes are enormous and in which little or no direct work has been done." (*The Bathroom,* p. 192.)

[25] See footnote 21 above.

[26] Simmel, "The Secret and the Secret Society," p. 373.

that index its depths.[27] The victim of a Peeping Tom is thus outraged not only at having been observed naked but also for having lost control of the number and type of people who may possess information about her body. To prove this we note that no nakedness need be observed to make Peeping Tomism intolerable.

"Alone, the visual feeling of the window," writes Simmel, "goes almost exclusively from inward to outward: it is there for looking out, not for seeing in." [28] This interdiction insures that the inhabitants of an establishment may have the outside world at their visual disposal, and at the same time it provides for control over their accessibility to this world. But, whereas the shade or curtain may be employed to regulate accessibility between the private and public spheres of action, situational proprieties are depended upon for protection in public. One such norm is that of "civil inattention" which has been elaborated by Goffman.[29]

Unlike the window, "the door with an in and out announces an entire distinction of intention." [30] There must be very clear rules as to who may open what doors at what times and under what conditions. The front and back doors are normally the only doors that any member of a family may enter at any time and under any circumstances. A parent may enter a child's room at any time and may inspect and replenish drawers, but visiting friends may not. But the parent must learn that some private doors (drawers) may not be opened (although they may be to friends); if they are, new receptacles for ego-indexes will be found, for example, the area between mattress and spring. The child, however, must never inspect the contents of the drawers of his parents nor enter their room at night. Thus the right of intrusion is seen to be an essential element of authority, whose legitimacy is affected by the degree to which it is exercised. Correspondingly, authority is dependent upon immunity against intrusion. Cooley notes that "authority, especially if it covers intrinsic personal weakness, has always a tendency to surround itself with forms and artificial mystery, whose object is to prevent familiar contact and so give the imagination a chance to idealize . . . self concealment serves, among other purposes, that of preserving a sort of ascendency over the unsophisticated." [31] In this same connection, Riesman writes:

> As compared with the one room house of the peasant or the "long house" of many primitive tribes, he (the inner directed child) grows up within walls that are physical symbols of the privacy of parental dominance. Walls separate parents from children, offices from home, and make it hard if not impos-

---

[27] The law recognizes the psychological effect of such criminal acts and provides additional penal sanction for them. Wolfgang and Sellin report that "the chain store is more outraged by theft from a warehouse, where the offender has no business, than from the store where his presence is legal during store hours." Moreover, "the victim of a house burglary is usually very disturbed by the fact that the offender had the effrontery to enter the house illegally. . . . For these and similar reasons, breaking and entering as well as burglary carry more severe sanctions in the law" (Marvin E. Wolfgang and Thorsten Sellin, *The Measurement of Delinquency* [New York: John Wiley & Sons, 1964], pp. 219–20).

[28] Simmel, "Brücke und Tür," p. 5.

[29] Goffman, *Behavior in Public Places,* pp. 83–88.

[30] Simmel, "Brücke und Tür," p. 4.

[31] Charles Horton Cooley, *Human Nature and the Social Order* (New York: Schocken Books, Inc., 1964), p. 351.

> sible for the child to criticize the parents' injunctions by an "undress" view of the parents or of other parents. What the parents say becomes more real in many cases than what they do. . . .[32]

Moreover, it is possible to map personal relations in terms of mutual expectations regarding intrusion. The invasion of various degrees of privacy may be a duty, a privilege, or a transgression, depending upon the nature of the interpersonal bond. And, clearly, expectations regarding such impositions may not be mutually agreed to.

Parental obligations concerning the care of a child override the child's rights to seclusion and place him in a position of social nakedness wherein he has no control over his appearance to others. However, to be subject to limitless intrusion is to exist in a state of dishonor, as implied in the rule against "coming too close." This point is made in Simmel's discussion of "discretion" as a quality which the person-in-private has a right to demand of another who is in a position to invade his seclusion.[33] Compromises between child and parent are therefore necessary and generally employed by the manipulation of the door. For example, the bedroom door may be kept half open while the child sleeps, its position symbolic of the parents' respect for the youngster's selfhood. Furthermore, a general temporal pattern might emerge if a large number of cases were examined. During infancy the door to self is generally fully open; [34] it closes perhaps halfway as a recogni-

---

[32] David Riesman, *The Lonely Crowd* (Garden City: Doubleday & Co., 1953), p. 61. Another characteriologist, William H. Whyte, suggests that "doors inside houses . . . marked the birth of the middle class" (*The Organization Man* [Garden City, N.Y.: Doubleday & Co., 1956], p. 389).

[33] Simmel, "The Secret and the Secret Society," pp. 320–24. Similarly, Erving Goffman writes, "There is an inescapable opposition between showing a desire to include an individual and showing respect for his privacy. As an implication of this dilemma, we must see that social intercourse involves a constant dialectic between presentational rituals and avoidance rituals. A peculiar tension must be maintained, for these opposing requirements of conduct must somehow be held apart from one another and yet realized together in the same interaction; the gestures which carry an actor to a recipient must also signify that things will not be carried too far" ("The Nature of Deference and Demeanor," *American Anthropologist* 58 [June 1956]: 488).

[34] The absence of ability among infants and children to regulate the appearance and disappearance of their audience does not mean that privacy or separateness is not an important feature of their development; the privacy need is simply expressed differently. The infant, for example, can sometimes remove himself from the field of stimulation by going to sleep or wriggling away from the adult who holds him. This is probably why pathology resulting from overcontact is less likely than that due to undercontact, for the former is far more easily regulated by the infant than the latter. At a later stage of development, the infant learns that he can hold back and let go in reference not only to sphincters but to facial expressions and general dispositions as well. He comes to view himself as a causal agent as he inherits the power of voluntary reserve. When the child is locomoting he first confronts privacy imposed against him by others and begins to define himself in terms of where he may and may not go. On the other hand, his ambulatory ability gives him enormous control over his audience, a power in which he delights by "hiding." Espionage is practiced as well and suspected in others—whereby the condition of shame begins to acquire meaning for the child. These incomplete comments suffice to illustrate the point that the privacy impulse is not at all inactive in infancy and childhood. They further suggest that each stage of development has its own mode of privacy, which may be defined in terms of the ego's relationship to those from whom privacy is sought and the manner in which withdrawal is accomplished.

tion of self development during childhood, it shuts but is left ajar at pre-puberty, and closes entirely—and perhaps even locks—at the pubertal and adolescent stages when meditation, grooming, and body examination become imperative. Parents at this time are often fully denied the spectatorship to which they may feel entitled and are kept at a distance by means of the privacy that a locked door insures.

There are also certain situations wherein husband and wife must remain separate from one another. A spouse, for example, must generally knock before entering a bathroom if the other is occupying it. This is a token of deference not to nudity but to the right of the other party to determine the way he or she wishes to present the self to the other. This rule insures that the self and its appearance will remain a controllable factor, independent of the whims of others, and it contributes to self-consciousness as well. This is seen most clearly in total institutions like the armed forces where open rows of toilets are used first with some measure of mortification and later with a complete absence of consciousness of self. In such doorless worlds we find a blurring of the distinction between "front and back regions," between those quarters where the self is put on and taken off and those in which it is presented.[35] In conventional society those who confuse these two areas are charged with vulgarity.

In contrast to the door, the wall symbolizes "separation" rather than "separateness" and denies the possibility of the encounter and withdrawal of social exchange. It strips away that element of freedom which is so clearly embodied in the door. "It is essential," notes Simmel, "that a person be able to set boundaries for himself, but freely, so that he can raise the boundaries again and remove himself from them." [36] In privacy, continues Simmel, "A piece of space is bound with himself and he is separated from the entire world." [37] But in enforced isolation man is bound *to* space. While the door separates outside from inside, the wall annihilates the outside. The door closes out; the wall encloses. Yet doors are converted into walls routinely, as is seen in the popular practice of "sending a child to his room" for misdeeds and the like. In this sense, many homes contain private dungeons or, rather, provisions for transforming the child's room into a cell—which forces upon us the distinction between formal and informal imprisonment.

Privacy is not dependent upon the availability of lockable doors. Goffman, for example, discusses "free places" in the institution where inmates may, free of surveillance, "be one's own man . . . in marked contrast to the sense of uneasiness prevailing on some wards." [38] In addition there is "personal territory" established by each inmate: for one a particular corner; for another a place near a window, etc. "In some wards, a few patients would carry their blankets around

---

[35] Goffman, *The Presentation of Self*, pp. 66–86.

[36] Simmel, "Brücke und Tür," p. 4.

[37] Ibid., p. 3.

[38] Erving Goffman, "The Underlife of a Public Institution," in *Asylums* (Garden City, N.Y.: Doubleday & Co., 1961), p. 231.

with them during the day and, in an act thought to be highly regressive, each would curl up on the floor with his blanket completely covering him; within the covered space each had some margin of control." [39] Thus do men withdraw from others to be at one with themselves and to create a world over which they reign with more complete authority, recalling Simmel's observation that "the person who erects a refuge demonstrates, like the first pathfinder, the typically human hegemony over nature, as he cuts a particle of space from continuity and eternity." [40]

In summary, islands of privacy exist in all establishments and throughout even the most intimate household. These islands are protected by an intricate set of rules. When these rules are violated secret places are sought after, discovered, and employed as facilities for secret action. These places and their permeability constitute one type of map, as it were, of interpersonal relationships and reveal the nature of the selves participating in them.

Privacy, property and self—Implied in any reference to a private place in its contents, personal property. One perhaps more often than not withdraws into privacy in order to observe and manipulate his property in some way, property which includes, of course, body and non-body objects.

There are two types of objects: those which may be observed by the public (and which may be termed personal objects) and those which are not available to public view (private property). Private property, as we are using the term, may be further delineated in terms of those intimate others who may have access to it in terms of visibility or use. Some private objectifications of self may be observed by family members, but some may be observed by *no one except the self.* There is no doubt that these latter objects have a very special meaning for identity; some of these are sacred and must not be contaminated by exposing them to observation by others; some are profane, and exposure will produce shame, but both are special and represent an essential aspect of self and, from the possessor's point of view, must not be tampered with.

It is because persons invest so much of their selves in private and personal things that total institutions require separation of self and material objects. When individualism must be minimized private ownership is always a vice worthy of constant surveillance. In such situations the acquisition and storage of personal things persist in the form of the "stash," which might be anything from a long sock to the cuff of one's pants.[41]

It follows that those who have direct or indirect access to the belongings of others or to articles which have been employed by them in private ways enjoy a certain amount of power which, if judiciously employed, may serve their interests well. Hughes observes:

---

[39] Ibid., p. 246. For more on norms regulating territorial conduct in face-to-face encounters, see Nancy Felipe and Robert Sommer, "Invasions of Personal Space," *Social Problems* 14 (May 1966): 206–14; and Robert Sommer, "Sociofugal Space," *American Journal of Sociology* 72 (May 1967): 654–60.

[40] Simmel, "Brücke and Tür," p. 3.

[41] Goffman, *Asylums*, pp. 248–54.

> It is by the garbage that the janitor judges, and, as it were, gets power over the tenants who high-hat him. Janitors know about hidden love affairs by bits of torn-up letter paper; of impending financial disaster or of financial four-flushing by the presence of many unopened letters in the waste. Or they may stall off demands for immediate service by an unreasonable woman of whom they know from the garbage that she, as the janitors put it, "has the rag on." The garbage gives the janitor the makings of a kind of magical power over that pretentious villain, the tenant. I say a kind of magical power, for there appears to be no thought of betraying any individual and thus turning his knowledge into overt power.[42]

But, certainly, power need not be exercised to be effective. The mere knowledge that another "knows" invokes in the treatment of that other certain amount of humility and deference.

Deprivatization

We have attempted to show that the possibility of withdrawal into well-equipped worlds which are inaccessible to others is that which makes intense group affiliations bearable. But we have also seen that men are not always successful in protecting their invisibility. Accidental leakages of information as well as the diverse modes of espionage threaten the information control that privacy is intended to maintain. But information control also consists of purposeful information leakage and even of the renunciation of secrecy. Just as men demand respite from public encounter they need periodically to escape themselves, for a privacy which lacks frequent remissions is maddening. The over-privatized man is he who is relieved of public demand only to become a burden to himself: He becomes his own audience to performances which are bound for tedium. Self-entertainment is thus a most exhausting business, requiring the simultaneous performance of two roles: actor and spectator. Both tire quickly of one another. When privacy thereby exhausts itself new and public audiences (and audienceships) are sought.

Moreover, we are led to relinquish our private information and activities by the expediencies and reciprocities routinely called for in daily life. We all know, for example, that in order to employ others as resources it is necessary to reveal to them something of ourselves, at least that part of ourselves which for some reason needs reinforcement. When this occurs (providing support is forthcoming), two things happen. First, we achieve some degree of gratification; second, and most important, our alter (or resource) reveals to us information which was heretofore withheld, for self-revelation is imbued with reciprocal power: It calls out in others something similar to that which we give of ourselves. There is both mutual revelation and mutual gratification. It is easy to see that when stress or need is prolonged this process may become institutionalized: Intimacy is then no longer an alternative; it is enforced, and private activity becomes clandestine and punishable. The deprivation process approaches completion when we are not

---

[42] Everett C. Hughes, *Men and Their Work* (Glencoe, Ill.: Free Press, 1958), p. 51.

only penalized for our withdrawals but feel guilty about them. A housewife who had probably undergone the deprivatization process confided to Whyte: "I've promised myself to make it up to them. I was feeling bad that day and just plain didn't make the effort to ask them in for coffee. I don't blame them, really, for reacting the way they did. I'll make it up to them somehow." [43]

But loss of privacy among conventional folk is free of many of the pains of social nakedness which are suffered by inmates and by others undergoing total surveillance. The civilian voluntarily subjects himself to publicity and is relatively free of the contamination of unwanted contacts. His unmaskings are selective and subject to careful forethought. The intruder is chosen rather than suffered; indeed, his resourcefulness depends upon his ability to "know" his client-neighbor. Therefore, in civil life, we find valid rationalization for our self-revelations. The demand that we "be sociable" is too compelling and too rewarding to be ignored by any of us.

But a substantial self-sacrifice is made by those who actually believe themselves to be what they present to public view. An awareness of the masquerades and deceptions that are part of good role performance is necessary to recall ourselves to our *own* selfhood and to our opposition to that of others. We must indeed deceive others to be true to ourselves. In this particular sense privacy prevents the ego from identifying itself too closely with or losing itself in (public) roles. Daily life is therefore sparked by a constant tension between sincerity and guile, between self-release and self-containment, between the impulse to embrace that which is public and the drive to escape the discomfort of group demands. Accordingly, our identities are maintained by our ability to hold back as well as to affiliate. Thus Goffman writes:

> When we closely observe what goes on in a social role, a spate of sociable interaction, a social establishment—or in any other unit of social organization—embracement of the unit is not all that we see. We always find the individual employing methods to keep some distance, some elbow room, between himself and that with which others assume he should be identified.
>
> Our sense of being a person can come from being drawn into a wider social unit; our sense of selfhood can arise through the little ways in which we resist the pull. Our status is backed by the solid buildings of the world, while our sense of personal identity often resides in the cracks.[44]

For Goffman, privacy is one of "the little ways in which we resist the pull" of group commitments and reinforce our selfhood.

---

[43] Whyte, *Organization Man,* p. 390.
[44] Goffman, *Asylums,* pp. 319–20.

2

Status of Frustrator as an Inhibitor of Horn-Honking Responses

ANTHONY N. DOOB · ALAN E. GROSS

The following selection can be profitably viewed from a number of perspectives. Substantively, the research report demonstrates the pervasive influence that status exerts on human behavior. When frustrated by another motorist, drivers' reactions are observed to vary significantly according to the apparent status of the frustrator. In this study the frustrating motorist was the experimenter, and his status was manipulated by changing the make of automobile he was driving. When the experimenter was driving an older model, low prestige automobile, other motorists were less hesitant to engage in horn-honking when he blocked traffic at an intersection than when was driving a newer model, high prestige automobile.

A second significant observation is that males are generally more aggressive in responding to both high status and low status frustrators than are females. This observation is consistent with the findings of numerous studies which indicate that males are more aggressive than are females in responding to frustration.

Methodologically, Doob and Gross's study is quite ingenious. It demonstrates how one can study a social psychological process by means of unobtrusive techniques. That is, the people who served as subjects in the research were not aware that they were participants in an experiment. The significance of this approach is underscored when the authors contrast their primary findings with the results of a questionnaire survey of a sample of college students. What the college students said they would do under the experimental circumstances differed markedly from what was actually observed among non-student motorists.

Anthony N. Doob and Alan E. Gross, "Status of Frustrator as an Inhibitor of Horn-Honking Responses," *Journal of Social Psychology* 76 (1968): 213–18.

Subjects may consciously attempt to present themselves in a favorable manner, they may cooperate with the experimenter or interviewer, and their reactions may be affected by the measurement process itself. In reviewing a number of such problems, Webb et al. point out that some of these sources of contamination can be avoided when field data are collected from people who are unaware that they are subjects participating in an experiment.[1] Although field procedures can reduce demand and reactivity effects, experimental manipulations outside of the laboratory may gain realism at the expense of control. The study reported here is an attempt to investigate unobtrusively some effects of frustration in a naturalistic setting without sacrificing experimental control.

Modern automobile traffic frequently creates situations which closely resemble classical formulations of how frustration is instigated. One such instance occurs when one car blocks another at a signal-controlled intersection. Unlike many traffic frustrations, this situation provides a clearly identifiable frustrator and a fairly typical response for the blocked driver: sounding his horn. Horn honking may function instrumentally to remove the offending driver and emotionally to reduce tension. Both kinds of honks may be considered aggressive, especially if they are intended to make the frustrator uncomfortable by bombarding him with unpleasant stimuli.

One factor that is likely to affect aggressive responses is the status of the frustrator.[2] The higher a person's status, the more likely it is he will have power to exercise sanctions, and although it is improbable that a high status driver would seek vengeance against a honker, fear of retaliation may generalize from other situations where aggression against superiors has been punished.

Aggression is not the only kind of social response that may be affected by status. High status may inhibit the initiation of any social response, even a simple informational signal. Although it is difficult in the present study to distinguish informational from aggressive motivation, it is hypothesized that a high status frustrator will generally inhibit horn honking.

Method

One of two automobiles, a new luxury model or an older car, was driven up to a signal-controlled intersection and stopped. The driver was instructed to remain stopped after the signal had changed to green until 15 seconds had elapsed, or until the driver of the car immediately behind honked his horn twice. Subjects

---

[1] E. J. Webb, D. T. Campbell, R. D. Schwartz, and L. Sechrest, *Unobtrusive Measures: Nonreactive Research in the Social Sciences* (Chicago: Rand McNally, 1956), pp. 13–27.

[2] R. A. Cohen, "Social Norms, Arbitrariness of Frustration, and Status of the Agent in the Frustration-Aggression Hypothesis," *Journal of Abnormal and Social Psychology* 51 (1955): 222–26. And, J. E. Hokanson and M. Burgess, "The Effects of Status, Type of Frustration and Aggression on Vascular Processes," *Journal of Abnormal and Social Psychology* 65 (1962): 230–37.

were the 82 drivers, 26 women and 56 men, whose progress was blocked by the experimental car. The experiment was run from 10:30 A.M. to 5:30 P.M. on a Sunday, in order to avoid heavy weekday traffic.

Status Manipulation

A black 1966 Chrysler Crown Imperial hardtop which had been washed and polished was selected as the high status car.[3] Two low status cars were used: a rusty 1954 Ford station wagon and an unobtrusive gray 1961 Rambler sedan. The Rambler was substituted at noon because it was felt that subjects might reasonably attribute the Ford's failure to move to mechanical breakdown. Responses to these two cars did not turn out to be different, and the data for the two low status cars were combined.

Location

Six intersections in Palo Alto and Menlo Park, California, were selected according to these criteria: (a) a red light sufficiently long to insure that a high proportion of potential subjects would come to a complete stop behind the experimental car before the signal changed to green, (b) relatively light traffic so that only one car, the subject's, was likely to pull up behind the experimental car, and (c) a narrow street so that it would be difficult for the subject to drive around the car blocking him. Approximately equal numbers of high and low status trials were run at each intersection.

Procedure

By timing the signal cycle, the driver of the experimental car usually managed to arrive at the intersection just as the light facing him was turning red. If at least one other car had come to a complete stop behind the experimental car before the signal had turned green, a trial was counted, and when the light changed, an observer started two stop watches and a tape recorder. Observers were usually stationed in a car parked close to the intersection, but when this was not feasible, they were concealed from view in the back seat of the experimental car. High and low status trials were run simultaneously at different intersections, and the two driver-observer teams switched cars periodically during the day. Drivers wore a plaid sport jacket and white shirt while driving the Chrysler, and an old khaki jacket while driving the older car.

---

[3] We have labeled this operation a "status manipulation" because a large expensive car is frequently associated with wealth, power, and other qualities which are commonly regarded as comprising high status. However, it could be argued that Chrysler is potentially inhibiting not because it is a status symbol, but because of some other less plausible attribute (e.g., physical size).

a. Dependent Measures At the end of each trial, the observer noted whether the subject had honked once, twice, or not at all. Latency of each honk and estimated length of each honk were recorded and later double-checked against tape recordings.

b. Subject Characteristics Immediately after each trial, the observer took down the year, make, and model of the subject's car. Sex and estimated age of driver, number of passengers, and number of cars behind the experimental car when the signal changed were also recorded.

Results and Discussion

Eight subjects, all men, were eliminated from the analysis for the following reasons: four cars in the low status condition and one in the high status condition went around the experimental car; on one trial the driver of the experimental car left the intersection early; and two cars in the low status condition, instead of honking, hit the back bumper of the experimental car, and the driver did not wish to wait for a honk. This left 38 subjects in the low status condition and 36 in the high status condition.

Although the drivers of the experimental cars usually waited for 15 seconds, two of the lights used in the experiment were green for only 12 seconds; therefore 12 seconds was used as a cutoff for all data. There were no differences attributable to drivers or intersections.

The clearest way of looking at the results is in terms of the percentage in each condition that honked at least once in 12 seconds. In the low status condition 84 percent of the subjects honked at least once, whereas in the high status condition, only 50 percent of the subjects honked ($\chi^2 = 8.37$, $df = 1$, $p < .01$). Another way of looking at this finding is in terms of the latency of the first honk. When no honks are counted as a latency of 12 seconds, it can be seen in Table 1 that the average latency for the new car was longer for both sexes. ($F = 10.71$, $p < .01$).

TABLE 1
FIELD EXPERIMENT (MEAN LATENCY OF FIRST HONK IN SECONDS)

	SEX OF DRIVER	
Frustrator	*Male*	*Female*
Low status	6.8 (23)	7.6 (15)
High status	8.5 (25)	10.9 (11)

Note: Numbers in parentheses indicate the number of subjects.

Thus, it is quite clear that status had an inhibitory effect on honking even once. It could be argued that status would have even greater inhibitory effects on more aggressive honking. Although one honk can be considered a polite way of calling attention to the green light, it is possible that subjects felt that a second honk would be interpreted as aggression.[4]

Forty-seven percent of the subjects in the low status condition honked twice at the experimental car, as compared to 19 percent of the subjects in the high status condition ($\chi^2 = 5.26$, $df = 1$, $p < .05$). This difference should be interpreted cautiously because it is confounded with the main result that more people honk generally in the low status condition. Of those who overcame the inhibitions to honk at all, 56 percent in the low status condition and 39 percent in the high status condition honked a second time, a difference which was not significant. First-honk latencies for honkers were about equal for the two conditions. The overall findings are presented in Table 2.

TABLE 2

NUMBER OF DRIVERS HONKING ZERO, ONE, AND TWO TIMES

	HONKING IN 12 SECONDS		
Frustrator	*Never*	*Once*	*Twice*
Low status	6	14	18
High status	18	11	7

Note: Overall $\chi^2 = 11.14$, $p < .01$.

Sex of driver was the only other measure that was a good predictor of honking behavior. In both conditions men tended to honk faster than women ($F = 4.49$, $p < .05$). The interaction of status and sex did not approach significance ($F = 1.17$). These data are consistent with laboratory findings that men tend to aggress more than women.[5]

Most experiments designed to study the effects of frustration have been carried out in the laboratory or the classroom, and many of these have employed written materials.[6]

It is undoubtedly much easier to use questionnaires, and if they produce the same results as field experiments, then in the interest of economy, they would have great advantage over naturalistic experiments. However, over 30 years ago, LaPiere warned that reactions to such instruments "may indicate what the responder would actually do when confronted with the situation symbolized in the question, but there is no assurance that it will." [7]

In order to investigate this relationship between actual and predicted behavior, an attempt was made to replicate the present study as a questionnaire experiment.

[4] Series of honks separated by intervals of less than one second were counted as a single honk.

[5] A. H. Buss, "Instrumentality of Aggression, Feedback, and Frustration as Determinants of Physical Aggression," *Journal of Personality and Social Psychology* 3 (1966): 153–162.

[6] R. A. Cohen, "Social Norms," pp. 222–26, and N. Pastore, "The Role of Arbitrariness in the Frustration-Aggression Hypothesis," *Journal of Abnormal and Social Psychology* 47 (1952): 728–31.

[7] R. T. LaPiere, "Attitudes vs. Actions," *Social Forces* 13 (1934): 236.

Obviously, the most appropriate sample to use would be one comprised of motorists sampled in the same way that the original drivers were sampled. Because this was not practicable, a questionnaire experiment was administered in a junior college classroom.

Subjects were 57 students in an introductory psychology class. Two forms of the critical item were included as the first of three traffic situations on a one-page questionnaire: "You are stopped at a traffic light behind a black 1966 Chrysler (gray 1961 Rambler). The light turns green and for no apparent reason the driver does not go on. Would you honk at him?" If subjects indicated that they would honk, they were then asked to indicate on a scale from one to 14 seconds how long they would wait before honking. Forms were alternated so that approximately equal numbers of subjects received the Chrysler and Rambler versions. Verbal instructions strongly emphasized that subjects were to answer according to what they actually thought they would do in such a situation. No personal information other than sex, age, and whether or not they were licensed to drive was required.

After the questionnaire had been collected, the class was informed that different kinds of cars had been used for the horn-honking item. The experimenter then asked subjects to raise their hands when they heard the name of the car that appeared in the first item of their questionnaire. All subjects were able to select the correct name from a list of four makes which was read.

One subject (a female in the high status condition) failed to mark the honk latency scale, and another subject in the same condition indicated that she would go around the blocking car. Both of these subjects were eliminated from the analysis, leaving 27 in the high status condition and 28 in the low status condition. The results were analyzed in the same manner as the latency data from the field experiment. Means for each condition broken down by sex are presented in Table 3. Males reported that they thought that they would honk considerably

TABLE 3

QUESTIONNAIRE EXPERIMENT (MEAN LATENCY OF HONKING IN SECONDS)

	SEX OF SUBJECT	
Frustrator	*Male*	*Female*
Low status	9.1 (18)	8.2 (10)
High status	5.5 (13)	9.2 (14)

Note: Numbers in parentheses indicate the number of subjects.

sooner at the Chrysler than at the Rambler, whereas this was slightly reversed for females (interaction of sex and status $F = 4.97$, $p < .05$). Eleven subjects, six males in the low status condition and five females in the high status condition indicated that they would not honk within 12 seconds.

It is clear that the behavior reported on the questionnaire is different from the behavior actually observed in the field. The age difference in the samples may account for this disparity. Median estimated age of subjects in the field was 38, compared to a median age of 22 in the classroom. In order to check the possibility that younger males would indeed honk faster at the high status car, the field data were reanalyzed by age. The results for younger males, estimated ages 16 to 30, fit the general pattern of the field results and differed from the results of the classroom experiment. In the field, young males honked sooner at the Rambler than at the Chrysler ($t = 2.74$, $df = 11$, $p < .02$).

Unfortunately, because these two studies differed in both sample and method, it is impossible to conclude that the differences are due to differences in the method of collecting data. However, it is clear that questionnaire data obtained from this often used population of subjects do not always correspond to what goes on in the real world.

3

The Hasher: A Study of Role Conflict

LOUIS A. ZURCHER · DAVID W. SONENSCHEIN · ERIC L. METZNER

During the course of a normal day a given individual typically moves into and out of a number of social positions (statuses). Each position he occupies is characterized by a distinctive set of behavioral expectations (role). Fortunately, structural barriers usually make it possible for one to confront these different sets of expectations serially. But what happens when a person finds himself occupying two positions simultaneously which are characterized by contradictory expectations? In the terminology of social psychology, what happens when one is confronted with role conflict? It is such a question that Zurcher and his colleagues examine in the following selection.

The research site selected to pursue this question was a number of sorority houses. Young men who work in sorority houses as hashers find that the expectations associated with their work position are incongruent with the expectations associated with their position as "college men." To cope with these contradictory expectations, the authors point out that the young men employ a number of defense mechanisms which are provided by and within the conflict engendering institution. For example, they rationalize that the job is only temporary, and the sorority itself concurs in this definition of the job. In view of the temporary nature of the job, the hasher does not use it as a basis for self identification. The physical features of the work place provide the hasher with a large backstage area (an area where his actions are not directly visible to his audience) where he can engage in a variety of verbal attacks on the girls he has to serve.

While the bases of the conflict described in this article and the modes of resolution discussed are by no means exhaustive, they are illustrative and informative.

Louis A. Zurcher, David W. Sonenschein, and Eric L. Metzner, "The Hasher: A Study of Role Conflict," *Social Forces* 44 (1966): 505–14.

The effect of role conflict upon personal and social adjustment has been of considerable interest to social scientists. Typically, the individual's reaction to a role conflict situation has been described in terms of traditional defense mechanisms. Burchard, for example, writing of the contradictory behavioral expectations facing the military chaplain, describes four representative solutions to the officer-clergyman conflict: (1) Rationalization (Someone has to carry the gospel to these boys), (2) Compartmentalization (Render therefore unto Caesar the things which are Caesar's and unto God the things that are God's), (3) Repression (I don't see any conflict), (4) Withdrawal (I'd rather not talk about it).[1] Cousins, reporting the behavior of subjects in experimentally contrived role conflict, observed "rationalization, displacements, and wish fulfilling fantasy" as modal responses.[2]

Role conflict, however, is experienced within the broad scope of perceived social environment. Defense mechanisms, as solutions to the conflict situation, are not isolated from the social context in which that conflict takes place. In fact, it is likely that a role conflict which has been perpetuated by a continuing set of social conditions will be accompanied by a similarly continuing, socially determined set of defense mechanisms. The individual who must enact the conflicting roles will be provided, usually informally, with the socially acceptable means whereby he can alleviate, at least temporarily, that conflict.

In this paper, the authors will present an example of perpetuated role conflict in a university setting. It will be seen that the informal organization supporting one of the role enactments provides each participant with a socially legitimized set of defenses (part of the role expectations) by which he can abate the conflict.

A number of studies have discussed the adjustment the college student must make to the conflicts between the behavioral expectations of college life and the behavioral expectations he has internalized from his family association.[3] Among the parental expectations for the college student are "good grades, conscientious study, writing home regularly, spending money carefully, and preparing for a future occupation." Conflicting with these are the peer-group expectations of "parties, campus politics, fraternity affairs, dating, athletics, and nights out with the boys." [4] Other sources of conflict, within the college life itself, are situations in which the individual must enact two college roles whose behavioral patterns are conflicting. The role of the fraternity man vs. the role of student has been discussed in that context.[5] A second example, which this paper presents, involves

---

[1] W. Burchard, "Role Conflicts of Military Chaplains," *American Sociological Review* 19 (August 1954): 528–35.

[2] A. N. Cousins, "Social Equilibrium and the Psychodynamic Mechanisms," *Social Forces* 30 (December 1951): 202–09.

[3] See, for example, E. Hartshorne, *Undergraduate Society and the College Culture* (Cambridge: Harvard University Press, 1943).

[4] A. R. Lindesmith and A. L. Strauss, *Social Psychology* (New York: Dryden Press, 1949), p. 616.

[5] D. Krech, R. S. Crutchfield, and E. L. Ballachey, *Individual In Society* (New York: McGraw-Hill Book Co., 1962), pp. 405, 496.

the role conflict inherent in the dual enactment of the roles of "college man" and "hasher" in a sorority.

The individual entering college for the first time has, through exposure to a popularized and dramatized stereotype, come to perceive the status of "college man" as incorporating the following characteristics and role expectations: (1) a young man who deserves a white-collar or "clean" occupation of more than average prestige, (2) a sophisticate, above average in intelligence, taste, and *savoir faire*—able to smoke a pipe with an air of casual indifference, (3) a "lover," "a man of the world" who dominates and manipulates the tender young coeds, (4) a "hail fellow well met" who can, at any time, spontaneously join in an impromptu frolicsome venture. These expectations are repeatedly reinforced in the informal academic setting.

Hashers at the subject university are male college undergraduate students who are employed as attendants in the kitchens of sororities and fraternities (in this paper, we will focus our attention on the unique social situation of the sorority hasher). In return for their work, hashers are given meals and, in some cases of additional responsibility, a few dollars a month. The job consists of setting tables; washing and drying dishes, silver, and utensils; cleaning up the kitchen; mopping floors; disposing of garbage; general handy work; and, on occasion, carrying luggage for the girls. As it can be seen, the tasks are in general very similar to those of the "K. P." of military fame.

Even though it is part-time work, the job of hasher can be classified as what Becker calls a "service occupation."[6] According to Becker, the service occupations are "distinguished by the fact that the worker in them comes into more or less direct and personal contact with the ultimate consumer of the product of his work, the client for whom he performs the service. Consequently, the client is able to direct or attempt to direct the worker at his task and to apply sanctions of various kinds . . ."[7] Becker sees as characteristic of such jobs that the workers consider "the client unable to judge the proper worth of the service and resent bitterly any attempt on his part to exercise control over the work. A good deal of conflict and hostility arises as a result, and methods of defense against outside interference become a preoccupation of the members."[8]

The hasher occupies the lowest level in the functional work hierarchy of the kitchen. At the top of the hierarchy is the house mother, then the cooks (in order of longevity), the head hasher, and finally, the hashers themselves (in order of longevity). This chain-of-command is rigidly enforced—a policy not unusual in an organized kitchen work setting. Whyte, for example, describes the elaborate restaurant kitchen status system in which even the kinds of vegetables worked with and the levels of food preparation are related to position in the staff hierarchy.[9] Orwell writes of the rigid caste system existing in the hotel restaurant

---

[6] Howard S. Becker, "The Professional Dance Musician and His Audience," *The American Journal of Sociology* 57 (September 1951): 136–44.

[7] Ibid., p. 136.

[8] Ibid., p. 136.

[9] W. F. Whyte, *Human Relations in the Restaurant Industry* (New York: McGraw-Hill Book Co., 1948).

where he was employed, in which the staff "had their prestige graded as accurately as that of soldiers, and a cook or waiter was as much above a kitchen helper as a captain above a private." [10] The hasher in the sorority house, since he is the low man on the totem pole, is expected to accept without question the assignments handed out by the cooks and by the head hasher (though there is considerably more latitude for complaining or "bitching" about a task assigned by the latter). Furthermore, as part of his job, the hasher is expected to be neat, quietly efficient, and at all times polite to the girls. He is not to speak with them when serving (unless asked a question), and, by house rule, he is not to attempt to date them during his off-duty hours.

The position of hasher in a sorority thus brings with it the behavioral expectations of (1) menial or "dirty" work, (2) low prestige, (3) a marked lack of sophistication, and (4) manifest subservience to and strict social distance from a group of college coeds.

It appears, therefore, that the individual who must enact both the role of college man and hasher experiences conflict, and it will be seen that this conflict manifests itself in the way the hashers perceive themselves, the way they behave in the work situation, their attitudes toward and behavior with the girls for whom they work, and the attitudes of the girls toward and their behavior with the hashers. Furthermore, components within the informal organization of the work situation will be observed to provide the individual with group-structured defenses to the role conflict. These defenses become an integral part of the hasher role enactment and are learned along with the formal requirements of the job.

Procedure

The two junior authors (one a senior in cultural anthropology and the other a senior in psychology), both of whom had been hashers in a total of five different sororities for three years previous to the present study, observed as participators [11] in the hasher group of a large, campus housed, nationally affiliated sorority (85 girls, ten hashers). The systematic observations were conducted during the course of ten months, a little more than the full academic year. The participant observers, cognizant of the hypotheses and familiar with role theory, kept daily records of relevant attitudes, behaviors, statements, and patterns of interaction of (1) the hashers, (2) the sorority girls, and (1) and (2) *vis-à-vis* each other. The three authors met several times a week to discuss the data and to focus attention for the periods of observation to follow.[12]

[10] George Orwell, *Down and Out in Paris and London* (London: Secker and Warburg, 1933), p. 70.

[11] The two junior authors occupied the role of "complete participator" in Gold's continuum of participant-observers. That is, they themselves were hashers, and members of the work group were not aware of the fact that they were being observed. See Raymond L. Gold, "Roles in Sociological Field Observations," *Social Forces* 36 (March 1958): 217–23.

[12] In addition to the work by Gold cited above, the authors are indebted to the following for various participant-observer techniques: Howard S. Becker, "Problems of Inferences

The subject sorority was one of the largest on the university campus. At the time of the study, and for a number of years before, the subject sorority was not among those considered by the students to be popular or "in," but rather among those considered to be "unreal." Furthermore, and perhaps to be expected because of the girls' awareness of the relatively low status of their house in the Panhellenic system, the social distance maintained between the members and the hashers was rigid and extreme.

The work setting of hashers in this particular sorority house would be, the authors felt, one in which there was a high degree of role conflict, and one in which the defenses to such conflict would be clearly manifested.

Conclusions based upon the data from participant observation in the subject sorority provided the framework for a series of open-ended interview questions.[13]

---

and Proof in Participant-Observation," *American Sociological Review* 23 (December 1958): 652–60; Mortimer Sullivan, Stuart Queen, and Ralph Patrick, "Participant Observation as Employed in the Study of a Military Training Program," *American Sociological Review* 23 (December 1958): 660–67; Jackson Toby, "Variables in Role Conflict Analysis," *Social Forces* 30 (March 1952): 323–27; Roger Heyns and Ronald Lippitt, "Systematic Observational Techniques," in Gardner Lindzey ed., *Handbook of Social Psychology,* Vol. 1 (Cambridge, Mass.: Addison-Wesley, 1954), pp. 370–404.

[13] The purpose of the open-ended interviews was to explore, in sororities other than the subject house, the following broad phenomena: What did the hashers think of their jobs? How did they get along with the girls? What did the girls think of the hashers? How did the house mothers and the cooks view the interaction between the hashers and the girls? What were the formal house rules and expectations relevant to the hasher work situation?

In each interview situation, at least the following questions were asked with the intent being to get the respondents talking, and to probe with further, more specific questions when the opportunity arose: (1) *Hashers:* What do you think of the job of hasher? Advantages? Disadvantages? When is the job most enjoyable? When is the job least enjoyable? Why did you choose hashing as a part-time job? Do you intend to continue hashing while you are a student? What do you think of the girls in this sorority? What do you think their attitude is toward the hashers? How do the hashers and girls get along, generally? Have you worked for any other houses? If so, how do the work situations compare? What is your idea of a "good house" for which to work? A "bad house?" Do you do any extra things for the girls in this house? Do you represent them in intramural sports? Do any of the hashers in the house date a member? Would you recommend the job of hasher to a good friend? (2) *Girls:* What do you think of the job of hasher for a college man? What do you think of the hashers in your own sorority? What is your idea of a "good hasher?" A "bad hasher?" How do you think the hashers and the members get along, generally? What are the names of the hashers who work in your sorority house? How do you think the hasher crew of your house compares with those of other houses? Do you think the members should date hashers? Have you ever dated a hasher? Do you ever find it difficult to get a hasher to do what you ask him to do? Do you have a "turn-about" day? Tell me about it. (3) *House Mothers* and *Cooks:* What do you think of the job of hasher for a college man? What is your idea of a good hasher employee? A bad hasher employee? Are there any particular work or disciplinary problems that you have with the hashers? How, in general, do the girls get along with the hashers? The hashers with the girls? What is your opinion of hashers and members dating? Is there a formal or informal house rule against such dating? What is the hasher turnover rate in this house? Have you worked for other houses? If so, how do the hashers here compare with those in the others? Are there any differences among the houses with which you have been associated in the way the hashers and the girls get along? In this sorority, do you have a "turn-about" day? Tell me about it.

Though the main focus of this investigation was the case study analysis of a specific conflict engendering work situation (in one sorority), interviews were conducted with 48 hashers, 50 members, and 21 staff personnel of seven of the remaining 13 sororities on the university campus, thus attempting to establish the degree, if any, to which the conclusions could be generalized. Including the subject sorority house, the sample consisted of: two "large" houses (65 or more members, eight to ten hashers, and two full-time cooks); three "medium" houses (50-65 members, six to eight hashers, and two cooks on separate shifts); and three "small" houses (less than 50 members, five or fewer hashers, and one full-time cook). Independent of size the eight sorority houses in the sample varied in prestige (indicated by the number of "rushees," number of student body and club offices held by members, number of queens, cheerleaders, pompom girls, etc., and by student opinion). Two were high prestige or "top" houses; four were of average prestige; and two were low prestige or "loser" houses. It was felt that this sample of sororities was fairly representative of the entire university population of houses, though at the onset, since the authors were aware of the limitations of participant observation and open-ended, informal interviews, no sweeping generalizations were intended.

Results and Discussion

It is immediately apparent to the observer that the hasher is not proud of his work and that he prefers not to be identified with the job. As MacIver has pointed out, men in our society tend to be judged according to the work which they pursue,[14] and the stereotype representing the occupational levels similar to that of the hasher is distasteful to the aspiring college man. Table 1 presents the mean prestige ranks assigned by 276 freshman and sophomore students in basic social science classes to ten part-time jobs typically held by male college students. As indicated in the table, the male students, on the average, rank the job of hasher last. The female students rank the jobs of off-campus restaurant helper and movie usher lower than the job of hasher. None of the student evaluators were fraternity or sorority members.

The college student has, in general, a middle-class view of work—that is, work should enhance one's prestige, provide for the realization of one's talents, and be satisfying and desirable in itself. This view is in contrast to that of the lower class which sees work as an unpleasant but necessary means of securing food and shelter, and as being neither interesting nor desirable in itself.[15] To the members of the lower class who must pursue such "drudgery," the college student imputes low intelligence, irresponsibility, and generalized inferiority.[16] The hasher then finds himself in the unique situation of having middle-class defini-

[14] R. M. MacIver, *Society: A Textbook of Sociology* (New York: Rinehart & Co., 1937).
[15] Krech, *et al., Individual in Society,* p. 283.
[16] Helen M. Davidson, F. Reissman, and Edna Meyers, "Personality Characteristics Attributed to the Worker," *Journal of Social Psychology* 57 (June 1962): 155–60.

TABLE 1

MEAN PRESTIGE RANKS ASSIGNED BY LOWER DIVISION STUDENTS TO TEN TYPICAL PART-TIME JOBS HELD BY MALE COLLEGE STUDENTS

	AVERAGE RANK BY SEX	
Part-time Job	*Males* (N = 112)	*Females* (N = 164)
Bellboy	6.8	6.8
Grocery Clerk	5.9	5.8
Life Guard	4.0	3.5
Hasher	7.4	7.0
Stock Clerk	4.9	5.0
Gas Station Attendant	6.1	6.0
Off-campus Restaurant Helper	7.1	7.1
Reader	2.8	2.6
Library Assistant	3.4	2.9
Movie Usher	6.6	7.5

tions and expectations of work, but performing tasks and conforming to expectations which clearly are representative of a lower-class job.

When in a position in which he must profess the nature of his employment, the hasher's admission is inevitably quickly followed by a qualifying statement: "It's a means to an end," "I'm just doing this until I find something more suitable," "It's the only job I could get with hours that won't interfere with my class schedule," and so on. The *temporary* nature of the job is stressed, and a point is made of demonstrating to the questioner that the hasher's primary role is that of student. (Table 1 indicates the high student ranking of the "scholarly" student related jobs of reader and library assistant.) The hasher's friends and acquaintances are often observed to ask him why he does such work, thus indicating a violation of their expectations of him as a college man. Sometimes a hasher will describe, with a leer, his job as an opportunity to "get near all those girls," and will gloss over the unpleasant realities of his task. In fact, some of the hashers interviewed stated that they initially took the job with the hope that they would "get the inside track" to a covey of coeds. This hope, of course, vanished in the face of the blunt reality of sorority girl-hasher social distance.

In the subject sorority house, there is a formal rule forbidding dating between the hashers and the sorority girls, and social intercourse within the house is maintained at as impersonal, employer-employee level as possible. Fraternization has been discouraged to the point where the girls and the hashers both feel uncomfortable if they have to interact on a level other than that called for by the job.

The no-dating rule in the subject sorority has been rigidly followed only for the last two years. The older hashers often speak of those "good old days a couple of years ago" when the girls were "somehow much nicer." Pertinent here is the hasher's definition of the sorority member who is a "good kid." In every case interviewed, the hasher's description of this ideal sorority girl centered on the attribute of "naturalness"—that is, a tendency to "be herself" and not to "look down" on the hasher, thus not stressing his subservient role. A good house to work for is one in which you are "treated like a human being." Good kids and good houses, then, are those that treat the individual less like a hasher and more like a college man. W. F. Whyte observed that a conflict situation resulted among restaurant personnel when persons of high status had their activities initiated by persons perceived by them to be of lower status.[17] Many of the hashers are upper classmen, yet they must take orders from and wait on freshman girls. Any sorority member who minimizes this status threat is appreciated by the hasher as a "good kid."

Whyte also noted that in the restaurant under his observation it was not uncommon for female employees to initiate the action of male employees—e.g., waitresses giving orders to male cooks. Since in our society the male sex role generally includes the expectation that he be the originator of action between the sexes, that he dominate in heterosexual interpersonal relations, Whyte saw the role reversal in the restaurant as a key source of employee dissatisfaction. He cites a number of occasions where male employees contrived ways to avoid having to receive direct orders from female employees.[18] Similarly, in an analysis of some of the factors contributing to alienation from work, Blauner observed that "jobs differ in the degree to which they permit the particular 'manly virtues' that in our society are deemed appropriate to a 'real man.' "[19] One of the factors Blauner emphasizes is the degree to which the job allows sexual expression and status dominance with respect to women. It can be seen that the job of hasher includes both the sex role reversal that Whyte viewed as disruptive of the work situation and the lack of sexual expression and status dominance over women that Blauner saw as being a contributing factor to alienation from work. (Note, as indicated in Table 1, the high prestige position of the life guard, a very masculine job.)

The kitchen, called "The Inside" by the hasher, is his stronghold—within it he is in close association with other like-situated individuals. In the dining room, "The Outside," are "them," the girls. Interaction through the swinging doors might best be described as studied aloofness on the part of the girls and overt hostility on the part of the hashers. Orwell writes of the "double door between us (kitchen help and waiters) and the dining room" and contrasts the spontaneity of emotion, the relative relaxation, and the we-feeling of the kitchen with the controlled, tense, and guarded interaction with the customers. "It is an instructive sight," continues Orwell, "to see a waiter going into a hotel dining room. The set of his shoulders alters; all the dirt and hurry and irritation have dropped off

---

[17] W. F. Whyte, "The Social Structure of the Restaurant," *American Journal of Sociology* 54 (January 1949): 302–10.

[18] Ibid., pp. 305–07.

[19] Robert Blauner, *Work, Self, and Manhood: Some Reflections on Technology and Identity,* paper read at the annual meeting of the American Sociological Association, Montreal, Canada, September, 1964.

in an instant. He glides over the carpet, with a solemn priest-like air." [20] Scott describes a similar phenomenon in the paddock, the private world of the professional jockeys and handlers. According to Scott, when in the paddock with his peers, the jockey or the handler "can no longer fake his behavior . . . The paddock represents that point where ordinary vigilance in role deception cannot be sustained." [21] Becker's description of the deliberately maintained self-isolation of the dance-band musician provides an interesting parallel to the hasher's kitchen stronghold. Becker observes that "the musician is, as a rule, spatially isolated from the audience, being placed on a platform barrier that prevents any direct interaction. This isolation is welcomed because the audience, being made up of squares, is felt to be potentially dangerous . . . Musicians, lacking the usually provided physical barriers, often improvise their own and effectively segregate themselves from their audience." [22]

The hasher, of course, is not able to isolate himself from the "clients" as readily as the dance-band musician or even the professional waiter. He must interact with the girls in the sorority house, on the campus, and often in the classroom. Neither is he so obligated, on the other hand, to restrain himself from insulting the "clients." Though hashers are formally expected to be polite to the girls "no matter what," and though they are still bound by the "gentleman" expectation for college men, they often are not subtle in their demonstrations of displeasure with the girls.

The girls very often refer to the individual as "hasher," rather than by given name, and are quite free with orders and criticism. Any praise usually takes on a condescending tone—"nice hasher," "nice boy," and so on. The girl's view of the hasher in the subject sorority house is revealed by the fact that one of the initiation requirements for a pledge is that she sing a love song to a hasher while he sits on her lap. This is taken to be one of the iniation rites that "humbles the pledges." (Ironically, the hashers themselves use this as a kind of initation rite for entrance into their informal work group. That is, the newest hasher is the one who is made available to the pledge for the love song, and after he has been so used, he is told by his fellow hashers that he now knows "what working in the sorority is really like.")

The hashers seem to get much satisfaction from "getting the girls' goats." The kitchen often resounds with gleefully shared exclamations like "Boy, did I get *her* mad!" and "I sure told *her* off!" Spilling of food while serving, ignoring an order, sharp answers to criticism, and any other verbal aggression is rewarded with the plaudits of the other hashers—"That'll show them"; "That'll shape her up!" While in the kitchen the hashers will often deliberately make noises (loud talking, whistling, banging of pots and pans) with the intent of disturbing the girls. In the subject sorority, the hashers will save the food scraps from the preparation phase of the meal, and while the girls are eating will overload the

---

[20] Orwell, *Down and Out,* p. 86.

[21] Marvin B. Scott, "A Note on the Place of Truth," *Berkeley Journal of Sociology* 8 (June 1963): 38.

[22] Becker, "Dance Musician," p. 142.

garbage disposal unit and convulse with laughter as the mechanism emits loud and excruciating gurgles, whines, and crunches. "It's hard to tell," reported one chuckling hasher, "which garbage disposals sound the worst—the ones out in the dining room, or the one in the kitchen."

Orwell describes the kitchen personnel's disdain for the customer of the hotel restaurant—a disdain developed as a defense against the "superiority" of the customer. One waiter told Orwell that, "as a matter of pride, he had sometimes wrung a dirty dishcloth into the customer's soup before taking it in, just to be revenged upon a member of the bourgeoisie." [23] Another waiter scolded Orwell, "Fool! Why do you wash that plate? Wipe it on your trousers. Who cares about the customers? They don't know what's going on. What is restaurant work? You are carving a chicken and it falls on the floor. You apologize, you bow, you go out; and in five minutes you come back by another door—with the same chicken. That is restaurant work!" [24] So also is it hasher revenge. Besides the deliberate casualness toward dropped food and the amused "what they don't know won't hurt them" attitude, on numerous other occasions in the subject sorority minor assaults were made on foods to be served to the girls—e.g., a marble tossed into a gelatin and grape salad mold; a small amount of grass thrown in with cooking spinach ("for those cows"); each dinner roll "thrown around the bases" from one hasher to another before it was placed in the serving basket; a drop or two of blood from the cut finger of a hasher splashed into a pot of soup ("This ought to make those bloodsuckers happy!"); green food coloring added to the milk; salt shaker tops loosened so they would fall off in the girls' plates; etc. The actions themselves are, of course, less significant than the glee with which they are shared by the hashers who are "getting to the girls."

An extremely interesting phenomenon revealed by the participant observation (and confirmed in other than the subject sorority by interviews) is the nature of the derisive terms the hashers have for the girls. Almost always, the names have animal referents, and the animal is most often the pig—"Here they come, let's slop the troughs"; "Soueee" and "Oink-Oink" grumbled (on the kitchen side of the swinging door) as the hashers walk out of the kitchen to serve the food; "What do the pigs want now"; "Let's go clean out the feeding pens"; "Mush, you huskies!" The records contain a startling number of this kind of statement, as well as many other derogatory comments about the girl's manners, breeding, and femininity. It would appear that the hashers are projecting feelings of their own "low born" position upon the girls. It is almost as if they are saying, "See, we aren't so bad, look at those slobs out in the dining room!"

The physical appearance of the sorority girls is also called into question by the hashers. "They've all had their faces remolded, and they still can't get dates." "A guy would have to be pretty hard up to take out one of these dogs." "They must have an 'ugly requirement' in order to get into this sorority." The hasher lets his peers know that even if he *could* date one of the girls in the sorority,

---

[23] Orwell, *Down and Out*, p. 113.

[24] Ibid., p. 114.

he wouldn't. Thus is some modicum of control gained by the hasher over the emasculating "no dating" situation.

Within the kitchen, escape mechanisms of various sorts are everywhere apparent. Horseplay is the order of the day, with episodic food throwing and water splashing bouts, word fads, running "in group" jokes, and general zaniness. Of particular interest are the sets of activities which the hashers in the subject sorority house referred to as "bits." A "bit" is a relatively organized session of play-acting, originally arising spontaneously, and having a central theme and roles for each of the hashers. During the "bit" everything in the work setting, people, actions, and utensils, would be made a part of the scene, and the hashers would adopt the argot relevant to the situation enacted. For example, the "bit" for one work session staged the kitchen and dining room as a hell ship, with the hashers cast as the mutineers, the girls as "Powdered Pirates," and the cooks as "Ahab" and "Bligh." Knives became "harpoons," the dinner meat became "salt horse," going out into the dining room was "walking the plank," one abundantly endowed sorority sister became the "treasure chest," and so on. In another session the kitchen was part of the Third Reich, with cooks "Goebbels" and "Goering" sending the hasher "Pots and Pans Panzer Corps" out to face the girls, who were now cast as "Storm Troopers" and "Girdled Gestapo." Serving the food was making a "Blitzkrieg," chicken was a "Luftwaffe Loser," and "bravery under fire" while in the dining room was rewarded with lettuce leaf medals at an "awards ceremony." "Bits," if contagious enough, would go on for more than one work session or even more than one day. Often the same "bit" would be recurrent, returning for replay every few months and year after year (e.g., the science fiction or horror movie "bit," the gangster "bit," and the western hero-villain "bit").

It would appear that the "bit" serves a number of functions for the hashers. It is, not unlike the therapeutic applications of psychodrama and role playing, an opportunity for a more or less legitimized expression of hostility. It serves also as a distraction from the repetitive drudgery and potential boredom of the hasher's work tasks, allowing him, in effect, to be more creative and expressive while on the job. Furthermore, the "bit," while affecting the hashers' enactment of an interconnecting and interdependent set of fantasy roles, serves to tighten the cohesion of the informal work group. As one hasher said, not without pride, "When we've got our own laughs going for us, this job is no sweat." Lastly, it would seem that the hasher welcomes the relatively clearly defined and uncomplicated roles of the "bit." Even if the play-acting roles are acknowledged fancy and are ephemeral, they are less ambiguous, less conflict-ridden, and less distasteful than his actual work role.

Other forms of symbolic withdrawal from the hasher work situation are also common. In the subject sorority house, the threats to quit, to leave the field, ran about 20 per week. Rarely did any hasher go through the entire week without stating his intention to quit the next week. Each new work day brought with it a new challenge to "finish up faster than yesterday, and get the hell out of here."

In the kitchen, stories of the "I am a great lover" variety are daily bantered about by the hashers, expressed in a fashion that seems to insist "away from here,

I really do manipulate and dominate the coeds." Many joking references and comic routines concerning homosexuality are observed, the hashers themselves using a falsetto voice or feigning homosexual cheracteristics. The homosexual routine does, in fact, at times represent itself with the elaborateness of a "bit." Such behavior is often seen in social environments where the masculine role is perceived by males to be threatened. Elkin, for example, describes clinically the need for overt erotic expression manifest among members of Army barracks.[25] Zurcher describes the "salty language" and "sea stories" of sexual conquest among recruits isolated in the Naval Training center.[26] Following Blauner's lead mentioned above, it may be that the emphasis on sexual topics during the work sessions is an effective means whereby the hashers can put some of their sex role expectations back into the job.

On those nights when the girls bring male guests to the sorority house, the hashers are especially belligerent. Venomously, the hashers comment about the dates the girls have—"I wonder if she's paying him a flat fee, or by the hour." "God, she must have robbed a grave to get him!" On such occasions, the role conflict of the hasher is exacerbated, since he must wait on college *couples*. Some hashers flatly refuse to work at these times. Others will agree to work in the kitchen, but refuse to wait on table.

The conflicts and resultant reactions thus far reported are seen, as indicated by the interview material, to be typical of the hasher-in-sorority situation, though the degree of conflict and defense varies from house to house. The interview material also revealed that two hasher groups would enter intramural athletic contests as representatives of their sororities, but the remaining six groups steadfastly refused to do so. The key variable influencing the degree to which the hashers would thus agree to identify with the sorority appeared to be the degree of status differentation in the house—those with more rigid "class" lines, thus with a situation that emphasized the hasher-college man conflict, are not identified with and are not represented. The two sorority houses represented in intramural sports by their hasher groups are more informal and relaxed in hasher-member interaction.

It appears that the degree of social distance between hashers and members is less a function of the size of the house than a function of its relative status on the campus. The "loser" sororities apparently have greater need to maintain class lines within their houses than do the "top" sororities. This relationship was difficult to assess and is cautiously presented, considering the techniques used in this study and the fact that the work setting of the hasher is affected by other variables—e.g., the managerial styles of the house mothers and the cooks. The significant point is that, in *all* the houses considered here, there was evidence of some degree of social distance between the hashers and the girls, of hasher role conflict, and of the hashers' need to abate that conflict.

---

[25] H. Elkin, "Aggressive and Erotic Tendencies in Army Life," *The American Journal of Sociology* 51 (March 1946): 408–13.

[26] Louis A. Zurcher, "The Naval Recruit Training Center: A Study of Role Behavior in a Total Institution," *Sociological Inquiry* 37 (1967): 85–98.

Most of the sororities permit a yearly "turn-about" day, during which the girls wait on the hashers. Such role reversals are seen in other social groups that have a sharp status differential and restricted social interaction—e.g., Naval vessels (enlisted men take over the ship for a few hours when it crosses the Equator); [27] military academies (lower classmen are allowed to command the upper classmen for a day); [28] asylums and prisons (skits in which patients and inmates mimic the staff members).[29] Such behavior can be taken to be a clear indicator of the awareness of and resentment of status inferiority.

Conclusion

The role conflict experienced by the individual who must enact both the roles of hasher in a sorority and college man is seen to be accompanied by a pattern of defense mechanisms that serve to abate the conflict. The defense pattern consists of: (1) rationalization (the job is only temporary); (2) denial (reluctance to identify with the job); (3) projection (the girls are "low born"); (4) aggression (verbal and mitigated physical hostility toward the girls); (5) withdrawal (horseplay, general zaniness on the job, and threats to quit); (6) compensation (emphasis on discussions of sexual dominance). These defense mechanisms are, however, clearly seen to be expectations of the informal organization of the hasher group. Like the "Rate Buster" of Mayo,[30] a hasher who works too hard, who tries to please the girls, or who does not join in the horseplay is branded as a "brown noser," and suffers group ostracism. This seldom happens, though, since on the first day of his job as a hasher, the individual experiences role conflict, and has need of some means for resolution of that conflict. Thus he is quite willing, in fact, eager, to accept the defense system that has become institutionalized in the informal work group. By enactment of these behaviors he not only implements functional defenses, but he gains the security of membership in the informal organization.

In summary, then, the role of hasher in a sorority house demands that the incumbent behave in a manner inconsistent with the expectations for a college man. The individual who must enact both of these roles must resolve the dissonance in the best way he can. He is aided in this resolution by an institutionalized defense pattern which is part of the expectations of the hasher informal organization. Thus in this case of perpetuated role conflict, defense mechanisms, though they are implemented by individuals, are socially delimited by and within the conflict engendering social situation.

---

[27] Louis A. Zurcher, "The Sailor Aboard Ship: A Study of Role Behavior in a Total Institution," *Social Forces* 43 (March 1965): 389–400.

[28] Sanford Dornbusch, "The Military Academy as an Assimilating Institution," *Social Forces* 33 (May 1955): 316–21.

[29] E. Goffman, *Asylums* (New York: Doubleday & Co., 1961).

[30] F. J. Roethlisberger and William J. Dickson, *Management and the Worker* (New York: John Wiley & Sons, 1964), p. 522.

4

Small Group Ecology

ROBERT SOMMER

Many people found it amusing and others found it disgusting that at the beginning of the Paris Peace Talks weeks of debate were devoted to the shape of the negotiating table and the seating arrangements of the various conferees. Regardless of our personal response to that sequence of events, its very occurrence underscores the symbolic significance of spatial arrangements in face-to-face groups. Further, at a very intuitive level, each of us "knows" that the way people are arranged spatially influences the way they behave. The spatial arrangement that we find most effective for a committee meeting is not necessarily the one we find most effective at a party.

In the reading which follows, Sommer reviews some of the research evidence that has accumulated concerning the causes and consequences of different spatial configurations in small groups. Data indicate that in those instances where spatial arrangements are not predetermined, the ecological structures that develop are a function of such factors as group task, personal characteristics of group members, the degree of liking among members, and the amount and kind of space available. These resulting arrangements in turn affect the extent to which positions in the group become differentiated, the nature, extent and direction of communication among members, task effectiveness, and satisfaction with participation in the group.

The reader should be aware that because the overlap between the ecological and other structural characteristics of groups is so extensive, some of the findings reviewed by Sommer are open to a variety of interpretations.

Robert Sommer, "Small Group Ecology," *Psychological Bulletin* 67 (1967): 145–52.

Systematic study of spatial arrangements in face-to-face groups, or small group ecology as the field has been termed, is a comparatively recent development. Typically, the arrangement of people has been an incidental or background variable in psychological experimentation. The use of spatial arrangements as an independent variable in small group research can be traced to Steinzor (1950), who noted some unusual spatial effects while he was doing a study on other aspects of interaction. This pattern persists to the present, since at least half the published studies of small group arrangements involve the reanalysis of data collected for other purposes. Despite consistent and clear data, psychologists seem reluctant to make the arrangement of people a major independent variable. As Hall (1959) put it, "We treat space somewhat as we treat sex, it is there but we don't talk about it." Yet, enough studies, experimental as well as ex post facto, have accumulated to warrant some attempt to integrate the findings and indicate what directions further studies may profitably take.

This review focuses upon the arrangement of individuals in face-to-face groups. Studies of residential living units such as dormitories, housing developments, and communities are omitted. These phenomena require a different level of analysis (community or societal) than the relationship between individuals in face-to-face groups. The study of larger stable human aggregations has fallen to the fields of demography, human ecology, and geography. Because of space limitations, studies of crowding and density are excluded from consideration since these important topics deserve treatment in their own right. This study concentrates instead on two aspects of small group ecology—the way groups arrange themselves under various conditions, and the ways in which the resulting arrangements affect communication, productivity, and social relationships.

Leadership and Spatial Arrangements

Many of the concepts used in discussion of leadership, such as central figure, dominant position, upper echelon, and high status are based on spatial analogies. Studies of group dynamics and leadership have shown that concepts such as social distance, inner circle, and isolate have some geographic reference but there is no simple isomorphism between psychological and geographic concepts. While investigating discussion groups, Steinzor noticed a participant changing his seat in order to sit opposite another person with whom he had recently had a verbal altercation. In an ex post facto design using data already collected, Steinzor found that when one person stopped speaking, someone opposite rather than alongside was next to speak, an effect he attributed to the greater physical and expressive value a person has for those opposite him in a circle. Following this, Bass and Klubeck (1952) reanalyzed their discussion group data to determine if leadership ratings varied as a function of location in an inverted V or a parallel row arrangement. Although they found that persons occupying end positions attained higher status than people in middle seats, there were so many confounding factors, including a nonrandom selection of seats by people of different status levels, that their results were equivocal. Hearn (1957) reanalyzed small group data collected for other purposes and found that leadership style had a significant influence on what was termed the "Steinzor effect." With minimal leadership, members of a discussion group would direct more comments to people sitting opposite than people adjacent; when a strong leader was present, people directed more comments to adjacent seats than to people opposite; and when direction of the group was shared equally among the members, no spatial effect appeared. These results may be explained in terms of eye contact. Since it is impermissible to look directly at a dominant individual at close quarters, the individual restricts his gaze to his immediate neighbors when a strong leader is close by. Steinzor's expressive contact hypothesis has been further refined by Argyle and Dean (1965), who studied the connection between eye contact, distance, and affiliation. A one-way mirror was used to chart interaction between a naïve subject and a confederate who gazed continually at the subject. There was less eye contact and glances were shorter when the people were close together, and this effect was most pronounced for mixed-sex pairs. The authors believed that eye contact is a component of intimacy, which is governed by both approach and avoidance forces kept in a state of equilibrium during any given encounter. When this equilibrium is disturbed by increasing physical proximity or decreasing eye contact, there are compensatory changes along the other dimensions.

Communication flow as a function of spatial relationship was emphasized by Leavitt (1951), who continued the work of Bavelas (1950). Leavitt used groups of five subjects each who were seated at a table but separated from one another by vertical partitions. Channels of communication could be changed by manipulating slots in the partitions. Group leadership was closely correlated with a member's position in the communication net. Centrally located individuals enjoyed the task most and those in the peripheral position enjoyed it least. Howells and Becker (1962) hypothesized that people who received greater numbers of messages would be more likely to be designated leaders than people who received fewer messages. They arranged groups of five subjects around small rectangular tables with three people on one side, two on the other. The results confirmed their predictions that more leaders than would be expected by chance would emerge from the two-man side of the table.

The studies described thus far have involved *relational* space, or the way people orient themselves toward one another. A second line of research has emphasized the cultural import of various fixed locations. In studies of leadership, the head chair at the table has a special significance. Sommer (1959) found that leaders in small discussion groups gravitated to the head position at rectangular tables. Strodtbeck and Hook (1961) reanalyzed data from experimental jury deliberations and found that people at end positions participated more and were rated as having greater influence on the decision process than people at the sides. It was also found that jurors from the managerial and professional classes selected the head chair more than did individuals of lower status. Hare and Bales (1963) did not work with leadership per se, but rather with dominance as measured by a paper-and-pencil personality test. Reanalyzing the data collected by Bales and his associates from five-man discussion groups, they found that subjects high on dominance tended to choose the central seats and do the most talking. Felipe (1966) used the semantic differential to assess dyadic seating arrangements along these dimensions: intimate-unacquainted, hostile-friendly, talkative-untalkative, and unequal-equal. The cultural influence of the head position was evident on the equality dimension—if one member of a pair was at the head of the table, this pair was rated significantly less equal than if members were both at ends of the table or only at the sides.

A weakness of all these studies is the limited range of cultures and populations sampled, almost all taking place in the United States. This would not be a serious limitation except that Hall indicated that leaders in other parts of the world use space differently. An equally serious problem concerns the confounding of location, status, and personality. All studies agreed that choice of seats is nonrandom with respect to status and personality. High status, dominant individuals in American culture gravitate to the head position, and people who occupy the head position participate more than people at the side positions (Strodtbeck & Hook, 1961), but there is no way to disentangle status from location in these studies. It is possible that occupancy of certain locations automatically raises an individual's status and/or dominance. On the other hand, it may be that dominant individuals choose these locations for reasons of tradition and would participate more wherever they sat, and thus their location has no essential connection with their participation. It may be that high status people tend to participate more *and* certain locations also increase participation, but the combination of the two results in greater participation than either by itself. The only way to disentangle these variables is to conduct experiments in which people are assigned randomly to various locations and their relative contributions noted. It must be recognized that these conditions are highly artificial in a society that typically allocates space according to status considerations. From the standpoint of designing experiments in natural settings, the policies of random assignments of location are not always adhered to in practice. In the prison camp studied by Grusky (1959), inmate leaders received the most desirable job assignments as well as the bottom bunks (which were status symbols in the dormitories) despite the official policy of random bed assignment. It is likely that the same pressures responsible for the connection between status and location operate against any assignment scheme in conflict with accepted spatial norms.

Task and Location

The quest for effective spatial arrangements in working units such as relay assembly teams, seminars, and buzz groups has been a subject of considerable concern to applied psychologists. Textbooks of group dynamics recommend horseshoe or semicircular rather than straight-row arrangements for discussion groups and classrooms, rectangular tables have been criticized for fostering authoritarian leadership, and the improper location of individuals has been blamed for the failure of the working teams. Intuitively it would seem that the proper arrangement of people would increase production, smooth the flow of communication, and reduce the "friction of space," but the data are largely of the anecdotal variety. Perhaps more convincing data lie buried somewhere in applied psychology or human engineering journals and, if so, a valuable service could be rendered by bringing them to light.

Several recent studies have explored the connection between spatial arrangement and group task. Sommer (1965) and Norum (1966) studied the arrangement of conversing, competing, coacting, and cooperating individuals. At a rectangular table, cooperating pairs sat side-by-side, conversing pairs sat corner-to-corner, and competing pairs sat across from one another, while coacting individuals sat in distant arrangements. In a separate study of cooperative and competitive working conditions using a like-sex decoy, the subjects sat opposite the decoy in the competitive condition and on the same side of the table in the cooperative condition.

The extent to which similar attitudes produce greater physical proximity remains in some dispute. Little, Ulehla, and Henderson (1965), using silhouette figures, found that pairs reputed to be Goldwater supporters were placed closer together than Goldwater-Johnson pairs, but the effect did not occur with Johnson-Johnson pairs. However, Elkin (1964), using actual discussion groups involving pro-pro, pro-anti, and anti-anti Medicare pairs of college students, found no differences in seating between concordant and discordant pairs. It is possible that the intensity of the discussion and the interest shown by each of the participants influences proximity more than attitude concordance or discordance.

Several psychiatrists and clinical psychologists have written speculative articles on the significance of various spatial arrangements in psychotherapy. Goodman (1959) made an intriguing comparison between the Freudian use of the couch, Sullivan's cross-the-table therapy, and the spatial freedom of the Gestalt therapists. Wilmer (1958), Winick and Holt (1961), and Horowitz (1965) all discussed seating position from the standpoint of nonverbal communication in group psychotherapy.

Individual Distance

The term individual distance was first used by Burkhardt (1944) to refer to the spacing that animals maintain between themselves and others of the same species. Several studies have been directed toward the question of how close people come to one another and to physical objects. Hall (1959) developed a detailed schema for conversational distance under various conditions of social and psychological closeness which ranged from 3–6 inches for soft intimate whispers to 8–20 feet for talking across the room in a loud voice. It is also likely that noise, bustle, or threat brings people together. To measure conversational distance, Sommer (1961) sent pairs into a large lounge where they could sit either side-by-side or across from one another to discuss designated topics. On the basis of previous work, it was assumed that people would sit across from one another rather than side-by-side unless the distance across was too great. It was found that the upper limit for comfortable conversation *under these specified conditions* was approximately 5.5 feet between individuals. A subsequent study used four chairs instead of couches so that the distance side-by-side as well as the distance across could be varied. Again the 5.5-foot conversational distance prevailed. However, a cursory examination of conversational distance in private homes revealed a much greater conversational range than this, something like 8–10 feet between chairs.

Other investigators have used paper-and-pencil or projective tests to study individual distance. Kuethe (1962, 1964) instructed students to pin yellow felt figures (a woman, man, child, dog, rectangles of various sizes) on a blue felt background in various combinations. Kuethe found that the woman and the child were placed closer together than the man and the child, while the dog was typically placed closer to the man than the woman. In all conditions, the people were placed closer together than the rectangles. Little (1965) used line drawings of males and females to examine concepts of individual distance. It was found that the degree of prior acquaintance attributed to cardboard figures influenced the distance they were placed apart. A replication using silhouettes and another using live actresses who were posed by the subject in scenes involving different activities also showed that the distance apart which the figures were placed was a function of the closeness of the relationship between them.

Horowitz, Duff, and Stratton (1964) investigated individual distance among schizophrenic and nonschizophrenic mental patients. Each subject was instructed to walk over to either another person or a hatrack, and the distance between his goal and his stopping place was measured. It was found that both groups approached the hatrack closer than they approached a person. Each subject tended to have a characteristic individual distance which was shorter for inanimate objects than for people. McBride, King, and James (1965) did a similar study testing GSR to varying amounts of closeness between subject and male or female experimenters. It was considered that GSR effects would provide an indication of the level of arousal associated with the proximity of neighbors. The authors found that GSR was greatest (skin resistance was least) when the subject was approached frontally, while a side approach yielded a greater response than a rear approach. The response to experimenters of the same sex was less than to experimenters of the opposite sex. Being touched by an object produced less of a GSR than being touched by a person. Argyle and Dean (1965) invited the subjects to participate in a perceptual experiment in which they were to "stand as close as comfortable to see well" to a book, a plaster head, and a cutout life-sized photograph of the senior author with his eyes closed and another with his eyes open. Among other results, the subjects placed themselves closer to the eyes-closed photograph than the eyes-open photograph.

Systematic violation of individual distance was undertaken by Garfinkel (1964) and Felipe and Sommer (1966). Garfinkel reported that the violation of individual distance produced avoidance, bewilderment, and embarrassment, and that these effects were most pronounced among males. Felipe and Sommer systematically staged invasion sequences under natural conditions (people seated on benches and at library tables) and demonstrated observable flight reactions. Two recent studies have dealt with the relationship between individual distance and personality variables. Williams (1963) showed that introverts placed themselves farther from other people than did extroverts. The same conclusion was reached by Leipold (1963), who noted the chair a person occupied vis-à-vis a seated decoy under anxiety and praise conditions. There was greater closeness under the praise than the anxiety conditions, and extroverts placed themselves closer to the decoy than introverts.

Sex differences in spacing have been found on a number of occasions, but the number of cultures sampled is limited. Several investigators (Elkin, 1964; Norum, 1966; Sommer, 1959) have found that females make more use of the side-by-side arrangement than do males. Side-by-side seating, which is generally considered to be the most intimate of all seating arrangements for people already acquainted, is comparatively rare among males if they are given the opportunity to sit across from one another. The idea that females can tolerate closer physical presence than males is underscored by observations of women holding hands or kissing one another, practices which are uncommon between males in this culture.

Campbell, Kruskal, and Wallace (1966) used seating arrangements of Negroes and whites as an index of attitude in three Chicago colleges. Clustering of Negroes and whites was found to be associated with differences in ethnic attitudes in the three schools. These authors and Strodtbeck and Hook (1951) attempted to develop appropriate statistical techniques for analyzing aggregation data. Tabulating the results of a single observation involving a large number of individuals whose behavior at times relates to one another and at times to aspects of the physical environment is no small achievement, but when one assembles the records of repeated osbervations of individuals, some observed many times and some just one, the difficulties multiply. It is fortunate that animal ecologists and zoologists have encountered these problems over the years and have developed useful methods for measuring aggregation, dispersion, home range, and social distance. McBride (1964) has developed computer programs to assess the degreee of nonrandomness within an aggregation. Esser (1965), working on a closed research ward of a mental hospital with the available area divided into squares so that the location of each patient can be charted during the entire working day, has obtained detailed records of individual spatial behavior similar to those of the better tracking studies by animal biologists, but he has not yet reached the same level of precision in relating the individual patient's locations one to another. The problems in analyzing the interdependency between a large number of individuals with $n(n-1)$ dyadic relationships has led some investigators to use physical aspects of the environment such as walls, partitions, and chairs as coordinates for locating individuals. A new approach (Bechtel & Srivastava, 1966) is the development of the Hodometer, an electronic recording device placed on the floor of a building to measure use of given areas as well as pathways. A much cruder index of area usage was suggested by Webb, Campbell, Schwartz, and Sechrest (1966), who examined the wear on floor tiles in front of different museum exhibits.

Discussion

Knowledge of how groups arrange themselves can assist in fostering or discouraging group relationships. A library which is intended to be *sociofugal space* (Osmond, 1957), aimed at discouraging interaction, requires knowledge of how to arrange people to minimize unwanted contact. It may be possible to use the rank order of preferred arrangements by interacting groups as arrangements *to be avoided* in sociofugal space. On this basis, corner-to-corner seating would be less satisfactory than opposite or distant seating in a sociofugal setting. An Emily Post or Amy Vanderbilt may know these principles intuitively, and diplomatic protocol may codify them, but there is value in making them explicit and subjecting them to empirical test. To an increasingly greater extent we find ourselves being arranged by impersonal environments in lecture halls, airports, waiting rooms, and lobbies. Many aspects of the proximate environment, including furniture and room dividers, have been placed for ease of maintenance and efficient cleaning with little cognizance to their social functions. These principles will be of most help in institutional settings such as schools, hospitals, public buildings, and old folks' homes where the occupants have little control over their surroundings. The straight-row arrangement of most classrooms has been taken for granted for too long. The typical long narrow shape of a classroom resulted from a desire to get light across the room. The front of each room was determined by window location, since pupils had to be seated so that window light came over the left shoulder. However, new developments in lighting, acoustics, ventilation, and fireproofing have rendered invalid many of the arguments for the boxlike room with straight rows. In mental hospitals, the isolation of schizophrenic individuals can be furthered by sociofugal settings which minimize social contact, or reduced through sociopetal buildings aimed at reinforcing social behavior. The former approach is valid if one wants to provide an optimal environment in terms of the individual's present needs, the latter if society desires to shape the patient's social behavior to facilitate his return to society. It is mindless to design mental hospitals without taking cognizance of the connection between physical environment and social behavior. The study of small group ecology is important not only from the standpoint of developing an adequate theory of relationships that takes into account the context of social relationships, but also from the practical standpoint of designing and maintaining functional contexts in which human relationships can develop.

Several problems of method must be resolved before a relevant theory of group ecology can be developed. Having reviewed the studies themselves, problems in recording and some special characteristics of the setting in which the studies have taken place should be mentioned. The studies described have generally tabulated gross categories of behavior without any real specificity or precision. A person's location has been plotted as if this described his orientation, head angle, arm position, etc. Stated another way the investigators whose work has been described here have relied almost exclusively on the eyeball technique of recording. Some, such as Esser and McBride, are moving into the electronic processing of observational data but the improved precision is in data analysis rather than the integration of various facets of spatial behavior. Very little use has been made of photographic recordings. One would hardly undertake the study of comparative linguistics without a tape recorder, but only a handful of investigators whose work we have discussed have used still photographs much less moving pictures. Twenty-five years ago, Efron (1941) hired a professional artist to sketch conversing groups. A few anthropologists, such as Birdwistell and Hall, are currently accumulating film libraries of interaction data. McBride found it necessary to photograph aggregations of fowl from small towers above the coops. It is difficult to get good photographs of the spatial arrangements of people from the horizontal plane, particularly if there are more than two individuals involved. Yet, it seems likely that the real breakthroughs in this field will occur when methods for monitoring angle of orientation eye contact, and various other nonverbal cues are developed for use in standard interaction situations. The arguments for and against laboratory studies of group behavior which involve one-way mirrors, microphones, and hidden photographic equipment compared to field studies in playgrounds, schools, and city streets will not be reviewed here. However a promising solution is the field-laboratory method used by Sherif (1954) in his camp studies where he employed a standard controlled situation, in the sense that relevant variables were specified in advance and introduced in specified ways by the experimenter but always under conditions that appeared natural and appropriate to the subjects. Another limiting element in the work to date is that almost all the studies have involved discussion groups around tables and chairs. We know little about the ecology of working groups (apart from sociometric data) or co-acting individuals, particularly if they are standing or moving. Again, the technical problems of recording interaction patterns of moving individuals are much greater than if the individuals are seated in a classroom or around a conference table.

Along with this is a disproportionate number of environmental studies that have taken place under conditions of confinement, particularly in mental hospitals. At this time there are at least seven studies underway on the use of space by mental patients. As far as the writer knows, this exceeds the number of current studies of spatial behavior of nonhospitalized individuals. Mental hospital studies allow greater control and environmental manipulation than can be achieved outside a total institution, but they also confound the effects of schizophrenia and institutionalization as a social process over time with the effects of captivity and locked doors as spatial variables.

REFERENCES

Argyle, M., & Dean, J. 1965. Eye contact, distance, and affiliation. *Sociometry* 28: 289–304.

Bass, B. M., & Klubeck, S. 1952. Effects of seating arrangements on leaderless group discussions. *Journal of Abnormal and Social Psychology* 47: 724–27.

Bavelas, A. 1950. Communication processes in task-oriented groups. *Journal of the Acoustical Society of America* 22: 725–30.

Bechtel, R. B., & Srivastava, R. 1966. Human movement and architectural environment. *Milieu* 2: 7–8.

Burckhardt, D. 1944. Mowenbeobachtungen in Basel. *Ornithologische Beobachter* 5: 49–76.

Campbell, D. T., Kruskal, W. H., & Wallace, W. P. 1966. Seating aggregation as an index of attitude. *Sociometry* 29: 1–15.

Efron, D. 1941. *Gesture and environment.* New York: Kings Crown Press.

Elkin, L. 1964. The behavioral use of space. Unpublished master's thesis, University of Saskatchewan.

Esser, A., et al. 1965. Territoriality of patients on a research ward. In, *Recent advances in biological psychiatry.* Vol. 7. New York: Plenum Press.

Filipe, N. 1966. Interpersonal distance and small group interaction. *Cornell Journal of Social Relations* 1: 59–64.

———, & Sommer, R. 1967. Invasions of personal space. *Social Problems* 14: 206–14.

Garfinkel, H. 1964. Studies of the routine grounds of everyday activities. *Social Problems* 11: 225–50.

Goodman, P. 1959. Meaning of functionalism. *Journal of Architectural Education* 14: 32–38.

Grusky, O. 1959. Organization goals and the behavior of informal leaders. *American Journal of Sociology* 65: 59–67.

Hall, E. T. 1959. *The silent language.* Garden City, N. Y.: Doubleday.

Hare, A. P., & Bales, R. F. 1963. Seating position and small group interaction. *Sociometry* 26: 480–86.

Hearn, G. 1957. Leadership and the spatial factor in small groups. *Journal of Abnormal and Social Psychology* 54: 269–72.

Horowitz, M. J. 1965. Human spatial behavior. *American Journal of Psychotherapy* 19: 20–28.

———, Duff, D. F., & Stratton, L. O. 1964. Body-buffer zone. *Archives of General Psychiatry* 11: 651–56.

Howells, L. T., & Becker, S. W. 1962. Seating arrangement and leadership emergence. *Journal of Abnormal and Social Psychology* 64: 148–50.

Kuethe, J. L. 1962. Social schemas. *Journal of Abnormal and Social Psychology* 64: 31–38.

———. 1964. Pervasive influence of social schemata. *Journal of Abnormal and Social Psychology* 68: 248–54.

Leavitt, H. J. 1951. Some effects of certain communication patterns in group performance. *Journal of Abnormal and Social Psychology* 46: 38–50.

Leipold, W. D. 1963. Psychological distance in a dyadic interview. Unpublished doctoral dissertation, University of North Dakota.

Little, K. B. 1965. Personal space. *Journal of Experimental Social Psychology* 1: 237–47.

———, Ulehla, J., & Henderson, C. 1965. Value homophily and interaction distance. Unpublished manuscript, University of Denver.

McBride, G. 1964. *A general theory of social organization and behaviour.* St. Lucia: University of Queensland Press.

———, King, M. G., & James, J. W. 1965. Social proximity effects on GSR in adult humans. *Journal of Psychology* 61: 153–57.

Norum, G. A. 1966. Perceived interpersonal relationships and spatial arrangements. Unpublished master's thesis, University of California, Davis.

Osmond, H. 1957. Function as a basis of psychiatric ward design. *Mental Hospitals* 8: 23–29.

Sherif, M. 1954. Integrating field work and laboratory in small group research. *American Sociological Review* 19: 759–71.

Sommer, R. 1959. Studies in personal space. *Sociometry* 22: 247–60.

———, 1961. Leadership and group geography. *Sociometry* 24: 99–110.

———, 1965. Further studies in small group ecology. *Sociometry* 28: 337–48.

Steinzor, B. 1950. The spatial factor in face to face discussion groups. *Journal of Abnormal and Social Psychology* 45: 552–55.

Strodtbeck, F. L., & Hook, L. H. 1961. The social dimensions of a twelve man jury table. *Sociometry* 24: 397–415.

Webb, E. J., Campbell, D. T. Schwartz, R. D., & Sechrest, L. 1966. *Unobtrusive measures: Nonreactive research in the social sciences.* Chicago: Rand McNally.

Williams, J. L. 1963. Personal space and its relation to extroversion-introversion. Unpublished master's thesis, University of Alberta.

Wilmer, H. A. 1958. Graphic ways of representing some aspects of a therapeutic community. In, *Symposium of preventive and social psychiatry.* Washington, D. C.: United States Government Printing Office.

Winnick, C., & Holt, H. 1961. Seating position as nonverbal communication in group analysis. *Psychiatry* 24: 171–82.

Group Structure:

Putting It into Perspective

The foregoing selections are merely indicative of the phenomena that social psychologists study under the rubric of "group structure." Actually, group structure is an inclusive term encompassing a range of phenomena such as the organization of positions (statuses) within a group and the varying expectations attached to them (roles), affective ties among members of a group, patterns of communication, and many more.

The social psychologist's interest in group structure is not simply descriptive, even though structural description may play an important part in his research activities. Instead, he is interested in structural variables as causal factors in human behavior. One does not have to observe social interaction long to realize that the nature of the relations among people is a function of more than the personal characteristics which the individuals bring with them to the situation. For example, one could not deduce the patterns of interaction that occur in a classroom from a knowledge of the personal characteristics of the students and teacher. He could, however, predict that the patterns of interaction that he would observe as he moved from one classroom to another would be very similar.

A number of structural factors contribute to this behavioral regularity. If one were to ask a group of students and a group of teachers to state their behavioral expectations of students vis-à-vis teachers and teachers vis-à-vis students, he would discover considerable agreement. Thus, much of the behavioral regularity observed in classrooms is a function of students and teachers responding to shared expectations regarding the behavior of people in different positions in the group. In social psychological terms, status and role considerations exert considerable influence on classroom behavior.

To appreciate the significance of status and role considerations for social interaction, we need only recall some instance in which we were "forced" to interact with another person without having any prior information about him. The early moments of such an initial encounter tend to be rather tense and to be characterized by a search for cues that would enable us to place him structurally. For example, we look at the way he is dressed, we scrutinize his diction, we estimate his age and, of course, are immediately sensitive to his sex, then we begin our verbal probes. What do you do? Where are you from? With these bits and pieces of information in hand, we then proceed to organize them in some fashion so that we can behave toward him as one in his position would expect one in our position to behave. Of course, in the meantime this stranger will be going through the same process. After all, he won't want to embarrass himself either.

In addition to their interest in the status structure of groups, social psychologists frequently focus on the affect structure, i.e., the patterns of interpersonal preference that emerge within groups. Whether one is studying a social fraternity or a community's physicians, he could probably identify a *pattern* of interpersonal preference among his subjects. Why is the social psychologist interested in who likes whom? He is interested in exploring the possible causal connections between interpersonal preference patterns and other behaviors.

Research evidence suggests that "liking" has consequences for a broad range of behaviors. For example, whether or not a physician will adopt a new drug has been demonstrated to be influenced significantly by the physician's friendship ties. In experimental task groups, liking influences group cohesion and, hence, group productivity and satisfaction. The precise nature of the relationships among those variables tends to be rather complex, but the affect structure of the group appears as a significant causal variable.

In those groups where there is a distinct status structure, there is generally a communication structure tied inextricably to it. In a large-scale organization, who communicates with whom is likely to be institutionalized. Anyone familiar with the military knows what is means to "go through channels." Even in small groups where status distinctions exist, the frequency, direction, and content of communication tends to be patterned and is influenced by one's position in the group. For example, higher status members initiate more communications, receive more communications, and devote more communications to giving information and expressing opinions than do lower status members.

In initially unstructured groups, the nature of the communication patterns that emerge has been found to vary according to the size of the group and the physical arrangement of members. A consistent finding in the study of communication patterns is that members differ in their rate of participation. When rates of participation are examined conjointly with group size, it is generally observed that the difference in the participation rate of the most active versus the least active member is greater as the size of the group gets larger. In other words, other things being equal, the larger the group, the more the activity tends to be dominated by a few members.

The study of group geography as it relates to communication structure has typically focused on the consequences of different physical arrangements for the content of information that is communicated, the efficiency with which communication can occur, the effectiveness with which the information possessed by the various members can be tapped, etc.

Except in those cases where group members are provided explicit information regarding appropriate channels of communication, a common assumption which members make is that their physical arrangement is a reflection of implicit expectations. For example, if a person walks into a meeting room in which there is a lectern located at the front with rows of chairs in front of and facing the lectern, his interpretation is likely to be that in this group it is expected that most of the communication will flow from, to, or through the person who stands behind the lectern. On the other hand, if the room were furnished with chairs placed about a round table, a very different interpretation would probably be rendered. When research evidence indicates that the person who occupies the chair at the head of the table in a jury room typically speaks first, is more frequently elected jury foreman, and participates disproportionately in the deliberations, the symbolic significance of group geography for communication, and hence, leadership and power, cannot be ignored.

It should be evident from the foregoing remarks that the different aspects of group structure tend to be highly interrelated. For example, status impinges upon affect so that interpersonal preferences tend to cluster within status levels. In groups with existing status structures, higher status members tend to initiate more communicative acts than do lower status members; on the other hand, in groups where the structure has not yet formed, those members who initiate more communicative acts tend to emerge as leaders (high status persons).

The student who is especially interested in pursuing some of these "group structure" topics should find the *Suggestions for Further Reading* quite helpful.

Suggestions for Further Reading

B. J. Biddle and E. J. Thomas, editors, *Role Theory: Concepts and Research.* New York: Wiley, 1966. Still the best single source available on role theory and research. While it is a book of readings, its organization is excellent.

B. E. Collins and B. H. Raven, "Group Structure: Attraction, Coalitions, Communication, and Power." Pp. 102–204 in G. Lindzey and E. Aronson, editors, *The Handbook of Social Psychology,* Second Edition, Volume 4. Reading, Massachusetts: Addison-Wesley, 1969. A review and analysis of specific group structures.

W. E. Moore, "Social Structure and Behavior." Pp. 283–322 in G. Lindzey and E. Aronson, editors, *The Handbook of Social Psychology,* Second Edition, Volume 4. Reading, Massachusetts: Addison-Wesley, 1969. An examination of some of the behavioral consequences of the structural characteristics of social relationships.

Marvin E. Shaw, *Group Dynamics: The Psychology of Small Group Behavior.* New York: McGraw-Hill, 1971. A systematic introduction to the study of small groups. Contains chapters dealing with structural characteristics of small groups and their consequences for group functioning.

Robert Sommer, *Personal Space.* Englewood Cliffs, New Jersey: Prentice-Hall, 1969. A highly readable book that students will find both intriguing and disturbing. It is intriguing to consider the extent to which behavior is affected by physical structures, but it is disturbing to discover that more is known about the spatial requirements of animals than for men.

CHAPTER II

Social Influence Processes

5 Thomas Scheff, *Negotiating Reality: Notes on Power in the Assessment of Responsibility* · 55

6 Stanley Milgram, *Some Conditions of Obedience and Disobedience to Authority* · 73

7 Jonathan L. Freedman and Scott C. Fraser, *Compliance Without Pressure: The Foot-in-the-door Technique* · 94

8 J. M. Darley and Bibb Latané, *Bystander Intervention in Emergencies: Diffusion of Responsibility* · 107

9 James H. Bryan and Mary Ann Test, *Models and Helping: Naturalistic Studies in Aiding Behavior* · 119

Putting It into Perspective · 131
Suggestions for Further Reading · 133

5

Negotiating Reality: Notes on Power in the Assessment of Responsibility

THOMAS SCHEFF

Before interaction can proceed smoothly, interactants must arrive at a "working consensus" on what sort of behavior is appropriate for each party. Said another way, the interactants must mutually define their relationship.

When people come together for the first time, the first thing they do is to try to "locate" one another with regard to social networks and thereby determine their respective identities. This is done by exchanging information about one another. They may volunteer information about themselves, ask questions about the others, and answer questions directed to them.

The exchange of information is by no means indiscriminate—it is highly selective. Whether consciously or not, the interactants know that the exchange of information in an initial encounter has significant implications for their emerging relationship. So, each party attempts to bias the flow of information in order to place himself in what he regards as a favorable position. In a very real sense, then, we may speak of the process of arriving at mutual behavioral expectations as a negotiation process.

We do not always enter such negotiations with an equal chance of coming out on top. For example, when we enter an encounter with someone with authority over us, we are at a disadvantage on two counts. First, as soon as our subordinate status is disclosed we are by definition "one down." But, we are also at a disadvantage in further negotiations because we must cede a good deal of control over the flow of information. Generally, the person with authority asks most of the questions, determines the topic of conversation, and sets the tone of the exchange.

In the following paper, Thomas Scheff specifies in greater detail the implications of a power differential between interactants for their identity

Thomas Scheff, "Negotiating Reality: Notes on Power in the Assessment of Responsibility," *Social Problems* 16 (1968): 3–17.

negotiations. The paper is not a report of empirical research. Rather, it is a thought-provoking piece intended to generate research. As illustrative data, the author employs (1) a transcript of an initial psychiatrist-patient interview, and (2) an excerpt of an attorney-client dialogue from a famous novel.

The use of interrogation to reconstruct parts of an individual's past history is a common occurrence in human affairs. Reporters, jealous lovers, and policemen on the beat are often faced with the task of determining events in another person's life, and the extent to which he was responsible for those events. The most dramatic use of interrogation to determine responsibility is in criminal trials. As in everyday life, criminal trials are concerned with both act and intent. Courts, in most cases, first determine whether the defendant performed a legally forbidden act. If it is found that he did so, the court then must decide whether he was "responsible" for the act. Reconstructive work of this type goes on less dramatically in a wide variety of other settings, as well. The social worker determining a client's eligibility for unemployment compensation, for example, seeks not only to establish that the client actually is unemployed, but that he has actively sought employment, i.e., that he himself is not responsible for being out of work.

This paper will contrast two perspectives on the process of reconstructing past events for the purpose of fixing responsibility. The first perspective stems from the common sense notion that interrogation, when it is sufficiently skillful, is essentially neutral. Responsibility for past actions can be fixed absolutely and independently of the method of reconstruction. This perspective is held by the typical member of society, engaged in his day-to-day tasks. It is also held, in varying degrees, by most professional interrogators. The basic working doctrine is one of *absolute* responsibility. This point of view actually entails the comparison of two different kinds of items: first, the fixing of actions and intentions, and secondly, comparing these actions and intentions to some predetermined criteria of responsibility. The basic premise of the doctrine of absolute responsibility is that both actions and intentions, on the one hand, and the criteria of responsibility, on the other, are absolute, in that they can be assessed independently of social context.[1]

[1] The doctrine of absolute responsibility is clearly illustrated in psychiatric and legal discussions of the issue of "criminal responsibility," i.e., the use of mental illness as an excuse from criminal conviction. An example of the assumption of absolute criteria of responsibility is found in the following quotation, "The finding that someone is criminally responsible means to the psychiatrist that the criminal must change his behavior before he can resume his position in society. *This injunction is dictated not by morality, but, so to speak, by reality.*" See Edward J. Sachar, "Behavioral Science and Criminal Law," *Scientific American* 209 (1963): 39–45 (emphasis added).

An alternative approach follows from the sociology of knowledge. From this point of view, the reality within which members of society conduct their lives is largely of their own construction.[2] Since much of reality is a construction, there may be multiple realities, existing side by side, in harmony or in competition. It follows, if one maintains this stance, that the assessment of responsibility involves the construction of reality by members; construction both of actions and intentions, on the one hand, and of criteria of responsibility, on the other. The former process, the continuous reconstruction of the normative order, has long been the focus of sociological concern.[3] The discussion in this paper will be limited, for the most part, to the former process, the way in which actions and intentions are constructed in the act of assessing responsibility.

My purpose is to argue that responsibility is at least partly a product of social structure. The alternative to the doctrine of absolute responsibility is that of relative responsibility: the assessment of responsibility always includes a process of negotiation. In this process, responsibility is in part constructed by the negotiating parties. To illustrate this thesis, excerpts from two dialogues of negotiation will be discussed: a real psychotherapeutic interview, and an interview between a defense attorney and his client, taken from a work of fiction. Before presenting these excerpts it will be useful to review some prior discussions of negotiation, the first in courts of law, the second in medical diagnosis.[4]

The negotiation of pleas in criminal courts, sometimes referred to as "bargain justice," has been frequently noted by observers of legal processes.[5] The defense attorney, or (in many cases, apparently) the defendant himself, strikes a bargain with the prosecutor—a plea of guilty will be made, provided that the prosecutor will reduce the charge. For example, a defendant arrested on suspicion of armed robbery may arrange to plead guilty to the charge of unarmed robbery. The prosecutor obtains ease of conviction from the bargain, the defendant, leniency.

Although no explicit estimates are given, it appears from observers' reports that the great majority of criminal convictions are negotiated. Newman states:

> A major characteristic of criminal justice administration, particularly in jurisdictions characterized by legislatively fixed sentences, is charge reduction to elicit pleas of guilty. Not only does the efficient functioning of criminal justice rest upon a high proportion of guilty pleas, but plea bargaining is closely linked with attempts to individualize justice, to obtain certain desirable conviction consequences, and to avoid undesirable ones such as "undeserved" mandatory sentences.[6]

---

[2] *Cf.* Peter L. Berger and Thomas Luckmann, *The Social Construction of Reality: A Treatise in the Sociology of Knowledge* (New York: Doubleday, 1966).

[3] The classic treatment of this issue is found in E. Durkheim, *The Elementary Forms of the Religious Life.*

[4] A sociological application of the concept of negotiation, in a different context, is found in Anselm Strauss, *et al.,* "The Hospital and its Negotiated Order," in Eliot Freidson, ed., *The Hospital in Modern Society* (New York: Free Press, 1963), pp. 147–69.

[5] Newman reports a study in this area, together with a review of earlier work, in "The Negotiated Plea," Part III of Donald J. Newman, *Conviction: The Determination of Guilt or Innocence Without Trial* (Boston: Little, Brown, 1966), pp. 76–130.

[6] Ibid., p. 76.

It would appear that the bargaining process is accepted as routine. In the three jurisdictions Newman studied, there were certain meeting places where the defendant, his client, and a representative of the prosecutor's office routinely met to negotiate the plea. It seems clear that in virtually all but the most unusual cases, the interested parties expected to, and actually did, negotiate the plea.

From these comments on the routine acceptance of plea bargaining in the courts, one might expect that this process would be relatively open and unambiguous. Apparently, however, there is some tension between the fact of bargaining and moral expectations concerning justice. Newman refers to this tension by citing two contradictory statements: an actual judicial opinion, "Justice and liberty are not the subjects of bargaining and barter"; and an off-the-cuff statement by another judge, "All law is compromise." A clear example of this tension is provided by an excerpt from a trial and Newman's comments on it.

> The following questions were asked of a defendant after he had pleaded guilty to unarmed robbery when the original charge was armed robbery. This reduction is common, and the judge was fully aware that the plea was negotiated:
>
> Judge: You want to plead guilty to robbery unarmed?
> Defendant: Yes, Sir.
> Judge: Your plea of guilty is free and voluntary?
> Defendant: Yes, Sir.
> Judge: No one has promised you anything?
> Defendant: No.
> Judge: No one has induced you to plead guilty?
> Defendant: No.
> Judge: You're pleading guilty because you are guilty?
> Defendant: Yes.
> Judge: I'll accept your plea of guilty to robbery unarmed and refer it to the probation department for a report and for sentencing Dec. 28.[7]

The delicacy of the relationship between appearance and reality is apparently confusing, even for the sociologist-observer. Newman's comment on this exchange has an Alice-in-Wonderland quality:

> This is a routine procedure designed to satisfy the statutory requirement and is not intended to disguise the process of charge reduction.[8]

If we put the tensions between the different realities aside for the moment, we can say that there is an explicit process of negotiation between the defendant and the prosecution which is a part of the legal determination of guilt or innocence, or in the terms used above, the assessment of responsibility.

In medical diagnosis, a similar process of negotiation occurs, but is much less self-conscious than plea bargaining. The English psychoanalyst Michael Balint refers to this process as one of "offers and responses":

---

[7] Ibid., p. 83.
[8] Ibid.

> Some of the people who, for some reason or other, find it difficult to cope with problems of their lives resort to becoming ill. If the doctor has the opportunity of seeing them in the first phases of their being ill, i.e., before they settle down to a definite "organized" illness, he may observe that the patients, so to speak, offer or propose various illnesses, and that they have to go on offering new illnesses until between doctor and patient an agreement can be reached resulting in the acceptance by both of them of one of the illnesses as justified.[9]

Balint gives numerous examples indicating that patients propose reasons for their coming to the doctor which are rejected, one by one, by the physician, who makes counter-proposals until an "illness" acceptable to both parties is found. If "definition of the situation" is substituted for "illness," Balint's observations become relevant to a wide variety of transactions, including the kind of interrogation discussed above. The fixing of responsibility is a process in which the client offers definitions of the situation, to which the interrogator responds. After a series of offers and responses, a definition of the situation acceptable to both the client and the interrogator is reached.

Balint has observed that the negotiation process leads physicians to influence the outcome of medical examinations, independently of the patient's condition. He refers to this process as the "apostolic function" of the doctor, arguing that the physician induces patients to have the kind of illness that the physician thinks is proper:

> Apostolic mission or function means in the first place that every doctor has a vague, but almost unshakably firm, idea of how a patient ought to behave when ill. Although this idea is anything but explicit and concrete, it is immensely powerful, and influences, as we have found, practically every detail of the doctor's work with his patients. It was almost as if every doctor had revealed knowledge of what was right and what was wrong for patients to expect and to endure, and further, as if he had a sacred duty to convert to his faith all the ignorant and unbelieving among his patients.[10]

Implicit in this statement is the notion that interrogator and client have unequal power in determining the resultant definition of the situation. The interrogator's definition of the situation plays an important part in the joint definition of the situation which is finally negotiated. Moreover, his definition is more important than the client's in determining the final outcome of the negotiation, principally because he is well trained, secure, and self-confident in his role in the transaction, whereas the client is untutored, anxious, and uncertain about his role. Stated simply, the subject, because of these conditions, is likely to be susceptible to the influence of the interrogator.

---

[9] Michael Balint, *The Doctor, His Patient, and The Illness* (New York: International Universities Press, 1957), p. 18. A description of the negotiations between patients in a tuberculosis sanitarium and their physicians is found in Julius A. Roth, *Timetables: Structuring the Passage of Time in Hospital Treatment and Other Careers* (Indianapolis: Bobbs-Merrill, 1963), pp. 48–59. Obviously, some cases are more susceptible to negotiation than others. Balint implies that the great majority of cases in medical practice are negotiated.

[10] Balint, *The Doctor,* p. 216.

Note that plea bargaining and the process of "offers and responses" in diagnosis differ in the degree of self-consciousness of the participants. In plea bargaining the process is at least partly visible to the participants themselves. There appears to be some ambiguity about the extent to which the negotiation is morally acceptable to some of the commentators, but the parties to the negotiations appear to be aware that bargaining is going on, and accept the process as such. The bargaining process in diagnosis, however, is much more subterranean. Certainly neither physicians nor patients recognize the offers and responses process as being bargaining. There is no commonly accepted vocabulary for describing diagnostic bargaining, such as there is in the legal analogy, e.g., "copping out" or "copping a plea." It may be that in legal processes there is some appreciation of the different kinds of reality, i.e., the difference between the public (official, legal) reality and private reality, whereas in medicine this difference is not recognized.

The discussion so far has suggested that much of reality is arrived at by negotiation. This thesis was illustrated by materials presented on legal processes by Newman, and medical processes by Balint. These processes are similar in that they appear to represent clear instances of the negotiation of reality. The instances are different in that the legal bargaining processes appear to be more open and accepted than the diagnostic process. In order to outline some of the dimensions of the negotiation process, and to establish some of the limitations of the analyses by Newman and Balint, two excerpts of cases of bargaining will be discussed: the first taken from an actual psychiatric "intake" interview, the second from a fictional account of a defense lawyer's first interview with his client.

The Process of Negotiation

The psychiatric interview to be discussed is from the first interview in *The Initial Interview in Psychiatric Practice.*[11] The patient is a thirty-four-year-old nurse, who feels, as she says, "irritable, tense, depressed." She appears to be saying from the very beginning of the interview that the external situation in which she lives is the cause of her troubles. She focuses particularly on her husband's behavior. She says he is an alcoholic, is verbally abusive, and won't let her work. She feels that she is cooped up in the house all day with her two small children, but that when he is home at night (on the nights when he *is* at home) he will have nothing to do with her and the children. She intimates, in several ways, that he does not serve as a sexual companion. She has thought of divorce, but has rejected it for various reasons (for example, she is afraid she couldn't take proper care of the children, finance the baby sitters, etc.). She feels trapped.[12]

In the concluding paragraph of their description of this interview, Gill, Newman, and Redlich give this summary:

---

[11] Merton Gill, Richard Newman, and Fredrick C. Redlich, *The Initial Interview in Psychiatric Practice* (New York: International Universities Press, 1954).

[12] Since this interview is complex and subtle, the reader is invited to listen to it himself, and compare his conclusions with those discussed here. The recorded interview is available on the first L.P. record that accompanies Gill, Newman, and Redlich, *The Initial Interview.*

> The patient, pushed by we know not what or why at the time (the children—somebody to talk to) comes for help apparently for what she thinks of as help with her external situation (her husband's behavior as she sees it). The therapist does not respond to this but seeks her role and how it is that she plays such a role. Listening to the recording it sounds as if the therapist is at first bored and disinterested and the patient defensive. He gets down to work and keeps asking, "What is it all about?" Then he becomes more interested and sympathetic and at the same time very active (participating) and demanding. *It sounds as if she keeps saying "This is the trouble." He says, "No! Tell me the trouble." She says, "This is it!" He says, "No, tell me," until the patient finally says, "Well I'll tell you." Then the therapist says, "Good! I'll help you."* [13]

From this summary it is apparent that there is a close fit between Balint's idea of the negotiation of diagnosis through offers and responses, and what took place in this psychiatric interview. It is difficult, however, to document the details. Most of the psychiatrist's responses, rejecting the patient's offers, do not appear in the written transcript, but they are fairly obvious as one listens to the recording. Two particular features of the psychiatrist's responses especially stand out: (1) the flatness of intonation in his responses to the patient's complaints about her external circumstances; and (2) the rapidity with which he introduces new topics, through questioning, when she is talking about her husband.

Some features of the psychiatrist's coaching are verbal, however:

T. 95: Has anything happened recently that makes it . . . you feel that . . . ah . . . you're sort of coming to the end of your rope? I mean I wondered what led you . . .

P. 95: (Interrupting.) It's nothing special. It's just everything in general.

T. 96: What led you to come to a . . .

P. 96: (Interrupting.) It's just that I . . .

T. 97: . . . a psychiatrist just now? (1)

P. 97: Because I felt that the older girl was getting tense as a result of . . . of my being stewed up all the time.

T. 98: Mmmhnn.

P. 98: Not having much patience with her.

T. 99: Mmmhnn. (Short pause.) Mmm. And how had you imagined that a psychiatrist could help with this? (Short pause.) (2)

P. 99: Mmm . . . maybe I could sort of get straightened out . . . straighten things out in my own mind. I'm confused. Sometimes I can't remember things that I've done, whether I've done 'em or not or whether they happened.

T. 100: What is it that you want to straighten out?
(Pause.)

P. 100: I think I seem mixed up.

T. 101: Yeah? You see that, it seems to me, is something that we really should talk about because . . . ah . . . from a certain point of view some-

---

[13] Ibid., p. 133. (Italics added.)

body might say, "Well now, it's all very simple. She's unhappy and disturbed because her husband is behaving this way, and unless something can be done about that how could she expect to feel any other way." But, instead of that, you come to the psychiatrist, and you say that you think there's something about you that needs straightening out. (3) I don't quite get it. Can you explain that to me? (Short pause.)

P. 101: I sometimes wonder if I'm emotionally grown up.

T. 102: By which you mean what?

P. 102: When you're married you should have one mate. You shouldn't go around and look at other men.

T. 103: You've been looking at other men?

P. 103: I look at them, but that's all.

T. 104: Mmmhnn. What you mean . . . you mean a grown-up person should accept the marital situation whatever it happens to be?

P. 104: That was the way I was brought up. Yes. (Sighs.)

T. 105: You think that would be a sign of emotional maturity?

P. 105: No.

T. 106: No. So?

P. 106: Well, if you rebel against the laws of society you have to take the consequences.

T. 107: Yes?

P. 107: And it's just that I . . . I'm not willing to take the consequences. I . . . I don't think it's worth it.

T. 108: Mmhnn. So in the meantime then while you're in this very difficult situation, you find yourself reacting in a way that you don't like and that you think is . . . ah . . . damaging to your children and yourself? Now what can be done about that?

P. 108: (Sniffs; sighs.) I dunno. That's why I came to see you.

T. 109: Yes. I was just wondering what you had in mind. Did you think a psychiatrist could . . . ah . . . help you face this kind of a situation calmly and easily and maturely? (4) Is that it?

P. 109: More or less. I need somebody to talk to who isn't emotionally involved with the family. I have a few friends, but I don't like to bore them. I don't think they should know . . . ah . . . all the intimate details of what goes on.

T. 110: Yeah?

P. 110: It becomes food for gossip.

T. 111: Mmmhnn.

P. 111: Besides they're in . . . they're emotionally involved because they're my friends. They tell me not to stand for it, but they don't understand that if I put my foot down it'll only get stepped on.

T. 112: Yeah.

P. 112: That he can make it miserable for me in other ways. . . .

T. 113: Mmm.

P. 113: . . . which he does.
T. 114: Mmmhnn. In other words, you find yourself in a situation and don't know how to cope with it really.
P. 114: I don't.
T. 115: You'd like to be able to talk that through and come to understand it better and learn how to cope with it or deal with it in some way. Is that right?
P. 115: I'd like to know how to deal with it more effectively.
T. 116: Yeah. Does that mean you feel convinced that the way you're dealing with it now . . .
P. 116: There's something wrong of course.
T. 117: . . . something wrong with that. Mmmhnn.
P. 117: There's something wrong with it.[14]

Note that the therapist reminds her *four times* in this short sequence that she has come to see a *psychiatrist.* Since the context of these reminders is one in which the patient is attributing her difficulties to an external situation, particularly her husband, it seems plausible to hear these reminders as subtle requests for analysis of her own contributions to her difficulties. This interpretation is supported by the therapist's subsequent remarks. When the patient once again describes external problems, the therapist tries the following tack:

T. 125: I notice that you've used a number of psychiatric terms here and there. Were you specially interested in that in your training, or what?
P. 125: Well, my great love is psychology.
T. 126: Psychology?
P. 126: Mmmhnn.
T. 127: How much have you studied?
P. 127: Oh (Sighs.) what you have in your nurse's training, and I've had general psych, child and adolescent psych, and the abnormal psych.
T. 128: Mmmhnn. Well, tell me . . . ah . . . what would you say if you had to explain yourself what is the problem?
P. 128: You don't diagnose yourself very well, at least I don't.
T. 129: Well you can make a stab at it. (Pause.) [15]

This therapeutic thrust is rewarded: the patient gives a long account of her early life which indicates a belief that she was not "adjusted" in the past. The interview continues:

T. 135: And what conclusions do you draw from all this about why you're not adjusting now the way you think you should?
P. 135: Well, I wasn't adjusted then. I feel that I've come a long way, but I don't think I'm still . . . I still don't feel that I'm adjusted.

---

[14] Ibid., pp. 176–82. (Numbers in parenthesis added.)
[15] Ibid., pp. 186–87.

T. 136: And you don't regard your husband as being the difficulty? You think it lies within yourself?
P. 136: Oh he's a difficulty all right, but I figure that even . . . ah . . . had . . . if it had been other things that . . . that is probably—this state—would've come on me.
T. 137: Oh you do think so?
P. 137: (Sighs.) I don't think he's the sole factor. No.
T. 138: And what are the factors within . . .
P. 138: I mean . . .
T. 139: . . . yourself?
P. 139: Oh it's probably remorse for the past, things I did.
T. 140: Like what? (Pause.) It's sumping' hard to tell, hunh? (Short pause.) [16]

After some parrying, the patient tells the therapist what he wants to hear. She feels guilty because she was pregnant by another man when her present husband proposed. She cries. The therapist tells the patient she needs, and will get, psychiatric help, and the interview ends, the patient still crying. The negotiational aspects of the process are clear: After the patient has spent most of the interview blaming her current difficulties on external circumstances, she tells the therapist a deep secret about which she feels intensely guilty. The patient, and not the husband, is at fault. The therapist's tone and manner change abruptly. From being bored, distant, and rejecting, he becomes warm and solicitous. Through a process of offers and responses, the therapist and patient have, by implication, negotiated a shared definition of the situation—the patient, not the husband, is responsible.

A Contrasting Case

The negotiation process can, of course, proceed on the opposite premise, namely that the client is not responsible. An ideal example would be an interrogation of a client by a skilled defense lawyer. Unfortunately, we have been unable to locate a verbatim transcript of a defense lawyer's initial interview with his client. There is available, however, a fictional portrayal of such an interview, written by a man with extensive experience as defense lawyer, prosecutor, and judge. The excerpt to follow is taken from the novel, *Anatomy of a Murder*.[17]

The defense lawyer, in his initial contact with his client, briefly questions him regarding his actions on the night of the killing. The client states that he discovered that the deceased, Barney Quill, had raped his wife; he then goes on to state that he then left his wife, found Quill and shot him.

> ". . . How long did you remain with your wife before you went to the hotel bar?"

---

[16] Ibid., pp. 192–94.
[17] Robert Traver, *Anatomy of a Murder* (New York: Dell, 1959).

"I don't remember."
"I think it is important, and I suggest you try."
After a pause. "Maybe an hour."
"Maybe more?"
"Maybe."
"Maybe less?"
"Maybe."

I paused and lit a cigar. I took my time. I had reached a point where a few wrong answers to a few right questions would leave me with a client—if I took his case—whose cause was legally defenseless. Either I stopped now and begged off and let some other lawyer worry over it or I asked him the few fatal questions and let him hang himself. Or else, like any smart lawyer, I went into the Lecture. I studied my man, who sat as inscrutable as an Arab, delicately fingering his Ming holder, daintily sipping his dark mustache. He apparently did not realize how close I had him to admitting that he was guilty of first degree murder, that is, that he "feloniously, wilfully and of his malice afore-thought did kill and murder one Barney Quill." The man was a sitting duck.[18]

The lawyer here realizes that his line of questioning has come close to fixing the responsibility for the killing on his client. He therefore shifts his ground by beginning "the Lecture":

The Lecture is an ancient device that lawyers use to coach their clients so that the client won't quite know he has been coached and his lawyer can still preserve the face-saving illusion that he hasn't done any coaching. For coaching clients, like robbing them, is not only frowned upon, it is downright unethical and bad, very bad. Hence the Lecture, an artful device as old as the law itself, and one used constantly by some of the nicest and most ethical lawyers in the land. "Who, me? I didn't tell him what to say," the lawyer can later comfort himself. "I merely explained the law, see." It is a good practice to scowl and shrug here and add virtuously: "That's my duty, isn't it?" . . .

"We will now explore the absorbing subject of legal justification or excuse," I said. . . .

"Well, take self-defense," I began. "That's the classic example of justifiable homicide. On the basis of what I've so far heard and read about your case I do not think we need pause too long over that. Do you?"

"Perhaps not," Lieutenant Manion conceded. "We'll pass it for now."

"Let's," I said dryly. "Then there's the defense of habitation, defense of property, and the defense of relatives or friends. Now there are more ramifications to these defenses than a dog has fleas, but we won't explore them now. I've already told you at length why I don't think you can invoke the possible defense of your wife. When you shot Quill her need for defense had passed. It's as simple as that."

"Go on," Lieutenant Manion said, frowning.

"Then there's the defense of a homicide committed to prevent a felony—say you're being robbed—; to prevent the escape of the felon—suppose he's getting away with your wallet—; or to arrest a felon—you've caught up with him and he's either trying to get away or has actually escaped." . . .

"Go on, then; what are some of the other legal justifications or excuses?"

"Then there's the tricky and dubious defense of intoxication. Personally I've

---

[18] Ibid., p. 43.

never seen it succeed. But since you were not drunk when you shot Quill we shall mercifully not dwell on that. Or were you?"

"I was cold sober. Please go on."

"Then finally there's the defense of insanity." I paused and spoke abruptly, airily: "Well, that just about winds it up." I arose as though making ready to leave.

"Tell me more."

"There is no more." I slowly paced up and down the room.

"I mean about this insanity."

"Oh, insanity," I said, elaborately surprised. It was like luring a trained seal with a herring. "Well, insanity, where proven, is a complete defense to murder. It does not legally justify the killing, like self-defense, say, but rather excuses it." The lecturer was hitting his stride. He was also on the home stretch. "Our law requires that a punishable killing—in fact, any crime—must be committed by a sapient human being, one capable, as the law insists, of distinguishing between right and wrong. If a man is insane, legally insane, the act of homicide may still be murder but the law excuses the perpetrator."

Lieutenant Manion was sitting erect now, very still and erect. "I see—and this—this perpetrator, what happens to him if he should—should be excused?"

"Under Michigan law—like that of many other states—if he is acquitted of murder on the grounds of insanity it is provided that he must be sent to a hospital for the criminally insane until he is pronounced sane." . . .

Then he looked at me. "Maybe," he said, "maybe I was insane." . . .

Thoughtfully: "Hm. . . . Why do you say that?"

"Well, I can't really say," he went on slowly. "I—I guess I blacked out. I can't remember a thing after I saw him standing behind the bar that night until I got back to my trailer."

"You mean—you mean you don't remember shooting him?" I shook my head in wonderment.

"Yes, that's what I mean."

"You don't even remember driving home?"

"No."

"You don't remember threatening Barney's bartender when he followed you outside after the shooting—as the newspaper says you did?" I paused and held my breath. "You don't remember telling him, 'Do you want some, too, Buster?' "

The smoldering dark eyes flickered ever so little. "No, not a thing."

"My, my," I said blinking my eyes, contemplating the wonder of it all. "Maybe you've got something there."

The Lecture was over; I had told my man the law; and now he had told me things that might possibly invoke the defense of insanity. . . .[19]

The negotiation is complete. The ostensibly shared definition of the situation established by the negotiation process is that the defendant was probably not responsible for his actions.

Let us now compare the two interviews. The major similarity between them is their negotiated character: they both take the form of a series of offers and responses that continue until an offer (a definition of the situation) is reached that is acceptable to both parties. The major difference between the transactions is that one, the psychotherapeutic interview, arrives at an assessment that the

[19] Ibid., pp. 46–47, 57, 58–59, and 60.

client is responsible; the other, the defense attorney's interview, reaches an assessment that the client was not at fault, i.e., not responsible. How can we account for this difference in outcome?

Discussion

Obviously, given any two real cases of negotiation which have different outcomes, one might construct a reasonable argument that the difference is due to the differences between the cases—the finding of responsibility in one case and lack of responsibility in the other, the only outcomes which are reasonably consonant with the facts of the respective cases. Without rejecting this argument, for the sake of discusssion only, and without claiming any kind of proof or demonstration, I wish to present an alternative argument; that the difference in outcome is largely due to the differences in technique used by the interrogators. This argument will allow us to suggest some crucial dimensions of negotiation processes.

The first dimension, consciousness of the bargaining aspects of the transaction, has already been mentioned. In the psychotherapeutic interview, the negotiational nature of the transaction seems not to be articulated by either party. In the legal interview, however, certainly the lawyer, and perhaps to some extent the client as well, is aware of, and accepts, the situation as one of striking a bargain, rather than as a relentless pursuit of the absolute facts of the matter.

The dimension of shared awareness that the definition of the situation is negotiable seems particularly crucial for assessments of responsibility. In both interviews, there is an agenda hidden from the client. In the psychotherapeutic interview, it is probably the psychiatric criteria for acceptance into treatment, the criterion of "insight." The psychotherapist has probably been trained to view patients with "insight into their illness" as favorable candidates for psychotherapy, i.e., patients who accept, or can be led to accept, the problems as internal, as part of their personality, rather than seeing them as caused by external conditions.

In the legal interview, the agenda that is unknown to the client is the legal structure of defenses or justifications for killing. In both the legal and psychiatric cases, the hidden agenda is not a simple one. Both involve fitting abstract and ambiguous criteria (insight, on the one hand, legal justification, on the other) to a richly specific, concrete case. In the legal interview, the lawyer almost immediately broaches this hidden agenda; he states clearly and concisely the major legal justifications for killing. In the psychiatric interview, the hidden agenda is never revealed. The patient's offers during most of the interview are rejected or ignored. In the last part of the interview, her last offer is accepted and she is told that she will be given treatment. In no case are the reasons for these actions articulated by either party.

The degree of shared awareness is related to a second dimension which concerns the format of the conversation. The legal interview began as an interrogation, but was quickly shifted away from that format when the defense lawyer realized the direction in which the questioning was leading the client, i.e., toward a legally unambiguous admission of guilt. On the very brink of such an admission, the defense lawyer stopped asking questions and started, instead, to make statements. He listed the principal legal justifications for killing, and, in response to the *client's* questions, gave an explanation of each of the justifications. This shift in format put the client, rather than the lawyer, in control of the crucial aspects of the negotiation. It is the client, not the lawyer, who is allowed to pose the questions, assess the answers for their relevance to his case, and most crucially, to determine himself the most advantageous tack to take. Control of the definition of the situation, the evocation of the events and intentions relevant to the assessment of the client's responsibility for the killing, was given to the client by the lawyer. The resulting client-controlled format of negotiation gives the client a double advantage. It not only allows the client the benefit of formulating his account of actions and intentions in their most favorable light, it also allows him to select, out of a diverse and ambiguous set of normative criteria concerning killing, that criteria which is most favorable to his own case.

Contrast the format of negotiation used by the psychotherapist. The form is consistently that of interrogation. The psychotherapist poses the questions; the patient answers. The psychotherapist then has the answers at his disposal. He may approve or disapprove, accept or reject, or merely ignore them. Throughout the entire interview, the psychotherapist is in complete control of the situation. Within this framework, the tactic that the psychotherapist uses is to reject the patient's "offers" that her husband is at fault, first by ignoring them, later, and ever more insistently, by leading her to define the situation as one in which she is at fault. In effect, what the therapist does is to reject her offers, and to make his own counter-offers.

These remarks concerning the relationship between technique of interrogation and outcome suggest an approach to assessment of responsibility somewhat different than that usually followed. The common sense approach to interrogation is to ask how accurate and fair is the outcome. Both Newman's and Balint's analyses of negotiation raise this question. Both presuppose that there is an objective state of affairs that is independent of the technique of assessment. This is quite clear in Newman's discussion, as he continually refers to defendants who are "really" or "actually" guilty or innocent.[20] The situation is less clear in Balint's discussion, although occasionally he implies that certain patients are really physically healthy, but psychologically distressed.

The type of analysis suggested by this paper seeks to avoid such presuppositions. It can be argued that *independently* of the facts of the case, the technique of

---

[20] In his Foreword the editor of the series, Frank J. Remington, comments on one of the slips that occurs frequently, the "acquittal of the guilty," noting that this phrase is contradictory from the legal point of view. He goes on to say that Newman is well aware of this, but uses the phrase as a convenience. Needless to say, both Remington's comments and mine can both be correct: the phrase is used as a convenience, but it also reveals the author's presuppositions.

assessment plays a part in determining the outcome. In particular, one can avoid making assumptions about actual responsibility by utilizing a technique of textual criticism of a transaction. The key dimension in such work would be the relative power and authority of the participants in the situation.[21]

As an introduction to the way in which power differences between interactants shape the outcome of the negotiations, let us take as an example an attorney in a trial dealing with "friendly" and "unfriendly" witnesses. A friendly witness is a person whose testimony will support the definition of the situation the attorney seeks to convey to the jury. With such a witness the attorney does not employ power, but treats him as an equal. His questions to such a witness are open, and allow the witness considerable freedom. The attorney might frame a question such as "Could you tell us about your actions on the night of ———?"

The opposing attorney, however, interested in establishing his own version of the witness' behavior on the same night, would probably approach the task quite differently. He might say: "You felt angry and offended on the night of ———, didn't you?" The witness frequently will try to evade so direct a question with an answer like: "Actually, I had started to . . . ." The attorney quickly interrupts, addressing the judge: "Will the court order the witness to respond to the question, yes or no?" That is to say, the question posed by the opposing attorney is abrupt and direct. When the witness attempts to answer indirectly, and at length, the attorney quickly invokes the power of the court to coerce the witness to answer as he wishes, directly. The witness and the attorney are not equals in power; the attorney used the coercive power of the court to force the witness to answer in the manner desired.

The attorney confronted by an "unfriendly" witness wishes to control the format of the interaction, so that he can retain control of the definition of the situation that is conveyed to the jury. It is much easier for him to neutralize an opposing definition of the situation if he retains control of the interrogation format in this manner. By allowing the unfriendly witness to respond only by yes or no to his own verbally conveyed account, he can suppress the ambient details of the opposing view that might sway the jury, and thus maintain an advantage for his definition over that of the witness.

In the psychiatric interview discussed above, the psychiatrist obviously does not invoke a third party to enforce his control of the interview. But he does use a device to impress the patient that she is not to be his equal in the interview, that is reminiscent of the attorney with an unfriendly witness. The device is to pose abrupt and direct questions to the patient's open-ended accounts, implying that

---

[21] Berger and Luckman, *Social Construction,* p. 100, also emphasizes the role of power, but at the societal level. "The success of particular conceptual machineries is related to the power possessed by those who operate them. The confrontation of alternative symbolic universes implies a problem of power—which of the conflicting definitions of reality will be 'made to stick' in the society." Haley's discussions of control in psychotherapy are also relevant. See Jay Haley, "Control in Psychoanalytic Psychotherapy," *Progress in Psychotherapy* (New York: Grune and Stratton, 1959), pp. 48–65; see also by the same author, "The Power Tactics of Jesus Christ" (New York: Grossman, 1969).

the patient should answer briefly and directly; and, through that implication, the psychiatrist controls the whole transaction. Throughout most of the interview the patient seeks to give detailed accounts of her behavior and her husband's, but the psychiatrist almost invariably counters with a direct and, to the patient, seemingly unrelated question.

The first instance of this procedure occurs at T6, the psychiatrist asking the patient, "What do you do?" She replies, "I'm a nurse, but my husband won't let me work." Rather than responding to the last part of her answer, which would be expected in conversation between equals, the psychiatrist asks another question, changing the subject: "How old are you?" This pattern continues throughout most of the interview. The psychiatrist appears to be trying to teach the patient to follow his lead. After some thirty or forty exchanges of this kind, the patient apparently learns her lesson; she cedes control of the transaction completely to the therapist, answering briefly and directly to direct questions, and elaborating only on cue from the therapist. The therapist thus implements his control of the interview not by direct coercion, but by subtle manipulation.

All of the discussion above, concerning shared awareness and the format of the negotiation, suggests several propositions concerning control over the definition of the situation. The professional interrogator, whether lawyer or psychotherapist, can maintain control if the client cedes control to him because of his authority as an expert, because of his manipulative skill in the transaction, or merely because the interrogator controls access to something the client wants, e.g., treatment, or a legal excuse. The propositions are:

1a. Shared awareness of the participants that the situation is one of negotiation. (The greater the shared awareness, the more control the client gets over the resultant definition of the situation.)

b. Explicitness of the agenda. (The more explicit the agenda of the transaction, the more control the client gets over the resulting definition of the situation.)

2a. Organization of the format of the transaction, offers and responses. (The party to a negotiation who responds, rather than the party who makes the offers, has relatively more power in controlling the resultant shared definition of the situation.)

b. Counter-offers. (The responding party who makes counter-offers has relatively more power than the responding party who limits his response to merely accepting or rejecting the offers of the other party.)

c. Directness of questions and answers. (The more direct the questions of the interrogator, and the more direct the answers he demands and receives, the more control he has over the resultant definition of the situation.)

These concepts and hypotheses are only suggestive until such times as operational definitions can be developed. Although such terms as offers and responses seem to have an immediate applicability to most conversation, it is likely that a thorough and systematic analysis of any given conversation would show the need for clearly stated criteria of class inclusion and exclusion. Perhaps a good place for such research would be in the transactions for assessing responsibility discussed above. Since some 90 percent of all criminal convictions in the United States are based on guilty pleas, the extent to which techniques of interrogation subtly influence outcomes would have immediate policy implication. There is considerable evidence that interrogation techniques influence the outcome of psychotherapeutic interviews also.[22] Research in both of these areas would probably have implications for both the theory and practice of assessing responsibility.

Conclusion: Negotiation in Social Science Research

More broadly, the application of the sociology of knowledge to the negotiation of reality has ramifications which may apply to all of social science. The interviewer in a survey, or the experimenter in a social psychological experiment, is also involved in a transaction with a client—the respondent or subject. Recent studies by Rosenthal and others strongly suggest that the findings in such studies are negotiated, and influenced by the format of the study.[23] Rosenthal's review of bias in research suggests that such bias is produced by a pervasive and subtle process of interaction between the investigator and his source of data. Those errors which arise because of the investigator's influence over the subject (the kind of influence discussed in this paper as arising out of power disparities in the process of negotiation), Rosenthal calls "expectancy effects." In order for these errors to occur, there must be direct contact between the investigator and the subject.

A second kind of bias Rosenthal refers to as "observer effects." These are errors of perception or reporting which do not require that the subject be influenced by investigation. Rosenthal's review leads one to surmise that even with techniques that are completely non-obtrusive, observer error could be quite large.[24]

The occurrence of these two kinds of bias poses an interesting dilemma for the lawyer, psychiatrist, and social scientist. The investigator of human phenomena is usually interested in more than a sequence of events, he wants to know why the events occurred. Usually this quest for an explanation leads him to deal with the motivation of the persons involved. The lawyer, clinician, social psychologist, or survey researcher try to elicit motives directly, by questioning the participants But in the process of questioning, as suggested above, he himself becomes involved in a process of negotiation, perhaps subtly influencing the informants

---

[22] Thomas J. Scheff, *Being Mentally Ill* (Chicago: Aldine, 1966).

[23] Robert Rosenthal, *Experimenter Effects in Behavioral Research* (New York: Appleton-Century-Crofts, 1966). Friedman, reporting a series of studies of expectancy effects, seeks to put the results within a broad sociological framework: Neil Friedman, *The Social Nature of Psychological Research: The Psychological Experiment as Social Interaction* (New York: Basic Books, 1967).

[24] Critics of "reactive techniques" often disregard the problem of observer effects. See, for example, Eugene J. Webb, Donald T. Campbell, Richard D. Schwartz, and Lee Sechrest. *Unobtrusive Measures: Nonreactive Research in Social Science* (Chicago: Rand-McNally, 1966).

through expectancy effects. A historian, on the other hand, might try to use documents and records to determine motives. He would certainly avoid expectancy effects in this way, but since he would not elicit motives directly, he might find it necessary to collect and interpret various kinds of evidence which are only indirectly related, at best, to determine motives of the participants. Thus, through his choice in the selection and interpretation of the indirect evidence, he may be as susceptible to error as the interrogator, survey researcher, or experimentalist—his error being due to observer effects, however, rather than expectancy effects.

The application of the ideas outlined here to social and psychological research need to be developed. The five propositions suggested above might be used, for example, to estimate the validity of surveys using varying degrees of open-endedness in their interview format. If some technique could be developed which would yield an independent assessment of validity, it might be possible to demonstrate, as Aaron Cicourel has suggested, the more reliable the technique, the less valid the results.

The influence of the assessment itself on the phenomena to be assessed appears to be an ubiquitous process in human affairs, whether in ordinary daily life, the determination of responsibility in legal or clinical interrogation, or in most types of social science research. The sociology of knowledge perspective, which suggests that people go through their lives constructing reality, offers a framework within which the negotiation of reality can be seriously and constructively studied. This paper has suggested some of the avenues of the problem that might require further study. The prevalence of the problem in most areas of human concern recommends it to our attention as a substantial field of study, rather than as an issue that can be ignored or, alternatively, be taken as the proof that rigorous knowledge of social affairs is impossible.

6

Some Conditions of Obedience and Disobedience to Authority

STANLEY MILGRAM

Instances where one person intentionally seeks to injure another cannot always be explained by personal motives, hatred, sadism, or psychological states of the aggressor. Quite often, injury is inflicted in response to the commands of a third party, someone "behind the scenes" directing the action. Some of the most dramatic examples of aggression in response to authority come from accounts of battlefield situations and war atrocities. During the trials at Nuremburg following World War II, the common plea of accused war criminals was: "I was only following orders!" More recently, the nature of official orders emerged as a central issue in the investigation of the My Lai incident in South Vietnam.

While the foregoing are extreme examples of a triadic relationship in aggressive behavior, they are not unique. What makes them dramatic is, of course, the large-scale loss of life and the scope of destruction involved. Yet, what may be equally appalling about such incidents is that the aggressor was apparently acting as an agent or "pawn." If we judge such incidents from the standpoint of our common sense morality, the agent appears more "inhuman" for "blindly" following someone's command to aggress.

Although we may readily label the agent's behavior as "inhumanity" or "blind obedience," such labels do not help us much in understanding the dynamics of the situation. As students of behavior, we need to know why or how the incident occurred. Stated in researchable form, the most basic question we need to ask is: "Under what conditions can we expect a person to obey a command to injure someone else?" In the following selection, Stanley Milgram describes a series of studies which were designed to explore this basic question. The author was able to simulate, in the laboratory, a situation in which a subject was directed to inflict pain upon an "innocent victim," a person the subject had never met before.

Stanley Milgram, "Some Conditions of Obedience and Disobedience to Authority," *Human Relations* 18 (1965): 57–76.

The situation in which one agent commands another to hurt a third turns up time and again as a significant theme in human relations. It is powerfully expressed in the story of Abraham, who is commanded by God to kill his son. It is no accident that Kirkegaard, seeking to orient his thought to the central themes of human experience, chose Abraham's conflict as the springboard to his philosophy.

War too moves forward on the triad of an authority which commands a person to destroy the enemy, and perhaps all organized hostility may be viewed as a theme and variation on the three elements of authority, executant, and victim.[1] We describe an experimental program, recently concluded at Yale University, in which a particular expression of this conflict is studied by experimental means.

In its most general form the problem may be defined thus: if *X* tells *Y* to hurt *Z*, under what conditions will *Y* carry out the command of *X* and under what conditions will he refuse? In the more limited form possible in laboratory research, the question becomes: if an experimenter tells a subject to hurt another person, under what conditions will the subject go along with this instruction, and under what conditions will he refuse to obey? The laboratory problem is not so much a dilution of the general statement as one concrete expression of the many particular forms this question may assume.

One aim of the research was to study behavior in a strong situation of deep consequence to the participants, for the psychological forces operative in powerful and lifelike forms of the conflict may not be brought into play under diluted conditions.

This approach meant, first, that we had a special obligation to protect the welfare and dignity of the persons who took part in the study; subjects were, of necessity, placed in a difficult predicament, and steps had to be taken to ensure their wellbeing before they were discharged from the laboratory. Toward this end, a careful, post-experimental treatment was devised and has been carried through for subjects in all conditions.[2]

---

[1] Consider, for example, J. P. Scott's analysis of war in his monograph on aggression: ". . . while the actions of key individuals in a war may be explained in terms of direct stimulation to aggression, vast numbers of other people are involved simply by being part of an organized society. . . .

"For example, at the beginning of World War I an Austrian archduke was assassinated in Sarajevo. A few days later soldiers from all over Europe were marching toward each other, not because they were stimulated by the archduke's misfortune, but because they had been trained to obey orders." (Slightly rearranged from J. P. Scott, *Aggression* [Chicago: University of Chicago Press, 1958], p. 103.)

[2] It consisted of an extended discussion with the experimenter and, of equal importance, a friendly reconciliation with the victim. It is made clear that the victim did not receive painful electric shocks. After the completion of the experimental series, subjects were sent a detailed report of the results and full purposes of the experimental program. A formal assessment of this procedure points to its overall effectiveness. Of the subjects, 83.7 percent indicated that they were glad to have taken part in the study; 15.1 percent reported neutral feelings; and 1.3 percent stated that they were sorry to have participated. A large number of subjects spontaneously requested that they be used in further experimentation. Four-fifths of

Terminology

If *Y* follows the command of *X* we shall say that he has obeyed *X;* if he fails to carry out the command of *X,* we shall say that he has disobeyed *X.* The terms *to obey* and *to disobey,* as used here, refer to the subject's overt action only, and carry no implication for the motive or experiential states accompanying the action.[3]

To be sure, the everyday use of the word *obedience* is not entirely free from complexities. It refers to action within widely varying situations, and connotes diverse motives within those situations: a child's obedience differs from a soldier's obedience, or the love, honor, and *obey* of the marriage vow. However, a consistent behavioral relationship is indicated in most uses of the term: in the act of obeying, a person does what another person tells him to do. *Y* obeys *X* if he carries out the prescription for action which *X* has addressed to him; the term suggests, moreover, that some form of dominance-subordination, or hierarchical element, is part of the situation in which the transaction between X and *Y* occurs.

A subject who complies with the entire series of experimental commands will be termed an *obedient* subject; one who at any point in the command series

---

the subjects felt that more experiments of this sort should be carried out, and 74 percent indicated that they had learned something of personal importance as a result of being in the study. Furthermore, a university psychiatrist, experienced in outpatient treatment, interviewed a sample of experimental subjects with the aim of uncovering possible injurious effects resulting from participation. No such effects were in evidence. Indeed, subjects typically felt that their participation was instructive and enriching. A more detailed discussion of this question can be found in Stanley Milgram, "Issues in the Study of Obedience: A Reply to Baumrind," *American Psychologist* 19 (1964): 848–52.

[3] *To obey* and *to disobey* are not the only terms one could use in describing the critical action of *Y*. One could say that *Y* is cooperating with *X,* or displays conformity with regard to *X*'s commands. However, *cooperation* suggests that *X* agrees with *Y*'s ends, and understands the relationship between his own behavior and the attainment of those ends. (But the experimental procedure, and, in particular, the experimenter's command that the subject shock the victim even in the absence of a response from the victim, precludes such understanding.) Moreover, cooperation implies status parity for the co-acting agents, and neglects the asymmetrical, dominance-subordination element prominent in the laboratory relationship between experimenter and subject. *Conformity* has been used in other important contexts in social psychology, and most frequently refers to imitating the judgments or actions of others when no explicit requirement for imitation has been made. Furthermore, in the present study there are two sources of social pressure: pressure from the experimenter issuing the commands, and pressure from the victim to stop the punishment. It is the pitting of a common man (the victim) against an authority (the experimenter) that is the distinctive feature of the conflict. At a point in the experiment the victim demands that he be let free. The experimenter insists that the subject continue to administer shocks. Which act of the subject can be interpreted as conformity? The subject may conform to the wishes of his peer or to the wishes of the experimenter, and conformity in one direction means the absence of conformity in the other. Thus the word has no useful reference in this setting, for the dual and conflicting social pressures cancel out its meaning.

In the final analysis, the linguistic symbol representing the subject's action must take its meaning from the concrete context in which that action occurs; and there is probably no word in everyday language that covers the experimental situation exactly, without omissions or irrelevant connotations. It is partly for convenience, therefore, that the terms *obey* and *disobey* are used to describe the subject's actions. At the same time, our use of the words is highly congruent with dictionary meaning.

defies the experimenter will be called a *disobedient* or *defiant* subject. As used in this report, the terms refer only to the subject's performance in the experiment, and do not necessarily imply a general personality disposition to submit to or reject authority.

Subject Population

The subjects used in all experimental conditions were male adults, residing in the greater New Haven and Bridgeport areas, aged 20 to 50 years, and engaged in a wide variety of occupations. Each experimental condition described in this report employed 40 fresh subjects and was carefully balanced for age and occupational types. The occupational composition for each experiment was: workers, skilled and unskilled: 40 percent; white collar, sales, business: 40 percent; professionals: 20 percent. The occupations were intersected with three age categories (subjects in 20s, 30s, and 40s, assigned to each condition in the proportions of 20, 40, and 40 percent respectively).

The General Laboratory Procedure [4]

The focus of the study concerns the amount of electric shock a subject is willing to administer to another person when ordered by an experimenter to give the "victim" increasingly more severe punishment. The act of administering shock is set in the context of a learning experiment, ostensibly designed to study the effect of punishment on memory. Aside from the experimenter, one naïve subject and one accomplice perform in each session. On arrival each subject is paid $4.50. After a general talk by the experimenter, telling how little scientists know about the effect of punishment on memory, subjects are informed that one member of the pair will serve as teacher and one as learner. A rigged drawing is held so that the naïve subject is always the teacher, and the accomplice becomes the learner. The learner is taken to an adjacent room and strapped into an "electric chair."

The naïve subject is told that it is his task to teach the learner a list of paired associates, to test him on the list, and to administer punishment whenever the learner errs in the test. Punishment takes the form of electric shock, delivered to the learner by means of a shock generator controlled by the naïve subject. The teacher is instructed to increase the intensity of electric shock one step on the generator on each error. The learner, according to plan, provides many wrong answers, so that before long the naïve subject must give him the strongest shock

[4] A more detailed account of the laboratory procedure can be found in Stanley Milgram, "Behavioral Study of Obedience," *Journal of Abnormal and Social Psychology* 67 (1963): 371–78. A similar and independently evolved experimental procedure, employing a shock generator, victim, and learning task, was reported by Arnold H. Buss, *The Psychology of Aggression* (New York: John Wiley, 1961). Buss used the technique for studying aggression, not obedience, and did not make use of the fundamental measure employed in the present study: break-off points. His investigation promises to be a useful complement to the present research.

on the generator. Increases in shock level are met by increasingly insistent demands from the learner that the experiment be stopped because of the growing discomfort to him. However, in clear terms the experimenter orders the teacher to continue with the procedure in disregard of the learner's protests. *Thus, the naïve subject must resolve a conflict between two mutually incompatible demands from the social field. He may continue to follow the orders of the experimenter and shock the learner with increasing severity, or he may refuse to follow the orders of the experimenter and heed the learner's pleas. The experimenter's authority operates not in a free field, but against ever-mounting countervailing pressures from the person being punished.*

A few technical points need to be considered before the findings of the study are described. For the purpose of delivering shock, a simulated shock generator is used, with 30 clearly marked voltage levels that range from 15 to 450 volts (and each activated by one of 30 individual lever switches set in a horizontal line). The naïve subject is given a sample shock of 45 volts to convince him of the authenticity of the instrument. The generator bears verbal designations that range from "Slight Shock" to "Danger: Severe Shock."

The responses of the victim are standardized on tape, and each protest is coordinated to a particular voltage level on the shock generator. Starting with 75 volts the learner begins to grunt and moan. At 150 volts he demands to be let out of the experiment. At 180 volts he cries out that he can no longer stand the pain. At 300 volts he refuses to provide any more answers to the memory test, insisting that he is no longer a participant in the experiment and must be freed. In response to this last tactic, the experimenter instructs the naïve subject to treat the absence of an answer as equivalent to a wrong answer, and to follow the usual shock procedure. The experimenter reinforces his demand with the statement: "You have no other choice, you must go on!" (This imperative is used whenever the naïve subject tries to break off the experiment.) If the subject refuses to give the next higher level of shock, the experiment is considered at an end. A quantitative value is assigned to the subject's performance based on the maximum intensity shock he administered before breaking off. Thus any subject's score may range from zero (for a subject unwilling to administer the first shock level) to 30 (for a subject who proceeds to the highest voltage level on the board). For any particular subject and for any particular experimental condition the degree to which participants have followed the experimenter's orders may be specified with a numerical value, corresponding to the metric on the shock generator.

This laboratory situation gives us a framework in which to study the subject's reactions to the principal conflict of the experiment. Again, this conflict is between the experimenter's demands that he continue to administer the electric shock, and the learner's demands, which become increasingly more insistent, that the experiment be stopped. The crux of the study is to vary systematically the factors believed to alter the degree of obedience to the experimental commands, to learn under what conditions submission to authority is most probable, and under what conditions defiance is brought to the fore.

Pilot Studies

Pilot studies for the present research were completed in the winter of 1960; they differed from the regular experiments in a few details: for one, the victim was placed behind a silvered glass, with the light balance on the glass such that the victim could be dimly perceived by the subject.[5]

Though essentially qualitative in treatment, these studies pointed to several significant features of the experimental situation. At first no vocal feedback was used from the victim. It was thought that the verbal and voltage designations on the control panel would create sufficient pressure to curtail the subject's obedience. However, this was not the case. In the absence of protests from the learner, virtually all subjects, once commanded, went blithely to the end of the board, seemingly indifferent to the verbal designations ("Extreme Shock" and "Danger: Severe Shock"). This deprived us of an adequate basis for scaling obedient tendencies. A force had to be introduced that would strengthen the subject's resistance to the experimenter's commands, and reveal individual differences in terms of a distribution of break-off points.

This force took the form of protests from the victim. Initially, mild protests were used, but proved inadequate. Subsequently, more vehement protests were inserted into the experimental procedure. To our consternation, even the strongest protests from the victim did not prevent all subjects from administering the harshest punishment ordered by the experimenter; but the protests did lower the mean maximum shock somewhat and created some spread in the subject's performance; therefore, the victim's cries were standardized on tape and incorporated into the regular experimental procedure.

The situation did more than highlight the technical difficulties of finding a workable experimental procedure: it indicated that subjects would obey authority to a greater extent than we had supposed. It also pointed to the importance of feedback from the victim in controlling the subject's behavior.

One further aspect of the pilot study was that subjects frequently averted their eyes from the person they were shocking, often turning their heads in an awkward and conspicuous manner. One subject explained: "I didn't want to see the consequences of what I had done." Observers wrote:

> . . . subjects showed a reluctance to look at the victim, whom they could see through the glass in front of them. When this fact was brought to their attention they indicated that it caused them discomfort to see the victim in agony. We note, however, that although the subject refuses to look at the victim, he continues to administer shocks.

This suggested that the salience of the victim may have, in some degree, regulated the subject's performance. If, in obeying the experimenter, the subject found it necessary to avoid scrutiny of the victim, would the converse be true? If the victim were rendered increasingly more salient to the subject, would obedience

---

[5] Stanley Milgram, "Dynamics of Obedience: Experiments in Social Psychology." Mimeographed report, *National Science Foundation,* January 25, 1961.

diminish? The first set of regular experiments was designed to answer this question.

Immediacy of the Victim

This series consisted of four experimental conditions. In each condition the victim was brought "psychologically" closer to the subject giving him shocks.

In the first condition (Remote Feedback) the victim was placed in another room and could not be heard or seen by the subject, except that, at 300 volts, he pounded on the wall in protest. After 315 volts he no longer answered or was heard from.

The second condition (Voice Feedback) was identical to the first except that voice protests were introduced. As in the first condition the victim was placed in an adjacent room, but his complaints could be heard clearly through a door left slightly ajar, and through the walls of the laboratory.[6]

The third experimental condition (Proximity) was similar to the second, except that the victim was now placed in the same room as the subject, and 1.5 feet from him. Thus he was visible as well as audible, and voice cues were provided.

The fourth, and final, condition of this series (Touch-Proximity) was identical to the third, with this exception: the victim received a shock only when his hand

---

[6] It is difficult to convey on the printed page the full tenor of the victim's responses, for we have no adequate notation for vocal intensity, timing, and general qualities of delivery. Yet these features are crucial to producing the effect of an increasingly severe reaction to mounting voltage levels. (They can be communicated fully only by sending interested parties the recorded tapes.) In general terms, however, the victim indicates no discomfort until the 75-volt shock is administered, at which time there is a light grunt in response to the punishment. Similar reactions follow the 90- and 105-volt shocks, and at 120 volts the victim shouts to the experimenter that the shocks are becoming painful. Painful groans are heard on administration of the 135-volt shock, and at 150 volts the victim cries out, "Experimenter, get me out of here! I won't be in the experiment any more! I refuse to go on!" Cries of this type continue with generally rising intensity, so that at 180 volts the victim cries out, "I can't stand the pain," and by 270 volts his response to the shock is definitely an agonized scream. Throughout, he insists that he be let out of the experiment. At 300 volts the victim shouts in desperation that he will no longer provide answers to the memory test; and at 315 volts, after a violent scream, he reaffirms with vehemence that he is no longer a participant. From this point on, he provides no answers, but shrieks in agony whenever a shock is administered; this continues through 450 volts. Of course, many subjects will have broken off before this point.

A revised and stronger set of protests were used in all experiments outside the Proximity series. Naturally, new baseline measures were established for all comparisons using the new set of protests.

There is overwhelming evidence that the great majority of subjects, both obedient and defiant, accepted the victims' reactions as genuine. The evidence takes the form of: (a) tension created in the subjects (see discussion of tension); (b) scores on "estimated pain" scales filled out by subjects immediately after the experiment; (c) subjects' accounts of their feelings in post-experimental interviews; and (d) quantifiable responses to questionnaires distributed to subjects several months after their participation in the experiments. This matter will be treated fully in a forthcoming monograph.

(The procedure in all experimental conditions was to have the naïve subject announce the voltage level before administering each shock, so that—independently of the victim's responses—he was continually reminded of delivering punishment of ever-increasing severity.)

rested on a shockplate. At the 150-volt level the victim again demanded to be let free and, in this condition, refused to place his hand on the shockplate. The experimenter ordered the naïve subject to force the victim's hand onto the plate. Thus obedience in this condition required that the subject have physical contact with the victim in order to give him punishment beyond the 150-volt level.

Forty adult subjects were studied in each condition. The data revealed that obedience was significantly reduced as the victim was rendered more immediate to the subject. The mean maximum shock for the conditions is shown in Figure 1.

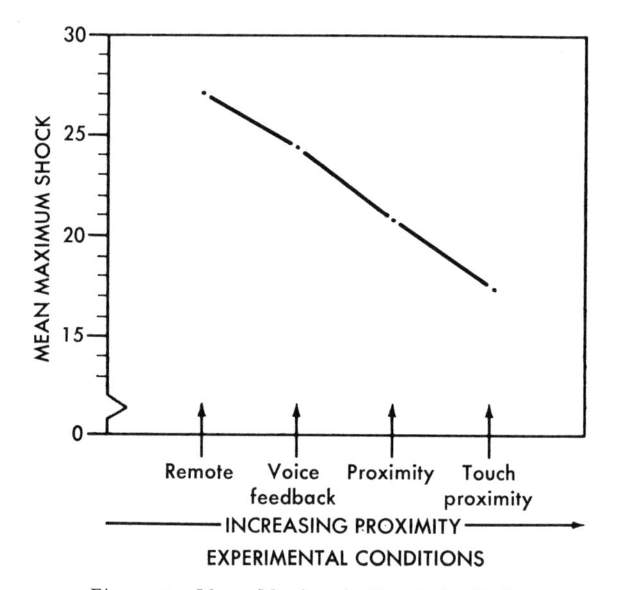

Figure 1 Mean Maxima in Proximity Series

Expressed in terms of the proportion of obedient to defiant subjects, the findings are that 34 percent of the subjects defied the experimenter in the Remote condition, 37.5 percent in Voice Feedback, 60 percent in Proximity, and 70 percent in Touch-Proximity.

How are we to account for this effect? A first conjecture might be that as the victim was brought closer the subject became more aware of the intensity of his suffering and regulated his behavior accordingly. This makes sense, but our evidence does not support the interpretation. There are no consistent differences in the attributed level of pain across the four conditions (i.e., the amount of pain experienced by the victim as estimated by the subject and expressed on a 14-point scale). But it is easy to speculate about alternative mechanisms:

Emphatic cues. In the Remote and to a lesser extent the Voice Feedback condition, the victim's suffering possesses an abstract, remote quality for the subject. He is aware, but only in a conceptual sense, that his actions cause pain to another person; the fact is apprehended, but not felt. The phenomenon is common enough. The bombardier can reasonably suppose that his weapons will inflict suffering and death, yet this knowledge is divested of affect, and does not move him to a felt, emotional response to the suffering resulting from his actions. Similar observations have been made in wartime. It is possible that the visual cues associated with the victim's suffering trigger empathic responses in the subject and provide him with a more complete grasp of the victim's experience. Or it is possible that the empathic responses are themselves unpleasant, possessing drive properties which cause the subject to terminate the arousal situation. Diminishing obedience, then, would be explained by the enrichment of empathic cues in the successive experimental conditions.

Denial and narrowing of the cognitive field. The Remote condition allows a narrowing of the cognitive field so that the victim is put out of mind. The subject no longer considers the act of depressing a lever relevant to moral judgment, for it is no longer associated with the victim's suffering. When the victim is close it is more difficult to exclude him phenomenologically. He necessarily intrudes on the subject's awareness since he is continuously visible. In the Remote condition his existence and reactions are made known only after the shock has been administered. The auditory feedback is sporadic and discontinuous. In the Proximity condition his inclusion in the immediate visual field renders him a continuously salient element for the subject. The mechanism of denial can no longer be brought into play. One subject in the Remote condition said: "It's funny how you really begin to forget that there's a guy out there, even though you can hear him. For a long time I just concentrated on pressing the switches and reading the words."

Reciprocal fields. If in the Proximity condition the subject is in an improved position to observe the victim, the reverse is also true. The actions of the subject now come under proximal scrutiny by the victim. Possibly, it is easier to harm a person when he is unable to observe our actions than when he can see what we are doing. His surveillance of the action directed against him may give rise to shame, or guilt, which may then serve to curtail the action. Many expressions of language refer to the discomfort or inhibitions that arise in face-to-face confrontation. It is often said that it is easier to criticize a man "behind his back" than to "attack him to his face." If we are in the process of lying to a person it is reputedly difficult to "stare him in the eye." We "turn away from others in shame" or in "embarrassment" and this action serves to reduce our discomfort. The manifest function of allowing the victim of a firing squad to be blindfolded is to make the occasion less stressful for him, but it may also serve a latent function of reducing the stress of the executioner. In short, in the Proximity condition, the subject may sense that he has become more salient in the victim's field of awareness. Possibly he becomes more self-conscious, embarrassed, and inhibited in his punishment of the victim.

Phenomenal unity of act. In the Remote condition it is more difficult for the subject to gain a sense of *relatedness* between his own actions and the consequences of these actions for the victim. There is a physical and spatial separation of the act and its consequences. The subject depresses a lever in one room, and protests and cries are heard from another. The two events are in correlation, yet they lack a compelling phenomenological unity. The structure of a meaningful act—*I am hurting a man*—breaks down because of the spatial arrangements, in a manner somewhat analogous to the disappearance of phi phenomena when the blinking lights are spaced too far apart. The unity is more fully achieved in the Proximity condition as the victim is brought closer to the action that causes him pain. It is rendered complete in Touch-Proximity.

Incipient group formation. Placing the victim in another room not only takes him farther from the subject, but the subject and the experimenter are drawn relatively closer. There is incipient group formation between the experimenter and the subject, from which the victim is excluded. The wall between the victim and the others deprives him of an intimacy which the experimenter and subject feel. In the Remote condition, the victim is truly an outsider, who stands alone, physically and psychologically.

When the victim is placed close to the subject, it becomes easier to form an alliance with him against the experimenter. Subjects no longer have to face the experimenter alone. They have an ally who is close at hand and eager to collaborate in a revolt against the experimenter. Thus, the changing set of spatial relations leads to a potentially shifting set of alliances over the several experimental conditions.

Acquired behavior dispositions. It is commonly observed that laboratory mice will rarely fight with their litter mates. Scott explains this in terms of passive inhibition. He writes: "By doing nothing under . . . circumstances [the animal] learns to do nothing and this may be spoken of as passive inhibition . . . this principle has great importance in teaching an individual to be peaceful, for it means that he can learn not to fight simply by not fighting."[7] Similarly, we may learn not to harm others simply by not harming them in everyday life. Yet this learning occurs in a context of proximal relations with others, and may not be generalized to that situation in which the person is physically removed from us. Or possibly, in the past, aggressive actions against others who were physically close resulted in retaliatory punishment which extinguished the original form of response. In contrast, aggression against others at a distance may have only sporadically led to retaliation. Thus the organism learns that it is safer to be aggressive toward others at a distance, and precarious to be so when the parties are within arm's reach. Through a pattern of rewards and punishments, he acquires a disposition to avoid aggression at close quarters, a disposition which does not extend to harming others at a distance. And this may account for experimental findings in the remote and proximal experiments.

Proximity as a variable in psychological research has received far less attention than it deserves. If men were sessile it would be easy to understand this neglect. But we move about; our spatial relations shift from one situation to the next, and the fact that we are near or remote may have a powerful effect on the psychological processes that mediate our behavior toward others. In the present situation, as the victim is brought closer to the man ordered to give him shocks, increasing numbers of subjects break off the experiment, refusing to obey. The concrete, visible, and proximal presence of the victim acts in an important way to counteract the experimenter's power and to generate disobedience.[8]

---

[7] Scott, *Aggression.*

[8] Admittedly, the terms *proximity, immediacy, closeness,* and *salience-of-the-victim* are used in a loose sense, and the experiments themselves represent a very coarse treatment of the variable. Further experiments are needed to refine the notion and tease out such diverse factors as spatial distance, visibility, audibility, barrier interposition, etc.

The Proximity and Touch-Proximity experiments were the only conditions where we were unable to use taped feedback from the victim. Instead, the victim was trained to respond in these conditions as he had in Experiment 2 (which employed taped feedback). Some improvement is possible here, for it should be technically feasible to do a proximity series using taped feedback.

Closeness of Authority

If the spatial relationship of the subject and victim is relevant to the degree of obedience, would not the relationship of subject to experimenter also play a part?

There are reasons to feel that, on arrival, the subject is oriented primarily to the experimenter rather than to the victim. He has come to the laboratory to fit into the structure that the experimenter—not the victim—would provide. He has come less to understand his behavior than to *reveal* that behavior to a competent scientist, and he is willing to display himself as the scientist's purposes require. Most subjects seem quite concerned about the appearance they are making before the experimenter, and one could argue that this preoccupation in a relatively new and strange setting makes the subject somewhat insensitive to the triadic nature of the social situation. In other words, the subject is so concerned about the show he is putting on for the experimenter that influences from other parts of the social field do not receive as much weight as they ordinarily would. This overdetermined orientation to the experimenter would account for the relative insensitivity of the subject to the victim, and would also lead us to believe that alterations in the relationship between subject and experimenter would have important consequences for obedience.

In a series of experiments we varied the physical closeness and degree of surveillance of the experimenter. In one condition the experimenter sat just a few feet away from the subject. In a second condition, after giving initial instructions, the experimenter left the laboratory and gave his orders by telephone; in still a third condition the experimenter was never seen, providing instructions by means of a tape recording activated when the subjects entered the laboratory.

Obedience dropped sharply as the experimenter was physically removed from the laboratory. The number of obedient subjects in the first condition (Experimenter Present) was almost three times as great as in the second, where the experimenter gave his orders by telephone. Twenty-six subjects were fully obedient in the first condition, and only 9 in the second (Chi square obedient vs. defiant in the two conditions, 1 d.f. $= 14.7$; $p < .001$). Subjects seemed able to take a far stronger stand against the experimenter when they did not have to encounter him face to face, and the experimenter's power over the subject was severely curtailed.[9]

Moreover, when the experimenter was absent, subjects displayed an interesting form of behavior that had not occurred under his surveillance. Though continuing with the experiment, several subjects administered lower shocks than were required and never informed the experimenter of their deviation from the correct procedure. (Unknown to the subjects, shock levels were automatically recorded by an Esterline-Angus event recorder wired directly into the shock generator; the instrument provided us with an objective record of the subjects' performance.) Indeed, in telephone conversations some subjects specifically assured the experi-

[9] The third condition also led to significantly lower obedience than this first situation, in which the experimenter was present, but it contains technical difficulties that require extensive discussion.

menter that they were raising the shock level according to instruction, whereas in fact they were repeatedly using the lowest shock on the board. This form of behavior is particularly interesting: although these subjects acted in a way that clearly undermined the avowed purposes of the experiment, they found it easier to handle the conflict in this manner than to precipitate an open break with authority.

Other conditions were completed in which the experimenter was absent during the first segment of the experiment, but reappeared at the point that the subject definitely refused to give higher shocks when commanded by telephone. Although he had exhausted his power via telephone, the experimenter could frequently force further obedience when he reappeared in the laboratory.

Experiments in this series show that the physical *presence* of an authority is an important force contributing to the subject's obedience or defiance. Taken together with the first experimental series on the proximity of the victim, it would appear that something akin to fields of force, diminishing in effectiveness with increasing psychological distance from their source, have a controlling effect on the subject's performance. As the victim is brought closer, the subject finds it harder to administer shocks to him. When the victim's position is held constant relative to the subject, and the authority is made more remote, the subject finds it easier to break off the experiment. This effect is substantial in both cases, but manipulation of the experimenter's position yielded the more powerful results. Obedience to destructive commands is highly dependent on the proximal relations between authority and subject.

Tensions

The description of final scores does not fully convey the character of the subjects' performance, and it would be useful to interrupt our reporting of quantitative relationships to remark on the subjects' general reaction to the situation.

One might suppose that a subject would simply break off or continue as his conscience and temperament dictated. Yet this is very far from what happened. There were powerful reactions of tension and emotional strain in a substantial proportion of the participants. Persons were observed to sweat, tremble, stutter, bite their lips, and groan as they found themselves increasingly implicated in the experimental conflict. Some sense of the subjects' mood can be gotten from a transcript of their remarks at break-off point. Here are the remarks of two defiant subjects:

> Is he banging? . . . Is he hurt out there? Well, I don't want to be responsible for anything that happens to him. No, I can't go on with it. I don't know whether he's all right or not. I mean he may have a heart condition or something; I wouldn't feel right doing it. He's banging for help. He's evidently in trouble or he wouldn't bang . . . I don't see any sense to this—to knocking him out or something. I just can't see it.
> (*Subject refuses to administer shocks*) [*Subject 0108*]

> The man is banging. He wants to get out . . . I'm sorry. If the man wants to get out I'd just as soon stop . . . I don't want to administer any more [extremely excited] . . . I will gladly refund the check, but I will not harm this man . . . I'm sorry. I will not give him any more if he obviously wants to get out. There is no money in the world that will make me hurt another individual. [*Subject 010 X*]

And here is a transcript from an obedient subject. He began the experiment calmly, but became increasingly tense as the experiment proceeded. After administering the 150-volt shock, he began to address the experimenter in agitated tones:

> *150 volts delivered.* You want me to keep going?
> *165 volts delivered.* That guy is hollering in there. There's a lot of them here. He's liable to have a heart condition. You want me to go on?
> *180 volts delivered.* He can't stand it! I'm not going to kill that man in there! You hear him hollering? He's hollering. He can't stand it. What if something happens to him? . . . I'm not going to get that man sick in there. He's hollering in there. You know what I mean? I mean I refuse to take responsibility. He's getting hurt in there. He's in there hollering. Too many left here. Geez, if he gets them wrong. There's too many of them left. I mean who is going to take responsibility if anything happens to that gentleman?
> [*The experimenter accepts responsibility.*] All right.
> *195 volts delivered.* You see he's hollering. Hear that. Gee, I don't know. [*The experimenter says: "The experiment requires that you go on."*]—I know it does, sir, but I mean—ugh—he don't know what he's in for. He's up to 195 volts.
> *210 volts delivered.*
> *225 volts delivered.*
> *240 volts delivered.* Aw, no. You mean I've got to keep going up with the scale? No sir. I'm not going to kill that man! I'm not going to give him 450 volts! [*The experimenter says: "The experiment requires that you go on."*]—I know it does, but that man is hollering in there, sir . . .

Despite his numerous, agitated objections, which were constant accompaniments to his actions, the subject unfailingly obeyed the experimenter, proceeding to the highest shock level on the generator. He displayed a curious dissociation between word and action. Although at the verbal level he had resolved not to go on, his actions were fully in accord with the experimenter's commands. This subject did not want to shock the victim, and he found it an extremely disagreeable task, but he was unable to invent a response that would free him from *E*'s authority. Many subjects cannot find the specific verbal formula that would enable them to reject the role assigned to them by the experimenter. Perhaps our culture does not provide adequate models for disobedience.

One puzzling sign of tension was the regular occurrence of nervous laughing fits. In the first four conditions 71 of the 160 subjects showed definite signs of nervous laughter and smiling. The laughter seemed entirely out of place, even bizarre. Full-blown, uncontrollable seizures were observed for 15 of these subjects. On one occasion we observed a seizure so violently convulsive that it was necessary to call a halt to the experiment. In the post-experimental interviews subjects took pains to point out that they were not sadistic types and that the laughter did not mean they enjoyed shocking the victim.

In the interview following the experiment subjects were asked to indicate on a 14-point scale just how nervous or tense they felt at the point of maximum tension (Figure 2). The scale ranged from "Not at all tense and nervous" to "Extremely

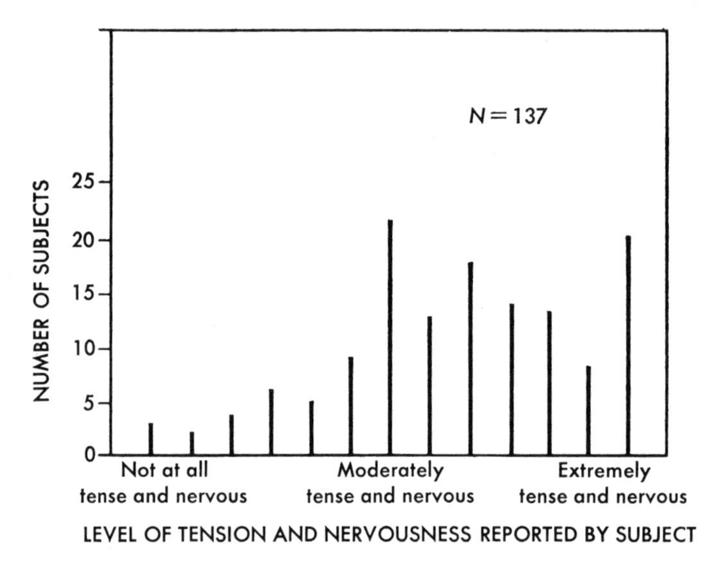

Figure 2 Level of Tension and Nervousness

Figure 2 shows the self-reports on "tension and nervousness" for 137 subjects in the Proximity experiments. Subjects were given a scale with 14 values ranging from "Not at all tense and nervous" to "Extremely tense and nervous." They were instructed: "Thinking back to that point in the experiment when you felt the most tense and nervous, indicate just how you felt by placing an X at the appropriate point on the scale." The results are shown in terms of mid-point values.

tense and nervous." Self-reports of this sort are of limited precision, and at best provide only a rough indication of the subject's emotional response. Still, taking the reports for what they are worth, it can be seen that the distribution of responses spans the entire range of the scale, with the majority of subjects concentrated at the center and upper extreme. A further breakdown showed that obedient subjects reported themselves as having been slightly more tense and nervous than the defiant subjects at the point of maximum tension.

How is the occurrence of tension to be interpreted? First, it points to the presence of conflict. If a tendency to comply with authority were the only psychological force operating in the situation, all subjects would have continued to the end and there would have been no tension. Tension, it is assumed, results from the simultaneous presence of two or more incompatible response tendencies.[10] If

[10] N. E. Miller, "Experimental Studies of Conflict," in J. McV. Hunt, ed., *Personality and the Behavior Disorders* (New York: Ronald Press, 1944).

sympathetic concern for the victim were the exclusive force, all subjects would have calmly defied the experimenter. Instead, there were both obedient and defiant outcomes, frequently accompanied by extreme tension. A conflict develops between the deeply ingrained disposition not to harm others and the equally compelling tendency to obey others who are in authority. The subject is quickly drawn into a dilemma of a deeply dynamic character, and the presence of high tension points to the considerable strength of each of the antagonistic vectors.

Moreover, tension defines the strength of the aversive state from which the subject is unable to escape through disobedience. When a person is uncomfortable, tense, or stressed, he tries to take some action that will allow him to terminate this unpleasant state. Thus tension may serve as a drive that leads to escape behavior. But in the present situation, even where tension is extreme, many subjects are unable to perform the response that will bring about relief. Therefore there must be a competing drive, tendency, or inhibition that precludes activation of the disobedient response. The strength of this inhibiting factor must be of greater magnitude than the stress experienced, else the terminating act would occur. Every evidence of extreme tension is at the same time an indication of the strength of the forces that keep the subject in the situation.

Finally, tension may be taken as evidence of the reality of the situations for the subjects. Normal subjects do not tremble and sweat unless they are implicated in a deep and genuinely felt predicament.

Background Authority

In psychophysics, animal learning, and other branches of psychology, the fact that measures are obtained at one institution rather than another is irrelevant to the interpretation of the findings, so long as the technical facilities for measurement are adequate and the operations are carried out with competence.

But it cannot be assumed that this holds true for the present study. The effectiveness of the experimenter's commands may depend in an important way on the larger institutional context in which they are issued. The experiments described thus far were conducted at Yale University, an organization which most subjects regarded with respect and sometimes awe. In post-experimental interviews several participants remarked that the locale and sponsorship of the study gave them confidence in the integrity, competence, and benign purposes of the personnel; many indicated that they would not have shocked the learner if the experiments had been done elsewhere.

This issue of background authority seemed to us important for an interpretation of the results that had been obtained thus far; moreover it is highly relevant to any comprehensive theory of human obedience. Consider, for example, how closely our compliance with the imperatives of others is tied to particular institutions and locales in our day-to-day activities. On request, we expose our throats to a man with a razor blade in the barber shop, but would not do so in a shoe store; in the latter setting we willingly follow the clerk's request to stand in our stockinged feet, but resist the command in a bank. In the laboratory of a great university, subjects may comply with a set of commands that would be resisted if given elsewhere. *One must always question the relationship of obedience to a person's sense of the context in which he is operating.*

To explore the problem we moved our apparatus to an office building in industrial Bridgeport and replicated experimental conditions, without any visible tie to the university.

Bridgeport subjects were invited to the experiment through a mail circular similar to the one used in the Yale study, with appropriate changes in letterhead, etc. As in the earlier study, subjects were paid $4.50 for coming to the laboratory. The same age and occupational distributions used at Yale, and the identical personnel, were employed.

The purpose in relocating in Bridgeport was to assure a complete dissociation from Yale, and in this regard we were fully successful. On the surface, the study appeared to be conducted by RESEARCH ASSOCIATES OF BRIDGEPORT, an organization of unknown character (the title had been concocted exclusively for use in this study).

The experiments were conducted in a three-room office suite in a somewhat run-down commercial building located in the downtown shopping area. The laboratory was sparsely furnished, though clean, and marginally respectable in appearance. When subjects inquired about professional affiliations, they were informed only that we were a private firm conducting research for industry.

Some subjects displayed skepticism concerning the motives of the Bridgeport experimenter. One gentleman gave us a written account of the thoughts he experienced at the control board:

> . . . Should I quit this damn test? Maybe he passed out? What dopes we were not to check up on this deal. How do we know that these guys are legit? No furniture, bare walls, no telephone. We could of called the Police up or the Better Business Bureau. I learned a lesson tonight. How do I know that Mr. Williams [the experimenter] is telling the truth? . . . I wish I knew how many volts a person could take before lapsing into unconsciousness . . .
>
> [*Subject 2414*]

Another subject stated:

> I questioned on my arrival my own judgment [about coming]. I had doubts as to the legitimacy of the operation and the consequences of participation. I felt it was a heartless way to conduct memory or learning processes on human beings and certainly dangerous without the presence of a medical doctor.
>
> [*Subject 2440 V*]

There was no noticeable reduction in tension for the Bridgeport subjects. And the subjects' estimation of the amount of pain felt by the victim was slightly, though not significantly, higher than in the Yale study.

A failure to obtain complete obedience in Bridgeport would indicate that the extreme compliance found in New Haven subjects was tied closely to the background authority of Yale University; if a large proportion of the subjects remained fully obedient, very different conclusions would be called for.

As it turned out, the level of obedience in Bridgeport, although somewhat reduced, was not significantly lower than that obtained at Yale. A large proportion of the Bridgeport subjects were fully obedient to the experimenter's commands (48 percent of the Bridgeport subjects delivered the maximum shock vs. 65 percent in the corresponding condition at Yale).

How are these findings to be interpreted? It is possible that if commands of a potentially harmful or destructive sort are to be perceived as legitimate they must occur within some sort of institutional structure. But it is clear from the study that it need not be a particularly reputable or distinguished institution. The Bridgeport experiments were conducted by an unimpressive firm lacking any credentials; the laboratory was set up in a respectable office building with title listed in the building directory. Beyond that, there was no evidence of benevolence or competence. It is possible that the *category* of institution, judged according to its professed function, rather than its qualitative position within that category, wins our compliance. Persons deposit money in elegant, but also in seedy-looking banks, without giving much thought to the differences in security they offer. Similarly, our subjects may consider one laboratory to be as competent as another, so long as it *is* a scientific laboratory.

It would be valuable to study the subjects' performance in other contexts which go even further than the Bridgeport study in denying institutional support to the experimenter. It is possible that, beyond a certain point, obedience disappears completely. But that point had not been reached in the Bridgeport office: almost half the subjects obeyed the experimenter fully.

Further Experiments

We may mention briefly some additional experiments undertaken in the Yale series. A considerable amount of obedience and defiance in everyday life occurs in connection with groups. And we had reason to feel in the light of many group studies already done in psychology that group forces would have a profound effect on reactions to authority. A series of experiments was run to examine these effects. In all cases only one naïve subject was studied per hour, but he performed in the midst of actors who, unknown to him, were employed by the experimenter. In one experiment (Groups for Disobedience) two actors broke off in the middle of the experiment. When this happened 90 percent of the subjects followed suit and defied the experimenter. In another condition the actors followed the orders obediently; this strengthened the experimenter's power only slightly. In still a third experiment the job of pushing the switch to shock the learner was given to one of the actors, while the naïve subject performed a subsidiary act. We wanted to see how the teacher would respond if he were involved in the situation but did not actually give the shocks. In this situation only three subjects out of forty broke off. In a final group experiment the subjects themselves determined the shock level they were going to use. Two actors suggested higher and higher shock levels; some subjects insisted, despite group pressure, that the shock level be kept low; others followed along with the group.

Further experiments were completed using women as subjects, as well as a set dealing with the effects of dual, unsanctioned, and conflicting authority. A final experiment concerned the personal relationship between victim and subject. These will have to be described elsewhere, lest the present report be extended to monographic length.

It goes without saying that future research can proceed in many different directions. What kinds of response from the victim are most effective in causing disobedience in the subject? Perhaps passive resistance is more effective than vehement protests. What conditions of entry into an authority system lead to greater or lesser obedience? What is the effect of anonymity and masking on the subject's behavior? What conditions lead to the subject's perception of responsibility for his own actions? Each of these could be a major research topic in itself, and can readily be incorporated into the general experimental procedure described here.

Levels of Obedience and Defiance

One general finding that merits attention is the high level of obedience manifested in the experimental situation. Subjects often expressed deep disapproval of shocking a man in the face of his objections, and others denounced it as senseless and stupid. Yet many subjects complied even while they protested. The proportion of obedient subjects greatly exceeded the expectations of the experimenter and his colleagues. At the outset, we had conjectured that subjects would not, in general, go above the level of "Strong Shock." In practice, many subjects were willing to administer the most extreme shocks available when commanded by the experimenter. For some subjects the experiment provides an occasion for aggressive release. And for others it demonstrates the extent to which obedient dispositions are deeply ingrained, and are engaged irrespective of their consequences for others. Yet this is not the whole story. Somehow, the subject becomes implicated in a situation from which he cannot disengage himself.

The departure of the experimental results from intelligent expectation, to some extent, has been formalized. The procedure was to describe the experimental situation in concrete detail to a group of competent persons, and to ask them to predict the performance of 100 hypothetical subjects. For purposes of indicating the distribution of break-off points judges were provided with a diagram of the shock generator, and recorded their predictions before being informed of the actual results. Judges typically underestimated the amount of obedience demonstrated by subjects.

In Figure 3, we compare the predictions of forty psychiatrists at a leading medical school with the actual performance of subjects in the experiment. The psychiatrists predicted that most subjects would not go beyond the tenth shock level (150 volts; at this point the victim makes his first explicit demand to be freed). They further predicted that by the twentieth shock level (300 volts; the victim refuses to answer) 3.73 percent of the subjects would still be obedient; and that only a little over one-tenth of one percent of the subjects would administer

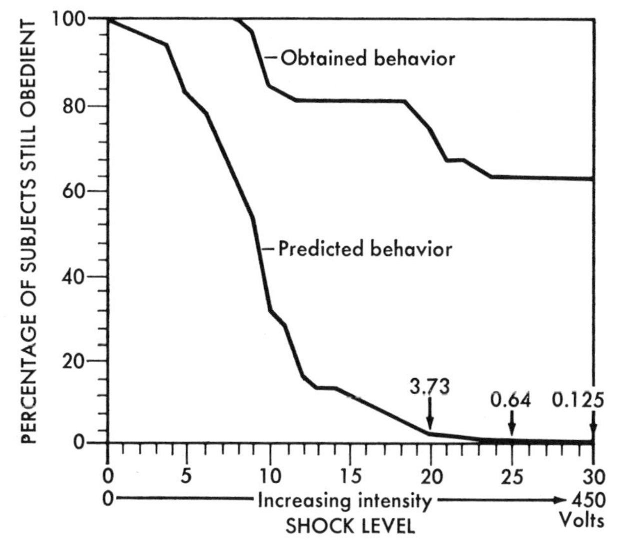

Figure 3 Predicted and Obtained Behavior in Voice Feedback

the highest shock on the board. But, as the graph indicates, the obtained behavior was very different. Sixty-two percent of the subjects obeyed the experimenter's commands fully. Between expectation and occurrence there is a whopping discrepancy.

Why did the psychiatrists underestimate the level of obedience? Possibly, because their predictions were based on an inadequate conception of the determinants of human action, a conception that focuses on motives *in vacuo.* This orientation may be entirely adequate for the repair of bruised impulses as revealed on the psychiatrist's couch, but as soon as our interest turns to action in larger settings, attention must be paid to the situations in which motives are expressed. A situation exerts an important press on the individual. It exercises constraints and may provide push. In certain circumstances it is not so much the kind of person a man is, as the kind of situation in which he is placed, that determines his actions.

Many people, not knowing much about the experiment, claim that subjects who go to the end of the board are sadistic. Nothing could be more foolish as an overall characterization of these persons. It is like saying that a person thrown into a swift-flowing stream is necessarily a fast swimmer, or that he has great stamina because he moves so rapidly relative to the bank. The context of action must always be considered. The individual, upon entering the laboratory, becomes integrated into a situation that carries its own momentum. The subject's problem then is how to become disengaged from a situation which is moving in an altogether ugly direction.

The fact that disengagement is so difficult testifies to the potency of the forces that keep the subject at the control board. Are these forces to be conceptualized as individual motives and expressed in the language of personality dynamics, or are they to be seen as the effects of social structure and pressures arising from the situational field?

A full understanding of the subject's action will, I feel, require that both perspectives be adopted. The person brings to the laboratory enduring dispositions toward authority and aggression, and at the same time he becomes enmeshed in a social structure that is no less an objective fact of the case. From the standpoint of personality theory one may ask: What mechanisms of personality enable a person to transfer responsibility to authority? What are the motives underlying obedient and disobedient performance? Does orientation to authority lead to a short-circuiting of the shame-guilt system? What cognitive and emotional defenses are brought into play in the case of obedient and defiant subjects?

The present experiments are not, however, directed toward an exploration of the motives engaged when the subject obeys the experimenter's commands. Instead, they examine the situational variables responsible for the elicitation of obedience. Elsewhere, we have attempted to spell out some of the structural properties of the experimental situation that account for high obedience, and this analysis need not be repeated here.[11] The experimental variations themselves represent our attempt to probe that structure, by systematically changing it and noting the consequences for behavior. It is clear that some situations produce greater compliance with the experimenter's commands than others. However, this does not necessarily imply an increase or decrease in the strength of any single definable motive. Situations producing the greatest obedience could do so by triggering the most powerful, yet perhaps the most idiosyncratic, of motives in each subject confronted by the setting. Or they may simply recruit a greater number and variety of motives in their service. But whatever the motives involved—and it is far from certain that they can ever be known—action may be studied as a direct function of the situation in which it occurs. This has been the approach of the present study, where we sought to plot behavioral regularities against manipulated properties of the social field. Ultimately, social psychology would like to have a compelling *theory of situations* which will, first, present a language in terms of which situations can be defined; proceed to a typology of situations; and then point to the manner in which definable properties of situations are transformed into psychological forces in the individual.[12]

Almost a thousand adults were individually studied in the obedience research, and there were many specific conclusions regarding the variables that control obedience and disobedience to authority. Some of these have been discussed briefly in the preceding sections, and more detailed reports will be released subsequently.

There are now some other generalizations I should like to make, which do not derive in any strictly logical fashion from the experiments as carried out, but which, I feel, ought to be made. They are formulations of an intuitive sort that have been forced on me by observation of many subjects responding to the pres-

[11] Stanley Milgram, "Behavioral Study of Obedience," *Journal of Abnormal and Social Psychology* 67 (1963): 371–78.

[12] My thanks to Professor Howard Leventhal of Yale for strengthening the writing in this paragraph.

sures of authority. The assertions represent a painful alteration in my own thinking; and since they were acquired only under the repeated impact of direct observation, I have no illusion that they will be generally accepted by persons who have not had the same experience.

With numbing regularity good people were seen to knuckle under the demands of authority and perform actions that were callous and severe. Men who are in everyday life responsible and decent were seduced by the trappings of authority, by the control of their perceptions, and by the uncritical acceptance of the experimenter's definition of the situation, into performing harsh acts.

What is the limit of such obedience? At many points we attempted to establish a boundary. Cries from the victim were inserted; not good enough. The victim claimed heart trouble; subjects still shocked him on command. The victim pleaded that he be let free, and his answers no longer registered on the signal box; subjects continued to shock him. At the outset we had not conceived that such drastic procedures would be needed to generate disobedience, and each step was added only as the ineffectiveness of the earlier techniques became clear. The final effort to establish a limit was the Touch-Proximity condition. But the very first subject in this condition subdued the victim on command, and proceeded to the highest shock level. A quarter of the subjects in this condition performed similarly.

The results, as seen and felt in the laboratory, are to this author disturbing. They raise the possibility that human nature, or—more specifically—the kind of character produced in American democratic society, cannot be counted on to insulate its citizens from brutality and inhumane treatment at the direction of malevolent authority. A substantial proportion of people do what they are told to do, irrespective of the content of the act and without limitations of conscience, so long as they perceive that the command comes from a legitimate authority. If in this study an anonymous experimenter could successfully command adults to subdue a fifty-year-old man, and force on him painful electric shocks against his protests, one can only wonder what government, with its vastly greater authority and prestige, can command of its subjects. There is, of course, the extremely important question of whether malevolent political institutions could or would arise in American society. The present research contributes nothing to this issue.

In an article titled "The Dangers of Obedience," Harold J. Laski wrote:

> . . . civilization means, above all, an unwillingness to inflict unnecessary pain. Within the ambit of that definition, those of us who heedlessly accept the commands of authority cannot yet claim to be civilized men.
>
> . . . Our business, if we desire to live a life, not utterly devoid of meaning and significance, is to accept nothing which contradicts our basic experience merely because it comes to us from tradition or convention or authority. It may well be that we shall be wrong; but our self-expression is thwarted at the root unless the certainties we are asked to accept coincide with the certainties we experience. That is why the condition of freedom in any state is always a widespread and consistent skepticism of the canons upon which power insists.[13]

---

[13] Harold Laski, "The Dangers of Obedience," *Harper's Monthly Magazine* 159 (June): 1–10.

7

Compliance Without Pressure: The Foot-in-the-Door Technique

JONATHAN L. FREEDMAN · SCOTT C. FRASER

In the absence of the use of force, how can a person be induced to do something he ordinarily would not do? This is the general question addressed by Freedman and Fraser in the following selection. The report describes two field experiments designed to test the assumption that once a person has been induced to comply with a small request, he is more likely to comply with a subsequent, larger request, i.e., the foot-in-the-door technique.

Data from the first of these experiments supported the research hypothesis. Specifically, Freedman and Fraser found that over 50 percent of the subjects who agreed to a small request also agreed three days later to a larger, related request, while less than 25 percent of the subjects asked to comply only with the larger request agreed to it. Because of the nature of the research design, however, the researchers were unable to make any firm statements about *why* people who first agreed to a small request were more likely to comply with a later, larger request. There are several plausible explanations for the increased compliance. Perhaps it can be attributed to some kind of involvement with or commitment to the person making the request. Since the same person made both requests in this experiment, no decision could be made as to the validity of this explanation. Alternatively, the increased compliance might be a function of involvement with the particular issue with which the requests were concerned. Because both requests dealt with the same issue, no decision could be made about this explanation.

The second experiment was designed to evaluate some of these alternative explanations. Freedman and Fraser found that whether the same or different experimenters made the two requests, subjects who agreed to

Jonathan L. Freedman and Scott C. Fraser, "Compliance Without Pressure: The Foot-in-the-Door Technique," *Journal of Personality and Social Psychology,* 4 (1966), 195–202.

comply with a small request were more likely to comply with a second, larger request than were subjects asked to comply only with the larger request. Further, this pattern of increased compliance held even when the first and second requests dealt with different issues and/or tasks. In light of these findings, the researchers suggest that the mechanism producing the increase in compliance is a general and diffuse one. "What may occur is a change in the person's feelings about getting involved or about taking action. . . . The change in attitude could be toward any aspect of the situation or toward the whole business of saying yes."

How can a person be induced to do something he would rather not do? This question is relevant to practically every phase of social life, from stopping at a traffic light to stopping smoking, from buying Brand X to buying savings bonds, from supporting the March of Dimes to supporting the Civil Rights Act.

One common way of attacking the problem is to exert as much pressure as possible on the reluctant individual in an effort to force him to comply. This technique has been the focus of a considerable amount of experimental research. Work on attitude change, conformity, imitation, and obedience has all tended to stress the importance of the degree of external pressure. The prestige of the communicator (Kelman & Hovland, 1953), degree of discrepancy of the communication (Hovland & Pritzker, 1957), size of the group disagreeing with the subject (Asch, 1951), perceived power of the model (Bandura, Ross, & Ross, 1963), etc., are the kinds of variables that have been studied. This impressive body of work, added to the research on rewards and punishments in learning, has produced convincing evidence that greater external pressure generally leads to greater compliance with the wishes of the experimenter. The one exception appears to be situations involving the arousal of cognitive dissonance in which, once discrepant behavior has been elicited from the subject, the greater the pressure that was used to elicit the behavior, the less subsequent change occurs (Festinger & Carlsmith, 1959). But even in this situation one critical element is the amount of external pressure exerted.

Clearly, then, under most circumstances the more pressure that can be applied, the more likely it is that the individual will comply. There are, however, many times when for ethical, moral, or practical reasons it is difficult to apply much pressure when the goal is to produce compliance with a minimum of apparent pressure, as in the forced-compliance studies involving dissonance arousal. And even when a great deal of pressure is possible, it is still important to maximize the compliance it produces. Thus, factors other than external pressure are often quite critical in determining degree of compliance. What are these factors?

Although rigorous research on the problem is rather sparse, the fields of advertising, propaganda, politics, etc. are by no means devoid of techniques designed to produce compliance in the absence of external pressure (or to maximize the effectiveness of the pressure that is used, which is really the same problem). One assumption about compliance that has often been made either explicitly or implicitly is that once a person has been induced to comply with a small request he is more likely to comply with a larger demand. This is the principle that is commonly referred to as the foot-in-the-door or gradation technique and is reflected in the saying that if you "give them an inch, they'll take a mile." It was, for example, supposed to be one of the basic techniques upon which the Korean brainwashing tactics were based (Schein, Schneier, & Barker, 1961), and, in a somewhat different sense, one basis for Nazi propaganda during 1940 (Bruner, 1941). It also appears to be implicit in many advertising campaigns which attempt to induce the consumer to do anything relating to the product involved, even sending back a card saying he does not want the product.

The most relevant piece of experimental evidence comes from a study of conformity done by Deutsch and Gerard (1955). Some subjects were faced with incorrect group judgments first in a series in which the stimuli were not present during the actual judging and then in a series in which they were present, while the order of the memory and visual series was reversed for other subjects. For both groups the memory series produced more conformity, and when the memory series came first there was more total conformity to the group judgments. It seems likely that this order effect occurred because, as the authors suggest, once conformity is elicited at all it is more likely to occur in the future. Although this kind of conformity is probably somewhat different from compliance as described above, this finding certainly lends some support to the foot-in-the-door idea. The present research attempted to provide a rigorous, more direct test of this notion as it applies to compliance and to provide data relevant to several alternative ways of explaining the effect.

Experiment I

The basic paradigm was to ask some subjects (Performance condition) to comply first with a small request and then 3 days later with a larger, related request. Other subjects (One-Contact condition) were asked to comply only with the large request. The hypothesis was that more subjects in the Performance condition than in the One-Contact condition would comply with the larger request.

Two additional conditions were included in an attempt to specify the essential difference between these two major conditions. The Performance subjects were asked to perform a small favor, and, if they agreed, they did it. The question arises whether the act of agreeing itself is critical or whether actually carrying it out was necessary. To assess this a third group of subjects (Agree-Only) was asked the first request, but, even if they agreed, they did not carry it out. Thus, they were identical to the Performance group except that they were not given the opportunity of performing the request.

Another difference between the two main conditions was that at the time of the larger request the subjects in the Performance condition were more familiar with the experimenter than were the other subjects. The Performance subjects had been contacted twice, heard his voice more, discovered that the questions were not dangerous, and so on. It is possible that this increased familiarity would serve to decrease the fear and suspicion of a strange voice on the phone and might accordingly increase the likelihood of the subjects agreeing to the larger request. To control for this a fourth condition was run (Familiarization) which attempted to give the subjects as much familiarity with the experimenter as in the Performance and Agree-Only conditions with the only difference being that no request was made.

The major prediction was that more subjects in the Performance condition would agree to the large request than in any of the other conditions, and that the One-Contact condition would produce the least compliance. Since the importance of agreement and familiarity was essentially unknown, the expectation was that the Agree-Only and Familiarization conditions would produce intermediate amounts of compliance.

Method

The prediction stated above was tested in a field experiment in which housewives were asked to allow a survey team of five or six men to come into their homes for 2 hours to classify the household products they used. This large request was made under four different conditions: after an initial contact in which the subject had been asked to answer a few questions about the kinds of soaps she used, and the questions were actually asked (Performance condition); after an identical contact in which the questions were not actually asked (Agree-Only condition); after an initial contact in which no request was made (Familiarization condition); or after an initial contact (One-Contact condition). The dependent measure was simply whether or not the subject agreed to the large request.

Procedure The subjects were 156 Palo Alto, California, housewives, 36 in each condition, who were selected at random from the telephone directory. An additional 12 subjects distributed about equally among the three two-contact conditions could not be reached for the second contact and are not included in the data analysis. Subjects were assigned randomly to the various conditions, except that the Familiarization condition was added to the design after the other three conditions had been completed. All contacts were by telephone by the same experimenter who identified himself as the same person each time. Calls were made only in the morning. For the three groups that were contacted twice, the first call was made on either Monday or Tuesday and the second always 3 days later. All large requests were made on either Thursday or Friday.

At the first contact, the experimenter introduced himself by name and said that he was from the California Consumers' Group. In the Performance condition he then proceeded:

> We are calling you this morning to ask if you would answer a number of questions about what household products you use so that we could have this information for our public service publication, "The Guide." Would you be willing to give us this information for our survey?

If the subject agreed, she was asked a series of eight innocuous questions dealing with household soaps (e.g., "What brand of soap do you use in your kitchen sink?"). She was then thanked for her cooperation, and the contact terminated.

Another condition (Agree-Only) was run to assess the importance of actually carrying out the request as opposed to merely agreeing to it. The only difference between this and the Performance condition was that, if the subject agreed to answer the questions, the experimenter thanked her, but said that he was just lining up respondents for the survey and would contact her if needed.

A third condition was included to check on the importance of the subject's greater familiarity with the experimenter in the two-contact conditions. In this condition the experimenter introduced himself, described the organization he worked for and the survey it was conducting, listed the questions he was asking, and then said that he was calling merely to acquaint the subject with the existence of his organization. In other words, these subjects were contacted, spent as much time on the phone with the experimenter as the Performance subjects did, heard all the questions, but neither agreed to answer them nor answered them.

In all of these two-contact conditions some subjects did not agree to the requests or even hung up before the requests were made. Every subject who answered the phone was included in the analysis of the results and was contacted for the second request regardless of her extent of cooperativeness during the first contact. In other words, no subject who could be contacted the appropriate number of times was discarded from any of the four conditions.

The large request was essentially identical for all subjects. The experimenter called, identified himself, and said either that his group was expanding its survey (in the case of the two-contact conditions) or that it was conducting a survey (in the One-Contact condition). In all four conditions he then continued:

> The survey will involve five or six men from our staff coming into your home some morning for about 2 hours to enumerate and classify all the household products that you have. They will have to have full freedom in your house to go through the cupboards and storage places. Then all this information will be used in the writing of the reports for our public service publication, "The Guide."

If the subject agreed to the request, she was thanked and told that at the present time the experimenter was merely collecting names of people who were willing to take part and that she would be contacted if it were decided to use her in the survey. If she did not agree, she was thanked for her time. This terminated the experiment.

Results

Apparently even the small request was not considered trivial by some of the subjects. Only about two thirds of the subjects in the Performance and Agree-Only conditions agreed to answer the questions about household soaps. It might be noted that none of those who refused the first request later agreed to the large request, although as stated previously all subjects who were contacted for the small request are included in the data for those groups.

Our major prediction was that subjects who had agreed to and carried out a small request (Performance condition) would subsequently be more likely to comply with a larger request than would subjects who were asked only the larger request (One-Contact condition). As may be seen in Table 1, the results support

TABLE 1
PERCENTAGE OF SUBJECTS COMPLYING WITH LARGE REQUEST IN EXPERIMENT I

Condition	%
Performance	52.8
Agree-Only	33.3
Familiarization	27.8*
One-Contact	22.2**

Note. $N = 36$ for each group. Significance levels represent differences from the Performance condition.
* $p < .07$.
** $p < .02$.

the prediction. Over 50 percent of the subjects in the Performance condition agreed to the larger request, while less than 25 percent of the One-Contact condition agreed to it. Thus it appears that obtaining compliance with a small request does tend to increase subsequent compliance. The question is what aspect of the initial contact produces this effect.

One possibility is that the effect was produced merely by increased familiarity with the experimenter. The Familiarization control was included to assess the effect on compliance of two contacts with the same person. The group had as much contact with the experimenter as the Performance group, but no request was made during the first contact. As the table indicates, the Familiarization group did not differ appreciably in amount of compliance from the One-Contact group, but was different from the Performance group ($\chi^2 = 3.70$, $p < .07$). Thus, although increased familiarity may well lead to increased compliance, in the present situation the differences in amount of familiarity apparently were not great enough to produce any such increase; the effect that was obtained seems not to be due to this factor.

Another possibility is that the critical factor producing increased compliance is simply agreeing to the small request (i.e., carrying it out may not be necessary). The Agree-Only condition was identical to the Performance condition except that in the former the subjects were not asked the questions. The amount of compliance in this Agree-Only condition feel between the Performance and One-Contact conditions and was not significantly different from either of them. This leaves the effect of merely agreeing somewhat ambiguous, but it suggests that the agreement alone may produce part of the effect.

Unfortunately, it must be admitted that neither of these control conditions is an entirely adequate test of the possibility it was designed to assess. Both conditions are in some way quite peculiar and may have made a very different and extraneous impression on the subject than did the Performance condition. In one case, a housewife is asked to answer some questions and then is not asked them; in the other, some man calls to tell her about some organization she has never heard of. Now, by themselves neither of these events might produce very much suspicion. But, several days later, the same man calls and asks a very large favor. At this point it is not at all unlikely that many subjects think they are being manipulated, or in any case that something strange is going on. Any such reaction on the part of the subjects would naturally tend to reduce the amount of compliance in these conditions.

Thus, although this first study demonstrates that an initial contact in which a request is made and carried out increases compliance with a second request, the question of why and how the initial request produces this effect remains unanswered. In an attempt to begin answering this question and to extend the results of the first study, a second experiment was conducted.

There seemed to be several quite plausible ways in which the increase in compliance might have been produced. The first was simply some kind of commitment to or involvement with the particular person making the request. This might work, for example, as follows: The subject has agreed to the first request and perceives that the experimenter therefore expects him also to agree to the second request. The subject thus feels obligated and does not want to disappoint the experimenter; he also feels that he needs a good reason for saying "no"—a better reason than he would need if he had never said "yes." This is just one line of causality—the particular process by which involvement with the experimenter operates might be quite different, but the basic idea would be similar. The commitment is to the particular person. This implies that the increase in compliance due to the first contact should occur primarily when both requests are made by the same person.

Another explanation in terms of involvement centers around the particular issue with which the requests are concerned. Once the subject has taken some action in connection with an area of concern, be it surveys, political activity, or highway safety, there is probably a tendency to become somewhat more concerned with the area. The subject begins thinking about it, considering its importance and relevance to him, and so on. This tends to make him more likely to agree to take further action in the same area when he is later asked to. To the extent that this is the critical factor, the initial contact should increase compliance only when both requests are related to the same issue or area of concern.

Another way of looking at the situation is that the subject needs a reason to say "no." In our society it is somewhat difficult to refuse a reasonable request, particularly when it is made by an organization that is not trying to make money. In order to refuse, many people feel that they need a reason—simply not wanting to do it is often not in itself sufficient. The person can say to the requester or simply to himself that he does not believe in giving to charities or tipping or working for political parties or answering questions or posting signs, or whatever he is asked to do. Once he has performed a particular task, however, this excuse is no longer valid for not agreeing to perform a similar task. Even if the first thing he did was trivial compared to the present request, he cannot say he never does this sort of thing, and thus one good reason for refusing is removed. This line of reasoning suggests that the similarity of the first and second requests in terms of the type of action required is an important factor. The more similar they are, the more the "matter of principle" argument is eliminated by agreeing to the first request, and the greater should be the increase in compliance.

There are probably many other mechanisms by which the initial request might produce an increase in compliance. The second experiment was designed in part to test the notions described above, but its major purpose was to demonstrate the effect unequivocally. To this latter end it eliminated one of the important problems with the first study which was that when the experimenter made the second request he was not blind as to which condition the subjects were in. In this study the second request was always made by someone other than the person who made the first request, and the second experimenter was blind as to what condition the subject was in. This eliminates the possibility that the experimenter exerted systematically different amounts of pressure in different experimental conditions. If the effect of the first study were replicated, it would also rule out the relatively uninteresting possibility that the effect is due primarily to greater familiarity or involvement with the particular person making the first request.

Experiment II

The basic paradigm was quite similar to that of the first study. Experimental subjects were asked to comply with a small request and were later asked a considerably larger request, while controls were asked only the larger request. The first request varied along two dimensions. Subjects were asked either to put up a small sign or to sign a petition, and the issue was either safe driving or keeping California beautiful. Thus, there were four first requests: a small sign for safe driving or for beauty, and a petition for the two issues. The second request for all subjects was to install in their front lawn a very large sign which said "Drive Carefully." The four experimental conditions may be defined in terms of the similarity of the small and large requests along the dimensions of issue and task. The two requests were similar in both issue and task for the small-sign, safe-driving group, similar only in issue for the safe-driving-petition group, similar only in task for the small "Keep California Beautiful" sign group, and similar in neither issue nor task for the "Keep California Beautiful" petition group.

The major expectation was that the three groups for which either the task or the issue were similar would show more compliance than the controls, and it was also felt that when both were similar there would probably be the most compliance. The fourth condition (Different Issue-Different Task) was included primarily to assess the effect simply of the initial contact which, although it was not identical to the second one on either issue or task, was in many ways quite similar (e.g., a young student asking for co-operation on a controversial issue). There were no clear expectations as to how this condition would compare to the controls.

Method

The subjects were 114 women and 13 men living in Palo Alto, California. Of these, 9 women and 6 men could not be contacted for the second request and are not included in the data analysis. The remaining 112 subjects were divided about equally among the five conditions (see Table 2). All subjects were contacted between 1:30 and 4:30 on weekday afternoons.

Two experimenters, one male and one female, were employed, and a different one always made the second contact. Unlike the first study, the experimenters actually went to the homes of the subjects and interviewed them on a face-to-face basis. An effort was made to select subjects from blocks and neighborhoods that were as homogeneous as possible. On each block every third or fourth house was approached, and all subjects on that block were in one experimental condition. This was necessary because of the likelihood that neighbors would talk to each other about the contact. In addition, for every four subjects contacted, a fifth house was chosen as a control but was, of course, not contacted. Throughout this phase of the experiment, and in fact throughout the whole experiment, the two experimenters did not communicate to each other what conditions had been run on a given block nor what condition a particular house was in.

The small-sign, safe-driving group was told that the experimenter was from the Community Committee for Traffic Safety, that he was visiting a number of homes in an attempt to make the citizens more aware of the need to drive carefully all the time, and that he would like the subject to take a small sign and put it in a window or in the car so that it would serve as a reminder of the need to drive carefully. The sign was 3 inches square, said "Be a safe driver," was on thin paper without a gummed backing, and in general looked rather amateurish and unattractive. If the subject agreed, he was given the sign and thanked; if he disagreed, he was simply thanked for his time.

The three other experimental conditions were quite similar with appropriate changes. The other organization was identified as the Keep California Beautiful Committee and its sign said, appropriately enough, "Keep California Beautiful."

Both signs were simply black block letters on a white background. The two petition groups were asked to sign a petition which was being sent to California's United States Senators. The petition advocated support for any legislation which would promote either safer driving or keeping California beautiful. The subject was shown a petition, typed on heavy bond paper, with at least 20 signatures already affixed. If she agreed, she signed and was thanked. If she did not agree, she was merely thanked.

The second contact was made about 2 weeks after the initial one. Each experimenter was armed with a list of houses which had been compiled by the other experimenter. This list contained all four experimental conditions and the controls, and, of course, there was no way for the second experimenter to know which condition the subject had been in. At this second contact, all subjects were asked the same thing: Would they put a large sign concerning safe driving in their front yard? The experimenter identified himself as being from the Citizens for Safe Driving, a different group from the original safe-driving group (although it is likely that most subjects who had been in the safe-driving conditions did not notice the difference). The subject was shown a picture of a very large sign reading "Drive Carefully" placed in front of an attractive house. The picture was taken so that the sign obscured much of the front of the house and completely concealed the doorway. It was rather poorly lettered. The subject was told that: "Our men will come out and install it and later come and remove it. It makes just a small hole in your lawn, but if this is unacceptable to you we have a special mount which will make no hole." She was asked to put the sign up for a week or a week and a half. If the subject agreed, she was told that more names than necessary were being gathered and if her home were to be used she would be contacted in a few weeks. The experimenter recorded the subject's response and this ended the experiment.

Results

First, it should be noted that here were no large differences among the experimental conditions in the percentages of subjects agreeing to the first request. Although somewhat more subjects agreed to post the "Keep California Beautiful" sign and somewhat fewer to sign the beauty petition, none of these differences approach significance.

The important figures are the number of subjects in each group who agreed to the large request. These are presented in Table 2. The figures for the four experimental groups include all subjects who were approached the first time, regardless of whether or not they agreed to the small request. As noted above a few subjects were lost because they could not be reached for the second request, and of course, these are not included in the table.

It is immediately apparent that the first request tended to increase the degree of compliance with the second request. Whereas fewer than 20 percent of the controls agreed to put the large sign on their lawn, over 55 percent of the experi-

TABLE 2
PERCENTAGE OF SUBJECTS COMPLYING WITH LARGE REQUEST IN EXPERIMENT II

ISSUE[a]	TASKS[a]			
	Similar	N	*Different*	N
Similar	76.0[c]	25	47.8[b]	23
Different	47.6[b]	21	47.4[b]	19
One-Contact 16.7 ($N = 24$)				

Note. Significance levels represent differences from the One-Contact condition.
[a] Denotes relationship between first and second requests.
[b] $p < .08$.
[c] $p < .01$.

mental subjects agreed, with over 45 percent being the lowest degree of compliance for any experimental condition. As expected, those conditions in which the two requests were similar in terms of either issue or task produced significantly more complicance than did the controls (χ^2s range from 3.67, $p < .07$ to 15.01, $p < .001$). A somewhat unexpected result is that the fourth condition, in which the first request had relatively little in common with the second request, also produced more compliance than the controls ($\chi^2 = 3.40$, $p < .08$). In other words, regardless of whether or not the two requests are similar in either issue or task, simply having the first request tends to increase the likelihood that the subject will comply with a subsequent, larger request. And this holds even when the two requests are made by different people several weeks apart.

A second point of interest is a comparison among the four experimental conditions. As expected, the Same Issue-Same Task condition produced more compliance than any of the other two-contact conditions, but the difference is not significant (χ^2s range from 2.7 to 2.9). If only those subjects who agreed to the first request are considered, the same pattern holds.

Discussion

To summarize the results, the first study indicated that carrying out a small request increased the likelihood that the subject would agree to a similar larger request made by the same person. The second study showed that this effect was quite strong even when a different person made the larger request, and the two requests were quite dissimilar. How may these results be explained?

Two possibilities were outlined previously. The matter-of-principle idea which centered on the particular type of action was not supported by the data, since the similarity of the tasks did not make an appreciable difference in degree of compliance. The notion of involvement, as described previously, also has difficulty accounting for some of the findings. The basic idea was that once someone has agreed to any action, no matter how small, he tends to feel more involved than he did before. This involvement may center around the particular person making the first request or the particular issue. This is quite consistent with the results of the first study (with the exception of the two control groups which as discussed previously were rather ambiguous) and with the Similar Issue groups in the second experiment. This idea of involvement does not, however, explain the increase in compliance found in the two groups in which the first and second request did not deal with the same issue.

It is possible that in addition to or instead of this process a more general and diffuse mechanism underlies the increase in compliance. What may occur is a change in the person's feelings about getting involved or about taking action. Once he has agreed to a request, his attitude may change. He may become, in his own eyes, the kind of person who does this sort of thing, who agrees to requests made by strangers, who takes action on things he believes in, who cooperates with good causes. The change in attitude could be toward any aspect of the situation or toward the whole business of saying "yes." The basic idea is that the change in attitude need not be toward any particular issue or person or activity, but may be toward activity or compliance in general. This would imply that an increase in compliance would not depend upon the two contacts being made by the same person, or concerning the same issue or involving the same kind of action. The similarity could be much more general, such as both concerning good causes, or requiring a similar kind of action, or being made by pleasant, attractive individuals.

It is not being suggested that this is the only mechanism operating here. The idea of involvement continues to be extremely plausible, and there are probably a number of other possibilities. Unfortunately, the present studies offer no additional data with which to support or refute any of the possible explanations of the effect. These explanations thus remain simply descriptions of mechanisms which might produce an increase in compliance after agreement with a first request. Hopefully, additional research will test these ideas more fully and perhaps also specify other manipulations which produce an increase in compliance without an increase in external pressure.

It should be pointed out that the present studies employed what is perhaps a very special type of situation. In all cases the requests were made by presumably nonprofit service organizations. The issues in the second study were deliberately noncontroversial, and it may be assumed that virtually all subjects initially sympathized with the objectives of safe driving and a beautiful California. This is in strong contrast to compaigns which are designed to sell a particular product, political candidate, or dogma. Whether the technique employed in this study would be successful in these other situations remains to be shown.

REFERENCES

Asch, S. E. 1951. Effects of group pressure upon the modification and distortion of judgments. In H. Guetzkow, ed., *Groups, leadership and men; research in human relations*. Pittsburgh: Carnegie Press, pp. 177–90.

Bandura, A., Ross, D., & Ross, S. A. 1963. A comparative test of the status envy, social power, and secondary reinforcement theories of identificatory learning. *Journal of Abnormal and Social Psychology* 67: 527–34.

Bruner, J. 1941. The dimensions of propaganda: German short-wave broadcasts to America. *Journal of Abnormal and Social Psychology* 36: 311–37.

Deutsch, M., & Gerard, H. B. 1955. A study of normative and informational social influences upon individual judgment. *Journal of Abnormal and Social Psychology* 51: 629–36.

Festinger, L., & Carlsmith, J. 1959. Cognitive consequences of forced compliance. *Journal of Abnormal and Social Psychology* 58: 203–10.

Hovland, C. I., & Pritzker, H. A. 1957. Extent of opinion change as a function of amount of change advocated. *Journal of Abnormal and Social Psychology* 54: 257–61.

Kelman, H. C., & Hovland, C. I. 1953. "Reinstatement" of the communicator in delayed measurement of opinion change. *Journal of Abnormal and Social Psychology* 48: 327–35.

Schein, E. H., Schneier, I., & Barker, C. H. 1961. *Coercive pressure.* New York: Norton.

8

Bystander Intervention in Emergencies: Diffusion of Responsibility

JOHN M. DARLEY · BIBB LATANÉ

When a person sees one of his fellows in a state of helplessness, it is generally expected that he will intervene in his behalf. The pervasiveness of this expectation is best exemplified by the public outcries which result when someone is victimized in the presence of others who make no attempt to intervene. Explanations for such "inhumane" behavior have taken a variety of forms, but they are generally cast in terms of characteristics of the observer, e.g., alienation, apathy, indifference.

In the selection which follows, Darley and Latané design and execute an experiment to test an alternative explanation of bystander nonintervention. They hypothesize that the more bystanders to an emergency, the less likely, or more slowly, any one bystander will intervene to provide aid. The basis for the hypothesis is that if only one bystander is present in an emergency, then he is the only source of help for the victim. He is the focal point of any pressure to intervene. If, on the other hand, there are a number of observers, the responsibility for intervention is diffused among all the onlookers. Consequently, either no one helps, or help is delayed.

In the experiment, subjects overheard an epileptic seizure. They were led to believe that they alone, or that one or four other subjects were also present and heard the seizure. While all subjects in the two-person groups reported the emergency to the experimenter, only two-thirds of those in the three-person groups and one-third of those in the six-person groups ever reported. Further, subjects in the two- and three-person groups responded significantly more rapidly than did subjects in the six-person groups. Selected personality and background factors had no significant influence on the likelihood or speed of bystander response. The authors conclude that the "explanation

John M. Darley and Bibb Latané, "Bystander Intervention in Emergencies: Diffusion of Responsibility," *Journal of Personality and Social Psychology* 8 (1968): 377–83.

of bystander 'apathy' may lie more in the bystander's response to other observers than in presumed personality deficiencies of 'apathetic' individuals."

Several years ago, a young woman was stabbed to death in the middle of a street in a residential section of New York City. Although such murders are not entirely routine, the incident received little public attention until several weeks later when *The New York Times* disclosed another side to the case: at least 38 witnesses had observed the attack—and none had even attempted to intervene. Although the attacker took more than half an hour to kill Kitty Genovese, not one of the 38 people who watched from the safety of their own apartments came out to assist her. Not one even lifted the telephone to call the police (Rosenthal, 1964).

Preachers, professors, and news commentators sought the reasons for such apparently conscienceless and inhumane lack of intervention. Their conclusions ranged from "moral decay," to "dehumanization produced by the urban environment," to "alienation," "anomie," and "existential despair." An analysis of the situation, however, suggests that factors other than apathy and indifference were involved.

A person witnessing an emergency situation, particularly such a frightening and dangerous one as a stabbing, is in conflict. There are obvious humanitarian norms about helping the victim, but there are also rational and irrational fears about what might happen to a person who does intervene (Milgram & Hollander, 1964). "I didn't want to get involved," is a familiar comment, and behind it lies fears of physical harm, public embarrassment, involvement with police procedures, lost work days and jobs, and other unknown dangers.

In certain circumstances, the norms favoring intervention may be weakened, leading bystanders to resolve the conflict in the direction of nonintervention. One of these circumstances may be the presence of other onlookers. For example, in the case above, each observer, by seeing lights and figures in other apartment house windows, knew that others were also watching. However, there was no way to tell how the other observers were reacting. These two facts provide several reasons why any individual may have delayed or failed to help. The responsibility for helping was diffused among the observers; there was also diffusion of any potential blame for not taking action; and finally, it was possible that somebody, unperceived, had already initiated helping action.

When only one bystander is present in an emergency, if help is to come, it must come from him. Although he may choose to ignore it (out of concern for his personal safety, or desires "not to get involved"), any pressure to intervene focuses uniquely on him. When there are several observers present, however, the pressures to intervene do not focus on any one of the observers; instead the responsibility for intervention is shared among all the onlookers and is not unique to any one. As a result, no one helps.

A second possibility is that potential blame may be diffused. However much we may wish to think that an individual's moral behavior is divorced from considerations of personal punishment or reward, there is both theory and evidence to the contrary (Aronfreed, 1964; Miller & Dollard, 1941; Whiting & Child, 1953). It is perfectly reasonable to assume that, under circumstances of group responsibility for a punishable act, the punishment or blame that accrues to any one individual is often slight or nonexistent.

Finally, if others are known to be present, but their behavior cannot be closely observed, any one bystander can assume that one of the other observers is already taking action to end the emergency. Therefore, his own intervention would be only redundant—perhaps harmfully or confusingly so. Thus, given the presence of other onlookers whose behavior cannot be observed, any given bystander can rationalize his own inaction by convincing himself that "somebody else must be doing something."

These considerations lead to the hypothesis that the more bystanders to an emergency, the less likely, or the more slowly, any one bystander will intervene to provide aid. To test this proposition it would be necessary to create a situation in which a realistic "emergency" could plausibly occur. Each subject should also be blocked from communicating with others to prevent his getting information about their behavior during the emergency. Finally, the experimental situation should allow for the assessment of the speed and frequency of the subjects' reaction to the emergency. The experiment reported below attempted to fulfill these conditions.

Procedure

Overview. A college student arrived in the laboratory and was ushered into an individual room from which a communication system would enable him to talk to the other participants. It was explained to him that he was to take part in a discussion about personal problems associated with college life and that the discussion would be held over the intercom system, rather than face-to-face, in order to avoid embarrassment by preserving the anonymity of the subjects. During the course of the discussion, one of the other subjects underwent what appeared to be a very serious nervous seizure similar to epilepsy. During the fit it was impossible for the subject to talk to the other discussants or to find out what, if anything, they were doing about the emergency. The dependent variable was the speed with which the subjects reported the emergency to the experimenter. The major independent variable was the number of people the subject thought to be in the discussion group.

Subjects. Fifty-nine female and thirteen male students in introductory psychology courses at New York University were contacted to take part in an unspecified experiment as part of a class requirement.

Method. Upon arriving for the experiment, the subject found himself in a long corridor with doors opening off it to several small rooms. An experimental assistant met him, took him to one of the rooms, and seated him at a table. After filling out a background information form, the subject was given a pair of headphones with an attached microphone and was told to listen for instructions.

Over the intercom, the experimenter explained that he was interested in learning about the kinds of personal problems faced by normal college students in a high pressure, urban environment. He said that to avoid possible embarrassment about discussing personal problems with strangers several precautions had been taken. First, subjects would remain anonymous, which was why they had been placed in individual rooms rather than face-to-face. (The actual reason for this was to allow tape recorder simulation of the other subjects and the emergency.) Second, since the discussion might be inhibited by the presence of outside listeners, the experimenter would not listen to the initial discussion, but would get the subjects' reactions later, by questionnaire. (The real purpose of this was to remove the obviously responsible experimenter from the scene of the emergency.)

The subjects were told that since the experimenter was not present, it was necessary to impose some organization. Each person would talk in turn, presenting his problems to the group. Next, each person in turn would comment on what the others had said, and finally, there would be a free discussion. A mechanical switching device would regulate this discussion sequence and each subject's microphone would be on for about 2 minutes. While any microphone was on, all other microphones would be off. Only one subject, therefore, could be heard over the network at any given time. The subjects were thus led to realize when they later heard the seizure that only the victim's microphone was on and that there was no way of determining what any of the other witnesses were doing, nor of discussing the event and its possible solution with the others. When these instructions had been given, the discussion began.

In the discussion, the future victim spoke first, saying that he found it difficult to get adjusted to New York City and to his studies. Very hesitantly, and with obvious embarrassment, he mentioned that he was prone to seizures, particularly when studying hard or taking exams. The other people, including the real subject, took their turns and discussed similar problems (minus, of course, the proneness to seizures). The naive subject talked last in the series, after the last prerecorded voice was played.[1]

When it was again the victim's turn to talk, he made a few relatively calm comments, and then, growing increasingly louder and incoherent, he continued:

---

[1] To test whether the order in which the subjects spoke in the first discussion round significantly affected the subjects' speed of report, the order in which the subjects spoke was varied (in the six-person group). This had no significant or noticeable effect on the speed of the subjects' reports.

I-er-um-I think I-I need-er-if-if could-er-er-somebody er-er-er-er-er-er-er give me a little-er-give me a little help here because-er-I-er-I'm-er-er-h-h-having a-a-a real problem-er-right now and I-er-if somebody could help me out it would-it would-er-er s-s-sure be-sure be good . . . because-er-there-er-er-a cause I-er-I-uh-I've got a-a one of the-er-cei-----er-er-things coming on and-and-and I could really-er-use some help so if somebody would-er-give me a little h-help-uh-er-er-er-er-er c-could somebody-er-er-help-er-uh-uh-uh (choking sounds. . . . I'm gonna die-er-er-I'm . . . gonna die-er-help-er-er-seizure-er-[chokes, then quiet].

The experimenter began timing the speed of the real subject's response at the beginning of the victim's speech. Informed judges listening to the tape have estimated that the victim's increasingly louder and more disconnected ramblings clearly represented a breakdown about 70 seconds after the signal for the victim's second speech. The victim's speech was abruptly cut off 125 seconds after this signal, which could be interpreted by the subject as indicating that the time allotted for that speaker had elapsed and the switching circuits had switched away from him. Times reported in the results are measured from the start of the fit.

Group size variable. The major independent variable of the study was the number of other people that the subject believed also heard the fit. By the assistant's comments before the experiment, and also by the number of voices heard to speak in the first round of the group discussion, the subject was led to believe that the discussion group was one of three sizes: either a two-person group (consisting of a person who would later have a fit and the real subject), a three-person group (consisting of the victim, the real subject, and one confederate voice), or a six-person group (consisting of the victim, the real subject, and four confederate voices). All the confederates' voices were tape-recorded.

Variations in group composition. Varying the kind as well as the number of bystanders present at an emergency should also vary the amount of responsibility felt by any single bystander. To test this, several variations of the three-person group were run. In one three-person condition, the taped bystander voice was that of a female, in another a male, and in the third a male who said that he was a premedical student who occasionally worked in the emergency wards at Bellevue hospital.

In the above conditions, the subjects were female college students. In a final condition males drawn from the same introductory psychology subject pool were tested in a three-person female-bystander condition.

Time to help. The major dependent variable was the time elapsed from the start of the victim's fit until the subject left her experimental cubicle. When the subject left her room, she saw the experimental assistant seated at the end of the hall, and invariably went to the assistant. If 6 minutes elapsed without the subject having emerged from her room, the experiment was terminated.

As soon as the subject reported the emergency, or after 6 minutes had elapsed, the experimental assistant disclosed the true nature of the experiment, and dealt with any emotions aroused in the subject. Finally the subject filled out a questionnaire concerning her thoughts and feelings during the emergency, and completed scales of Machiavellianism, anomie, and authoritarianism (Christie, 1964), a social desirability scale (Crowne & Marlowe, 1964), a social responsibility scale (Daniels & Berkowitz, 1964), and reported vital statistics and socioeconomic data.

Results

Plausibility of Manipulation

Judging by the subjects' nervousness when they reported the fit to the experimenter, by their surprise when they discovered that the fit was simulated, and by comments they made during the fit (when they thought their microphones were off), one can conclude that almost all of the subjects perceived the fit as real. There were two exceptions in different experimental conditions, and the data for these subjects were dropped from the analysis.

Effect of Group Size on Helping

The number of bystanders that the subject perceived to be present had a major effect on the likelihood with which she would report the emergency (Table 1). Eighty-five percent of the subjects who thought they alone knew of the victim's plight reported the seizure before the victim was cut off, only 31 percent of those who thought four other bystanders were present did so.

TABLE 1
EFFECTS OF GROUPS SIZE ON LIKELIHOOD AND SPEED OF RESPONSE

Group size	N	*Percent responding by end of fit*	*Time in sec.*	*Speed score*
2 (*S* & victim)	13	85	52	.87
3 (*S*, victim, & 1 other)	26	62	93	.72
6 (*S*, victim, & 4 others)	13	31	166	.51

Note. *p* value of differences: $\chi^2 = 7.91$, $p < .02$; $F = 8.09$, $p < .01$, for speed scores.

Every one of the subjects in the two-person groups, but only 62 percent of the subjects in the six-person groups, ever reported the emergency. The cumulative distributions of response times for groups of different perceived size (Figure 1) indicates that, by any point in time, more subjects from the two-person groups had responded than from the three-person groups, and more from the three-person groups than from the six-person groups.

Ninety-five percent of all the subjects who ever responded did so within the first half of the time available to them. No subject who had not reported within 3 minutes after the fit ever did so. The shape of these distributions suggest that had the experiment been allowed to run for a considerably longer time, few additional subjects would have responded.

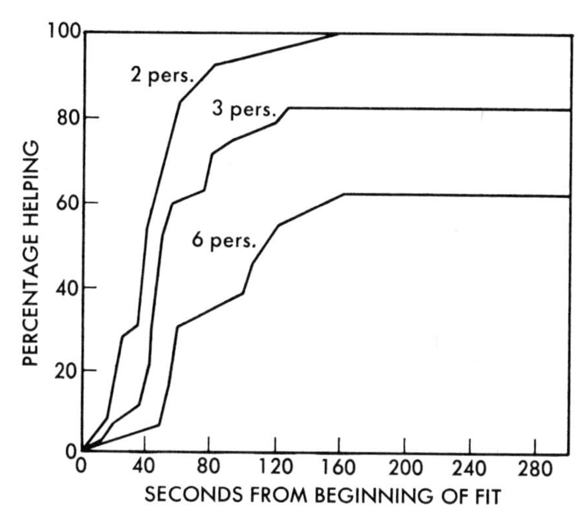

Figure 1 Cumulative Distributions of Helping Responses

Speed of Response

To achieve a more detailed analysis of the results, each subject's time score was transformed into a "speed" score by taking the reciprocal of the response time in seconds and multiplying by 100. The effect of this transformation was to deemphasize differences between longer time scores, thus reducing the contribution to the results of the arbitrary 6-minute limit on scores. A high speed score indicates a fast response.

An analysis of variance indicates that the effect of group size is highly significan ($p < .01$). Duncan multiple-range tests indicate that all but the two- and three-person groups differ significantly from one another ($p < .05$).

Victim's Likelihood of Being Helped

An individual subject is less likely to respond if he thinks that others are present. But what of the victim? Is the inhibition of the response of each individual strong enough to counteract the fact that with five onlookers there are five times as many people available to help? From the data of this experiment, it is possible mathematically to create hypothetical groups with one, two, or five observers.[2] The calculations indicate that the victim is about equally likely to get help from one bystander as from two. The victim is considerably more likely to have gotten help from one or two observers than from five during the first minute of the fit. For instance, by 45 seconds after the start of the fit, the victim's chances

[2] The formula for the probability that at least one person will help by a given time is $1-(1-P)^2$ where n is the number of observers and P is the probability of a single individual (who thinks he is one of n observers) helping by that time.

of having been helped by the single bystanders were about 50 percent, compared to none in the five-observer condition. After the first minute, the likelihood of getting help from at least one person is high in all three conditions.

Effect of Group Composition on Helping the Victim

Several variations of the three-person group were run. In one pair of variations, the female subject thought the other bystander was either male or female; in another, she thought the other bystander was a premedical student who worked in an emergency ward at Bellevue hospital. As Table 2 shows, the variations in sex and medical competence of the other bystander had no important or detectable affect on speed of response. Subjects responded equally frequently and fast whether the other bystander was female, male, or medically experienced.

TABLE 2
EFFECTS OF GROUP COMPOSITION ON LIKELIHOOD AND SPEED OF RESPONSE [a]

Group composition	N	*Percent responding by end of fit*	*Time in sec.*	*Speed score*
Female *S*, male other	13	62	94	74
Female *S*, female other	13	62	92	71
Female *S*, male medic other	5	100	60	77
Male *S*, female other	13	69	110	68

[a] Three-person group, male victim.

Sex of the Subject and Speed of Response

Coping with emergencies is often thought to be the duty of males, especially when females are present, but there was no evidence that this was the case in this study. Male subjects responded to the emergency with almost exactly the same speed as did females (Table 2).

Reasons for Intervention or Nonintervention

After the debriefing at the end of the experiment each subject was given a 15-item checklist and asked to check those thoughts which had "crossed your mind when you heard Subject 1 calling for help." Whatever the condition, each subject checked very few thoughts, and there were no significant differences in number or kind of thoughts in the different experimental groups. The only thoughts checked by more than a few subjects were "I didn't know what to do" (18 out of 65 subjects), "I thought it must be some sort of fake" (20 out of 65), and "I didn't know exactly what was happening" (26 out of 65).

It is possible that subjects were ashamed to report socially undesirable rationalizations, or, since the subjects checked the list *after* the true nature of the experiment had been explained to them, their memories might have been blurred. It is our impression, however, that most subjects checked few reasons because they had few coherent thoughts during the fit.

We asked all subjects whether the presence or absence of other bystanders had entered their minds during the time that they were hearing the fit. Subjects in the three- and six-person groups reported that they were aware that other people were present, but they felt that this made no difference to their own behavior.

Individual Difference Correlates of Speed of Report

The correlations between speed of report and various individual differences on the personality and background measures were obtained by normalizing the distribution of report speeds within each experimental condition and pooling these scores across all conditions ($n = 62–65$). Personality measures showed no important or significant correlations with speed of reporting the emergency. In fact, only one of the 16 individual difference measures, the size of the community in which the subject grew up, correlated ($r = -.26$, $p < .05$) with the speed of helping.

Discussion

Subjects, whether or not they intervened, believed the fit to be genuine and serious. "My God, he's having a fit," many subjects said to themselves (and were overheard via their microphones) at the onset of the fit. Others gasped or simply said "Oh." Several of the male subjects swore. One subject said to herself, "It's just my kind of luck, something has to happen to me!" Several subjects spoke aloud of their confusion about what course of action to take, "Oh God, what should I do?"

When those subjects who intervened stepped out of their rooms, they found the experimental assistant down the hall. With some uncertainty, but without panic, they reported the situation. "Hey, I think Number 1 is very sick. He's having a fit or something." After ostensibly checking on the situation, the experimenter returned to report that "Everything is under control." The subjects accepted these assurances with obvious relief.

Subjects who failed to report the emergency showed few signs of the apathy and indifference thought to characterize "unresponsive bystanders." When the experimenter entered her room to terminate the situation, the subject often asked if the victim was "all right." "Is he being taken care of?" "He's all right isn't he?" Many of these subjects showed physical signs of nervousness; they often had trembling hands and sweating palms. If anything, they seemed more emotionally aroused than did the subjects who reported the emergency.

Why, then, didn't they respond? It is our impression that nonintervening subjects had not decided *not* to respond. Rather they were still in a state of indecision and conflict concerning whether to respond or not. The emotional behavior of these nonresponding subjects was a sign of their continuing conflict, a conflict that other subjects resolved by responding.

The fit created a conflict situation of the avoidance-avoidance type. On the one hand, subjects worried about the guilt and shame they would feel if they did not help the person in distress. On the other hand, they were concerned not to make fools of themselves by overreacting, not to ruin the ongoing experiment by leaving their intercom, and not to destroy the anonymous nature of the situation which the experimenter had earlier stressed as important. For subjects in the two-person condition, the obvious distress of the victim and his need for help were so important that their conflict was easily resolved. For the subjects who knew there were other bystanders present, the cost of not helping was reduced and the conflict they were in more acute. Caught between the two negative alternatives of letting the victim continue to suffer or the costs of rushing in to help, the non-responding bystanders vacillated between them rather than choosing not to respond. This distinction may be academic for the victim, since he got no help in either case, but it is an extremely important one for arriving at an understanding of the causes of bystanders' failures to help.

Although the subjects experienced stress and conflict during the experiment, their general reactions to it were highly positive. On a questionnaire administered after the experimenter had discussed the nature and purpose of the experiment, every single subject found the experiment either "interesting" or "very interesting" and was willing to participate in similar experiments in the future. All subjects felt they understood what the experiment was about and indicated that they thought the deceptions were necessary and justified. All but one felt they were better informed about the nature of psychological research in general.

Male subjects reported the emergency no faster than did females. These results (or lack of them) seem to conflict with the Berkowitz, Klanderman, and Harris (1964) finding that males tend to assume more responsibility and take more initiative than females in giving help to dependent others. Also, females reacted equally fast when the other bystander was another female, a male, or even a person practiced in dealing with medical emergencies. The ineffectiveness of these manipulations of group composition cannot be explained by general insensitivity of the speed measure, since the group-size variable had a marked effect on report speed.

It might be helpful in understanding this lack of difference to distinguish two general classes of intervention in emergency situations: direct and reportorial. Direct intervention (breaking up a fight, extinguishing a fire, swimming out to save a drowner) often requires skill, knowledge, or physical power. It may involve danger. American cultural norms and Berkowitz's results seem to suggest that males are more responsible than females for this kind of direct intervention.

A second way of dealing with an emergency is to report it to someone qualified to handle it, such as the police. For this kind of intervention, there seem to be no norms requiring male action. In the present study, subjects clearly intended to report the emergency rather than take direct action. For such indirect intervention, sex or medical competence does not appear to affect one's qualifications or responsibilities. Anybody, male or female, medically trained or not, can find the experimenter.

In this study, no subject was able to tell how the other subjects reacted to the fit. (Indeed, there were no other subjects actually present.) The effects of group size on speed of helping, therefore, are due simply to the perceived presence of others rather than to the influence of their actions. This means that the experimental situation is unlike emergencies, such as a fire, in which bystanders interact with each other. It is, however, similar to emergencies, such as the Genovese murder, in which spectators knew others were also watching but were prevented by walls between them from communication that might have counteracted the diffusion of responsibility.

The present results create serious difficulties for one class of commonly given explanations for the failure of bystanders to intervene in actual emergencies, those involving apathy or indifference. These explanations generally assert that people who fail to intervene are somehow different in kind from the rest of us, that they are "alienated by industrialization," "dehumanized by urbanization," "depersonalized by living in the cold society," or "psychopaths." These explanations serve a dual function for people who adopt them. First, they explain (if only in a nominal way) the puzzling and frightening problem of why people watch others die. Second, they give individuals reason to deny that they too might fail to help in a similar situation.

The results of this experiment seem to indicate that such personality variables may not be as important as these explanations suggest. Alienation, Machiavellianism, acceptance of social responsibility, need for approval, and authoritarianism are often cited in these explanations. Yet they did not predict the speed or likelihood of help. In sharp contrast, the perceived number of bystanders did. The explanation of bystander "apathy" may lie more in the bystander's response to other observers than in presumed personality deficiencies of "apathetic" individuals. Although this realization may force us to face the guilt-provoking possibility that we too might fail to intervene, it also suggests that individuals are not, of necessity, "non-interveners" because of their personalities. If people understand the situational forces that can make them hesitate to intervene, they may better overcome them.

REFERENCES

Aronfreed, J. 1964. The origin of self-criticism. *Psychological Review* 71: 193–219.

Berkowitz, L., Klanderman, S., & Harris, R. 1964. Effects of experimenter awareness and sex of subject on reactions to dependency relationships. *Sociometry* 27:327–29.

Christie, R. 1964. The prevalence of machiavellian orientations. Paper presented at the meeting of the American Psychological Association, Los Angeles.

Crowne, D., & Marlowe, D. 1964. *The approval motive.* New York: Wiley.

Daniels, L., & Berkowitz, L. 1963. Liking and response to dependency relationships. *Human Relations* 16: 141–48.

Milgram, S., & Hollander, P. 1964. Murder they heard. *Nation* 198: 602–04.

Miller, N., & Dollard, J. 1941. *Social learning and imitation.* New Haven: Yale University Press.

Rosenthal, A. M. 1964. *Thirty-eight witnesses.* New York: McGraw-Hill.

Whiting, J. W. M., & Child, I. 1953. *Child training and personality.* New Haven: Yale University Press.

9

Models and Helping: Naturalistic Studies in Aiding Behavior

JAMES H. BRYAN · MARY ANN TEST

The following selection by Bryan and Test explores further the question of how social influence operates in helping or altruistic behavior. Unlike Darley and Latané, who observed subjects' reactions in the presence of presumably apathetic bystanders, the present authors sought to determine whether conformity operates as a "positive" factor in altruistic behavior. That is, they pose the question, "Will the presence of an altruistic model increase the likelihood of altruistic behavior in others?"

In addition to their substantive contributions, the four studies described by Bryan and Test are important as illustrations of carefully executed field experiments.

Recently, concern has been evidenced regarding the determinants and correlates of altruistic behavior, those acts wherein individuals share or sacrifice a presumed positive reinforcer for no apparent social or material gain. Studies addressed to these behaviors have explored both individual differences in the tendency to be altruistic and the situational determinants of such responses. Gore and Rotter (1963) found that students at a southern Negro college were more likely to volunteer for a social protest movement if they perceived sources of reinforcement as internally rather than externally guided. Subjects high on internal control were more likely to volunteer as freedom riders, marchers, or petition signers than subjects who perceived others as primary

James H. Bryan and Mary Ann Test, "Models and Helping: Naturalistic Studies in Aiding Behavior," *Journal of Personality and Social Psychology* 6 (1967): 400–07.

agents of reinforcement. Experimental evidence has been generated supporting the often-made assumption that guilt may serve as a stimulus to altruistic activity Darlington and Macker (1966) found that subjects led to believe that they had harmed another through incompetent performances on the experimental tasks (three paper-and-pencil tests) were more willing than control subjects to donate blood to a local hospital. Aronfreed and Paskal [1] and Midlarsky and Bryan (1967) found that children exposed to treatment conditions designed to produce empathy were more willing to donate M&M candies than subjects given control conditions, while Handlon and Gross (1959), Ugurel-Semin (1952), Wright (1942), and Midlarsky and Bryan have found sharing to be positively correlated with age among school-age children. Lastly, Berkowitz and Friedman (1967) have demonstrated that adolescents of the working class and the bureaucratic middle class are less affected in their helping behaviors by interpersonal attraction than adolescents of the entrepreneur middle class.

Three hypotheses have emerged regarding the situational determinants of self-sacrificing behaviors. One suggests that individuals behave in an altruistic fashion because of compliance to a norm of reciprocity. That is, individuals are aware of the social debts and credits established between them, and expect that ultimately the mutual exchange of goods and services will balance (Gouldner, 1960). Berkowitz and Daniels (1964) have suggested that individuals might show a generalization of such obligatory feelings and thus aid others who had not previously assisted them.

A second hypothesis was put forth by Berkowitz and his colleagues (Berkowitz, 1966; Berkowitz & Daniels, 1963; Berkowitz, Klanderman & Harris, 1964; Daniels & Berkowitz, 1963) who have postulated the social responsibility norm. They have contended that dependency on others evokes helping responses even under conditions where the possibility of external rewards for the helper are remote. Using supervisor's ratings of an unknown and absent other to produce dependency, and a box-construction task as the dependent variable, considerable support has been generated for the suggestion that dependency increases helping.

A third major determinant of helping may be the presence of helping (or nonhelping) models. While attention to the effects of models has generally been directed toward antisocial behaviors (cf. Bandura & Walters, 1963; Freed, Chandler, Mouton, & Blake, 1955; Lefkowitz, Blake, & Mouton, 1955), some recent evidence suggests that observation of self-sacrificing models may lead to subsequent succorant behavior by children. For example, Rosenhan and White (1967) have demonstrated that children are more likely to donate highly valued gift certificates to residents of a fictitious orphanage if they have seen an adult do so. Hartup and Coates [2] found that nursery school children who have been exposed to a self-sacrificing peer were more likely to be altruistic than children

[1] J. Aronfreed & V. Paskal, "Altruism, Empathy and the Conditioning of Positive Affect." Unpublished manuscript, 1965.

[2] W. W. Hartup & B. Coates, "Imitation of Peers as a Function of Reinforcement from the Peer Group and Rewardingness of the Model." Unpublished manuscript, 1966.

not so exposed. Test and Bryan [3] found that female college students were more likely to render aid to another in computing arithmetic problems if they saw other people so doing.

The present series of experiments was designed to test the effects of models in natural settings on subject samples other than college or high school students, and in contexts other than a school-room or university setting. The first three experiments reported are concerned with the impact of observing helping models upon subsequent helping behaviors, while the fourth is addressed to the influence of interpersonal attraction upon donation behavior.

Experiment I: Lady in Distress: A Flat Tire Study

Few studies have been concerned with the effects of models upon *adults,* and fewer still with the impact of *prosocial* models upon them (Wheeler, 1966). Those that have been concerned with such behaviors have invariably employed college students as subjects. For example, Rosenbaum and Blake (1955) and Rosenbaum (1956) have found that college students exposed to a model who volunteered, upon the personal request of the experimenter, to participate in an experiment would be more likely to consent than subjects not exposed to such a model or than subjects who observed a model refuse to cooperate. Pressures toward conformity in these experiments were great, however, as the request was made directly by the experimenter and in the presence of a large number of other students.

Test and Bryan found that the observation of helping models significantly increased the subsequent offers of aid by observers. However, in that study, subjects were given the task of solving arithmetic problems and then rating their difficulty, a task ordinarily requiring autonomous efforts. Furthermore, the experiment was conducted within a university setting, a context where independence of thought is often stressed. The effects of the model may have been simply to increase the subjects' faith that assisting others was allowed. While questionnaire data of the study did not support this interpretation, such effects could not be ruled out entirely. Thus, it is possible that the model impact was simply a propriety-defining activity which reduced the inhibitions associated with such helping behavior.

In general, then, investigations of modeling that employ adults as subjects and that demand self-sacrifice on the part of subjects are limited in number, exploit strong pressures toward conformity, and rely upon college students as subjects. The present experiment was designed to assess the impact of models upon subsequent spontaneous offers of help in other than a university setting.

Method

The standard condition consisted of an undergraduate female stationed by a 1964 Ford Mustang (control car) with a flat left-rear tire. An inflated tire was

---

[3] M. A. Test & J. H. Bryan, "Dependency, Models and Reciprocity." Unpublished manuscript, 1966.

leaned upon the left side of the auto. The girl, the flat tire, and the inflated tire were conspicuous to the passing traffic.

In the model condition, a 1965 Oldsmobile was located approximately 1/4 mile from the control car. The car was raised by jack under the left rear bumper, and a girl was watching a male changing the flat tire.

In the no-model condition, the model was absent; thus, only the control car was visible to the passing traffic.

The cars were located in a predominantly residential section of Los Angeles, California. They were placed in such a manner that no intersection separated the model from the control car. No turnoffs were thus available to the passing traffic. Further, opposite flows of traffic were divided by a separator such that the first U turn available to the traffic going in the opposite direction of the control car would be after exposure to the model condition.

The experiment was conducted on two successive Saturdays between the hours of 1:45 and 5:50 P.M. Each treatment condition lasted for the time required for 1000 vehicles to pass the control car. While private automobiles and trucks, motorscooters, and motorcycles were tallied as vehicles, commercial trucks, taxis, and buses were not. Vehicle count was made by a fourth member of the experiment who stood approximately 100 feet from the control car hidden from the passing motorists. On the first Saturday, the model condition was run first and lasted from 1:45 to 3:15 P.M. In order to exploit changing traffic patterns and to keep the time intervals equal across treatment conditions, the control car was moved several blocks and placed on the opposite side of the street for the no-model condition. The time of the no-model treatment was 4:00 to 5:00 P.M. On the following Saturday, counterbalancing the order and the location of treatment conditions was accomplished. That is, the no-model condition was run initially and the control car was placed in the same location that it had been placed on the previous Saturday during the model condition. The time of the no-model condition was 2:00 to 3:30 P.M. For the model condition, the control car was placed in that locale where it had been previously during the no-model condition. The time of the model condition was 4:30 to 5:30 P.M.

Individuals who had stopped to offer help were told by the young lady that she had already phoned an auto club and that help was imminent. Those who nonetheless insisted on helping her were told the nature of the experiment.

Results

The dependent variable was the number of cars that stopped and from which at least one individual offered help to the stooge by the control car. Of the 4000 passing vehicles, 93 stopped. With the model car absent, 35 vehicles stopped; with the model present, 58 halted. The difference between the conditions was statistically significant ($\chi^2 = 5.53$, corrected for continuity, $df = 1$, $p < .02$, two-tailed). Virtually all offers of aid were from men rather than women drivers.

The time of day had little impact upon the offering of aid. Fifty vehicles stopped during the early part of the afternon; 43 during the later hours. Likewise, differences in help offers were not great between successive Saturdays, as 45 offers of aid were made on the first Saturday, 48 on the second Saturday.

The results of the present study support the hypothesis that helping behaviors can be significantly increased through the observation of others' helpfulness. However, other plausible hypotheses exist which may account for the findings. It is possible to account for the differences in treatment effects by differences in sympathy arousal. That is, in the model condition, the motorist observed a woman who had had some difficulty. Such observations may have elicited sympathy and may have served as a reminder to the driver of his own social responsibilities.

Another explanation of the findings revolves around traffic slowdown. It is possible that the imposition of the model condition served to reduce traffic speed, thus making subsequent stopping to help a less hazardous undertaking. While the time taken for 1000 autos to pass the control car was virtually identical in the model and no-model condition and thus not supportive of such an explanation, the "slowdown" hypothesis cannot be eliminated. Assuming the model effect to be real, one might still argue that it was not a norm of helping that was facilitated by the model, but rather that inhibitions against picking up helpless young ladies were reduced. That is, within the model condition, the passing motorists may have observed a tempted other and thus felt less constrained themselves regarding similar efforts. Indeed, the insistence of some people to help in spite of the imminent arrival of other aiders suggested the operation of motives other than simply helping. Indeed, while the authors did not index the frequency of pick-up attempts, it was clear that a rather large number were evidenced.

Because of the number of alternative explanations, the evidence supporting the hypothesis that the observation of helpers per se will increase subsequent aiding is weak. Experiment II was designed to test further the prediction that the perception of another's altruistic activity would elicit similar behavior on the part of the observer.

Experiment II: Coins in the Kettle

The investigation was conducted on December 14, between the hours of 10:00 A.M. and 5:00 P.M. The subjects were shoppers at a large department store in Princeton, New Jersey. Observations made on the previous day indicated that the shoppers were overwhelmingly Caucasian females.

A Salvation Army kettle was placed on the sidewalk in front of the main entrance to the store. Two females, both in experimenter's employ, alternatively manned the kettle for periods of 25 minutes. One solicitor was a Negro, the other a Caucasian. Each wore a Salvation Army cape and hat. Although allowed to ring the Salvation Army bell, they were not permitted to make any verbal plea or to maintain eye contact with the passing shoppers, except to thank any contributor for his donation.

The model condition (M) was produced as follows: Once every minute on the minute, a male dressed as a white-collar worker would approach the kettle from within the store and contribute 5 cents. As the model donated, he started a stopwatch and walked from the kettle toward a parking lot as if searching for someone. He then returned to the store. The following 20-second period constituted the duration of the treatment condition.

Following a subsequent lapse of 20 seconds, the next 20-second period defined the no-model condition (NM). Within any one minute, therefore, both M and NM treatments occurred. There were 365 occasions of each treatment.

It should be noted that it was possible that some subjects in the NM condition observed the contribution of the model or a donor affected by the model. If that hypothesis is correct, however, the effects of such incidents would be to reduce rather than enhance the differences between treatments.

Results

The dependent variable was the number of people who independently donated to the Salvation Army. People obviously acquainted, as for example, man and wife, were construed as one potential donating unit. In such conditions, if both members of a couple contributed, they were counted as a single donor.

Since there were no differences in model effects for the Negro or Caucasian solicitor, data obtained from each were combined. The total number of contributors under the NM condition was 43; under the M condition, 69. Assuming that the chance distribution of donations would be equal across the two conditions, a chi-square analysis was performed. The chi-square equaled 6.01 ($p < .01$).[4]

In spite of precautions concerning the elimination of correlated observations within a treatment condition, it was possible for subjects in any one observational period to influence one another. Such influence may have been mediated through acquaintances not eliminated by our procedures or the observations of others as well as the model donating. A more conservative analysis of the data, insuring independent observation, was therefore made. Instead of comparing treatments by analyzing the number of donors, the analysis used, as the dependent variable, the number of observation periods in which there was a contribution, that is, those periods in which more than one donation occurred were scored identically to those in which only a single contribution was received. Occasions of donations equaled 60 in the M treatment, 43 in the NM condition. The chi-square equaled 2.89 ($p < .05$).

The results of Experiment II further support the hypothesis that observation of altruistic activity will increase such behavior among observers. But the matter is not yet entirely clear, for when the observer saw the model donate he saw two things: first, the actual donation, and second, the polite and potentially reinforcing interaction that occurred between the donor and solicitor. Conceivably, the observation of an altruistic model, per se, who was not socially reinforced for his behavior, would have little or no effect on an observer. The third experiment was designed to examine this possibility.

---

[4] All chi-square analyses were corrected for continuity and all tests of significance were one-tailed.

Experiment III: Coins in the Kettle II

The experiment was conducted at a Trenton, New Jersey, shopping center from the hours of 10:00 A.M. to 5:00 P.M. Again, the majority of the patrons were Caucasian females. It is likely, however, that these shoppers were of a lower socioeconomic status than those in the Princeton group.

Salvation Army kettles were placed before the main entrance of a large department store (Kettle 1) and a large food center (Kettle 2). The kettles were separated by more than 200 yards. During the first 120 observations (10:00 A.M. to 12:00 P.M.), two male college students, employed by the Salvation Army and wearing its uniform, manned the kettles. The site of the experiment was Kettle 1, except on those occasions where the worker took his "coffee break." At those times, data collection was centered at Kettle 2. An equal number of M and NM conditions were run at each site, although approximately two-thirds of the observational time was spent at Kettle 1. During the remaining 240 observational periods (1:00 P.M. to 5:00 P.M.) the same male worker and his spouse alternately manned Kettle 1. The wife was stationed by the kettle for 136 minutes, the male for 104 minutes. The experiment was conducted only at Kettle 1 during the afternoon period.

Solicitors were told to make no verbal appeals for donations or responses to the model upon his contribution. While they were not informed of the hypothesis underlying the experiment, they may well have deduced it. The model was the same as Experiment II, and again was dressed as a white-collar worker.

The imposition of the treatment conditions were identical to those described in Experiment II with the following exceptions. Since the kettle was more visible at this site than at the previous one, 30-second rather than 20-second periods were used for each treatment. To simplify the procedures, no waiting periods between treatments occurred. Additionally, after donating, the model would return to the parking lot. There were a total of 360 occasions of each of the M and NM conditions.

Results

The criteria defining a donor were identical to those outlined in Experiment II, Under the M condition, 84 donors were tallied; under the NM treatment, 56. The chi-square value was 4.86 ($p < .025$).

Since it was possible that one donor might have seen a donor other than the model receive social approval from the solicitor, the more conservative comparison of the treatments as outlined in Experiment II was made. That is, treatments were compared by noting the number of observational periods in which any donation occurred. Therefore, those donors who may have been influenced by a contributor receiving the solicitor's thanks were excluded. Of the 360 observational periods under the M condition, there were 75 in which some donation was made. Of the 360 periods, 51 were marked by contributions. Chi-square yielded a value of 5.09 ($p < .025$).

Experiment IV: Ethnocentrism and Donation Behavior

While Experiment III was conducted to eliminate the solicitor's explicit social approval as a mechanism underlying donation behavior, it is possible that the model's impact was due to the information communicated to the observer regarding the consequence of donations. Work by Bandura, Ross, and Ross (1963), for example, found that children observing a model rewarded for aggression would be more aggressive than children who had observed a model being punished for such behavior. Additionally, considerable data have been gathered within the university laboratory suggesting that interpersonal attraction may greatly influence the helping response. Berkowitz and Friedman (1967), Daniels and Berkowitz (1963), and Goranson and Berkowitz (1966) have suggested that positive affect increases the probability of low payoff helping behavior.

The present experiment was designed to assess the impact of the solicitor's race upon the donation behavior of shoppers. It was assumed that a Negro solicitor would be held in less esteem by Caucasian shoppers than a solicitor of their own race, and that such attitudes would affect contributions. While the applicability of the "consequence to the model" hypothesis in accounting for the model's effect was not tested directly, the study assesses the importance of interpersonal attraction in eliciting charitable behavior.

Method

The experiment was conducted on December 2 and 3 between the hours of 10:00 A.M. and 6:00 P.M. at the Trenton area site. The subjects were Caucasian shoppers at a large department store.[5] Three thousand seven hundred and three shoppers were observed; 2154 females and 1549 males. In order to reduce the possibility of including the same subject in the experiment on more than one occasion, tallies were made only of exiting shoppers.

Two Salvation Army kettles were placed at two store exits, their location being separated by approximately 75 yards. Two female solicitors, a Negro and a Caucasian, manned the kettles. Both were in their early twenties, wore the uniform of the Salvation Army, and were in the employ of the experimenter. Each was instructed to make no verbal appeals for donations and to avoid eye contact with the shoppers. After a period of 25 minutes, the girls rotated kettle assignments, and during the last 10 minutes of the hour were allowed to take a coffee break. Hence, during a single hour, each solicitor manned both kettles. Each solicitor manned each kettle on seven occasions per day. Thus, each solicitor was observed for a total of 28 observational periods; 14 on each day (seven on each kettle) over a period of two days.

Two observers, each assigned to a particular kettle, tallied the number and sex of the exiting shoppers and contributors during each of the 25-minute periods.

---

[5] As there were very few Negro donors ($N = 70$) analysis was confined to the behavior of Caucasian shoppers.

In addition, records were kept of the amount of money donated within any period, although it was impossible on this measure to separate those donations made by incoming from outgoing customers.

Results

The dependent variable was the percentage of donors contributing to the kettle within an observational period. That is, observational periods were assigned a percentage donor score. Shoppers within an observational period were treated as a single group, with differences between groups on percentage donor score forming the critical comparisons. The total N of the study was then the 56 observational periods, rather than the 3703 shoppers. Since the mean group size for the Negro solicitor was 70.32 and for the Caucasian 61.93 (standard deviations equal to 53.33 and 42.98, respectively), it was assumed that the percentage score was relatively stable.

The effects of race, kettle location, and day and their interactions were analyzed by analysis of variance.

As can be seen from Table 1, both the main effect of race and of day were significant. As predicted, the Negro solicitor elicited a statistically significant lower percentage of donors than did the Caucasian. For the Negro solicitor, the average percentage donor score for observational periods was 2.22 ($SD = 2.36$), while for the Caucasian solicitor the average percentage donor score was 3.89 ($SD = 3.60$). Additionally, Saturday shoppers were by and large less generous than Friday customers. The average percentage donor score of the group was 1.73 ($SD = 1.97$) for the Saturday shopper, and 4.38 for the Friday shopper ($SD = 3.52$).

TABLE 1

ANALYSIS OF VARIANCE OF PERCENTAGE DONOR SCORES

	df	*MS*	*F*
Race (A)	1	38.778	4.84*
Day (B)	1	98.315	12.28**
Kettle (C)	1	.018	
A × B	1	1.511	
A × C	1	11.340	
B × C	1	1.031	
A × B × C	1	3.206	
Error	48	8.009	

* $p < .05$ (2-tailed).
** $p < .01$ (2-tailed).

A second dependent variable was the amount of money donated during each time period. No significant differences were found for race, day, or kettle location.

The present investigation does support, albeit equivocally, the notion that interpersonal attraction may affect donations even when the solicitors are not the eventual recipients of such contributions. While it is possible that race differences simply fail to remind observers of their social responsibilities, it is also feasible that the subjects wanted to avoid interpersonal contact with a minority group member. If this is true, then it is interesting to note that interpersonal attraction may play an important role even in those situations where personal anonymity is high and escape from unpleasant situations easy.

Discussion

The results of the first three experiments clearly replicate those of Test and Bryan and extend the findings over a variety of subject populations, settings, and tasks. The results hold for college students, motorists, and shoppers; in the university laboratory, city streets, and shopping centers; and when helping is indexed by aiding others solve arithmetic problems, changing flat tires, or donating money to the Salvation Army. The findings then are quite consistent: the presence of helping models significantly increases subsequent altruistic behavior.

That generosity breeds generosity is interesting in light of the recent concern with helping behaviors in emergency contexts. Darley and Latané [6] and Latané and Darley [7] have found that subjects are less inclined to act quickly in emergency situations when in the presence of other potential helpers. Whether faced with a medical emergency (a simulated epileptic seizure) or a dangerous natural event (simulated fire), the rapidity with which students sought to aid was reduced by the presence of others. These findings have been interpreted in three ways: as reflecting the subjects' willingness to diffuse responsibility (others will aid); as reflecting their diffusion of blame (others didn't aid either); or as reflecting conformity to the nonpanicked stooges. It is clear that the results of the first three experiments in the present series do not follow that which might be predicted by the diffusion concepts. A giving model apparently does not lend credibility to the belief that others than the self will make the necessary sacrifices. The helping other did not strengthen the observer's willingness to diffuse his social obligations, but rather stimulated greater social responsibility. In light of these results, the delayed reaction exhibited by the subjects tested by Darley and Latané might be best attributable to conformity behavior. As they have suggested, subjects faced with a unique and stressful situation may have been either reassured by the presence of calm others or fearful of acting stupidly or cowardly. Additionally, it is possible that diffusion of responsibility is only associated with anxiety-inducing situations. The current data fail to indicate that such diffusion occurs in non-stressful situations which demand fulfillment of social obligations.

While it appears clear that the behavior of the motorists and shoppers was not dictated by a variety of situational and social pressures usually associated with

[6] J. Darley & B. Latané, "Diffusion of Responsibility in Emergency Situations." Unpublished manuscript, 1966.

[7] B. Latané & J. Darley, "Group Inhibition of Bystander Intervention in emergencies." Unpubished manuscript, 1966.

the study of modeling in adults or experiment in academic settings (Orne, 1962), the mechanisms underlying the effects are not obvious. While the presence of the model in the flat-tire study may have reminded the motorists as to the social responsibility norm, a hypothesis does not appear reasonable in accounting for the results in the coins-in-the-kettle series. The bell-ringing Salvation Army worker, with kettle and self placed squarely in the pathway of the oncoming pedestrian, would seem to be reminder enough of one's obligation toward charity. A priori, it would not appear necessary to superimpose upon that scene the donating other for purposes of cognitive cueing (Wheeler, 1966).

One hypothesis to account for the model effect is that the observer is given more information regarding the consequences of such donation behavior. Experiment IV suggested that solicitor status or personal attraction might operate on donation behaviors even under conditions of personal anonymity and few social constraints. It is possible that the model serves to communicate to the potential donor relevant information concerning the consequences of his act. That is, the model may demonstrate that an approach to the solicitor does not involve an unwanted interpersonal interaction (e.g., lectures on religion).

A second hypothesis to account for the data pertains to the shame-provoking capacities of the model. It is reasonable to assume that most people feel that they are, by and large, benevolent and charitable. Furthermore, it is likely that such a self-image is rarely challenged: first, because charitable acts are not frequently required; second, at least in the street scenes employed in the current series of studies, solicitations are made in the context of many nongiving others. That is, a multitude of negative models—of noncharitable others—surround the solicitations in the current series of studies. Indeed, the contexts are such that most people are not helping; many more cars pass than stop to offer aid to the lady in distress; and there are many more people who refuse to put coins in the kettle than those who do. However, the witnessing of a donor, an individual who not only recognizes his social responsibility but in fact acts upon it, may produce a greater challenge to the good self-image of the observer. Acts rather than thoughts may be required of the observer in order to maintain the self-image of benevolence and charity. If such is the case, then the model characteristics most effective in producing prosocial behavior by socialized adults would be those directed toward shame or guilt production (e.g., donations from the poor), rather than those reflecting potential reinforcement power (e.g., donations from the high status).

Whatever the mechanism underlying the model effect, it does appear quite clear that prosocial behavior can be elicited through the observation of benign others.

REFERENCES

Bandura, A., Ross, D., & Ross, S. 1963. Vicarious reinforcement and imitative learning. *Journal of Abnormal and Social Psychology* 66: 601–07.

Bandura, A., Ross, D., Ross, S., & Walters, R. M. 1963. *Social learning and personality development.* New York: Holt, Rinehart & Winston.

Berkowitz, L. 1966. A laboratory investigation of social class and national differences in helping behavior. *International Journal of Psychology* 1: 231–40.

———, & Daniels, L. 1963. Responsibility and dependency. *Journal of Abnormal and Social Psychology* 66: 429–36.

———, 1964. Affecting the salience of the social responsibility norm: Effects of past help on the response to dependency relationships. *Journal of Abnormal and Social Psychology* 68: 275–81.

———, & Friedman, P. 1967. Some social class differences in helping behavior. *Journal of Personality and Social Psychology* 5: 217–25.

———, Klanderman, S. B., & Harris, R. 1964. Effects of experimenter awareness and sex of subject and experimenter on reactions to dependency relationships. *Sociometry* 27: 327–37.

Daniels, L., & Berkowitz, L. 1963. Liking and response to dependency relationships. *Human Relations* 16:141–48.

Darlington, R. B., & Macker, C. E. 1966. Displacement of guilt-produced altruistic behavior. *Journal of Personality and Social Psychology* 4: 442–43.

Freed, A., Chandler, P., Mouton, J., & Blake, R. 1955. Stimulus and background factors in sign violation. *Journal of Personality,* 23: 499.

Goranson, R., & Berkowitz, L. 1966. Reciprocity and responsibility reactions to prior help. *Journal of Personality and Social Psychology* 3: 227–32.

Gore, P. M., & Rotter, J. B. 1963. A personality correlate of social action. *Journal of Personality* 31: 58–64.

Gouldner, A. 1960. The norm of reciprocity: A preliminary statement. *American Sociological Review* 25: 161–78.

Handlon, B. J., & Gross, P. 1959. The development of sharing behavior. *Journal of Abnormal and Social Psychology* 59: 425–28.

Lefkowitz, M., Blake, R., & Mouton, J. 1955. Status factors in pedestrian violation of traffic signals. *Journal of Abnormal and Social Psychology* 51: 704–06.

Midlarsky, E., & Bryan, J. H. 1967. Training charity in children. *Journal of Personality and Social Psychology* 5: 408–15.

Orne, M. 1962. On the social psychology of the psychological experiment: With particular reference to demand characteristics and their implications. *American Psychologist* 17: 776–83.

Rosenbaum, M. 1956. The effect of stimulus and background factors on the volunteering response. *Journal of Abnormal and Social Psychology* 53: 118–21.

———, & Blake, R. 1955. Volunteering as a function of field structure. *Journal of Abnormal and Social Psychology* 50: 193–96.

Rosenhan, D., & White, G. M. 1967. Observation and rehearsal as determinants of prosocial behavior. *Journal of Personality and Social Psychology* 5: 424–31.

Ugurel-Semin, R. 1952. Moral behavior and moral judgment of children. *Journal of Abnormal and Social Psychology* 47: 463–74.

Wheeler, L. 1966. Toward a theory of behavioral contagion. *Psychological Review* 73: 179–92.

Wright, B. A. 1942. Altruism in children and perceived conduct of others. *Journal of Abnormal and Social Psychology* 37: 218–33.

Social Influence Processes:

Putting It into Perspective

The selections included in the present section have dealt mainly with compliance and conforming behavior. They have variously explored the relevance of power and authority, models, and what might be called interpersonal skills for affecting a person's definition of the situation and his actions. While all of the selections fall in the mainstream of studies in social influence, there are a number of other forms of influence that were not represented.

In addition to compliance and conformity, the term social influence can apply to (1) socialization, (2) social perception, (3) persuasion and attitude change, and (4) social facilitation. The first two areas have been assigned to separate sections, since each constitutes a rather broad specialty in its own right. The article by Thomas Scheff can be considered as a member of the third category, social perception, although it is hardly representative of the major research traditions in this area. Finally, no selection dealing with social facilitation was included. The latter two categories unfortunately fell prey to lack of space, but will be given at least passing mention below.

Social or interpersonal influence can be said to be operating whenever the behavior of individuals is modified by the action or mere presence of others. It is clearly the central problem of social psychology.

Speculation and theorizing about social influence processes pre-dates any systematic research in social psychology. And, perhaps the first experimental study that can be called social psychological dealt with social influence. Publishing his findings in the *American Journal of Psychology* in 1897, Norman Triplett conducted a study in which forty boys, aged 10 to 12, were given the task of winding line onto fishing reels. Each boy performed the task both alone and in the presence of other boys. Triplett found that 20 of the boys performed better in the group situation, 10 worked at about the same rate, while the remaining 10 worked better alone. This group effect on individuals' task performance was given a special name, "social facilitation," by Floyd Allport, who conducted a good deal of research on the phenomenon during the 1920s.

Probably every introductory textbook in social psychology contains an account of Muzafer Sherif's studies employing the autokinetic effect and the somewhat later studies by Solomon Asch employing the line-matching problem. These classic studies explored the effects of the judgments of others on an individual's (reported) visual perception. These two studies have served as points of departure for a vast number of studies in social perception as well as studies of compliance and conformity in overt behavior of various types. However, while the Sherif and Asch studies are among the best known studies in social psychology, they are only two examples of the literally hundreds of studies in social influence that are published each year.

Students exposed to the social influence literature for the first time often react by judging such processes as undesirable or even dehumanizing. Individualism is highly valued in certain segments of our society and is currently in vogue among college students. One hears a good deal about "doing your own thing," working free from "social hangups," and so on. From such a value position the very notion of social influence processes is repugnant.

Ignoring for the moment the fact that those who are telling us to do our own thing are also attempting to influence our behavior, it is safe to say that the assumption that social influence processes are inherently bad is misguided. That is, such a blanket appraisal reflects a lack of understanding of how social influence processes operate in our everyday lives.

Social influence can have beneficial as well as undesirable effects. As indicated by the Bryan and Test studies, for example, the influence of a model can stimulate altruistic behavior. Just as aggressive behavior resulted from the action of others in Milgram's studies, so can influence serve to attenuate aggressive behavior. And, as pointed out above, social facilitation can lead to greater productivity on certain types of tasks and often results in superior individual achievement.

Moreover, it is inaccurate to view social influence as purely a coercive force, operating to get people to do what they don't want to do. Often, the influence of others can free us from inhibitions, so that we end up acting as we really wanted to in the first place. Our motives do not always run counter to what others want or expect us to do.

Social influence is much more pervasive than the foregoing list of desirable effects would suggest. We could go much further and observe that what is distinctly human about a human being is the accumulated effects of social influence. Phenomenologically, we experience ourselves as distinct individuals, but paradoxically we could not be individuals without socialization. One's identity, self-esteem, and aspirations emerge through a long history of "reflected self-appraisals," i.e., perceptions of how others evaluate one's behavior.

Another important point to consider about social influence is that in real-life situations it is almost without exception a reciprocal process. If we stop to analyze what happens in face-to-face encounters, for example, it becomes clear that "all leaders are led by their followers."

Interaction proceeds as a sequence of acts, each of which is dependent upon preceding acts. Consider a conversation between two people, A and B. If they are interacting in any sense of the word, they will at least be taking turns in speaking—first A, then B, then A, and so on. Moreover, if they are taking into account what one another say, each party will "construct" his next act in such a way that it builds logically upon his partner's preceding act.

Say, for example, that A commands B to do something. B has a number of alternative responses to A. He may comply with the command, reject it, ignore it, or perhaps ask for a clarification of what A expects him to do. Each alternative that B may choose now has implications for A's next act. If B has rejected the original command, A may become more forceful and reassert his command; or he may withdraw the command, give B an alternative command, terminate the encounter, and so on. If B ignored the original command, A has a similar set of alternatives from which to choose, with appropriate modifications for the manner in which B acted. And, if B has asked for a clarification, A is obligated to provide it before the focus of interaction can switch to something else.

Suppose, however, that B complies readily to A's original command. As we might infer from the articles by Scheff, and by Freedman and Scott, B's very compliance may encourage A to issue additional commands. Through a sequence of command-compliance acts, A and B may negotiate a clear-cut dominance-subordinance relationship. Under such conditions, one may at first expect to find A doing nearly all of the "initiating" and B merely "responding." However, while B is in the one-down position, he still has a good deal of potential to influence A. It would be unlikely for A to respond to a direct command from B, but A can be manipulated quite readily by more indirect person-control strategies. B can employ ingratiation techniques, "prostitution" behavior, or initiate a course of action for A disguised as an appeal for help, and so forth.

It was noted previously that social influence is not necessarily the same as coercion. It is not some impersonal force that "society" imposes on individuals. People influence people, and reciprocal influence operates whenever interaction takes place.

For students interested in pursuing the topic of social influence further, the following sources will serve well as ports of entry to this fascinating literature.

Suggestions for Further Reading

Darwin Cartwright and Alvin Zander, *Group Dynamics: Research and Theory.* Third Edition. New York: Harper and Row, 1968. An important collection of essays, many of which deal with interpersonal influence processes. Theoretical articles and research reports explore such topics as social facilitation, pressures toward uniformity in small groups, influence through ingratiation, and power.

Erving Goffman, *Interaction Ritual: Essays on Face-to-Face Behavior.* Garden City, New York: Anchor Books, 1967. A collection of highly provocative essays dealing with face-to-face behavior in "natural settings." A distinctly different approach from those represented by the other sources in this list.

Charles A. Kiesler and Sara B. Keisler, *Conformity.* Reading, Massachusetts:

Addison-Wesley, 1970. An overview of the conformity literature. Prepared especially for undergraduates, this brief volume reviews and organizes the findings from more than one hundred empirical studies.

Edward C. Simmel, Ronald A. Hoppe, and G. Alexander Milton, *Social Facilitation and Imitative Behavior.* Boston: Allyn and Bacon, 1968. A collection of papers reporting on some of the most recent research developments in the area.

Ladd Wheeler, *Interpersonal Influence.* Boston: Allyn and Bacon, 1970. Another condensed overview of the field, prepared with the undergraduate in mind.

CHAPTER III

Perception: Self, Object, and Other

10 Gary T. Marx, *The White Negro and the Negro White* · 137

11 Rex A. Lucas, *The Influence of Kinship upon Perception of an Ambiguous Stimulus* · 149

12 Paul R. Wilson, *The Perceptual Distortion of Height as a Function of Ascribed Academic Status* · 164

13 Richard deCharms, Virginia Carpenter, and Aharon Kuperman, *The "Origin-Pawn" Variable in Person Perception* · 170

Putting It into Perspective · 187
Suggestions for Further Reading · 189

10

The White Negro and the Negro White

GARY T. MARX

The image(s) that people have of themselves stems from the responses they elicit from others in the course of day-to-day interaction. It is erroneous to think, however, that a person has no control over the responses that he elicits. It is not infrequent that people consciously alter their behavior or otherwise manipulate the cues they provide others in order to create a desired image.

The reading which follows focuses on two groups in our society who dislike their public images and explores the processes by which these groups attempt to alter those images. The first group is composed of those members of the black middle class who have frequently been called the black bourgeoisie. These blacks are very critical of the average black and their values, and they attempt to dissociate themselves from such blacks in the eyes of society. This attempt takes the form of unconditional acceptance of white middle-class norms, values, and behavior patterns. Lower-class blacks are used as a negative reference group, while middle-class whites become a positive reference group. That is, the groups whose responses and valuations are used in establishing a self conception are altered. The subsequent alteration in self conception produces what Marx calls the black white.

In contrast to the black bourgeoisie are some whites who view their public image as WASPs as undesirable and, consequently, disdain the very middle-class norms and values which the black bourgeoisie attempt to emulate. These whites take their cues for behavior from working-class blacks. They attempt to put down their whiteness by adopting what they view as the carefree lifestyle of the black hipster. Middle-class whites constitute a negative reference group, while working-class blacks become a positive reference group. As in the case of the black bourgeoisie, this represents a reversal of

Gary T. Marx, "The White Negro and the Negro White," *Phylon* 28 (1967): 168–77.

the general reference group patterns. The subsequent alteration in self-conception produces what Marx calls the white black.

As Marx develops the foregoing thesis, he points out that in the case of both groups, there is a distorted image of both the group they seek to identify with and the group they seek to leave. Some of the sources of these misperceptions are explored.

James Baldwin has stated, "We take our shape, it is true, within and against that cage of reality bequeathed us at our birth; . . . black is the color of evil" and Negroes must live with this. This paper is concerned with a segment of those who must live with the stigma of being black. It is also concerned with the behavior of some whites who would perhaps say, "White is the color of evil; must middle-class Caucasians live with this?"

That part of the Negro middle class which Frazier, in his polemical account, has called the black bourgeoisie is in many ways opposed in its behavior to those whites who adhere to a beat philosophy of life.[1] In this paper, I compare these two groups to suggest that in spite of their obvious differences certain important similarities may be noted. One of the most significant is that as groups in transition both have a distorted image of both the group they seek to identify with and the group they seek to leave. The existence of myths and distorted images about other social groups of course gives no cause for surprise. However, what is of interest here is the reversal of both positive and negative reference groups which has taken place. An understanding of either white beats or the black bourgeoisie requires consideration of both the white middle class and the Negro working class.

As has often been noted, the black bourgeoisie take a very positive stand toward middle-class values and are very critical of averages Negroes. Frazier has written, "they have accepted unconditionally the values of the white bourgeois world: its morals and its canons of respectability, its standards of beauty and

[1] This paper was originally written when the "beat movement" was at its peak. Since that time the beat movement has dwindled and eventually fused into the contemporary "hippy" scene. Many of the original beats have rejoined conventional society, while others have remained on the scene as elder statesmen. Hippies are not ideologically committed to poverty, are more involved with drugs, have more of a communal love emphasis, and draw from a younger group than did beats. Nevertheless, much of the discussion in this article about beats would apply to the contemporary hippies.

The term *beat* is used to refer to individuals who willfully disaffiliated and lived together in communities such as those that flourished in Venice West, North Beach, and the Village some years ago. This distinction is made to separate beats from what one might term *fellow traveling beats* of college communities who still care enough to go to school. The fellow traveling beats might be said by some to have the best of all possible worlds since they are getting a few kicks on the side while keeping one foot in the doorway of the middle-class world via their education.

consumption. In fact, they have tended to overemphasize their conformity to white ideals." [2] They have strongly internalized middle-class values emphasizing self-control, deferred gratification, achievement, extreme cleanliness and rigid moral standards. With their strong acceptance of these middle-class values, these Negroes are attempting to separate themselves from the supposed values of the Negro lower class and hipsters, i.e., the stereotyped values with which many whites still would identify them.

Beats, on the other hand, reject middle-class values and take their cues for behavior from working class Negroes. Norman Mailer, in a much criticized article, has pointed out that Negroes are the source of hip for beats.[3] Beats with a middle-class background attempt to put down their whiteness and adopt what they believe is the carefree, spontaneous, cool life style of Negro hipsters: their manner of speaking and language, their use of milder narcotics, their appreciation of jazz and the blues, and their supposed concern with the good orgasm.[4] Furthermore,

---

[2] E. Franklin Frazier, *Black Bourgeoisie* (Glencoe, Ill.: Free Press, 1957), p. 24. The controversy around Frazier's work rages on, partly because there has been little effort at systematic data collection to ascertain how widespread are the patterns he noted. While the civil rights struggle and the related pride in blackness and increased questioning of the nature of white society have no doubt resulted in some changes, many observers have recently noted patterns similar to those reported by Frazier. For example: N. Hare, *The Black Anglo-Saxons* (New York: Marzani & Munsell, 1965); Broadus N. Butler, "The Negro Self-Image" in A. Rose and C. Rose, *Minority Problems* (New York: Harper & Row, 1965); Nat Hentoff, *The New Equality* (New York: Viking Press, 1964), pp. 85–93; LeRoi Jones, *Blues People* (New York: W. Morrow, 1963); and to a lesser extent some of the cases reported in John H. Rohrer and Munro S. Edmonson (eds.), *The Eighth Generation Grows Up* (New York: Harper & Row, 1960).

The Negro middle class is of course diverse. Without offering any precise quantitative judgment, the patterns noted by Frazier (particularly the exaggeration of white standards and negative attitudes toward the Negro masses) certainly occur frequently enough to warrant discussion. In addition, some of the issues considered in this paper have relevance for all middle-class Negroes.

[3] Norman Mailer, "The White Negro," *Dissent* 4 (Spring 1957). While Mailer has popularized the term *white Negro,* it does not owe its origin to him. The term has been used for several centuries in the West Indies to describe white men who had become submerged among their Negro servants and concubines. A. C. Carmichael, *Domestic Manners of the West Indies* (London: Whittaker, Treacher & Co., 1833), I, 59, as referred to in Frank Tannenbaum, *Slave and Citizen* (New York: Knopf, 1963), p. 123.

[4] Their poverty, unemployment, support by women and welfare are further similarities. However, this view of Negroes as the source of hip should not be taken too far. Much of what has come to be identified as Negro behavior patterns are in a larger sphere patterns of the working class.

It should be recalled that while drugs are held by most to be squarely in the domain of Negroes, their use by American bohemians can be traced back to Edgan Allan Poe, who took them over from the French. Marijuana and peyote were introduced into this country by Mexicans and Indians in the Southwestern United States. Bohemians were showing similar behavior patterns long before the advent of Negroes on the scene, as a look at Albert Parry, *Garrets and Pretenders* (New York: Dover, 1960) will clearly show. Furthermore, as Jean Malaquais has noted in *Dissent* 5 (Winter 1958), the equivalent of American beats is found in Russia, Japan, and Sweden, where no Negroes exist. It has been suggested that a characteristic of bohemian movements everywhere is a populist identification with a disinherited folk group, in this instance Negroes. See David Matza, "Subterranean Traditions of Youth," *Annals of American Academy of Political and Social Science* 338 (November, 1961).

The stance of Negro hipsters further differs from that of beats in that the latter's life is organized around modes of behavior considered criminal by the dominant society. However, with their cultivated irresponsibility, spontaneity, emotionalism, immediate impulse gratification, slovenly and often dirty dress, occasional use of drugs, more liberal and open attitudes toward sex, interracial friendships and the use of four letter words, beats are attempting to separate themselves from the middle-class culture with which they are identified and in which they were brought up.

By stretching matters a bit, both groups may be seen to be socially mobile, although their mobility ethos and the actual direction of their mobility are very different. The extreme quest for status of the black bourgeoisie is a central theme of many studies. On the other hand, the perspective of beats is expressed by Ferlinghetti in the following excerpt from his poem, "Junkman's Obbligato":

> *I wish to descend in the social scale.*
> *High society is low society.*
> *I am a social climber*
> *climbing downward*
> *And the descent is difficult.*
> *The Upper Middle Class Ideal*
> *is for the birds*
> *but the birds have no use for it*
> *having their own kind of pecking order.*[5]

Beats are from a middle-class background and have been downwardly mobile.[6] Negroes are more likely to be from a working-class background and to have been upwardly mobile.[7]

---

this is done to obtain goals valued by the larger society—such as financial success and high living. If hipsters happen to be poor, this is not voluntary. While both hipsters and beats were cynical about the larger society, hipsters actively tried to manipulate that society and to beat it at its own game, while cynicism among beats simply led to withdrawal. While beats occasionally broke laws, this was not a defining characteristic of their mode of existence and was usually not directed towards obtaining the ends of the larger society. Beats tended to have the means (education and savoir faire) required to obtain legitimately the ends of the larger society, but chose to reject the ends. Their poverty was voluntary. R. Merton, *Social Theory and Social Structure* (Glencoe, Ill.: Free Press, 1962), pp. 121–94.

[5] Lawrence Ferlinghetti, "Junkman's Obbligato," in *Coney Island of the Mind* (Norfolk: New Directions, 1958), pp. 57–58.

[6] In their study of the San Francisco North Beach community Rigney and Smith note that beats "came from middle-class backgrounds with a distribution heavily askew in favor of the upper end of the class scale. Many were unemployed and received veterans' pensions, and others were supported by unemployment compensation and welfare." F. Rigney and L. Smith, *The Real Bohemia* (New York: Basic Books, 1961), pp. 21–33.

[7] In contrast to the backgrounds of beats, Edwards, in his study of Negro professionals, notes that his respondents were much more likely to have come from a lower-class background than their white counterparts, and if they were from a middle-class background this is unlikely to be as many generations old. Franklin Edwards, *The Negro Professional Class* (Glencoe, Ill.: Free Press, 1959), p. 49.

Using a more refined index of mobility, there is a sense in which middle-class Negro professionals have not been upwardly mobile—at least when compared to working-class Negro beats. In considering mobility we might distinguish between culture-class mobility and racial-ethnic mobility. The former refers to changes in a person's economic position and cultural dowry, while the latter refers to changes in the racial or ethnic group with which an individual interacts socially. Those Negroes who have been upwardly mobile and whose baggage is filled with middle-class equipment are not the Negroes who interact with whites. Negro beats who are working-class economically and certainly not middle-class in their cultural en-

Beats avoid employment while middle-class Negroes seek it. For the black bourgeoisie jobs are seen as an important means of obtaining status and a means to bigger and better conspicuous consumption. A French sociologist has even called this group "colored babbits." [8] Popular mythology suggests that beats will not work, and statements like the following support this: "Me earn money? Never. All you earn the government takes and what you got left, man? I'll tell you. What the little boy urinated at, that's what. The hole in the fence, man, that's what you got left." [9]

Middle-class Negroes are constantly engaged in deferring gratification, an activity which beats abhor. For Negroes who are upwardly mobile deferred gratification is of the utmost importance. Obtaining middle-class status requires hard work and often great sacrifices, as well as planning for the future. For beats, on the other hand, what counts is the "here and now"; it makes no sense to defer any satisfaction since world destruction seems so imminent. Means become all important. Thus in *On the Road,* Dean says, "We Sal, we gotta go and never stop going till we get there." "Where we going, man?" "I don't know but we gotta go." [10]

While differing in the direction of their mobility, beats and middle-class Negroes show a similarity with respect to the acceptance they are granted. People who have been upwardly or downwardly mobile often have trouble being accepted. That Negroes who have moved up from a working-class position may experience difficulty being accepted by middle-class whites (and even old middle-class Negroes) because they are both new arrivals and Negroes is well known. The difficulties often faced by this group in attempting to join country clubs, yacht clubs, some professional associations, and in finding places to live outside of the ghetto all suggest this. However, beats, who have been downwardly mobile, may also experience difficulty in being accepted by their working-class neighbors. Ned Polsky notes that in New York many young Italians "make violent efforts to roll back the beat invasion"; [11] they resent the beats because of their extreme behavior, which the beats assume to be typical of Italians. Beats may have difficulty finding employment when they seek it. In a study of one of the original beat communities, in Venice West, Lipton notes, "those who choose manual labor soon find out that so far as the trades are concerned, breaking into the ranks of labor is never easy or cheap. Joining the proletariat is like trying to join an exclusive club and often quite as expensive, what with trade union initiation fees and

---

dowment are making it socially with whites and in this sense they have been mobile while middle-class Negroes have not. A similar phenomenon may be seen in the case of Jews. Those Jews who are "nice middle-class people" tend not to be the Jews who interact socially to any meaningful extent with gentiles, while Jewish bohemians who reject much of the bourgeois way of life are making it socially with gentiles. There is irony in the fact that those who fall down the farthest from the dominant group's ideal cultural package are the very ones who manage to interact with the dominant group on the basis of social equality.

[8] Georges Friedmann, *Ou Va Le Travail Humain?* (Paris: Gallimard, 1950), as reported in Frazier, *Black Bourgeoisie,* p. 109.

[9] J. Shock, *Life is a Lousy Drag* (San Francisco: 1958), p. 9.

[10] Jack Kerouac, *On the Road* (New York: Viking Press, 1957), p. 196.

[11] Ned Polsky, "The Village Beat Scene," *Dissent* 7 (Summer 1960).

numerous qualifications and restrictions." [12] With a change in a few words this quote would be applicable to Negroes attempting to break into the white middle-class world.

The sexual behavior and morality of Negroes differ from those of beats. Some have suggested that the black bourgeoisie take up where the white middle-class leaves off. Frazier has called this group the "black puritans." [13] Things of a bohemian, off-beat or unusual nature are steadfastly avoided. A negative attitude is taken publicly toward interracial marriages [14] and many aspects of Negro culture, such as spirituals, blues and jazz, are rejected.[15] The ethical and legal standards of society are accepted as valid and the use of violence and narcotics is strongly condemned. Kenneth Clark reports rigid control of behavior and at times the maintaining of "unrealistically high standards of personal and sexual conduct." [16] Kardiner notes that with respect to "white ideals, the Negro often overshoots the mark. He overdoes the sex mores. . . ." [17] And in one case he reports, "the sexual mores were puritanical to such an extent that boys were not even allowed in the house." [18] Family stability and fidelity may often be more pronounced among these individuals than among their white counterparts.

In great contrast are the attitudes and behavior of those involved in the beat milieu. Beats reject traditional middle-class morality. For them the search for unconventional and exotic kinds of experience is important whether in the realm of drugs or sex. Homosexual relationships, extra-marital heterosexual relationships, illegitimacy and abortions occur frequently.[19] Beats have idolized the easy relationships which developed in some Negro families as a result of slavery. Beats also value interracial romances and social contact with Negroes as a supreme way of rejecting the middle-class mess.[20] Beats are likely to be cynical and skeptical about what are to them phony bourgeois or square ethics. Violence, at least in

---

[12] Lawrence Lipton, *The Holy Barbarians* (New York: Messner, 1962), p. 152.

[13] E. Franklin Frazier, *The Negro Family in the United States* (New York: Macmillan, 1949).

[14] Martin Luther King, although not representative of the black bourgeoisie, shows their attitude on this issue when he states that the aim of Negroes is to be "the white man's brother, not his brother-in-law." *Stride Toward Freedom* (New York: Harper & Row, 1958), p. 168.

[15] This was true even in the 1920s. Note Garvin Bushell's report about New York: "They were trying to forget the traditions of the South; they were trying to emulate the whites. . . . You usually weren't allowed to play blues and boogie woogie in the average Negro middle-class home. That music supposedly suggested a low element." "Garvin Bushell and New York Jazz in the 1920's," *Jazz Review* (January, 1959): 12, as quoted in Jones, *Blues People,* p. 128.

[16] Kenneth Clark, *Prejudice and Your Child* (Boston: Beacon Press, 1955), p. 59.

[17] Abraham Kardiner and Lionel Ovesey, *The Mark of Oppression* (Cleveland: Meridian Books, 1962), p. 316.

[18] Ibid., p. 215.

[19] Rigney and Smith, *Real Bohemia,* pp. 46 and 48. It may be that transgressions of America's murky code of sexual morality do not occur any more frequently among beats than in square society but rather that beats are just more open and honest about what they do. Note Kinsey's findings on the extensiveness of homosexuality and recent studies of sexual morality on the campus.

[20] In commenting on mixed marriages a Venice West resident asks, "What's mixed about two people getting married?" Lipton, *Holy Barbarians,* p. 141.

theory, is valued as the expression of a primitive life force and assertion of man's individuality.

In the area of personal demeanor the lack of worldly goods, the shabby dress, and often the beard and sandals of beats may be seen as their means of symbolizing their disaffiliation with and rejection of the middle-class world with which they were associated originally. Thus a resident of Venice West comments about his beard, "it's my letter of resignation from the rat [white] race." [21] Similarly, a whitewardly mobile Negro might say, "My straightened hair, my use of skin bleaching creams, and my strong emphasis on middle-class values are signs of my resignation from the Negro race." One observer has noted that many in this group refuse to buy watermelon and are hesitant to be seen purchasing chitterlings and black eyed peas, and the color red, Negro dolls, and "Negro" names (particularly middle names such as Mae or Ann) are strongly avoided.[22] It has often been noted by middle-class liberals that the home of their lone Negro neighbor is always the most meticulously kept, and the Negro children are the cleanest and least likely to be misbehaved.

In their political values beats and middle-class Negroes are again at opposite ends of the pole. Beats are cynical: "elections are rigged and the whole political game is a shuck." [23] However, when beats express their political ideas they are likely to be pacifist and to espouse a philosophy of nonviolence,[24] to be strong in their support of civil liberties and civil rights, to be internationalist in outlook, and to be economically on the left.

In marked contrast to the radical attitudes of beats are the political values of the black bourgeoisie, whom one might imagine would be driven to a radical view of the existing society given their subordinate racial position. However, excluding civil rights issues, they tend to be a conservative group.[25] While segments of the black middle class have played an important role in the conventional civil rights movement, rarely have they been driven toward radicalism in race matters, as the failure of the Garvey movement, the communist and socialist parties, and the contemporary black nationalists to gain appreciable support from them suggests. Some members of this group, with their vested interest in the status quo, have no doubt impeded civil rights change.

The political beliefs of beats serve to further differentiate them from the middle class, just as the conservative position of the black bourgeoisie is adopted partly to gain their acceptance into the middle class.

While beats and the black bourgeoisie travel in very different circles, when they do come infrequently into contact the reversal of roles in the situation is

---

[21] Ibid., p. 50.

[22] Hare, *Black Anglo-Saxons,* pp. 38, 85, 91.

[23] Lipton, *Holy Barbarians,* p. 306.

[24] There is an interesting contrast between the sanctioning of violence as a form of personal expression by beats and their abhorrence of it in its collective forms such as war.

[25] Many observers have commented on the conservatism of this group. A study of Negro college graduates notes that "In the popular political terminology of the day, the Negro graduates constitute a conservative rather than a liberal or radical group." Ernest Haverman and Patricia West, *They Went to College* (New York: Harcourt, 1952), p. 197.

similar to that seen in the contact of poor whites and the Negro elite in the South. A white girl, who might be termed a fellow traveling beat, told of the conflict that occurred between herself and the high-school-educated, property-owning, middle-class Negro woman who took care of the girl's children part time while she was in school. The Negro had rigid ideas about child rearing which conflicted with the more carefree ones of the beat. Conflict developed when the employee attempted to undermine the mother's authority, and the relationship was soon terminated. In this situation the Negro was indignant at the white's behavior patterns, instead of the reverse.

Both the middle-class Negro and the beat had feelings of righteous indignation and subjectively gained status from the behavior of the other. The Negro saw herself as a normal middle-class person and the white as a deviant; the white saw herself as more hip than the Negro, who was seen as the original source of hip, and she gained status through viewing the Negro as very square.

Both beats and middle-class Negroes may arouse the dominant society's hostility, although perhaps for opposite reasons. Beats incur middle class society's wrath because they do what it often would really like to do, and perhaps would do, were it not restrained by anxiety-producing inhibitions. As in the case of Jews, fastidiously conforming Negroes may draw condemnation because they are often a reflection of what middle-class society "really" should be. Negroes are breaking into the system and are feared, while beats are hated for the opposite reason—breaking out of the system. It may be more than coincidental that those rejecting the system the most furiously are those who have thoroughly experienced it, and those so eagerly accepting it are those to whom it is the newest.

Thus far I have been concerned primarily with contrasting these two groups in terms of their very different attitudes toward the values of the white middle class and the Negro working class. In pursuing this contrast further, I note the similarity between them with respect to the distorted image each has of the groups it is oriented toward and away from and the occurrence of behavior which is seen as exaggerated or unauthentic.

The Negro characteristics which Kerouac reverences are clearly stated in a well-known passage from *On the Road:*

> At lilac evening I walked with every muscle aching among the lights of 27th and Welton in the Denver colored section, *wishing I were a Negro, feeling that the best the white world had offered was not enough life, joy, kicks, darkness, music, not enough nights*. . . . I passed the dark porches of Mexican and Negro homes; soft voices were there, occasionally the dusky knee of some *mysterious sensual gal;* and dark faces of the men behind rose arbors. Little children sat like sages in ancient rocking chairs. A gang of colored women came by, and one of the young ones detached herself from the motherlike elders and came to me fast—"Hello Joe"—and suddenly saw it wasn't Joe, and ran back blushing. I wished I were Joe. I was only myself Sal Paradise, sad, strolling in this violent dark, this unbearably sweet night, *wishing I could exchange worlds with the happy true-hearted ecstatic Negroes of America.*[26]

[26] Kerouac, *On the Road,* pp. 148–49. Negroes are not the only symbol of the disinherited urban slum proletariat that beats identify with. Kerouac also states, "I wished I were a

Mailer shares a similar view of the primitivism and sexuality of Negroes. In their view of Negroes, Mailer and Kerouac draw on a stereotype shared by such noted analysts of human behavior as Rankin, Bilbo, and Eastland. Mailer and Kerouac differ from them only on the emotive dimension of prejudice; they like super-sexed, narcotics-using, primitive, easy-going, spontaneous, irresponsible, violent Negroes, while racists dislike them. Their conception of what it means to be a Negro probably differs greatly from the experience of most black people.[27]

In this racial glorification of black men irrespective of their individual attributes, beats seek out Negroes simply because they are black.[28] In observing how readily beats identify with Negroes, use their jargon, assume that they understand what it means to be a black man in America, think that they can even speak for them, and that they are accepted by them (all the while ignoring or being unaware of the hatred many Negroes have for whites at some level of consciousness), we may note the phenomena of misplaced intimacy and identification. Part of the current negative reaction against liberal, and even radical, whites must be understood in these terms.[29]

In commenting on his associations with Mailer in Paris, James Baldwin has

---

Denver Mexican, or even a poor overworked Jap." The stereotype involved in the reference to the latter group as well as the use of what is to many the derogatory word *Jap* is itself worthy of attention. (All italics in the paper are added.)

[27] With respect to Kerouac's view of Negro life, Norman Podhoretz "doubts if a more idyllic picture of Negro life has been painted since certain Southern ideologues tried to convince the world that things were just as fine as fine could be for the slaves on the old plantation." "The Know-Nothing Bohemians," *Partisan Review* 25 (Fall 1958).

[28] While the search of whites for blackness may result in their making slight distinctions between Negroes, the same may be true of Negro beats in their search for whiteness. In such relationships mutual exploitation goes on, with whites proving their liberalism, rebelliousness, and wildness by being with a Negro, and Negroes becoming un-Negro through being with a valued white. This can be clearly seen in the following passage, in which a Negro girl is speaking about her experience in meeting her Caucasian boy friend's father.

> "I'll never forget or forgive the look on that old man's face when he opened his hotel room door and saw me. The horror. His inability to believe that it was his son standing there holding my hand. . . . Nor can I forget Bob's laugh in the elevator afterwards, the way he kept repeating: 'Did you see his face when he saw you? Did you. . . ?' He had used me, you see. I had been the means, the instrument of revenge. And I wasn't any better. I used him . . . trying, you see, through him to get at the white world which had not only denied me, but had turned my own against me. . . . I went numb all over when I understood what we were doing to and with each other." Paule Marshall, "Reena," *Harper's* 29 (October 1952): 159.

[29] For example, note the strained relations between Negroes and whites on the Berkeley campus of the University of California over a conference on Black Power called by a white student group, or the presumptuousness of a poem written by a white entitled "Spade Answers Moderate" that appeared recently in a "radical quarterly."

White civil rights workers in a Negro movement of course face many problems. Some whites have reacted like beats in becoming as Negro as possible in their language and dress. They seem to meet with both amusement and resentment. In commenting on this Carmichael states, "they say things without realizing what they're saying. You know—'Yeah, man, I really dig that.' They use words out of context. He suggests that they seem to say, 'Look, I'm not like the other whites you know. I dig you.' Snap their fingers out of tune: 'I dig Ray Charles.' The white boy putting on a show was resented. As much as I would be resented if I put on a show to show how white I was." As reported in Robert Penn Warren, "Two for SNCC," *Commentary* 39 (April 1965): 45.

written, "The Negro jazz musicians among whom we sometimes found ourselves did not for an instant consider him [Mailer] as being remotely 'hip' and Norman didn't know this and I couldn't tell him." [30]

A similar phenomenon can be seen in the reverence which some black bourgeoisie hold for everything middle class and white and their condemnation of things black. Note the following case reported by Kardiner: "She rejects totally her identification with Negroes." This person states, "Ugh, black is dirty, bad, no-good, evil. . . . Why do people [Negroes] have to be like this?" Throughout her interview she says, "Negroes are ill-clad, dirty, loud, boisterous, coarse, ill-mannered, odoriferous, drunk and stupid." The assumption here is that whites are completely opposite, just as beats assume that middle-class "respectable" people are selfless mechanized automatons and that Negroes represent all that is good. Kardiner reports, "She is engaged in a ceaseless effort to remake them [her children] in terms of the perfectionist white image she desires for herself." She reports, "I'm supersensitive about things like that [her children giggling]. I don't want them to do anything wrong. I want them to be perfect." She is continuously criticizing her children, "they don't read well, they can't eat properly, they are too loud." [31]

In her view she expresses in a marked form traditional stereotypes about Negroes, as well as about "proper" white people. Implicit in her view of whiteness is something which approaches perfection. She ignores the fact that whites are often ill-mannered, loud, drunk, stupid, and that their children often do not read well, do not eat properly and may even occasionally giggle. Even in cases where middle-class ideals are observed in white homes, the behavior falls short of her perfectionist view of these standards. In terms such as *exaggerated Americans, over-compensation,* and *over-assimilation,* numerous observers have commented on such aspects of black bourgeois behavior.

---

[30] James Baldwin, "The Black Boy Looks at the White Boy, Norman Mailer," *Esquire* (May 1961): 104. However, elsewhere Baldwin sounds a little like the beats. In writing about the "zest and joy" of Negro life he remembers parties "where rage and sorrow sat in the darkness and did not stir, and we ate and drank and talked and laughed and danced and forgot all about 'the man.' We had the liquor, the chicken, the music, and each other. . . . This is the freedom that one hears in some gospel songs. . . ." *The Fire Next Time* (New York: Dial, 1963), p. 56.

Other black writers culturally and economically marginal to the Negro masses occasionally sound like beats. For example, Jones, *Blues People,* pp. 122–26 and H. Keil, *Urban Blues* (Chicago: University of Chicago Press, 1966), p. 192.

[31] Kardiner and Ovesey, *Mark of Oppression,* pp. 252–54. In noting this group's reference to the lower-class as "niggers," Hare reports a frequently heard comment that "you can take a Nigger out of the country, but you can't take the country out of a Nigger." Hare, *Black Anglo-Saxons,* p. 81.

While it is increasingly fashionable to criticize the black bourgeoisie, it is important to note that many attitudes often attributed to them are held to an even greater extent by lower-status Negroes. For example, data from a nation-wide non-Southern metropolitan area sample of Negroes reveal that 68 percent of working-class persons as against 46 percent of those in middle-class positions agreed with the statement "Before Negroes are given equal rights, they have to show that they deserve them." The percentages agreeing with the statement "Poor people have no one to blame but themselves" were 33 and 15 respectively. Gary T. Marx, *Protest and Prejudice: A Study of Belief in the Black Community* (New York: Harper and Row, 1967).

The images held by both beats and black bourgeoisie thus tend to be extreme and to some extent they miss the mark in terms of the behavior models they imitate.

The issues of identity and authenticity which emerge in considering these two groups are complex and involve moral evaluations as well as social and psychological factors. My point has certainly not been to suggest that individuals should be bound rigidly to the culture of their hereditary class, ethnic, racial, or religious group.[32] But rather it has been to suggest that in making such changes both beats and black bourgeoisie sometimes behave in an exaggerated fashion relative to the sets of expectations held by the groups they are oriented toward. These distortions emerge partly from their inadequate grasping of the nature of what is being copied. In the case of Negroes in particular there is the failure to differentiate the normative as ideal from the normative as usual or anticipated. In the case of beats there is the lack of experience which gives substance and meaning to the cultural forms emulated. In addition to these cognitive factors, for both groups the social process which Goffman has called *deminstrelization* is relevant.[33] Deminstrelization occurs when an individual goes out of his way to show that the set of behavioral expectations held for him are the very ones which do not apply to him. Thus a middle-class Negro parent says about her child, "I always tell him he has to behave wherever he goes, because Negro children are expected not to behave." [34] In one sense Negroes are trapped and their behavior is more easily understood than that of beats because they start with a stigma of identity which, by their behavior, they try to overcome.[35] Like Jews, middle-class Negroes are on trial, and although their guilt is often a foregone conclusion, both may attempt to improve their position and to conform more than anyone else, for if they do not they are guilty of being dirty Jews or Negroes.[36] While deminstrelization may be a common enough feature of social life, it is interesting to note that in their deminstrelization beats and black bourgeoisie have in a sense switched roles.

Both are initially identified with the values they reject—Negroes as a result of their skin color and frequently lower-class background and beats as a result of

---

[32] Specifically in the case of the black bourgeoisie I do not mean to argue that a glorious African past or the golden tradition of the Southern rural black gentlemen has been betrayed, as some critics implicitly argue.

[33] Erving Goffman, *Stigma* (New York: Prentice-Hall, 1963), p. 110.

[34] Kardiner and Ovesey, *Mark of Oppression,* p. 221.

[35] On the other hand, white middle-class beats with their expressive deviance may be said to be *in search of a stigma to differentiate themselves*. In attempting to understand the behavior of beats, one must keep in mind the alienation and dehumanization many associate with modern mass society, the boredom and complacency of a welfare state society that is affluent for the majority of its members, rampant social hypocrisy and injustice, and fear of world destruction. In addition, changes in technology and an economy of abundance are conducive to new attitudes toward work, sex and drugs. In this sense in some ways beats and hippies are in the vanguard of social change.

[36] Jean-Paul Sartre, *Anti-Semite and Jew* (New York: Schocken Books, 1961). This behavior of course has been noted on the part of many ethnic groups that have been upwardly mobile. In a more general sense it may be a characteristic response of those in insecure status positions.

their skin color and middle-class background. In their attempt to avoid identification with their presumed past both may go out of their way to show that they are in fact the opposite. Negroes will show how middle class they are and beats what white Negroes they are. What Negroes embrace wholeheartedly beats reject just as furiously. The hipster behavior patterns which beats embrace and go out of their way to be identified with are the very behavior patterns that middle-class Negroes strongly reject. They have switched drummers and in so doing both may be hearing the beat not quite right, resulting in the misconception by Negroes of what it really means to be middle-class white and the misconception by beats of what it really means to be Negro.

11

The Influence of Kinship upon Perception of an Ambiguous Stimulus

REX A. LUCAS

Social psychologists have frequently used ambiguous stimuli in experimental studies of perception in an attempt to elucidate the influence of various social and psychological factors upon the perceptual process. In general, the evidence suggests that both individual and interpersonal variables must be taken into account.

The following selection is a significant addition to the perception literature because it examines perceptual responses to a natural ambiguous stimulus in a field setting. The ambiguous stimulus was a severe earth tremor that destroyed a coal mine and shook the adjacent community. Immediately after the coal mine disaster, a research team went into the community to collect data. In the analysis of these data it was noticed that half the off-shift workers interviewed immediately interpreted the ambiguous stimulus as a "bump" in the mine, whereas the remaining interviewees attributed it to some other phenomenon. What could account for these different perceptions?

Very systematically, Lucas evaluates and subsequently rejects plausible explanations involving factors that might be expected to influence the ambiguity of the stimulus properties of the tremor, and hence, account for the different perceptions as well as psychological factors and explanations involving social background characteristics. The only consistent difference between those who perceived the tremor as a mine bump and those who rendered other interpretations of the tremor was that all but one of the former group had relatives in the mine, while none of the latter group had relatives in the mine. This observation led to the formulation of the following hypothesis: status occupants whose relatives are engaged in a potentially dangerous activity are more apt to identify an ambiguously threatening

Rex A. Lucas, "The Influence of Kinship upon Perception of an Ambiguous Stimulus," *American Sociological Review* 31 (1966): 227–36.

stimulus as affecting their relatives than status occupants without such relatives. An examination of further data related to this and a subsequent tremor in the same community provided additional support for this hypothesis.

This study demonstrates that kinship role relationships influence perception. The discussion is based upon a secondary analysis of data from a coal mine disaster. The natural ambiguous stimulus, a severe earth tremor, shattered the mine and shook the adjacent community. This paper grew out of the search for and testing of a hypothesis to account for the unexpected finding that respondents with similar socioeconomic background and work experience immediately perceived the tremor in widely different ways.

The complexity of perception, embracing as it does cortical activity, memory trace, neural mechanisms and inner motivation, as well as the outer social order, involves considerations that normally lie in the diverse fields of neurology, physiology, psychology and sociology. This breadth of interdisciplinary involvement has led to a diversity of meanings for the term "perception." [1] The problem arises because some researchers regard perception as a process affected by social and psychological factors while others concentrate upon the stimulus pattern itself. Allport notes that "the application of the term perception in social disciplines has thus shifted from mere object-awareness, physical-world relations and biological adaptation to a cognitive and perhaps even phenomenological *modus operandi* for collective activities and role playing and for concepts of self and society, cultural significance and the alignments and conflicts of human associations." [2] For the purposes of this paper, the broadest connotation of perception will be used; the concept of perception will be expanded to include one of Tolman's specifications that " 'perception' (and hence the behavior space) may also include entities of which the actor is not then and there consciously aware. Any concrete particular objects of relations which govern the actor's immediate action are said to be in the behavior space—that is, to be also 'perceived' whether or not in introspective terms the actor is then and there consciously aware of them." [3] In the analysis to follow, the social background and relationships of the respondents are important considerations. We turn to the conditions and characteristics of social life relevant to the situation.

---

[1] See J. Gould and W. L. Kolb, *A Dictionary of the Social Sciences* (New York: Free Press, 1964), pp. 491–92. Reviews of the field are found in F. H. Allport, *Theories of Perception and the Concept of Structure* (New York: Wiley, 1955); and M. D. Vernon, *A Further Study of Visual Perception* (Cambridge, England: Cambridge University Press, 1951).

[2] Allport, *Theories of Perception,* p. 368.

[3] E. C. Tolman, "A Psychological Model," in T. Parsons and E. A. Shils, eds., *Toward a General Theory of Action* (Cambridge: Harvard University Press, 1959), p. 297.

The Setting

Minetown [4] (population 7,500), a small isolated community with a single industry, had a coal mine work force of about 1,000, served by a small professional and proprietor group. The community had never had the transient labor, dormitory accommodation or work force instability found in many coal towns in North America.[5] Eighty percent of the town's families were home owners. Many families were linked by ties of kinship; a full 88 percent of the families interviewed in the present study had extended kin in Minetown.

The single industry had a high accident rate. Mining accounted for 18.2 percent of the fatal industrial accidents in Canada in 1958, second only to the construction industry.[6] In Minetown itself only six years had been free of fatal mining accidents since 1900. The average frequency of death from individual accidents was two per year; these isolated individual accidents have killed 176 men. A major mine explosion in 1891 killed 125 men [7] and another in 1956 killed 38.[8] There is no complete record of deaths caused by occupational disease from the long term effects of methane, carbon monoxide poisoning, dust particles or serious injury.[9]

In the mine, the threats to life were of three types. First, there were individual fatalities and explosions caused by human error and accordingly humanly preventable. Second, there were dangers such as methane which were not man-made and so not always preventable, but they could be detected (predicted) and defensive action taken. The third type of danger is most relevant to the present study: the Minetown mine was threatened by bumps, a characteristic of only a few mining areas in the world. A bump is an unpredictable upheaval caused by sudden underground bursting of the coal or of the strata immediately in contact with it. In Minetown some underground bumps dislodged stones that required the combined efforts of five or six men to move; bumps have buried or killed large groups of men. Bigger bumps have resulted in major shifts of the strata, heaving underground roadways against the roof. In all, some 500 bumps

---

[4] This pseudonym was adopted to protect the anonymity of respondents.

[5] H. R. Luntz, *People of Coaltown* (New York: Columbia University Press, 1958).

[6] Dominion Bureau of Statistics, *Canada Year Book, 1962–63* (Ottawa: Queen's Printer). In 1958 construction accounted for 22.1 percent of the total fatal industrial accidents, mining and quarrying 18.2 percent and manufacturing 13.1 percent.

[7] R. A. H. Morrow, *The Story of the [Minetown] Disaster,* published by R. A. H. Morrow, and entered according to Act of Parliament of Canada in the year 1891 in the office of the Minister of Agriculture, Ottawa.

[8] *Report of the Royal Commission appointed to inquire into the explosion and fire in No. 4 Mine [Minetown]* on the last day of November, 1956 (Halifax: Queen's Printer, 1957).

[9] The mortality rate of coal miners in Canada from causes other than accidents is somewhat above that of the general male population. (*Report of the Royal Commission on Coal, 1946* [Ottawa: King's Printer, 1947], p. 296.) The same report suggests fatality rates can be expressed in average numbers of fatalities per million man-hours worked for a ten-year period. In the ten years ending 1931 the rate was 1.64; in the ten years ending 1945 it was 1.17. This rate was lower than that of the United States, but higher than that of the United Kingdom.

have been recorded in the Minetown mine.[10] Between March and October, 1958, underground personnel recorded seventeen bumps, and although they were all small bumps which could not be detected above ground, fifty men were injured, one fatally.[11]

The miners themselves were aware of the dangers they faced—"That mine is a man killer," "We are all scared of it . . . ," and the miners' wives were apprehensive—"I wondered every morning when I said goodbye whether I would see him that night." The miners, their families, the townspeople, the mining company and the labor union were all alert to the threat of death and injury in the mine.

Minetown is therefore a community that is especially conscious of danger, injury and accidental death. When a recurrent problem or threat persists through many years, common expectations and social arrangements tend to emerge. To the miners themselves, great support and reassurance came from fellow miners. The informal but sacred miners' code was a common understanding that in case of a mine disaster [12] the miners not directly involved worked ceaselessly at digging and clearing operations until the last man or the last body was found in the mine. This pact was carried out regardless of the difficulty or futility of the operation or of the danger to the rescuers. In Minetown as in many mining communities rescue work was a sacred duty to friends and co-workers, a part of the traditional work discipline and responsibility.[13] The obligations were strongly supported by the wives and families of the miners.[14]

Whenever the mine whistle sounded the alarm, off-shift miners in town stopped

---

[10] W. F. Campbell, "Deep Coal Mining in [Minetown] No. 2 Mine," *Mining Engineering* (September 1958).

[11] *Report of the Royal Commission on the Upheaval or Fall or Other Disturbance Sometimes Referred to as a Bump in No. 2 Mine at [Minetown] . . . on the 23rd day of October, 1958* (Halifax: Queen's Printer, 1959).

[12] "We define disaster as a severe, relatively sudden and frequently unexpected disruption of normal structural arrangements within a social system or subsystem, resulting from a force, 'natural' or 'social,' 'internal' to a system or 'external' to it, over which the system has no firm 'control.' " G. Sjoberg, "Disaster and Social Change," in G. W. Baker and D. W. Chapman, eds., *Man and Society in Disaster* (New York: Basic Books, 1962), p. 357. The term "disaster" tends to be somewhat misleading. The objective definition is often sociologically and psychologically superfluous because people act on the basis of their own definition of what constitutes a disaster. It is probable that many people have contended with what they felt were disasters without these being officially designated as "disaster areas." Nevertheless, disaster usually implies that the phenomenon affects a number of people, i.e., "a social system" or "subsystem."

[13] This is common to most mining communities. Similar data from the West Frankfort Mine disaster are quoted by C. E. Fritz, "Disaster," in R. K. Merton and R. A. Nisbet, *Contemporary Social Problems* (New York: Harcourt Brace, 1961), pp. 569–661.

[14] Minetown presented a situation of naturally supported loyalties rather than one of conflicting loyalties reported by L. M. Killian, "The Significance of Multiple-Group Membership in Disaster," *American Journal of Sociology* 57 (November 1952): 309–14. See also the discussion in A. H. Barton, *Social Organization under Stress: A Sociological Review of Disaster Studies,* Disaster Study No. 17 (Washington: National Academy of Sciences–National Research Council, 1963), pp. 20–72. Also J. D. Thompson and R. W. Hawkes, "Disaster, Community Organization and Administrative Process" in Baker and Chapman, *Man and Society,* pp. 268–303; S. H. Prince, *Catastrophe and Social Change* (New York: Columbia University Press, 1920).

whatever they were doing to report to the mine to await word of the trouble and if necessary volunteer their services for rescue operations. In Minetown the patterned and permanent shift-working hours of all miners were known, and when the off-shift miners left for the dangerous rescue work at the mine, their wives telephoned or visited the wives of relatives or friends whose husbands and sons worked on the shift caught in the accident.

At 8:05 P.M. on October 23, 1958, an underground upheaval devastated the Minetown Mine. There were 174 men working in the mine at the time.[15] It was the most severe bump that ever occurred in Minetown; at the surface the bump was experienced as a severe ground tremor that shook houses and rattled dishes, accompanied by a loud explosive sound. The bump was felt as a distinct tremor in communities 15 or 20 miles away. The shock was registered on a seismograph 800 miles distant.

Despite the fact that it occurred in a community whose population was familiar with bumps and constantly alert to danger, the district bump presented a unique, severe, and ambiguous stimulus. It was unique because of its intensity. It was ambiguous because it was unique and because the alarm whistle at the mine was not sounded.[16] This paper is concerned with the different ways in which the severe and threatening but ambiguous stimulus of the earth tremor was perceived.

The Problem

Shortly after the mine disaster, an interdisciplinary research team [17] entered Minetown. In the course of the research, interviews were conducted with miners who had been trapped in the mine by the bump, the wives of the trapped miners, citizens of the community and off-shift miners.[18] During the analysis of the taped

---

[15] Seventy-four died in the mine; 100 were rescued. One of the rescued died of injuries two weeks later.

[16] The term "ambiguous" raises semantic problems. In the strict sense, no stimulus can be "objectively" ambiguous because ambiguity is a "subjective" quality in the mind of the perceiver. As will be seen shortly, few if any of the respondents thought the stimulus ambiguous—whether or not they correctly identified it. But the Minetown situation is different from the structure of social responses to unanticipated air raid warnings. In the three situations analyzed by Mack and Baker the air raid siren itself (the signal) was heard and perceived as an air raid siren; the study concentrates on the ambiguous meaning and behavioral response to a known signal. See R. W. Mack and G. W. Baker, *The Occasion Instant* (Washington: National Academy of Sciences–National Research Council Pub. 945, 1961). In contrast, in Minetown, the stimulus was ambiguous, but, once established, there was no ambiguity as to its meaning and the appropriate behavioral response.

[17] H. D. Beach, L. Denton (Psychology); R. J. Weil, P. N. Murphy (Psychiatry); Nellen Armstrong, R. A. Lucas (Sociology). The project was supported by the Disaster Research Group, National Academy of Sciences–National Research Council, Washington, D.C.

[18] As this study is based upon a secondary analysis of data, the respondents do not represent a sample in relation to present considerations. Two groups of miners were trapped in the mine for a week, and the off-shift miners were a matched sample to provide a control base in relation to the trapped miners. The wives under consideration were the wives of the trapped men. The citizens were roughly representative of the non-mining population. Within the context of the present study, reference will be made to bodies of data rather

interviews of twelve off-shift miners, one unexpected fact was noticed. When the impact of the bump was felt, six of the twelve off-shift miners immediately interpreted it as a bump, but five off-shift miners attributed it to some other phenomenon, and one was not aware of the tremor (he was driving a vehicle at the time).

The five off-shift miners who did not interpret the tremor as a bump attributed it to a variety of causes, including a bomb:

> I thought some kids had put a bomb under Jim Brown's house. I said, "What in the hell is that?" And my friend said, "I don't know." Then a neighbor came out and she hollered, "What was that?" and I said, "I don't know."

The other four attributed the shock to various phenomena: "I thought a stool had fallen," "I thought a transfer truck had hit the house," "I thought it was the kids upstairs," "My first thought was that the furnace had blown up."

In direct contrast, the other six off-shift miners immediately identified the tremor as a bump in the mine: "I said, 'There's a big bump' "; "It has happened"; "I knew immediately what it was." The majority of these respondents went on to describe and explain the physical sensation in terms of similes which they thought the interviewer would understand: "It felt as if the whole world had hit the house, it was terrific"; "It shook the house just like a truck hit it"; "It felt as if the house had fallen off its foundation."

All miners confirmed or respecified their original perception within a few minutes of the tremor. Some carried out this social confirmation in the group in which they found themselves at the time of the impact. Others who were mystified telephoned friends or went out of doors and gathered with neighbors to discuss the phenomenon, while those who were sure it was a bump provided information and interpretation to others as they hurried to the mine to volunteer their services. These activities, typical of disasters, have been called convergence behavior by Fritz and Mathewson.[19] This phenomenon has been interpreted as serving a number of functions: it provides group communication and evaluation,[20] it aids in individual and social management of an acute situation,[21] it restructures an important but ambiguous situation,[22] and provides an opportunity to assess the social implications of the physical phenomenon.[23]

---

than to "samples." The interviews with off-shift and trapped miners were largely unstructured. Each miner was asked to give a chronological account of what he had thought and done from shortly before the bump. These accounts were tape-recorded. An interview schedule was used for the wives and citizens.

[19] C. E. Fritz and J. H. Mathewson, *Convergence Behavior in Disasters: A Problem in Social Control,* Disaster Study Number 9 (Washington: National Academy of Sciences-National Research Council, 1957). Mack and Baker, *Occasion Instant.*

[20] J. Reusch and A. Prestwood, "Anxiety—Its Initiation, Communication and Interpersonal Management," *Archives of the Neurological Psychiatrist* 62 (1949): 527–50.

[21] J. S. Tyhurst, "Individual Reactions to Community Disaster," *American Journal of Psychiatry* 197 (1950–51): 764–69.

[22] G. W. Allport and L. Postman, *The Psychology of Rumor* (New York: Henry Holt, 1947).

[23] J. S. Tyhurst, "Research on Reactions to Catastrophe," in I. Galdston, ed., *Panic and Morale* (New York: International Universities Press, 1958).

The focus of attention in this paper, however, is upon the immediate perception of the ambiguous stimulus rather than the subsequent reconfirmation or respecification of this perception.

The Development of a Hypothesis

It has been noted that five off-shift miners did not immediately recognize the earth tremor as a bump. This is surprising because they had the orientation and experience which equipped them to recognize mine disaster or accident cues. Why had the single ambiguous stimulus been interpreted as a disastrous bump by some miners while others attributed it to some other unusual event? Kilpatrick suggests that conflicting accounts of disaster may be accounted for by individuals' perceptions of the situation. "If I have one suggestion to make . . . it is that more study of the factors involved in this complex relational process of perception be included in future disaster research." [24] The Minetown facts suggested a search for the variable or variables that influenced the diverse meanings the men gave to the single stimulus.

There seemed to be a number of plausible explanations for the different perceptions of the stimulus. These explanations fall into five broad categories or levels: (1) physical and geographical; (2) social activities; (3) social background and social characteristics; (4) psychological; (5) social interpersonal role relationships. Although the list is in no way exhaustive, it provides a number of plausible explanations to be checked against the facts. Such a checking procedure, if nothing else, provides a safeguard against spurious findings.

Physical and Geographical. The diverse meanings of the single stimulus could be explained in terms of sheer physical distance. The men nearest to the mine might have been able to identify the bump because of the intensity of the shock emanating from the mine. This explanation has to be discarded because ten of the twelve men were within ten city blocks of the mine at the time of the bump. Further, the off-shift miner who was one and a half miles from the mine felt the tremor with such force that it "felt as if the house had fallen off its foundation." This same man identified the stimulus as a bump. The distances involved do not seem to have affected the shock of impact nor the perception of the men involved. In addition, the fact that ten of the twelve men were within a few hundred yards of the mine discounts another possible explanation that close physical association to a potential source (and explanation) of the stimulus affected the perception of some but not others.

It could be argued that the meaning given to the stimulus was affected by the immediate surroundings. The data show that six of the off-shift miners were in their own homes at the time; six were in less familiar surroundings. The explanation that familiar contexts provide a known bench mark from which to evaluate the stimulus has to be discarded because three men in their own homes recognized

[24] F. P. Kilpatrick, "Problems of Perception in Extreme Situations," *Human Organization* 16 (1947): 20–22.

the tremor as a bump and three did not. Three who were in less familiar surroundings identified the tremor as a bump and three did not.

Social Activities. It could be maintained that differences in perception were affected by the degree of each man's absorption in the matter of the moment. When the tremor was felt, for instance, five miners were talking, each with a different type of partner in a different setting—at home, in the garden, at lodge meeting, in the home of a friend, at a store. Despite the fact that four of the five men who were talking identified the tremor as a bump, the variety of settings and conversations suggests that the crucial factor was not the level of concentration. Of the five men who were watching television ("I Love Lucy"), three did not identify the tremor while two watchers immediately identified it as a bump. This suggests little convincing support for the thesis that different levels of preoccupation affected the perception of the phenomenon.

Social Background and Social Characteristics. The tendency to interpret new cues within a framework of normal expectations has been reported in virtually every disaster studied.[25] This has meant, for instance, that the roar of an approaching tornado was interpreted as a train, and flood water in the living room was attributed to a broken pipe.[26] In Minetown, mining formed a framework of normal expectations, and one off-shift miner suggested the inevitability of any ambiguous stimulus being associated with the mine:

> There's not much else you could figure it being in a town like this—to get that sound and vibration. It don't matter what kind of sound [there is] in this town—it is the mine anyway.

This does not explain why some miners thought it was a mine disaster but others a truck running into the house, or a bomb.

It seems plausible that some men were more skilled at interpreting the stimulus than others. The older men, for instance, had experienced more minor bumps and had more practice in identifying them. The ages of the off-shift miners who identified the bump ranged from 30 to 50, with a median age of 43; those who identified the shock as some other phenomenon ranged from 33 to 42, with a median age of 39. The difference of four or five years in terms of experience does not seem to be a strategic one. In like manner education, ethnic groupings, and rank did not account for the differences.

It has been found that people who have recently had direct experience with disaster become hypersensitive to signs of its recurrence.[27] This might be tested

---

[25] Mack and Baker, *Occasion Instant,* p. 52. See also E. S. Marks and C. E. Fritz, *Human Reaction in Disaster Situations* (3 vols.), unpublished report, National Opinion Research Center, 1954. For a discussion see Fritz, "Disaster," in Merton and Nisbet, *Social Problems,* pp. 668–70; I. L. anis, "Psychological Effects of Warnings"; and S. B. Withey, "Reaction to Uncertain Threat," in Baker and Chapman, *Man and Society,* pp. 55–123.

[26] Fritz, "Disaster," in Merton and Nisbet, *Social Problems,* p. 669.

[27] Mack and Baker, *Occasion Instant,* p. 52. See also H. E. Moore, *Tornadoes Over Texas* (Austin: University of Texas Press, 1958), pp. 271–72; Martha Wolfenstein, *Disaster: A Psychological Essay* (New York: Free Press, 1957), pp. 42–3.

on the basis of involvement in the Minetown mine explosion two years before the present study. None of the twelve off-shift miners interviewed were directly involved in that explosion.

Psychological. Denial might seem to be an obvious psychological explanation of the phenomenon. If we used a theory of "defense-against-anxiety" to explain the behavior of the men, we would assert that perception in response to threat may take the form of denial, exaggeration, or personalization of the source of threat.[28] The difficulty of this general theory is that it "explains" everything but nothing—it does not suggest why some men resorted to denial while others did not.

In terms of the future, a serious bump meant that many off-shift miners would have to fulfill their obligations by performing the arduous, dangerous and unpleasant work of rescue. Could the different interpretations be, in effect, a misreading of the stimulus, a conscious or unconscious mechanism of defense? Perhaps perceptual defense is at work—"the manner in which organisms utilize their perceptual readiness to ward off events that are threatening but about which there is nothing they can do"—either through lack of perceiving or through interference with perceiving.[29]

Evidence on this question is highly circumstantial. For instance, although it was a moral obligation to take part in rescue operations, there were always more off-shift miners than could be used at any one time. If a man was reluctant to act as rescuer, there were many ways of avoiding his duty with impunity.[30] It is fairly safe to assume that the majority of the off-shift miners who actually worked on rescue teams (except those assigned permanent rescue jobs) had little hesitancy about undertaking rescue work. The men who did not take part in rescue operations formed a residual category containing eager rescuers who could not be accommodated, as well as reluctant rescuers. Eight of the twelve men under study subsequently performed rescue work. Among the four who did not, two identified the tremor as a bump and two identified it as some other phenomenon. Half of the rescue workers identified the bump and half did not. The men's subsequent activities do not support the hypothesis that the perception of the stimulus as something other than a bump was a conscious or unconscious mechanism of defense.

---

[28] D. W. Chapman, "Dimensions of Models in Disaster Behavior," in Baker and Chapman, *Man and Society,* p. 313.

[29] J. S. Bruner and L. Postman, "Emotional Selectivity in Perception and Reaction," *Journal of Personality* 16 (1947): 69–77; L. Postman, J. S. Bruner and E. M. McGinnies, "Personal Values as Selective Factors in Perception," *Journal of Abnormal and Social Psychology* 43 (1946): 142–54. For a bibliography and later appraisals of the concept see L. Postman, et al., "Is There a Mechanism of Perceptual Defense?" and J. S. Bruner, "On Perceptual Readiness," in D. C. Beardslee and M. Wertheimer, eds., *Readings in Perception* (New York: Van Nostrand, 1958). See also F. H. Allport, *Theories of Perception and the Concept of Structure* (New York: Wiley, 1955), chapters 12–15.

[30] H. D. Beach and R. A. Lucas, eds., *Individual and Group Behavior in a Coal Mine Disaster,* Disaster Study Number 13 (Washington: National Academy of Sciences–National Research Council, 1960), pp. 18–20.

Interpersonal Role Relationships. The idea of role relationship shifts attention from the individual perceiver to the relationship between the perceiver and others with whom he carries on patterned interaction. Whether the shock was experienced while alone, among friends or family, had little effect upon immediate perception. This suggests that the individual perceptions may have been influenced by the presence of particular men in the mine at the time of the bump. The size of Minetown meant that every miner knew almost everyone who worked for the Minetown Mine Company. The fact that the shifts were permanent (rather than rotating) had the effect of restricting close working friendships to men on the same shift if for no other reason than that being on different shifts ruled out on- and off-duty interaction for at least sixteen hours of each day. Few off-shift miners had close friends on the working shift in question. These facts—that all off-shift miners were acquainted with miners in the mine at the time of the bump, but few had close friends in the mine—supply little basis for distinguishing between the different perceptions of the tremor.

The kinship structure provides a second set of primary role relationships. The data were checked to see if having a relative in the mine at the time of the bump made any difference to the man's perception. Five of the six who identified the stimulus as a bump had relatives in the mine at the time. None of the men who interpreted the tremor as something unconnected with the mine had relatives [31] in the mine when the bump occurred. This variable strongly discriminated between those who recognized the bump and those who identified it as some other phenomenon.

The data discounted plausible explanations involving physical, geographical, and social activities at the time of the bump as well as psychological factors and explanations involving social background and social characteristics. Previous research provides no clues about differential perception and evaluation of first disaster clues. The fact that having a relative working in the mine when the bump occurred seemed to affect the perception of the tremor suggests that there is a social link between family role partners and the perception.

This finding indicates that certain primary role relations affected the initial perception and evaluation of disaster. The importance of primary role relations has been noted in studies of convergence behavior,[32] and multiple group affiliation [33] but it has not been directly considered in terms of the significance for perception. Most people would acknowledge that once a disaster has been identified, it takes on particular significance for the individual when a relative is or may be involved. "An individual . . . who knows that his family is in the area potentially covered by the signal is more likely to interpret the signal as valid

---

[31] Relatives for the main part include father or brother on both the male and the female sides of the family. Sons, of course, were included. In a total of 48 interviews there were two instances in which a cousin was the closest relative in the mine. One individual had six close relatives in the mine at the time of the bump.

[32] Fritz and Mathewson, *Convergence*.

[33] Killian, "Multiple Group Membership."

than one whose family is not in the area potentially covered." [34] The pattern that has been identified in Minetown involves a different phenomenon—that family role relationships affect the definition of the situation, the *meaning* and *perception* of an ambiguous stimulus.

It seems possible to state a tentative hypothesis in general terms: status occupants whose relatives are engaged in a potentially dangerous activity are more apt to identify an ambiguously threatening stimulus (as affecting their relatives) than status occupants without such relatives.

The Testing of the Hypothesis

Two additional bodies of information on the Minetown disaster were available to test the hypothesis. In the course of the original field work a different interviewer conducted structured interviews with seventeen wives whose husbands were in the mine at the time of the bump. These women had less than expert mining knowledge but a high involvement with role partners in the mine. One of the questions included in the schedule was: "How did you first hear about the bump?" A typical rely was: "I *felt* it, of course! I *knew* it was a bump immediately." (After the tenth interview the question was almost dropped from the schedule as being inappropriate—the persistence of the reply and the tone of astonishment expressed by the respondents convinced the interviewer that it was a "silly" question. The question was retained because it permitted the respondent to discuss a range of local expert knowledge.) The following is a characteristic description of the bump by a woman whose husband was at work in the mine at the time:

> I was sitting alone in the house—in the dining room watching television—and I knew exactly what had happened. It is hard to explain, but it felt like the whole world hit the house—it was terrific. I knew it was a bump and I thought of my husband in the mine. I remember hearing myself say in the empty house, "My God above, it happened!"

Of the seventeen wives who had husbands in the mine at the time of the tremor, fifteen immediately identified the shock as a bump. One woman thought that her television aerial had fallen onto the roof, and one was driving her car at the time and did not feel the impact. The experience of these women who all had husbands in the mine at the time of the shock lends considerable support to the hypothesis.

The data supplied by the women also permit the tentative establishment of two other important points. First, it is clear that the identification of the bump

---

[34] Mack and Baker, *Occasion Instant,* p. 48. See also the N.O.R.C. study, "A Series of Home Explosions in Brighton, New York," pp. 141–42, and "An Airplane Crash in Flager, Colorado," pp. 174–75, in *Conference on Field Studies of Reactions to Disasters* (Chicago: National Opinion Research Center, 1953). See also L. M. Killian, *A Study of Response to the Houston, Texas, Fire-works Explosion* (Washington: National Academy of Sciences–National Research Council, 1956).

was not dependent upon expert mining knowledge. The second point is that sex differences do not seem to be strategic ones in terms of the perception of the ambiguous stimulus. Males and females alike interpreted the shock both as a bump and as some other phenomenon.

A second body of information was available. Ten citizens—bank managers, clergy, school teachers, nurses, store managers and the like—whose occupations were unrelated to coal mining were interviewed. Included in the schedule was the question, "How did you first hear about the bump?" Among the ten citizens, six immediately recognized the tremor as a bump while four attributed the shock to some cause other than the mine. One who did not immediately recognize the bump said, "*After* checking everything in the house (that could account for the tremor) I decided it must be a bump." These citizens whose occupations seemed so far removed from coal mining were not as disinterested in the mine as was first thought, for six had close relatives working in the mine at the time of the bump. The six with relatives in the mine were the same six who immediately identified the bump. The four with no relatives in the mine attributed the tremor to some other cause. Again these findings support the original hypothesis.

The findings seemed so promising that when, at a later date, an interviewer returned to Minetown he took the opportunity of interviewing nine additional miners who were off-shift at the time of the bump. Six of the men immediately recognized the bump. Five of the six who recognized the bump had relatives in the mine at the time,[35] and one had no relatives in the mine. The three who did not immediately recognize the bump had no relatives in the mine.

If all 48 cases are combined (see Table 1)—the off-shift miners, the wives of the miners, the non-miners and the second group of off-shift miners—it is found that 97 percent of those who immediately identified the bump had relatives

TABLE 1

IDENTIFICATION OF AN AMBIGUOUS STIMULUS BY INVOLVEMENT OF RELATIVES

(N = 48)

	Relative in the Mine	*No Relative in the Mine*
Identified the bump	31	1
Identified some other phenomenon	4*	12

* Includes the two who were driving vehicles and were unaware of the stimulus.

[35] Of course it was not the presence of the relative in the mine, but the conviction (definition) that he was that had the social and perceptual consequences. One respondent immediately recognized the tremor as a bump and (or because) he *knew* his brother worked on that shift. In fact, his brother had not gone to work that evening. The respondent was not aware of this until six hours later when the two brothers met in the same rescue party. The meaning of the stimulus and the respondent's subsequent behavior were influenced by the idea that his brother was in the mine.

in the mine at the time. On the other hand, 86 percent of those who attributed the bump to some other phenomenon had no relatives in the mine.

Four small but separate bodies of data related to the perception of the meaning given to the underground upheaval in Minetown support the hypothesis that status occupants whose family role partners are engaged in a potentially dangerous activity are more apt to define an ambiguously threatening stimulus as affecting their family role partners than status occupants without such partners. Although the evidence was compelling, there was no way of knowing if the respondents who identified the bump were individuals who traditionally attributed any out-of-the-way event to the mine. Another related problem was that because 74 percent of the respondents had relatives in the mine at the time of the bump it was not possible to support or refute the allegation of the off-shift miner who said . . . "It don't matter what kind of sound [there is] in this town—it is in the mine anyway."

After the Minetown disaster, the mine was closed and sealed and the community was left without an industry. Eighteen months later Minetown was shaken by a second intense tremor attributed to a bump in the then abandoned mine. It was possible to schedule additional interviews shortly after this second ambiguous stimulus. Respondents were closely questioned on their immediate perception of it.

Interviews were carried out with sixteen men who had been interviewed about the first bump in order to establish whether there were miners who habitually attributed any untoward incident to the mine. Nine of the respondents in the repeat interviews had identified the first tremor as a bump and seven had identified it as some other phenomenon. None of these men immediately perceived the second tremor as a bump. The fact that eight of the nine (one was out of town at the time of the second tremor) who originally identified the first bump when they had relatives in the mine failed to identify the second bump when there was no one in the mine adds to the confidence that these men did not "automatically" attribute all ambiguous stimuli to the mine.

No one in Minetown had relatives in the mine at the time of the second tremor. If the hypothesis held it would be expected that few would immediately identify the stimulus as arising from an underground bump. In all, 31 ex-miners were interviewed on this subject. Of these, four were out of town at the time of the second incident, three recognized the stimulus as a bump, but 24 (89 percent) of the respondents in town at the time attributed the simulus to some other cause:

> I was walking up the street . . . and when it let go, the first thing I thought of was a blast of dynamite. But then I got to thinking a little, and the more I kept thinking about it, the more I thought maybe it was bump in the old workings. Afterwards they claimed it was a jet breaking the sound barrier . . . But there were fellows out picking [up] coal [near the sealed mine] that day, and they claim it [the tremor] was right below them—that it definitely was a bump in the old workings.

> He said, "What's that?" and I said, "I don't know," and I looked at the sky and the sky was all bright and the sun was out and all lovely so it couldn't be thunder, but we heard it again—the rumble—and I said, "That's under my feet!" "Oh," he said, "I believe that's somebody firing dynamite."

The shock was variously perceived as "a jet plane breaking the sound barrier," "blasting," "a tank exploding," "a truck had hit the side of the garage," "thunder." One man added:

> Oh, I didn't think anything of it because I knew it couldn't do no damage now—nobody there [in the mine] or anything like that.

The data gathered on the perception of this second incident in the same community upheld the hypothesis.

Discussion

Perception is part of all social behavior but sociologically it is usually treated as an implicit intervening variable or as a general unspecified explanatory variable. Between the extremes of sociology and neurophysiology, clinical and social psychologists have been interested in the relationship of perception to individual values, needs, personality characteristics and other psychological variables. This led Allport to observe: "Its emphasis has lain not upon perception as a means of biological adaptation to a common environment, but upon the way the *individual* perceives his world." [36] Both the physiological and psychological approaches to perception are valid and necessary; the purpose of this paper has been to demonstrate that there is a third area of concern that must be taken into account, the network of social relations in which the perceiver perceives.

This relationship between perception and family roles was brought to our attention by the very special circumstances in Minetown. It would be difficult if not foolhardy to make generalizations beyond Minetown; we need to know more about the effect of family role relationships upon perception of other types of ambiguous stimuli. It remains to be established if these roles also influence perception of non-ambiguous stimuli. From there curiosity leads to the study of the effect of multiple and conflicting roles upon perception.

Although the data demonstrate that family roles influence perception of ambiguous stimuli, they do not suggest why this should be so. Why, for instance, are kinship primary roles more important than friendship primary roles? This is particularly perplexing because kinship roles involve such a wide range of intensity of affect and meaning. There must be many situations in which the loss of a friend in a mine disaster has a much greater emotional impact than the loss of a brother-in-law. This wide range of possible affect within family relationships suggests a possible explanation. Kinship relations in our society carry normative obligations; these reciprocal responsibilities are particularly important when the

---

[36] Allport, *Theories of Perception,* p. 363.

kin are close at hand geographically. The death of a son, father, brother, brother-in-law or father-in-law usually involves a reorganization of kinship roles and responsibilities. Widowhood often necessitates short-term and sometimes long-term assistance from other male kin. The death of a friend, on the other hand, may well involve a deep emotional loss but seldom necessitates a reorganization of life roles and responsibilities. It is possible to speculate that the cogency of family roles may be due partly to affect but more importantly to the role obligations involving a life reorganization of major proportions. This conjecture requires systematic investigation.

12

The Perceptual Distortion of Height as a Function of Ascribed Academic Status

PAUL R. WILSON

Social psychologists have frequently emphasized the social nature of the perceptual process. The thesis is that factors other than the stimulus properties of the perceptual object impinge upon the perception. In the language of the layman, what one sees in his environment depends upon what's out there, but only partially so.

In the research report which follows, Wilson demonstrates that the status which is ascribed to a stimulus person influences others' perception of his height. The same stimulus person was introduced successively to five groups of students, but in each group a different academic status was ascribed to the stimulus person. In one group he was introduced as a student from Cambridge, in the second group as a demonstrator in psychology at Cambridge, then as a lecturer, a senior lecturer, and finally, as a professor.[1] The person making the introduction was the same for all groups, and in each instance he was the students' course director. After the introduction, the students were requested to estimate the height (to the nearest half-inch) of both the stimulus person and the course director. The course director presented a contrived rationale for his request. An analysis of the data revealed that with each increment in ascribed status, the students perceived the stimulus person as taller. In fact, he was perceived as approximately 2½ inches taller as a professor than as a student. In contrast, the students' estimation of the course director's height varied no more than three-fourths an inch from one group to another.

[1] The subjects for this study were students in an Australian university. While the status designations of demonstrator, lecturer, and senior lecturer are not commonly used in United States colleges and universities, they had meaning for the subjects.

Paul R. Wilson, "The Perceptual Distortion of Height as a Function of Ascribed Academic Status," *Journal of Social Psychology* 74 (1968): 97–102.

Thus, even in the perception of the physical properties of a person, the social characteristics of that person exert a significant influence. Similar findings have been reported by others using non-student subjects and different social characteristics. Because of the primary role of perception in social interaction, the implications of this research are numerous.

The influence that motivational or value factors can have on the perceptual judgment of magnitude has been noted by a number of investigators. *Ss* have been found to estimate the size of coins as larger than discs of the same size,[1] to overestimate the size of cards in accordance with monetary value given to them,[2] and to perceive discs associated with high and low social value as larger than discs of the same size associated with neutral symbols.[3] Dukes and Bevan [4] and Beams [5] have shown that value factors related to food objects also influence perceptual judgments.

In a recent study Dannenmaier and Thumin further investigated the relationship between value and perceptual distortion of size.[6] Forty-six nursing students were asked to estimate the heights of the assistant director of their school, their instructor, their class president, and a specified fellow student. Results indicated a significant relationship between authority status and perceptual distortion of size: the two staff members were overestimated in height and the two student figures were judged shorter than they actually were.

While Dannenmaier and Thumin's study represents a valuable addition to the literature on perceptual judgment as a function of stimulus values, their results have to be treated with some caution. Their stimulus figures—fellow staff and students of the nursing college—varied along other dimensions besides social status. The systematic over- and underestimation could be related not to status but to general body somatypes, facial characteristics, personality attributes, or to numerous unknown and uncontrolled for aspects of the authority figures used.

---

[1] J. S. Bruner and C. C. Goodman, "Value and Need as Organizing Factors in Perception," *Journal of Abnormal and Social Psychology* 42 (1947): 33–44.

[2] W. F. Dukes and W. Bevan, "Size Estimation and Monetary Value: A Correlation," *Journal of Psychology* 34 (1952): 43–53.

[3] S. J. Bruner and L. Postman, "Symbolic Value as an Organizing Factor in Perception," *Journal of Social Psychology* 27 (1948): 203–08.

[4] W. F. Dukes and W. Bevan, "Accentuation and Response Variability in the Perception of Personally Relevant Objects," *Journal of Personality* 20 (1952): 457–65.

[5] H. L. Beams, "Affectivity as a Factor in the Apparent Size of Pictured Objects," *Journal of Experimental Psychology* 47 (1954): 197–200.

[6] W. D. Dannenmaier and F. J. Thumin, "Authority Status as a Factor in Perceptual Distortion of Size," *Journal of Social Psychology* 63 (1964): 361–65.

Furthermore, the relationship between authority status and perceptual distortion of size obtained could result simply from the actual heights of the people used in the study or to an interaction between status, actual height, and the many other personality and physical attributes along which people vary.

The present study was a further investigation of the relationship between authority status and height estimation. Like Dannenmaier and Thumin's experiment, living persons rather than physical objects acted as stimuli; but unlike their study, the present one used a single stimulus figure who was a person unknown to the *S*s making height estimations and who had been ascribed an imaginary status. Furthermore this investigation attempted to control for all other factors besides the one under investigation: viz., status of the authority figure. Specifically, the purpose of this study was to determine whether perceptual judgments of height would be influenced by the ascribed status of the person being evaluated. It was hypothesized that as ascribed academic status increased, there would be a related tendency to increase the height of the stimulus figure.

Method

One hundred and ten undergraduate students divided into five equal groups were asked to estimate, to the nearest half inch, the height of a man presented before them. The academic status of the man changed with each of the five groups. After writing down their estimates, *S*s had then to estimate the height of a member of the staff who was the students' course director. The procedure used was as follows. The course director on entering the room where the students were assembled introduced the person standing next to him by saying:

"This is Mr. England, a student in psychology from the University of Cambridge. He will be in the department for a period and may be giving a talk to your class. I thought I'd introduce him to you so if you see him again in the laboratory classes you will know him."

Mr. England was presented to the five groups of *S*s, but his status changed with each group. In the first group it was Mr. England, a student from Cambridge; in the second, Mr. England, demonstrator in psychology from Cambridge; third, Mr. England, lecturer in psychology from Cambridge; fourth, Dr. England, senior lecturer from Cambridge; and, finally, Professor England from Cambridge.

After Mr. England was introduced according to his status, he left and the course director continued:

"Well, as later on in the year we will have to do a number of statistical tests, let's get some data to analyze. I want you on the sheet provided to estimate the height of Mr. England (or whatever the status was for the particular group of *S*s) to the nearest ½ inch."

The course director then asked the students to estimate his own height. The course director, known to the students, naturally had the same status for each of the five groups of *S*s. Care was taken to see that *S*s worked independently of each other and did not begin to make their estimates until the figures being judged had left the room.

The person whom *Ss* were asked to estimate and whose status changed with each of the five groups was selected for two reasons. First, having just arrived from Great Britain he was unknown to the students and, second, his general features were such that he could plausibly be anyone of the statuses ranging from student through to professor.

Results

Mean height estimations were calculated for each group of *Ss* on the course director's estimated height and the authority figure's estimated height, the latter's status changing with each of the five groups of *Ss*. An examination of Table 1 shows that the mean estimated height of Mr. England was directly related to his ascribed status. His height increased with increasing academic status. On the other hand the mean estimated height of the course director (who had the same status for all *Ss*) showed no significant change between groups.

TABLE 1

ESTIMATED MEAN HEIGHT OF ACADEMIC FIGURE AND COURSE DIRECTOR ACCORDING TO STATUS ASCRIBED TO ACADEMIC FIGURE

Group [a]	*Ascribed status of academic figure*	*Estimated height of academic figure according to ascribed status*	*Estimated height of course director*
I	Student	139.727	137.863
II	Demonstrator	140.772	138.045
III	Lecturer	141.727	137.060
IV	Senior lecturer	143.138	138.909
V	Professor	144.636	137.861

Note: All values expressed in half inches.
[a] Each group based on N of 22.

An analysis of variance was performed on the differences for all *Ss* between their estimates for the authority figure and their estimates for the course director. The differences between groups were highly significant ($F = 6.779$, $p < .001$). The mean differences between *Ss*' estimate for the authority figure and the course director for all five groups were then compared by t-test, the results of which are presented in Table 2.

An examination of the table shows that mean differences were statistically significant (.05 level) between status levels one level apart: i.e., between, for

TABLE 2

CRITICAL DIFFERENCES BETWEEN MEAN DIFFERENCE SCORES FOR FIVE DIFFERENT STATUS GROUPS

Status of stimulus figure	*Student*	*Demon-strator*	*Lecturer*	*Senior lecturer*	*Professor*
Student		1.045	2.0	3.591*	4.660*
Demonstrator			.955	2.546*	3.864*
Lecturer				1.591	2.909*
Senior lecturer					1.318

Note: All values expressed in half inches.
* $p < .05$.

example, the authority figure as a student and then as a lecturer, but not between him as a student and then a demonstrator. This pattern was the same for all other status levels.

Discussion

As hypothesized, there was a significant relationship between ascribed status and estimation of height. The results showed quite conclusively that as ascribed academic status of a person increased, estimates of height increased. However, even though estimated height of the stimulus figure increased in proportion to this status, as Table 1 indicates, there was not a statistically significant difference between adjacent status level. For example, as Table 2 shows, the mean difference between the estimated height of the stimulus figure as a student and then as a demonstrator was not significant, but there was a statisically significant difference in the estimated height of the stimulus figure as a student when compared with the estimated height as a lecturer. Similar patterns held for all comparisons of all five different status groups with each other.

The results of the significance tests appear to indicate that there are no differences between population means at successive status levels, while there are differences between alternate status levels. This is numerically impossible; there must be differences for at least some of the successive status levels. In these cases the insignificant results must be due to Type II errors.

It is also noteworthy that the height of the authority figure, regardless of his status, was underestimated. The authority figure's real height was 73 inches; while, as Table 1 indicates, the estimate made by subjects judging the stimulus figure as a professor was only 72 inches. The height of the course director was 69 inches, and the biggest estimate of his height made by any group was 69.5 inches.

This underestimation of height of the stimulus figure could be a function of the body width of the authority figure or some other such physical attribute. It is possible, though, that this result is due to the fact that *S*s were not judging objects in a series. Dannenmaier and Thumin [7] noted that heights of two student figures were underestimated, whereas those of two staff figures were overestimated; while Bruner and Rodrigues [8] and Carter and Schooler [9] found a tendency for small coins to be underestimated and for large coins to be overestimated. In all these studies the stimulus objects were in a series and all objects were judged by all *S*s. Thus, as Tajfel [10] has indicated, the objects influence one another in such a way as to maximize differences between them and, therefore, *S*s, to avoid confusion, accentuate size or height estimations between objects.

Finally, it is interesting to note that, when stimulus objects are not presented in a series as in previous studies and when all other variables except status level are controlled for, *S*s increase their estimates of perceived height according to the ascribed status of the stimulus figure. In other words, support is given to Dannenmaier and Thumin's hypothesis that, as authority status increases, there will be an increasing tendency to perceive the individual as taller than a person of lesser status.

Summary

The aim of the present investigation was to determine whether perceptual judgment of height would be influenced by the ascribed academic status of a stimulus figure when all other factors except for the status level of the person being evaluated were controlled for.

Five separate groups each containing 22 students were asked to estimate to the nearest half inch the height of a man presented before them whose academic status changed with each of the five groups. *S*s also had to estimate height of their course director whose status remained constant over all groups of subjects.

Results indicated a significant relationship between ascribed status and perceptual distortion of height. As the ascribed academic status increased, students' estimation of height increased. The course director's perceived height remained constant over the five groups of *S*s.

However, all groups underestimated the actual height of the stimulus figure evaluated. This finding was briefly discussed in relation with Tajfel's hypothesis of accentuation of differences.

---

[7] Ibid.

[8] J. S. Bruner and J. S. Rodrigues, "Some Determinants of Apparent Size," *Journal of Abnormal and Social Psychology* 48 (1953): 17–24.

[9] F. L. Carter and K. Schooler, "Value, Need and Other Factors in Perception," *Psychological Review* 56 (1949): 200–07.

[10] H. Tajfel, "Value and Judgment of Magnitude," *Psychological Review* 64 (1957): 192–204.

13

The "Origin-Pawn" Variable in Person Perception

RICHARD deCHARMS · VIRGINIA CARPENTER
AHARON KUPERMAN

We are continuously processing new information about others, making judgments and evaluations of them, and making predictions about their future behavior. This largely unconscious activity is, of course, a significant determinant of our actions toward others.

One of the most important factors in evaluating another's behavior is the attribution of responsibility for his actions. That is, before we can praise or blame a person for his behavior, we must first decide whether he was the "origin" of his own behavior or a "pawn" executing the will of an external agent.

Placing a person on the origin-pawn dimension is not always a straightforward task, since some influence from external agents is nearly always evident if we care to look for it. On what basis, then, are attributions of responsibility made? What factors determine whether an actor is seen as an origin or a pawn? The following research report by deCharms, Carpenter, and Kuperman explores the significance of three such factors: (1) the judged person's liking or dislike for the persuasive agent, (2) whether the persuasive agent is an individual, a small group, or an organization, and (3) whether the person making the judgment sees himself generally as having strong control or weak control over his own fate.

Albert Schweitzer is usually seen as a man who is voluntarily working for the good of mankind in Africa. Our perception of him is that of a man who is free, is pursuing what he has chosen as his contribution to humanity,

Richard deCharms, Virginia Carpenter, and Aharon Kuperman, "The Origin-Pawn Variable in Person Perception," *Sociometry* 28 (1965): 241–58.

and is happy in doing it. If anything is seen as constraining him to this work it is his own dedication to the value of working for the good of mankind. We see Albert Schweitzer as the *origin* of his behavior.

Joe Doe has just been drafted into the Army, preventing him from going to college as he had wished. He is peeling potatoes on KP while his buddies are out "on the town." Our perception of him is that of a man who is completely constrained, pursuing an activity not of his own choosing. He is probably miserable and finds little to value in the constraining force—the Army. We see John Doe, not as the origin of his behavior, but as a *pawn.*

Behavior is readily interpreted along the "origin-pawn" dimension, and the interpretation may have important effects. If we ask ourselves in a specific instance "What made him do that?" the interpretation of the word "made" can be very important. If force is implied, especially from an external personal source, we may absolve the person who was forced to behave in a socially disapproved way of all responsibility. We locate the "cause" of his behavior as external to him, and say he is "merely a pawn in the game."

If we interpret the question "What made him do that?" in terms of intentions, we assume that the "cause" or "origin" of the behavior lies in the intention and a person is held personally responsible for his intentions. The motivational implications of the attribution of intention are developed by Urmson and by Anscombe.[1] The importance of such attribution in person perception probably derives from the personal experience of the person attributing intentions to another. In the past he may be assumed to have felt strongly under some conditions that he freely initiated his behavior, and under other conditions that he was constrained by direction from some external force. Thus, personal knowledge of being treated like a pawn or feeling like an origin enter into the attribution of intention.

It seems reasonable to assume that different external sources of influence on the behavior of a person will be seen as differentially constraining his behavior. A person who is caught in the web of a large organization which has absolute power to control his behavior in ways which he does not like or approve, is a pawn. A pawn is relatively powerless compared to an origin, and power relationships are most certainly entailed when inferences are made along the origin-pawn dimension.

At the societal level alienation may be involved, for, as Seeman, and Rotter, Seeman, and Liverant [2] have shown, feelings of powerlessness may reflect alienation from society. Alienation, in turn, may be a consequence to the worker of

---

[1] J. O. Urmson, R. S. Peters and D. J. McCracken, "Symposium: Motives and Causes," *Aristotelian Society* 26 (1952): 139–94; G. E. M. Anscombe, *Intention* (Oxford: Basil Blackwell, 1957).

[2] Melvin Seeman, "On the Meaning of Alienation," *American Sociological Review* 24 (December 1959): 783–91; Julian B. Rotter, Melvin Seeman and Shephard Liverant, "Internal versus External Control of Reinforcements: A Major Variable in Behavior Theory," in N. F. Washburne, ed., *Decisions, Values, and Groups,* Vol. 2 (New York: Macmillan Co., 1962), pp. 473–516.

industrialization, as pointed out by Marx, or of bureaucratization as suggested by Max Weber.

In this connection it is also relevant to mention Merton's [3] analysis of Durkheim's concept of anomie which stresses the lack of overlap between values of an anomic individual and those of the culture or organization of which he is a part. The anomalous situation arises of a person who is a deviant from the norms of the group either as to the ends which he values or as to the approved means by which he seeks the ends. Under such conditions the person will not have access to the means of achieving his life goals, as Meier and Bell [4] have shown, and will be perceived as a pawn.

The person who is seen as the origin of his behavior is assumed to be personally responsible for it. He has found means within his group of achieving some of his life goals, and has initiated the appropriate behavior. One example of such behavior in our culture is that of the entrepreneur. McClelland [5] sees entrepreneurial behavior as most appropriate and conducive to the goal of economic development of the culture, and one of the major characteristics which McClelland attributes to entrepreneurs is the desire for individual responsibility for their actions.

Evidence presented by McClelland indicates that individual responsibility is not necessarily precluded in working for a group or an organization, as long as the individual can feel free to initiate action and make decisions contributing to group success. Clearly such innovative behavior would be seen as originating within the person. Apparently we cannot assume that all persons working in a bureaucratic structure will feel like or be seen as pawns. Overlap between the goals of the organization and those of the individual might lead to the inference that he is more of an origin despite the fact that he is working for a bureaucratic organization.

The "origin-pawn" concept derives its social psychological roots from Heider's [6] discussion of the perception of the locus of causality of behavior. Research showing the importance of the locus of causality concept has been reported by Thibaut and Riecken, Pepitone, and Wilkins and deCharms,[7] among others. From these studies we can assume that when people attempt to infer

---

[3] Robert K. Merton, *Social Theory and Social Structure* (Glencoe, Ill.: Free Press, 1957).

[4] Dorothy L. Meier and Wendell Bell, "Anomia and Differential Access to the Achievement of Life Goals," *American Sociological Review* 24 (April 1959): 189–202.

[5] David C. McClelland, *The Achieving Society* (Princeton: Van Nostrand, 1961).

[6] Fritz Heider, *The Psychology of Interpersonal Relations* (New York: John Wiley, 1958).

[7] John W. Thibaut and Henry W. Riecken, "Authoritarianism, Status, and the Communication of Aggression," *Human Relations* 8 (1955): 95–120; J. W. Thibaut and H. W. Riecken, "Some Determinants and Consequences of the Perception of Social Causality," *Journal of Personality* 24 (December 1955): 113–33; Albert Pepitone, "Attributions of Causality, Social Attitudes, and Cognitive Matching Processes," in Renato Tagiuri and Luigi Petrullo, eds., *Person Perception and Interpersonal Behavior* (Stanford, California: Stanford University Press, 1958), pp. 258–76; Edward J. Wilkins and Richard deCharms, "Authoritarianism and Response to Power Cues," *Journal of Personality* 30 (September 1962): 439–57.

motives from a person's behavior they often take into account to what extent the behavior may be considered to be "his own" and to what extent he "was forced" into it. They probably arrive at some estimate which reaches neither extreme of the origin-pawn dimension for the underlying concept involves a continuous dimension rather than a discrete dichotomy. The evidence from which one draws inferences probably has to do with such things as (a) whether or not an agent of persuasion is trying to get the person to act in a prescribed way; (b) whether the person likes or dislikes the agent; and (c) "what's in it for him" (reward or punishment for the person). Ultimately the judgment is probably made in terms of an estimate of how the observer making the judgment would feel under such circumstances.

The purpose of this study is to investigate some of the personal and situational aspects which affect the perception that a person is acting as an origin or is being pushed around like a pawn. From the broader context sketched above we can derive the generalization that a large impersonal bureaucratic organization fosters a feeling of powerlessness in its members. From this we may predict that people involved in the network of a large bureaucratic organization may be seen as pawns vis-à-vis the organization. The perception may be tempered by information about the person's attitudes toward the organization. If overlap may be assumed between the individual's and the organization's goals, he will be seen as more of an origin.

Specifically, we presented our subjects with a series of stories in all of which the principal character (hero) is being influenced to do something by another character or group (the persuasive agent). The persuasive agent is presented as either very attractive or very unattractive to the hero, and is variously an individual, a small group, or a large organization.

On the assumption that inferences about an observed person's behavior are affected by the perceiver's estimate of how *he* would feel in the situation, we have attempted to measure a generalized characteristic of the subjects along a dimension of feeling in control of fate or of being controlled by it. As an outgrowth of Rotter's [8] social learning theory, Rotter, Seeman, and Liverant have developed a scale to measure the perception of internal vs. external control of reinforcements: "External control refers to the perception of positive and/or negative events as being unrelated to one's own behaviors in certain situations and therefore beyond personal control." [9] A form of the internal-external control (I-E) scale developed by these authors was used here to measure a personal aspect of subjects which was hypothesized to be related to their perception of the hero along the origin-pawn dimension.

The choice of the independent variable of attractiveness of the persuasive agent was guided by the hypothesis (I) that the hero would be perceived more as an origin when he was being persuaded by an agent that he liked and more as

[8] Julian B. Rotter, *Social Learning and Clinical Psychology* (New York: Prentice-Hall, 1954).

[9] Rotter, Seeman, and Liverant, "Internal vs. External Control," p. 499.

a pawn when being persuaded by an agent that he disliked, when all other factors were held constant.

The type of persuasive agent was varied from individual to small group to large organization to test the hypothesis (II) that a hero reacting to a large organization would be seen as more of a pawn than a hero reacting to a small group or an individual. The feeling of control over fate (as measured in each subject) was included to test the hypothesis (III) that subjects who feel that they have internal control over the consequences of their own actions will perceive the hero as more of an origin than subjects who feel external control over their own behavior.

The variation of type of persuasive agent to test Hypothesis II is really a composite variable. The agents used were an individual, a small group, and a large organization. The major difference may be seen as size of group, but as size of group increases several other aspects are also likely to change in real groups. The individual and the small group can be personally known, the large organization cannot, and the type of power wielded by an individual, a small group, or a large organization may be quite different. In the present study, an attempt was made to to select typical agents in the real world rather than to try to assure that the *only* difference between agents was the number of people included. Although it might be argued that it would be more precise to vary the size alone, we followed the assumption that it would be more meaningful and realistic to investigate the effects of typical agents despite their composite nature.

Method

Forty-two vignettes about seven different heroes were composed around a basic design which always presented a hero who was being persuaded to do something. Each vignette explained (a) who the hero was; (b) what his relationship with and attitude toward the persuasive agent was; (c) what the hero was being asked to do; and (d) what extra reward he would get for doing it well in each case. The seven different heroes varied as to occupation and social status, and each of them appeared in six different vignettes in which the major independent variables of positive vs. negative agent by individual, small group, large organization appeared in all six combinations. This formed a 2 x 3 design.

Six of the heroes were being asked to do something which was over and above routine duty but not extreme—something which they would not do without some incentive. Thus, the Army private was asked to stand "extra" guard duty. These six heroes were considered examples of extrinsic incentive situations and constituted the major part of the study. As a comparison, one hero was presented who was to be intrinsically motivated. He was a professor who needed no help, but was vitally interested in studying cancer with the goal of "helping mankind." In this version he was encouraged to do it by the six types of agents contained in the independent variables. The six versions of this intrinsically motivated hero were "tacked on" to the basic design.

The six extrinsic heroes and the six varations of the independent variables were arranged to form a 6^2 Latin Square. In such a design all subjects responded to six vignettes in which the hero was always different (plus the seventh of the intrinsic professor). Each subject reacted to each of the six independent variations paired with a separate hero. In order to get a complete replication, six subjects were needed since they produced thirty-six responses, one under each of the six variations of type and attractiveness of agent for each of the six different heroes. The "intrinsic professor" vignette was "tacked on" to the design to vary as one of the other heroes. The resulting data can be analyzed for variance attributable to subjects, blocks of subjects (the specific combination of hero and independent variable they received), I-E score of a subject, the six heroes, attractiveness of agent, and type of agent.

Table 1 condenses the content of the forty-two vignettes into the various relevant categories. All subjects reviewed the vignette containing the political party precinct worker first, etc., in the order of the first column, except that the professor was inserted in ordinal position three for all subjects. Table 2 presents the Latin Square design.

After each vignette the subject responded to six Likert-type items on a scale from strong agreement to strong disagreement. The responses were converted into a seven-point scale. The items were slightly reworded to adapt them to each vignette but the basic phrases were identical. Four of the items constituted the Origin-Pawn Scale, two worded so that a high score indicated that the hero would feel like an origin. These items follow:

(The name of the hero) will feel that all decisions are being made for him by (the name of the agent).

In this situation (the name of the hero) will feel that (the name of the agent) is arbitrarily controlling him like a pawn.

(Hero) will feel that he is completely free to make his own decisions in carrying out (name of task).

In carrying out (name of task), (hero) will feel completely free.

Two of the items after each vignette constituted the Task Enjoyment Scale:

(Hero) will very much enjoy his (name of task).

(Name of task) will seem very unpleasant to (hero).

After giving responses to these six items after all seven vignettes, subjects completed a form of the I-E scale consisting of the twelve items given in the article by Rotter, Seeman, and Liverant.[10] Responses were again on a seven-point agree-disagree scale, and the items were in couplets of two (one to be reverse scored) from six diverse areas, namely (a) academic recognition; (b) social recognition; (c) love and affection; (d) dominance; (e) social-political; (f) general life philosophy. In each of these areas the items attempt to measure how much the

[10] Rotter, Seeman, and Liverant, "Internal vs External Control."

TABLE 1

OUTLINE OF STIMULUS MATERIALS

	PERSUASIVE AGENT			
Hero	*Individual*	*Small group*	*Large group*	*Reward*
1. Political party precinct worker	Precinct committeeman	Fellow precinct workers	Republocrat party	Appointment in recorder's office
2. Army private	C.O. (Major)	Men in his platoon	The Army	Special 3-day pass
3. Salesman, General Machines, Inc.	Office sales manager	Other salesmen	The Company	Paid delegate to convention
4. Clerk, U.S. Embassy Moscow (Protocol Sec.)	Chief of Protocol Section	Embassy Protocol Section	State Department	"Hitch-hike" flight to Switzerland
5. Medical intern	Chief resident in pediatrics	His fellow interns	American Medical Association	Residency appointment
6. Member, Shoe Worker's Union	Union shop steward	His work crew	Amalgamated Shoe Worker's Union	Requested shift, and slight pay increase
7. University professor	Another professor	A few colleagues	His university	None—hopes to help mankind
a) Positive attractiveness	"a man whom he likes and admires very much"	"they are his friends off the job as well as on"	Hero has high regard for the record of the organization	
b) Negative attractiveness	"a man whom he considers an opportunist, and so does not respect"	"lazy and incompetent; not the kind of men he would want as close personal friends"	Hero is disgusted with the organization; feels that it does not accomplish anything worthwhile	

TABLE 2
LATIN SQUARE DESIGN

	ORDER OF PRESENTATION						
Block of Subjects	*1 Political*	*2 Army*	*4 Business*	*5 Govern't*	*6 Doctor*	*7 Union*	*3 Professor**
1	+L**	−s	−i	+s	−L	+i	+s
2	+i	+L	−s	−i	+s	−L	−i
3	−L	+i	+L	−s	−i	+s	−s
4	+s	−L	+i	+L	−s	−i	+L
5	−i	+s	−L	+i	+L	−s	+i
6	−s	−i	+s	−L	+i	+L	−L

* The professor was the same treatment as Government for any subject.
** *L* = large organization; *s* = small group; *i* = individual.
+ = positive attractiveness; − = negative attractiveness.

subject feels in control of his reinforcement or how much he feels controlled by others. The total scale scores indicate a general attitude toward internal or external control in a broad spectrum of life situations. In our terms the scale may be said to measure how much the subject feels like an origin or a pawn of fate in many situations.

The total score was computed for each subject (possible range 12–84, actual range 38–80) and the scores within each of the six blocks of subjects were split at the median score of that block. The median within the blocks varied from 60.5 to 64.5 (overall median = 63.5). The greatest discrepancy produced by this procedure was one subject who was classified as high who was 2.5 points below the overall median. In all, ten subjects would have been classified differently by an overall median split but only one varied from the overall median by more than 1.5. The within-blocks split seems justified on these grounds and is necessary to maintain the advantages of the Latin Square.

The subjects were 216 college students enrolled in introductory psychology classes, who read the vignettes and responded to the scales in the classroom setting. Each block of subjects contained 18 who were high on the I-E scale and 18 who were low. Excluding the "intrinsic professor" vignette, the basic analyses of variance were carried out on 1296 scores (one from each of the six vignettes for each subject representing his total on the Origin-Pawn or the Task-Enjoyment Scales). The total represents 18 complete replications of the design above the median I-E score and 18 replications below the median.

Results

The Appropriate Error Term. Table 3 presents the basic data from the Origin-Pawn scale, which takes the form of 36 means based on 36 scores in each cell formed by the 2 x 3 x 6 design. The table is composed in such a way that the

TABLE 3

MEAN SCORES ON ORIGIN-PAWN SCALE

PERSUASIVE AGENT		THEME						I-E SCORE		
Attractiveness	*Type*	*Political*	*Army*	*Business*	*Govern't*	*Doctor*	*Union*	*High*	*Low*	*Total*
Positive	Individual	4.34	4.59	4.22	5.49	5.45	4.85	5.00	4.65	4.82
	Small group	4.58	4.85	5.38	5.42	5.59	4.94	5.38	4.87	5.12
	Large group	4.27	3.98	5.06	5.14	5.44	4.65	4.99	4.52	4.75
	Subtotal	4.40	4.47	4.89	5.35	5.49	4.81	5.12	4.67	4.89
Negative	Individual	3.43	3.23	3.58	3.75	3.93	3.19	3.58	3.44	3.51
	Small group	4.36	3.70	4.55	5.09	3.74	3.42	4.22	4.07	4.14
	Large group	2.87	2.26	3.97	3.73	3.60	3.14	3.26	3.26	3.26
	Subtotal	3.55	3.06	4.03	4.18	3.76	3.25	3.68	3.59	3.64
	Total	3.97	3.77	4.46	4.76	4.62	4.03	4.40	4.13	4.26

Note: N in each cell = 36.

significant comparisons of means representing independent variables are displayed. Table 4 presents the results of the analysis of variance.

TABLE 4

ANALYSIS OF VARIANCE OF ORIGIN-PAWN AND TASK-ENJOYMENT SCALES

		ORIGIN-PAWN			TASK-ENJOYMENT		
Source of variation	*df*	*Mean square*	*F*	*p*	*Mean square*	*F*	*p*
Between Subjects	215						
Between blocks	5	181.3	3.5	<.01	32.4	2.5	<.05
I-E level	1	371.6	7.1	<.01	22.4	1.7	—
Blocks x I-E	5	86.2	1.6	—	10.9	0.8	—
Within block	204	52.3	—	—	12.9	—	—
Within Subjects	1080						
(1) Group attractiveness	1	8,260.8	182.7	<.0005	5,492.5	337.0	<.0005
(2) Type of group	2	735.3	16.3	<.001	64.3	3.9	<.10
(3) Theme	5	554.1	12.3	<.001	94.8	5.8	<.01
1 x 2	2	116.7	2.6	—	66.1	4.1	<.05
1 x 3	5	107.7	2.4	—	25.1	1.5	—
2 x 3	10	97.7	2.2	—	17.6	1.1	—
1 x 2 x 3	10	45.2*	—	—	16.3*	—	—
Residual	1050	23.7	—	—	8.5	—	—

* Used as error term in computing F ratios for within subjects comparisons.

Of first concern is the fact that using the within cells variance (1050 *d.f.*) as error variance results in a significant interaction ($p < .05$) between all three independent variables. Such a finding may be interpreted as indicating that the general pattern of the effects of attractiveness and type of persuasive agent is not constant across the six various themes. The amount of variance attributable to the interaction, however, is small ($F = 1.9$, *d.f.* 10/1050) compared to the variance attributable to the major variables (Attractiveness $F = 347.8$, 1/1050 *d.f.;* type of groups $F = 31.0$, 2/1050 *d.f.;* theme $F = 23.3$, 5/1050 *d.f.*). Statistically, it is feasible to use the variance attributable to the highest order interaction as the error term. In essence, this reduces the analysis of variance to one which treats the 36 means in Table 3 as the basic scores. The residual variance degree of freedom reduces from 1050 to 10. Ordinarily this would be too stringent a restriction, but in the present case, the main effects remain highly significant.

Such a drastic curtailment of the analysis seems justified conceptually since it does not reduce below significance level any results which were involved in the major hypotheses. All results which lose significance are tenuous at best since they are reactions to specific aspects of the various themes or persuasive agents. For instance, the hero who disliked his position in the Moscow Embassy's protocol section was seen as an origin far out of proportion to any of the other com-

TABLE 5

MEAN SCORES ON TASK-ENJOYMENT SCALE

PERSUASIVE AGENT		THEME						I-E SCORE		
Attractiveness	*Type*	*Political*	*Army*	*Business*	*Govern't*	*Doctor*	*Union*	*High*	*Low*	*Total*
Positive	Individual	6.12	5.67	4.38	6.10	6.10	5.33	5.73	5.51	5.62
	Small group	5.94	5.88	5.47	5.97	6.07	5.97	6.00	5.77	5.88
	Large group	5.54	5.99	5.72	6.22	5.94	5.55	6.00	5.66	5.83
	Subtotal	5.87	5.84	5.19	6.10	6.04	5.62	5.91	5.65	5.78
Negative	Individual	3.74	3.85	3.06	4.38	4.03	3.81	3.92	3.69	3.81
	Small group	4.35	4.17	3.68	4.88	3.72	3.36	4.00	4.05	4.03
	Large group	3.40	2.75	3.16	3.82	3.46	3.32	3.22	3.42	3.32
	Subtotal	3.83	3.59	3.30	4.36	3.74	3.50	3.71	3.72	3.72
	Total	4.85	4.72	4.25	5.23	4.89	4.56	4.81	4.69	4.75

Note: N in each cell = 36.

parable situations. The unique combination of the three independent variables (Moscow Embassy, disliked protocol section) contributed to the significant highest order interaction. Speculation about why this combination should be unique would seem to be useless theoretically. The danger of discarding theoretically meaningful results by the stringent analysis, therefore, seems slight.

Origin-Pawn Results Results indicate that the hero is seen as more of a pawn when the persuasive agent is presented as unattractive. The hero is seen as reacting most as a pawn to large organizations and least to small groups. Subjects with scores below the median on the I-E scale (who perceive the control of their own reinforcements as primarily external to themselves) perceive the hero as more of a pawn under all conditions than do subjects above the I-E scale median. These findings confirm the major hypotheses of the study and are graphically presented in Figure 1.

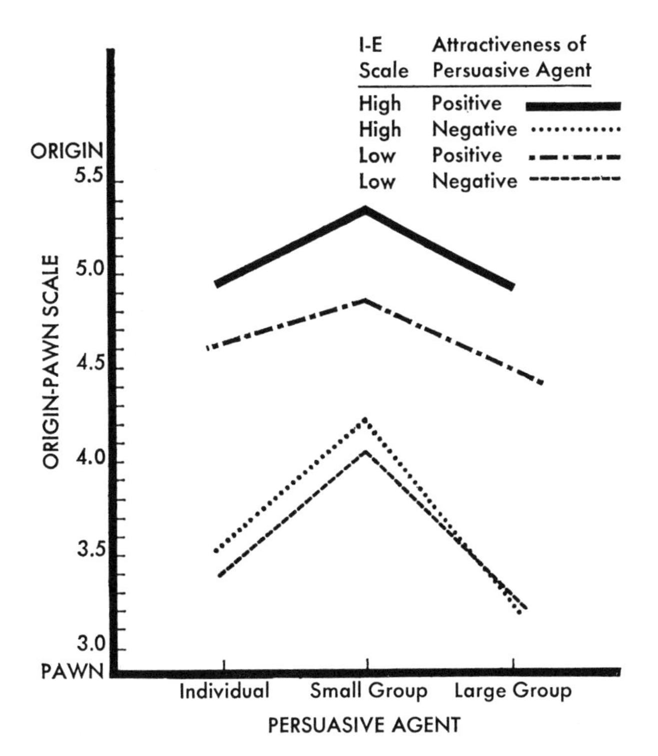

Figure 1 Mean rating on the Origin-Pawn scale for subjects high and low on Internal and External control (I-E) for various stimulus persons

Significant variation between the means representing the themes indicates that the hero who is seen as most like an origin is the U. E. Embassy clerk in Moscow. In descending rank order to the Army private the order is as follows: (a) U. S. Embassy clerk in Moscow; (b) medical intern; (c) business salesman; (d) member of the shoe-worker's union; (e) political party precinct worker; (f) Army private.

Task-Enjoyment Results Table 5 presents the results from the task-enjoyment scale. The analysis of variance using the overall interaction as the error term is again employed. The hero is seen as enjoying the task more when the persuasive agent is attractive. There is an interaction between attractiveness and type of agent. The task is enjoyed less when the attractive agent is an individual than when it is either a small group or a large organization. On the other hand, the task is enjoyed less when the unattractive agent is a large organization than when it is either a small group or an individual.

There is no significant relationship between the I-E scale and task-enjoyment. The significant relationship between task-enjoyment and theme indicates the following descending order of task-enjoyment: (a) U. S. Embassy clerk; (b) medical intern; (c) political party precinct worker; (d) Army private; (e) member of the shoe-worker's union; (f) business salesman.

Intrinsic-Professor Results Table 6 presents means on the origin-pawn scale for the "tacked-on" theme involving the professor who was intrinsically motivated to work on cancer research. As was expected the ratings were extremely high on the origin-pawn scale. This resulted in a ceiling effect and consequent inhomogeneity of variance.[11]

TABLE 6

MEAN SCORES ON THE ORIGIN-PAWN SCALE FOR THE INTRINSIC PROFESSOR

		TYPE OF PERSUASIVE AGENT			
Attractiveness of agent	*I-E Level*	*Individual*	*Small group*	*Large organization*	*Total*
	High	6.33	5.69	6.76	6.25
Positive	Low	6.19	6.21	5.94	6.11
	Subtotal	6.26	5.95	6.35	6.18
	High	5.39	6.03	5.91	5.77
Negative	Low	5.49	5.60	4.92	5.35
	Subtotal	5.44	5.82	5.42	5.56
	High	5.86	5.86	6.34	6.01
Combined	Low	5.84	5.91	5.43	5.73
	Total	5.85	5.89	5.89	5.87

Note: N in each cell = 18.

[11] Analysis of variance in the face of inhomogeneity may be justified on two counts. In the present case, the danger is not that significant findings will be erroneous, but that findings will be masked by the ceiling effect. Statistically, the restriction of analysis of variance to cases where homogeneity obtains is no longer considered necessary. See, for instance, G. E. P. Box, "Nonnormality and Tests on Variance," *Biometrika* 40 (December 1953): 318–35, and B. J. Winer, *Statistical Principles in Experimental Design* (New York: McGraw-Hill, 1962).

It is clear without any resort to statistical analysis that the professor is seen as far more an origin than any of the other heroes. In addition, the analysis of variance indicates that when the attractive agent encourages him he is perceived as freer (more an origin) than when the unattractive agent does. The type of group and level of the I-E scale do not account for significant variance alone, but the I-E scale interacts with type of group significantly. This interaction may be seen at the bottom of Table 6 and indicates that when the persuasive agent is an individual or a small group, no differences are perceived by subjects high as opposed to low on the I-E scale. When the agent is a large organization, however, high I-E subjects see the hero as freer (more like an origin) whereas low I-E subjects see him as constrained (more like a pawn).

The task-enjoyment scale means were also extremely high for the intrinsic professor, higher for the attractive agent than for the unattractive. Neither type of group nor level of I-E scale accounted for significant variance.

Discussion

This study was designed to demonstrate that a variable derived from Heider's [12] concept of the perceived locus of causality is an important dimension in person perception. The results unambiguously support the conclusion that persons are perceived as acting more like pawns under certain conditions, and under others they are seen more as origins of their own behavior. Put another way, the perception that a person is "pushed around" under certain conditions and more freely acting from his own volition under others is apparently an inference which subjects make reliably. The inference is a function of information given about the person, the situation, and the personal characteristics of the subject making the inference. The data are consistent with the assumption that the origin-pawn inference is a continuous bi-polar variable although no attempt was made to test this assumption in contrast to some other alternative.

It is clear from the data that persons who are being persuaded to engage in "extra-duty" activity are perceived as more the origin of their own behavior when they like and respect the persuasive agent than when the persuasive agent is disliked. The inference might be drawn that a person feels freer when working for an attractive agent than when working for an unattractive one, even when all other conditions more relevant to freedom are constant. This hypothesis may seem like common sense, but theoretically the connection between the attractiveness of an agent who is attempting to control a person's behavior and the person's feeling of freedom is not immediately obvious. The reasoning which led to the present experiment was that a person who likes and respects another probably accepts the other's goals more readily than he would accept the goals of a disliked person, and he may assume more overlap between his and a liked person's goals. He will therefore feel that compliance to the persuasion of an attractive agent is

---

[12] Heider, *Interpersonal Relations.*

behavior directed toward goals of his own choosing, i.e., that he is actually the origin of his own behavior. It could be said that in this situation he feels more intrinsically than extrinsically motivated, since the rather vague concept of intrinsic motivation probably has a strong component of the origin feeling. When a person is intrinsically motivated he feels like an origin.

The data show that the professor who freely chose the task and did not have to be persuaded is seen as the extreme case of an origin. If an attractive agent encourages him, he is seen as more an origin than if an unattractive agent encourages him. This is interesting in that the agent here was not presented as influencing or in a position to reward the behavior.

It was hypothesized that a persuasive agent consisting of a large organization would lead to the strongest inference that the hero was a pawn compared with small group or individual agents. According to Marx, Weber, and Durkheim large organizations engender feelings of alienation, anomie, and powerlessness, with the consequent feelings of being pushed around like a pawn. On the other hand, one might expect that the feeling of being an origin vis-à-vis a large organization might be strong if the individual can use the power of the organization to attain his own goals. The evidence indicates that the large organization is seen as treating the individual more as a pawn than is the small group or the individual under all conditions where the job to be done is not chosen by the person but by the agent. When the task is freely chosen, however, as in the "intrinsic professor" vignette, subjects high on the I-E scale perceive the professor as more of an origin when encouraged by the university than when encouraged by his colleagues. The reverse holds for subjects low on the I-E scale.

In general, large organizations as compared to individuals or small groups are seen as tending to make pawns out of people. There is some evidence, however, that subjects who feel that they can control their environment in order to gain reinforcements see a person who is pursuing something of his own choosing as freer when he is encouraged by a large organization. Perhaps these subjects feel that they can use the power of the organization to give them greater freedom.

When the persuasive agent is an individual the person is seen as slightly less a pawn than when the agent is a large organization. When the agent is a small group, however, the person is seen as least constrained (least like a pawn) even when the small group members are disliked.

The measure of task-enjoyment was included in the experiment to test the assumption that a person is perceived as not enjoying the task to the extent that he is seen as a pawn. A high relationship between the origin-pawn and the task-enjoyment scales was expected and found. As would be predicted, task-enjoyment is perceived as much higher when the persuasive agent is liked than when disliked. The hero is assumed to dislike the task most when working for a large disliked organization, but the task is not seen as so odious to the hero when he is working for a disliked small group. The more positive attitude toward the small group even when disliked as compared to the large organization is again in evidence.

The task-enjoyment scale may be used to check whether the origin-pawn scale merely reflects a general affective reaction to the various conditions or is measuring something unique. There are two pieces of evidence to indicate that the origin-pawn scale has validity in its own right. The results for the origin-pawn and the task-enjoyment scales are similar (but not identical) in the variables of type and attractiveness of group—as would be expected. The various situations or themes, however, are rated differently on the two scales. For instance, the army private induces the strongest inference that the person is a pawn whereas the salesman is seen as much less of a pawn. Task-enjoyment is lowest for the salesman and third from lowest for the Army private. Statistical analysis of these themes indicates that the scales are giving significantly different results and can be considered to be measuring different things.[13]

Perhaps the most convincing evidence for the validity of the origin pawn scale is the fact that results on it are predictable from the I-E scale, but the task-enjoyment results are not predictable by this scale. This result shows that subjects who themselves feel in control of their destinies (as opposed to those who do not) make greater distinctions along the origin-pawn scale, but do not differ on the task-enjoyment scale. Without such evidence the results with the origin-pawn variable might be attributable to a generalized "halo" effect. With such evidence the variable appears to be validly related to the theoretical concepts attributed to it.

Finally, the fact that aspects of the hero and the personal characteristics of the perceiver both affect the responses on the origin-pawn variable needs elaboration. It is impossible to trace empirically exactly how a personal characteristic affects the perception of a person as an origin or as a pawn. Taking a lead from Polanyi's [14] concept of personal knowledge, we felt it probable that in drawing inferences from the behavior of others, a person's personal knowledge of how he might feel in such a situation would affect his inference. Thus a person who feels that he has control over the valued outcomes in his life would assume that this kind of personal knowledge is an integral part of the person he is observing. He might then be expected to see other persons who are like him more as origins than would a person who feels little control of outcomes. The data presented here are consistent with this hypothesis.

To the extent that a person differentiates others from himself, however, he may not see them in ways congruent to his own feelings of control. A power oriented person who feels little control may see himself as a pawn to others to whom he attributes origin characteristics, especially if they are of higher status than he (see Thibaut and Riecken [15]). Under conditions where power is of primary concern it may be possible to classify people as origins and pawns, but it

[13] The four means were tested for interaction using the largest error term, i.e., the highest order interaction variance for the task-enjoyment scale ($F = 5.58$, $p < .05$, 1/10 *d.f.*). This is the most conservative test.

[14] Michael Polanyi, *Personal Knowledge* (Chicago: University of Chicago Press, 1958).

[15] Thibaut and Riecken, "Authoritarianism."

would be a mistake to conceive of the origin-pawn variable as a general trait. Rather, it will probably be more useful to follow the assumption that under different conditions a person will perceive himself and/or others as more or less the origin of his behavior. It is even quite possible that some people conceive of themselves as origins only when they are subjugating others as pawns whereas other people conceive of themselves primarily as an origin only when they can treat others as origins.

Perception: Self, Object, and Other:

Putting It into Perspective

Perception does not mean simply seeing, touching, hearing, or smelling. Although our senses are involved in perception, cognitive processes mediate between what is "out there" and what we experience. We impose order on the array of objects within our visual field at any given moment. We place objects mentally into relationships with one another and organize them in relation to ourselves. We focus our attention on only a limited number of objects at one time, letting the greater portion of impinging sense-data pass unnoticed. What we expect to see, what we consider important, and what others around us report that they see, are all important in determining what we experience.

In the strict sense, perception refers to the interpretation of a stimulus at the moment that it impinges on the senses. However, the term perception is also used to refer to such processes as the inferences one person draws from the behavior of another, the evaluations he makes about the other, and the formulation of attitudes he will assume toward the other. While these latter would be more aptly termed "conceptions," we shall follow traditional usage and include them under the heading of perception.

Social psychologists have long been interested in how a person's perception of physical objects is influenced by culture or prior social learning. For example, a number of early studies explored the effects of such factors as social class, race, sex, and ethnicity on the estimation of the size of objects. Other studies explored variation across social groupings in tendency to classify a set of objects according to shape as opposed to color. Studies of this sort focus on what the individual brings to a situation in the form of sets, predispositions, or conceptual categories. Approaching more closely the central problems of social psychology are the numerous studies on how an individual's perception of objects is influenced by the presence of others. These latter studies, like those dealing with the effects of prior learning, are somewhat limited in advancing our understanding of how people interact in real-life situations, the primary concern of social psychologists today.

Perhaps the most important aspect of perception, from the standpoint of social psychology, is the perception of people, i.e., the perception of self, the perception of others, and the perception of social relationships. How we perceive someone has significant implications for our actions toward that person. Throughout an interaction encounter, we constantly collect and process cues that the other person is giving off. We attempt to judge his mood, his intentions, and his expectations for us. These important pieces of information enable us to plan our next move in an encounter.

We do not see another person as simply a physical object. We see him as a being who thinks, evaluates, and feels emotions just as we do. Moreover, we do not merely take the cues he gives off at face value. We use these cues as bases for making inferences about him. Often, with only scanty information we may gather in a brief encounter with a stranger, we may construct an elaborate set of inferences about his identity, his personality characteristics, his probable future behavior, and even such things as his political ideology.

Among the most important inferences we make about another person are those which concern that person's feelings about us. In order to continue interacting, we must know how he is evaluating our behavior, whether he is getting the impression of us that we are trying to give off, and how he intends to act toward us. Further, as studies of interpersonal attraction suggest, we are usually quite concerned with whether or not he likes us. This latter judgment is crucial for our own decision about whether or not we like him. Since etiquette restrains him from expressing most of his judgments of us directly, we must infer most of what we need to know from indirect and often very subtle cues he gives us. If he appears bored, we might infer that he does not find our conversation engaging. If he appears to be laughing sincerely at our jokes, we may infer that he enjoys our company. Or, if he resists disclosing information about himself, we might infer that he wishes to maintain social distance, i.e., avoid intimacy. All these inferences, of course, will help us to construct our actions and to make our actions fit appropriately with his.

The judgments we make about another person can be derived from practically any cue or configuration of cues he gives off. Depending upon the situation, we may attend to such qualities as physical attractiveness, manner of dress, speech mannerisms, or posture—especially if there is something about these things which strikes us as out of the ordinary. Notwithstanding this infinite variety of occasionally relevant bases for judgment, most people are fairly consistent in what qualities in others that they attend to. Moreover, the characteristics of others that we most consistently single out tend to correspond to those which we see as most important in ourselves.

The judgments we make about others are probably never completely accurate, since we can never share another person's phenomenal world completely. However, our success in interacting with others depends largely upon our ability to *approach* perfect accuracy in reading others. There is a good deal of evidence to suggest that people differ considerably in general ability to empathize, and that empathy goes hand in hand with one's accuracy of self-perception. However, in real-life encounters, empathy is contingent upon so many other factors that one's general empathic ability may be of secondary importance for constructing appropriate responses, for controlling the flow interaction, or even for evaluating reflected self-appraisals. For example, our reading of a person may agree quite well with a number of other judges; but if the person we are judging has made no self-disclosures, chances are our inferences about him are wrong. Inaccurate person perception is most likely in situations where behavior is structured by formal role considerations, or where casual acquaintances spend the duration of their encounter exchanging pleasantries or discussing meteorological principles.

Most social psychologists would agree that the perception of self and others is an important key to understanding interpersonal behavior. However, most of the large body of empirical data in this area derive from studies in which one person is considered the judge while another is the "object." In most cases the judge does not even interact with the object person. He may be asked for his evaluations of someone he has merely seen briefly, or of someone who has merely read a prepared statement before him. In some cases, the judge may even be asked to react to photographs or written biographies.

In real-life encounters, each person is at once perceiver and object. While one person's act is influenced by his perception of the other, the other person's next act is influenced by his own perception of the first person's act, and so forth. This reciprocal sequence of acts and perceptions of acts is exceedingly difficult to capture with traditional research designs. However, studies aimed at the analysis of interaction sequences are beginning to appear, and we can expect to find studies of person perception taking this form in the near future.

Suggestions for Further Reading

Kenneth J. Gergen, *The Concept of Self.* New York: Holt, Rinehart and Winston, 1971. An abbreviated textbook providing a fine introduction to self-concept research and theory.

Don E. Hamacheck, *Encounter with the Self.* New York: Holt, Rinehart and Winston, 1971. A fairly broad overview of research and theory dealing with self-concept. The emphasis in the volume is on developmental processes.

Albert Hastorf, David Schneider, and Judith Polefka, *Person Perception.* Reading, Massachusetts: Addison-Wesley, 1970. Intended primarily for undergraduates, this brief volume brings together the findings of nearly two hundred empirical studies in person perception.

Renato Tagiuri, "Person Perception" in G. Lindzey and E. Aronson, editors, *Handbook of Social Psychology.* Second Edition, Volume Three. Reading, Massachusetts: Addison-Wesley, 1969, 395–449. An excellent "state of the field" review, indicating major issues and possible directions for future research in person perception. Written with the professional social psychologist in mind, this review presupposes more previous exposure to the literature than the other volumes on this list.

Peter Warr and Christopher Knapper, *The Perception of People and Events.* London: John Wiley and Sons, 1968. This volume combines an excellent review of the literature with detailed reports of numerous empirical studies conducted by the authors themselves.

CHAPTER IV

Communication

14 Paul Watzlawick, Janet H. Beavin, and Don D. Jackson, *Some Tentative Axioms of Communication* · 193

15 Wendell Johnson, *Stuttering: How the Problem Develops* · 202

16 Jay M. Davis and Amerigo Farina, *Humor Appreciation as Social Communication* · 212

17 Norman Goodman and Richard Ofshe, *Empathy, Communication Efficiency, and Marital Status* · 218

18 Edgar H. Schein, *Interpersonal Communication, Group Solidarity, and Social Influence* · 231

Putting It into Perspective · 244
Suggestions for Further Reading · 246

14

Some Tentative Axioms of Communication

PAUL WATZLAWICK · JANET H. BEAVIN
DON D. JACKSON

The study of communication can be divided into three major areas: syntactics, semantics, and pragmatics. Syntactics is the domain of information theory, and deals with the transmission of information. Here, the focus of study is on problems of coding and decoding messages, channels and channel capacity, "noise" and signal competition, and such statistical properties of language as redundancy. On the other hand, the main object of study in semantics is the meaning of messages. In this area, such notions as "universe of discourse" are central. The third and final area, pragmatics, is concerned with the question of how communication affects behavior. Said another way, pragmatics is the study of the reciprocal influence people have on one another through communication.

In the following excerpt from their book on the pragmatic aspect of communication, Watzlawick, Beavin and Jackson present five axioms which they believe are crucial for the understanding of the behavioral effects of communication. The axioms do not constitute a theory, nor do they exhaust the possibly relevant assumptions that might be included in a well-developed theory. However, the basic insights which the axioms represent are intended to sensitize the student of communication to problems and issues that have been neglected heretofore. More importantly, since they concern the reciprocal influence of people on one another's behavior, the axioms deal directly with the core problem of social psychology.

The Impossibility of Not Communicating

First of all, there is a property of behavior that could hardly be more basic and is, therefore, often overlooked: behavior has no opposite. In other words, there is no such thing as nonbehavior or, to put it even more simply: one cannot *not* behave. Now, if it is accepted that all behavior in an interactional situation has message value, i.e., is communication, it follows that no matter how one may try, one cannot *not* communicate. Activity or inactivity, words or silence all have message value: they influence others and these others, in turn cannot *not* respond to these communications and are thus themselves communicating. It should be clearly understood that the mere absence of talking or of taking notice of each other is no exception to what has just been asserted. The man at a crowded lunch counter who looks straight ahead, or the airplane passenger who sits with his eyes closed, are both communicating that they do not want to speak to anybody or be spoken to, and their neighbors usually "get the message" and respond appropriately by leaving them alone. This, obviously, is just as much an interchange of communication as an animated discussion.

Neither can we say that "communication" only takes place when it is intentional, conscious, or successful, that is, when mutual understanding occurs. Whether message sent equals message received is an important but different order of analysis, as it must rest ultimately on evaluations of specific, introspective, subject-reported data, which we choose to neglect for the exposition of a behavioral theory of communication. On the question of misunderstanding, our concern, given certain formal properties of communication, is with the development of related pathologies aside from, indeed in spite of, the motivations or intensions of the communicants.

. . . . .

The impossibility of not communicating is a phenomenon of more than theoretical interest. It is, for instance, part and parcel of the schizophrenic "dilemma." If schizophrenic behavior is observed with etiological considerations in abeyance, it appears that the schizophrenic tries *not to communicate*. But since even nonsense, silence, withdrawal, immobility (postural silence), or any other form of denial is itself a communication, the schizophrenic is faced with the impossible task of denying that he is communicating and at the same time denying that his denial is a communication. The realization of this basic dilemma in schizophrenia is a key to a good many aspects of schizophrenic communication that would otherwise remain obscure. Since any communication, as we shall see, implies commitment and thereby defines the sender's view of his relationship with the receiver, it can be hypothesized that the schizophrenic behaves as if he would avoid commitment by not communicating. Whether this is his purpose, in the causal sense, is of course impossible of proof. . . .

To summarize, a metacommunicational axiom of the pragmatics of communication can be postulated: *one cannot* not *communicate.*

The Content and Relationship Levels of Communication

Another axiom was hinted at in the foregoing when it was suggested that any communication implies a commitment and thereby defines the relationship. This is another way of saying that a communication not only conveys information, but that at the same time it imposes behavior. Following Bateson (1951, pp. 179–81), these two operations have come to be known as the "report" and the "command" aspects, respectively, of any communication. Bateson exemplifies these two aspects by means of a physiological analogy: let *A, B,* and *C* be a linear chain of neurons. Then the firing of neuron *B* is both a "report" that neuron *A* has fired and a "command" for neuron *C* to fire.

The report aspect of a message conveys information and is, therefore, synonymous in human communication with the *content* of the message. It may be about anything that is communicable regardless of whether the particular information is true or false, valid, invalid, or undecidable. The command aspect, on the other hand, refers to what sort of a message it is to be taken as, and, therefore, ultimately to the *relationship* between the communicants. All such relationship statements are about one or several of the following assertions: "This is how I see myself . . . this is how I see you . . . this is how I see you seeing me . . ." and so forth in theoretically infinite regress. Thus, for instance, the messages "It is important to release the clutch gradually and smoothly" and "Just let the clutch go, it'll ruin the transmission in no time" have approximately the same information content (report aspect), but they obviously define very different relationships. To avoid any misunderstanding about the foregoing, we want to make it clear that relationships are only rarely defined deliberately or with full awareness. In fact, it seems that the more spontaneous and "healthy" a relationship, the more the relationship aspect of communication recedes into the background. Conversely, "sick" relationships are characterized by a constant struggle about the nature of the relationship, with the content aspect of communication becoming less and less important.

. . . . .

The reader will have noticed that the relationship aspect of a communication, being a communication about a communication, is, of course, identical with the concept of metacommunication. . . . The ability to metacommunicate appropriately is not only the *conditio sine qua non* of successful communication, but is intimately linked with the enormous problem of awareness of self and others. These . . . messages can be constructed, especially in written communication, which offers highly ambiguous metacommunicational clues. As Cherry (1961, p. 120), points out, the sentence "Do you think that one will do?" can have a variety of meanings, according to which word is to be stressed—an indication that written language usually does not supply. Another example would be a sign in a restaurant reading "Customers who think our waiters are rude should see the manager," which, at least in theory, can be understood in two entirely different ways. Ambiguities of this kind are not the only possible complications arising out of the level structure of all communication; consider, for instance, a notice that reads "Disregard This Sign." As we shall see in the chapter on paradoxical communication, confusions or contaminations between these levels—communication and metacommunication—may lead to impasses identical in structure to those of the famous paradoxes in logic.

For the time being let us merely summarize the foregoing into another axiom of our tentative calculus: *Every communication has a content and a relationship aspect such that the latter classifies the former and is therefore a metacommunication.*

The Punctuation of the Sequence of Events

The next basic characteristic of communication we wish to explore regards interaction—exchanges of messages—between communicants. To an outside observer, *a series of communications can be viewed as an uninterrupted sequence of interchanges.* However, the participants in the interaction always introduce what Bateson and Jackson have termed the "punctuation of the sequence of events." They state:

> The stimulus-response psychologist typically confines his attention to sequences of interchange so short that it is possible to label one item of input as "stimulus" and another item as "reinforcement" while labelling what the subject does between these two events as "response." Within the short sequence so excised, it is possible to talk about the "psychology" of the subject. In contrast, the sequences of interchange which we are here discussing are very much longer and therefore have the characteristic that every item in the sequence is simultaneously stimulus, response and reinforcement. A given item of A's behavior is a stimulus insofar as it is followed by an item contributed by B and that by another item contributed by A. But insofar as A's item is sandwiched between two items contributed by B, it is a response. Similarly A's item is a reinforcement insofar as it follows an item contributed by B. The ongoing interchanges, then, which we are here discussing, constitute a chain of overlapping triadic links, each of which is comparable to a stimulus-response-reinforcement sequence. We can take any triad of our interchange and see it as a single trial in a stimulus-response learning experiment.
>
> It is still true, however, that in a long sequence of interchange, the organisms concerned—especially if these be people—will in fact punctuate the sequence so that it will appear that one or the other has initiative, dominance, dependency or the like. That is, they will set up between them patterns of interchange (about which they may or may not be in agreement) and these patterns will in fact be rules of contingency regarding the exchange of reinforcement. While rats are too nice to re-label, some psychiatric patients are not, and provide psychological trauma for the therapist! (1964, pp. 273–74)

It is not the issue here whether punctuation of communicational sequence is, in general, good or bad, as it should be immediately obvious that punctuation *organizes* behavioral events and is therefore vital to ongoing interactions. Culturally, we share many conventions of punctuations which, while no more or less accurate than other views of the same events, serve to organize common and important interactional sequences. For example, we call a person in a group behaving in one way the "leader" and another the "follower," although on reflection it is difficult to say which comes first or where one would be without the other.

Disagreement about how to punctuate the sequence of events is at the root of countless relationship struggles. Suppose a couple have a marital problem to which he contributes passive withdrawal, while her 50 percent is nagging criticism. In explaining their frustrations, the husband will state that withdrawal is his only *defense against* her nagging, while she will label this explanation a gross and willful distortion of what "really" happens in their marriage: namely, that she is critical of him *because of* his passivity. Stripped of all ephemeral and fortuitous elements, their fights consist in a monotonous exchange of the messages "I withdraw because you nag" and "I nag because you withdraw."

. . . . .

Thus we add a third metacommunicational axiom: *The nature of a relationship is contingent upon the punctuation of the communicational sequences between the communicants.*

Digital and Analogic Communication

In the central nervous system the functional units (neurons) receive so-called quantal packages of information through connecting elements (synapses). Upon arrival at the synapses these "packages" produce excitatory or inhibitory postsynaptic potentials that are summed up by the neuron and either cause or inhibit its firing. This specific part of neural activity, consisting in the occurrence or nonoccurrence of its firing, therefore conveys binary digital information. The humoral system, on the other hand, is not based on digitalization of information. This system communicates by releasing discrete quantities of specific substances into the bloodstream. It is further known that the neural and the humoral modes of intraorganismic communication exist not only side by side, but that they complement and are contingent upon each other, often in highly complex ways.

The same two basic modes of communication can be found at work in the field of man-made organisms: there are computers which utilize the all-or-none principle of vacuum tubes or transistors and are called *digital,* because they are basically calculators working with digits; and there is another class of machines that manipulate discrete, positive magnitudes—the analogues of the data—and hence are called *analogic.* In digital computers both data and instructions are processed in the form of numbers so that often, especially in the case of the instructions, there is only an arbitrary correspondence between the particular piece of information and its digital expression. In other words, these numbers are arbitrarily assigned code names which have as little resemblance to actual magnitudes as do the telephone numbers assigned to the subscribers. On the other hand, as we have already seen, the analogy principle is the essence of all analogic computation. Just as in the humoral system of natural organisms, the carriers of information are certain substances and their concentration in the bloodstream, in analogue computers data take the form of discrete and, therefore, always positive quantities, e.g., the intensity of electrical currents, the number of revolutions of a wheel, the degree of displacement of components, and the like.

In human communication, objects—in the widest sense—can be referred to in two entirely different ways. They can either be represented by a likeness, such as a drawing, or they can be referred to by a name. Thus, in the written sentence "The cat has caught a mouse" the nouns could be replaced by pictures; if the sentence were spoken, the actual cat and the mouse could be pointed to. Needless to say, this would be an unusual way of communicating, and normally the written or spoken "name," that is, the word, is used. These two types of communication—the one by a self-explanatory likeness, the other by a word—are, of course, also equivalent to the concepts of the analogic and the digital respectively. Whenever a word is used to *name* something it is obvious that the relation between the name and the thing named is an arbitrarily established one. Words are arbitrary signs that are manipulated according to the logical syntax of language. There is no particular reason why the three letters "c-a-t" should denote a particular animal. In ultimate analysis it is only a semantic convention of the English language, and outside this convention there exists no other correlation between any word and the thing it stands for, with the possible but insignificant exception of onomatopoeic words. As Bateson and Jackson point out: "There is nothing particularly five-like in the number five; there is nothing particularly table-like in the word 'table' " (1964, p. 271).

In analogic communication, on the other hand, there *is* something particularly "thing-like" in what is used to express the thing. Analogic communication can be more readily referred to the thing it stands for. The difference between these two modes of communication may become somewhat clearer if it is realized that no amount of listening to a foreign language on the radio, for example, will yield an understanding of the language, whereas some basic information can fairly easily be derived from watching sign language and from so-called intention movements, even when used by a person of a totally different culture. Analogic communication, we suggest, has its roots in far more archaic periods of evolution and is, therefore, of much more general validity than the relatively recent, and far more abstract, digital mode of verbal communication.

What then is analogic communication? The answer is relatively simple: it is virtually all nonverbal communication. This term, however, is deceptive, because it is often restricted to body movement only, to the behavior known as kinesics. We hold that the term must comprise posture, gesture, facial expression, voice inflection, the sequence, rhythm, and cadence of the words themselves, and any other nonverbal manifestation of which the organism is capable, as well as the communicational clues unfailingly present in any *context* in which an interaction takes place.[1]

. . .

[1] The paramount communicational significance of context is all too easily overlooked in the analysis of human communication, and yet anyone who brushed his teeth in a busy street rather than in his bathroom might be quickly carted off to a police station or to a lunatic asylum—to give just one example of the pragmatic effects of nonverbal communication.

In short, if we remember that every communication has a content and a relationship aspect, we can expect to find that the two modes of communication not only exist side by side but complement each other in every message. We can further expect to find that the content aspect is likely to be conveyed digitally whereas the relationship aspect will be predominantly analogic in nature.

. . . . .

To summarize: *Human beings communicate both digitally and analogically. Digital language has a highly complex and powerful logical syntax but lacks adequate semantics in the field of relationship, while analogic language possesses the semantics but has no adequate syntax for the unambiguous definition of the nature of relationships.*

Symmetrical and Complementary Interaction

In 1935 Bateson reported on an interactional phenomenon which he observed in the Iatmul tribe in New Guinea and which, in his book *Naven,* published a year later, he dealt with in greater detail. He called this phenomenon *schismogenesis* and defined it as *a process of differentiation in the norms of individual behavior resulting from cumulative interaction between individuals.* This concept, which, as we can see, has a heuristic value beyond the confines of any one discipline, was elaborated by Bateson in *Naven* as follows:

> When our discipline is defined in terms of the reactions of an individual to the reactions of other individuals, it is at once apparent that we must regard the relationship between two individuals as liable to alter from time to time, even without disturbance from outside. We have to consider, not only *A*'s reactions to *B*'s behaviour, but we must go on to consider how these affect *B*'s later behaviour and the effect of this on *A.*
>
> It is at once apparent that many systems of relationship, either between individuals or groups of individuals, contain a tendency towards progressive change. If, for example, one of the patterns of cultural behaviour, considered appropriate in individual *A,* is culturally labelled as an assertive pattern, while *B* is expected to reply to this with what is culturally regarded as submission, it is likely that this submission will encourage a further assertion, and that this assertion will demand still further submission. We have thus a potentially progressive state of affairs, and unless other factors are present to restrain the excesses of assertive and submissive behavior, *A* must necessarily become more and more assertive, while *B* will become more and more submissive; and this progressive change will occur whether *A* and *B* are separate individuals or members of complementary groups.
>
> Progressive changes of this sort we may describe as *complementary* schismogenesis. But there is another pattern of relationships between individuals or groups of individuals which equally contains the germs of progressive change. If, for example, we find boasting as the cultural pattern of behaviour in one group, and that the other group replies to this with boasting, a competitive situation may develop in which boasting leads to more boasting, and so on. This type of progressive change we may call *symmetrical* schismogenesis. (1958, pp. 176–77)

The two patterns just described have come to be used without reference to the schismogenetic process and are now usually referred to simply as symmetrical and complementary interaction. They can be described as relationships based on either equality or difference. In the first case the partners tend to mirror each other's behavior, and thus their interaction can be termed *symmetrical*. Weakness or strength, goodness or badness, are not relevant here, for equality can be maintained in any of these areas. In the second case one partner's behavior complements that of the other, forming a different sort of behavioral Gestalt, and is called *complementary*. Symmetrical interaction, then, is characterized by equality and the minimization of difference, while complementary interaction is based on the maximization of difference.

There are two different positions in a complementary relationship. One partner occupies what has been variously described as the superior, primary, or "one-up" position, and the other the corresponding inferior, secondary, or "one-down" position. These terms are quite useful as long as they are not equated with "good" or "bad," "strong" or "weak." A complementary relationship may be set by the social or cultural context (as in the cases of mother and infant, doctor and patient, or teacher and student), or it may be the idiosyncratic relationship style of a particular dyad. In either case, it is important to emphasize the interlocking nature of the relationship, in which dissimilar but fitted behaviors evoke each other. One partner does not impose a complementary relationship on the other, but rather each behaves in a manner which presupposes, while at the same time providing reasons for, the behavior of the other: their definitions of the relationship fit.

A third type of relationship has been suggested—"metacomplementary," in which *A* lets or forces *B* to be in charge of him; by the same reasoning, we could also add "pseudosymmetry," in which *A* lets or forces *B* to be symmetrical. This potentially infinite regress can, however, be avoided by recalling the distinction made earlier between the observation of behavioral redundancies and their inferred explanations, in the form of mythologies; that is, we are interested in *how* the pair behave without being distracted by why (they believe) they so conduct themselves. If, though, the individuals involved avail themselves of the multiple levels of communication in order to express different patterns on different levels, paradoxical results of significant pragmatic importance may arise.

. . . . .

For the present, we can state simply our last tentative axiom: *All communicational interchanges are either symmetrical or complementary, depending on whether they are based on equality or difference.*

Summary

Regarding the above axioms in general, some qualifications should be reemphasized. First, it should be clear that they are put forth tentatively, rather informally defined and certainly more preliminary than exhaustive. Second, they are, among themselves, quite heterogeneous in that they draw from widely ranging observations on communication phenomena. They are unified not by their origins but by their *pragmatic* importance, which in turn rests not so much on their particulars as on their *interpersonal* (rather than monadic) reference. Birdwhistell has even gone so far as to suggest that

> an individual does not communicate; he engages in or becomes part of communication. He may move, or make noises . . . but he does not communicate. In a parallel fashion, he may see, he may hear, smell, taste, or feel—but he does not communicate. In other words, he does not originate communication; he participates in it. Communication as a system, then, is not to be understood on a simple model of action and reaction, however complexly stated. As a system, it is to be comprehended on the transactional level. (1959, p. 104)

Thus, the impossibility of not communicating makes all two-or-more-person situations *interpersonal,* communicative ones; the relationship aspect of such communication further specifies this same point. The pragmatic, interpersonal importance of the digital and analogic modes lies not only in its hypothesized isomorphism with content and relationship, but in the inevitable and significant ambiguity which both sender and receiver face in problems of translation from the one mode to the other. The description of problems of punctuation rests precisely on the underlying metamorphosis of the classic action-reaction model. Finally, the symmetry-complementary paradigm comes perhaps closest to the mathematical concept of *function,* the individuals' positions merely being variables with an infinity of possible values whose meaning is not absolute but rather emerges only in relation to each other.

REFERENCES

Bateson, G. 1958. *Naven.* Stanford: Stanford University Press (2nd Edition).

———, and Jackson, D. D., 1964. "Some varieties of pathogenic organization." In D. Rioch, ed., *Disorders in communication.* Volume 42, Research Publications. Association for Research in Nervous and Mental Disease, pp. 270–83.

Birdwhistell, R. L. 1959. "Contribution of linguistic-kinesic studies to the understanding of schizophrenia." In A. Auerback, ed., *Schizophrenia: an integrated approach.* New York: Ronald Press, pp. 99–123.

Cherry, C. 1961. *On human communciation.* New York: Science Editions, 1961.

Ruesch, J., and G. Bateson 1951. *Communication: the social matrix of psychiatry.* New York: Humanities Press.

15

Stuttering: How the Problem Develops

WENDELL JOHNSON

In the following selection, Wendell Johnson describes the interpersonal processes through which a child may be identified by his parents as "a stutterer" and subsequently, though unintentionally, be coerced into adopting disfluency as a characteristic communications pattern. While his discussion is rather informal, his interpretations are based on extensive and careful research including (1) "depth interviews" with parents who had brought their children to a speech clinic because they were "stuttering," and (2) a comparative analysis of the tape-recorded speech of children identified as "stutterers" versus a carefully matched sample of "normal" children who constituted a control group.

Through his interviews with parents, Johnson is able to isolate the circumstances under which a child is originally labeled as a "stutterer" and gain insight into the effects of corrective actions taken by parents once they had decided that their child had a speech problem. And, his comparisons of the frequency and type of speech disfluencies displayed by "stutterers" and "normal" children supports his thesis that the "problem" develops through interaction with significant others.

While Johnson focuses on a somewhat limited speech problem, his insights shed light on the socialization process in general. He provides a particularly vivid account of the role of interpersonal communication in the emergence of the self-concept and self-identity. And, his discussion lends substance to the more abstract treatment by Thomas Scheff ("Negotiating Reality") of the significance of power in the assessment of responsibility for one's actions.

Wendell Johnson, "Stuttering: How the Problem Develops," excerpts from Chapters 8 and 9 of *Stuttering and What You Can Do About It,* Minneapolis, Minnesota: University of Minnesota Press, 1961.

The research we have done indicates that in the most representative case the problem of stuttering arises under quite ordinary circumstances. It arises when the child involved is between three and four years old, and at the moment when the child's mother begins to doubt that he is speaking all right. What sort of speaking is the child doing at this time and in these circumstances?

Though most parents say they can't recall the very first time they thought the child was stuttering, nearly all can give some account of the way the youngster was talking during the general period when they felt he was beginning to stutter. The accounts they give are much like those of the few parents who do claim to be describing the child's speech as it was the first time they looked upon him as a stutterer. In general, as we have already seen, in the most representative case the youngster, when his parents think he is starting to stutter, is repeating words, or the first sounds or syllables of words, or occasionally whole phrases, or he is hesitating by saying something like "uh uh uh." He is doing these things with no apparent awareness that he is doing them or that they are of any significance, and he is showing no notable tension or effort. Moreover, he is apparently doing these things only about as often or as much as most other children of his age do.

. . . . .

Sometimes, of course, it is impossible to establish just what did happen. Our memories are not always good enough. The parents cannot say just when the problem first arose and they cannot describe the first instance of it or say for sure what the child's speech was like at the time. We can't be absolutely sure whether such cases are exceptions to our most representative case, and yet the clearest indication is that they are not exceptions in any important sense, because they appear not to involve anything very much out of the ordinary.

. . . . .

Close examination of all the data we have collected strongly suggests that the major reason parental memories of the beginnings of the problem are so dim is that there is as a rule not much to be remembered.

. . . . .

The common view seems to be that more or less suddenly one day stuttering begins in the form of a tense speech block of some sort. We took special pains, therefore, to determine in each case whether the child had been speaking with noticeable tension, or having what might be called a severe speech block, or suffering an "inability to get the word out" when he was first thought to be stuttering.

We asked the parents in the clinical group this question: At the time when stuttering was first noticed, was the child using force or more effort than usual "to get his words out"? Was there more than usual muscular tension? We put the same question to those parents in the control group who said their children had spoken with hesitations and repetitions, except that for them we did not use the word "stuttering." The two groups of parents gave answers that were remarkably similar. About a third of the mothers in the clinical group answered yes to this question—but so did one out of every five of those in the control group. Most of the stuttering group mothers who reported tension said it was slight.

We also asked these five questions: Did the child seem indifferent to his very first stoppages? When the stuttering was first noticed did the child seem to be aware of the fact that he was speaking in a different manner or doing something wrong? Did the child show surprise or bewilderment after having had trouble on a word? Did the very first stoppages seem to be unpleasant to the child? Do you think the child felt irritated when the very first stoppages occurred?

Roughly nine out of ten of the parents in both groups indicated that the children seemed oblivious or indifferent to what they were doing and showed no emotionality about it.

In my series of tape-recorded research interviews I have not yet had a parent tell me that the stuttering began with a tense blockage or anything of that sort. In [our study], however, we found nine out of 300 parents whose responses seemed to indicate that they had observed some kind of block or breakdown in speech as the first evidence of the stuttering problem. The reports of these nine mothers and fathers may be summarized in these words: (1) complete block on the first sound of a word; (2) repetition of a whole word and of the first syllable or sound of a word; complete block on the first sound of a word; (3) repetition of a word; block on the initial sound of a word; (4) block before a word, with guttural sounds; (5) repetition of the first syllable of a word; block on the initial sound of a word; (6) repetition of the first sound or syllable of a word; complete block on the first sound of a word; prolongation of the initial vowel or consonant of a word; (7) repetition of a whole word, or of the first sound or syllable of a word; complete block on the first sound of a word; prolongation of the first consonant of a word; interjection of "uh uh"; (8) repeated gasps; (9) block before a word.

. . . . .

I think it is likely that the nine parents were trying to tell us about something that they had observed their children doing which in their judgment was important. I should prefer to regard these, for present purposes, as exceptions to our "most representative case." At any rate, I think there are exceptions to it and that it is important to account for them.

One explanation of apparent exceptions is the one we have already considered, that we don't always say quite what we mean—we say "every time" when we mean "once in a while" or "five minutes" when we mean "a few seconds." In the same vein, we undoubtedly sometimes say that a child had a "complete block" when we mean something much less dramatic or serious. In other words, what there is to be explained is what there is left after our ways of saying things sometimes have been properly discounted.

That still leaves some things to be explained, in my opinion. One explanation to be noted and put to one side is that children do a good deal of playing with the sounds they discover they can make. They try to sound like geese and chickens, and trains and tugboats—and they make a lot of sounds that are seemingly quite original. In experimenting with sound-making they sometimes tense up their mouths and throats and twist their tongues and huff and puff and generate a good deal of tension. Sometimes they do these things when they are talking—or instead of getting on with the talking their parents think they should be doing. We don't know as much about the vocal play of young children as we should, but on the basis of what we do know I think some of the things that parents occasionally refer to as "difficulty" or even "complete blocks" in speaking turn out, on a closer look, to be a kind of unusual playfulness, or vocal experimenting and exploring.

What is rather more important, in my judgment, is that there are many conditions under which young children—as well as older children and adults—speak with tension, excessive hesitation, and indeed in ways that give the appearance of "complete stoppage." In fact, I think that moderate to severe blockages in speech are sufficiently common that we might well expect more of them to be reported by parents in describing what they remember as their children's first stutterings. It is as necessary to explain the large majority of cases in which no such blockages are reported among the "first stutterings" as it is to account for the small minority in which they are. And the best explanation I can draw from our data is that parents, provided they notice the disfluencies in their children's speech and take them seriously, are most likely to regard them as stuttering *if they can see no reason for them.*

To me, this is one of the most surprising and fascinating conclusions that our data suggest. You see, our dictionaries, our speech authorities, and just about everyone else define "stuttering" as a disturbance in the rhythm or fluency of speech, marked by repetitions and hesitations, associated in some instances at least with tension or strain. It is a curious fact that although this definition is so widely taken for granted, it is also all but universally ignored or disregarded in certain cases.

. . . . .

Parents are most likely to decide their children are stuttering when they are hesitating and repeating *for no reason that the parents can detect.* And these are precisely the hesitations and repetitions that are not associated with anything obvious like great fright, excessive fatigue, great mortification, muscular paralysis, or incoordination. "No reason" can be any one of the reasons that the parents do not recognize or understand.

What reasons might these be? There are probably two major kinds. Under one may be grouped all the things that make children generally repeat and hesitate as much as they do when speaking under ordinary conditions. There are many such factors, some inborn, some learned, and some that are environmental in a passing or at least unremarkable sense. The human brain just doesn't work perfectly in transforming experience into spoken words. And some normal brains perform this amazing function less smoothly than other brains do—for reasons about which no one really knows very much. Moreover, any young child still has a lot to learn about using the language, and some children have more to learn than others.

The other reason children speak disfluently—the other reason, that is, that parents usually don't notice—is traceable to anything and everything that the parents themselves do that make a child doubt that he can speak well or smoothly enough to be accepted and approved by them, and that makes him feel concerned or uneasy about not being able to speak that well.

Most mothers and fathers have not been sufficiently prepared while in school, or by any other means, to recognize or understand very well either of these reasons for a child's disfluent speech.

Whenever the child repeats and hesitates for these reasons, then, to his parents he is doing so "for no reason" and, since they can see nothing wrong with anything else, they are likely to conclude that there must be something wrong *with his speech.* They are likely to do this, of course, only if they happen to notice the disfluency in the first place and give it a second troubled thought.

. . . . .

One of the most crucial facts in connection with this matter is the age at which the child is most likely to be first regarded as a stutterer. Our investigations have shown that very few parents report the onset of stuttering before the age of two and a half years. The average age falls between three and three and a half, and in the large majority of cases the onset occurs before the age of four years. About the only time it is said to occur after that is when the child enters school, and whenever this is the case it is practically always a teacher who first decides that the child is beginning to stutter, even though no one else has thought so up to that time.

Parents are pleased with their child's speech so long as they think that he is *learning* to talk. So long as they are listening for the signs of learning and development, they do not focus on imperfections. What they notice is that he is saying new words that he has never said before, that he is making longer and longer sentences, asking more and more questions, speaking to more and more people, and making more and more sense in one way or another. Then there comes a time, usually around the child's third birthday, when their attitude gradually changes because it becomes harder and harder for them to notice whether any learning is going on. By the time the youngster is three or so his vocabulary has become so large that it is not easy to tell when he has used a new word, none of his sentences stand out anymore as being a great deal longer than the longest ones he has previously uttered, he has already talked to everybody in the neighborhood, and in general he is talking so much that now, as far as the parents are concerned, he is no longer *learning* to speak. He has learned.

The youngster is now a speaker—and so the parents begin to judge him as a speaker. It is at this point, then, that they may notice that he repeats and hesitates. They had not previously noticed his repetitions and hesitations, and so they can say in all honesty that so far as they know he had never done these things before. They take for granted, therefore, that he is *beginning* to do them. If they think that children who are normal speakers do not repeat and hesitate, they conclude that their tike is not speaking normally. And if they can see no reason for his repeating and hesitating—and if they have the necessary motivations for doing so—they call what he is doing "stuttering." Actually, he was doing more repeating and hesitating six months previously, and even more six months before that, but then either the parents didn't notice his disfluencies at all, or else they accepted them as all right, or as "nothing," because they were more or less aware of a reason for them. The reason, which they took for granted, was that he was then too young to talk any better. For a little fellow of one and a half, or two, or two and a half, he was doing just fine, his parents thought, no matter how he was talking, because what they noticed above all else was that month by month, or week by week, even day by day he was talking better and better, and this pleased and delighted them.

The parents' decision, then, that the child is beginning to "stutter" is one thing; the ways in which the child actually talks, in the meantime, is something else again. There may be some relationship between these two, and there may not be. It depends not only on what the youngster does when he talks, but also on the circumstances in which he does it, and precisely what his parents are paying attention to while he is talking. Some parents pay attention to the circumstances and think nothing of the child's repetitions and hesitations; others pay attention to the hesitations and repetitions and ignore the circumstances; and some don't pay much attention to either one. Moreover, some parents worry about the circumstances and some don't; others worry about the child's speech and others don't; and the rest see nothing to worry about in either the child's speech or the circumstances in which he speaks.

. . . . .

In addition to soliciting the parents' own observations of their children's speech, we attempted to obtain tape-recorded samples of the speech of the youngsters. Even though we worked in the homes of many of the children, particularly those in the control group, and in several different clinical centers, we managed to obtain clear and usable tape-recorded samples of the speech of most of the 150 pairs of children in our study. By a pair I mean a control group child and a clinical group child, matched for age, sex, and social and economic level of family. We analyzed these speech samples and compared the two groups of children on several different measures of disfluency.

This analysis revealed certain differences between the two groups; there were also some interesting similarities; and there was much overlapping on most aspects of the comparison. For example, the two groups differed somewhat in the kinds of disfluency they showed most and least. For the control group most of the disfluencies were interjections ("uh uh uh") and revisions ("I was—I am going"); for the clinical group most of them were interjections and syllable and word repetitions. The two groups did about the same amount of interjecting of sounds like "uh uh," and, as has been noted, this was one of the most common types of disfluency for both groups. The two groups also showed about the same numbers of revisions, incomplete phrases, and broken words (the speaker starts to say a word, stops, pauses briefly, and then goes on to finish the word). They differed most in syllable and word repetitions and prolonged sounds and somewhat less in phrase repetitions, with the clinical group doing more of all these than the control group.

For the "stutterers" the median number of repetitions that involved either words or syllables was approximately six per hundred words, and for the "nonstutterers" the median number was between one and two per hundred words. The median numbers of all other kinds of disfluency were about seven for the clinical group and five for the control group per hundred words. No child in either group was perfectly fluent. The most disfluent child of those who were looked upon as normal speakers had eighteen breaks in fluency of one kind or another every hundred words, and half of them had over seven such breaks per hundred words. Half or more of those classified as stutterers had over thirteen disfluencies per hundred words.

The overlapping of the two groups was impressive. Taking the boys only (there were no statistically significant differences in speech fluency between the boys and girls in either group), and considering all types of disfluency combined, the most disfluent "nonstutterer" spoke less fluently than two thirds of the "stutterers." Twenty percent of the "nonstutterers" were more disfluent than 30 percent of the "stutterers." There was practically complete overlapping of the two groups for interjections, revisions, incomplete phrases, and broken words. There was more overlapping for phrase repetitions and prolonged sounds than for syllable and word repetitions. Even in syllable repetition, however, for which there was the largest average difference between the groups, the "nonstutterer" who did the most of this kind of repeating did more of it than 40 percent of the "stutterers," and 20 percent of all the "nonstutterers" did more repeating of syllables than did 20 percent of all the "stutterers."

Thus, even though a child's parents regard him as a stutterer he may speak more fluently than many children who are looked upon by their parents as normal speakers. The problem called stuttering is not the same as the problem—when it is a problem—of disfluency. They are not completely different, or completely unrelated, but they are not one and the same.

The findings we obtained by analyzing the tape-recordings are all the more striking because the speech samples we analyzed were not taken at the moment when, in each case, someone first regarded the child as a stutterer. The problem had been developing for a year and a half, on the average. For that period of time the children in the clinical group had been speaking in the face of parental concern and implied or expressed disapproval of the way they were talking, while those in the control group had been speaking presumably under normally favorable conditions.

Allowing for the possibility of some exceptions, certainly the majority of the children in the two groups were speaking with about equal fluency at the beginning of the eighteen-month period. The differences between the two groups that we observed at the end of that period indicate, therefore, the contrasting effects of the different conditions under which they had been talking during that time. Most of those whose attempts at speech had been regarded as stuttering and disapproved by their parents, however subtly and gently for the most part, had paid a price of some sort in increasing hesitancy, particularly in the form of more frequent repetition of the first parts of words and of whole words. Even so, many of them were still talking as fluently as were a considerable proportion of those who had not been classified as stutterers.

Our fluency analysis revealed one additional fact of major importance: in both groups the boys and girls were about equally fluent—or disfluent. Some girls speak more fluently than some boys, but substantial numbers of boys speak more fluently than a large proportion of girls. Traditionally it has been assumed that boys are not as fluent as girls, and that this accounts for the larger number of male stutterers. Now it turns out, according to our data, that there is apparently no greater disfluency in boys. This finding, moreover, agrees essentially with such other data as are available. All the relevant studies done to date have indicated that either there is no difference or else a relatively slight difference in speech fluency between very young members of the two sexes.

It is necessary, therefore, to explain on some other ground the fact that many more boys than girls are classified as stutterers. A good possibility is that we do not follow exactly the same policies and practices in raising boys and girls. The double standard may very well start in the cradle. If girls speak fully, or very nearly, as disfluently as boys do, and yet from about two and a half to four times more boys than girls are regarded as stutterers by their parents, this would seem to mean that parents do not judge the early speech of their little girls in quite the same way that they judge the early speech of their little boys. Here is something that requires further and very thorough investigation. Whatever it is that we are doing to little girls that results in fewer of them getting caught up in the problem of stuttering we should find out exactly what it is and start doing it to little boys too!

The problem called stuttering begins, then, when the child's speech is felt, usually by the mother, to be not as smooth or fluent as it ought to be. There seems as a rule to be a quality of puzzlement mixed with slight apprehension and dread about the mother's feeling. She uses the only name she knows for what she thinks must be the matter with her youngster's speech, and that word is "stuttering"—or, if she has grown up in England or certain other parts of the world, "stammering." Her first use of this word, however, may be rather loose and not very definite in meaning, at least as far as she is concerned. After all, as we have seen, in the most representative case the hesitations and repetitions she is calling "stuttering" are not very striking.

It is particularly to be noted that she had not noticed the disfluencies before, and so she thinks the youngster has just begun to do them. If he is doing the average number of about 50 every 1,000 words, they are likely to sound to her like a great—and sudden—lack of fluency. She may not be sure of herself at first in deciding that her child is stuttering, but her use of the word serves to crystallize her feelings and to focus her attention on the hesitations in the speech of her child. The more she attends to them and thinks about them as "stuttering," the more firm and deep becomes her conviction that the youngster is, indeed, a "stutterer" and that he has a grave problem.

All the while her feelings are becoming more and more clear to the child, and by a kind of process that we all commonly experience in one form or another but seldom try to put into words, he takes from his mother the feelings she has about his speech. In such a way he comes, slowly and by offs and ons, to doubt that he can get his words out "soon enough" and keep them coming smoothly one after another, and he learns to feel uneasy about this. Gradually, over a period of several months, in the usual case, this doubt and uneasiness affect him so that he loses some of his spontaneity in speaking and feels less like speaking at all and attempts it a little more hesitantly. In fact, after a while he no longer talks as much as he did before, especially to certain persons in certain places where his doubt and uneasiness are greatest.

Eventually he becomes hesitant enough in trying to say some things to some people that he holds back so much he has to force himself to go ahead, and this seems to be why he begins to speak with some degree of effort or strain. But to exert this effort he tenses up the muscles of his lips or tongue or throat and when he does this he talks even more hesitantly and less smoothly, and with some sense of difficulty, and as a result his doubt and uneasiness increase all the more. As a consequence he becomes more hesitant and holds back still more, and so he forces himself harder to go ahead, and in doing this he tenses his muscles increasingly, so that he speaks still less smoothly and with a greater sense of difficulty. On this distressing merry-go-round—or sad-go-round—his doubts and dreads are fed by his hesitations and tensions, which in turn are fed by his doubts and dreads.

While all this is happening to the child, his mother and father, and his sisters and his uncles and his aunts, and his playmates and his doctor and the ice cream man do not stand by idly and calmly. The less smoothly he speaks the more they worry, and the more they worry the more he senses their concern with the way he is speaking. The more he senses their concern the more uneasy he feels, and the more hesitantly and tensely he talks, the more they all worry—and this is an ever expanding spiral that carries everyone farther and farther from where they all want to be.

An unlucky seven out of every thousand children ride this sad-go-round into the adolescent years and beyond. They carry with them into adulthood the possibility of unhappiness and handicap that they would otherwise never know. The most sobering fact of all is that in all likelihood they—and their mothers and fathers and all their other companions in distress—need never have gone on this journey to nowhere that they had ever wanted to go. The best scientific information we have indicates, as I interpret it, that the problem we call stuttering is an avoidable accident.

We are left, however, with a most heartening prospect: through our continuing research and public education we may very well succeed in time in tearing down the old, old sad-go-round on which so many millions of the world's children and grownups are at this moment making their unrewarding way to ever more doubt and dread and tension. The glad promise of our findings to date is that the problem called stuttering can be prevented, and the learning of speech can be for every child a wonderful, wonderful ride on a merry-go-round of understanding and love and laughter.

16

Humor Appreciation as Social Communication

JAY M. DAVIS · AMERIGO FARINA

It was pointed out in a previous selection by Watzlawick, Beavin, and Jackson that much of our communications with others about our relationships occurs in the form of analogic language. Said another way, we communicate such things as availability, dominance, and attraction by our demeanor and manner of speaking as well as through what we actually say.

One special form of analogic communication is laughter or humor appreciation. We may laugh to show deference—as when students laugh appreciatively at a professor's characteristically corny jokes. We may laugh at the misfortune of others to indicate that we are one-up on them in terms of adaptation—as when a companion is doused with soup by a passing waiter. Or, we may use humor to communicate intimacy and solidarity—picture a newly engaged couple who bewilder and exclude third parties with constant giggling over *double entendres* which only they can appreciate.

The following report by Davis and Farina explores the function of humor appreciation in communicating sexual attraction to a stranger of the opposite sex. This is one of the few experimental studies of humor and one of the even more rare studies of the communication function of humor.

In a society that spends vast sums to make itself laugh, where to be labeled "humorless" is a dire indictment, and where one study (Allport, 1961) found 94 percent of the subjects rating their sense of humor as equal to or

Jay M. Davis and Amerigo Farina, "Humor Appreciation as Social Communication," *Journal of Personality and Social Psychology* 15 (1970): 175–78.

above average, it is clear that humor is something viewed as very important. There have been numerous attempts to explain this phenomenon and the results of such efforts make interesting, if arduous, reading. The history of these attempts can be traced back at least as far as Aristotle, and is filled with philosophical speculation, psychoanalytic pronouncement, and myriad psychological studies. Yet one who reads this accumulation of written material cannot help but feel that the phenomenon still remains far from understood.

Early writers on the subject—philosophers and psychologists alike—sought to find unifying principles with which to explain all of humor (Bliss, 1915; Carpenter, 1922; Kline, 1907), although the trend in recent humor research has been to focus on smaller and more manageable variables. Studies have been made of joke contents, individual differences affecting humor appreciation—including focus on such surprising variables as height and weight (Stump, 1939), personality characteristics, and interactions between these variables (Landis & Ross, 1933; Murray, 1934). The limited goal of these recent studies is certainly understandable if one considers the signal lack of success of the generalists. Of all the general theories, only Freud's continues to generate research interest, and often the findings are not too kind to the theory (Byrne, 1957; Epstein & Smith, 1956). But there is another, more compelling reason for being wary of theories which attempt to explain all of humor in a single stroke. What is referred to as "humor" appears to be a whole composite of different behaviors rather than a single one, and any explanation which attempts to explain them equally would appear doomed to do so by explaining them marginally. A careful reconsideration of the various behaviors labeled as "humor" may well prove the most useful strategy in the long run, and an obvious first step is a categorization and delineation of these behaviors and their function.

In considering the roles of humor, it seems apparent that one function it serves is that of interpersonal communication. And while many writers recognize the social nature of humor (Coser, 1959; Wallis, 1922), little research has been done along these lines (Doris & Fierman, 1956; Perl, 1933) and probably no research attention has been paid to the communication function of humor. Yet common experience indicates that the presence and degree of laughter is very often a function of what people wish to communicate. Consider, for example, the situation where a new member of a group offers his first (but, alas, poor) joke. If he is liked, his joke is apt to meet with laughter from his listeners. In this situation, the laughter implies acceptance of his offering and—by extension—acceptance of him. To seek explanations for this laughter in terms of personality characteristics of his listeners, the libidinous content of the joke, or any of the other variables which have been so tediously studied, seems to miss the point. Instead, it is suggested that humor appreciation in this case has served the function of social communication.

Presumably humor appreciation can serve to convey other messages besides acceptance. Thus, the individual who laughs at a racially biased joke while in racially mixed company *may* be viewed as communicating agreement with the derogatory implications of the jest. In both of the examples cited, it is suggested that the listeners chose to communicate through humor appreciation because a direct communication would be socially awkward. It is poor social form to make openly prejudiced remarks, and usually awkward to tell a relative stranger directly that he is liked.

As a final example, consider the situation which occurs in the study to be discussed. Male undergraduates participating in a required experiment find themselves confronted with a very attractive female experimenter whose dress and demeanor are sexually stimulating. Their task, they discover, is to rate for funniness a number of cartoons, some of which are clearly sexual in nature. The social communication hypothesis predicts that subjects may attempt to convey their interest in the experimenter via increased appreciation of the sexual cartoons.

Of course, one needn't employ the social communication hypothesis to predict that sexually aroused subjects will show a heightened appreciation of sexually toned humor. As early as 1959, Strickland showed that arousal of specific motives (sex or aggression) led to increased appreciation of humorous stimuli related to the aroused drive. Unfortunately, however, subsequent unsuccessful attempts to replicate this finding (Byrne, 1961; Davis, 1966; Lamb, 1963) have cast doubt on the apparently simple relationship between motivation arousal and humor appreciation. Nevertheless, this is a widely known and cogent alternative hypothesis. For that reason, the present study is so designed that the effects on humor appreciation of both motivation arousal and social communication can be evaluated independently.

Method

Subjects

Sixty male undergraduates enrolled in an introductory psychology course served as volunteer subjects. Participating in experiments was a course requirement, although students could choose freely from a large number of experiments.

Procedure

Subjects were randomly assigned to one of four experimental conditions: nonarousal/noncommunication; nonarousal/communication; arousal/noncommunication; or arousal/communication.

In all conditions, subjects were met by the same attractive female experimenter who explained that she was working for a member of the English Department who was compiling an anthology of cartoons and was sampling college students to find their tastes in cartoon humor.[1] All subjects rated the 24 cartoons on a 5-point scale of funniness.

[1] The authors would like to express their thanks to Sherry Friedman who acted as the experimenter in this study.

For subjects in the arousal condition, the experimenter was dressed in such a way as to maximize her (considerable) sexual attractiveness, and she behaved in a flirtatious manner—a routine which was practiced and standardized as much as possible.

For subjects in the nonarousal condition, her manner and dress were proper, polite, and formal.

To subjects in the communication condition, the experimenter showed the cartoons to the subject one at a time, and she recorded his verbal evaluations herself.

Subjects in the noncommunication condition were given the cartoons and a rating sheet and told to rate the cartoons for funniness. They were instructed to give the completed rating sheet—unsigned—to the departmental secretary. As subjects made their ratings, the experimenter busied herself with a book, obviously taking no interest in—and presumably having no knowledge of—their ratings.

There were 24 cartoons culled from mass circulation magazines and anthologies. They were judged as to content by a group of clinical psychologists. Eight of the cartoons were sexual in nature, while the other 16 were either hostile (7) or other (9). As an example, one of the sexual cartoons shows an attractive, buxom young woman speaking to a pharmacist in a drug store. The caption reads, "A sedative for my husband. He can't sleep." In a previous study, similar experimental subjects had rated the cartoons in the three content categories as approximately equally funny.

Results

Table 1 shows the mean funniness ratings of sexual and nonsexual cartoons in each of the four experimental conditions.

TABLE 1
MEAN FUNNINESS RATINGS OF SEXUAL AND NONSEXUAL CARTOONS BY EACH GROUP OF SUBJECTS

	NONAROUSED		AROUSED	
Condition	*Sexual*	*Non-sexual*	*Sexual*	*Non-sexual*
Noncommunication	2.8	2.8	2.9	2.6
Communication	3.3	2.9	3.8	3.0

These same ratings were analyzed by means of a three-variable analysis of variance as described by Winer (1962, pp. 337–49). The results of the analysis are shown in Table 2. As may be seen, the effect of sexual arousal on appreciation of sexual and nonsexual humor is not statistically significant. This result contradicts some earlier research (Lamb, 1963; Strickland, 1959) where sexual arousal was reported to enhance the appreciation of all types of humor. However, sexual arousal does have a clearly measurable impact upon humor appreciation. It increases the rated funniness of sexual relative to nonsexual cartoons, and enhances the impact of communication. These effects can be seen in the Arousal × Communication and the Arousal × Cartoons interactions. Additionally, Tukey tests indicate that appreciation of sexual over nonsexual cartoons is significantly greater for aroused than nonaroused subjects ($p < .05$), and that within the communication condition, the sexual cartoons are described as significantly funnier ($p < .05$) by aroused than by nonaroused subjects.

As predicted, providing an opportunity to communicate through humor has a striking influence on humor appreciation as shown by the main effect of communication. Communication enhances the effect of arousal, as previously indicated, and increases the appreciation for sexual cartoons significantly more than for nonsexual ones as show in the Communications × Cartoons interaction. Table 2 also indicates that the sexual cartoons were rated funnier overall than the nonsexual cartoons. This effect is presumably due to the fact that subjects in three of the four conditions were manipulated in such a way as to raise their appreciation for sexual humor. As Table 1 shows, those subjects in the nonarousal/noncommunication condition rated sexual and nonsexual humor cartoons very similarly.

TABLE 2
SUMMARY OF ANALYSIS OF VARIANCE OF FUNNINESS RATINGS

Source	*df*	*MS*	*F*
Between *S*s			
Arousal (A)	1	32.03	2.22
Communication (B)	1	440.83	30.59**
A × B	1	66.01	4.58*
Error (b)	56	14.41	
Within *S*s			
Cartoons (C)	1	316.87	31.48**
A × C	1	64.53	6.41*
B × C	1	90.13	8.95**
A × B × C	1	3.67	.36
Error (w)	56	10.07	

* $p < .05$.
** $p < .01$.

Discussion

The results presented quite clearly demonstrate that social variables play a role in humor appreciation, and, specifically, that a principal role of humor can be communication with another person. In the present study, the focus was on the recipient of the humor who could communicate his sexual interest by selectively responding to the offered humorous stimuli. It has been suggested, however

(Davis, 1966), that in the usual course of social interaction, both the offering of humor and the response thereto provide a potent sub rosa means of communication. Consider the problem of defining limits of acceptable social intercourse. When relative strangers meet there is presumably a range of mutually acceptable topics of conversation, although neither party knows the limits set by the other. A number of strategies may be used to cope with this problem, the most common of which appears to be the selection of obviously banal and inoffensive topics. Another strategy, it is suggested, is to broach the potentially taboo subjects by incorporating them within the fabric of a joke. The listener, by providing or withholding laughter, may then indicate whether the topic falls outside the range of topics acceptable to him. This indirect method clearly smoothes the process of designating limits, since in this way the listener may reject the offered jest on the pretext that it is simply a poor joke. Had the taboo remark been made openly, it would have been more difficult for the listener to reject the remark without rejecting the speaker at the same time.

One specific implication of the present findings deals with studies relating motivation arousal to humor appreciation. An example of such a study might be one where experimental subjects are systematically angered and their responses to hostile humor are compared to those of control subjects. When the procedure permits communication through humor appreciation, interpretation of the data will become unnecessarily difficult if ability to communicate is not varied. In view of this, researchers should devise procedures which either control for or eliminate the variable of communication.

Finally, although the emphasis has been on the social communication function of humor, it must be recalled that motivation arousal was found to affect appreciation of sexual relative to nonsexual humor. Furthermore, although arousal significantly potentiated the effectiveness of communication, it was shown to be effective independently. Obviously the finding that motivation arousal affects humor appreciation is not incompatible with the finding that humor serves a communication function. Rather, as was suggested earlier in this article, it highlights the proposition that humor comprises a number of phenomena, serving diverse and sometimes unrelated functions.

REFERENCES

Allport, G. W. 1961. *Pattern and growth in personality.* New York: Holt, Rinehart & Winston.

Bliss, S. H. 1915. The origin of laughter. *American Journal of Psychology* 26: 236–46.

Byrne, D. 1957. Response to humor as a function of drive arousal and psychological defenses. Unpublished doctoral dissertation, Stanford University.

Byrne, D. 1961. Some inconsistencies in the effect of motivation arousal on humor preferences. *Journal of Abnormal and Social Psychology* 62: 158–60.

Carpenter, R. 1922. Laughter, a glory in sanity. *American Journal of Psychology* 33: 419–22.

Coser, R. R. 1959. Some social functions of laughter. A study of humor in a hospital setting. *Human Relations* 12: 171–82.

Davis, J. 1966. Appreciation of hostile humor: Some relationships to motivational and personality variables. Unpublished doctoral dissertation, University of Connecticut.

Doris, J., & Fierman, E. 1956. Humor and anxiety. *Journal of Abnormal and Social Psychology* 53: 59–62.

Epstein, S., & Smith, R. 1959. Repression and insight as related to reactions to cartoons. *Journal of Abnormal and Social Psychology* 59: 278–81.

Kline, L. W. 1907. The psychology of humor. *American Journal of Psychology* 18: 421–41.

Lamb, C. 1963. Personality correlates of humorous behavior following motivation arousal. Unpublished master's thesis, Ohio State University.

Landis, C., & Ross, J. 1933. Humor and its relation to other personality traits. *Journal of Social Psychology* 4: 156–75.

Murray, H. A. 1934. Mirth responses to disparagement jokes as a manifestation of an aggressive disposition. *Journal of Abnormal and Social Psychology* 29: 66–81.

Perl, R. E. 1933. The influence of a social factor upon the appreciation of humor. *American Journal of Psychology* 45: 308–14.

Strickland, J. 1959. The effect of motivation arousal on humor preferences. *Journal of Abnormal and Social Psychology* 59: 278–81.

Stump, N. F. 1939. Sense of humor and its relationship to personality, scholastic aptitudes, emotional maturity, height and weight. *Journal of General Psychology* 20: 25–32.

Wallis, W. D. 1922. Why do we laugh? *Scientific Monthly* 15: 343–47.

Winer, B. J. 1962. *Statistical principles in experimental design.* New York: McGraw-Hill.

17

Empathy, Communication Efficiency, and Marital Status

NORMAN GOODMAN · RICHARD OFSHE

When a message is communicated between two people, the receiver is faced with the problem of "decoding" the message, i.e., making an interpretation of the message and ascribing some meaning to it. According to George Herbert Mead, empathy or understanding is possible because of the ability of the receiver to "take the role of the other." By this phrase, he means that the receiver puts himself mentally in the place of another person and imagines how the latter perceives the situation. Through interaction over a period of time, people develop a set of symbols whose meanings are mutually agreed upon. And it is this set of symbols, the "universe of discourse," which facilitates empathy. As interaction continues, certain symbols may be "enriched" greatly by the interacting parties, assigned broader denotative and connotative meaning, so that more information may be communicated with fewer symbols.

Following Mead's reasoning, Norman Goodman and Richard Ofshe hypothesize that empathy and communication efficiency should be greater for married couples than for newly engaged couples, and that the latter should display greater empathy and efficiency than randomly paired strangers. They further hypothesize that the relationship between empathy and communication efficiency should be strongest for married couples and weakest for newly acquainted pairs. Since not all commonly shared symbols are necessarily "enriched" in meaning by a given pair of interactants, the authors expected to find that differences in empathy and efficiency would be especially evident when issues of some importance to the couples were involved, e.g., family matters and experiences during courtship. The situation they employ in testing the hypotheses is the game of "Password," adopted from the popular T.V. game show of the same name.

Norman Goodman and Richard Ofshe, "Empathy, Communication Efficiency, and Marital Status," *Journal of Marriage and the Family* 30 (1968): 597–603.

Communication and understanding has always been central to courtship and marriage; in addition, they have been pivotal concepts in symbolic interaction theory in social psychology. It is the intention in this paper to bring the data and methods of a sociological social psychology to bear upon these persistent problems in the study of marital behavior.

Understanding, i.e., empathy, arises out of the ability of one member of a pair to see the situation as his partner sees it; in George Herbert Mead's [1] felicitous phrase, the person is able to "take the role of the other." Empathy develops out of and is rendered possible by the communication process. In turn, the more empathic two people are vis-à-vis each other, the more short-circuited their communication becomes. Put otherwise, the more two people are "in tune with" one another, the fewer units of information are required to transmit meaning between them. In addition, this gain in communication efficiency is likely to take place in those areas which are central to the pair's existence as a unit.[2]

This general social psychological orientation may be used to examine communication and empathy in courtship and marriage. In the early stages of courtship involvement, two people are likely to increase their communication with one another. As the commitment to each other deepens, the interaction becomes more intense and typically with a resultant increase in mutual empathy—especially in those areas of greatest concern (e.g., the wedding, married life, sex, children, etc.). This improved empathy leads to the transmission of more meaning per message unit of information than was originally the case, since gestures—verbal and non-verbal—rather than completed acts can be understood.[3] Once more, this gain in communication efficiency is primarily around those issues that are of some importance to the couple.

Several investigators [4] have studied various aspects of these issues without concern for courtship or marriage processes. Within the family field, Kirkpatrick and Hobart,[5] in a cross-sectional study, demonstrated that increasing involvement in the courtship process was associated with greater empathy. However, the possibility of the less empathic being weeded-out between the stage of casual dating

---

[1] George Herbert Mead, *Mind, Self and Society* (Chicago: University of Chicago Press, 1934).

[2] Though this is a brief statement of the social psychology of interpersonal interaction, it is sufficient for the purposes at hand. A more extended discussion in a somewhat similar vein may be found in Tamotsu Shibutani, *Society and Personality* (Englewood Cliffs, New Jersey: Prentice-Hall, 1961), especially chap. 5.

[3] For a discussion of the concept of gestures, see Mead, *Mind, Self and Society,* especially pp. 12–51; and Shibutani, *Society and Personality,* pp. 142–45.

[4] For example, see among others, Sheldon Stryker, "Conditions of Accurate Role Taking: A Test of Mead's Theory," in *Human Behavior and Social Processes,* ed. by Arnold M. Rose (Boston: Houghton-Mifflin, 1962), pp. 41–61; Harry C. Triandis, "Cognitive Similarity and Communications in a Dyad," *Human Relations* 13 (May 1960): 175–83; and Philip Runkel, "Cognitive Similarity in Facilitating Communication," *Sociometry* 19 (September 1956): 178–91.

[5] Clifford Kirkpatrick and Charles Hobart, "Disagreement, Disagreement Estimate, and Non-empathetic Imputation for Intimacy Groups Varying from Favorite Date to Married," *American Sociological Review* 19 (February 1954): 10–19.

to the point of marriage could account for these data. Moreover, Udry, Nelson, and Nelson[6] failed to find any relationship between degrees of empathy and length of acquaintance or marriage. The numerous studies of the relationship between empathy and marital happiness (e.g., Dymond;[7] and Locke, Sabagh, and Thomas[8]) yielded complex and conflicting results. However this study is concerned with communication efficiency and empathy and not with the issue of marital success.

From the authors' reading of the literature, it is clear that most of the relevant studies are indeterminate at crucial points and this is true, in large part, because of the cross-sectional nature of their research designs. Since this type of design is more efficient than a longitudinal one, the authors have attempted to use the cross-sectional approach to study the courtship and marital process in a somewhat more effective manner. Consequently, they expect to be able to conclude that (a) both empathy and communication efficiency increase from the period of being strangers through engagement to marriage and (b) the relationship between empathy and communication efficiency deepens as couples increase their intimacy from being strangers through being engaged to being married.

Method

Subjects

The 45 men and 45 women used as subjects for this study were chosen to provide 15 cross-sex dyads of males and females in each of three categories reflecting differential marital status: couples who met for the first time in the research situation (i.e., strangers), engaged couples, and married couples. The subjects were either seniors or graduate students in a large municipal college; their spouses were themselves either college students or college graduates.

The three sets of subjects clearly differ with regard to the length of time each person had known the other member of the pair. Strangers obviously had not known one another at all before the research situation. The engaged couples had, on the average, begun to date one another approximately two years before the experiment and had been engaged for the last six months of this period. Married couples, on the average, had begun dating slightly more than five years before the research, become engaged about one and a half years after that, and been married for almost three years prior to the experiment. On the basis of the time over which members of engaged and married couples had intimately associated, one can assume that forces toward coorientation between them already existed before

[6] J. Richard Udry, Harold A. Nelson, and Ruth Nelson, "An Empirical Investigation of Some Widely Held Beliefs about Marriage Interaction," *Marriage and Family Living* 23 (November 1961): 388–90.

[7] Rosalind Dymond, "Interpersonal Perception and Marital Happiness," *Canadian Journal of Psychology* 8 (1954): 164–71.

[8] Harvey J. Locke, George Sabagh, and Mary H. Thomas, "Correlates of Primary Communication and Empathy," *Research Studies of the State College of Washington* 24 (1956): 116–24.

they entered the experiment and that these would certainly be greater than those that could conceivably develop between strangers during the experiment.

Procedures

Each subject was required to perform two tasks, the first to provide information on communication efficiency and the second on a more static measure of empathy (the ability "to take the role of the other").

Communication efficiency. To examine the effect of prior interaction on communication efficiency in as "natural" an interactive situation as possible, the investigators used a variation of the popular parlor game "Password." The game required one member of the dyad to give cue words to the other in order to suggest to him the particular goal word. The unit of communication consisted of one English word. The only other restraint on the interaction was that there be no talking outside the prescribed exchange.

Because the purpose of each individual's cue was to produce a particular response in the other, the task would be more efficiently performed if the ability of a person to predict the other's response to these cues were high. Conversely, the ability of the second (recipient) person to analyze the cue and respond as expected by the first was also crucial. We would therefore say that each cue word demanded that the players empathize with ("take the role of") the other. When they succeeded, the game was over.

The subjects continued the cue-response sequence in each case until the goal word was correctly identified. Each dyad was given a mean communication efficiency score based on the average number of *in*correct responses to cue words for the same 12 goal words. Therefore, a low score indicated greater communicative efficiency.

In order to vary the relevance of the words to the interactive situation, the investigators used goal words which, on an a priori basis, they divided into two classes. *Family-related words* designated objects which the authors believe are more relevant than the second type to the activities of an ongoing family of procreation and hence are salient to engaged and married couples. The words in this group were: birth, family, hospital, house, in-laws, and marriage. The second type consisted of more *general words* that could not be so easily classified as either related to courtship and marriage or used more frequently in these kinds of relationships. The words selected for this group were: beef, bite, hope, party, sin, and symphony. In effect, the general words were used as a control. If empathy and communication efficiency preceded serious involvement in courtship and marriage, then there should be no difference between these words and the "family-related" words. If, however, empathy and communication efficiency grow out of courtship and marital interaction, then empathy and communication efficiency should be greater on those issues around which courtship and marriage revolve—the "family-related" words. The possible effects of word order, word-type order, and sex of starter were removed by rotating all three.

Empathy. In the second phase of the study, the investigators utilized a more rigorously controlled analytic design in order to isolate and examine the mechanism of role-taking ability and its relationship to communication efficiency. They were concerned here with the effect of interaction on one's empathic accuracy. The measure of empathy they used was derived from Osgood's semantic differential technique.[9]

The procedure called for the subjects to differentiate the 12 goal words, i.e., to place them at some point on a semantic differential scale. Initially the subjects were given the standard set of instructions for the use of the semantic differential. After a brief pause, during which time background data were collected, all subjects were asked to differentiate the same words a second time. This time, however, each individual was asked to differentiate the words as he thought his partner had. Empathic ability, then, was measured by the difference between the response of the subject to a word on a given set of scales when asked to act as his partner and the actual response of his partner to the same word.

The numerical scores for empathic ability were derived by taking the mean absolute squared difference between the two differentiations of the same words. For example, if a female rated the word "birth" as very pleasurable and the male rated it as moderately painful, he was given a score for this particular differentiation of 16, the square of the number of steps (in this case, four) that separated the two ratings. For each word there was a total of ten bipolar adjectival scales used for the differentiation.

The semantic differential is particularly well suited for use in the study of empathy because of its flexibility. Since both the concept to be differentiated and the bipolar adjectival scales may be chosen completely at the discretion of the experimenter, it is possible to study any act or role-taking situation.

Results and Discussion

Communication Efficiency

The data on all words do not support the view that communication efficiency is significantly greater for those groups in which the participants have interacted over longer periods of time (see Table 1). This is as expected and is due to the differential results on the two types of words that the investigators have used. The means and t values presented for family-related words reveal that greater efficiency is associated with marital status; but for the general words, the strangers were found to be more efficient at communication than the engaged couples, though the difference was not significant.

The relationship between the communication efficiency of the different word types and marital status emerges even more clearly in other data (Table 2). Thus when one turns to the difference between the two word types, one notes that communication efficiency was greater on family-related words for those who were

[9] Charles Osgood, George Suci, and Percy Tannenbaum, *The Measurement of Meaning* (Urbana, Illinois: University of Illinois Press, 1957).

TABLE 1

MEAN COMMUNICATION EFFICIENCY SCORES[a] AND t VALUES OF COMPARISONS[b]

	MARITAL STATUS		
Words communicated	*Strangers*	*Engaged*	*Married*
All Words	7.75	7.67	6.31
Family-Related Words	7.46	6.66	5.27
General Words	8.04	8.68	7.34
	GROUPS COMPARED		
t Value of comparisons	*Strangers versus engaged*	*Engaged versus married*	*Strangers versus married*
All Words	+.09	+2.09*	+1.80*
Family-Related Words	+.59	+2.05*	+1.94*
General Words	−.51	+1.30	+ .63

[a] The greater the score, the more cues and incorrect responses occurred in eliciting the goal word; hence, the lower the efficiency.
[b] A positive sign indicates greater communication efficiency for the group with the longer period of interaction.
* Significant at the .05 level or less, using a one-tailed test.

TABLE 2

VALUES OF t FOR DIFFERENCES IN FAMILY-RELATED AND GENERAL WORDS BY MARITAL STATUS[a]

Communication efficiency	MARITAL STATUS *Strangers*	*Engaged*	*Married*
Famly-Related Versus General Words	+.53	+3.17*	+3.38*

[a] A positive sign indicates greater communication efficiency on family-related words.
* Significant at the .05 level or less, using a one-tailed test.

engaged or married, but the difference between strangers was small and not statistically significant. The latter point illustrates a baseline effect; i.e., the two word types are equal as far as their initial level of difficulty is concerned, and the divergence of the two reflects the influence of courtship and marital processes.

It appears that words that are central and thus are used frequently in courtship and marriage develop, on the basis of mutual conditioning of the two members of the pair, into a special universe of discourse through which meaning can be transmitted more efficiently than between those not so conditioned. How does this come about?

During the 45 experimental sessions the investigators observed, they gained some insight as to how common experience fosters accurate role taking and, consequently, communication efficiency. First, they found communication patterns in which specific common knowledge is used to elicit the proper goal word. However, it is not *only* the *amount* of common knowledge the subjects have but their ability to use and interpret this information as they think the other does (i.e., to empathize with the other). One of the married couples arrived at the goal word "hospital" in the following manner, with the female giving the cues:

	Cue		*Response*
She—	1. Ulcer	He—	1. Aggravation
	2. Summer		2. Hospital

Married couples, not unexpectedly, tend to rely on specific knowledge they have in common more than the strangers. They have the assurance that specific reference will be understood in terms of a shared context. The communication patterns employed by the strangers are influenced by inadequacies in the ability of one to take the perspective of the other; in some cases a breakdown in communication results among subjects who lack this common pool of information on which to draw. Their responses are too dissimilar and hence too unpredictable to one another. One dyad of strangers attempted to communicate the word "family" as follows:

	Cue		*Response*
She—	1. Nuclear	He—	1. Warfare
	2. Group		2. Atoms
	3. Primary		3. Electrons
	4. Father		4. Einstein
	5. Primary		5. Reactor
	6. Children		6. Molecules
	7. Human		7. Matter
	8. Mother		8. Family

Based primarily on the interactive pattern observed during the experimental sessions, the authors suggest a typology of four modes of empathic behavior. These modes are not mutually exclusive, and, in fact, there is good reason to conceive of them as being interdependent.

The first of these modes is the *"shared cultural mode"* in which communication takes place solely through common denotative meaning. This mode requires only a knowledge of the meanings of the standard universe of symbols that make up the formal language within a particular social system. Though this mode accounts for the bulk of interpersonal communication, it requires the least amount of empathy in relation to a specific other; thus it leads to the most error in transmitting meaning from one person to another. Since this mode is so general it is not related to marital status. The remaining three modes are of greater theoretical interest and of more use in the analysis of significant problems in the process of interpersonal communication.

The second mode is the *"sub-group mode,"* for which associations provide the means of communication. Here, the authors suggest that the degree of empathy vis-à-vis a specific other that is necessary is only slightly greater than that employed in the "shared cultural mode." For this mode, judgments of ethnicity, social class, religion, educational level, sex and/or any other factors which allow for the categorization of the individual are crucial. The knowledge that a person is a Jew, for example, opens the door to a variety of possible meanings or associations beyond those which are part of the formal language. An individual who is attempting to communicate through this mode is able to make use of somewhat more specific knowledge of the other than someone working through the "shared cultural mode." He may more accurately "take the role of the other" in a greater number of possible situations and therefore achieve greater communication efficiency. The following are two examples of communication patterns for the word "hope" which were produced by two pairs of strangers. The first pattern illustrates the "shared cultural," or denotative, mode of communication.

	Cue		*Response*
He—	1. Desire	She—	1. Wish
	2. Chest		2. Passion
	3. Wish		3. Want
	4. Future		4. Imagine
	5. Pray		5. Aspire
	6. Desire		6. Hope

The second illustrates the "subgroup mode." In this illustration the subject made the decision that his partner was familiar with a certain phase.

	Cue		*Response*
He—	1. Faith	She—	1. God
	2. Charity		2. Hope

He obviously expected that his partner who belonged to sufficiently similar subgroups would make the association "faith, hope and charity."

The third mode that the authors propose may best be referred to as the *"self-other mode."* In communication based on this mode, it is possible for each member of the system to call out in himself the responses of the other as a consequence of having interacted with the other in specific situations and internalized particular response patterns of the other. The authors suggest that, in the "self-other" mode of communication, people use empathy exactly as Cottrell [10] suggests it in his concept of the self-other pattern. An example provided by one of the married couples illustrates this mode of communication. The goal word in this case was "bite."

	Cue		*Response*
She—	1. Piece (Peace)	He—	1. Corps
	2. Todd		2. Bite

After the session was completed, questioning of the subjects revealed that their son Todd always said "piece" when he was about to take a bite of food or, for that matter, one of his parents, friends, or relatives.

---

[10] Leonard S. Cottrell, "The Analysis of Situational Fields in Social Psychology," *American Sociological Review* 7 (June 1942): 370–82.

The fourth type may be termed the *"inferential" mode,* since inference is the key mechanism here. For this mode, ego uses either his general knowledge of alter or specific knowledge of alter's interaction with a third party in order to predict alter's response to a novel stimulus. It is necessary for ego to be able to use this information as the basis for predicting, specifically, some future behavior pattern for alter. This is perhaps the most difficult of the four modes in that ego must act as alter in a manner which is not based simply on a continuation of alter's past performance in the same situation but on an extension of it. One illustration of this mode of role taking was provided by an engaged couple. The female gave the cues to the word "in-laws."

Cue	*Response*
She— 1. Trouble	He— 1. In-laws

In this case the female was able to use her knowledge of her partner's complex of attitudes, values, and cognitions in deciding to select this cue and not on any specific situation (or so she told the investigators).

Clearly, the first two modes are available to, and actually used by, all people in each and every interpersonal situation. The last two modes are alternate ways in which one may have obtained more specific information concerning the other in an interactive situation. Consequently, use of these latter modes increases the predictability of alter's responses by permitting the individual to reach beyond the level of denotative understanding available to most other people. In a sense, the latter two modes are dependent on the person also using the former two. Those who share a great deal of time and experience—i.e., engaged and married couples—are in a position to use the "self-other" and "inferential" modes of role taking and thus communicate to one another in a much more efficient fashion than those who do not (strangers).

Empathy

The degree of accurate empathy exhibited by the strangers was used as a baseline for all later analyses. As expected, Table 3 reveals that both the married and the engaged subjects were significantly better at taking the roles of their partners than were the strangers.

Surprisingly, married subjects were less able to take the partner's role than were the engaged subjects. Though this difference is neither substantial nor statistically significant, it does call attention to the possibility that the relationship between empathy and marital status may not be linear. If this is the case, then sex differences within each marital status level may shed some necessary light on the issue.[11]

When the sex of the subjects within each marital status level was controlled,

[11] Since the procedures from which the communication efficiency scores were derived established an interactive situation between members of a cross-sex dyad, sex differences in these scores would be meaningless and hence were not examined.

intriguing variations in empathy were apparent. No significant sex difference in empathy occurs for the strangers. In Table 3 the authors have already demonstrated that the engaged males and females exhibited significantly more accurate empathy than males and females who were strangers, and this difference was relatively equivalent for the two sexes. Further, the males showed the expected linear relationship of empathy to marital status; i.e., the engaged males scored between the strangers and the husbands. However, for the females, the data were clearly discordant with the authors' expectations; the mean score for wives revealed that they were less accurate at role taking than were the engaged females. The consequence of this nonparallel sex difference is clearly revealed in the statistically significant sex difference for married couples that is evident in Table 4.

There are a number of possible explanations of this anomalous finding. However, an analysis in terms of the sex-role differentiation of the conjugal unit is

TABLE 3

MEAN SCORES ON EMPATHY AND t VALUES OF ALL COMPARISONS

Empathy scores[a]	MARITAL STATUS *Strangers*	*Engaged*	*Married*
Dyad	57.39	43.29	45.62
Male	58.53	43.20	42.14
Female	56.24	43.51	49.10

t Value of comparisons[b]	GROUPS COMPARED *Strangers versus engaged*	*Engaged versus married*	*Strangers versus married*
Dyad	+2.68*	−.53	+2.18*
Male	+2.52*	+.25	+2.79*
Female	+2.00*	−.91	+1.16

[a] The lower the score, the greater the empathy (i.e., the less difference between ego rating the words as he believes alter rates them and alter's actual rating).
[b] A positive sign indicates greater empathy with increased marital status.
* Significant at the .05 level or less using a one-tailed test.

TABLE 4

VALUES OF t FOR SEX DIFFERENCES IN EMPATHY

Empathy[a]	MARITAL STATUS *Strangers*	*Engaged*	*Married*
Male Versus Female	−.50	+.22	+2.10*

[a] A positive sign indicates more accurate empathy for the male.
* Significant at the .05 level or less using a two-tailed test.

compelling, as it is both in accord with the data and consistent with the authors' general theoretical stance. Obviously, the writers are not attempting to use the present data as a "test" of this explanation, since this is clearly post hoc analysis. The validity and utility of this interpretation must be sought elsewhere.

As Zelditch[12] has shown, most societies differentiate the adult roles in the nuclear family along the instrumental-expressive dimension, with the former generally allocated to the male and the latter to the female. The authors suggest that this differentiation in sex roles is less clearcut during the period of engagement than both before and after this stage. During the engagement period the male exhibits more expressive behavior than is customary since, among other things, there is no fully independent unit for which he may assume responsibility and perform a full range of instrumental tasks. At the same time the male is permitted, if not required by the norms governing the situation, to be highly affectionate and supportive (expressive) to his future wife.

Thus, the authors suggest that the general equality in terms of expressive behavior is a tenable explanation of why engaged males and females, *relatively equally,* exhibit more empathy than do strangers. The authors base this proposition on the simple fact that during this period the male has an unprecedented opportunity to understand the expressive role of his fiancée by following Dewey's admonition to "learn by doing." Also, his enactment of a more expressive role facilitates his fiancée's ability to take his role and empathize with him. It is clear that the more similar two actor's roles are, the easier will it be for one actor to learn the other's role and this, of course, includes the cognitions of the other actor.

With the advent of marriage, the range of instrumental functions required of the male increases while there often is a simultaneous reduction in his expressive behavior—much to the dismay of his wife. This makes the learning of the male's role during this period more difficult for the female as compared to the previous period of engagement. During this period of time, the male is undergoing more change in his cognitive structure because of his greater involvement in activities outside the home, which makes it more difficult for the married female to learn the male's role. This is reflected in her having a less accurate role-taking score vis-à-vis her husband than he has in relation to her role as well as that which the engaged female has in relation to her partner.

Thus, the authors have what appears to be another piece of scientific evidence to substantiate the claim of many men that their wives just do not understand them. Systematic study of this phenomenon would come under the heading of applied research, though some might term it basic.

Communication Efficiency, Empathy, and Marital Status

The data in Table 5 reveal that the relationship between empathy and communication efficiency depends on marital status. No relationship exists between the

---

[12] Morris Zelditch, Jr., "Role Differentiation in the Nuclear Family: A Comparative Study," in *Family, Socialization, and Interaction Process,* ed. by Talcott Parsons and Robert F. Bales (Glencoe, Illinois: Free Press, 1955), pp. 307–31.

two for strangers. The data on the engaged couples approach but do not attain statistical significance. Finally, for married couples, the relationship is substantial and statistically significant. Thus the degree of empathy and communication efficiency go hand in hand as couples move from being strangers to "almost-marrieds" to husbands and wives. Moreover, the reader should recall that communication efficiency was associated with marital status only for the family-related words and not for the general words.

TABLE 5
SPEARMAN'S RANK CORRELATION (RHO) BETWEEN EMPATHY AND COMMUNICATION EFFICIENCY FOR EACH MARITAL STATUS

	MARITAL STATUS		
Variable	*Strangers*	*Engaged*	*Married*
Communication Efficiency and Empathy	.07	.31*	.59**

* $.10 < P < .15$, two-tailed test.
** $p < .05$, two-tailed test.

Taken together, these data suggest that, even though this study was cross-sectional in design, the authors may make inferences of a developmental nature about the relationship of empathy to communication efficiency and of both variables to marital status. Specifically, increasing commitment of two people to each other in courtship typically leads to increased communication between them, especially about matters that relate to courtship and marriage. This intense and intimate communication ordinarily results in heightened possibilities for each to observe and understand the perspective of the other, i.e., to empathize with the other. This increase in mutual empathy leads to greater communication efficiency, since meaning can be transmitted in gestures as well as in complete behavioral acts and the former is more efficient than the latter.

This approach to courtship and marriage points to the usefulness of viewing a family (or near-family) as a social system. As in the larger society, shared symbol systems (language, or argot in subgroups) facilitate communication and promote in-group identity. The particular study reported here suggests that special universes of gestures, as a subcategory of language and communication, arise through intimate interaction in a cooperative enterprise such as courtship and marriage.[13] The present data merely whet the appetite for further research along these lines.

---

[13] Cottrell, "Situational Fields."

18

Interpersonal Communication, Group Solidarity, and Social Influence

EDGAR H. SCHEIN

Many of the POWs returning to America after the Korean war displayed astonishing changes in their belief systems. A large portion of them were accused of collaborating with the enemy during imprisonment, and many had apparently rejected repatriation. When the public first became aware of this situation, many were shocked and outraged. Mass media accounts of what had occurred in POW camps contained a good deal of exaggeration and misinformation, contributing little to our understanding of the situation. A special word, 'brainwashing," was commonly used to designate the presumably mystical and diabolical powers of persuasion that the Chinese had employed. Brainwashing became a common theme in novels, TV dramas, and movies of the period, the most famous of which was *Manchurian Candidate.* Such bizarre fictional accounts hardly ever hit on the methods of persuasion actually employed by the Chinese.

In the following paper, Edgar Schein provides a systematic analysis of the processes which led to such dramatic changes in American POWs. His analysis recognizes the interrelatedness of interpersonal communication, group solidarity, personal integration, and susceptibility to social influence. He argues that the control of interpersonal communication by the Chinese was the key factor in their success at persuasion. By manipulating interpersonal communication, they were able to destroy social solidarity, upon which personal integration is based. Once POWs were alienated from one another, they became personally disorganized. The POWs were thus deprived of their most important sources of resistance to persuasion and were primed for the induction of new beliefs.

Edgar H. Schein, "Interpersonal Communication, Group Solidarity, and Social Influence," *Sociometry* 23 (1960): 148–61.

The purpose of this paper is to examine some relationships between communication, group solidarity, and influenceability. Few topics in psychology have received as much attention as communication. We have looked at the nature of communication systems, at the flow of information within them, at the structural properties of languages, and at the function which communication plays in organized systems, be they groups, individuals, or neural networks. Only more recently, however, have we begun to consider some of the more subtle semantic and communication problems which, I believe, lie at the root of social relationships. In particular, except in the study of psychotherapy, we have not given enough attention to that aspect of communication which relates to the *maintenance* of social relationships, roles, and self-images. It is this maintenance of social relationships, roles, and self-images which, I believe, accounts in large measure for the stability both of groups and of individual personalities, and which represents, therefore, one of the greatest forces against change or influenceability. When we see behavior change and social influence occurring, or when we think it should be occurring, yet it is not, we might well focus our analysis on the interpersonal communication processes which are occurring and consider their implication for the social situation and the individuals within it.

The conceptual model which I will attempt to spell out below grew out of my studies of Chinese Communist techniques of controlling civilian and military prisoners during and after the Korean conflict (Schein 1956, 1960; Strassman, 1956). Most of my examples will be drawn, therefore, from the experiences of the prisoners. These experiences highlight the role which interpersonal communication plays in the destruction of the subject's social and personal integration and in his subsequent increase in influenceability. My aim in presenting these examples is not limited, however, to providing a socio-psychological explanation of what has popularly come to be termed as "brainwashing." An additional and perhaps more fundamental purpose is to provide some bases for a more general theory of influence which could encompass the kinds of attitude and value changes which we can witness in our own society.

A Conceptual Model: Creating Influenceability through Social Alienation [1]

In any ongoing situation the things that people *say* to each other, and nonverbally *do* with respect to each other carry two kinds of information: one, information directly relevant to the task that they are engaged in, and two, information about their feelings toward each other and toward the task, reflecting in particular the value they attach to each other and to the task. In order for people to accomplish any kind of task together they must have a certain level of regard for each other, which is usually reflected in the degree of attention they give to each other, and

---

[1] For many of the ideas in this formulation, I am indebted to the sociologist Erving Goffman (1955, 1957, 1957a, 1958).

they must have a certain level of involvement in the situation. If such regard or involvement is improperly low or high, it is a signal that the person cannot be trusted to fulfill his proper function, or worse, cannot be trusted not to take advantage of the other participants in the situation.

Such information is usually communicated through a host of gestures and non-verbal cues as well as through the content of what is said. For example, the way we dress, our social manners, the degree of deference we pay to the high status people, and the degree of energy with which we approach a task all serve to communicate to others whether we are properly involved or motivated, and therefore, whether we can be counted on to fulfill our role, be it in an office, on a combat mission, or at a party.

The importance of this type of interpersonal communication is twofold: *First,* the flow of cues which indicate that we have proper regard for each other and are properly involved in situations is critical for the maintenance of organized activity and group solidarity. *Second,* it is also critical for the maintenance of personal identity and security. Much of our personality is learned in and supported by a social context through the information which our significant others communicate to us concerning their evaluation of us. Because of this fact, we become susceptible to change when our social supports are destroyed or removed. Such potential influenceability can be hypothesized at the following levels of psychological functioning:

1. We become more influenceable at the level of *opinions and beliefs,* particularly in regard to those beliefs which are socially shared and operate as norms or standards of conduct. If we cease to have the kinds of relationships which imply mutual trust and regard, we cease to have access to each others' opinions and beliefs which, in turn, makes it virtually impossible for us to establish, check, or enforce social norms or standards.

2. Our *image of ourselves,* both its conscious and unconscious components, depends to a great extent on the confirmation provided to us by others through interpersonal communication. A good example is given by Goffman: In order for a girl to perceive herself as "beautiful" she must obtain from others a whole range of communication cues such as compliments, invitations to dates, "passes" made at her, etc., because beauty has no absolute standard against which it can be judged. The same sort of cues are, of course, required for us to see ourselves as intelligent, witty, manly, or what have you. In most of our daily life we operate in situations and groups which are fairly well integrated, hence we are largely unaware of the constant flow of such interpersonal communication and the confirmation of our selves which it provides. Only when such cues are absent or are manipulated in a destructive manner, as they were by the Chinese Communists, do we realize their importance.

3. Our *fundamental values,* whether we think of them in terms of super-ego, or moral conscience, or some other concept, probably depend to a great extent on the social support of individuals or institutions which operate as surrogates for the parents or the significant others from whom they were learned. One would at least suspect this conclusion from the frequent statements by psychotherapists that change can be produced in the patient only when such surrogate relationships are exposed

and re-evaluated. Again, it is difficult to see this process in ordinary social life; only when marked social disorganization occurs do we see the manner in which morals are supported by social relationships.

In summary, the ongoing integrity of the individual is at several levels of his functioning dependent on adequate social integration which, in turn, is based on adequate interpersonal communication. When interpersonal cues cease to confirm the social relationships upon which the individual depends, he becomes socially alienated and susceptible to change at the level of opinion, belief, self-image, or basic value; the degree and depth of influenceability depend on the degree of alienation, the degree of pressure to change, and the availability of new opinions, beliefs, self-images, or values.

Social relationships here are not meant to be limited to face-to-face relationships. This term applies as well to the symbolic relationships which are implied by identifications with others who are absent or identifications with groups and organizations.

Interpersonal cues which cease to confirm social relationships can be of two kinds: (a) cues which tend to be destructive—that is, cues which tell us that we are held in contempt by others, that our social value is very low; and (b) cues which tend to be neutral—that is, cues which tell us that we are not regarded highly enough to be allowed to participate in intimate relationships or share confidences, but which do not devaluate us except as potential friends or confidants. Both kinds of cues tend to destroy the kind of social integration which is required to sustain high personal integration, but there is a difference in degree, if not in kind, between the destructive effect of being held in contempt and the destructive effect of being merely mistrusted.

Thus far I have tried to argue that the reduction of confirming interpersonal cues makes a person more influenceable because it removes some of the forces which ordinarily operate to make him resist being influenced; in effect, such reduction "unfreezes" him by removing some of the "restraining forces," to use Lewin's terminology (1947). If such unfreezing occurs, what is the probability that it will be followed by influence or change? The probability is high for two reasons: First, social alienation is an unsatisfying psychological state which induces strong motives toward regaining old or finding new social relationships. Such social reintegration can probably not occur without some personal change. Second, social alienation, by cutting off the individual from accustomed sources of information on which to base his judgment, heightens his susceptibility to cognitive re-definition. By cognitive re-definition I mean a process of accepting new definitions for existing concepts, placing concepts into new scales of evaluation, or shifting the anchors or neutral points on such scales. Whichever of these processes occurs, the individual's judgments and consequently his behavior will change as a result. The adoption of new definitions, scales, or anchors occurs through the process of learning to pay attention to how others in the environment view the alienated individual and the total situation, and by identifying with them. If no alternative models are available and the situation is ambiguous, the individual probably redefines it in a direction which maximizes his immediate chances of socal reintegration and also minimizes other stresses to which he is exposed.

Creating Social Alienation in POWs

In the case of the Chinese Communist treatment of United Nations prisoners of war, we have excellent examples of undermining without completely destroying the bonds which hold groups together, thus reducing the flow of confirming interpersonal cues, and thereby heightening social alienation and the individual prisoner's susceptibility to being influenced to collaborate with his captor (Biderman 1957, Schein 1956). This result was accomplished by manipulating the overall situation, the communication channels and the communication content.

One basic device was to destroy the authority structure of the group by systematically segregating leaders and other key personnel from the remainder of the group, or systematically undermining their own authority. As examples of the latter may be cited the rather frequent choice of low ranking enlisted men as squad leaders in prison camp, on the grounds that under Communism rank no longer had any significance and that it was the workingman who should get all the breaks. A further device was to threaten the higher ranking officers with punishment of their group if they failed to cooperate with the Chinese by providing slanted radio broadcasts or other kinds of propaganda. Attempts by the higher ranking officers to work out compromises which would satisfy the Chinese, yet which would provide increased chances of survival for their men, would often appear to the lower ranking officers like collaboration. They would then either covertly or overtly fail to obey orders, thus destroying the chain of command.

This process of social decay was aided by the fact that the first months of captivity had been marked by extreme physical privation and a high prisoner death rate which stimulated some competition for the very scarce supplies of food, medicine, and other means of survival. From the very beginning, the Chinese indicated to the prisoners that, if they were cooperative in re-educating themselves and learning the "truth" about the Korean war, they could expect better treatment. Of course, being cooperative meant being willing to give radio broadcasts and other propaganda to the effect that being a prisoner of war in Chinese hands was a pleasant affair, and so on.

In any *large* group of men such as an army, there will be a few opportunists, psychopaths, and psychotics who will take advantage of any situation for personal gain. The willingness of these men to compete and to collaborate, and the rewarding of such behavior by the Chinese, began to create a general atmosphere of mutual mistrust which was heightened by several additional techniques of manipulating the POWs. For example, a sizeable group of men would be told that, if they cooperated by giving propaganda broadcasts, they would be repatriated; then the group would be split up into smaller groups some of which would be marched off in the direction of the front lines and then taken to another collection point for prisoners, leaving the impression that they had cooperated, given broadcasts, and been repatriated or rewarded in some other fashion. Also, Chinese guards would spy intensively on conversations of the most trivial and intimate nature, look for infractions of camp rules, pull in the culprit and accuse him, force him to confess, then leave him in a state of wondering how they could have known of his words or deeds unless there were more informers in camp than he had previously suspected. During interrogations a man would often be asked a question and after continued refusal to answer would be shown that the Chinese already had the answer. Then he would be asked if he would copy the answer out of the Chinese document. If he did so to get the Chinese "off his back" for a little while, his copy would be shown to another man who was being interrogated with the statement: "Why do you continue to hold out; look, your friend so-and-so has already given us the answer." These and many other devices were used to create the image that almost everyone else was collaborating, so why not you?

The Communists also prohibited any organized activity not specifically sanctioned by them. For example, religious services, social gatherings, athletic events, and so on were prohibited for most of the first two years of captivity. Thus, not even by shared rituals could prisoners reaffirm their solidarity. Any attempt at organized resistance or escape was severely punished and the group responsible split up.

The most striking examples of actual interference in the communication process were the uses of what might be called testimonials. I have already cited the example of tricking an individual into writing out material in interrogation and presenting this to another prisoner as if it had been spontaneously given. In the same category fell the utilization of a small number of men who had made germ-warfare confessions and who were then sent to various camps to give lectures and answer questions. The sincerity of their answers and the small details of their confessions were very convincing to many a prisoner. Still another device was to offer prizes like fruit or cigarettes for essays or articles in the camp newspaper. Of course, the winning essay was usually the one which most agreed with the Communist line. Once obtained by the Chinese, such an essay would be circulated widely among the other prisoners. Those few men who found themselves in a position of cooperating regularly with the Chinese would be used to try to get other prisoners to be more cooperative as well.

Identifications with groups and individuals outside of prison camp also became the targets of Chinese Communist manipulation. The best example was the selective delivery of mail. In some cases, the Chinese did not give a man any of his mail, at the same time solicitously pointing out that there had been no mail for him, which could only mean that his loved ones at home no longer cared about him. In other cases, they only delivered mail which contained bad news or was completely devoid of anything meaningful, and withheld mail which was either directly reassuring or contained news which could be reassuring. At the same time, the mass media of communication were completely saturated by Communist propaganda. Most prisoners did not see a Western non-Communist newspaper or hear a non-Communist radio broadcast during their entire captivity, unless, of course, such a medium contained news which played into Communist hands. Our manifest lack of concern about the Korean war would be a good example of the kind of news which the prisoners were surely given.

Of course the most obvious example of cutting communication channels was solitary confinement which was used for varying lengths of time up to two years or more in the case of some prisoners. However, the effects of solitary confinement were by no means clearcut. In many men it led to a tremendous need to communicate with someone, a need which interrogators have played upon for centuries; in such men it sometimes also led to real loss of assurance about their personal identity and self-image, particularly if they were deprived of the means of living in a civilized fashion, for example if they were deprived of any means of keeping clean. For other men, however, the total lack of interpersonal cues was less threatening to their integrity and sense of integration with reference groups than being systematically given cues that they were not trusted by others or were not worthy of any regard. In particular, men whose reference group identifications were very strong and whose self-images were in part organized around solitude and meditation, for example highly religious individuals, welcomed solitary confinement as a relief from pressure. This fact, by the way, highlights the superiority of actively manipulating interpersonal communication over a mere cutting of the communication channels for the production of social alienation. A man can be most alienated in the very midst of many others, as the examples below will show.

The systematic manipulation of communication and social relationships among prisoners of war produced a degree of social alienation which was characterized in most men by a systematic withdrawal of involvement from *all* social situations (Strassman 1956). They lived increasingly in a shell, going through certain of the motions of cooperating with the Chinese without getting over-involved, or so they believed, at the same time giving up attempts to establish relationships with other prisoners whom they did not really trust or regard highly. However, the social alienation was not sufficient in most instances to disconfirm the prisoners' self-image or destroy his basic values. At most, the process made a man doubtful and insecure.

Creating Social Alienation in Civilians in Chinese Communist Prisons

To find examples of a more intensive destruction of identification with family and reference groups, and the destruction of social role and self-image, we must turn to the experiences of civilian political prisoners interned within Chinese Communist prisons. In such prisons the total regimen, consisting of physical privation, prolonged interrogation, total isolation from former relationships and sources of information, detailed regimentation of all daily activities, and deliberate humiliation and degradation, was geared to producing a complete confession of alleged crimes, and the assumption of a penitent role depicting the adoption of a Communist frame of reference. The prisoner was not informed what his crimes were, nor was it permissible to evade the issue by making up a false confession. Instead, what the prisoner learned he must do was re-evaluate his past from the point of view of the Communists and recognize that most of his former attitudes and behavior were actually criminal from this point of view. For example, a priest who had dispensed food to needy peasants in his mission church had to recognize that he was actually a tool of imperialism and was using his missionary activities as a cover for exploitation of the peasants. Even worse, he may have had to recognize that he was using food as blackmail to accomplish his aims.

The key technique used by the Communists to produce social alienation to a degree sufficient to allow such re-definition and re-evaluation to occur was to put the prisoner into a cell with four or more other prisoners who were somewhat more advanced in their "thought reform" than he. Such a cell usually had one leader who was responsible to the prison authorities, and the progress of the whole cell was made contingent upon the progress of the least "reformed" member. This condition meant in practice that four or more cell members devoted all their energies to getting their least "reformed" member to recognize the truth about himself and to confess. To accomplish this they typically swore at, harangued, beat, denounced, humiliated, reviled, and brutalized their victim twenty-four hours a day, sometimes for weeks or months on end. If the authorities felt that the prisoner was basically uncooperative they manacled his hands behind his back and chained his ankles, which made him completely dependent on his mates for the fulfillment of his basic needs. It was this reduction to an animal-like existence in front of other humans which, I believe, constituted the ultimate humiliation and led most reliably to the destruction of the prisoner's image of himself. Even in his own eyes he became something which was not worthy of the regard of his fellow man.

If, to avoid complete physical and personal destruction, the prisoner began to confess in the manner desired of him, he was usually forced to prove his sincerity by making irrevocable behavioral commitments, such as denouncing and implicating his friends and relatives in his own newly recognized crimes. Once he had done this he became further alienated from his former self, even in his own eyes, and could seek security only in a new identity and new social relationships. Aiding this process of confessing was the fact that the crimes gave the prisoner something concrete to which to attach the free-floating guilt which the accusing environment and his own humiliation usually stimulated.[2]

Influence through Identification and Social Reintegration

As I indicated previously, I am assuming that adult humans are powerfully motivated to know themselves, to have some kind of positive viable self-image and a set of social roles which are confirmed in interaction with others. A state of social alienation, therefore, implies powerful motives toward personal and social integration, and initiates searching behavior on the part of the alienated individual

[2] The number of cases in which such a process occurred is extremely small. The description presented here is included to illustrate the model of influence, not as a typical account of how prisoners fared in Chinese Communist prisons. In many such prisons the thought reform program was ineffective and could be successfully resisted by the prisoner.

for some meaningful relationship, role, and self-image. The usual case, both in the prisoner of war camps and in the political prisons, was that the only relationships which were permitted to grow were with the Communists or with prisoners who were cooperating with them. Such relationships were strongly encouraged and facilitated by a variety of means. A good example was the plight of the sick and wounded prisoners of war who, because of their physical confinement, were unable to escape from continual contact with their interrogator or instructor, and who therefore often ended up forming a close relationship with him. Chinese Communist instructors often encouraged prisoners to take long walks or have informal talks with them and offered as incentives cigarettes, tea, and other rewards. If the prisoner was willing to cooperate and become a "progressive," he could join with other "progressives" in an active group life.

Within the political prison, the group cell provided not only the forces toward alienation but also offered the road to a "new self." Not only were there available among the fellow prisoners individuals with whom the prisoner could identify because of their shared plight,[3] but, once he showed any tendency to seek a new identity by truly trying to re-evaluate his past, he received again a whole range of rewards of which perhaps the most important was the interpersonal information that he was again a person worthy of respect and regard. The force of the motivation to have some identity can be deduced from the fact that positive relationships typically formed in the group cell in spite of the ever present atmosphere of mutual hostility.

Influence through Cognitive Re-definition

When groups become disorganized through the kinds of manipulation cited above for POW groups, not only does it become impossible to communicate and enforce existing norms, but it becomes impossible to share in the formation of new norms for situational contingencies not previously encountered. Being a prisoner of war, in the first place, and being handled in the pseudo-benevolent manner which characterized the Chinese Communist approach, in the second place, were for most men highly novel and highly ambiguous situations to which our cultural norms and standards of conduct did not readily apply. The problem, then, was not that a man became unsure of his moral principles, such as the wrongness of collaborating with the enemy. Rather, the new and ambiguous situation made it difficult to determine that sort of behavior would actually be a violation of such moral principles.[4] The Chinese put considerable effort into

[3] Any degree of communication with either cell mates or interrogators heightened susceptibilities to identification, because even minimum communication requires some degree of taking the role of the other person. Some prisoners reported, by way of confirmation of this point, that they had a tougher time resisting thought reform if they knew the Chinese language.

[4] This ambiguity is actually still present after the fact, as evidenced by the difficulty in our own country of enunciating a clear policy toward POW behavior. Accounts in the press and popularized analyses have shifted markedly in the last few years from blaming collaboration on Communist mistreatment to blaming it on POW misconduct (Biderman 1958).

providing the prisoner with suitable rationales for collaborative behavior, which would allow him to re-define his situation in a manner that would absolve him. Such re-definition might take the form of not recognizing that his behavior was in fact helping the enemy, or might take the form of re-evaluating relative priorities where conflicting values were involved. An officer might see less harm in giving the Chinese propaganda than in risking having his men shot; a prisoner might see greater importance in letting his loved ones at home know that he was alive by making a radio broadcast than in preventing the Chinese from getting a bit of propaganda out of him; or to put the matter more extremely, a man might see less harm in collaborating than in letting a friend die because the Chinese would not give him medicine unless he collaborated.

The important point about these examples is that they all involve some cognitive evaluations and some judgments concerning the consequences of a given course of action. The ambiguity of the situation, the Chinese saturation of the informational environment with their concept of the "truth," and the physical pressures on the men made it quite likely that some shifts in scales of judgment would occur, and that errors in assessing the consequences of collaborative behavior would also occur. However, it was also quite likely that in the whole prisoner population there were many who, because of previous experience or specialized knowledge, could have made more accurate assessments which could have become the basis for shared norms and standards of conduct. However, in a situation in which men were prevented from communicating with each other, did not trust each other, or had low regard for each other, there was no opportunity to share such knowledge. This statement is confirmed by the accounts of many men that successful resistance was usually organized around a few key individuals, often non-commissioned officers with broad experience, who were able to maintain clandestine relationships with other prisoners of war, and who would advise them how far they could cooperate with the Chinese without giving them anything of real propaganda value or getting involved with them in an irrevocable fashion. These instances of failure to produce alienation highlight the importance of effective communication channels as prerequisites to resistance.

In the political prison the pressure toward cognitive re-definition was, of course, present to an even more intense degree. Not only was there unremitting pressure on the prisoner to shift his frame of reference and to re-evaluate his own self-image and past behavior, but there were available ever present models of how to do this, combined with complete isolation from all contacts which could in any manner affirm the old self-image or social norms. Through identifying with cell mates, the prisoner came to pay attention to their point of view which led to a re-defining of his own. Behavior previously seen as innocent could then be judged as criminal, and a past life based on capitalist premises could be seen as evil.[5]

---

[5] The degree of permanence of the change which was produced in a few individuals by a process such as that described depended, of course, on the kinds of interpersonal cues they were exposed to following their repatriation. If their newly acquired identity and set of attitudes were not acceptable to their "significant others" back home, a new and com-

Recapitulation and Conclusions

Social and personal integration depend on interpersonal cues which confirm social norms and the individual's beliefs, self-image, basic values, and social role. When such cues are absent or disconfirming, the individual becomes socially alienated, which makes him susceptible to influence for three reasons: First, forces against change are reduced or removed; second, motives toward re-integration are induced; and third, cognitive re-definitions are facilitated.

My reasons for emphasizing this kind of influence model are twofold. First, we need a better understanding of the technique employed by the Communists in attempting to influence captives and their potential or actual effects. Certainly we need to go beyond some of the thinking often expressed in our mass media—that the behavior of prisoners of the Communists is either the result of mysterious occult devices or is the result of personal weakness reflecting social pathology in our society. Second: we need conceptual tools with which to explore further those institutions within our own society which are presumably geared to producing profound and lasting changes in their adult inmates, students, or patients.

When one examines institutions such as prisons, mental hospitals, basic training centers, intensive educational workshops, and so on, one is struck by the need to conceptualize what goes on in them at a level somewhat broader than is reflected in most experimental studies of social influence. In particular, one is struck by the number of similarities in such institutions with respect to the manipulation of social relationships. For example, a frequent practice in prisons, mental hospitals, educational workshops, reformatories, religious retreats, basic training centers, monasteries, nunneries, academies, and so on is to isolate the inmates from their former social relationships, either by physically confining them or by regimenting their daily routine to such an extent that they do not have time to maintain such relationships.

In authoritarian institutions, like prisons, to which inmates are sent involuntarily, there also tend to be systematic efforts on the part of the staff to destroy the internal organization of the inmate group. This fact has been noted in the prison situation and is embodied in the admonition to prisoners to "serve their *own* time" (Cressey 1958). Evidences of internal organization among prisoners result in punishment for some men, removal to another cell block for others. At the same time, social alienation is fostered by the bestowing of special favors, rewards, or privileges for cooperation with the authorities. In reformatories in which there is a reasonably high rate of success of reform, one finds the key to this success in the identification of the inmates with one or more members of the staff through whom they learn new norms, self-images, and values. Such identifications can only occur when old social bonds have been undermined.

---

parable influence process was set into motion. In the few cases where such changes have persisted, there is good evidence that the individuals sought out and attached themselves emotionally to others who would support the new identity and attitude structure. These observations are based on a recent follow-up study of some of the civilian repatriates (Schein 1960).

In the mental hospital we have recognized that therapy operates through the medium of forming a relationship with a psychiatrist or some other member of the staff. What we have recognized less often is that sometimes the hospital staff will, in a number of subtle ways, destroy the internal organization of the patient group, usually by moving patients from one ward to another, thus preventing stable friendships. Whether the alienation of the patient from other patients is an aid or hindrance to therapy I am not prepared to say, but it would seem to be a problem worthy of investigation. In many of these institutions, a major function of reducing inmate organization is to maintain better control over the inmate population, but perhaps such practices have other functions as well.

By focusing on social alienation, I do not wish to bypass the fact that in many change-producing institutions social organization among inmates is encouraged and is considered to heighten rather than weaken influenceability. This emphasis would certainly be true of educational workshops, religious revivals, voluntarily entered group therapy, and so on. The fact that these institutions are voluntary would appear to be one common feature which differentiates them from prisons and mental hospitals. They also differ in that the participants presumably are motivated to change or be influenced, and that the staff does not feel it necessary to impose its own authority coercively over the inmates. Instead, participants themselves are expected to assume a certain amount of responsibility and authority. An interesting middle ground is found in institutions which are entered voluntarily and with motivation to change, but which involve total submission to authority—for example, monasteries and academies. The fact that such institutions initially tend to destroy the internal organization of inmates would suggest that such destruction is more closely related to the nature of authority in the institution than to the degree of voluntariness of entry or motivation to change.

It is my hope that a model of influence such as is presented here will provide a useful approach both to the comparative study of influence within organizations and to the study of those influence processes which have major consequences for the personalities of the individuals who become its targets.

REFERENCES

Biderman, A. D. 1957. Communist attempts to elicit false confessions from air force prisoners of war. *Bulletin of the New York Academy of Medicine* 33: 616–25.

———, and J. L. Monroe 1958. Reactions to the Korean pow episode. Paper read before the American Psychological Association Meetings, Washington, D. C.

Bonnichon, A. 1965. Cell 23—Shanghai. *The Month* (March): 1–32.

Bull, Geoffrey T. 1955. *When iron gates yield.* Chicago: Moody Press.

Cressey, D. L., and W. Krassowski 1958. Inmate organization and anomie in American prisons and Soviet labor camps. *Social Problems* 5: 217–30.

Ford, R. W. 1957. *Wind between the worlds.* New York: David McKay Company.

Goffman, E. 1955. On face-work. *Psychiatry* 18: 213–31.

——— 1957. Alienation from interaction. *Human Relations* 10: 47–60.

——— 1957. On the characteristics of total institutions. *Proceedings of the Sympo-*

sium on Preventive and Social Psychiatry. Washington, D. C.: Walter Reed Army Institute of Research.

——— 1958. The structure and function of situational properties. Unpublished manuscript.

Lewin, K. 1947. Frontiers in group dynamics: concept, method, and reality in social sciences. *Human Relations* 1: 5–42.

Lifton, R. J. 1956. "Thought reform" of western civilians in Chinese Communist prisons. *Psychiatry* 19: 173–95.

——— 1957. Thought reform of Chinese intellectuals: a psychiatric evaluation. *Journal of Social Issues* 13: 5–20.

Rickett, A., and Adele Rickett 1957. *Prisoners of liberation.* New York: Cameron Associates.

Rigney, Harold 1956. *Four years in a red hell.* Chicago: Henry Regnery.

Schein, E. H. 1956. The Chinese indoctrination program for prisoners of war. *Psychiatry* 19: 149–72.

———, Inge Schneier, and C. Barker 1960. *Coercive persuasions: A socio-psychological analysis of Chinese Communist treatment of American civilian prisoners.* Cambridge: Center for International Studies, Massachusetts Institute of Technology.

Strassman, H., Margaret Thaler, and E. H. Schein 1956. A prisoner of war syndrome: apathy as a reaction to severe stress. *American Journal of Psychiatry* 112: 998–1003.

Yen, Maria 1954. *The umbrella garden.* New York: Macmillan.

Communication:

Putting It into Perspective

Whenever we speak of human interaction, we imply that communication is taking place. In fact, it is impossible to conceive of interaction without communication. Communication is the medium through which interaction occurs, and a complete understanding of the latter presupposes our understanding of communication processes. Consequently, social psychologists have devoted a good deal of their research energies to the exploration of communication per se. This research has touched upon nearly every conceivable facet of communication.

It has already been noted that the study of communication can be divided into three main areas—semantics, syntactics, and pragmatics. Semantics is the study of the meaning of messages, and is mainly concerned with the content of communications. Syntactics, on the other hand, deals with the transmission of information, i.e., how messages are exchanged, the channels employed, and sources of message distortion. Finally, pragmatics is concerned with the behavioral effects of communication. As the sampling of articles in the present section indicates, social pychologists are active in all three of these areas.

In its everyday .sense, the term human communication is used almost exclusively to refer to the exchange of verbal messages, as in speaking, listening, reading, and writing. And, when we say that someone is communicating with someone else, we usually imply that they *intend* to convey certain information to each other. However, as Watzlawick, et al., suggest, the reciprocal influence that occurs in interpersonal situations cannot be very well understood if we limit our attention to what people say to one another, much less limit our attention to only what they intend to say. Implicit in their discussion of the five axioms of communication is a broader view of communicative behavior.

From this broader perspective, communication may be defined as any transfer of information from one person to another. Information may be transferred without any intent on the sender's part and without regard to the way in which the receiver interprets the information. "Accurate" exchange of messages is not a necessary quality of communication. The ultimate test of whether communication has occurred is some sort of response on the part of a receiver. Information that goes unnoticed has not been communicated. In interpersonal communication, the receiver seeks information, selectively perceives cues as information, and constructs a response based on the meaning he ascribes to it.

Man's reality is a world of meanings. He acts toward objects as he defines them. Most of our meanings are shared with others, and most of them have been transmitted to us in the form of language symbols. But, meaning can be attached to almost anything, and we obtain information from others through a wide variety of objects, actions, and relationships to which we ascribe meaning.

Since language is a set of symbols with agreed upon meanings, we can exchange abstract ideas most accurately through this medium. However, language is not always the most effective means for communicating such things as feelings and emotions. In communication of this latter sort of information, we rely heavily on what has been called "body language." Hand gestures, gross body movements, posture, facial expressions, and spatial distance all may serve as cues through which a receiver gauges another person's emotional state. To this list we should also add variations in voice quality such as loudness, pitch, inflection, and cadence. Along with other forms of body language, voice quality contains information about how the content of a verbal message is supposed to be interpreted.

As a number of the articles in the present section point out, communication is crucial for the emergence of interpersonal relationships and for the maintenance of some degree of stability in these relationships. Social relationships, in turn, serve as a basis for personal orientation, for personal integration, and even for one's feeling of individuality. As we watch people negotiate interpersonal relationships, it becomes apparent again that the content of verbal exchanges tells only part of the story. We constantly communicate about our relationships with others through what Watzlawick, et al., refer to as analogic communication, i.e., through nonverbal cues such as body language. Our communications about relationships may be even more subtle than such things as voice inflection or facial expression. They may involve, as one author has suggested, the repetitive acting out of social dramas or games which impress upon all parties their relationship to one another. A perceptive student, for example, might be able to gauge the rank of a faculty member, and his willingness to involve himself in student's problems, through the simple drama of knocking on his office door and waiting to be admitted. The length of time elapsed between the knock and the message, "Come in," is probably a fairly good indicator of the social distance the faculty member wishes to maintain between himself and students.

The social psychological implications of communication extend beyond interpersonal situations. We have not even mentioned the study of mass media communications thus far, although social psychologists have done extensive work in this area. Rather than covering the entire range, we have attempted to present selected aspects of communication which are central to the social psychological enterprise. The *Suggestions for Further Reading* list some key sources which will allow the student to expand his exposure to the social psychological study of communication.

Suggestions for Further Reading

Dean C. Barnlund, ed., *Interpersonal Communication: Survey and Studies.* Boston: Houghton Mifflin, 1968. A collection of theoretical articles and research reports, gathered together from a variety of disciplines.

James H. Campbell and Hal W. Helper, *Dimensions of Communication.* Belmont, California: Wadsworth Publishing Company, 1965. A symposium composed mainly of theoretical articles. Focuses on the functions of communication in persuasion and aspects of verbal and nonverbal language which affect the communication process.

Melvin L. DeFleur, *Theories of Mass Communication.* Second Edition. New York: David McKay Company, 1970. A review of contemporary theoretical perspectives on mass communication along with a historical sketch of the development of the mass media.

Hugh D. Duncan, *Communication and the Social Order.* New York: Oxford University Press, 1962. A provocative analysis of communication as the basic "cement" and determinant of social order. The author's major thesis is that symbolic communication does not merely reflect social hierarchy but determines it.

Gerald M. Phillips, *Communication in the Small Group.* Indianapolis, Indiana. Bobbs-Merrill, 1966. Presents a framework for analyzing communication in small groups. A valuable source for students engaged in their first attempt at an observational study of communicative acts.

Kenneth K. Sereno and C. David Mortensen, *Foundations of Communication Theory.* New York: Harper and Row, 1970. A superb collection of theoretical articles dealing with communication on four levels of analysis: viz., communication as a system of behavior, the "co-orientation" of communicators, the individual as a processor of messages, and the importance of the context or situation in which communication proceeds.

CHAPTER V

Attitudes

19 Philip Goldberg, *Are Women Prejudiced Against Women?* · 249

20 James M. Fendrich, *A Study of the Association Among Verbal Attitudes, Commitment and Overt Behavior in Different Experimental Situations* · 254

21 John Colombotos, *Physicians and Medicare: A Before-After Study of the Effects of Legislation on Attitudes* · 268

22 Robert E. Knox and James A. Inkster, *Postdecision Dissonance at Post Time* · 292

Putting It into Perspective · 300
Suggestions for Further Reading · 302

19

Are Women Prejudiced Against Women?

PHILIP GOLDBERG

An attitude that predisposes a person to think, feel, or act in favorable or unfavorable ways toward a group or its individual members is commonly referred to as *prejudice.* In the following selection, Goldberg describes a study which was designed to determine whether women are prejudiced against women. A sample of female college students were asked to read excerpts of six articles written by six different authors in six different professional fields (art history, dietetics, education, city planning, linguistics, and law). For half the sample a given article was ascribed to a male author; for the other half it was attributed to a female author. After reading each excerpt, the subjects were asked to rate the articles for value, persuasiveness, and profundity, and to rate the authors for writing style, professional competence, professional status, and ability to sway the reader.

Goldberg's findings reveal an unmistakable tendency for women to be biased against women. That is, subjects consistently found an article more valuable and its author more competent when the article bore the name of a male than when the same article was ascribed to a female author. This tendency was stronger in those occupations that traditionally have been viewed as "masculine," but it was also present in traditionally "female" fields. In other words, "Women seem to think that men are better at *everything.*"

These findings are curious in their own right, and they are of special interest in light of current discussions of sexism. If Goldberg's data are representative, anti-feminism is very pervasive in our society. While he does not address the question in this study, a determination of the causes of such prejudice would seem to warrant research attention.

Philip Goldberg, "Are Women Prejudiced Against Women?" *Trans-action* 5 (1968): 28–30.

"Woman," advised Aristotle, "may be said to be an inferior man."

Because he was a man, Aristotle was probably biased. But what do women themselves think? Do they, consciously or unconsciously, consider their own sex inferior? And if so, does this belief prejudice them against other women—that is, make them view women, simply because they *are* women, as less competent than men?

According to a study conducted by myself and my associates, the answer to both questions is Yes. Women *do* consider their own sex inferior. And even when the facts give no support to this belief, they will persist in downgrading the competence—in particular, the intellectual and professional competence—of their fellow females.

Over the years, psychologists and psychiatrists have shown that both sexes consistently value men more highly than women. Characteristics considered male are usually praised; those considered female are usually criticized. In 1957 A. C. Sheriffs and J. P. McKee noted that "women are regarded as guilty of snobbery and irrational and unpleasant emotionality." Consistent with this report, E. G. French and G. S. Lesser found in 1964 that "women who value intellectual attainment feel they must reject the woman's role"—intellectual accomplishment apparently being considered, even among intellectual women, a masculine preserve. In addition, ardent feminists like Simone de Beauvoir and Betty Friedan believe that men, in important ways, are superior to women.

Now, is this belief simply prejudice, or are the characteristics and achievements of women really inferior to those of men? In answering this question, we need to draw some careful distinctions.

Different or Inferior?

Most important, we need to recognize that there are two distinct dimensions to the issue of sex differences. The first question is whether sex differences exist at all, apart from the obvious physical ones. The answer to this question seems to be a unanimous Yes—men, women, and social scientists agree that, psychologically and emotionally as well as physically, women *are* different from men.

But is being different the same as being inferior? It is quite possible to perceive a difference accurately but to value it inaccurately. Do women automatically view their differences from men as *deficiencies?* The evidence is that they do, and that this value judgment opens the door to anti-female prejudice. For if someone (male or female) concludes that women are inferior, his perceptions of women—their personalities, behavior, abilities, and accomplishments—will tend to be colored by his low expectations of women.

As Gordon W. Allport has pointed out in *The Nature of Prejudice,* whatever the facts about sex differences, anti-feminism—like any other prejudice—

distorts perception and experience. What defines anti-feminism is not so much believing that women are inferior, as allowing that belief to distort one's perceptions of women. More generally, it is not the partiality itself, but the distortion born of that partiality, that defines prejudice.

Thus, an anti-Semite watching a Jew may see devious or sneaky behavior. But, in a Christian, he would regard such behavior only as quiet, reserved, or perhaps even shy. Prejudice is self-sustaining: It continually distorts the "evidence" on which the prejudiced person claims to base his beliefs. Allport makes it clear that anti-feminism, like anti-Semitism or any other prejudice, consistently twists the "evidence" of experience. We see not what is there, but what we *expect* to see.

The purpose of our study was to investigate whether there is real prejudice by women against women—whether perception itself is distorted unfavorably. Specifically, will women evaluate a professional article with a jaundiced eye when they think it is the work of a woman, but praise the same article when they think its author is a man? Our hypotheses were:

Even when the work is identical, women value the professional work of men more highly than that of women.

But when the professional field happens to be one traditionally reserved for women (nursing, dietetics), this tendency will be reversed, or at least greatly diminished.

Some 140 college girls, selected at random, were our subjects. One hundred were used for the preliminary work; 40 participated in the experiment proper.

To test the second hypothesis, we gave the 100 girls a list of 50 occupations and asked them to rate "the degree to which you associate the field with men or with women." We found that law and city planning were fields strongly associated with men, elementary school teaching and dietetics were fields strongly associated with women, and two fields—linguistics and art history—were chosen as neutrals, not strongly associated with either sex.

Now we were ready for the main experiment. From the professional literature of each of these six fields, we took one article. The articles were edited and abridged to about 1500 words, then combined into two equal sets of booklets. The crucial manipulation had to do with the authors' names—the same article bore a male name in one set of booklets, a female name in the other set. An example: if, in set one, the first article bore the name John T. McKay, in set two the same article would appear under the name Joan T. McKay. Each booklet contained three articles by "men" and three articles by "women."

The girls, seated together in a large lecture hall, were told to read the articles in their booklets and given these instructions:

"In this booklet you will find excerpts of six articles, written by six different authors in six different professional fields. At the end of each article you will find several questions. . . . You are not presumed to be sophisticated or knowledgeable in all the fields. We are interested in the ability of college students to make critical evaluations. . . ."

Note that no mention at all was made of the authors' sexes. That information was contained—apparently only by coincidence—in the authors' names. The girls could not know, therefore, what we were really looking for.

At the end of each article were nine questions asking the girls to rate the articles for value, persuasiveness, and profundity—and to rate the authors for writing style, professional competence, professional status, and ability to sway the reader. On each item, the girls gave a rating of from 1 (highly favorable) to 5 (highly unfavorable).

Generally, the results were in line with our expectations—but not completely. In analyzing these results, we used three different methods: We compared the amount of anti-female bias in the different occupational fields (would men be rated as better city planners, but women as better dieticians?); we compared the amount of bias shown on the nine questions that followed each article (would men be rated as more competent, but women as more persuasive?); and we ran an overall comparison, including both fields and rating questions.

Starting with the analysis of bias by occupational field, we immediately ran into a major surprise. (See box below.) That there is a general bias by women

Law: A Strong Masculine Preserve

	MEAN	
Field of article	*Male*	*Female*
Art History	23.35	23.10
Dietetics	22.05	23.45
Education	20.20	21.75
City Planning	23.10	27.30
Linguistics	26.95	30.70
Law	21.20	25.60

These are the total scores the college girls gave to the six pairs of articles they read. The lowest possible score—9—would be the most favorable; the highest possible score—54—the most critical. While male authors received more favorable ratings in all occupational fields, the differences were statistically significant only in city planning, linguistics, and—especially—law.

against women, and that it is strongest in traditionally masculine fields, was clearly borne out. But in other fields the situation seemed rather confused. We had expected the anti-female trend to be reversed in traditionally feminine fields. But it appears that, even here, women consider themselves inferior to men. Women seem to think that men are better at *everything*—including elementary-school teaching and dietetics!

Scrutiny of the nine rating questions yielded similar results. On all nine questions, regardless of the author's occupational field, the girls consistently found an article more valuable—and its author more competent—when the article bore a male name. Though the articles themselves were exactly the same, the girls felt that those written by the John T. McKays were definitely more impressive, and reflected more glory on their authors, than did the mediocre offerings of the Joan T. McKays. Perhaps because the world has accepted female authors for a long time, the girls were willing to concede that the female professionals' writing styles were not *far* inferior to those of the men. But such a concession to female competence was rare indeed.

Statistical analysis confirms these impressions and makes them more definite. With a total of six articles, and with nine questions after each one, there were 54 points at which comparisons could be drawn between the male authors and the female authors. Out of these 54 comparisons, three were tied, seven favored the female authors—and the number favoring the male authors was 44!

Clearly, there is a tendency among women to downgrade the work of professionals of their own sex. But the hypothesis that this tendency would decrease as the "femaleness" of the professional field increased was not supported. Even in traditionally female fields, anti-feminism holds sway.

Since the articles supposedly written by men were exactly the same as those supposedly written by women, the perception that the men's articles were superior was obviously a distortion. For reasons of their own, the female subjects were sensitive to the sex of the author, and this apparently irrelevant information biased their judgments. Both the distortion and the sensitivity that precedes it are characteristic of prejudice. Women—at least these young college women—are prejudiced against female professionals and, regardless of the actual accomplishments of these professionals, will firmly refuse to recognize them as the equals of their male colleagues.

Is the intellectual double-standard really dead? Not at all—and if the college girls in this study are typical of the educated and presumably progressive segments of the population, it may not even be dying. Whatever lip service these girls pay to modern ideas of equality between men and women, their beliefs are staunchly traditional. Their real coach in the battle of the sexes is not Simone de Beauvoir or Betty Friedan. Their coach is Aristotle.

20

A Study of the Association Among Verbal Attitudes, Commitment and Overt Behavior in Different Experimental Situations

JAMES M. FENDRICH

Studies reporting little or no correspondence between verbal attitudes and overt behavior are quite numerous, and a variety of explanations to account for attitude-behavior discrepancies have been offered. In the following reading, Fendrich proposes that a major determinant of the correspondence, or lack thereof, between racial attitudes and overt behavior is the structure of the experimental situation in which racial attitudes are measured. Expressing one's attitudes in a testing situation is generally unlike expressing one's attitudes in the course of everyday activities. For example, in day-to-day interaction people are held accountable for what they say and what they do. In a testing situation, such contingencies are seldom operative.

To evaluate the foregoing ideas, Fendrich created an experimental research design with two conditions. In the first condition, subjects responded to a standard racial attitude scale and their overt behavior was measured by the degree to which they voluntarily became involved in a campus civil rights organization. In the second condition, subjects were required to express their willingness to participate in certain interracial activities at some future time prior to responding to the attitude and behavior measures. Thus, in this situation subjects responded to the attitude items in the context of anticipated future interaction. As predicted, Fendrich found that the correspondence between the attitude and behavior measures was quite strong under the second (commitment) condition, but almost non-existent under the first condition.

The author discusses a number of implications of these findings, both theoretical and practical.

James M. Fendrich, "A Study of the Association Among Verbal Attitudes, Commitment and Overt Behavior in Different Experimental Situations," *Social Forces* 45 (1967): 347–55.

Studies examining racial attitudes and overt behavior have often reported inconsistency between the measure of verbal attitudes and overt behavior.[1] One explanation for the disprepancy is that characteristics of the overt situation, rather than attitudes, determine the action toward the attitude object.[2] Another way of interpreting the finds involves the recognition that situational factors influence behavior in both measurement situations. When measuring verbal attitudes, the situational characteristics can be markedly different than characteristics in the overt situation. The disparity between the situational characteristics which influence respondents' role-playing in each setting may contribute to the inconsistency.

The present study examines the relationship between expressed racial attitudes and overt behavior, looking at characteristics of the research setting which influence the expression of attitudes and affect the consistency between verbal attitudes and overt behavior. The objectives are: (1) to manipulate the definition of the situation while measuring verbal attitudes in order to explore the extent to which different definitions of the situation influence the degree of association between verbal attitudes and overt behavior; and (2) to compare the relative power of verbal attitudes and commitment in predicting overt behavior.

The definition of the situation is used to refer to the respondent's subjective attempt to orient himself to the context in which he finds himself, ascertain his interest, and then proceed to cope with the circumstances.[3] The definition of the situation is a process whereby present stimuli and past experience are synthesized in some meaningful whole to facilitate interaction. When a situation has been defined "decisions can be made as to what behavior and objects can be appro-

---

[1] There are numerous articles on this topic: Douglas W. Bray, "The Prediction of Behavior From Two Attitude Scales," *Journal of Abnormal and Social Psychology* 45 (1950): 6–84; Wilbur Brookover and John Holland, "An Inquiry Into the Meaning of Minority Group Attitude Expressions," *American Sociological Review* 17 (April 1952): 196–202; Lewis M. Killian, "The Adjustment of Southern White Migrants to Northern Urban Norms," *Social Forces* 32 (October 1953): 66–69; Bernard Kutner, Carol Wilkins and Penny Yarrow, "Verbal Attitudes and Overt Behavior Involving Racial Prejudice," *Journal of Abnormal and Social Psychology* 47 (1952): 649–52; Richard T. LaPiere, "Attitudes vs. Actions," *Social Forces* 13 (December 1934): 230–37; Lawrence S. Linn, "Verbal Attitudes and Overt Behavior: A Study of Racial Discrimination," *Social Forces* 45 (1965): 353–64; Milton Malof and Albert Lott, "Ethnocentrism and the Acceptance of Negro Support in a Group Situation," *Journal of Abnormal and Social Psychology* 65 (October 1962): 254–58; Gerhart H. Saenger and Emily Gilbert, "Customer Reactions to the Integration of Negro Sales Personnel," *Public Opinion Quarterly* 4 (1950): 57–76.

[2] Herbert Blumer, "Research on Race Relations in the United States of America," *International Social Science Journal* 10 (1958): 403–47; Melvin L. DeFleur and Frank A. Westie, "Attitude as a Scientific Concept," *Social Forces* 42 (October 1963): 17–31; Earl Raab and Seymour Martin Lipset, "The Prejudiced Society," *American Race Relations Today,* ed., Earl Raab (New York: Doubleday & Co., 1962), pp. 29–55; Dietrich C. Reitzes, "Institutional Structures and Race Relations," *Phylon* (Spring 1959): 48–66; and Arnold M. Rose, "Intergroup Relations vs. Prejudice: Pertinent Theory for the Study of Social Change," *Social Problems* 4 (1956): 173–76.

[3] Tamotsu Shibutani, *Society and Personality* (Englewood Cliffs, New Jersey: Prentice-Hall, 1961), pp. 41–42.

priately woven into the interaction sequence and what cannot." [4] Role-playing is considered to be the overt manifestation of a set of perceived normative expectations resulting from defining the situation.[5] By altering the definition of the research setting, the role-playing involved in expressing attitudes was expected to vary. Verbal attitudes were considered to be the outward manifestation of two internal processes. One is the acquired behavioral dispositions toward a class of objects. The other is the definition of the situation. Both processes shape the expression of attitudes. Commitment was considered as the act of making perceived voluntary decisions to participate in a consistent pattern of action that involves some risk.[6] The perceived voluntary decisions refer to the choices between a limited set of possible alternatives that will affect subsequent behavior. The consistent activity involves a series of acts which are not easily reversible. The risk of commitment results from making decisions to engage in a particular pattern of overt behavior. Thus, the committed person by acting out his decisions exposes himself to the sanctioning of significant others. Overt behavior refers to observable acts directed toward the attitude object.

A number of authors have suggested the usual testing situation has unique characteristics which influence respondents' role-playing. Hyman states the inconsistency between verbal attitudes and overt behavior results from inconsistencies between the interpretations researchers put upon attitude measurements and the measurements' relation to behavior. In attempting to account for the lack of a one-to-one relationship between verbal attitudes and overt behavior, Hyman states that in the typical testing situation respondents are not subject to the normal coercive forces of everyday life. In contrast, outside the testing situation respondents are held to account for what they have said or how they have acted.[7] Cicourel and Back et al. outline game theory models to explain behavior in the testing situation. They stress the researcher tries to create a testing situation that is considered a special kind of interpersonal system, very similar to play.[8] The behavior is separate in time and space, uncertain, unproductive, free and governed by rules

---

[4] Glenn M. Vernon, *Human Interaction* (New York: The Ronald Press, 1965), p. 154.

[5] Shibutani, *Society,* pp. 46–50.

[6] This short definition was derived from Jack W. Brehm and Arthur Cohen, *Explorations in Cognitive Dissonance* (New York: John Wiley & Sons, 1962), pp. 8–9, 198, 217; Amitai Etzioni, *A Comparative Analysis of Complex Organizations* (New York: The Free Press, 1961), pp. 8–11; Kurt Lewin, "Frontiers in Group Dynamics," *Field Theory in Social Science,* ed. Dorwin Cartwright (New York: Doubleday & Co., 1965), pp. 227–35; Carl I. Hovland, Enid H. Campbell and Timothy Brock, "The Effects of 'Commitment' on Opinion Change Following Communication," *The Order of Presentation in Persuasion* (New Haven: Yale University Press, 1957), pp. 23–32; Harold B. Gerald, "Deviation, Conformity and Commitment," *Current Studies in Social Psychology,* ed. Ivan D. Steiner and Martin Fishbein (New York: Holt, Rinehart & Winston, 1965), pp. 263–76; Leon Festinger, *Conflict, Decision, and Dissonance* (Stanford: Stanford University Press, 1964), pp. 155–56.

[7] Herbert H. Hyman, "Inconsistencies as a Problem of Attitude Measurement," *Journal of Social Issues* 5 (1959): 38–42.

[8] Aaron V. Cicourel, *Method and Measurement in Sociology* (New York: The Free Press, 1964), pp. 203–09; Kurt W. Back, Thomas C. Hood, and Mary L. Brehm, "The Subject Role in Small Group Experiments," *Social Forces* 43 (December 1964): 181–87.

of make-believe.[9] Linn has described the characteristics of role-playing when measuring racial attitudes of students. While attending a university which has a reputation for being more politically and racially liberal than many other institutions, there is a social and cultural norm held by most *S*s to take a liberal position on racial integration. In the usual testing situation many *S*s actively play, or attempt to play, their social role of the liberal college student; consequently, they express favorable attitudes toward Negroes.[10] Linn's description of active role-playing suggests that *S*s in trying to cooperate, may bias the results of the attitude measure.

The association between verbal attitudes and overt behavior was not expected to be highly correlated in the usual research setting due to its play-like characteristics. In this type of setting it was assumed that subjects would define the situation as an attempt to find out how prejudiced they were toward Negroes. In actively trying to cooperate some subjects would try to demonstrate they were not prejudiced while others would cooperate in revealing how they *felt* toward Negroes. In neither interpretation would they be revealing how they would *act* toward the attitude object.

Hyman states if the aim is to predict a given kind of behavior in a given social setting, tests should be designed to incorporate the fundamental aspects of the overt setting into the testing situation.[11] One of the most important characteristics of overt behavior is the sanctioning of significant others.[12] A commitment measure was designed to incorporate this fundamental aspect of the overt setting into the testing situation. Since committing one's self involves volunteering to engage in future acts that will be sanctioned by significant others, it was hypothesized the commitment would be significantly related to overt behavior.

Measurement of verbal attitudes does not normally tap commitment. Verbal attitudes are statements of preference that have no specific consequences for subsequent behavior. Definite decisions are not made to interact with the attitude object outside the testing situation. Therefore, attitudes can be expressed without consideration of the sanctioning of significant others. Thus, the relationship between commitment and overt behavior was expected to be greater than verbal attitudes and overt behavior.

If expressed commitment preceded verbal attitudes in the testing situation, the role-playing in the research setting was expected to change. Role-playing in the measurement of verbal attitudes would no longer retain its play-like characteristics, but would be played within a framework of previous commitment. When

[9] Back, Hood, and Brehm, "Subject Role," p. 181.

[10] Linn, "Verbal Attitudes," p. 359.

[11] Hyman, "Inconsistencies," p. 40.

[12] DeFleur and Westie, "Attitude," p. 672 and Linn, "Verbal Attitudes," pp. 363–64 have indicated that the overt behavior toward members of minority groups is strongly influenced by significant others. As another part of this study it was found that perceived support from significant others was significantly related to attitude, commitment and overt behavior. See James M. Fendrich, "A Study of White Attitudes, Commitment and Overt Behavior Toward Members of a Minority Group," unpublished Ph.D. dissertation, Michigan State University, 1965.

the attitude measurement immediately followed the measurement of commitment, verbal attitudes were expected to be consistent with the expressed level of commitment. Therefore, the relationship between verbal attitudes and overt behavior was expected to be greater in the research setting involving previous commitment to the attitude object. In summary, three hypotheses were tested:

1. *The greater the degree of favorable commitment, the greater the degree of overt behavior.*

2. *The degree of relationship between commitment and overt behavior will be greater than the relationship between verbal attitude and overt behavior.*

3. *The greater the extent to which attitudes are expressed in a research setting involving previous commitments to the attitude object, the greater the relationship between verbal attitudes and overt behavior.*

Experimental Methodology

Research Design

The attitude and commitment data were gathered in face-to-face interviews. There were two experimental treatments. The two treatments were designed to create different definitions of the attitude measurement situation. Treament A was similar to the usual testing situation. Students were asked to express their attitudes toward Negroes. They were not told they would later be asked to commit themselves to interaction with Negroes. In essence a play-like environment was created. In Treatment B *S*s were asked to commit themselves to interaction with Negroes before they responded to the attitude items. Commitment involved interacting with Negroes in the future, creating the risk of being sanctioned by significant others. The commitment scale was designed to reduce sharply the play-like conditions of the testing situation. After taking the risk of committing themselves, *S*s were asked to respond to the attitude scale. In Treatment B role-playing was expected to be consistent with commitment.

After responding to both the attitude and commitment questions, respondents were asked if they would be willing to attend a small group discussion with Negro and white members of a campus chapter of the National Association for the Advancement of Colored People (NAACP).[13] The discussions were planned for the week following the administration of the instruments. The expressed purpose of the discussions was to improve interracial understanding in the college community.

---

[13] The NAACP was chosen for its saliency to the respondents. At the time the study was conducted, the NAACP was the only effective civil rights organization on campus. It held regular meetings and the group activities were frequently reported in the school daily. Membership in the organization varied from timid support to advocators of strong militancy.

Sample

The interview data were gathered by sampling from the undergraduate population at a large "Big Ten" university. The university was not considered solely as an institution of higher learning; it was considered to be a community. Within this community *S*s interact with people directly and indirectly involved with the academic institution. Sampling criteria were used to select those most likely to be participants in the university community. Freshmen were excluded because they were relatively new arrivals on campus and were not familiar with the prevalent attitudes and sanctions governing the patterns of interracial interaction. With the assistance of the university's Data Processing Center a small representative sample of 65 sophomores, juniors and seniors was drawn. From this sample *S*s were selected if they were U.S. citizens, white, full-time students who lived on campus or in the community surrounding the university. Foreign *S*s were excluded because their familiarity with interracial activities in the United States was considered to be either limited or viewed from a different perspective. Students who lived outside the community and *S*s who were not attending the university on a full-time basis were excluded because of their often minimal contact with other *S*s outside of the classroom. Six *S*s who did not complete all of the scales were excluded. The remaining 46 *S*s were interviewed at their place of residence. Randomization procedures were used in order that each *S* would have the same probability of falling into either treatment.

Attitude Scale

The operational definitions consist of scales designed to measure three variables—verbal attitudes, commitment and overt behavior. A 32-item scale was developed to measure verbal attitudes toward Negro *S*s.[14] A variety of campus experiences were included in the items, e.g., dating, student government, housing, athletics, academic abilities, militancy, etc. Thirteen items expressed a favorable attitude toward Negro *S*s and 19 expressed an unfavorable attitude. To be consistent *S*s had to both agree and disagree with items. All of the attitude scale items had a range of five possible responses—"strongly agree," "agree," "undecided," "disagree," and "strongly disagree." The estimated split-half reliability of the study was .91. Item-total score correlations indicated that the scale was internally consistent. Twenty-eight of the 32 items were significantly correlated with the total score. The remaining four approached significance. The following 32 items were used to construct the attitude scale:

1. I think there are Negroes qualified to be class presidents.
2. Negro students all look alike.

---

[14] It was felt that the class of social objects should be clearly specified and they should be similar to the object of the commitment and overt behavior.

3. I think research would show that Negroes definitely get much poorer grades than white students.
4. I wouldn't want Negroes in positions of responsible student leadership on campus.
5. I wouldn't mind at all if I lived in an area that was integrated.
6. I find some Negroes attractive.
7. Negroes on campus want too much.
8. I would like to go on a double date with a Negro couple.
9. I would feel extremely uncomfortable dancing with a Negro student.
10. Negroes are better in sports because they come from more primitive backgrounds.
11. Eating at the same table with a Negro wouldn't bother me.
12. It would be a good experience to get to know more Negroes on campus.
13. Negro students don't take care of their personal hygiene.
14. I'd hate to be seen walking across campus alone with a Negro.
15. Negroes should stick to themselves.
16. Any white student is better than a Negro student.
17. No one forgets so easily as a Negro student.
18. When given a chance Negroes can do just as well in school as anyone else.
19. I wouldn't want to see a Negro president of student government.
20. Only unprincipled students would go on an interracial date.
21. I would like to see Negroes get equal treatment in all areas of campus life.
22. Negroes want the same things out of life that I do.
23. The more Negroes come to this university the lower the standards get.
24. I wouldn't mind working with Negroes on some campus project.
25. I hate to see a white and Negro going steady together.
26. I would prefer sharing living quarters with any white rather than with a Negro student.
27. I think the only thing that Negroes can contribute to campus life is better athletics.
28. The only way that Negro students can obtain full equality on campus is through the help of white students.
29. The more Negro professors we get on campus the lower will be the quality of teaching.
30. The reason why Negroes want fraternities and sororities of their own is so they can stay by themselves.
31. I think there are Negroes on campus who will be more successful in the future than I will.
32. Some Negro students are smarter than I am.

Commitment Scale

A 10-item scale was developed to measure commitment.[15] Questions were designed to imply participation in interracial activities with Negro *S*s. The interviewer stated the questions involved possible interaction with Negro *S*s in the

---

[15] It was unrealistic to create a longer scale. The longer the scale, the more students would have become skeptical of the manifest function of the commitment items.

future. Following this introduction, *Ss* were asked if they would be willing to commit themselves to nine different forms of activities. If they committed themselves to any of the nine activities, they were then asked to give their phone number. This last item was included in the scale to reinforce the idea of being committed to future interaction. Care was taken to construct items that would appear realistic to the *Ss*. Items varied in the extent of personal involvement in the interracial activities. The following 10 items were used to construct the commitment scale:

1. Would you agree to go to coffee or lunch with a mixed racial group of students to talk about interracial problems on campus?
2. Would you agree to have a Negro as a roommate next year or next term?
3. Would you agree to spend a weekend at the home of a Negro attending the university if he or she invited you?
4. Would you agree to invite a Negro at the university to spend a weekend at your home?
5. Would you agree to participate in a small group discussion on the topic of white students' social relations with Negroes on campus?
6. Would you agree to attend a lecture or conference on the topic of white students' social relations with Negroes on campus?
7. Would you agree to protest against segregated housing in the city with Negro students?
8. Would you agree to attend a meeting of the Campus Chapter of the NAACP?
9. Would you, if asked, agree to contribute $1.00 to help finance the activities of a Negro action group (SNCC) (NAACP) or (CORE)?
10. (If respondent says yes to any of the above items) Would you give your phone number?

No. . . . .

The *Ss* were given three choices of responses to each of the ten items—"yes," "maybe," and "no." Since the primary interest was the degree of positive commitment, it was decided to score the "yes" responses as one and the remaining two responses as zero. The estimated split-half reliability was .82. Every item was significantly correlated to the total score.

Overt Behavior Scale

The overt behavior scale was developed to measure behavior congruent with verbal attitudes and commitment toward Negro *Ss*. After responding to the attitude and commitment scales, *Ss* were asked if they were willing to attend small group discussions with members of the NAACP that were scheduled in the near future. During the five-day period following the administration of the attitude and commitment scales, *Ss* were contacted to determine if they still definitely planned to attend the discussions. The NAACP representatives tried to obtain firm decisions and answer any questions. The *Ss* were given the opportunity to attend one of four discussions.[16] If the *S*s declined, the representatives did not force the issue and noted either a refusal or acceptance to attend the discussions. At the small group discussions every *S* was asked to give his name in order that name-tags could be used to facilitate interaction. This information was used to associate *S*s with their interview data. At the beginning of each meeting the researcher defined himself as a member of the NAACP and he introduced other members who had previously volunteered to take part in the discussions. At each session the campus history of the organization was presented, particular areas of discrimination on- and off-campus were cited, and future activities were brought to the students' attention. Afterwards *S*s participated in lively and pointed conversation with the members of the NAACP. At the end of the discussions they were asked if they were willing to sign up to participate further in interracial activities. The activities involved a number of committees of the NAACP, e.g., publicity, program of research, entertainment, membership, direct action, housing, and the NAACP Newsletter. Besides these activities *S*s were given the opportunity to help organize a talent show to raise money for projects in southern states, volunteer to work in Mississippi during the summer, or recruit students for summer work, take part in a civil rights program sponsored by student government, assist in a campus fund raising drive for students volunteering for summer projects and circulate a petition in the local community to obtain signatures of residents which would be used as evidence to support a "Fair Housing Ordinance" being considered by the City Council.

The overt behavior scale measures behavior outside of the research setting. The scale has four discrete points:

0 = Refusing invitation to attend small group discussions designed to improve race relations on campus.

1 = Accepting invitation to attend small group discussions designed to improve race relations on campus.

2 = Participating in small group discussions.

3 = Signing up for ongoing civil rights activities.

Inspection of the scale revealed very few inconsistencies. The time ordering of responses that increased in degree of involvement in interracial activities reduced the possibility of inconsistency. Using scalogram analysis procedures, resulted in a coefficient of reproducibility of .99.

Table 1 reports the scores of the *S*s on the three scales. The *S*s in both treatments had favorable attitudes toward Negro *S*s. The commitment scores were

---

[16] The scheduling of the small group discussions was designed to provide every student the opportunity to attend; however, the students independently selected the evening discussions. Some of the students brought friends who did not take part in the interviews.

TABLE 1

SCORES ON THE ATTITUDE, COMMITMENT AND OVERT BEHAVIOR SCALES, BY STUDENT

TREATMENT A				TREATMENT B			
Student	*Attitude*	*Commitment*	*Overt* behavior	*Student*	*Attitude*	*Commitment*	*Overt* behavior
1	131	5	3	23	118	4	0
2	127	7	2	24	118	4	0
3	138	2	1	25	108	0	0
4	118	6	1	26	141	8	2
5	106	3	0	27	127	5	1
6	113	6	1	28	131	10	1
7	113	4	0	29	110	4	1
8	118	4	0	30	144	8	3
9	149	8	0	31	144	10	3
10	131	10	3	32	132	6	1
11	118	6	1	33	159	10	2
12	143	8	1	34	126	5	0
13	137	7	0	35	116	3	0
14	123	6	0	36	139	6	1
15	117	10	0	37	124	6	0
16	146	9	1	38	136	6	2
17	137	7	0	39	129	8	0
18	127	8	1	40	133	6	1
19	124	5	0	41	128	10	1
20	149	10	0	42	136	10	2
21	124	6	0	43	113	7	1
22	132	3	0	44	123	5	0
				45	111	7	1
				46	123	7	1

widely dispersed and the overt behavior scores were more varied in Treatment B than Treatment A.

Statistical Treatment

In contrast to other studies on verbal attitudes and overt behavior, this study does not employ a theoretical model that posits there will be a linear one-to-one association between the independent and dependent variables. This type of model for testing hypotheses is artificially stringent. It was felt that a better theoretical and methodological approach would be to consider verbal attitudes and commitment as contributory causes of overt behavior, i.e., they are important independent variables but not the sole determinants of overt behavior. The most useful measures for testing the consistency hypothesis are measures reporting the "predictability" of the dependent variable from known values of the independent variable.

Since interest was primarily in the proportional-reduction-in-error variance of overt behavior from knowledge of attitude and commitment, a measure was chosen that meets Costner's criteria for proportional-reduction-in-error measures.[17] The overt behavior scale was an ordinal scale and the data were not normally distributed. Therefore, *gamma* was chosen as the measure of association. If the explained variance was ≧.50 the independent variable was considered a good predictor of overt behavior.

Results

Test of Hypothesis 1

Table 2 reports the results of the measures of association by treatment. In Treatment A the attitude scale preceded the commitment scale. The order was reversed in Treatment B. Hypothesis 1 states that the level of commitment is an effective predictor of overt behavior. In Treatment B the relationship between

TABLE 2
ASSOCIATION AMONG VERBAL ATTITUDES, COMMITMENT AND OVERT BEHAVIOR, BY TREATMENT

Relationship	TREATMENT A *Attitude measured before commitment* gamma	TREATMENT B *Commitment measured before attitude* gamma
Attitude-Commitment	.37*	.66†
Attitude-Overt Behavior	.12	.69†
Commitment-Overt Behavior	.18	.72†
	N = 22	N = 24

* P < .05
† P < .01

commitment is significant beyond the .01 confidence level. The level of commitment explains .72 of the variance of overt behavior scores. In Treatment B *Ss* responded to the experimental design, engaging in acts of commitment that were consistent with their overt behavior.

In Treatment A the relationship was not significant at the .05 level of confidence. The level of commitment explains only .18 of the variance of overt

[17] Herbert L. Costner, "Criteria for Measures of Association," *American Sociological Review* 30 (June 1965): 341–53. Computation of a confidence interval for *gamma* takes ties into account. The magnitude of *gamma* is not affected by ties, but a large proportion of ties affects sampling variability. For more information on *gamma* see Leo A. Goodman and William H. Kruskal, "Measures of Association for Cross-Classification: III Approximate Sampling Theory," *Journal of the American Statistical Association* 58 (1963): 322–30.

behavior scores. The proportion of explained variance in Treatment A did not meet perceived expectations. It was felt that the threat of sanctions from significant others would make acts of commitment consistent with overt behavior. Evidently there were two major types of social pressures operating in the interview situation. The first was to respond in a consistent manner to the interviewer. The second social pressure was to be consistent with the expectations of significant others outside of the testing situation. Recent research on cognitive dissonance theory has demonstrated the extent to which respondents strain to act consistently in a voluntary experimental situation.[18] This strain to act consistently was expected to be greater in Treatment B when measuring attitudes after commitment, but it was not expected to operate as strongly in Treatment A when measuring commitment after verbal attitudes. Thus, the strain to give consistent response patterns within the testing situation was underestimated in Treatment A. One conclusion that can be drawn is that commitment is a useful predictor of overt behavior if the research setting is not contaminated by previous acts unrelated to overt behavior with which the respondent is forced to be consistent.

Test of Hypothesis 2

Hypothesis 2 states commitment will be a better predictor of overt behavior than verbal attitudes. Since the pressure to be consistent with the first expression of either commitment or verbal attitudes strongly influenced the second expression, the measure of association between verbal attitudes and overt behavior in Treatment A and commitment and overt behavior in Treatment B were used to test the hypothesis. The research situations in which these two measures were obtained were comparable. Both measures were presented first in the respective treatments, and therefore were unaffected by interaction with the second variable. In Treatment B the level of commitment explains .69 of the variance of overt behavior. In Treatment A the degree of favorable attitudes explains only .12 of the variance of overt behavior. Under comparable research conditions commitment is a much stronger predictor of overt behavior than verbal attitudes.

Test of Hypothesis 3

Hypothesis 3 states the greater the extent to which attitudes are expressed in a research setting involving previous commitment to the attitude object, the greater the relationship between verbal attitudes and overt behavior. In Treatment B verbal attitudes were expected to be consistent with commitment, and therefore significantly related to overt behavior. Data from Treatments A and B support the hypothesis. The difference between $gamma_1$-$gamma_2$ was .57, i.e., verbal attitudes in Treatment B explained 57 percent more of the variance in overt behavior than verbal attitudes in Treatment A. This great a difference of

---

[18] Brehm and Cohen, *Explorations,* p. 303.

gammas was considered to be significant. The results suggest the definitions of the research settings were markedly different, producing one set of responses that were consistent with overt behavior and one set of inconsistent responses.

Discussion

The results of this study caution against simplistic explanations of either consistency or inconsistency between verbal attitudes and overt behavior. The expression of attitudes is not simply an expression of an orientation toward action with the attitude object, and thus, consistent with overt behavior. The definition of the measurement situation influences the way respondents express their attitudes. Previous research that explains the inconsistency between verbal attitudes and overt behavior as being due to different situational factors in the overt situation and the attitude measurement situation appears to be correct. The researchers, however, did not recognize the flexibility of the research setting. Verbal attitudes can be useful predictors of overt behavior, if the artificial play atmosphere of the testing situation is reduced. Hyman's suggestion that fundamental aspects of the overt setting should be incorporated in the testing situation, which is designed to predict behavior, is useful advice. In this study a measure of commitment to interaction with the attitude object did incorporate the fundamental aspects of overt behavior. When the expression of attitudes immediately followed the measured commitment, attitudes were consistent with overt behavior.

The findings of this study add to the growing body of literature on social behavior in the research process.[19] It is dangerous to assume that participants are willing but docile subjects in social research, rather, they are active agents who define a social situation and play what they perceive to be the appropriate role. The results of this study suggest that recognition of the social psychology of the research process can contribute to designing experiments to collect reliable and valid predictors of overt behavior. Lacking this knowledge researchers may draw false conclusions from their findings.

In criticizing a recent article that tended to polarize conceptualizations of attitudes into "probability conceptions" and "latent process conceptions," Weissberg made a point that is well taken. The effects of attitudes in behavior should not be considered from a perspective of theoretical monism. Verbal attitudes are, "simply one of the terms in the complex regression equation we use to predict behavior." [20] One possible way of solving this equation is to adopt a field theory orientation, considering behavior both in and outside an experimental environ-

[19] Cicourel, *Method and Measurement,* pp. 39–72; Back, Hood, and Brehm, "Subject Role," pp. 181–87; M. T. Orne, "On the Social Psychology of the Psychological Experiment: With Particular Reference to Demand Characteristics and Their Implications," *American Psychologist* 17 (1962): 776–83; Robert Rosenthal, "On the Social Psychology of the Psychological Experiment," *American Scientist* 51 (1963): 268–83; and William H. Form, "On the Sociology of Social Research," *Rassegna di Sociologia* (September 1963): 463–81.

[20] Norman C. Weissberg, "On DeFleur and Westie's 'Attitude as a Scientific Concept,' " *Social Forces* 43 (March 1965): 422.

ment as being a function of both personality and environmental factors. Such an approach prevents positing theories of contemporaneity or theories of predispositional determinism.

Summary

The data for this study were gathered from 46 randomly selected college sophomores, juniors and seniors at a "Big Ten" university. The *S*s were randomly distributed between two experimental treatments. Under Treatment A *S*s were encouraged to define the research setting as the usual play-like experiment. In Treatment B *S*s were encouraged to define the research setting as a situation where current acts would have consequences for future behavior. In Treatment A verbal attitudes toward Negroes were not found to be good predictors of the degree of involvement in a campus chapter of the NAACP. In contrast verbal attitudes in Treatment B were good predictors of the same overt behavior.

This study demonstrates the importance of the social psychology of the research process. The way respondents define a situation, and consequently, play the corresponding role, significantly affects the relationship between independent and dependent variables. *Verbal attitudes can be either consistent or inconsistent with overt behavior, depending upon the way respondents define the attitude measurement situation.* The results caution against simplistic interpretations of verbal attitudes relationship to overt behavior. As Hyman has stated the inconsistency between verbal attitudes and overt behavior frequently results from inconsistencies between the interpretations researchers put upon attitude measurements and the measurements' relationship to behavior, rather than from evidence of measures of association.

Data also suggest that measures of commitment may be better predictors of overt behavior than measures of attitude, if the measurement situation is not contaminated by role-playing unrelated to overt behavior with which respondents feel forced to be consistent. Unlike attitude measures, commitment incorporates in the measurement situation the fundamental aspect of overt behavior—the possible sanctioning of significant others. Since the measurement of commitment involves the reduction of the play-like atmosphere of the usual testing situation, it serves the function of providing a good predictor for overt behavior.

21

Physicians and Medicare: A Before-After Study of the Effects of Legislation on Attitudes

JOHN COLOMBOTOS

One of the most frequently used concepts in social psychology is *attitude*. Underlying much of the concern with this construct is the assumption that there is a high degree of correspondence between attitudes and behavior. While researchers are aware that the linkage between the two is actually highly conditional, and thus in everyday situations is frequently weak, much social action and the existence of some professions are predicated on their assumed correspondence. For example, many efforts to alter intergroup relations have been based on efforts to change intergroup attitudes. The assumption is, of course, that if the efforts to change attitudes are successful, the desired changes in behavior will follow. Similarly, the support of the advertising industry is based on the supposition that consumers' behavior can be manipulated by means of creating certain attitudes or altering existing ones.

The significance of the following selection is that rather than focusing on the impact of attitudes on behavior, Colombotos examines changes in attitudes resulting from (1) changes in law, and (2) changes in behavior to comply with the law. Data were collected from a sample of physicians at three points in time concerning their attitudes toward Medicare. The results led the investigator to conclude that changes in the law produced changes in physicians' attitudes toward Medicare even before the law was implemented. After the law was implemented and the physicians altered their behavior accordingly, further changes in their attitudes were observed.

These data suggest that the popular notion that "you can legislate behavior, but you can't legislate beliefs and feelings" is probably invalid.

John Colombotos, "Physicians and Medicare: A Before-After Study of the Effects of Legislation on Attitudes," *American Sociological Review* 34 (1969): 318–34.

Seldom has a law been more bitterly opposed by any group than was Medicare by the medical profession (see Harris, 1966; Feingold, 1966; Rose, 1967: 400–55). Just before Medicare was passed by Congress in 1965, there was even talk about a "boycott" of the program by physicians. This paper examines how individual physicians reacted, in their behavior and in their thinking, to Medicare after it became law.[1] The more general issue raised by this question is the role of law as an instrument of social change, an old sociological problem.

Law as an Instrument of Social Change. One view, attributed to early sociologists such as Herbert Spencer and William Graham Sumner, is that law can never move ahead of the customs or mores of the people, that legislation which is not rooted in the folkways is doomed to failure. Social change must be slow, and change in public opinion must precede legislative action. In brief, "stateways cannot change folkways." This view was expressed by Senator Barry Goldwater in the 1964 Presidential campaign (*New York Times,* Nov. 1, 1964:1): "I am unalterably opposed to . . . discrimination, but I also know that government can provide no lasting solution. . . . The ultimate solution lies in the hearts of men."

Others see law as a positive force in initiating social change (Allport, 1954: 471): "It is a well known psychological fact that most people accept the results of an election or legislation gladly enough after the furor has subsided. . . . They allow themselves to be re-educated by the new norm that prevails." [2]

These are oversimplified statements of the role of law as an instrument of social change and miss the complexity of the problem. The question must be specified: under what conditions do laws have what effects?

Effects: Behavior vs. Attitudes. Sumner's negative position on law as an instrument of social change has been distorted, according to one reappraisal of his writings (Ball et al., 1962: 235–40). Sumner (1906: 68), in distinguishing between the effects of law on behavior and on attitudes, did not reject the power of law to influence men's behavior: "Men can always perform the prescribed act, although they cannot always think or feel prescribed thoughts or emotions."

This is in agreement with the views of the majority of contemporary politically liberal social scientists, who see law primarily as a way of changing behavior, not attitudes. For example: "[Legal action] cannot coerce thoughts or instill subjective tolerance. . . . Law is intended only to control the outward expression of intolerance" (Allport, 1954: 477). And according to MacIver (1954: viii),

---

[1] It is of course necessary to distinguish between the attitudes of individual physicians toward Medicare and official AMA policy. The AMA leadership is commonly regarded as more conservative than the rank-and-file; however, the opposition of the AMA to Medicare before its passage apparently was supported by the majority of its membership. In a national poll of private practitioners in 1961, less than 20 percent were in favor of the program "to provide hospital and nursing home care for the aged through the Social Security System" (*Medical Tribune,* May 15, 1961).

[2] Allport qualifies this remark elsewhere in his book. It is quoted here to state the issue in its sharpest form.

"No law should require men to change their attitudes. . . . In a democracy we do not punish a man because he is opposed to income taxes, or to free school education, or to vaccination, or to minimum wages, but the laws of a democracy insist that he obey the laws that make provisions for these things. . . ."

The distinction between the effects of law on attitudes and on behavior is supported by empirical studies showing a discrepancy between the two (see Deutscher, 1966: 235–54). In race relations, for example, study after study has shown that in concrete situations—in hotel accommodations (La Piere, 1934: 230–37), restaurant service (Kutner et al., 1952: 649–52), department store shopping (Saenger and Gilbert, 1950: 57–76), hospital accommodations, and school desegregation (Clark, 1953: 47–50)—expressions of prejudice are not necessarily accompanied by discriminatory behavior. There are undoubtedly instances of the opposite, that is, verbal expressions of tolerance accompanied by discriminatory behavior, but they are not as well documented. The flight of white, liberal, middle-class families from the cities to the suburbs may be such an instance (Scott and Scott, 1968: 46 ff.).

But to say that attitudes and behavior are not perfectly correlated is not to say they are unrelated, and there is evidence that change in behavior leads to change in attitudes. Studies of integrated army units, housing projects, and children's camps show that white people in these situations develop more favorable attitudes toward Negroes (Swanson et al., 1952: 502; Deutsch and Collins, 1951; Yarrow, 1958). In an analysis of school desegregation, Hyman and Sheatsley (1964: 6) describe the process thus:

> "There is obviously some parallel between public opinion and official action. . . . Close analysis of the current findings . . . leads us to the conclusion that in those parts of the South where some measure of school integration has taken place official action has preceded public sentiment, and *public sentiment has then attempted to accommodate itself to the new situation* [emphasis added]."

Other studies (Mussen, 1950: 423–41; Campbell, 1958: 335–40), however, have found that social contact has little effect in reducing prejudice.[3]

If indeed behavioral change does lead to attitudinal change, then law, by first changing behavior, may ultimately lead to changes in attitudes. As Allport says: "Outward action, psychology knows, has an eventual effect upon inner habits of thought and feeling. And for this reason we list legislative action as one of the major methods of reducing, not only public discrimination [behavior], but private prejudice [attitudes] as well" (1954: 477). Berger, too, writes: "Law does not change attitudes directly, but by altering the situations in which attitudes and

[3] In Campbell's study of a desegregating school system, the results were mixed. White students who claimed Negroes as personal friends were more likely to show a reduction of prejudice than those without Negro friends, but the time order of these factors is ambiguous: those who became less prejudiced may then have chosen Negro friends. Also, those who had many classes with Negroes were no more likely to become less prejudiced than those with few classes with Negroes.

opinions are formed, law can indirectly reach the more private areas of life it cannot touch directly in a democratic society" (Berger, 1954: 187). Clark (1953: 72), among others, states the issue in more problematic terms: "Situationally determined changes in behavior [as in response to a law] *may or may not* be accompanied by compatible changes in attitudes or motivation of the individuals involved [emphasis added]."

Others, however, see law exerting a *direct* influence on attitudes, without necessarily changing behavior first. Law is conceived as a legitimizing and educational force, supporting one value or set of values against another. For example, according to Dicey (1914: 465): "No facts play a more important part in the creation of opinion than laws themselves." And according to Bonfield (1965: 111):

> "Past the change in attitude which may be caused by legally mandated and enforced nondiscriminatory conduct, *the mere existence of the law itself affects prejudice* [emphasis added]. People usually agree with the law and internalize its values. This is because considerable moral and symbolic weight is added to a principle when it is embedded in legislation."

The results of the few studies done on the effects of law on behavior and attitudes are mixed. Cantril (1947: 228) notes: "When an opinion is held by a slight majority or when opinion is not solidly structured, an accomplished fact tends to shift opinion in the direction of acceptance. Poll figures show that immediately after the repeal of the arms embargo, immediately after the passage of the conscription laws, and immediately after favorable Congressional action on lend-lease and on the repeal of the neutrality laws [just before the United States' entry into World War II] there was invariably a rise of around ten percent in the number of people favorable to these actions." And Muir (1967) found that the Supreme Court decision banning religious exercises in the nation's schools had an over-all positive effect on the attitudes and behavior of 28 officials in one public school system, though there was some evidence of a backlash.

Other studies, however, show that laws and court decisions have negligible effects on relevant attitudes. Hyman and Sheatsley (1964: 3) and Schwartz (1967: 11–12, 28–41) interpret the increasing acceptance of integration between 1942 and 1964 as a complex of long-term trends that are not easily modified by specific, even highly dramatic events, such as the Supreme Court decision of 1954. The physicians' strike against the province's medical care plan in Saskatchewan, Canada, in 1962 (Badgley and Wolfe, 1967) is an extreme case of noncompliance with a program implemented by a law.[4]

Conditions for Effectiveness of Law. Three commonly cited factors determining the effectiveness of law are: (1) the degree of compatibility of the law with

[4] In an experimental study, information that a behavior was illegal did not change the subjects' attitudes toward that behavior (Walker and Argyle, 1964: 570–81). In a follow-up experiment, however, it was found that knowledge of the law and knowledge of peer consensus did change attitudes, and, furthermore, these effects depended on the authoritarianism of the subjects (Berkowitz and Walker, 1967: 410–22).

existing values, (2) the enforceability of the law, (3) the clarity of public policy and the diligence of enforcement.[5]

1. To say that a law must be compatible with some major existing values is not to say that it must be compatible with all values. In any society, especially in modern, industrial society, values themselves "are full of inconsistencies and strains, unliberated tendencies in many directions, responsive adjustments to new situations well conceived or ill conceived" (MacIver, 1948: 279). A law, then, "maintains one set of values against another" (Pound, 1944: 25). Thus desegregation and civil rights laws find support in the democratic creed and due process; Medicare finds support in the principle that adequate medical care is a right, rather than a privilege. This position appears to be in agreement with Sumner's principle of a "strain toward consistency." There is an important difference, however. Whereas Sumner posed the question of compatibility between a new law and existing mores as one of all or nothing, the current view emphasizes conflicts and strains among a system of mores and poses the question of compatibility as a matter of degree (Myrdal, 1944: 1045–57).

2. In order for a law to be enforceable, the behavior to be changed must be observable. It is more difficult to enforce a law against homosexual behavior, for example, than a law against racial discrimination in public transportation.

3. The authorities responsible must be fully committed to enforcing the new law. One reason for the failure of Prohibition was the failure, or disinclination, of law enforcement agents to implement the law. Civil rights legislation runs into the same problem where local authorities, especially in the deep South, look the other way.

The Medicare Law. Medicare, signed into law in July, 1965, is a major piece of social legislation. It is often compared in importance with the original Social Security Act of 1935.

Medicare, Title 18 of the Social Security Amendments Act of 1965 (Public Law 89–97), established a new program of health insurance for people 65 years old or over. It has two parts: hospital insurance (Part A), applying automatically to almost all people 65 or over, which covers inpatient hospital services, outpatient hospital diagnostic services, and posthospital care in the patient's home or in an extended care facility (such as a nursing home); and medical insurance (Part B),

[5] These conditions are discussed in the following: Berger, 1954: 173–77; Clark, 1953: 53–59; Allport, 1954: 469–73; Roche and Gordon, 1955: 10, 42, 44, 49; Rose, 1959: 470–81; Evan, 1965: 285–93; Bonfield, 1965: 107–22; Mayhew, 1968: 258–84. Problems of implementation, specifically, the work and effects of antidiscrimination enforcement agencies, are analyzed by Berger (1954) and Mayhew (1968).

Less commonly cited factors determining the effectiveness of law are: (1) The amount of opposition to the law and the distribution of this opposition. The stronger and the more concentrated the opposition in politically relevant units, along geographical or occupational lines, for example, the more effectively it can oppose the law (Roche and Gordon, 1955: 341). (2) The quality of support. A law is more likely to be effective if supported than if it is opposed by community leaders (see Killian, 1958: 65–70). (3) The tempo of change. It is argued that the less the transition time, the easier the adaptation to the change enacted by the law (see Clark, 1953: 43–47; Evan, 1965: 290; Badgley and Wolfe, 1967: 45).

a voluntary plan elected by over 90 percent of those eligible for Part A, which covers physicians' services wherever they are furnished, home health services, and a number of other medical services. Part A is financed by the same method that finances retirement, disability, and death benefits under Social Security, i.e., special Social Security contributions by employees and their employers. Part B is financed by a monthly premium of $3.00 from each participant who elects to pay, matched by $3.00 from the general revenues of the Federal Government.[6]

For twenty years the American Medical Association fought bitterly and effectively against such a Federal program of health insurance under Social Security. Now, however, that the program has become law, the question is: How have individual physicians reacted, in their behavior and in their attitudes, to Medicare?

Research Design

Our data come from standardized interviews in 1964 and early 1965, before Medicare was passed, with 1,205 physicians in private practice in New York State (about 80 percent of a probability sample), and from reinterviews with subsamples of these physicians at two different points in time after Medicare was passed. The interviews were conducted mainly by telephone. An experimental comparison of telephone and personal interviews with small, random subsamples of physicians showed that the responses obtained by the two methods were essentially similar.[7]

The purpose of the first wave of interviews was to study physicians' political attitudes, their attitudes toward issues in the organization of medical practice, and their career values, and to examine the relationship between background characteristics, such as their social origins and specialties, and their attitudes.[8] Among the questions in the first wave of interviews was: "What is your opinion about the bill that would provide for compulsory health insurance through Social Security to cover hospital costs for those over 65—Are you personally in favor of such a plan, or are you opposed to it?"

The bill referred to was passed, as noted above, in July, 1965, as Part A of Title 18. Part B of Title 18, the voluntary insurance plan that pays for physicians' bills and other services, and Title 19, which provides for Federal matching funds to states for medical care for the "medically indigent," were not covered in the first wave of interviews because they were not introduced in the bill until the spring of 1965. Title 19, as a matter of fact, received little publicity until after the bill was passed. Title 19 is commonly called *Medicaid;* Title 18, parts A and B, *Medicare.*

---

[6] Amendments to the Social Security Act in 1967 made some minor changes in the Medicare program and included an increase in the monthly premium.

[7] Reported in "The Effects of Personal vs. Telephone Interviews on Socially Acceptable Responses," presented by the author at the annual meeting of the American Association for Public Opinion Research, Groton, Connecticut, May 14, 1965.

[8] Some of these data are reported in the following papers: Colombotos, 1968; Colombotos, 1969a; Colombotos, 1969b.

Thus, before the law was passed, measures were available of physicians' attitudes toward what was generally considered the major feature of the bill, hospital insurance for the elderly, and many related issues, providing a unique opportunity for a natural experiment of the effects of legislation on attitudes.

The 1,205 physicians were stratified on their initial attitude toward Title 18A (i.e., before it was passed) and on geographic area, religious background, and political ideology, all of which were highly correlated with their initial attitude toward Title 18A,[9] and randomly divided into two subsamples, one with 804 and the other with 401 physicians.

The first subsample of 804 physicians was contacted between the middle of May, 1966, and the end of June, 1966, nearly one year after Medicare was passed and just before it was to go into effect. The second subsample of 401 doctors was contacted between the end of January and April, 1967, a little over six months after the main provisions of the Medicare program had gone into effect. More than 80 percent of each of these subsamples—676 and 331, respectively—were successfully reinterviewed.

To summarize, 1,205 doctors were interviewed before Medicare was passed (call this Time 1). Of these, 676 were reinterviewed about ten months after the law was passed and just before its implementation (call this Time 2),[10] and another 331 were reinterviewed a little over six months after its implementation (call this Time 3).[11] Thus, differences in attitudes between Time 1 and Time 2 would reflect the effects of the Medicare law before actual experience with it; differences between Time 1 and Time 3 would reflect the combined effects of the Medicare law and short-term experience with the program. This design makes it possible to separate the effects on attitudes of the law itself from the effects of its implementation, that is, short-term experience with the program. The design is represented in Figure 1.

---

[9] Physicians in New York City were more pro-Medicare than physicians in upstate New York; Jewish physicians were more pro-Medicare than Protestant physicians, with Catholics in between; and those who were Democrats and took a liberal position on economic-welfare issues were more pro-Medicare than those who were Republicans and took a conservative position (see Colombotos, 1968: 320–31).

[10] Actually, the 676 physicians interviewed at Time 2 include 100 who could not be reached by June 30 and were interviewed between July and October, after Medicare went into effect. Those interviewed after June 30 were a little better informed than those interviewed before June 30 about the services covered by the Medicare program, which is not surprising, but the patterns of change in the attitude toward Title 18A of the two groups were practically the same. The specific month within the Time 2 or Time 3 periods when respondents were interviewed also made no difference in the pattern of change in their attitude toward Title 18A.

[11] The original plan of this phase of the study was to reinterview all 1,205 physicians just before Medicare went into effect and again three to four years after it had been in effect. It was decided, however, to set aside a third of this sample (401) to be reinterviewed six months after the law was implemented in order to test the *short-run* effecs of implementation. The original sample of 1,205 was not reinterviewed both before and immediately after Medicare's implementation because of the financial cost and because, with the two interviews coming so close together, of a concern about a high refusal rate in the third interview. Reinterviews with all 1,007 (676 plus 331) physicians, interviewed both before and after Medicare, are planned for 1970.

FIGURE 1
RESEARCH DESIGN

MEDICARE BECOMES LAW (JULY 30, 1965)		MEDICARE PROGRAM IS IMPLEMENTED (JULY 1, 1966)
Time 1	*Time 2*	*Time 3*
January to April, 1964; November, 1964, to March, 1965	May to June, 1966	January to April, 1967
Interviews with 1,205 physicians in private practice	Reinterviews with 676 of a stratified subsample of 804 from 1,205 interviewed at Time 1 [330 of a control sample of 472 also interviewed]	Reinterviews with 331 of remaining stratified subsample of 401 from 1,205 interviewed at Time 1

The Findings

Physicians' Behavior. As the Medicare bill was going through its final stages in Congress in June, 1965, resolutions were introduced at the semiannual meeting of the AMA's House of Delegates calling for a "boycott," or "nonparticipation," when it was passed (*New York Times,* June 22, 1965: 1). Immediately after the law was passed, the president of the AMA predicted that "quite a few" physicians throughout the country would refuse to participate in the program (*New York Times,* August 18, 1965: 55). By the following March, however, it was reported that "threats of a boycott, if not dead, are at least moot" (*New York Times,* March 28, 1966: 1). When the AMA House of Delegates met in June, 1966, a month before Medicare was to go into effect, there was little, if any, talk of a boycott.

There has been no boycott, that is, no concerted noncooperation on a large scale, to date.

Responses from the New York State private practitioners interviewed in this study are consistent with the evidence of nationwide compliance by physicians. In the fall of 1965, just a few months after the law was passed, the New York State Medical Society issued a statement that "now that 'Medicare' is an accomplished fact, [the Society] will cooperate in every way possible with the government. . . . As citizens and as physicians, the members of the State Society will obey, and assist in the implementation of the law of the land . . ." (*New York State Journal of Medicine,* 1965: 2779).

The physicians interviewed were asked if they agreed or disagreed with their Society's policy of cooperation. (Note that the answers to this question indicate physicians' *attitudes* toward cooperation with Medicare. They are not reports of actual cooperation.) Ninety percent agreed at Time 2; 91 percent agreed at Time 3 (see Table 1).

TABLE 1

RESPONSES OF PHYSICIANS INDICATING COMPLIANCE WITH MEDICARE AT TIME 2 AND TIME 3[a]

	Time 2	*Time 3*
Last fall the New York State Medical Society said it would cooperate with the government on Medicare—do you agree or disagree with this policy?[b]		
Agree	90%	91%
Disagree	8	8
Don't know, no answer	2	1
	100%	100%
Weighted totals	(10,214)	(4,954)
Unweighted totals	(676)	(331)
(If the physician had been asked to serve on a utilization review committee under Title 18): Have you agreed to serve?		
Yes	87%	94%
No	10	6
Not decided	4	0
	101%	100%
Weighted totals	(1,810)	(1,441)
Unweighted totals	(156)	(123)
(If the physician had not been asked to serve on a utilization review committee under Title 18): If you were asked, would you agree to be a member of such a committee?		
Yes	66%	71%
No	27	26
Don't know	7	3
	100%	100%
Weighted totals	(8,323)	(3,513)
Unweighted totals	(516)	(208)
According to your present thinking, do you plan to accept patients who get benefits under Medicare, or not?[c]		
Accept (have treated)	93%	93%
Will not accept (have not treated)	4	6
Don't know, no answer	4	1
	101%	100%
Weighted totals	(8,941)	(4,345)
Unweighted totals	(609)	(299)

[a] "Time 1" in these tables refers to interviews conducted before the passage of Medicare, from January to April, 1964, and from November, 1964, to March 1965; "Time 2," to interviews done after the passage of Medicare but before its implementation, from May to June, 1966; "Time 3," to interviews done after the implementation of Medicare, from January to April, 1967.

All percentages in these tables are based on the weighted figures, which estimate the total number of private practitioners in New York State. The weighted figures do not add up to the actual number of private practitioners in the State because of noninterviews. The sampling design was stratified on geographic area, size of city, and part-time participation in a health department. The unweighted totals represent the number of physicians in a given category actually interviewed.

[b] This is the Time 2 question. The Time 3 question was: "The New York State Medical Society has said it would cooperate with the government on both Titles 18 and 19. Regarding Tittle 18, do you agree or disagree with this policy?"

[c] This is the Time 2 question. The Time 3 question was: "Have you treated any patients who get benefits under Part B of Title 18, or not?" The figures for both questions exclude those physicians who indicated in a previous question that they had no patients 65 years of age or over.

Of the 18 physicians with patients 65 or over who had not treated any of these patients under Title 18B at Time 3, only one had actually refused. The others reported that no elderly patients had come to them for treatment since Medicare.

At Time 2, 87 percent of those who had been asked to serve on a hospital utilization review committee for Medicare patients had agreed to serve; and of those not asked, 66 percent said they would serve if asked. Slightly higher proportions indicated willingness to serve at Time 3. Furthermore, a physician's refusal to serve on such a committee does not necessarily indicate protest against Medicare. He may refuse for other reasons (see Footnote 12, below).

At Time 2, less than 5 percent said they would not accept patients who get benefits under Medicare. At Time 3, 6 percent of those who had any patients 65 or over had not treated any patients under Title 18B, but only one of the 331 physicians interviewed at that time had actually *refused* to treat any patients under Title 18B. That doctor explained he was in "semi-retirement" (he was 73 years old), and he wasn't "going to bother with this." The remainder of the 6 percent indicated that none of their elderly patients had come to them for treatment yet.

To sum up, despite what appeared to be threats of a boycott before Medicare was passed, practically all physicians complied after it became "the law of the land."[12]

[12] Our measures of compliance, apart from being reports of own behavior rather than observations of actual behavior, are admittedly simple measures of a complex variable. Consider the following: (1) A physician may provide some services under Medicare, but refuse to provide other services; (2) He may provide services to some patients, but refuse to provide them to other patients; (3) He may cooperate at one point in time after the program goes into effect, and not cooperate at another; (4) He may sabotage the program by "over-complying," that is, by providing more services than are medically indicated. Also, the question of compliance is irrelevant for physicians without patients 65 or over, such as pediatricians.

As a matter of fact, when the specific behaviors required of physicians under Medicare are examined, it is difficult to conceive what form a physicians' boycott of Medicare could have taken. What is a physician asked to do under Medicare?

(1) He must certify that the diagnostic or therapeutic services for which payment is claimed are "medically necessary." Such certification can be entered on a form or order or prescription the physician ordinarily signs.

(2) Under Title 18, Part B, the physician can choose between two methods of payment for his services: he can accept an assignment and bill a designated carrier (such as Blue

Physicians' Attitudes. It is possible, of course, for physicians to comply with Medicare without changing their minds about it. What effects has Medicare had on physicians' attitudes toward the program? In 1964 and early 1965, before Medicare was passed (Time 1), 38 percent of the private practitioners in New York State were "in favor" of "the bill that would provide for compulsory health insurance through Social Security to cover hospital costs for those over 65," the bill that became Title 18A. This is a sizeable number, but nevertheless, a minority.

At Time 2, ten months after the law was passed, even before it went into effect, the proportion "in favor" jumped to 70 percent. At Time 3, a little over six months after the program went into effect, the proportion "in favor" again jumped, to 81 percent. At both Time 2 and Time 3, more than half of those in favor felt "strongly," rather than only "somewhat" in favor (see Table 2).

Table 3 shows that of those opposed to Title 18A at Time 1, more than half (59 percent) had switched by Time 2; 70 percent had switched by Time 3.[13] Very few switched from favoring it to opposing it.

Although the absolute percentage increase favoring Title 18A of Medicare is greater between Time 1 and Time 2 (from 38 to 70 percent), than between Time 2 and Time 3 (from 70 to 81 percent), it might be misleading, because of the operation of a "ceiling effect," to argue that the Medicare law itself had a

---

Shield, or another private insurance company, depending on the geographic area), or he can bill the patient directly. If he takes an assignment, he agrees that the "reasonable charge" determined by the carrier will be his full charge and that his charge to the patient will be no more than 20 percent of that reasonable charge. If the physician refuses to take an assignment and bills the patient directly, the patient pays the physician, and then applies to the carrier for payment. Under this method, a physician is not restricted by the "reasonable charge" for a given service. The patient, however, will be reimbursed only 80 percent of the reasonable charge by the carrier. Although the Social Security Administration had hoped for wide use of the assignment method, the AMA's House of Delegates adopted a resolution at its 1966 meeting recommending the use of the direct billing method (*New York Times,* June 30, 1966: 1). Use of the direct billing method cannot be called "non-cooperation," however, since the law provides for either method.

(3) In order to promote the most efficient use of facilities, each participating hospital and extended care facility is required to have a utilization review plan. A committee set up for such a purpose must include at least two physicians. Many hospitals already had such review procedures before Medicare went into effect. One way in which a physician can protest against Medicare is to refuse to serve on such a committee if asked. But refusal to serve does not necessarily mean a protest against Medicare, anymore than unwillingness to run for a local Board of Education is an indication of protest against the public school system.

To sum up, the direct and immediate effects of Medicare on a physician's day-to-day practice are minimal. For the vast majority of services under Medicare, the physician is not required to do anything more or differently in treating patients than he did before Medicare was passed. One form a boycott of Medicare could have taken would be for physicians to have refused to treat patients 65 or over, most of whom are eligible for benefits under both Part A and Part B of Medicare. This, apparently, few physicians chose to do. Furthermore, it would be difficult to interpret such acts as "non-cooperation," unless the physician himself said so. A physician's refusal to admit an elderly patient to the hospital, for example, could mean that, in his medical judgment, hospitalization was not necessary.

[13] Physicians' attitudes toward Title 18B, highly correlated with their attitudes toward Title 18A, were also very favorable. Seventy-eight percent were "in favor" at Time 2 and 83 percent at Time 3.

TABLE 2

ATTITUDES OF PHYSICIANS TOWARD MEDICARE (TITLE 18A) AT TIME 1, TIME 2, AND TIME 3[a]

	Time 1	*Time 2*	*Time 3*
Favor	38%	70%	81%
Strongly		38	45
Somewhat		31	33
Don't know, no answer		1	3
Oppose	54	26	19
Strongly		14	10
Somewhat		11	9
Don't know, no answer		1	*
Don't know, no answer	8	5	*
	100%	101%	100%
Weighted totals	(18,044)	(10,214)	(4,954)
Unweighted totals	(1,205)	(676)	(331)

[a] At Time 1, the question was: "What is your opinion about the bill that would provide for compulsory health insurance through Social Security to cover hospital costs for those over 65—are you personally in favor of such a plan, or are you opposed to it?" Respondents were not asked whether they were "strongly" or "somewhat" in favor or opposed at Time 1. At Time 2, the questions were: "What is your opinion of Part A of Medicare—the part that provides for compulsory health insurance through Social Security to cover hospital costs for those over 65—are you personally in favor of this plan, or opposed to it?" "Would you say strongly (in favor) (opposed) or somewhat (in favor) (opposed)?" At Time 3 the words "Part A of Title 18" were substituted for the words "Part A of Medicare."
* Less than 0.5 percent.

stronger impact than experience of the physicians with the program implemented by the law.[14] What can be asserted, however, is that the law itself had

[14] The effect of an experimental variable on a group is limited by the initial frequency giving a certain response before exposure to that variable. Since the percentage in favor of Medicare is higher at Time 2 than at Time 1, there is "less room" for an increase in the percentage in favor between Time 2 and Time 3 than between Time 1 and Time 2. The statistical effect of this "ceiling" may be "corrected" by dividing the actual percentage difference by the maximum possible increase. Hovland et al. (1949: 285–89) call such a measure the "effectiveness index." Such an index for the Time 1-Time 2 change is .52 [(70–38)/(100–38) = .52]. For the Time 2-Time 3 change it is .37[(81–70)/(100–70) = .37]. The fact that the Time 1-Time 2 index is larger than the Time 2-Time 3 measure indicates that the larger increase in the percentage of those in favor of Medicare between Time 1 and Time 2 than between Time 2 and Time 3 cannot be explained away as being entirely due to a statistical ceiling effect.

There is another type of ceiling effect, this one due to *selection.* Those still opposed to Medicare at Time 2 are likely to include a higher proportion of "hard-core" opponents of Medicare than those opposed at Time 1. We found, however, that the Time 2 opponents of Medicare were no more conservative on other measures of political ideology at Time 1 than the Time 1 opponents.

The study design has a limitation, too. Since it provides for only one measure of the physicians' attitudes after the law was passed and before its implementation, it is not possible to assess the effect of time alone. It is possible that the change in attitude toward Medicare between Time 2 and Time 3 is a function of time alone and has nothing to do with the implementation of the program. As a matter of fact, the "transition probabilities" between Time 2 and Time 3 are the same as those between Time 1 and Time 2.

TABLE 3
ATTITUDES OF PHYSICIANS TOWARD MEDICARE (TITLE 18A) AT TIME 2 AND TIME 3 BY THEIR ATTITUDES AT TIME 1

	TIME 1 ATTITUDE TOWARD MEDICARE			
	Favor		*Oppose*	
Time 2 attitude toward Medicare				
Favor		90%		59%
Strongly	59		25	
Somewhat	30		33	
Don't know, no answer	1		1	
Oppose		11		40
Strongly	5		22	
Somewhat	6		16	
Don't know, no answer	0		2	
		101%		99%
Weighted totals	(3,757)		(5,098)	
Unweighted totals	(193)		(411)	
Time 3 attitude toward Medicare				
Favor		98%		70%
Strongly	84		19	
Somewhat	10		48	
Don't know, no answer	4		3	
Oppose		2		30
Strongly	*		17	
Somewhat	2		13	
Don't know, no answer	0		*	
		100%		100%
Weighted totals	(1,877)		(2,787)	
Unweighted totals	(95)		(213)	

* Less than 0.5 percent.

a large effect on physicians' attitudes toward Medicare even before it was implemented.

The Effects of Implementation on Attitudes. Consistent with the increase in the level of physicians' support for Medicare between Time 2 and Time 3 is the fact that they were less worried about the consequences of Medicare at Time 3 than at Time 2. Their earlier fears simply did not materialize.[15]

For example, the proportion who thought that the quality of care physicians

[15] Clark (1953: 47–50) reports a similar pattern in cases of desegregation.

give their elderly patients would be "not as good" under Medicare dropped from percent at Time 2 to 8 percent at Time 3 (see Table 4). The proportion who thought there would be "a great deal" or "a fair amount" of unnecessary hospitalization under Medicare dropped from 69 percent at Time 2 to 38 percent at

TABLE 4

PERCEIVED EFFECTS OF MEDICARE (TITLE 18A) AT TIME 2 AND AT TIME 3

	Time 2	*Time 3*
Weighted totals	(10,214)	(4,954)
Unweighted totals	(676)	(331)
In your opinion, how will Medicare (Title 18) affect the *quality* of care doctors give their elderly patients—in general, will doctors give *better medical* care, or *not as good* care, or won't Medicare (Title 18) make any difference?		
Better	14	30
Not as good	28	8
No difference	54	60
Don't know	5	2
	100%	100%
In your opinion, will there be a great deal of *unnecessary hospitalization* under Medicare (Title 18), or a fair amount, or very little, or none at all?		
Great deal	32	12
Fair amount	37	26
Very little	18	38
None at all	9	20
Don't know	4	4
	100%	100%
Will there be a great deal of *unnecessary* utilization of *doctors' services* under Medicare (Title 18), or a fair amount, or very little, or none at all?		
Great deal	39	8
Fair amount	38	28
Very little	15	39
None at all	4	20
Don't know	4	5
	100%	100%
In your opinion, will doctors *earn more* money under Medicare (Title 18) than before, or less money, or won't Medicare (Title 18) make any difference?		
More	35	42
Less	12	11
No difference	41	38
Don't know	12	9
	100%	100%

TABLE 4 (*cont'd*)

In your opinion, will the Federal Government, under Medicare (Title 18), interfere with the individual doctor's professional freedom—Would you say a great deal, or a fair amount, or very little, or not at all?		
Great deal	17	21
Fair amount	37	26
Very little	25	31
Not at all	15	16
Don't know	6	6
	100%	100%

Time 3 (27 percent thought there had actually been "a great deal" or "a fair amount" of unnecessary hospitalization up to Time 3). The proportion who thought there would be "a great deal" or "a fair amount" of unnecessary utilization of physicians' services under Medicare also dropped from 77 percent to 36 percent (25 percent thought there had actually been "a great deal" or "a fair amount" up to Time 3). It is only in the questions about government interference under Medicare and its effects on physicians' income that there were not significant changes, but only 12 percent at Time 2 and 11 percent at Time 3 thought that they would earn less money under Medicare than before, compared with more than a third who thought they would earn more money.[16]

Alternative Interpretations

Let us consider some alternative explanations of the large shifts in attitude toward Title 18A:

1. It could be argued that the changes described above could have taken place without the Medicare law and its implementation; that the shift in physicians' attitudes toward Medicare is part of a general, long-term liberal trend in their thinking. Obviously, there is not available a control group of physicians from whom the facts of the passage of the Medicare law and its implementation could be withheld. The argument that the changes in attitude toward Medicare are due to the law, however, is supported by the following observations:

a. The change in attitude toward Title 18A is a large change—from 38 percent in favor to 70 to 81 percent in a period of no longer than three years. It is not plausible to argue that this is due to a general ideological trend unrelated to the passage and implementation of Medicare.

b. The attitudes that do change are highly specific to Medicare. Physicians'

[16] There is no increase in the level of physicians' knowledge about the details of Medicare between Times 2 and 3—they are poorly informed at both times—and there is no association between their level of knowledge and the amount of experience with Medicare, on the one hand, and change in their attitude toward Medicare, on the other.

responses to questions indicating their position on economic-welfare issues, political party preference, group practice, and colleague controls, all of which strongly related to their attitudes toward Title 18A at Time 1 (Colombotos, 1968), are relatively stable at Time 1, Time 2, and Time 3 compared with their responses to the question on Medicare. If the change in attitudes toward Medicare was part of a more general trend in physicians' thinking and unrelated to the passage of Medicare, then one would expect changes in attitudes toward these other issues as well.

2. It could be argued that the increasingly favorable medical opinion about Medicare and the passage of the Medicare law were both the result or part of a third factor occurring immediately before Medicare was passed. Strong public support for Medicare, for example, could have influenced both medical and legislative opinion. Data in the present study from two independent samples of Manhattan doctors who were interviewed at two different times before Medicare was passed are inconsistent with such an argument. The first sample of 70 physicians was interviewed from January to April in 1964, about 18 months before Medicare was passed. The second sample of 61 physicians was interviewed from November, 1964, to March, 1965, scarcely six months before the law was passed. There was essentially no difference in the proportion in favor of Title 18A in the two samples—53 percent in the first sample, 57 percent in the second.

3. It is possible that New York State physicians' acceptance of Medicare after the enactment of the law was influenced by their opposition to the State's Medicaid program. The New York State implementation of Medicaid was one of the most liberal in the country. The first version of the New York State program was signed into law on April 30, 1966. The program was amended and curtailed two months later after strong opposition in upstate New York and threatened boycotts by county medical societies.

At Time 2, just after the first version of Medicaid was passed by the state legislature, 42 percent of the doctors interviewed said they were in favor of the law. At Time 3, despite, or perhaps because of, the fact the program had been curtailed six months earlier, it was still only 42 percent.

On all other questions about Medicaid asked at Time 3, it was less well received than Medicare:

a. Forty-six percent thought that the government would interfere "a great deal" with the individual physicians' professional freedom under Medicaid, compared with 21 percent for Medicare.

b. Fifty-nine percent thought that the State Medical Society should cooperate with the Government on Medicaid, compared with 91 percent on Medicare.

c. Fifty-five percent said they planned to accept or had already accepted patients under Title 19, compared with all but one physician under Title 18B.

It could be argued that the opposition to Medicaid in New York State had a "contrast" effect on physicians' responses to Medicare; that Medicare looked better to physicians than it would have looked had Medicaid not been passed, and that this "contrast" inflated the size of the oppose-favor switchers on Medicare. For example, at the height of the furor over Medicaid in the state, one county medical society in an advertisement in *The New York Times* agreed to "co-operate" with the "Federal Medicare Law, which provides a sensible and reasonable plan of medical care for all people over 65 . . . ," but found it "impossible to cooperate with the implementation of this State law [Medicaid] . . . as it is presently proposed. . . ." (June 10, 1966: 36). It called Medicaid "socialized medicine."

There is no evidence of such a contrast effect in our data. Rather, among those physicians who opposed Title 18A at Time 1, those who were in favor of Medicaid at Time 2 and Time 3 were much more likely to switch and favor Title 18A than those who opposed Medicaid.[17]

4. It could be argued that the physicians' attitudes toward Medicare expressed at Time 1, before its passage, were superficial and equivocal, and merely reflected official AMA policy, and that once the program became law, physicians felt freer to express their "real" attitudes toward Medicare. But this argument misses the point that law may "legitimate" opinion. The fact that the Medicare program was not law is as significant a part of the social situation at Time 1 as the fact that it had become law at Time 2 and Time 3. One could just as plausibly argue for the superficiality of attitudes expressed after the law, because of a "band-wagon effect," as for the superficiality of attitudes expressed before the law.

As a matter of fact, neither the attitudes toward Medicare at Time 1 nor at Time 2 and Time 3 appear superficial. The sub-question on intensity of feeling was not asked at Time 1. In the Time 1 measure, however, less than 8 percent were "don't knows." Also, attitude toward Medicare at Time 1 was strongly related to other political questions and issues in the organization of medical practice, as noted above (Colombotos, 1968), which argues against its being superficial. In the Time 2 and 3 measures, the number of "don't knows" was even smaller than at Time 1: at Time 2, it was 5 percent, and at Time 3, it was less than 0.5 percent. Also, of those in favor, more than half responded they felt "strongly" in favor, rather than only "somewhat" in favor.

5. Finally, a number of methodological problems in panel surveys may be involved:

a. *Reinterview Effect.* It could be argued that the Time 1 interview generated an interest in Medicare, thus influencing physicians' responses in the Time 2 interview. We found no difference between the responses to selected questions, including the one on Medicare, obtained from the reinterviewed sample at Time 2 and from a control sample of 330 physicians not interviewed before.

b. *Change in the Interview Instrument,* specifically in the sequence of the questions. The items preceding the question on Medicare in the Time 2 interview were different from those in the Time 1 interview. We found no difference

---

[17] Another test of the effects of Medicaid on attitude change toward Title 18A would be to examine the problem in a state where physicians' attitudes toward Title 18A were similar to those in New York State, but where the Medicaid program did not arouse as much opposition as the one in New York State. Unfortunately, such data are not available.

between the responses obtained in two different versions of the interview at Time 2: one in which the repeat (retest) questions were mixed with new questions and one in which the repeat (retest) questions were asked first, followed by the new questions.

c. *Mortality Effect.* It could be argued that physicians in the panel not interviewed at Time 2 and Time 3 were less likely to be pro-Medicare than those who were interviewed. We found that physicians who could not be reinterviewed at Time 2 and Time 3 did not differ from those who were reinterviewed in either background characteristics or attitudes, including their attitude toward Medicare, expressed at Time 1.

Summary and Conclusions

Despite their opposition to Medicare before the law was passed in 1965, physicians are complying with the program. There may be individual instances of noncooperation, but they are rare, at least in New York State, and there has been no boycott in the sense of concerted noncompliance.

Consistent with their compliance with Medicare, a large number of physicians who were opposed to Medicare before it became law switched and accepted it after it became law. In New York State, the proportion in favor rose from 38 percent before the law was passed to 70 percent less than a year after it was passed, even before it was implemented, and once again to 81 percent six months after the program went into effect.[18] The first increase, from 38 to 70 percent, argues that for law to influence attitudes it does not necessarily have to change relevant behavior first. We have in physicians' response to Medicare a case in which attitudes adapted to the law even before it went into effect.

The ready accommodation, both in deed and in mind, of these physicians to Medicare contrasts sharply with their continuing opposition to Medicaid and, to take a more extreme example, with physician strikes, such as the one in Saskatchewan, Canada, in 1962, against the province's medical care program.

What accounts for such differences in response to a law? The following differences between Medicare and the New York State Medicaid law illustrate some of the conditions listed above and suggest others that promote the effectiveness of a law:

1. *The Content of the Program.* The direct impact on physicians' practice of Medicaid in New York State is much greater than that of Medicare.

a. The number of people covered under Medicare in the state (those 65 or over) is less than two million. Estimates in May, 1966, of the number eligible under Medicaid ranged from 3.5 to 7 million. Furthermore, the number covered by Medicaid could be increased by liberalizing the definition of eligibility.

---

[18] The proportion of private practitioners in favor of Medicare was higher in New York State than in the country as a whole before Medicare was passed (see Footnote 1). No post-Medicare data from a national sample of physicians are available, however. Note also that our New York State study sample excludes physicians on full-time salary, who are more likely to be politically liberal and in favor of Medicare than private practitioners. (For data supporting the latter point, see Lipset and Schwartz, 1966: 304).

b. The clients of Medicare are the aged and the program is based on the insurance principle. The clients of Medicaid are the "medically indigent" and the program is based on the welfare principle. Physicians may be more sympathetic to a program serving the medical needs of the aged through insurance than to a program serving the "(medically) indigent," classified with "welfare cases."

c. Medicaid provides more services than Medicare, including drugs, dental bills, and other services not covered by Medicare.

d. New York State's Medicaid affects the physicians' practice more directly than Medicare. Medicaid attempts to control the quality and cost of medical care: the quality, by establishing criteria for determining who can render care, thus limiting the free choice of physicians; and the cost, by paying physicians fixed fees rather than "usual and customary" charges. Medicare has attempted neither. The direct effects of Medicare on physicians' practice, as a matter of fact, are minimal. Somers and Somers (1967: 1) put it this way:

> The 1965 enactment of Medicare was heralded as "revolutionary." But, in fact, it was neither a sudden nor radical departure from the march of events in the organization and financing of medical care and government's growing participation. No existing institutions were overturned or seriously threatened by the new legislation. On the contrary, Medicare responded to the needs of the providers of care as well as those of the consumers. It was primarily a financial underpinning of the existing health care industry—with all that implies in terms of strengths and weaknesses.

As a matter of fact, Medicare supports the stability of physicians' income under Title 18B, without controlling their fees. As noted above, more than a third of New York State physicians interviewed thought that under Medicare physicians would earn more money than before, and only about 10 percent thought they would earn less; the remainder thought it would not make any difference.

Both in terms of consistency with their ideology and in terms of their self-interest, then, Medicare is more acceptable to New York State physicians than Medicaid.

2. *Degree of Popular Support.* Medicare was passed with overwhelming popular support. Two-thirds of the public were in favor of Medicare, according to a nationwide Gallup poll in January, 1965, six months before it was passed. The percentage was probably higher in New York State. In contrast, there was little awareness about Medicaid before it was passed, and there was strong opposition, particularly in upstate New York, from industry, farm organizations, and in the press, after the first version of the New York Medicaid law was passed in April, 1966.

3. *Medicare is the Same Throughout the Country, Whereas Medicaid Varies Greatly from State to State.* It is possible that the opposition of New York physicians to their state's Medicaid program, the most liberal in the country, is reinforced by their feeling "worse off" than their colleagues in other states where the Medicaid programs are not as ambitious. A plausible hypothesis, setting aside

regional and local differences in values that may or may not be congruent with a given law, is that a national law is more "legitimate" and more likely to be effectively complied with than a state or local law.[19]

Outside the area of medical care, public response in many parts of the country to statutes and judicial decisions requiring the desegration of schools and other institutions contrasts sharply with physicians' response to Medicare. The issues of desegregation and civil rights will not be taken up here in any detail, but some obvious differences between them and Medicare come to mind:

1. Despite the "American creed" and trends showing a reduction of prejudice and discrimination, at least up to 1964, "white racism" may be more firmly entrenched among large segments of the American public than the fear of government participation in health care among physicians.

2. The distributions of opposition to desegration and to Medicare are different. Social supports to segregationists are more widely available than social supports to physicians opposed to Medicare. The general public strongly supported Medicare, and it was the medical profession that was out of step.

3. Desegregation, like Medicaid, runs into a hodgepodge of inconsistent and contradictory local, state, and Federal laws concerning different facilities and institutions—schools, transportation, recreation, housing, employment, marriage. Some of these laws actually *prescribe* segregation. Consider a hypothetical situation in which some states had laws that made it illegal to provide hospitalization and medical care under the terms ultimately provided by the Federal Medicare law! [20]

Having established in this paper the fact that the passage and implementation of Medicare had a sharp effect in changing the attitudes of physicians toward the program, the next steps will be (1) to examine the *conditions* under which physicians make both short-term and long-term changes in their attitudes toward

---

[19] In terms of these conditions, the prospects of the plan that physicians struck against in Saskatchewan in 1962 were, in retrospect, not good: (1) the plan's impact on physicians' practice was much greater than Medicare's, providing for universal coverage for all residents in the province and a comprehensive range of services; (2) public opposition to the plan appeared to be stronger and better organized than the opposition to Medicare; and (3) it was a provincial, not a national plan.

[20] The effects of law on behavior and attitudes are interpretable in terms of cognitive dissonance theory. According to this theory, the greater the dissonance between an individual's continued opposition to a program, behaviorally and attitudinally, and other elements in his cognitive structure, the greater is the probability of his complying and accepting the program. If we conceive as elements in an individual's cognitive structures the passage of a law and the specific conditions for its effectiveness, then it follows that the more of these conditions that apply, the greater the dissonance and the greater the probability of compliance and attitudinal acceptance.

That part of the theory that focuses on the effects of compliance on attitude change and the conditions under which dissonance between these two elements is aroused, however, is not particularly relevant to our case, since we found a large shift in attitudes toward Medicare even before physicians had an opportunity to comply (unless planning to comply is seen as equivalent to complying). The effects of compliance on attitude change in terms of dissonance theory is explicitly applied to desegregation in Brehm and Cohen (1962: 269–85).

Medicare, (2) to examine the long-term effects of Medicare on physicians' attitudes toward the program and toward other related political and health care issues, and (3) to compare the long-term and short-term responses of physicians to Medicare and Medicaid. A fourth wave of interviews with our physician panel is being planned in 1970—five years after the passage of Medicare—to answer these questions.

1. The two major sets of conditions of individual change in attitudes toward Medicare we shall examine are attitude-structural and social-structural variables. The general assumption is that there is pressure toward both intrapersonal and interpersonal consistency. For example, among those opposed to Medicare before the law was passed, it is predicted that Democrats are more likely to change their attitudes toward Medicare than Republicans; that physicians in areas where support for Medicare was initially strong are more likely to change than those in areas where support was weak; and that physicians who perceive themselves as having different opinions from their colleagues are more likely to change than those who see themselves as being in agreement. Other variables such as physicians' knowledge about Medicare, their experience with it, and their perceptions of its effects on their practice will also be studied as conditions of change in their attitudes toward Medicare.

2. a. The short-term effects of the Medicare law and program on physicians' attitudes toward it were indeed dramatic. What will be the long-term effects—five years later? Will opposition to Medicare continue to wither away, or will it stiffen?

b. We have found that the Medicare law had little short-term effect on physicians' attitudes toward other related political and health care issues. The stability of these attitudes, as a matter of fact, was offered to support the argument that the change in attitude toward Medicare was indeed an effect of the Medicare law and program rather than a part of a more general liberal trend in physicians' thinking. Katz observes that "it is puzzling that attitude change seems to have slight generalization effects, when the evidence indicates considerable generalization in the organization of a person's beliefs and values" (Katz, 1960: 199). But our results, and Katz' observation, refer to the short-run. It is plausible to expect that a change in one part of an attitude structure will produce changes in other parts of the structure, but the generalization of change *may not take place immediately.* It may take some time for the structure to become reintegrated. Will physicians' acceptance of Medicare make them more liberal in the longer run in their thinking about political issues and about changes in the organization of medical practice, or will it make them more conservative and resistant to such changes, or will it simply have no effects? [21]

---

[21] Note that "short-term" and "long-term" in attitude change research mean quite different things depending on the perspective of the investigator and the design used. In experimental studies, "short-term" effects are measured within minutes, hours, or at most, a few days after the introduction of the experimental variable; "long-term" effects usually mean no more than a few weeks later. In panel surveys, the time intervals are longer.

3. In contrast to the ready acceptance of Medicare, physicians continued to oppose Medicaid in New York State nearly a year after it was implemented. How will they feel four years later? What will be the conditions under which physicians make long-term changes in their attitudes toward Medicaid, and how will these conditions differ from those that distinguish changers and non-changers on Medicare? A comparison of the dynamics of the short-term and long-term responses of physicians to Medicare and Medicaid represents a modest test of the conditions under which laws influence behavior and attitudes.

REFERENCES

Allport, Gordon W. 1954. *The Nature of prejudice.* Cambridge, Mass.: Addison-Wesley Publishing Co.

Badgley, Robin F. and Samuel Wolfe. 1967. *Doctors' strike, medical care and conflict in Saskatchewan.* New York: Atherton Press.

Ball, Harry V., George Eaton Simpson and Kiyoshi Ideda. 1962. Law and social change: Sumner reconsidered. *American Journal of Sociology* 67 (March): 532–40.

Berger, Morroe. 1954. *Equality by statute.* New York: Columbia University Press.

Berkowitz, Leonard and Nigel Walker. 1967. Laws and moral judgments. *Sociometry* 30 (December): 410–22.

Bonfield, Arthur Earl. 1965. The role of legislation in eliminating racial discrimination. *Race* 7 (October): 108–09.

Brehm, Jack W. and Arthur R. Cohen. 1962. *Explorations in cognitive dissonance.* New York: John Wiley and Sons.

Campbell, Ernest Q. 1958. Some social psychological correlates of direction in attitude change. *Social Forces* 36 (May): 335–40.

Cantril, Hadley. 1947. *Gauging public opinion.* Princeton: Princeton University Press.

Clark, Kenneth (issue ed.) 1953. Desegregation: an appraisal of the evidence. *The Journal of Social Issues* 9: 47–50.

Colombotos, John. 1968. Physicians' attitudes toward Medicare. *Medical Care* 6 (July–August): 320–31.

———. 1969a. Physicians' attitudes toward a county health department. *American Journal of Public Health* 59 (January): 53–59.

———. 1969b. Social origins and ideology of physicians: a study of the effects of early socialization. *Journal of Health and Social Behavior* 10 (March): 16–29.

Deutsch, Morton and Mary E. Collins. 1951. *Interracial housing: a psychological evaluation of a social experiment.* Minneapolis: University of Minnesota Press.

Deutscher, Irwin. 1966. Words and deeds. *Social Problems* 13 (Winter): 235–54.

Dicey, Albert Venn. 1914. *Law and opinion in England during the nineteenth century.* Second Edition, London: Macmillan and Co., Ltd. [Printing used, 1963]

Evans, William M. 1965. Law as an instrument of social change. Pp. 291–92 in A. W. Gouldner and S. M. Miller (eds.), *Applied sociology.* New York: The Free Press.

Feingold, Eugene. 1966. *Medicare: Policy and politics.* San Francisco, Cal.: Chandler Publishing Co.

Harris, Richard. 1966. *A sacred trust.* New York: The New American Library.

Hovland, Carl I., Arthur A. Lumsdaine and Fred D. Sheffield. 1949. *Experiments on mass communication, vol. III, studies in social psychology in World War II.* Princeton: Princeton University Press.

Hyman, Herbert H. and Paul B. Sheatsley. 1964. Attitudes toward desegregation. *Scientific American* 211 (July): 6.

Katz, Daniel. 1960. The functional approach to the study of attitudes. *Public Opinion Quarterly* 24 (Summer): 163–204.

Killian, Lewis M. 1958. *The Negro in American society.* Florida State University Studies, No. 28: 65–70.

Kutner, Bernard, Carol Wilkins and Penney B. Yarrow. 1952. Verbal attitudes and overt behavior involving racial prejudice. *Journal of Abnormal and Social Psychology* 47: 649–52.

LaPiere, Richard T. 1934. Attitudes vs. actions. *Social Forces* 13 (March): 230–37.

Lipset, Seymour Martin and Mildred A. Schwartz. 1966. The politics of professionals. Pp. 299–310 in Howard M. Vollmer and Donald L. Mills, eds., *Professionalization.* Englewood Cliffs, New Jersey: Prentice-Hall.

MacIver, Robert M. 1948. *The more perfect union.* New York: Macmillan.

———. 1954. Foreword. P. viii in Morroe Berger, *Equality by statute.* New York: Columbia University Press.

Mayhew, Leon H. 1968. *Law and equal opportunity.* Cambridge, Massachusetts: Harvard University Press.

Muir, William K., Jr. 1967. *Prayer in the public schools: law and attitude change.* Chicago: The University of Chicago Press.

Mussen, Paul H. 1950. Some personality and social factors related to changes in children's attitudes toward Negroes. *Journal of Abnormal and Social Psychology* 45 (July): 423–41.

Myrdal, Gunnar. 1944. *An American dilemma.* New York: Harper and Row.

New York State Journal of Medicine. 1965. Editorial. Vol. 65 (November 15): 2779.

Opinions about Negro infantry platoons in white companies of seven divisions. 1952. P. 502 in Guy E. Swanson et al. eds., *Readings in social psychology.* New York: Holt.

Pound, Roscoe. 1944. *The task of law.* Lancaster, Pa.: Franklin and Marshall College.

Roche, John P. and Milton M. Gordon. 1955. Can morality be legislated? *New York Times Magazine* (May 22): 10, 42, 44, 49. In Kimball Young and Raymond W. Mack eds., *Principles of sociology: a reader in theory and research.* New York: American Book Co., 1966.

Rose, Arnold M. 1959. Sociological factors in the effectiveness of projected legislative remedies. *Journal of Legal Education* 11: 470–81.

———. 1967. *The power structure: political processes in American society.* New York: Oxford University Press. Chap. xii, pp. 400–55, "The passage of legislation: the politics of financing medical care for the aging."

Saenger, Gerhart and Emily Gilbert. 1950. Customer reactions to the integration of Negro sales personnel. *International Journal of Opinion and Attitude Research* 4 (Spring): 57–76.

Schwartz, Mildred A. 1967. *Trends in white attitudes toward Negroes.* Chicago: National Opinion Research Center, University of Chicago.

Scott, John Finley and Lois Heyman Scott. 1968. They are not so much anti-Negro as pro-middle class. *The New York Times Magazine* (March 24): 46 ff.

Somers, Herman M. and Anne R. Somers. 1967. *Medicare and the hospitals: issues and prospects.* Washington, D.C.: The Brookings Institution.

Sumner, William Graham. 1906. *Folkways.* New York: The New American Library [Printing used, 1960].

Walker, Nigel and Michael Argyle. 1964. Does the law affect moral judgments? *British Journal of Criminology* 5: 570–81.

Yarrow, Marion Radke. 1958. Interpersonal dynamics in a desegregation process. Special Issue. *Journal of Social Issues,* 14.

Young, Kimball and Raymond W. Mack. 1960. *Principles of sociology: a reader in theory and research.* New York: American Book Company.

22

Postdecision Dissonance at Post Time

ROBERT E. KNOX · JAMES A. INKSTER

Much of the attitude-behavior research in social psychology focuses on the question of consistency. That is, do people behave in accord with their attitudes? One of the most common theoretical perspectives for examining the attitude-behavior relationship today is dissonance theory. This perspective emphasizes the linkages between attitudes and/or beliefs and behavior in decision situations. The significance of the decision situation is that minimally the actor is faced with two alternative courses of behavior and he has some attitudes and beliefs consistent with both the alternatives. Dissonance theory predicts that the actor will decide on the alternative with which most of his attitudes and beliefs are consistent. But when a person commits himself to a decision, what happens to his attitudes toward that alternative? Do they remain comparable to what they were before the decision was made, or do they undergo change. Dissonance theory predicts that attitudes toward the alternatives foregone will become less favorable after a decision is made and that attitudes toward the chosen alternative will become more favorable.

In the reading that follows, Knox and Inkster report the results of two ingenious field experiments designed to evaluate attitude change in small bettors at a race track. The researchers asked bettors what chance they thought the horse they were about to bet on had of winning the race. The general response (based on a rating scale) was that the horse had a *fair* chance to win. Another sample of bettors who had already placed their bets were asked a similar question. The average response was that their horse had a *good* chance to win. Knox and Inkster conclude, therefore, that in a real life setting, dissonance reducing processes may occur very shortly after commiting oneself to a decision.

Robert E. Knox and James A. Inkster, "Postdecision Dissonance at Post Time," *Journal of Personality and Social Psychology* 8 (1968): 319–23.

In the last decade there have been numerous laboratory experiments conducted to test various implications of Festinger's (1957) theory of cognitive dissonance. In spite of sometimes serious methodological faults (cf. Chapanis & Chapanis, 1964), the laboratory evidence as a whole has tended to support Festinger's notions. Confidence in the theory, as Brehm and Cohen (1962) had previously suggested, can now be further strengthened by extending empirical tests from lifelike to real life situations. The present study investigates the effects of postdecision dissonance on bettors in their natural habitat, the race track.

Festinger (1957) had originally contended that due to the lingering cognitions about the favorable characteristics of the rejected alternative(s), dissonance was an inevitable consequence of a decision. Subsequently, however, Festinger (1964) accepted the qualification that in order for dissonance to occur, the decision must also have the effect of committing the person. A favorite technique for reducing postdecisional dissonance, according to the theory, is to change cognitions in such a manner as to increase the attractiveness of the chosen alternative relative to the unchosen alternative(s). At the race track a bettor becomes financially committed to his decision when he purchases a parimutuel ticket on a particular horse. Once this occurs, postdecisional processes should operate to reduce dissonance by increasing the attractiveness of the chosen horse relative to the unchosen horses in the race. These processes would be reflected by the bettor's expression of greater confidence in his having picked a winner after his bet had been made than before.

In order to test this notion, one need only go to a race track, acquire a prebet and postbet sample, and ask members of each how confident they are that they have selected the winning horse in the forthcoming race. The two samples should be independent since the same subjects in a before-after design could contravene the observed effects of dissonance reduction by carrying over consistent responses in the brief interval between pre- and postmeasurements. In essence, this was the approach employed in the two natural experiments reported here. More formally, the experimental hypothesis in both experiments was that bettors would be more confident of their selected horse just after betting $2 than just before betting.

Experiment I

Subjects

Subjects were 141 bettors at the Exhibition Park Race Track in Vancouver, British Columbia. Sixty-nine of these subjects, the prebet group, were interviewed less than 30 seconds *before* making a $2 Win bet. Seventy-two subjects, the postbet group, were interviewed a few seconds after making a $2 Win bet. Fifty-one subjects, interviewed before the fourth and fifth races, were obtained in the exclusive Clubhouse section. Data from the remaining 90 bettors were collected prior to the second, third, sixth, and seventh races at various betting locations in the General Admission or grandstand area.

No formal rituals were performed to guarantee random sampling, but instead, every person approaching or leaving a $2 Win window at a time when the experimenters were not already engaged in an interview was contacted. Of those contacted, approximately 15 percent refused to cooperate further because they could not speak English, refused to talk to "race touts," never discussed their racing information with strangers, or because of some unexpressed other reason. The final sample consisted of white, Negro, and Oriental men and women ranging in estimated age from the early twenties to late sixties and ranging in style from ladies in fur to shabby old men. The final sample was felt to be reasonably representative of the Vancouver racetrack crowd.

Procedure

The two experimenters were stationed in the immediate vicinity of the "Sellers" window during the 25-minute betting interval between races. For any given race, one experimenter intercepted bettors as they approached a $2 Win window and the other experimenter intercepted different bettors as they left these windows. Prebet and postbet interview roles were alternated with each race between the two experimenters.

The introductory appeal to subjects and instructions for their ratings were as follows:

> I beg your pardon. I am a member of a University of British Columbia research team studying risk-taking behavior. Are you about to place a $2 Win bet? [Have you just made a $2 Win bet?] Have we already talked to you today? I wonder if you would mind looking at this card and telling me what chance you think the horse you are going to bet on [have just bet on] has of winning this race. The scale goes from 1, a slight chance, to 7, an excellent chance. Just tell me the number from 1 to 7 that best describes the chance that you think your horse has of winning. Never mind now what the tote board or professional handicappers say; what chance do *you* think your horse has?

It was, of course, sometimes necessary to give some of the subjects further explanation of the task or to elaborate further on the cover story for the study.

The scale, reproduced here in Figure 1, was prepared on 8½ × 11-inch posterboard. The subjects responded verbally with a number or, in some cases, with the corresponding descriptive word from the scale.

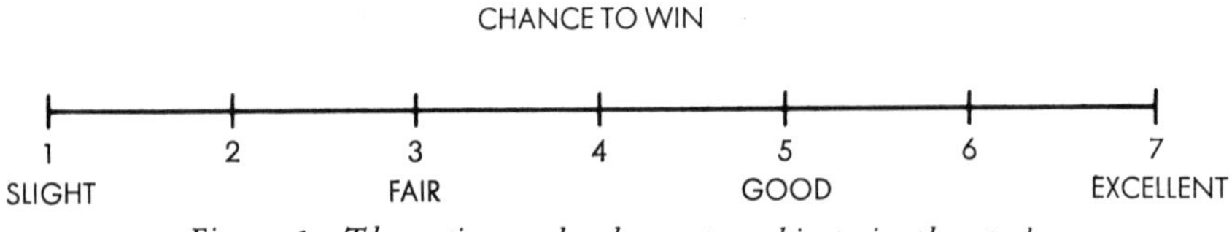

Figure 1 The rating scale shown to subjects in the study

After each prebet rating the experimenter visually confirmed that his subject proceeded directly to a $2 Win window. In the few instances that subjects did wander elsewhere, their data were discarded. No effort was made to collect data in the 3 frantic minutes of betting just prior to post time.

Results

Since no stronger than ordinal properties may be safely assumed for the rating scale, nonparametric statistics were employed in the analysis. Several χ^2 approximations of the Kolmogorov-Smirnov test (Siegel, 1956) were first performed to test for distributional differences between the ratings collected by the two experimenters. For prebet ratings ($\chi^2 = .274$, $df = 2$, $p > .80$) and for the combined pre- and postbet ratings ($\chi^2 = 2.16$, $df = 2$, $p > .30$) the differences in the two distributions may be considered negligible according to these tests. Distributional differences on postbet rating ($\chi^2 = 3.14$, $df = 2$, $p > .20$) were greater but still did not meet even the .20 probability level.[1] On the basis of these tests the two experimenters were assumed to have collected sufficiently comparable ratings to justify pooling of their data for the subsequent test of the major hypothesis of the study.

The median for the 69 subjects in the prebet group was 3.48. In qualitative terms they gave their horse little better than a "fair" chance of winning its race. The median for the 72 subjects in the postbet group, on the other hand, was 4.81.

TABLE 1
DIVISION OF SUBJECTS WITH RESPECT TO THE OVERALL MEDIAN FOR THE PREBET AND POSTBET GROUPS: EXPERIMENT I

	Prebet group	*Postbet group*
Above the *Mdn*	25	45
Below the *Mdn*	44	27

They gave their horse close to a "good" chance in the race. The median test for the data summarized in Table 1 produced a χ^2 of 8.70 ($df = 1$), significant beyond the .01 level.

These results, in accord with our predictions from dissonance theory, might also have arisen, however, had a substantial number of bettors simply made last-minute switches from relative long shots to favorites in these races. Although this possibility was not pursued with the above sample of subjects, two follow-up inquiries on another day at the same race track indicated that the "switch to favorites" explanation was unlikely. The first of these inquiries involved 38 $2

[1] The χ^2 approximation for Kolmogorov-Smirnov is designed for one-tailed tests, whereas the hypothesis tested here is nondirectional. However, since the differences were insignificant by a one-tailed test they would necessarily be insignificant by the two-tailed test.

bettors who were contacted prior to the first race and merely asked if they ever changed their mind about which horse to bet on in the last minute or so before actually reaching a Sellers window. Nine of the 38 indicated that they sometimes changed, but among the 9 occasional changers a clear tendency to switch to long shots rather than to favorites was reported. Additional evidence against a "switch to favorites" explanation was obtained from a sample of 46 bettors for whom the prebet procedure of Experiment I was repeated. Each of these bettors was then contacted by a second interviewer just as he was leaving the $2 Win window and asked if he had changed to a different horse since talking to the first interviewer. All 46 responded that they had not changed horses in midinterviews.

In order to investigate the robustness of the findings in Experiment I a second study was undertaken which was like the first study in its essentials but employed different experimenters, a different response scale, and a different population of subjects. It also provided for a test of the "switch to favorites" explanation among subjects in a postbet group.

Experiment II

Subjects and Procedure

Ninety-four subjects were interviewed at the Patterson Park Harness Raceway in Ladner, British Columbia. Forty-eight of these subjects, the prebet group, were interviewed prior to the first six races as they approached one of the track's four $2 Win windows. This contact was usually completed just a few seconds before the subject actually reached the window to make his bet, but occasionally, when the betting lines were long, up to ¾ minute elapsed between interview and bet. Forty-six subjects, the postbet group, were interviewed a few seconds after leaving one of the $2 Win windows. As in Experiment I, all persons approaching or leaving a $2 Win window at a time when the experimenters were not already engaged were contacted. Of those contacted, fewer than 10 percent refused to cooperate, thus producing a heterogeneous and, presumably, representative sample of $2 Win bettors.

The overall design was the same as in the first study. Two experimenters, different from those who interviewed bettors in Experiment I, were located in the immediate area of the Sellers windows. One of these experimenters would intercept bettors as they approached a $2 Win window and the other intercepted different bettors as they left a $2 Win window. The prebet and postbet interview roles were alternated between the two experimenters as in the first study.

After a brief introductory preamble, the experimenter established whether a bettor was about to make a $2 Win bet (or had just made such a bet) and whether he had been previously interviewed. The experimenters proceeded only with those $2 bettors who had not already provided data. These subjects were then asked to indicate on a 23-centimeter scale how confident they felt that they had picked the winning horse. The mimeographed response scales were labeled with the words "No confidence" at the extreme left and "Complete confidence" at the extreme right. Although no other labels were printed on the scale, the experimenters made explicit that mild confidence would fall in the middle of the scale and ". . . the more confident that a person felt, the further along he should put his mark on the scale." When subjects indicated understanding, they were handed a pencil and a mimeographed scale and directed to ". . . just draw a line across the point in the scale that best corresponds to your own confidence." All bettors in the postbet sample were also asked if they changed their mind about which horse to bet while waiting in line or while on the way to the window.

Within the limits permitted by extremely crowded conditions, the prebet experimenter visually confirmed that subjects in his sample proceeded to a $2 Win window. Data collection was suspended during the last minute before post time.

Confidence scores for each subject were determined by laying a ruler along the 23-centimeter scale and measuring his response to the nearest millimeter.

TABLE 2
DIVISION OF SUBJECTS WITH RESPECT TO THE OVERALL MEDIAN FOR THE PREBET AND POSTBET GROUPS: EXPERIMENT II

	Prebet group	*Postbet group*
Above the *Mdn*	19	28
Below the *Mdn*	29	18

Results

On the strength of insignificant Kolmogorov-Smirnov tests for distributional differences between ratings collected by the two experimenters, data from the two experimenters were combined to test the major hypothesis of the study. The median rating for the 48 subjects in the prebet group was 14.60, and for the postbet group it was 19.30. The median test for these data, summarized in Table 2, produced a χ^2 of 4.26 ($df = 1$), significant at less than the .05 level.

Since data in Experiment II might reasonably be assumed to satisfy interval scale assumptions, a t test between pre- and postbet means was also performed. The difference between the prebet mean of 14.73 and the postbet mean of 17.47 was also significant ($t = 2.31$, $p < .05$).

No subject in the postbet sample indicated that he had changed horses while waiting in line or, if there were no line, just before reaching the window.

Discussion

These studies have examined the effects of real life postdecisional dissonance in the uncontrived setting of a race track. The data furnished by two relatively heterogeneous samples of bettors strongly support our hypothesis derived from

Festinger's theory. The reaction of one bettor in Experiment I well illustrates the overall effect observed in the data. This particular bettor had been a subject in the prebet sample and had then proceeded to the pari-mutuel window to place his bet. Following that transaction, he approached the postbet experimenter and volunteered the following:

> Are you working with that other fellow there? [indicating the prebet experimenter who was by then engaged in another interview] Well, I just told him that my horse had a fair chance of winning. Will you have him change that to a good chance? No, by God, make that an excellent chance.

It might reasonably be conjectured that, at least until the finish of the race, this bettor felt more confortable about his decision to wager on a horse with an excellent chance than he could have felt about a decision to wager on a horse with only a fair chance. In the human race, dissonance had won again.

The results also bear upon the issue of rapidity of onset of dissonance-reducing processes discussed by Festinger (1964). On the basis of an experiment by Davidson described in that work, Festinger argued that predecisional cognitive familiarity with the characteristics of alternatives facilitated the onset of dissonance reduction. It is reasonable to assume that most bettors in the present studies were informed, to some extent, about the virtues and liabilities of all the horses in a race before making a $2 commitment on one. Since never more than 30 seconds elapsed between the time of commitment at the window and confrontation with the rating task, the present results are consistent with the notion that the effects of dissonance reduction can, indeed, be observed very soon after a commitment is made to one alternative, providing that some information about the unchosen alternatives is already possessed. Furthermore, the exceedingly short time span here suggests that the cognitive reevaluation process could hardly have been very explicit or as deliberate as conscious rationalization.

Finally, these studies, like the earlier Ehrlich, Guttman, Schonbach, and Mills (1957) study which showed that recent new car buyers preferred to read automobile advertisements that were consonant with their purchase, demonstrate that meaningful tests of dissonance theory can be made in the context of real life situations. Insofar as real life studies are unaffected by contrived circumstances, improbable events, and credibility gaps, they may offer stronger and less contentious support for dissonance theory than their laboratory counterparts. It is also clear that such studies will help to define the range of applicability of the theory in natural settings.

REFERENCES

Brehm, J. W., & Cohen, A. R. 1962. *Explorations in cognitive dissonance.* New York: Wiley.

Chapanis, N. P., & Chapanis, A. 1964. Cognitive dissonance: Five years later. *Psychological Bulletin* 61: 1–22.

Ehrlich, D., Guttman, I., Schonbach, P., & Mills, J. 1957. Postdecision exposure to relevant information. *Journal of Abnormal and Social Psychology* 54: 98–102.
Festinger, L. 1957. *A theory of cognitive dissonance.* Evanston, Ill.: Row, Peterson.
———. *Conflict, decision, and dissonance.* 1964. Stanford, Calif.: Stanford University Press.
Siegel, S. 1956. *Nonparametric statistics for the behavioral sciences.* New York: McGraw-Hill.

Attitudes:

Putting It into Perspective

Few topics have received more attention from social psychologists than have attitudes. The focus has frequently been upon the *description* of the attitudes of particular populations about everything from toothpaste to sex. The implicit assumption in such studies is that a knowledge of a population's attitudes provides a basis for anticipating that population's future behavior. Other attitudinal research focuses on the processes of *attitude formation and change.* Researchers probe such queries as: How is it that children from different social classes come to hold different attitudes toward religion, politics, etc.? What distinguishes a successful from an unsuccessful propaganda campaign? Again, ultimately much of the concern with attitudes is linked to their assumed consequences for behavior. Further, social psychologists have developed a number of systematic and rather general *theories about the relationship between attitudes and behavior.* Much academic research has been devoted to testing and refining these theories, which subsequently have often provided bases for applied programs of attitude and/or behavior change. While these categories of attitudinal research are neither mutually exclusive nor exhaustive, they provide a reasonably accurate reflection of the major research foci.

In general, the descriptive work on attitudes has focused on major social issues of the time. For example, in the past many scholarly studies were published concerning attitudes toward Fascism, McCarthyism, democracy, unionization of workers, etc. More recently, the major attitude objects receiving attention include racial integration, the war in Southeast Asia, pollution of the environment, and sexism. Indeed, you will note that three of the four readings in this section concentrate on such socially significant topics—medicare, black-white relations, and sexism. Goldberg's study, "Are Women Prejudiced Against Women?", is illustrative of what we have called descriptive attitude research.

It is rare that social psychologists gather information about attitudes in order to simply "pass the word." Instead, their objectives generally take one of the following forms. On the one hand, the researcher may be attempting to identify the factors that lead different groups of people to hold different sets of attitudes. In research terminology, attitudes may constitute dependent variables, the causes of which are sought among plausible independent variables. On the other hand, the researcher may be describing the attitudes of his subjects in an attempt to predict their future behavior. In this instance, attitudes are employed as independent variables, with some behavior(s) constituting the dependent variable.

Perhaps this is an appropriate point to alert you to the fact that many efforts to predict behavior from a knowledge of attitudes have met with failure. This fact has, itself, led to a rather voluminous literature attempting to explain attitude-behavior discrepancies. The explanations generally fall into one of the following categories: measurement imprecision, conceptual confusion, or theoretical naïveté. In the first case, it is argued that the inability to predict behavior from attitudes is largely the result of inadequate measures of attitudes. In fact, research evidence indicates that the correspondence between attitudes and behaviors is higher when attitudes are measured by means of Likert Scales than when measured by Thurstone, Guttman, or Semantic Differential Scales. Even in these methodological studies, however, the link between attitude scores and behavior scores is typically quite weak. Therefore, factors other than measurement imprecision must be operating.

Some of our colleagues have suggested that the weak relationships reported between attitudes and behavior are a function of conceptual confusion surrounding the concept attitude. A long-standing debate continues concerning the nature of this concept. For example, are attitudes real phenomena or are they analytical constructs created for theoretical use in predicting other things? The more cynical of these critics suggest that it would be advantageous to scrap the concept attitude altogether.

It is our opinion that the most likely explanation for the frequent lack of correspondence between attitudes and behavior is theoretical naïveté. That is, some researchers seem to be of the opinion that they should be able to predict complex behavior patterns by means of a single independent variable—attitudes. In other areas of social psychology, single factor explanations were discarded years ago. We have found from our own research experience that when attitudes are incorporated as one of a number of independent variables in a prediction equation, they have predictive value.

Now, to return to our original objective of characterizing current attitudinal research. Social psychological inquiry into the formation and change of attitudes is linked to a number of key theoretical and practical issues. The formation of attitudes can be viewed as a specific instance of the more general processes of learning. Of course, learning the attitudes, beliefs, values, and behavior patterns of one's group(s) is referred to as socialization. Thus, the study of attitude formation may be carried out in the context of learning research or socialization research.

In the case of attitude change, the practical concern is with the behavioral consequences of attitudes. The generally untested assumption is that people behave in accord with their attitudes and beliefs. If this assumption is granted, the importance of determining the factors which can effectively produce changes in attitudes is obvious. By undertaking programs of attitude change, changes in personal and interpersonal relations can be produced. Many community organizations have been established on the premise that if members of different groups can "understand" each other, they will behave toward each other in a more civil manner. Of course, in the reading in this section by Colombotos, it was noted that changes in attitudes might be the result of changes in law and/or behavior.

The reader who wishes to pursue the topic of attitudes further will find that there are a number of theories dealing directly with the relationship between attitudes and behavior. The most popular of these in recent years has been Festinger's theory of cognitive dissonance. The research report in this section by Knox and Inkster, "Postdecision Dissonance at Post Time," examined some prediction from dissonance theory. Dissonance theory may be considered a special case of a more general category of theories referred to as balance or consistency theories. While they differ in detail, they are very similar in principle. In addition, many systematic theories about processes such as interpersonal attraction incorporate attitudes as major independent variables. Some of these theories will be discussed briefly in the section on *Interpersonal Attraction.*

Finally, social psychologists have developed highly sophisticated techniques for measuring attitudes. One might call attitude measurement a specialty within the area of attitudes. While we cannot characterize the frequently technical work in this area in a few brief paragraphs, we have provided some selective references to this literature in the *Suggestions for Further Reading.*

Suggestions for Further Reading

H. J. Ehrlich, "Attitudes, Behavior, and the Intervening Variables," *American Sociologist* 4 (1969): 29–34. A thoughtful examination of the link between attitudes and behavior. Theoretical explanations are offered for those cases where researchers report no relationship between attitudes and behavior.

Leon Festinger, *A Theory of Cognitive Dissonance.* Evanston, Illinois: Row, Peterson, 1957. The original statement of dissonance theory. A major work in social psychology.

Marie Jahoda and Neil Warren, editors, *Attitudes: Selected Readings.* Baltimore, Maryland: Penguin Books, 1966. A collection of papers representing the diversity in conceptualization, theory and research characterizing the study of attitudes.

C. A. Kiesler, B. E. Collins, and N. Miller, *Attitude Change: A Critical Analysis of Theoretical Approaches.* New York: John Wiley, 1969. The authors' critical evaluations provide the reader with considerable insight into the major theoretical approaches to attitude change. The book presupposes some knowledge of the attitude change literature on the part of the reader.

W. J. McGuire, "The Nature of Attitudes and Attitude Change." Pp. 136–314 in G. Lindzey and E. Aronson, editors, *The Handbook of Social Psychology,* Second Edition, Volume 3. Reading, Massachusetts: Addison-Wesley, 1969.

The student will find this a tedious piece, but for reference purposes, it is invaluable.

Milton Rokeach, *Beliefs, Attitudes, and Values.* San Francisco: Jossey-Bass, 1968. A collection of papers representing a critical examination of the differences and relationships among the concepts *beliefs, attitudes,* and *values.* A book that has great theoretical significance and is presented in a style that is relaxed and lucid.

P. G. Zimbardo and E. B. Ebbersen, *Influencing Attitudes and Changing Behavior.* Reading, Massachusetts: Addison-Wesley, 1969. A brief volume that holds the reader's attention because of its emphasis on the applications and implications of attitude change theory and research.

CHAPTER VI

Interpersonal Attraction

23 Elliot Aronson and Vernon Cope, *My Enemy's Enemy Is My Friend* · 307

24 Elaine Walster, Vera Aronson, Darcy Abrahams, and Leon Rottmann, *Importance of Physical Attractiveness in Dating Behavior* · 316

25 Milton Rokeach and Louis Mezei, *Race and Shared Belief as Factors in Social Choice* · 330

Putting It into Perspective · 343

Suggestions for Further Reading · 344

23

My Enemy's Enemy Is My Friend

ELLIOT ARONSON · VERNON COPE

A variety of responses have been framed for the question: Why do you like some people and don't like others? In the research report which follows, Aronson and Cope evaluate the very interesting proposition that people like those who punish their enemies and reward their friends.

There are actually a number of bases for this expectation. For example, if I observe someone punishing my enemy, I might assume that we dislike him for the same reason and, therefore, that we have common beliefs and attitudes. Considerable research evidence indicates that the more similar people are in their beliefs and attitudes, the more strongly they are attracted to each other. On the other hand, I might interpret the punishment of my enemy as indicative of this other person's liking for me. Other studies in attraction suggest that people come to like those whom they perceive to like them.

But are such mediating events as those specified above necessary for the proposition to hold? Aronson and Cope contend that they are not necessary and, consequently, structure their research design to eliminate the influence of such factors. The results of their investigation support their contention. Specifically, the data indicate that even in the absence of mediating phenomena, (a) we like others who like our friends; (b) we like others who dislike our enemies; (c) we dislike others who dislike our friends; and (4) we dislike others who like our enemies. Thus, as these authors state the matter, there is apparently something good about seeing one's enemy punished and one's friend rewarded—in and of itself, and that the observation of such behaviors on the part of a third party exerts a significant influence on the feelings that we develop for that person.

Elliot Aronson and Vernon Cope, "My Enemy's Enemy Is My Friend," *Journal of Personality and Social Psychology* 8 (1968): 8–12.

It makes sense to assume that, all other things being equal, if two people discover that they share a common enemy, their mutual attractiveness will increase. This proposition is a simple derivation from balance theory (Heider, 1958). But such a situation may consist of one or more underlying factors. For example, if I know nothing about the reason why another person dislikes my enemy, I might assume that we dislike him for the same reasons and, therefore, that we share similar beliefs and attitudes. Thus, suppose that Person *X*'s most outstanding characteristic is that he is a pompous ass, and I dislike him for it. If I learn that Person *Y* also dislikes *X*, I might assume that *Y* dislikes *X* for the same reason. A similarity of beliefs and attitudes has been shown to increase attractivenesss (Byrne, 1961; Newcomb, 1961). Accordingly, I might like *X* because I feel that we both dislike people who exhibit "pompous assiness." Second, I might believe that this other person dislikes my enemy because he knows that I dislike him. This would suggest that my enemy's enemy likes me. Since people generally like those who like them (Aronson & Linder, 1965; Backman & Secord, 1959), I might come to like him. Finally, this relationship may have certain concrete practical advantages. Specifically, if I dislike *X* and I discover that *Y* dislikes *X* also, I may feel that it is conceivable that *Y* and I might band together and beat *X* up or plot strategy against him or at least engage in some satisfying malicious gossip. Thus, I might like *Y* purely because he can do me some tangible good.

One may wonder whether the above criteria are essential for the phenomenon to occur. For example, suppose *X* behaved harshly to me. If *Y* behaved negatively to *X*, would I increase my liking for *Y* even if (*a*) he were unaware that *X* had behaved harshly toward me, (*b*) his nasty behavior toward *X* was inspired by a totally different set of events, and (*c*) there was no opportunity for us to socialize and commiserate? For example, if *X* had insulted me at a cocktail party, and 2 weeks later I noticed a police officer (*Y*) issuing a summons to *X* for a traffic violation, would that police officer become dear to my heart? The authors' guess is that he would. It is the authors' contention that Heider's proposition is a general one, not limited to such mediating events; that is, there is something good about seeing one's enemy punished—in and of itself. Consequently, it is predicted that individuals will like their enemy's punisher even if the two events are noncontingent and unrelated, that is, even if the punisher's behavior implies neither attitude similarity nor utility. By the same token, individuals will come to like a person who rewards someone who treated them kindly—even if the two events are noncontingent and unrelated.

Method

General Overview

The general procedure involved placing the subject in a situation in which he was treated either harshly or pleasantly by an experimenter and then allowing the subject to overhear the experimenter being treated either harshly or pleasantly by the latter's supervisor. The subject was then given an opportunity to express his feelings for the supervisor. It was obviously essential that the supervisor's evaluation of the experimenter be separate from and unrelated to the experimenter's evaluation of the subject.

Subjects and Design

The subjects were 40 male and 40 female introductory psychology students at the University of Texas. They were randomly assigned to one of four conditions designed to test the hypothesis: pleasant experimenter-pleasant supervisor, pleasant-experimenter-harsh supervisor, harsh experimenter-pleasant supervisor, harsh experimenter-harsh supervisor.[1]

Procedure

The subjects volunteered for participation in a study of creativity. When the subject arrived, the experimenter[2] led him into a cubicle and introduced himself as a graduate student who was assisting Dr. Cope in his creativity project. The experimenter explained that the purpose of the study was to determine the relationship between creativity and college performance. He informed the subject that he would present him with a series of three pictures and that the subject's task would be to write a story about each picture—what the situation is, what led to the situation, what the people are thinking or feeling, and what they will do. The subjects were told that they would have only 4 minutes to write each story.

After the subject had written a story, the experimenter silently read it and marked it with various coded grading signals. During his reading of each story and after the reading of all three stories, the manipulation of either pleasant experimenter or harsh experimenter was put into effect. In order to reduce opportunities for bias, the experimenter was kept ignorant of the condition in which the subject was to be run until this point in the experiment. This was determined randomly. When it was essential to ensure equal numbers of subjects per condition, the senior author determined the condition of each subject in advance and handed the experimenter a folded slip of paper before each subject was run. The slip contained the word "harsh" or "pleasant." After delivering the initial instructions and while the subject was writing the first story, the experimenter simply reached into his pocket, unfolded the paper, and determined the subject's condition. Thus, the initial instructions were delivered in ignorance of the subject's condition. At this point the manipulation commenced.

---

[1] In actuality, 86 subjects were run. Because of suspiciousness, 2 subjects were discarded in each of Conditions 2, 3, and 4, respectively.

[2] Two different experimenters were used in the experiment. They ran an equal proportion of subjects in all conditions; the results were not influenced by the identity of the experimenter.

Harsh condition. While he read each story, the experimenter occasionally emitted a displeased and condescending grunt, sigh, or grumble. After reading all three stories, the experimenter stated that although the final scoring was not completed and would take more time he would give the subject a tentative evaluation. He then proceeded to tell the subject that his stories were unimaginative and uncreative. The evaluation was given starkly and somewhat brutally, with no punches pulled. The experimenter acted as if he enjoyed making these negative statements.

Pleasant condition. In this condition the evaluation was essentially the same. The experimenter told the subject that although the final scoring was not completed and would take more time he would give the subject a tentative evaluation. He then told the subject that his stories were uncreative and unimaginative. But in this condition the experimenter treated the subject very gently. Specifically, he told him not to be too worried about it—that although the test was a good measure of creativity, it *was* only one test. In short, although the experimenter told the subject that according to his analysis of the test results the subject was uncreative, he let the subject down gently rather than harshly; he allowed the subject to save face.

A few seconds before the experimenter finished his evaluation, he casually leaned against the door of the testing room and rubbed his foot against the air vent. This served as a signal to the "supervisor" who, although waiting some distance from the door, was able to see it move. After waiting a few seconds, the supervisor knocked on the door, entered, excused himself for interrupting, told the experimenter that he must talk to him for a moment, and asked the experimenter to step into the hall. The experimenter stood up and introduced the supervisor to the subject. The supervisor shook hands with the subject and escorted the experimenter into the corridor.

Although they were careful to close the door behind them (so as not to arouse the subject's suspicions), the situation was such that the subject could easily overhear their conversation through the air vent at the bottom of the door.

At this point the second variable was manipulated: the supervisor's treatment of the experimenter. Half of the subjects were randomly assigned to the pleasant-supervisor condition, half were randomly assigned to the harsh-supervisor condition. The conversations in each condition are presented in that order below:

> I read that report you wrote for me, and, well, I think it's one of the finest analyses of the articles I've seen in a long, long time. In particular, I thought you made an excellent selection of references. I don't think I could have done a better job myself—and I know that area pretty well! Also, I think I'll make up another copy of your paper so I can show it to my other research assistants as an example of the sort of work I want from them and just as an example of good, creative work. Uh, I'm on my way to see the department chairman right now and, well, because I'm so impressed with the sort of work you've been doing here, I'm going to ask him if we can get you an increase in salary. Well, I have to run now so you can get back to your subject.

> I read that report you wrote for me, and I think it's, well, virtually worthless. It's sloppy and somewhat stupid. I can see no logical reason for using the

references you cited. They have absolutely no relevance to the topics you were supposed to write about. I have an idea you were just using those references as filler material. Well, there's a lot of irrelevant material, and the quality and the organization are both very poor. OK, I'm going to give you a couple of days to do it over. As a matter of fact, I'm on my way right now to see the department chairman, and I'm going to ask him if there's anyone else we have who could replace you if you continue to do bad work. OK, I've got to run now so you can get back to your subject.

After he had been "evaluated," the experimenter reentered the room with a gloomy face if he had been negatively evaluated and a smile if positively evaluated. He told the subject that that was all they had time for and instructed him to go upstairs to the psychology office where the secretary would give him credit for the experiment.

It should be noted that at the time the supervisor was acting either harshly or pleasantly to the experimenter, the supervisor was ignorant as to whether the experimenter had been pleasant or harsh to the subject. Similarly, while the experimenter was acting either pleasantly or harshly to the subject, the experimenter was unaware as to whether the supervisor was about to treat him pleasantly or harshly. Thus, since an interaction is being predicted, this technique of "partial ignorance" effectively guards against the systematic bias described by Rosenthal (1966). For a greater elaboration of the applicability of this partial ignorance technique, see Aronson and Carlsmith (1968).

Dependent variable. The dependent variable was administered by the departmental secretary who was, of course, ignorant of the subject's experimental condition. As she prepared to give the subject credit for participation in the experiment, she said that she had a request to make on behalf of the supervisor of the experiment the subject had just participated in. After ascertaining that the subject recalled having met the supervisor, she proceeded to tell him that he (Dr. Cope) was spending 1 year at the University to do research for the National Science Foundation. In regard to a different project he was directing, she continued, the National Science Foundation had recently informed him that he must use a different body of subjects taken from the local community instead of the college students he had been using as subjects. The result was that the supervisor needed hundreds of nonuniversity people within the next 2 weeks and that the job of contacting people and convincing them to volunteer was enormous. She said that the supervisor did not have the staff to do this work, and he could not afford to pay for it; he was really desperate and needed a favor. Specifically, he had requested that she ask anyone to help him by making phone calls. She said that she had a long list of several thousand phone numbers randomly selected from the Austin telephone directory. She asked:

Would you be willing to help Dr. Cope by making some phone calls and asking people to serve as subjects? Other people have volunteered to call anywhere from 2 to 50 people—would you be willing to help him out?

The number of phone calls served as the dependent variable, being a reflection of the positive feelings the subjects held for the supervisor.

After the subject made his decision, the secretary thanked him. She then handed him a short questionnaire which she introduced as a departmental questionnaire designed to determine the effectiveness and viability of the departmental requirement that all introductory psychology students serve as subjects. The significant item on the questionnaire was an evaluation of the experimenter. The secretary was ignorant of the subject's experimental treatment while she was soliciting his aid in making phone calls and administering the questionnaire. Thus, the inevitable minor variations in her tone and manner could not have had a systematic effect on the results.

After the subject completed the questionnaire, Dr. Cope entered the office and debriefed him. Because all of the subjects had received a rather negative evaluation, they were delighted to learn that the evaluation was preprogrammed rather than an accurate reflection of their creative ability.

Results and Discussion

Before presenting the primary data, it is necessary to determine if the major manipulation worked: Did the subjects like the harsh experimenter less than the pleasant experimenter? Recall that the subjects were asked to complete a series of rating scales which were introduced as a departmental questionnaire aimed at determining their reaction to the experiment. Included in this questionnaire was a direct evaluation of the experimenter: "How much did you enjoy working with the experimenter?" The results indicate that the manipulation was effective. Subjects were more favorably disposed to the experimenter in the pleasant conditions than in the harsh conditions ($p < .005$).[3]

The hypothesis was that the subject would like his enemy's enemy more than his enemy's friend, and that he would like his friend's friend better than his friend's enemy. Specifically, it was predicted that the subject would volunteer to make the most phone calls as a favor to the supervisor if the latter had acted either harshly to the experimenter who treated the subject harshly or pleasantly to the experimenter who had treated the subject kindly. The results are presented in Table 1. Inspection of the table reveals that the subjects were willing to make more phone calls for a supervisor who was his enemy's enemy than for one who was his enemy's friend. Similarly, subjects were willing to make more phone calls for a friend's friend than for a friend's enemy. The data were analyzed by analysis of variance (Table 2). The prediction is reflected in the interaction between the experimenter's behavior toward the subject and the supervisor's behavior toward the experimenter. The interaction is highly significant ($p < .005$). Separate con-

[3] A rather interesting serendipitous finding should be reported. Specifically, there was an interaction between the sex of the subject and the behavior of the supervisor as it affected the liking of the subject for the experimenter ($p < .005$). Generally, males tended to like the experimenter if he was pleasantly treated by the supervisor; females liked the experimenter better if he was harshly criticized by the supervisor, irrespective of how the experimenter behaved toward the subject. This may reflect a tendency for women to be more nurturant and/or less impressed by success than men.

TABLE 1
MEAN NUMBER OF PHONE CALLS VOLUNTEERED ON BEHALF OF SUPERVISOR

	SUPERVISOR	
E	*Harsh*	*Pleasant*
Harsh	12.1	6.2
Pleasant	6.3	13.5

TABLE 2
ANALYSIS OF VARIANCE

Source	MS	F
E's evaluation (A)	12.03	.12
Supervisor's evaluation (B)	8.53	.09
Sex of *S* (C)	122.00	1.26
Identity of *E* (D)	1.00	.01
A × B	816.40	8.42*
A × C	4.03	.04
A × D	140.83	1.45
B × C	48.13	.50
B × D	128.13	1.32
C × D	.40	.00
A × B × C	49.40	.51
A × B × D	25.20	.26
A × C × D	17.63	.18
B × C × D	.53	.00
A × B × C × D	143.00	1.47
Error	96.95	

* $p < .005$, $df = 1/64$.

trasts were performed between the harsh supervisor and the pleasant supervisor within the pleasant-experimenter condition and between the harsh supervisor and the pleasant supervisor within the harsh-experimenter condition. Both were significant ($p < .05$). As expected, there were no main effects due to the behavior of the experimenter or the behavior of the supervisor. Likewise, neither sex of the subject nor the identity of the person playing the role of experimenter affected the results to a significant degree.

The results, then, would seem to indicate that a person's hostility toward our enemy or pleasantness toward our friend is, in and of itself, sufficient to bring about an increase in our liking for him. In the present experiment, as far as the subject was concerned, the supervisor was unaware of the fact that the experimenter had been kind or unkind to the subject. Thus, the supervisor's treatment of the experimenter could in no way be construed as being caused by the experimenter's treatment of the subject. In addition, it was clear that the supervisor's reasons for being nice or nasty to the experimenter were unrelated to the subject's reasons for liking or disliking the experimenter. The subjects liked or disliked the experimenter because he was either kind or harsh during their encounter. On the other hand, the supervisor rewarded or punished the experimenter for his prior performance on a written report which had no relevance to the nature of the experimenter's behavior to the subject. Moreover, the vast difference in status between the subject and the supervisor made it extremely unlikely that the two would ever discuss their mutual feelings about the experimenter.

At the same time, it should be noted that all alternative explanations have not been ruled out. Although the subject and the supervisor clearly dislike the experimenter for different reasons, it is conceivable that the supervisor's negative evaluation of the experimenter could have had an effect on the impact of the experimenter's negative evaluation of the subject; that is, in the harsh-supervisor conditions, the supervisor told the experimenter that he wrote a poor report. This could imply that the experimenter is stupid and incompetent. If the subject had just received harsh criticism from a person, learning that he (that person) is stupid and incompetent could reduce the impact of this harsh treatment. Consequently, it is possible that the subject came to like the supervisor who treated the unpleasant experimenter harshly, not simply because we like people who punish our enemies, but, more specifically, because we like people who help us believe that a person who judged us harshly may be a stupid and incompetent person, and that, consequently, his harsh judgment may be erroneous. This alternative explanation is unlikely, however, because it is not symmetrical; that is, it does not apply in the pleasant experimenter-pleasant supervisor condition. Recall that, like the harsh experimenter, the pleasant experimenter rated the subject as uncreative—his manner was simply more pleasant as he made this negative evaluation of the subject. Consequently, when the pleasant supervisor implied that the pleasant experimenter was intelligent and competent, he was, in effect, offering support to the experimenter's evaluation of the subject as an uncreative person. In short, if we like someone because he questions the intelligence of someone who has recently judged us as uncreative, then we should have discovered a main effect due to the behavior of the supervisor. The fact that the data show a clear interaction and significant contrasts sharply reduces the plausibility of this alternative explanation.

The results suggest that balance theory applies in a behavioral context even in the absence of specific opinion similarity; that is, the data indicate that: (*a*) We like someone who likes someone that we like; (*b*) we like someone who dislikes someone we dislike; (*c*) we dislike someone who likes someone we dislike; and (*d*) we dislike someone who dislikes someone we like. This follows even though it is clear that the respective reasons for liking or disliking the target person are unrelated. The primary contribution of this experiment, then, is in the demonstration that the basic proposition of balance theory is true in a very general sense and is not limited to situations which are mediated by other phenomena, for example, by specific opinion similarity.

REFERENCES

Aronson, E., & Carlsmith, J. M. 1968. Experimentation in social psychology. In G. Lindzey & E. Aronson, eds., *Handbook of social psychology.* (Rev. ed.) Vol. 2. Reading, Mass.: Addison-Wesley.

Aronson, E., & Linder, D. 1965. Gain and loss of esteem as determinants of interpersonal attractiveness. *Journal of Experimental Social Psychology* 1: 156–71.

Backman, C. W., & Secord, P. F. 1959. The effect of perceived liking on interpersonal attraction. *Human Relations* 12: 379–84.

Byrne, D. 1961. Interpersonal attraction and attitude similarity. *Journal of Abnormal and Social Psychology* 62: 713–15.

Heider, F. 1958. *The psychology of interpersonal relations.* New York: Wiley.

Newcomb, T. M. 1961. *The acquaintance process.* New York: Holt, Rinehart & Winston.

Rosenthal, R. 1966. *Experimenter effects in behavioral research.* New York: Appleton-Century-Crofts.

24

Importance of Physical Attractiveness in Dating Behavior

ELAINE WALSTER · VERA ARONSON
DARCY ABRAHAMS · LEON ROTTMANN

One of the more interesting variants of interpersonal attraction is what can be called romantic attraction. The nature and determinants of romantic attraction have been subjects for poets, novelists, and philosophers throughout history, and in recent years, they have come under the scrutiny of social psychologists.

One variable that is commonly assumed to influence romantic attraction is physical attractiveness. But what is the nature of the relationship between physical attractiveness and romantic attraction? Is it the case that a person is most attracted romantically to another whom he perceives as most attractive physically? If a person sees himself as unattractive, will this influence the level of physical attractiveness that he will seek in a romantic partner?

These are some of the questions that Walster and her associates address in the following selection. Specifically, these researchers hypothesized that an individual would most often expect to date, would try to date, and would most like a partner of approximately his own social desirability. This prediction is based on level of aspiration theory which suggests that one's choice behavior is affected both by the objective desirability of the object and by one's perception of the possibility of attaining the object. An ingenious field study was designed to test the research hypothesis—a "Computer Dance." The data, however, failed to confirm the level of aspiration hypothesis. Regardless of a person's own physical attractiveness, the major determinant of how much he liked his partner, how much he wanted to date the partner again, and how often he actually asked the partner out was the physical attractiveness of the partner. A variety of personality measures failed to influence this relationship.

Elaine Walster, Vera Aronson, Darcy Abrahams, and Leon Rottmann, "Importance of Physical Attractiveness in Dating Behavior," *Journal of Personality and Social Psychology* 4 (1966): 508–16.

In one of his delightful articles Goffman (1952: 456) said that: "A proposal of marriage in our society tends to be a way in which a man sums up his social attributes and suggests to a woman that hers are not so much better as to preclude a merger or a partnership in these matters." Goffman's proposal suggests that one's romantic feelings and choices are affected both by the objective desirability of the romantic object and by one's perception of the possibility of attaining the affection of the other. Rosenfeld (1964) has demonstrated that an individual's choice of a *work partner* was affected by his assumptions about whether or not the partner would reciprocate his choice.

The following field experiment was conducted to see if one's romantic aspirations are influenced by the same factors that affect one's level of aspiration in other areas. (Level of aspiration theory is presented in Lewin, Dembo, Festinger, & Sears, 1944.) We wish to point out that this study concentrates on *realistic* social choices. In their discussion of *"ideal choices"* Lewin et al. conclude that an individual's ideal goals are usually based entirely on the desirability of the goal, with no consideration of the possibility of attaining this goal. Probably an individual's fantasy romantic choices are also based entirely on the desirability of the object. One's *realistic* level of aspiration, on the other hand, has been shown by Lewin et al. to depend both on the objective desirability of the goal and on one's perceived possibility of attaining that goal.

We propose that one's realistic romantic choices will be affected by the same practical considerations that affect other realistic goal setting. Lewin et al. note that since the attractiveness of a goal and the probability of attaining that goal are negatively correlated, the goal an individual can expect to attain is usually less attractive than the one he would desire to attain. In romantic choices, attractiveness and availability would also seem to be negatively correlated. The more abstractly desirable a potential romantic object is, the more competition there probably is for him (or her), and the less likely it is that a given individual will be able to attain his friendship. Thus, one's *realistic* social choices should be less "socially desirable" than one's fantasy social choices. In addition, Lewin et al. note that one's realistic level of aspiration is affected by his perception of his own skills. In the romantic area, we would expect that the individual's own social attractiveness would affect his level of aspiration. On the basis of the above reasoning, we would propose the following specific hypotheses:

1. Individuals who are themselves very socially desirable (physically attractive, personable, or possessing great material assets) will require that an appropriate partner possess more social desirability than will a less socially desirable individual.

2. If couples varying in social desirability meet in a social situation, those couples who are similar in social desirability will most often attempt to date one another.

3. In addition, we propose that an individual will not only *choose* a date of approximately his own social desirability, but also that after actual experience with

potential dates of various desirabilities an individual will express the most *liking* for a partner of approximately his own desirability. This prediction is not directly derived from level of aspiration formulations. Lewin et al. predict only that an individual will choose a goal of intermediate attractiveness and difficulty; they do not propose that an individual will come to *like* goals of intermediate difficulty.

We thought that unattainably desirable individuals might be derogated (although inappropriately difficult tasks are not) for the following reasons:

1. If a man chooses an inappropriately difficult task and then fails to attain it, all he suffers is defeat. The task cannot point out to him that he has been presumptuous in choosing a goal so far beyond his level of ability. We speculated, however, that an extremely desirable date can be counted on to make it clear to a somewhat undesirable individual that he is foolish to try to win her friendship and that he should not embarrass her by asking her out.

2. We thought that perhaps an extremely attractive date would not be as considerate of an unattractive date as with a date more average in appearance.

Procedure

Subjects were 376 men and 376 women who purchased tickets to a Friday night dance held on the last day of "Welcome Week." (Welcome Week is a week of cultural, educational, and social events provided for incoming University of Minnesota freshmen.) The dance was advertised along with 87 other events in a handbook all incoming freshmen received. In fact, however, the dance was not a regular Welcome Week event and had been set up solely to test our hypotheses. The handbook advertisement describing a Computer Dance said: "Here's your chance to meet someone who has the same expressed interests as yourself." Freshmen were told that if they would give the computer some information about their interests and personalities, the computer would match them with a date. Tickets were $1.00 per person; both men and women purchased their own tickets. Long lines of subjects appeared to buy tickets on the opening day—only the first 376 male and 376 female students who appeared were accepted.

For experimental purposes, ticket sales and information distribution were set up in extremely bureaucratic style: The subject walked along a table in the foyer of the Student Union. First, a student sold him a ticket. He moved down the table, and a second student checked his identification card to make sure he was a student and told him to report to a large room two flights above. When the subject arrived at the upstairs room, a third student met him at the door and handed him a questionnaire with his student code number stamped on it and asked him to complete the questionnaire at an adjoining table. A fourth student directed him to a seat. (Proctors around the room answered the subject's questions and discouraged talking.)

Physical Attractiveness Rating

The four bureaucrats were actually college sophomores who had been hired to rate the physical attractiveness of the 752 freshmen who purchased tickets to the dance.[1]

We assumed that one's social desirability would include such attributes as physical attractiveness, personableness, and material resources and that these aspects would be positively correlated with one another. We chose physical attractiveness to be the indicator of the subject's social desirability since this trait was more quickly assessed under standard conditions.

As each subject passed, the four raters rapidly and individually evaluated the subject's physical attractiveness on an 8-point scale, going from 1 ("Extremely unattractive") to 8 ("Extremely attractive"). Obviously, these attractiveness ratings had to be made very quickly; usually the rater had less than 1 or 2 seconds to look at the subject before making his evaluation, and rarely did the rater get to hear the subject say more than "OK" or "Thank you." The briefness of this contact was by design. Since we had chosen to use one aspect of social desirability as an index of total desirability, as far as possible, we wanted to be sure that the raters were assessing only that aspect. We did not want our ratings of attractiveness to be heavily influenced by the subject's personableness, intelligence, voice quality, etc.

Once the subjects were seated in the large upstairs room, they began filling out the questionnaire. The subject first answered several demographic questions concerning his age (nearly all were 18), height, race, and religious preference. The next measures were designed to assess how considerate the subject felt he would be of a fairly attractive date.

The remainder of the booklet contained material which we wanted to encourage the subjects to answer honestly. For this reason, a section prefacing the questions assured participants that their answers to the questions would not be used in selecting their date. We explained that we were including these questions only for research purposes and not for matching purposes. In addition, the subjects were reassured that their statements would be kept confidential and associated only with their ticket number, never their name. Four pages of questions followed this introduction. In the pages following this introduction, four variables were measured:

Subject's popularity (self-report). The subject was asked how popular he was with members of the opposite sex, how easy it was to get a date with someone he thought was exceptionally attractive, and how many dates he had had in the last 6 months.

Subject's nervousness. The subject was asked how nervous or awkward he felt about the idea of going on a blind date.

---

[1] David Kushner, John B. Kelly, Susan Lampland, and Victoria Noser rated the attractiveness of all the subjects. These students were simply told to use their own judgment in rating the subjects and to be careful not to communicate their ratings to the other raters.

Measure of the subject's expectations in a computer date. The subject was asked how physically attractive, how personally attractive, and how considerate he expected his date to be.

Subject's self-esteem. Questions from a scale developed by Berger (1952) ended the questionnaire. The subject was asked how true 36 different statements were of himself. The subject was once again reassured that this information was confidential and would not be used in selecting his computer date. (A typical question is: "When I'm in a group, I usually don't say much for fear of saying the wrong things.") This test was scored so that a high score indicated high self-acceptance and high self-esteem.

From the University's state-wide testing service program at the University of Minnesota,[2] several additional measures were secured for the subject whenever possible. The subject's high school academic percentile rank, his Minnesota Scholastic Aptitude Test (MSAT) score, and his score on the MMPI or the Minnesota Counseling Inventory (MCI) were secured.

Two days after the subject completed his questionnaire, he was assigned to a date. Dates were randomly assigned to the subjects with one limitation: a man was never assigned to a date taller than himself. On the few occasions when the assigned female date would have been taller than the male, the IBM card next in the shuffled deck was selected as the partner. When subjects picked up their dates' name, the experimenter advised them to meet their dates at the dance. Many couples, however, met at the girl's home.

The dance was held in a large armory. In order to be admitted to the armory, the subjects had to turn in their numbered tickets at the door. In this way, we could check on whether or not a given couple had attended the dance. Of the 376 male and 376 female students who signed up for the dance and were assigned a partner, 44 couples did not attend.[3] The subjects generally arrived at the dance at 8:00 P.M. and danced or talked until the 10:30 P.M. intermission.

Assessing Subjects' Attitudes toward One Another

Subjects' attitudes toward their dates were assessed during intermission. Several times during Welcome Week, we had advertised that couples should hold onto their ticket stubs until intermission, because these stubs would be collected during intermission and a $50 drawing would be held at that time. When the subjects bought their tickets, we reminded them that they would need to save their tickets for an intermission lottery. They were also told that during the dance they would have a chance to tell us how successful our matching techniques had been.

During the 10:30 P.M. intermission, the subjects were reminded that tickets for

[2] We would like to thank Theda Hagenah and David Wark of the Student Counseling Bureau, University of Minnesota, for providing access to this information.

[3] By far the most common reason given by the subjects for not attending the dance was that the date was of a different religion than the subject and that their parents had objected to their dating.

the lottery would be collected while they filled out a brief questionnaire assessing their dates and the dance. The purpose of the lottery was simply to insure that the subjects would retain their ticket stubs, which contained an identifying code number, and would report to an assigned classroom during intermission to evaluate their dates. Men were to report to one of seven small rooms to rate their dates and to turn in their stubs; women were to remain in the large armory to evaluate their partners.

The forms on which the subjects rated their partner were anonymous except that the subjects were asked to record their ticket numbers in the right-hand corner. This number, of course, identified the subjects perfectly to us, while not requiring the subjects to sign their name to their evaluation. A crew of experimenters rounded up any subjects who had wandered to rest rooms, fire escapes, or adjoining buildings and asked them to turn in their ticket stubs and to complete the evaluation questionnaires.

In the eight rooms where the subjects were assembled to evaluate their dates, the experimenters [4] urged the subjects to take the questionnaire seriously and to answer all questions honestly. All but 5 of 332 couples attending the dance completed a questionnaire, either during intermission or in a subsequent contact 2 days later.

The intermission questionnaire asked the subject about the following things: (*a*) how much the subject liked his date, (*b*) how socially desirable the date seemed to be ("How physically attractive is your date?" "How personally attractive is your date?"), (*c*) how uncomfortable the subject was on this blind date, (*d*) how much the date seemed to like the subject, (*e*) how similar the date's values, attitudes, and beliefs seemed to the subject's own, (*f*) how much of an effort the subject made to insure that the date had a good time, and how much of an effort the date made on the subject's behalf, (*g*) whether or not the subject would like to date his partner again.

How often couples actually dated was determined in a follow-up study. All participants were contacted 4–6 months after the dance and asked whether or not they had tried to date their computer date after the dance. If the experimenter was unable to contact either the subject or the subject's date in 2 months of attempts, the couple was excluded from the sample. Only 10 couples could not be contacted.

Results

Physical Attractiveness and Social Desirability

We assumed that we could use our ratings of physical attractiveness as a rough index of a person's social desirability. Is there any evidence that these outside

[4] Darcy Abrahams, James Bell, Zita Brown, Eugene Gerard, Jenny Hoffman, Darwyn Linder, Perry Prestholdt, Bill Walster, and David Wark served as the experimenters. Male experimenters interviewed male subjects; female experimenters interviewed female subjects.

ratings are related to the subject's own perception of his social desirability? When we look at the data, we see that there is. The more attractive an individual is, the more popular he says he is. The correlation between physical attractiveness and popularity for men is .31 and for women is .46. (Both of these *r*'s are significant at $p < .001$.) [5]

Hypothesis 1

Our first prediction was that a very socially desirable (attractive) subject would expect a "suitable" or "acceptable" date to possess more physical and personal charm and to be more considerate than would a less socially desirable subject.

We had two ways of testing whether or not attractive subjects did, in fact, have more rigorous requirements for an acceptable date than did less attractive individuals. Before the subject was assigned a date, he was asked how physically attractive, how personally attractive, and how considerate he expected his date to be. His answers to these three questions were summed, and an index of degree of the perfection he expected was computed. From the data, it appears that the more attractive the subject is, the more attractive, personable, and considerate he expects his date to be. The correlation between physical attractiveness and total expectations in a date is .18 for men and .23 for women.

A second way an individual's stringency of requirements could have been tested was by seeing whether or not the subject refused to go out with an "unsuitable" date. We wanted to eliminate the possibility that attractive and unattractive subjects would attend the dance with different frequencies, so we encouraged subjects to meet one another at the dance. However, it is possible that a few individuals were ingenious enough to get a preview of their dates before their public appearance together. We tried to determine whether or not attractive individuals rejected their partners *before* the dance more often than did unattractive ones.

It will be recalled that four raters rated each subject on an 8-point scale of attractiveness. We then separated subjects into three approximately equal-sized groups on the basis of these ratings. Men receiving an average rating of from 1.50 to 4.00 and women rated 1.50 to 4.75 were classified as *Ugly* individuals; men receiving an average rating of from 5.25 to 6.00 and women rated 5.00–5.75 were classified as *Average* individuals; and men rated 6.25–8.00 and women rated 6.00–8.00 were classified as *Attractive* individuals. We then contacted the 44 couples who did not attend the computer dance and interviewed them about their reasons for not attending. Attractive subjects did not reject their dates before the dance any more often than did unattractive subjects.

---

[5] With an *N* of 327, a correlation of .10 is significant at $p < .05$, a correlation of .15 at $p < .01$, and a correlation of .18 at $p. < .001$.

Behavioral Measures of Rejection

After men had arrived at the dance, or at their date's home, they met the partner who had been randomly assigned to them. Then during intermission, the subjects rated their liking for their dates. Since partners were randomly assigned, very attractive individuals should be assigned to just as attractive partners, on the average, as are average or ugly individuals. Thus, if during intermission, very handsome individuals rate their dates as less attractive, less personable, and less considerate than do less attractive men, this would indicate that attractive men are more harsh in their standards and ratings than are less attractive men. Also, if attractive individuals are more harsh in their standards they should, on the average, like their dates less, express less of a desire to date their partner again, and should actually try to date their computer partner less often than do less attractive individuals. When we look at the data, we see that this first hypothesis is confirmed.

The more attractive a man is, the less physically and personally attractive he thinks his date is ($F = 8.88$, $df = 1/318$, $p < .01$), the less he likes her ($F = 6.69$, $p < .01$), the less he would like to date her again ($F = 14.07$, $p < .001$), and the less often the date says he actually did ask her out again ($F = 3.15$, *ns*). Similarly, the more attractive a woman is, the less physically and personally attractive she thinks her date is ($F = 5.71$, $df = 1/318$, $p < .05$), the less she likes her date ($F = 2.23$, *ns*), and the less she would like to date him again ($F = 13.24$, $p < .001$).

Though it is clear that the more attractive subjects do appear to judge their dates more harshly than do unattractive subjects, we would like to note that this variable does *not* account for a very large portion of the total variance. For example, the relationships we have demonstrated between the subject's attractiveness and his expectations and evaluations of a date are strongly significant in five of the seven cases reported. However, correlations for the above variables range from only .07 to .20.

Hypothesis II proposed that an individual would most often choose to date a partner of approximately his own attractiveness. Hypothesis III stated that if individuals were to interact with partners of varying physical attractiveness, in a naturalistic setting, an individual would be better liked and would more often want to continue to date a partner similar to himself in attractiveness. Figure 1 depicts graphically the theoretical expectation that subjects will most often choose and most often like dates of approximately their own attractiveness.

Statistically, we test Hypotheses II and III by testing the significance of the interaction between date's attractiveness and subject's attractiveness in influencing the subject's *attempts* to date the partner, his *desire* to date the partner, and his liking for his date.

In Table 1, as in Figure 1, the subjects who supplied information to us were divided into three groups—Ugly subjects, Average subjects, and Attractive subjects. Unlike Figure 1, however, the actual attractiveness of the dates the subjects

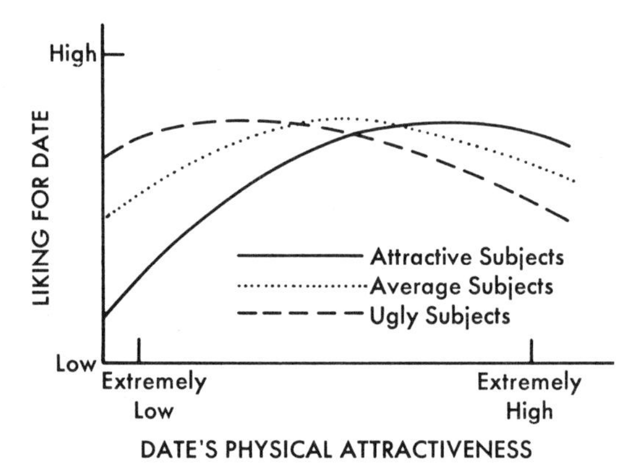

Figure 1 Amount of liking predicted for dates of various attractiveness by Ugly, Average, and Attractive subjects

are rating is not allowed to vary continuously; for the sake of clarity, the dates were also divided into three attractiveness groups.

So that we could very precisely assess whether or not the interaction we predicted was significant, we also examined the data by dividing subjects and their dates into five attractiveness levels. When the 5×5 interaction is examined, however, the conclusions and *F*s are identical to those we form on the basis of the less fine discriminations (3×3) reported in Table 1. For this reason, the smaller breakdown is presented.

Hypotheses II and III are not supported. The subject's attractiveness does not significantly interact with the date's attractiveness in determining his attempt to date her, his desire to date her, or his liking for her. In *no case* is there a significant interaction. If we look at the *actual* attempts of men to date their partners (Table 1:I), we find that men did not more often ask out dates similar to themselves in attractiveness. (These data were secured in a follow-up study.) The only important determinant of whether or not the date was asked out again was how attractive the *date* was. The most attractive girls are most often asked out ($F = 12.02$, $df = 1/318$, $p < .001$). This is generally true *regardless of the attractiveness of the man* who is asking her out. There is *not* a significant tendency for subjects to try to date partners of approximately their own physical desirability. The interaction *F* which is necessary to demonstrate such a tendency is very small ($F = .07$).

Our hypothesis (III) that individuals would best *like* dates similar to themselves in attractiveness also fails to be supported by the data. During intermission, individuals indicated how much they liked their dates on a scale ranging from 2.5 ("Like extremely much") to −2.5 ("Dislike extremely much"). From Table 1, Sections II and III, it is apparent that by far the greatest determinant of how much liking an individual feels for his partner is simply how attractive the partner is. The more attractive the female date is, the better liked she is ($F =$

TABLE 1

VARIOUS MEASURES OF THE SUBJECTS' LIKING FOR THEIR DATES AND SUBJECTS' DESIRE TO DATE THEIR PARTNERS

	DATE'S PHYSICAL ATTRACTIVENESS		
	Ugly	*Average*	*Attractive*
I. Percent *S*s actually asking date out			
According to ugly male *S*s	.16	.21	.40
According to average male *S*s	.12	.25	.22
According to attractive male *S*s	.00	.26	.29
II. How much *S* says he liked his date			
According to ugly male *S*s	.06[a]	.57	.90
According to average male *S*s	−.10	.58	1.56
According to attractive male *S*s	−.62	.16	.82
According to ugly female *S*s	.03	.71	.96
According to average female *S*s	−.10	.61	1.50
According to attractive female *S*s	−.13	.21	.89
III. Percent *S*s saying they wanted to date partner again			
According to ugly male *S*s	.41	.53	.80
According to average male *S*s	.30	.50	.78
According to attractive male *S*s	.04	.37	.58
According to ugly female *S*s	.53	.56	.92
According to average female *S*s	.35	.69	.71
According to attractive female *S*s	.27	.27	.68
IV. How many subsequent dates couples had			
Ugly male *S*s	.09	1.23	.73
Average male *S*s	.30	.94	.17
Attractive male *S*s	.00	2.08	.53
V. Amount *S* thinks date likes him			
Guesses by ugly male *S*s	.47[b]	.52	.43
Guesses by average male *S*s	.55	.64	.65
Guesses by attractive male *S*s	.77	.53	.58
Guesses by ugly female *S*s	.41	.41	.35
Guesses by average female *S*s	.38	.58	.55
Guesses by attractive female *S*s	.63	.65	.61
VI. No. of *S*s in each cell			
Ugly male *S*s	(32)	(43)	(30)
Average male *S*s	(43)	(36)	(41)
Attractive male *S*s	(26)	(38)	(38)

[a] The higher the number, the more the subject says he liked his date.
[b] The higher the number, the more the subject thinks his date liked him.

59.26, $df = 1/318$) and the more often the man says that he would like to date her ($F = 49.87$). Men do not overrate women at their own attractiveness level. (Interaction Fs for liking and desire to date = 2.53 and .69, respectively.) Very surprising to us was the fact that a *man's* physical attractiveness is also by far the largest determinant of how well *he* is liked. We had assumed that physical attractiveness would be a much less important determinant of liking for men than for women. However, it appears that it is just as important a determinant. The more attractive the man, the more his partner likes him ($F = 55.79$, $df = 1/318$) and the more often she says she wants to date him again ($F = 37.24$). As before, we see that women do not tend to overrate partners at their own attractiveness level. (Interaction *F*s for liking and desire to date = .07 and .08, respectively.)

In order to get a better idea of the extent to which liking was related to the date's physical attractiveness, we examined the correlation between these two variables. The correlations between date's attractiveness and the partner's liking is almost as high as the reliability of the attractiveness ratings.

Our measure of physical attractiveness is not highly reliable. When rating the subject's physical attractiveness, raters saw the subject for only a few seconds as the subject moved along in a line. In addition, raters had to devise their own standards of attractiveness. Probably as a consequence of the preceding factors, the attractiveness ratings made by the four raters of the same individual intercorrelate .49–.58. In addition, there is a factor which may further reduce the reliability of our attractiveness measure from the time of the rating to the time of the dance. At the time of the rating, the subjects were in school clothes, casually dressed, while on the day of the dance they were dressed for a date. It is possible that this difference would have produced a change in the subject's relative attractiveness orderings. In spite of these limitations, the correlation between a *woman's* average physical attractiveness rating and her male partner's liking for her is .44; the correlation between her attractiveness and whether or not he wants to continue to date her is .39; and between her attractiveness and how much he actually does ask her out subsequently is .17. The correlations between a *man's* average physical attractiveness rating and his partner's liking for him and desire to date him are .36 and .31, respectively.

When we examine the relationship between the *individual's* own estimation of the date's physical attractiveness and his expression of liking for her, the correlations are still higher. The correlation between liking of the date and evaluation of the date's physical attractiveness is .78 for male subjects and .69 for female subjects.

It appears that the more attractive the date, the more he was liked, and the more the subject desired to date him regardless of how attracted the date was to the subject. The happy accommodation that we proposed between what an individual desires and what he can realistically hope to attain appears not to exist. The lack of symmetry between the individual's liking for his date and the date's liking for the individual is striking. The correlation between how much the man says he likes his partner and how much she likes him is virtually zero: $r = .03$. Nor is there a significant correlation between whether or not the subject wants to date his partner again and whether she wants to date him: $r = .07$. Clearly, a variable that we assumed would be very important—how much the date likes individual—does not appear to be an important determinant of the individual's ratings. Sheer physical attractiveness appears to be the overriding determinant of liking.

How can we account for the singular importance of physical attractiveness in determining the individual's liking for the other? There seem to be several plausible explanations:

1. Perhaps it could be argued that in the relationships we have discussed it is not really physical attractiveness that is so crucial, but one of the *correlates* of attractiveness. For example, we know from developmental studies of intelligent individuals (Terman, 1925, 1947, 1959) that intelligence, physical attractiveness, creativity, and certain personality traits are often positively correlated. Perhaps it is one of these correlated variables that is really important in determining liking.

From the other evidence we have on this point and which we will present in the next paragraphs, it appears that "intelligence" and "personality" are *not* better predictors of liking than physical attractiveness.

Intelligence and Achievement Measures

Students' high school percentile ranks and MSAT scores are undoubtedly much more reliable measures than is our measure of physical attractiveness. Yet, these measures have only a very weak relationship to liking. The higher the male's high school percentile rank, the less his partner likes him ($r = -.18$) and the less she wants to date him again ($r = -.04$) ($N = 303$). Male's MSAT scores correlate .04 with both the woman's liking for him and her desire to date him ($N = 281$). The higher the female's high school percentile rank, the less her partner likes her ($r = -.07$) and the less he desires to date her again ($r = -.09$). High school rank is uncorrelated with his actual attempt to date her again ($r = .00$) ($N = 323$). Females' MSAT scores correlate −.05, −.06, and −.06 with these same variables ($N = 306$). It is clear then that intelligence is clearly not a variable of the same importance as physical attractiveness in determining liking. In no case did a subject's intellectual achievement or ability test scores have a significant relationship to the liking his date expressed for him.

Personality Measures

The subjects also completed several personality measures which could reasonably be expected to predict the liking one would engender in a social situation.[6]

MCI: Social relationships (SR). Low scorers are said to have good social skills, have acceptable manners, and be courteous, mature individuals (Berdie, Layton, Swanson, Hagenah, & Merwin, 1962).

[6] MCI scores were secured for 234 of the male subjects and 240 of the female subjects during freshman testing. In addition, the MMPI had been administered to a sample including 50 of the men and 41 of the women.

MMPI: Masculinity-femininity (Mf). Low scorers are said to be more masculine in their values, attitudes, and interest, styles of expression and speech, and in their sexual relationships than high scorers (Dahlstrom & Welsh, 1962).

MMPI: Social introversion (Si). Low scorers are said to be more extroverted in their thinking, social participation, and emotional involvement.

Berger's Scale of Self-Acceptance (1952). When we look at the correlations between an individual's scores on these personality measures and the liking his date expresses for him, we see that these personality measures are not as good predictors of liking as is our crude measure of physical attractiveness. When we look at the data, we see that the low scoring individuals on the MCI (SR), on the MMPI (*Mf*), and on the MMPI (*Si*) or high scorers on Berger's Scale of Self-Acceptance are only slightly better liked by their dates than are high scoring individuals. Men's scores on these tests correlate −.11, −.12, −.10, and .14 with their dates' liking for them. Women's scores on these tests correlate only −.18, −.10, −.08, and .03 with their dates' liking. Our personality measures, then, like our intelligence measures, appear to be very inadequate predictors of liking.

It is, of course, possible that intelligence and personality determinants would have been more important had individuals had more time to get acquainted. It may be that 2½ hours is too short a time for individuals to discover much about their partners' intelligence or personality, while physical attractiveness is obvious from the start. It is not likely, however, that intelligence or personality variables are "really" underlying the correlations we obtained between attractiveness and romantic liking.

2. It may be that in this situation, individuals were not very affected by their dates' liking for them because the dates were so polite that it was impossible for the individual to know if he was accepted or rejected. Or, perhaps individuals were so eager to be liked that they did not want to correctly perceive the available cues.

The only available evidence for this position is ambiguous. The correlation between the partner's stated liking for the subject and the subject's perception of the partner's liking for him is .23 for male subjects and .36 for female subjects. The subject, thus, has some, though not a great deal of, ability in estimating how much his partner likes him. The reader may see subjects' guesses concerning how much their date likes them in Table 1:V. Possible answer to the question, "How much does your partner like you?" could range from (2.5) "Date likes me extremely much" to (−2.5) "Date dislikes me extremely much."

3. It may be that our findings are limited to large group situations, where young people are in very brief contact with one another. Perhaps if individuals had been exposed to one another for *long* periods of time, similarity of interests, beliefs, and reciprocal liking would come to be more important than physical appearance in determining liking. Finally, it might also be true that physical attractiveness loses some of its importance as individuals get to be *older* than the 18-year-olds interviewed in our study.

We should note that, even though further contact may have decreased the importance of physical attractiveness, whether or not the subject attempted to continue to date his partner depended on the partner's physical attractiveness. Similarly, though our findings may well be limited to the youthful population that we interviewed (average age: 18 years), it is also true that this is the age at which many individuals make their lifelong romantic choices.

4. Finally, it may be that if we had arranged more conventional single dates, the date's personality and conversational abilities would have been more important. It may have been that just getting to display a very attractive date compensated for any rejection on the date's part.

REFERENCES

Berdie, R. F., Layton, W. L., Swanson, E. O., Hagenah, T., & Merwin, J. C. 1962. *Counseling and the use of tests.* Minneapolis: Student Counseling Bureau.

Berger, E. M. 1952. The relation between expressed acceptance of self and expressed acceptance of others. *Journal of Abnormal and Social Psychology* 47: 778–82.

Dahlstrom, W. G., & Welsh, G. S. 1962. *An MMPI handbook: A guide to use in practice and research.* Minneapolis: University of Minnesota Press.

Goffman, E. 1952. On cooling the mark out: Some aspect of adaptation to failure. *Psychiatry* 15: 451–63.

Lewin, K., Dembo, T., Festinger, L., & Sears, P. 1944. Level of aspiration. In J. McV. Hunt, ed. *Personality and the behavior disorders.* Vol. 1. New York: Ronald Press, pp. 333–78.

Rosenfeld, H. M. 1964. Social choice conceived as a level of aspiration. *Journal of Abnormal and Social Psychology* 68: 491–99.

Terman, L. M. 1925. *Genetic studies of genius.* Vol. 1. Stanford: Stanford University Press.

———. 1947. *Genetic studies of genius.* Vol. 4. Stanford: Stanford University Press.

———. 1959. *Genetic studies of genius.* Vol. 5. Stanford: Stanford University Press.

25

Race and Shared Belief as Factors in Social Choice

MILTON ROKEACH · LOUIS MEZEI

Numerous studies have indicated that a major factor influencing interpersonal choice is similarity of attitudes and beliefs. Apparently, people tend to prefer others whom they think have beliefs similar to their own. But what happens when the other person is of a different race or ethnic group? Is a difference in race important enough to cause people to prefer racially similar others with dissimilar beliefs? As surprising as it may seem, the evidence indicates that of these two factors, similarity of beliefs is the more important.

Most of the research bearing on the foregoing questions, however, has relied on pencil-and-paper tests of interpersonal choice, rather than on choice in actual social situations. One might reasonably ask, then, if the same results would hold in everyday encounters with other people.

The significance of the following research report is that Rokeach and Mezei present the results of not one, but three, real-life experiments designed (1) to determine the relative importance of race and beliefs in interpersonal choice, (2) to see if differences existed in this regard for blacks versus whites, and (3) to determine whether the relative influence of race and beliefs differed for highly prejudiced versus relatively unprejudiced people. The results, which we will let you discover for yourself, are even more impressive in that they are based on data from very different populations—college students and workers applying for a job at an employment agency.

The reader would find it interesting and enlightening to trace some of the implications of this research for the acquaintance process and for intergroup relations.

Milton Rokeach and Louis Mezei, "Race and Shared Belief as Factors in Social Choice," *Science* 14 (1966): 167–72.

Several recent studies support the hypothesis that differences in belief on important issues are a more powerful determinant of prejudice or discrimination than differences in race or ethnic membership. White college students in the North and South [1] and white teen-agers in California [2] have been found in questionnaire-type studies to prefer Negroes with beliefs, values, and personalities perceived to be similar to their own (for example, a Negro who believes in God) to whites with beliefs, values, and personalities perceived to be dissimilar to their own (for example, a white atheist). More generally, these subjects are observed to rate less favorably those, regardless of race, whose belief systems are incongruent with their own than those, regardless of race, whose belief systems are congruent with their own. Rokeach, Smith, and Evans [3] have reported comparable results with Jewish children; the children of their study rated gentiles whose belief systems were seen as congruent with their own (for example, a gentile who is for Israel) more favorably than they did Jews whose belief systems were seen as incongruent with their own (a Jew who is against Israel). Stein [4] has recently reported confirmatory results in studies of Negro, Jewish, and gentile teen-agers in a Northeastern city, as has Martin [5] in a study of the differential preferences of English Canadians for English Canadians, French Canadians, and Canadian Indians of varied beliefs.[6]

Generalization from these findings is, however, severely limited by the fact that in all these studies the social stimuli were "paper-and-pencil" stimuli and the discriminatory responses elicited were "paper-and-pencil" responses. To overcome this limitation, we conducted three experiments in which subjects were given the opportunity to discriminate on the basis of race or belief, or both, in real-life situations. These experiments are all alike in basic design. A naive subject engages four strangers, confederates of the experimenter, in a group discussion about an important or situationally relevant topic. Two of the confederates are

---

[1] M. Rokeach, P. W. Smith, R. I. Evans, *The Open and Closed Mind* (New York: Basic Books, 1960); D. Byrne and T. J. Wong, "Racial Prejudice, Interpersonal Attraction, and Assumed Dissimilarity of Attitudes," *Journal of Abnormal and Social Psychology* 65 (1962): 246; M. Rokeach and G. Rothman, "The Principle of Belief Congruence and the Congruity Principle as Models of Cognitive Interaction," *Psychological Review* 72 (1965): 128.

[2] D. D. Stein, J. A. Hardyck, M. B. Smith, "Race and Belief: An Open and Shut Case," *Journal of Personality and Social Psychology* 1 (1965): 281.

[3] Rokeach et al., *Open and Closed Mind.*

[4] D. D. Stein, "Similarity of Belief Systems and Interpersonal Preference: A Test of Rokeach's Theory of Prejudice," Ph.D. dissertation, University of California at Berkeley, 1965.

[5] Bette Mary Evans Martin, "Ethnic Group and Beliefs as Determinants of Social Distance," M.A. thesis, Department of Psychology, University of Western Ontario, 1964.

[6] The only exception to the cited findings is a study by H. C. Triandis, "A Note on Rokeach's Theory of Prejudice," *Journal of Abnormal and Social Psychology* 62 (1961): 184–86. For a critique of this study see M. Rokeach, "Belief versus Race as Determinants of Social Distance: A Comment on Triandis' Paper," *Journal of Abnormal and Social Psychology* 62 (1961): 187–88, and for a reconciliation of findings see Stein et al., "Race and Belief."

white and two are Negro. One white and one Negro agree with the subject, and one white and one Negro disagree with him. The subject is then asked to state a preference for two of the four confederates.

In two of the experiments, conducted on a university campus, the subject chose two of the confederates to join him for a coffee break. In the third experiment, which was conducted in the natural field setting of an employment office, the subjects were actually applying for jobs; each chose two of four "job applicants" he would most like to work with. This third experiment provides the strongest test of our major hypothesis. For one thing, these subjects were unemployed workers (or, occasionally, employed workers seeking to change jobs), not college students. More important, they were under the impression that the procedures to which they were subjected were an integral part of a normal interview procedure, and they were totally unaware that they were participating in an experiment—a condition that can rarely be assured with college students participating in psychological experiments.

Within the basic framework of these experiments we were interested in three additional questions:

(1) *Comparison between white and Negro subjects.* The field experiment in the employment office included Negro as well as white applicants, and the results obtained from these two groups can be compared. This study was carried out during the winter of 1963–64, a period during which civil rights demonstrations and clashes provided many daily headlines. In this charged atmosphere, would Negroes and whites pick working partners along race lines, or would beliefs relevant to the working situation be a more important determinant of interpersonal choice?

(2) *Comparison between subjects high and low in anti-Negro prejudice.* Rokeach, Smith, and Evans found that, "whether a person is high or low in prejudice against Jews and Negroes [as determined by scores on anti-Semitism and anti-Negro attitude scales], he responds to belief rather than racial or ethnic cues when given an opportunity to do so." [7] In our two campus experiments we also studied the extent to which racial attitudes predict social choice.

(3) *Comparison between public and private conditions.* If discrimination on the basis of race is institutionalized or if there exists extreme social pressure to discriminate along racial lines (as is most clearly the case in the South or in South Africa), there is virtually no likelihood that social discrimination will occur on the basis of similarity of belief. All the experiments to be reported here were conducted in the state of Michigan, where patterns of racial discrimination are less institutionalized and less subject to social pressure than they are in the South. Nevertheless, it is reasonable to assume that such pressures are far from absent in Michigan and consequently that our subjects would choose partners differently under public and private conditions. This assumption was tested in the two campus experiments.

---

[7] Rokeach, *Open and Closed Mind,* p. 155.

Procedure in the Campus Experiments

Two virtually identical experiments were performed, one in 1961 with 20 white male subjects drawn from an introductory sociology class,[8] the second in 1963–64 with 48 white male subjects drawn from an introductory psychology class. At least 10 days before the respective experiments, instructors (not the experimenters) administered a six-item anti-Negro Scale.[9] "High-prejudice" subjects were defined as those who obtained plus scores and "low-prejudice" subjects as those who obtained minus scores on this scale.

The experiment was conducted in two adjacent rooms—one for receiving and interviewing the subjects, the other for group discussion—situated in an isolated wing of a campus building. To avoid suspicion, the confederates arrived separately. After all five participants had arrived, they were seated around a conference table and were told that their task was to discuss a controversial topic, to be selected from a list of five topics by their chairman, who was to be chosen by election. The topics were: (i) invasion of Cuba, (ii) elimination of fraternities from campus, (iii) allowing girls to visit men's dormitories, (iv) Bible reading in the schools, and (v) the grading system.

Each participant was first asked to introduce himself; then the subject, by prearrangement, was elected chairman. He selected the topic and then led a 15-minute discussion. One white and one Negro confederate agreed with the subject, and one white and one Negro disagreed. Identification was facilitated by printed name cards, as in TV panel shows. Personality effects on interpersonal choice were randomized by rotating the assignments of each confederate so that if he agreed with one subject he disagreed with the next. On terminating the discussion, the experimenter took the subject into the next room for a private interview. The experimenter displayed a seating chart of the participants and, under the guise of checking his written notes against the subject's judgment, asked the subject to identify the opinions expressed by the participants, thus assuring that the subject remembered their opinions as well as their names.

While the subject looked at the seating chart, the experimenter remarked that the participants would be interviewed individually and that therefore there would be enough time for several of them to take a coffee break; he then asked the subject, as chairman, to select two of the participants to join him for coffee. In half the cases the experimenter specified that they would be served coffee in a private room next door (the *private* condition), in the other half that they would go to the grill in the Student Union Building (the *public* condition), where the coffee would be paid for from research funds. After the subject made his choices he was asked how he had decided on them. The experimenter then explained the purpose of the experiment and pledged the subject to secrecy.

---

[8] We thank Joe Smucker and Del Dyer, who conducted this experiment and analyzed the data.

[9] T. W. Adorno, E. Frenkel-Brunswik, D. J. Levinson, R. N. Sanford, *The Authoritarian Personality* (New York: Harper & Row, 1950), p. 142.

Procedure in the Field Experiment

The subjects in the field experiment were 26 Negro and 24 white male applicants for the positions of janitor, laundry worker, attendant, and recreational director at two mental hospitals in Michigan. The level of positions applied for was the same for Negro and white applicants. Experimental sessions were scheduled at the employment offices of the two hospitals on days when several job applicants were to appear for job interviews by prior appointment. All such applicants were included in the sample.

After an applicant had filled out the usual application form, the experimenter, posing as a staff member of the personnel office, accompanied him to a "waiting room" in which the four confederates, posing and dressed and previously trained to play their roles as job applicants, were already "waiting to be interviewed." As the experimenter and the subject entered, two confederates were looking intently at a mimeographed sheet entitled "Problems of working with mental patients," on which five topics were listed: what to do if a patient (i) misses dinner, (ii) refuses to shave because of a delusion, (iii) takes off his clothes, or (iv) asks to change his dining-room seat, and (v) what to do with juvenile offenders. In each case two specific courses of action were provided—one based on a rule, the other a more permissive alternative. The experimenter handed mimeographed sheets to the subject and to those confederates who did not already have them, explaining that "they are used in the training program" and suggesting that the applicants look at them while waiting their turns to be interviewed.

The experimenter then left the room, and the four confederates initiated a "spontaneous" discussion of at least three of the five topics. One white and one Negro confederate defended the permissive position, and one white and one Negro confederate defended the rule-oriented position. As in the campus experiments, confederates alternated positions from one applicant to another. The subject was gradually drawn into the discussion, his opinion being directly solicited if necessary. If the subject was not consistent in choosing either the rule or the permissive course of action in the several situations (and this was true of about half the subjects), the confederates tried to follow him, agreeing or disagreeing with him according to their predetermined assignments.

The experimenter returned after about 12 minutes, announcing that the interviewers were not quite ready yet. He then passed out 2 by 4 cards and asked each participant to write the names of the two people in the group whom he would most prefer to work with. Since the applicants did not yet "know" one another's names, they introduced themselves. The experimenter then assured the applicants that their choices would be kept confidential and that this part of the interview procedure was "something new and has nothing to do with your employment interview." While the subject wrote down the two preferred names, each of the other four wrote down the names of the two confederates who agreed with the subject most of the time. This was done to check on whether there had been a slip-up in carrying out the assignments. (There were none.) The experimenter then collected the cards, thanked the applicants, and left. He or the personnel assistant returned shortly afterwards to escort the subject to his real interview.

The Choices

Under the experimental conditions described, there are six possible combinations of partners among which the subject can choose:

1) S+O+: two persons who agree with him, one of each race.

2) S−O−: two persons who disagree with him, one of each race.

3) S+S−: two persons of the same race (as the subject), one agreeing, the other disagreeing with him.

4) O+O−: two persons of the other race, one agreeing, the other disagreeing.

5) S+O−: one person of his own race who agrees and a second person of the other race who disagrees.

6) S−O+: one person of his own race who disagrees and a second person of the other race who agrees.

It is reasonable to assume that the more frequently our subjects choose pattern 1 or 2 over the remaining patterns, the more probable it is that they are discriminating (that is, choosing preferentially) on the basis of belief criteria alone; the more frequently they choose pattern 3 or 4 over the remaining patterns, the more probable it is that they are discriminating on the basis of racial criteria alone; and the more frequently they choose pattern 5 or 6 over the remaining patterns, the more probable that they are not choosing preferentially on the basis of either race or belief criteria alone.

It is immediately obvious from Table 1 that the six patterns do not appear equally often. This is true for each of the three experiments considered separately, and when the data from all experiments are combined we see that patterns 1 through 6 were chosen by 47, 4, 7, 7, 22, and 31 subjects, respectively.

The most direct way of assessing the relative effects of congruence of belief and congruence of race, as determinants of personal choice, is to compare the number of subjects who chose two persons of the same belief (pattern 1) with the number who chose two persons of the same race (pattern 3). Pattern 1 (S+O+) was chosen twice as often as pattern 3 (S+S−) in the campus 1961 study, four times as often in the campus 1963–64 study, and 15 times as often in the field study. When the data from all three experiments are combined, we find that pattern 1 was chosen by 47 subjects and pattern 3 by only 7—a ratio of almost 7 to 1. Under the conditions described, similarity of belief is clearly a more powerful determinant of interpersonal choice than similarity of race.

Additional support for the initial hypothesis is obtained when we compare pattern 1 with pattern 2 and pattern 3 with pattern 4. Our subjects preferred two partners who agreed with them to two partners who disagreed with them 4 to 1, 13 to 0, and 30 to 3 in the three experiments, respectively. Of the 118 subjects in the three experiments, 47 chose two partners who agreed with them and only 4 chose two partners who disagreed with them. In contrast, 7 subjects (out of 118) preferred two partners of their own race (S+S−), and 7 preferred two partners of the other race (O+O−).

TABLE 1

FREQUENCY OF CHOICE OF VARIOUS RACE AND BELIEF PATTERNS IN THREE EXPERIMENTS. EACH PATTERN CONSISTS OF TWO PARTNERS. S, SAME RACE AS SUBJECT; O, OTHER RACE; +, AGREED WITH SUBJECT; −, DISAGREED WITH SUBJECT.

Experimental group	PATTERN						
	(1) *S+O+*	*(2)* *S−O−*	*(3)* *S+S−*	*(4)* *O+O−*	*(5)* *S+O−*	*(6)* *S−O+*	*Total*
Campus 1961	4	1	2	1	3	9	20
High prejudice	2	1	2	0	2	3	10
Low prejudice	2	0	0	1	1	6	10
Private	0	0	1	0	1	8	10
Public	4	1	1	1	2	1	10
Campus 1963–64	13	0	3	3	15	14	48
High prejudice	5	0	1	2	6	7	21
Low prejudice	8	0	2	1	9	7	27
Private	7	0	1	1	8	7	24
Public	6	0	2	2	7	7	24
Field 1963–64	30	3	2	3	4	8	50
Negro	15	3	1	2	3	2	26
White	15	0	1	1	1	6	24
All groups	47	4	7	7	22	31	118

Clearly, similarity of belief is a far more important basis for choosing partners than dissimilarity of belief; only 4 subjects out of 118 (instead of the 19 that would be expected by pure chance) chose two partners who disagreed with them (pattern 2). More surprising is that (i) only 14 subjects (instead of a theoretically expected 39) chose partners of one race (patterns 3 and 4), and (ii) of these 14, as many chose two partners from the other race as from their own.

Let us consider next the findings with respect to patterns 5 and 6. A sizable proportion of our subjects—53 of the 118—chose coffee- and work-partners varying in both belief and race; 22 chose pattern 5 (S+O−) and 31 chose pattern 6 (S−O+). But with respect to these two patterns we note an important difference between the two campus studies on the one hand and the field study on the other. In each of the campus studies, 60 percent apparently preferred partners differing from one another in both race and belief. But this was so of only 24 percent of the subjects in the field study; 60 percent in the field study chose two partners with beliefs congruent with their own, one white and one Negro. It is not possible to say whether these differences are due to sampling differences between college students and workers; or to the fact that choice of coffee-partners is a "one-shot deal," while choice of work-partners has longer-range implications; or to the fact that the particular issues discussed were related to work in the one case but not in the other. Another interpretation which would seem to fit the data equally well is that while a majority of the work-applicants preferred partners with congruent beliefs (S+O+), a majority of the campus subjects preferred the mixed racial patterns 1, 5, and 6 (S+O+, S+O−, S−O+), their choices among these patterns being about evenly distributed. But this preference for SO patterns must be qualified by the fact that the campus subjects avoided pattern 2 (S−O−).

No matter how one chooses to state the differences between the subjects in the campus and field studies, it is clear that in all three experiments (i) similarity of belief is a considerably more frequent basis of choice than dissimilarity of belief; (ii) similarity of race is rarely a basis of choice—considerably less often even than chance, and no more frequently than dissimilarity of race; and (iii) similarity of belief is a considerably more frequent basis of choice than similarity of race.

In the campus 1963–64 and field studies, we obtained additional data on the order in which the two confederates were chosen. These data (Table 2) generally confirm the findings already presented. Considering first the campus 1963–64 results, note that, although a large proportion of the subjects chose a partner who disagreed as well as one who agreed, two-thirds of those who did so chose first the partner who agreed. In contrast, the first choices of all the subjects were exactly evenly divided between the two races. The comparable findings in the field study are even more decisively in favor of belief rather than race congruence as a determinant of choice. Here a much smaller proportion chose a

TABLE 2

ORDER OF CHOICE OF PARTNERS IN TWO EXPERIMENTS

CHOICE		NO. OF SUBJECTS	
First	*Second*	*Campus study**	*Field study*
+	+	13	30
+	−	23	13
−	+	12	4
−	−	0	3
S	S	3	2
S	O	21	18
O	S	21	27
O	O	3	3

* 1963–64.

disagreeing as well as an agreeing partner, and three-quarters of those who did so chose the agreeing partner first. Again, these results are in sharp contrast to those concerning race. All but a few subjects chose partners of both races, and only 40 percent of them chose the partner of their own race first. These findings are quite consistent for the Negro and white subjects considered separately.

Another interesting finding shown in Table 2 is that in both studies the proportion of choices on the basis of belief congruence decreases from the first to the second choice (in the campus 1963–64 study $\chi^2 = 4.50$, $P < .05$; in the field study $\chi^2 = 3.61$, $P < .10$). No such decreases are, of course, observed with respect to race in the campus study, since the racial choices, being exactly equal on the first choice, are already balanced. But in the field study we again note a tendency to balance out the unequal racial choices as the subjects proceed from the first to the second partner. These results enable us to understand better the choice patterns shown in Table 1. It would seem as if many of the subjects, especially the campus subjects, were somehow aware of the basis on which they made their first preferential choice, and motivated by considerations of fair-mindedness they were more likely to choose a second partner possessing both belief and racial characteristics opposite to those of the first partner. At the same time the results show that more of the subjects were fair-minded about race than about belief.

Comparison between white and Negro subjects. Under the experimental conditions described, that is, when a person possesses situationally relevant information about another person's beliefs, there is little evidence indeed that he will discriminate on the basis of race per se. The question may now be raised whether Negro subjects respond any differently from white subjects when choosing others. James Baldwin, perhaps the most eloquent spokesman of the Negro people today, has insisted that white people, even well-meaning liberal white people, cannot understand the perceptions, thoughts, feelings, and desires of the Negro who lives in a white society which oppresses him from birth; as a result of life-long oppression, the Negro's psychological processes are inevitably different from the white's. If Baldwin's contentions are correct we should find our Negro subjects choosing partners in ways which are significantly different from the ways whites choose.

But the results presented in Table 1 show that in this experimental situation, at least, Negroes chose partners in ways which were indistinguishable from whites. Fifteen Negro applicants (out of 26) and 15 white applicants (out of 24) chose two partners who agreed with them, one white and one Negro. Only three of the Negro subjects and only two of the white subjects chose two partners of one race, and these were not necessarily of their own race.

Comparison between subjects high and low in prejudice. In the two campus studies the subjects had been classified before the experiment as high or low in prejudice on the basis of an anti-Negro scale. The results of both studies are essentially the same for high- and low-prejudice groups (Table 1). It would seem that scores on an anti-Negro scale are not necessarily related to real-life discrimination.

Comparison between public and private conditions. In neither campus study did privacy appear to have an effect on racial choice. In 1961, only one out of 10 subjects in the private condition and two out of 10 in the public condition chose two partners of their own race or of the other race; in 1963–64, two out of 24 in the private condition and four out of 24 in the public condition chose two partners of their own race or of the other race. If we look further at the campus 1963–64 data, it is also evident that the frequency of choice of all six patterns is remarkably similar under the public and private conditions. But certain unanticipated differences in choice patterns appear between the two conditions in the campus 1961 study. Four subjects in the public condition but none in the private condition chose pattern 1—two partners who agreed with them; eight subjects in the private condition but only one in the public condition chose pattern 6—one partner of the same race who disagreed and one of the other race who agreed with the subject. The variability of patterns chosen is generally greater for the public than for the private condition, but it makes for a difference only in the belief choices, not the racial choices. While the difference between conditions is statistically significant ($\chi^2 = 7.27$), we are nevertheless inclined to discount this difference for methodological reasons [10] and to conclude tentatively that the social pressures in a northern campus community were not sufficiently great to produce consistent differences between public and private choices. In this connection and in support of this interpretation it should be pointed out that the naive subjects were undoubtedly aware that they were participating in interactions with the four others, within a university context or an employment-interview context in the State of Michigan (a state which took an early lead in developing nondiscriminatory laws and policies in employment and in education). This may have been sufficient to indicate to the subjects that there existed no strong external social pressures to discriminate along racial lines. In other words, the conditions under which the studies were conducted must have suggested to the subjects that they were more or less free to choose partners in any way they wanted to.

It is conceivable, of course, that, given the social context, the subjects may have felt some external pressure *not* to discriminate along racial lines. We had no way of determining which or how many subjects may have felt such pressure. In any event, our data show little or no discrimination along racial lines; and, whether or not external pressures not to discriminate along racial lines existed, the subjects were free to choose from among the remaining five patterns.

[10] It is tempting to suggest that these differences are somehow due to the existence of social pressures in the campus community in 1961 and to their disappearance in 1963–64, perhaps as a result of changing social norms concerning civil rights. If this interpretation were valid we would expect to find the campus 1963–64 results under both private and public conditions looking very much like the campus 1961 results found under private conditions. But this does not appear to be the case. A more likely possibility is that the difference between public and private conditions in the campus 1961 study are, because of the small number of cases, unreliable, despite the fact that they turn out to be statistically significant. We are inclined to discount these results because we determined the significance level by first looking at the data and then combining patterns 1–5 (in order to eliminate small frequencies) and, more important, because we have not been able to replicate them.

Our main interest in studying differences in discrimination patterns under public and private conditions stems from the assumption that the crucial social-psychological difference between them is the presence or absence of social pressures to coerce discrimination along racial lines. It is interesting to speculate about the results we might have obtained had we been able to to replicate our studies in the deep South. An attempt by one of us to set up such a study in the deep South was unsuccessful, mainly because of anticipated reprisals toward research collaborators, confederates, and co-operating subjects. But had such a study proven feasible we would have predicted results considerably different from those reported here, namely, that, because of greater social pressures existing under public than under private conditions, choice of coffee- and work-partners would have been more uniformly along racial rather than belief lines.

Regarding the role of belief versus race as a determinant of discrimination, Triandis [11] and Stein, Hardyck, and Smith [12] have raised the objection that in the vast majority of social situations where discrimination is practiced (for example, in employment, education, public transportation and accommodation, and housing) white people do not stop to inquire into the beliefs of Negroes in order to determine whether they are congruent or incongruent with their own. The person discriminated against is a total stranger whose belief system is unknown to the person doing the discriminating. We have already suggested that discrimination along racial lines can be expected to occur whenever there is sufficient social pressure or when it is institutionally sanctioned. Under such conditions beliefs are irrelevant as a basis for discrimination. What should be added is that white persons in general and prejudiced white persons in particular, as a result of living within a social system in which racial discrimination is socially reinforced, come to assume that Negro strangers possess beliefs, values, and personalities dissimilar to their own. Thus, Byrne and Wong [13] found in a group of white subjects in Texas that those with anti-Negro prejudice more frequently than those without assumed that Negroes' beliefs are dissimilar to their own. And Stein, Hardyck, and Smith have reported that "the correlations presented . . . seem to indicate that the inference made by most subjects about a Negro teenager, in the absence of other information, is that he is *unlike* them." [14]

A final point concerns the issue of equal-status social contacts. Brink and Harris's [15] public-opinion data show that whites who have had previous social contact with Negroes are less prejudiced and have fewer stereotypes than whites with no such contact. Many others have pointed out that racial prejudice can be overcome or eliminated if individuals get to know one another in equal-status contacts. Our studies lead to the same conclusion but with one important quali-

---

[11] See footnote 6.
[12] See footnote 2.
[13] See footnote 1.
[14] See footnote 2.
[15] W. Brink and L. Harris, *The Negro Revolution in America* (New York: Simon & Schuster, 1964).

fication. In the field study especially, all contacts were equal-status contacts, but not all individuals who interacted with one another had congruent beliefs. It should therefore be pointed out that the concept of "equal-status contacts" is not necessarily equivalent to the concept of "contact between individuals with congruent belief systems." And recent research by Stein[16] shows that the latter variable is more crucial than the former as a determinant of interpersonal choice.

Subjects' reports on reasons for choice. At the end of the campus 1963–64 study the subjects were invited to give their reasons for choosing as they did. Four types of reasons were given (Table 3). Since there were no differences between high- and low-prejudice subjects or between subjects in the public and private conditions, these breakdowns are not shown. The most frequent reason given—by 20 out of 48 subjects—was to "keep the discussion going" or some variant thereof ("interesting guys to talk with," "keep things going," "best talkers"). The majority of these 20 subjects had chosen patterns 5 and 6, combinations in which both race and belief are varied. Four additional subjects who had chosen patterns 5 and 6 said more or less explicitly that they chose one of each race and one of each belief. When asked why, they responded with such reasons as "because of my Army experience" or "I did not want to leave two Negroes" or "I picked one on color and one on belief."

TABLE 3

REASONS FOR CHOICE IN CAMPUS 1963–64 STUDY, BY PATTERN OF CHOICE

Reason	PATTERN (1) S+O+	(2) S−O−	(3) S+S−	(4) O+O−	(5) S+O−	(6) S−O+
Quality of discussion	2	0	3	2	7	6
Race and belief	0	0	0	0	3	1
Personality	4	0	0	1	4	3
Other	7	0	0	0	1	4

A third type of reason was "Nice personality" or "I liked them." And a fourth type, which we have classified as "Other," may be interpreted as "evasive." The subject said he "didn't know" or "it didn't matter" or "I picked any two guys" or "I just picked two guys sitting next to me." It is interesting to note that 11 of the 13 subjects who chose pattern 1 (S + O +) but only 12 of the 29 who chose patterns 5 and 6 gave the third and fourth kinds of reason. This suggests that different processes underlie different choice patterns and, perhaps more important, that those who chose on the basis of belief congruence were generally more evasive about or unaware of the real reasons for their choices, possibly because

[16] See footnote 4.

choosing others on the basis of belief congruence violates religious and social ideals of tolerance toward those with opposing viewpoints.

Conclusion

Our three experiments and some of the others we have referred to suggest that the importance of racial attitudes per se as determinants of racial discrimination have been greatly overestimated and the importance of congruence of beliefs correspondingly underestimated. Whatever racial attitudes our subjects may have had seem to have exerted little or no influence on actual choices in social situations where external pressures to discriminate along racial lines were slight or absent (and pressures *not* to discriminate along racial lines possibly present). One of us has speculated elsewhere [17] on the basis of earlier findings with paper-and-pencil tests, now reinforced by the experiments here described, that "in those actions not subject to social sanction discrimination along racial or ethnic lines would not take place, not even in the South . . . the *locus* of racial and ethnic discrimination is to be sought in society, not in the individual's psyche. If society's constraints were altogether removed . . . man would still discriminate, if discriminate he must, not in terms of race or ethnic grouping, but in accord with his basic psychological predisposition, characteristic of all human beings, to organize the world of human beings in terms of the principle of belief congruence."

It remains to be seen whether the results of these experiments can be replicated with other kinds of subjects, in other kinds of situations, and in other kinds of cultural and subcultural contexts. And another task for future research is to explore in more detail the personal and social determinants of all the choice patterns we observed.

---

[17] Rokeach, "Comment on Triandis' Paper."

Interpersonal Attraction:

Putting It into Perspective

Two questions have dominated the research in interpersonal attraction. First, why do we like some people and not others? Second, what consequences does liking have for other aspects of interpersonal behavior? The readings in this section were devoted almost exclusively to the first of these questions, but it is the second question that prevents the first from being vacuous. If liking had no behavioral or psychological consequences, then the pursuit of its causes could justifiably be dubbed as an elitist, ivory-tower activity. Because liking serves as a basis for much recurrent interaction, its personal and social significance is immense.

While we do not propose to catalogue the variables that have been considered to influence attraction, those which have received most research attention and have yielded the most consistent results are similarity of orientations (attitudes, beliefs, values), similarity of personality, reciprocity of liking, and, in the case of opposite sex pairs, physical attractiveness. Each of the foregoing variables have been observed in multiple studies to exert a significant positive effect on attraction.

Different researchers have used different theoretical perspectives in their efforts to account for interpersonal preference patterns. Most research has been from the perspective of either consistency theory or reinforcement theory. Consistency theorists emphasize the symmetry of attitudes, beliefs, values, etc. of interactants with respect to each other and/or objects in their environment about which they communicate. In contrast, reinforcement theorists stress the reward-punishment consequences of the different ingredients of an interaction situtation. While researchers of both theoretical persuasions frequently investigate the same variables and make the same predictions about their effects on attraction, at some points the theories diverge. Reinforcement theory is the more general of the two, but as a result of its generality, it is of limited utility in informing the selection of independent variables. The reader who wishes to pursue these matters further will find some assistance in the *Suggestions for Further Reading*.

Another variable that has been demonstrated to influence interpersonal attraction is physical proximity. Because the practical implications of the link between proximity and attraction are so numerous, research in this tradition deserves some comment. In general, evidence from a variety of settings indicates that people like others who are physically proximate more frequently and/or more intensely than they like others who are physically distant. For example, demographic data indicate that mate selection (a special case of attraction) tends to occur within rather restricted geographical limits. When Cupid shoots his arrows into the air, they have a tendency to land amazingly close to home. In the more formal setting of work organizations too, data indicate that people in close physical proximity more frequently like each other than they like workers physically removed from them in the organization. Studies of interracial housing yield similar evidence. Living in physical proximity to people of other races or ethnic groups increases the likelihood of attraction.

Of course, proximity per se may have little significance for attraction. Certainly much of the influence of proximity on liking is due to the tendency for people of similar social backgrounds (race, social class, religion, etc.) to live in the same neighborhoods. Within socially homogeneous areas, there tends also to be considerable homogeneity of attitudes, beliefs, values, etc. As was pointed out earlier, both similarity of backgrounds and similarity of orientations contribute to liking. In addition, physical proximity increases the frequency with which people interact. One could predict from reinforcement theory that the more frequently people interact, the greater the likelihood that they will become attracted to each other. In the vernacular, you can come to like some strange birds, if you are around them long enough.

It should not be surprising that most of the research concerning the consequences of liking has been conducted in those areas of social psychology with strong applied interests, e.g., organizational social psychology. Patterns of liking in organizations influence who communicates with whom, the content of what is communicated, the bases for and the exercise of power, and the effectiveness and efficiency with which tasks are performed. The practical significance of these links for the organization man should be apparent.

While the implications of interpersonal attraction for contemporary social issues such as intergroup relations, care for the indigent and aged, co-operative political and social action, etc. have only recently begun to be explored, the logic of the linkages between attraction and these issues is obvious. Most of these issues have as a prerequisite to their solution the development of meaningful, recurrent interaction with others. Outside the constraints of formal organizations, one of the most common bases for the establishment of such interaction patterns is interpersonal liking. The researchable questions concerning attraction consequences far outnumber the questions researched to date.

Suggestions for Further Reading

Ellen Berscheid and Elaine H. Walster, *Interpersonal Attraction.* Reading, Massachusetts: Addison-Wesley, 1969. A nice summary of the theory and research in interpersonal attraction. Contains an excellent bibliography.

Don Byrne, "Attitudes and Attraction." Pp. 35–89 in L. Berkowitz, editor, *Advances in Experimental Social Psychology*. Volume 4. New York Academic Press, 1969. A comprehensive review of theory and research linking attitudes to patterns of interpersonal preference. A good presentation of the reinforcement model of attraction.

T. M. Newcomb, *The Acquaintance Process*. New York: Holt, Rinehart and Winston, 1961. The report of a field study which examines attraction from the perspective of a balance model. Must reading for any serious student of the area.

Mary L. Northway, *A Primer of Sociometry*. Second Edition. Toronto, Canada: University of Toronto Press, 1967. An introduction to a specific approach to the identification of preference patterns in social groups. Its major significance has been of a methodological nature.

Stanley Schachter, *The Psychology of Affiliation: Experimental Studies of the Sources of Gregariousness*. Stanford, California: Stanford University Press, 1959. A report of a series of experiments examining an interesting variety of independent variables related to affiliation. Stress is placed upon internal states of the individual which lead him to seek the presence of others.

CHAPTER VII

Aggression, Hostility, and Conflict

26 James L. Hoyt, *Effect of Media Violence "Justification" on Aggression* · 349

27 Leonard Berkowitz, *The Study of Urban Violence: Some Implications of Laboratory Studies of Frustration and Aggression* · 357

28 Richard H. Walters, *Implications of Laboratory Studies of Aggression for the Control and Regulation of Violence* · 366

29 H. Edward Ransford, *Isolation, Powerlessness, and Violence: A Study of Attitudes and Participation in the Watts Riot* · 380

Putting It into Perspective · 395
Suggestions for Further Reading · 397

26

Effect of Media Violence "Justification" on Aggression

JAMES L. HOYT

Does mass media violence have any significant effects on its viewers? This is a question that has received considerable popular and scholarly attention in recent years, and the apparent answer to the question is yes. A variety of research has demonstrated that people who witness violence or aggression are more likely to display aggression subsequently than are people who have not observed such behavior. But does all violence have the same effect on its viewers? The evidence to date suggests that the answer to this latter question is no. For example, viewing violence that is defined as "justified" leads to a higher degree of subsequent aggression among viewers than does watching the same violence which is defined as "unjustified."

In the following selection, Hoyt examines the effects of two types of violence justification on viewers' subsequent behavior. The first form of justification is "vengeance"—the motive of someone, previously harmed by another, for his later retaliation. The second form is "self-defense"—kill-or-be-killed. The major research findings are (1) that subjects who heard vengeance justification for violence in a film exhibited more subsequent aggression than did subjects who viewed violence for which no justification was offered and (2) that subjects in the self-defense condition showed significantly less aggression than did those in the vengeance condition.

What are the implications of these findings? At least one implication is that the media code position that violence should be shown only in a justified context may not produce the desired results. Justification increases rather than decreases the likelihood that the observer will subsequently engage in aggression.

James L. Hoyt, "Effect of Media Violence 'Justification' on Aggression," *Journal of Broadcasting* 14 (1970): 455–64.

For a number of years mass media critics have been concerned about possible adverse effects of of violence in the media. As early as 1949, phrases such as "Hollywood's new violence" were being used to describe film content.[1] By the mid-50s at least one well-known film quarterly, *Sight and Sound,* joined religious and parents' groups to decry what it termed "meaningless acts of violence" appearing too regularly in feature films.[2] At the same time, television also was being accused of having unfavorable influences on its viewers by presenting too much violence. More specifically, TV was charged with unconsciously conditioning viewers to commit destructive and vicious acts.[3]

In recent years, discussion of similar issues has increased dramatically, and a number of researchers systematically have been analyzing the question of the influence that violence in the mass media might have on audiences.[4] Although research in this area has been stimulated by the million-dollar "television and social behavior" project of the National Institute of Mental Health, a number of researchers have been studying such questions for a number of years. Among them are Leonard Berkowitz of the University of Wisconsin, Seymour Feshbach of the University of California at Los Angeles, Albert Bandura of Stanford University, Arnold Buss of Rutgers University, Russell Geen of the University of Missouri, and Dolf Zillmann of the University of Pennsylvania.

Feshbach has advanced a "symbolic catharsis" doctrine,[5] maintaining that participation in a vicarious aggressive activity, such as watching a violent film, can cause a release of aggressiveness in the viewers, and act as a substitute for the direct act of aggression. Thus he claims that the viewing of violence, by "draining off" previously aroused aggressive tendencies, can be beneficial.

Theoretical positions which predict opposite effects have been developed by others, particularly Berkowitz.[6] He argues that watching a violent film can produce instigational effects, especially if the viewer has been angered prior to seeing the film. According to Berkowitz, when a person is frustrated an anger arousal is

---

[1] Gershorn Legman, *Love and Death, A Study in Censorship* (New York: Breaking Point, 1949).

[2] Penelope Houston, "Rebels Without Causes," *Sight and Sound* 25 (1956): 178–81.

[3] United States Senate, Committee on the Judiciary. *Television Programs and Juvenile Delinquency.* Hearings before the Subcommittee to Investigate Juvenile Delinquency, 84th Congress, First Session (1955).

[4] The present author is a Ph.D. candidate in the University of Wisconsin School of Journalism. This paper is based on his Master's thesis at Wisconsin, done under the direction of Dr. Percy H. Tannenbaum. The study was supported by grant G-23963 from the National Science Foundation to Prof. Tannenbaum. The author also expresses his appreciation to Dr. Leonard Berkowitz of the University of Wisconsin Department of Psychology for the use of research facilities and equipment.

[5] Seymour Feshbach, "The Drive-Reducing Function of Fantasy Behavior," *Journal of Abnormal and Social Psychology* 50 (1955): 3–11; Seymour Feshbach, "The Stimulating Versus Cathartic Effects of a Vicarious Aggressive Activity," *Journal of Abnormal and Social Psychology* 63 (1961): 381–85.

[6] Leonard Berkowitz, "The Concept of Aggressive Drive: Some Additional Considerations." In Leonard Berkowitz, ed., *Advances in Experimental Social Psychology,* Vol. 2. (New York: Academic Press, 1965), pp. 301–29.

created. Then, when exposed to a violent film sequence, the individual's response sequence is heightened. Generally this arousal state is quite weak, rarely leading to overt action, but rather resulting only in discomfort and tension in the individual.

However, adults have learned that certain responses are required to relieve these states of arousal. While the individual is in the arousal state he is particularly sensitive to cues in his environment which are associated with his tensions, and when the cues are present the aggressive behavior can be elicited, that is, pulled from the organism. In Berkowitz' conception of aggressive drive, even given a state of arousal (frustration) and an eliciting cue in the environment, a third component—low inhibitions—is needed for an aggressive act to erupt.[7]

Much of Berkowitz' research on this topic has been directed toward defining and isolating certain variables which might contribute to the three components in his model. Whereas frustration and cue associations have been quite successfully manipulated in laboratory situations, it has been more difficult to lower the relatively high inhibitions individuals have against displaying aggressive tendencies. However, Berkowitz and Rawlings devised a successful method to overcome these restraints.[8] Before showing their subjects (*S*s) an aggressive film, they suggested to half the *S*s that the violence in the film was justified, or positively evaluated. They found that previously angered *S*s who saw the film containing justified violence displayed a higher degree of subsequent aggression than those *S*s who saw the same film, but without the justification.

Berkowitz has explained this result by reasoning that *S*s who saw socially approved (justified) aggressive behavior in the film may have become convinced, at least for the moment, that they too would be justified in aggressing against their own frustrater—an examiner who had angered them by insult before they saw the film.[9] Thus, Berkowitz argues, the *S*'s inhibitions against aggression were lowered by justifying the film's aggressive action, thereby facilitating aggressive behavior.

The Berkowitz and Rawlings study used the seven-minute prize fight scene from the 1949 movie *Champion,* in which the protagonist, played by Kirk Douglas, received a severe beating. The degree of justification was manipulated by varying a tape recorded introduction to the film which purportedly explained what had happened up to the time of the scene. The justified introduction portrayed Douglas as a scoundrel, while the less justified version depicted him in a rather sympathetic manner. The measure of aggression was a scaled rating of the insulting examiner.

In subsequent research Berkowitz has continued to use the justified film introduction of the Berkowitz and Rawlings study as the method to elicit optimum

---

[7] Leonard Berkowitz, "Impulse, Aggression, and the Gun," *Psychology Today* 2 (1968): 18–22.

[8] Leonard Berkowitz and Edna Rawlings, "Effects of Film Violence on Inhibitions Against Subsequent Aggression," *Journal of Abnormal and Social Psychology* 66 (1963): 405–12.

[9] Leonard Berkowitz, *Aggression: A Social Psychological Analysis* (New York: McGraw-Hill, 1962), p. 242.

aggression from *S*s. However, there are conditions under which violent acts can appear to be justified other than by describing the victim as a scoundrel. Other types of justification appear in the media today, and are normally more specific than the Berkowitz and Rawlings justification. That is, rather than create an overall disposition to sympathize with or to dislike a character, the media justifications deal more directly with the situation at the time the potential aggressor is confronted with the opportunity to aggress. Certain characteristics of the situation cause some actions to appear justified, while others do not.

If Berkowitz is correct in arguing that justification per se is crucial in determining the response, two types of justification appearing regularly on television and in films, characterized as "vengeance" and "self-defense," should yield the same results if substituted for the more general Berkowitz and Rawlings justification. Vengeance is the motive of someone, previously harmed by another, for his later retaliation, whereas the self-defense justification philosophy is "kill-or-be-killed."

The second component, as mentioned in the Berkowitz conception, is the cue association between the film scene and the experimental setting. In testing this phenomenon experimentally, Berkowitz used a Confederate (*C*) posing as a second *S* to anger *S*, then, after viewing the film, *S* was given a sanctioned opportunity to electrically shock *C*. In a number of studies,[10] it has been demonstrated that if *C*'s name or description was associated with the victim in the film violence or with the film violence generally, he would receive stronger shocks after *S* had seen the film than if his name or label was unrelated to the film scene. Berkowitz and LePage successfully used a weapon "incidentally" placed in the experimental room as an aggressive cue.[11] And Geen more recently demonstrated that the boxing film could be used merely as an aggression-related cue to enhance *S*'s aggressive activity.[12]

The current study considers a cue property of a different sort. Of the two manipulated variables (vengeance and self-defense), the vengeance justification described a situation in the film which was very similar to the situation *S* was in during the experimental session. That is, *S* had been angered by *C*, posing as another *S*, and after seeing the film, *S* was given sanctioned opportunity to shock *C*. In this case there was a cue present which tied the vengeance introduction more closely to the postfantasy setting than the self-defense introduction. The current study sought to determine if the Berkowitz notion of interconnecting cue properties was applicable to this more indirect situation.

---

[10] Leonard Berkowitz, "Some Aspects of Observed Aggression," *Journal of Personality and Social Psychology* 2 (1965): 359–69; Leonard Berkowitz and Russell Geen, "Film Violence and the Cue Properties of Available Targets," *Journal of Personality and Social Psychology* 3 (1966): 525–30; Leonard Berkowitz and Russell Geen, "Stimulus Qualities of the Target of Aggression: A Further Study," *Journal of Personality and Social Psychology* 5 (1967): 364–68; Russell Geen and Leonard Berkowitz, "Name-Mediated Aggressive Cue Properties," *Journal of Personality* 34 (1966): 456–65.

[11] Leonard Berkowitz and Anthony LePage, "Weapons as Aggression-Eliciting Stimuli," *Journal of Personality and Social Psychology* 7 (1967): 202–07.

[12] Russell Geen, "Effects of Frustration, Attack, and Prior Training in Aggressiveness upon Aggressive Behavior," *Journal of Personality and Social Psychology* 9 (1968): 316–21.

The experimental design involved both the presence and absence of the two critical variables—vengeance and self-defense justifications for the film violence. The vengeance justification explained that the protagonist, a boxer named Midge Kelly (Kirk Douglas), had previously defeated the opposing boxer, named Johnny Dunne, and in so doing had ruthlessly injured Dunne. Thus Dunne was motivated by vengeance to retaliate against Kelly. The self-defense justification simply called Kelly a fighter with a "killer instinct," battling with a "kill-or-be-killed" philosophy. In this case Dunne was motivated by self-defense to protect himself against the powerful Kelly. Additionally, a neutral condition containing neither of the two justifications was used. It was similar in length to the other two introductions, but without justification. The final condition was a combination, using key information from both the vengeance and self-defense justifications. This condition was included to determine the relative effectiveness of adding information to an already complete justification, and to assess possible interactions.

Methods

The *S*s were 60 male volunteers from introductory psychology courses at the University of Wisconsin. Each *S* attended one testing session, lasting about 35 minutes. The experiment employed the same basic procedures used by Berkowitz and Geen in their recent studies, but with some modifications. The entire experiment was disguised as an experiment dealing with the effects of punishment on learning.

The *C*, a male undergraduate assistant, and the *S* were given preliminary instructions in the same room, after which *C* was moved to an adjoining room. Thus *C* and *S* were placed in separate rooms much earlier in the session than in the Berkowitz studies. This procedure aimed to minimize possible unintended influences *C* may have had on the behavior of *S*, a problem emphasized by Rosenthal.[13]

Anger was aroused in the following manner. *S* was given a list of twelve items and told to give his opinion on each into a microphone for *C* to hear. The items were topics of general interest to college males or were somewhat related to the movie topic. This procedure was used to supposedly establish a "base-line comparison" between *S* and *C* to be used in evaluating the learning techniques.

Among the items used were: "Professional boxing is a cruel sport which should be outlawed," and, "All full-time college students should receive automatic draft deferments." *S* was told that *C* would administer an electric shock to *S* if he disagreed with *S*'s opinions. By a previously determined schedule, *C* shocked *S* on nine of the twelve items.

In addition, *S* was told he would see a portion of the film to help him gain

[13] Robert Rosenthal, *Experimenter Effects in Behavioral Research* (New York: Appleton-Century-Crofts, 1966).

some of the "flavor" of it. *C* had supposedly seen the film the previous day, and was to recall relationships from the film during the experiment. *S* then heard the appropriate introduction (justification) before the film, then saw the film scene. After the film *S* was seated at an aggression machine,[14] and given some "coded relationships" (actually just combinations of three letters) to transmit for *C* to "learn." *S* was told to shock *C* each time *C* responded incorrectly to the relationships. Of the 20 trials, *C* made twelve "wrong" responses, each one giving *S* an opportunity to administer his choice of ten intensities of electric shock. The shocks were described to him as ranging "from a relatively weak shock at button one to quite a painful one at button ten." The mean intensity of the shocks given by *S* thus was the operational definition of aggressive activity in the study. (*S*, of course, did not actually shock *C*, but rather his shock intensity *selections* were recorded.) [15]

Results

It was predicted that *S*s would act more aggressively if the aggression in the film they witnessed was justified, and that aggression would be greater if the justification were vengeance than if it were self-defense. The results of the analysis of variance, and accompanying cell means, reported in Table 1, shows that this prediction was generally upheld.

TABLE 1
SUMMARY OF ANALYSIS OF VARIANCE OF MEAN SHOCK INTENSITIES

Source of variance	*Degrees of freedom*	*Mean square*	*F ratio*
Vengeance (A)	1	18.497	11.94**
Self-Defense (B)	1	.006	<1.00
A x B	1	4.990	3.22
Within	56	1.549	
TOTAL	59		

** $= p < .01$.

MEAN SHOCK INTENSITIES

	Vengeance absent	*Vengeance present*
Self-Defense Absent	3.90_{c}	5.59_{a}
Self-Defense Present	4.47_{bc}	5.00_{ab}

Note: Cells having a subscript in common are not significantly different (at the .05 level) by Duncan Multiple Range Test. There were 15 subjects in each condition.

---

[14] Arnold Buss, *The Psychology of Aggression* (New York: Wiley, 1961); K. M. Shemberg, D. B. Leventhal, and L. Allman, "Aggression Machine Performance and Rated Aggression," *Journal of Experimental Research in Personality* 3 (1968): 117–19.

[15] A complete transcript of experimental instructions and materials may be obtained from the author (School of Journalism, University of Wisconsin, Madison, Wis. 53706).

*S*s who heard the vengeance justification for the film exhibited the most aggression while those who heard the neutral introduction displayed the least. In addition, *S*s in the self-defense condition showed significantly less aggression than did those in the vengeance condition; however, there was no significant difference between aggression scores in the self-defense and neutral conditions.

Scores in the combination condition, which used basic elements from both the vengeance and self-defense conditions, were midway between the means of the individual vengeance and self-defense conditions. The subjects' aggression in this condition was significantly greater than that in the neutral condition, but was not different from that in the vengeance and self-defense conditions alone.

Discussion

The significant difference between the aggression displayed in the vengeance and self-defense conditions was specifically predicted through the extension of Berkowitz' notion of eliciting cue properties. Thus the similarity between the justification for the film violence and the justification for *S*s' aggression in the experimental situation could be interpreted as a disinhibition to *S*s' potential aggression. Aggression in the combination condition was midway between that in the vengeance and self-defense conditions, with no interaction evident.

The generally higher aggression scores in the various justification conditions substantiate and extend the finding of Berkowitz and Rawlings. Whereas Berkowitz formulated a general notion concerning the effects of justification for violence, the present study has demonstrated that this prediction is revelant and can be appropriately applied to specific justifications derived from current media drama plots. In demonstrating the increase in disinhibition in *S*s exposed to the vengeance justification, these results suggest a potential paradox facing the media in their current attempts at self-regulation. The Television Code of the National Association of Broadcasters points out the industry's position in such matters by saying, "Crime should not be presented as attractive or as a solution to human problems, and the inevitable retribution should be made clear." [16] In other words, the favorable treatment of crime should be avoided, but when crime or violence does occur, the offender should receive his "just deserts."

A 60-second promotional film recently being used by NAB-member television stations makes the same point, only more dramatically. The audio track contains this message: "Kids are impressionable. That's why at this station we watch the programs and commercials your child watches—carefully. He may see bad guys, but not in the role of heroes. He'll learn that crime doesn't pay."

As for why aggression in the combination condition, contrary to that in the vengeance condition, was not significantly different from that in the self-defense condition, it can be argued that the combination simply did not justify the film violence identically to the experimental situation. That is, the addition of part of

---

[16] Television Code of the National Association of Broadcasters, in *1969 Broadcasting Yearbook,* p. D-3.

the self-defense justification to the basic elements of the vengeance justification may have resulted in the combination condition being dissimilar enough from the experimental setting to result in insufficient disinhibition to *Ss'* aggression. Only the vengeance condition had this strong cue similarity between the justification and the experimental setting, and it, therefore, resulted in the highest level of aggression by the *Ss*.

The vengeance condition may have yielded significantly higher aggression scores than the self-defense condition for another reason besides its cue property connection. It may be that vengeance is a more powerful form of justification than is self-defense, particularly when it is used in the context of a boxing match. That is, boxing, by definition, is a sport based on self-defense. Thus a boxing film probably has an inherent self-defense justification to begin with, making an additional self-defense justification redundant. However, the vengeance justification was able to add to this implicit self-defense rationale, and demonstrate what may have been the only real justification effect in the study. Unfortunately, the present study is unable to precisely evaluate this question. Further investigation into the nature of justification is required.

In interpreting the results of the current study, two key points should be kept in mind. First, the study deals only with the short term effects of viewing violence. A study of longer range effects to more specifically determine the generality of the observed phenomena remains to be done. And second, the reported effects attributed to justification have been observed using only one film—the prize fight from *Champion.* The rationale under which the effects due to justification have been predicted can only gain power if similar results are obtained using a broader sample of films.

Nevertheless, the current results do suggest that the media code position that violence should be shown in a justified context may not be appropriate. By placing specific justifications derived from the media into an experimental setting, it has been found that, at least under the circumstances employed, the witnessing of justified violence tends to increase, rather than to decrease, the probability that subsequent aggression will occur. Thus the critical assumption made by the codes has not been supported. As Tannenbaum and Greenberg have recently pointed out; the media, in emphasizing the crime doesn't pay philosophy, "may actually be undermining the very moral and behavioral qualities they seek to promote." [17]

---

[17] Percy Tannenbaum and Bradley Greenberg, "Mass Communication," in *Annual Review of Psychology* 19 (1968): 351–86.

27

The Study of Urban Violence: Some Implications of Laboratory Studies of Frustration and Aggression

LEONARD BERKOWITZ

Year after year, an ever increasing number of American cities are faced with outbreaks of widespread violence. The costs of urban violence, both in human and economic terms, are so great and its implications for social life are so far-reaching that it has become a major public and academic concern.

In the selection which follows, Berkowitz identifies and evaluates some of the more common explanations offered by students of human behavior for the mob violence in contemporary America. Subsequently, he traces the implications of these different explanations for social policy decisions. The fact that different explanations may lead to diametrically opposed "solutions" means that the layman must be familiar with the rudiments of scientific criticism if he is to act responsibly as a member of society.

The specific explanations which Berkowitz contrasts are: (1) Lorenz' psychophysiological theory and (2) frustration-aggression theory, presented initially by Dollard and his associates at Yale some three decades ago. He is rather severe in his criticism of Lorenz' explanation of and solution for human aggression. He clearly finds the frustration-aggression model more insightful, but he insists upon some alterations in it in order to account for historical variations in human violence.

The author offers no easy solution to this growing social problem, but he does point out some of the policy implications of current social psychological knowledge. Before one labels the suggestions "common sense," he might attempt to explain why they are so seldom acted upon. Or, if one considers the theoretical ideas on which the suggestions are based to be

Leonard Berkowitz, "The Study of Urban Violence: Some Implications of Laboratory Studies of Frustration and Aggression," in L. H. Masotti and D. R. Bowen, eds., *Riots and Rebellion: Civil Violence in the Urban Community.* Beverly Hills, California: Sage Publications, Inc., 1968, pp. 39–49. By permission of the publisher, Sage Publications, Inc., Beverly Hills, California.

faulty, it would be an exciting and worthwhile exercise to lay out those criticisms in a logical form and to evaluate them.

The frustration-aggression hypothesis is the easiest and by far the most popular explanation of social violence—whether political turmoil, the hot summers of riot and disorder, or robberies and juvenile delinquency. We are all familiar with this formulation, and there is no need to spell out once again the great number of economic, social, and psychological frustrations that have been indicted as the source of aggression and domestic instability. Espoused in the social world primarily by political and economic liberals, this notion contends that the cause of civil tranquility is best served by eliminating barriers to the satisfaction of human needs and wants. Indeed, in the version that has attracted the greatest attention, the one spelled out by Dollard and his colleagues at Yale in 1939, it is argued that "aggression is always the result of frustration." [1]

The widespread acceptance of the frustration-aggression hypothesis, however, has not kept this formula safe from criticism. Since we are here concerned with the roots of violence, it is important to look closely at the relationship between frustration and aggression and consider the objections that have been raised. These criticisms have different, sometimes radically divergent, implications for social policy decisions. Before beginning this discussion, two points should be made clear. One, I believe in the essential validity of the frustration-aggression hypothesis, although I would modify it somewhat and severely restrict its scope. Two, with the Yale psychologists I prefer to define a "frustration" as the blocking of ongoing, goal-directed activity, rather than as the emotional reaction to this blocking.

One type of criticism is today most clearly associated with the ideas and writings of the eminent ethnologist, Konrad Lorenz. Throughout much of his long and productive professional career Lorenz has emphasized that the behavior of organisms—humans as well as lower animals, fish, and birds—is largely endogenously motivated; the mainsprings of action presumably arise from within. Behavior, he says, results from the spontaneous accumulation of some excitation or substance in neural centers. The external stimulus that seems to produce the action theoretically only "unlocks" inhibitory processes, thereby "releasing" the response. The behavior is essentially not a reaction to this external stimulus, but is supposedly actually impelled by the internal force, drive, or something, and is only let loose by the stimulus. If a sufficient amount of the internal excitation or substance accumulates before the organism can encounter a releasing stimulus,

[1] John Dollard et al., *Frustration and Aggression* (New Haven: Yale University Press, 1939), p. 3.

the response will go off by itself. In his latest book, *On Aggression,* Lorenz interprets aggressive behavior in just this manner. "It is the spontaneity of the [aggressive] instinct," he maintains, "that makes it so dangerous." [2] The behavior "can 'explode' without demonstrable external stimulation" merely because the internal accumulating *something* had not been discharged through earlier aggression. He strongly believes that "present-day civilized man suffers from insufficient discharge of his aggressive drive. . . ." [3] Lorenz's position, then, is that frustrations are, at best, an unimportant source of aggression.

We will not here go into a detailed discussion of the logical and empirical status of the Lorenzian account of behavior. I should note, however, that a number of biologists and comparative psychologists have severely criticized his analysis of animal behavior. Among other things, they object to his vague and imprecise concepts, and his excessive tendency to reason by crude analogies. Moreover, since Lorenz's ideas have attracted considerable popular attention, both in his own writings and in *The Territorial Imperative* by Robert Ardrey, we should look at the evidence he presents for his interpretation of human behavior. Thus, as one example, he says his views are supported by the failures of "an American method of education" to produce less aggressive children, even though the youngsters have been supposedly "spared all disappointments and indulged in every way." [4] Since excessively indulged children probably expect to be gratified most of the time, so that the inevitable occasional frustrations they encounter are actually relatively strong thwartings for them, Lorenz's observation must leave the frustration-aggression hypothesis unscathed. His anthropological documentation is equally crude. A psychiatrist is quoted who supposedly "proved" that the Ute Indians have an unusually high neurosis rate because they are not permitted to discharge the strong aggressive drive bred in them during their warlike past.[5] Nothing is said about their current economic and social frustrations. Again, we are told of a psychoanalyst who "showed" that the survival of some Bornean tribes is in jeopardy because they can no longer engage in head-hunting.[6] In this regard, the anthropologist Edmund Leach has commented that Lorenz's anthropology is "way off," and reports that these Bornean tribes are actually having a rapid growth in population.

Another citation also illustrates one of Lorenz's major cures for aggressive behavior. He tells us that quarrels and fights often tear apart polar expeditions or other isolated groups of men. These people, Lorenz explains, had experienced an unfortunate damming up of aggression because their isolation had kept them from discharging their aggressive drive in attacks on "strangers or people outside their own circle of friends." [7] In such circumstances, according to Lorenz, "the

---

[2] Konrad Lorenz, *On Aggression* (New York: Harcourt, Brace & World, 1966), p. 50.
[3] Ibid., p. 243.
[4] Ibid., p. 50.
[5] Ibid., p. 244.
[6] Ibid., p. 261.
[7] Ibid., p. 55.

man of perception finds an outlet by creeping out of the barracks (tent, igloo) and smashing a not too expensive object with as resounding a crash as the occasion merits." [8] According to this formulation, then, one of the best ways to prevent people from fighting is to provide them with "safe" or innocuous ways of venting their aggressive urge. Efforts to minimize their frustrations would presumably be wasted or at least relatively ineffective.

I must strongly disagree with Lorenz's proposed remedy for conflict. Informal observations as well as carefully controlled laboratory experiments indicate that attacks upon supposedly safe targets do not lessen, and can even increase, the likelihood of later aggression. We know, for example, that some persons have a strong inclination to be prejudiced against almost everyone who is different from them. For these prejudiced personalities, the expression of hostility against some groups of outsiders does not make them any friendlier toward other persons. Angry people may perhaps feel better when they can attack some scapegoat, but this does not necessarily mean their aggressive tendencies have been lessened. The pogroms incited by the Czar's secret police were no more successful in preventing the Russian Revolution than were the Russo-Japanese and Russo-Germanic wars. Attacks on minority groups and foreigners did not drain away the hostility toward the frustrating central government. Aggression can stimulate further aggression, at least until physical exhaustion, fear, or guilt inhibits further violence. Rather than providing a calming effect, the destruction, burning, and looting that take place during the initial stages of a riot seem to provoke still more violence. Further, several recent laboratory studies have demonstrated that giving children an opportunity to play aggressive games does not decrease the attacks they later will make upon some peer, and has a good chance of heightening the strength of these subsequent attacks.[9]

These misgivings, it should be clear, are not based on objections to the notion of innate determinants of aggression. Some criticisms of the frustration-aggression hypothesis have argued against the assumption of a "built-in" relationship between frustration and aggression, but there is today a much greater recognition of the role of constitutional determinants in human behavior. However, we probably should not think of these innate factors as constantly active instinctive drives. Contemporary biological research suggests these innate determinants could be likened to a "built-in wiring diagram" instead of a goading force. The "wiring" or neural connections makes it easy for certain actions to occur, but only in response to particular stimuli.[10] The innate factors are linkages between stimuli and responses—and an appropriate stimulus must be present if the behavior is to be elicited. Frustrations, in other words, may inherently increase the likelihood of aggressive reactions. Man might well have a constitutional

---

[8] Ibid., p. 56.

[9] For example, S. K. Mallick and B. R. McCandless, "A Study of Catharsis of Aggression," *Journal of Personality and Social Psychology* 4 (1966): 591–96.

[10] See L. Berkowitz, "The Concept of Aggressive Drive," in L. Berkowitz, ed., *Advances in Experimental Social Psychology,* Vol. 2 (New York: Academic Press, 1965).

predisposition to become aggressive after being thwarted. Clearly, however, other factors—such as fear of punishment or learning to respond in non-aggressive ways to frustrations—could prevent this potential from being realized.

It is somewhat easier to accept this interpretation of the frustration-aggression hypothesis, if we do not look at frustration as an emotionally neutral event. Indeed, an increasing body of animal and human research suggests that the consequences of a severe thwarting can be decidedly similar to those produced by punishment and pain. In the language of the experimental psychologists, the frustration is an aversive stimulus, and aversive stimuli are very reliable sources of aggressive behavior. But setting aside the specific emotional quality of the frustration, more and more animal and human experimentation has provided us with valuable insights into the frustration-aggression relationship.

This relationship, first of all, is very widespread among the various forms of life; pigeons have been found to become aggressive following a thwarting much as human children and adults do. In a recent experiment by Azrin, Hutchinson, and Hake,[11] for example, pigeons were taught to peck at a key by providing them with food every time they carried out such an action. Then after the key-pressing response was well established, the investigators suddenly stopped giving the bird food for his behavior. If there was no other animal present in the experimental chamber at the time, the pigeon exhibited only a flurry of action. When another pigeon was nearby, however, this burst of responding did not take place and the thwarted bird instead attacked the other pigeon. The frustration led to aggression, but only when a suitable target was present. This last qualification dealing with the nature of the available target is very important.

Before getting to this matter of the stimulus qualities of the target, another aspect of frustrations should be made explicit. Some opponents of the frustration-aggression hypothesis have assumed a person is frustrated whenever he has been deprived of the ordinary goals of social life for a long period of time. This assumption is not compatible with the definition of "frustration" I put forth at the beginning of this paper or with the results of recent experimentation. Contrary to traditional motivational thinking and the motivational concepts of Freud and Lorenz, many psychologists now insist that deprivations alone are inadequate to account for most motivated behavior. According to this newer theorizing, much greater weight must be given to anticipations of the goal than merely to the duration or magnitude of deprivation per se. The stimulation arising from these anticipations—from anticipatory goal responses—is now held to be a major determinant of the vigor and persistence of goal-seeking activity. As one psychologist (Mowrer) put it, we cannot fully account for goal-striving unless we give some attention to "hope." Whether a person's goal is food, a sexual object, or a color TV set, his goal-seeking is most intense when he is thinking of the goal and anticipating the satisfactions the food, sexual object, or TV set will bring. But

---

[11] N. H. Azrin, R. R. Hutchinson, and D. F. Hake, "Extinction-Induced Aggression," *Journal of Experimental Animal Behavior* 9 (1966): 191–204.

similarly, his frustration is most severe when the anticipated satisfactions are not achieved.[12]

The politico-social counterpart of this theoretical formulation is obvious; the phrase "revolution of rising expectations" refers to just this conception of frustration. Poverty-stricken groups who had never dreamed of having automobiles, washing machines, or new homes are not frustrated merely because they had been deprived of these things; they are frustrated only after they had begun to hope. If they had dared to think they might get these objects and had anticipated their satisfactions, the inability to fulfill their anticipations is a frustration. Privations in themselves are much less likely to breed violence than is the dashing of hopes.

James Davies has employed this type of reasoning in his theory of revolutions.[13] The American, French, and Russian Revolutions did not arise because these people were subjected to prolonged, severe hardships, Davies suggests. In each of these revolutions, and others as well, the established order was overthrown when a sudden, sharp socioeconomic *decline* abruptly thwarted the hopes and expectations that had begun to develop in the course of gradually improving conditions. Some data recently reported by Feierabend and Feierabend[14] can also be understood in these terms. They applied the frustration-aggression hypothesis to the study of political instability in a very impressive cross-national investigation. Among other things, they observed that rapid change in modernization within a society (as indicated by changes in such measures as the percentage of people having a primary education and the per capita consumption of calories) was associated with a relatively great increase in political instability (p. 265).[15] It could be that the rapid socioeconomic improvements produce more hopes and expectations than can be fulfilled. Hope outstrips reality, even though conditions are rapidly improving for the society as a whole, and many of the people in the society are frustrated. Some such process, of course, may be occurring in the case of our present Negro revolution.

Let me now return to the problem of the stimulus qualities of the target of aggression. Recall that in the experiment with the frustrated pigeons the thwarted birds did not display their characteristic aggressive behavior unless another pigeon was nearby. The presence of an appropriate stimulus object was evidently necessary to evoke aggression from the aroused animals. Essentially similar findings have been obtained in experiments in which painful electric shocks were administered to rats.[16] Here too the aroused animals only attacked certain targets; the shocked

---

[12] See Berkowitz, *Advances*, for a further discussion, and also L. Berkowitz, ed., *Roots of Aggression: A Re-examination of the Frustration-Aggression Hypothesis* (New York: Atherton Press, 1968).

[13] J. C. Davies, "Toward a Theory of Revolution," *American Sociological Review* 27 (1962): 5–19.

[14] I. K. Feierabend and R. L. Feierabend, "Aggressive Behaviors Within Polities, 1948–1962: A Cross-National Study," *Journal of Conflict Resolution* 10 (1966): 249–71.

[15] Ibid., p. 265.

[16] R. E. Ulrich and N. H. Azrin, "Reflexive Fighting in Response to Aversive Stimulation," *Journal of Experimental Animal Behavior* 5 (1962): 511–20.

rats did not attack a doll placed in the experimental chamber, whether the doll was moving or stationary. Nor did they attack a recently deceased rat lying motionless in the cage. If the dead animal was moved, however, attacks were made. Comparable results have been obtained when electrical stimulation was applied to the hypothalamus of cats.[17] Objects having certain sizes or shapes were attacked, while other kinds of objects were left alone.

This tendency for aroused animals to attack only particular targets can perhaps be explained by means of Lorenz's concept of the releasing stimulus. The particular live and/or moving target "releases" the animal's aggressive response. But note that the action is not the product of some gradually accumulating excitation or instinctive aggressive drive. The pigeon, rat, or cat, we might say, was first emotionally aroused (by the frustration, pain, or hypothalamic stimulation) and the appropriate stimulus object then released or evoked the action.

Similar processes operate at the human level. A good many (but not all) aggressive acts are impulsive in nature. Strong emotional arousal creates a predisposion to aggression, and the impulsive violent behavior occurs when an appropriate aggressive stimulus is encountered. Several experiments carried out in our Wisconsin laboratory have tried to demonstrate just this. Simply put, our basic hypothesis is that external stimuli associated with aggression will elicit relatively strong attacks from people who, for one reason or another, are ready to act aggressively. A prime example of such an aggressive stimulus, of course, is a weapon. One of our experiments has shown that angered college students who were given an opportunity to attack their tormentor exhibited much more intense aggression (in the form of electric shocks to their frustrator) when a rifle and pistol were nearby than when a neutral object was present or when there were no irrelevant objects near them.[18] The sight of the weapons evidently drew stronger attacks from the subjects than otherwise would have occurred in the absence of these aggressive objects. Several other experiments, including studies of children playing with aggressive toys, have yielded findings consistent with this analysis.[19] In these investigations, the aggressive objects (guns) acquired their aggressive stimulus properties through the use to which they were put. These stimulus properties can also come about by having the object associated with aggression. Thus, in several of our experiments, people whose name associated them with violent films shown to our subjects later were attacked more strongly by the subjects than were other target-persons who did not have this name-mediated connection with the observed aggression.[20]

These findings are obviously relevant to contemporary America. They of course argue for gun-control legislation, but also have implications for the riots that have torn through our cities this past summer. Some of our political leaders

[17] P. K. Levinson and J. P. Flynn, "The Objects Attacked by Cats During Stimulation of the Hypothalamus," *Animal Behavior* 13 (1965): 217–20.

[18] L. Berkowitz and A. Le Page, "Weapons as Aggression-Eliciting Stimuli," *Journal of Personality and Social Psychology* 7 (1967): 202–07.

[19] E.g., Mallick and McCandless, "Catharsis of Aggression."

[20] See Berkowitz, "Concept of Aggressive Drive," for a summary of some of this research.

seem to be looking for single causes, whether this is a firebrand extremist such as Stokely Carmichael or a history of severe social and economic frustrations. Each of these factors might well have contributed to this summer's rioting; the American Negroes' frustrations undoubtedly were very important. Nevertheless, a complete understanding of the violence, and especially the contagious spread from one city to another, requires consideration of a multiplicity of causes, all operating together. Some of these causes are motivational; rebellious Negroes may have sought revenge, or they may have wanted to assert their masculinity. Much more simply, a good deal of activity during these riots involved the looting of desirable goods and appliances. Not all of the violence was this purposive, however. Some of it arose through the automatic operation of aggressive stimuli in a highly emotional atmosphere.

This impulsive mob violence was clearly not part of a calculated war against the whites. Where a deliberate anti-white campaign would have dictated attacks upon whites in all-white bastions, it was often Negro property that was destroyed. Moreover, aggressive stimuli had an important role. A lifetime of cruel frustrations built up a readiness for aggression, but this readiness had to be activated and inhibitions had to be lowered in order to produce the impulsive behavior. Different types of aggressive stimuli contributed to the aggressive actions. Some of these stimuli originated in the news reports, photographs, and films from other cities; research in a number of laboratories throughout this country and Canada indicates that observed aggression can stimulate aggressive behavior. This media-stimulated aggression may not always be immediately apparent. Some aggressive responses may operate only internally, in the form of clenched fists and violent ideas, but they can increase the probability and strength of later open aggression. The news stories probably also lower restraints against this open violence. A person who is in doubt as to whether destruction and looting are safe and/or proper behavior might have his doubts resolved; if other people do this sort of thing, maybe it isn't so bad. Maybe it is a good way to act and not so dangerous after all. And again the likelihood of aggression is heightened.

Then a precipitating event occurs in the Negro ghetto. The instigating stimulus could be an attack by whites against Negroes—a report of police brutality against some Negro—or it might be the sight of aggressive objects such as weapons, or even police. Police probably can function as stimuli automatically eliciting aggression from angry Negroes. They are the "head thumpers," the all-too-often hostile enforcers of laws arbitrarily imposed upon Negroes by an alien world. Mayor Cavanagh of Detroit has testified to this aggression-evoking effect. Answering criticisms of the delay in sending in police reinforcements at the first sign of rioting, he said experience in various cities around the country indicates the presence of police can inflame angry mobs and actually increase violence (*Meet the Press,* July 30, 1967). Of course the events in Milwaukee the week after Mayor Cavanagh spoke suggest that an army of police and National Guardsmen swiftly applied can restrain and then weaken mob violence fairly effectively. This rapid, all-blanketing police action obviously produces strong inhibitions, allowing time for the emotions inflamed by the precipitating event to cool down. Emptying the streets also removes aggression-eliciting stimuli; there is no one around to see other people looting and burning. But unless this extremely expensive complete inhibition can be achieved quickly, city officials might be advised to employ other law-enforcement techniques. Too weak a display of police force might be worse than none at all. One possibility is to have Negroes from outside the regular police department attempt to disperse the highly charged crowds. There are disadvantages, of course. The use of such an extra-police organization might be interpreted as a weakening of the community authority or a sign of the breakdown of the duly constituted forces of law and order. But there is also at least one very real advantage. The amateur law enforcers do not have a strong association with aggression and arbitrary frustration, and thus are less likely to draw out aggressive reactions from the emotionally charged people.

There are no easy solutions to the violence in our cities' streets. The causes are complex and poorly understood, and the possible remedies challenge our intelligence, cherished beliefs, and pocketbooks. I am convinced, however, that the roots of this violence are not to be found in any instinctive aggressive drive, and that there is no easy cure in the provision of so-called "safe" aggressive outlets. The answers can only be found in careful, systematic research free of the shopworn, oversimplified analogies of the past.

28

Implications of Laboratory Studies of Aggression for the Control and Regulation of Violence

RICHARD H. WALTERS

Social scientists seldom explore the practical implications of their research findings, but emphasize instead the theoretical significance that might be attached to them. Since many of the findings seem contradictory to the untrained eye of the layman, he will either ignore the work of social scientists altogether, act on the basis of those selected findings that he "understands," or voice the query: What does it all mean? Each of these courses of action is easily exemplified in regard to studies of aggression. There are those who argue that since "the experts" can't agree about the consequences of viewing media violence, the punishment of aggressive behavior, etc., the consequences must not be very important anyway. On the other hand, there are those who read that a social scientist found that subjects faced with a threat of punishment were less likely to behave aggressively than were subjects who faced no threat. Subsequently, these laymen support corporal punishment on "scientific grounds." Others, however, ask the social scientist to "make sense" out of his and his colleagues' work, so that they can make more rational decisions in the area on a day-to-day-basis.

In the selection which follows, Walters spells out some of the implications of numerous laboratory studies in the area of aggression. The reader would find it profitable to evaluate some of our social practices such as mass media codes, movie ratings, child discipline, physical-contact sports, etc., in light of Walters' observations.

Richard H. Walters, "Implications of Laboratory Studies of Aggression for the Control and Regulation of Violence," *The Annals of the American Academy of Political and Social Science* 364 (March 1966): 60–72.

During the present decade there has been considerable interest among child and social psychologists in the problem of the control and regulation of violence. This period, also, has yielded a relatively large number of laboratory studies aimed at determining conditions under which aggressive behavior is learned and at identifying motivational and environmental factors that increase or decrease the probability that aggression will be displayed. Representative samples of these studies, as well as a few earlier studies, are briefly described in this paper, and an attempt is made to assess their implications for the problem of the social control of aggression in real-life situations.[1]

Exposure to Aggressive Models

Field studies of delinquency [2] and of the effects of parental child-training practices on the behavior of children [3] have yielded findings that strongly suggest that aggressive parents are more likely to have aggressive children than are parents who are relatively nonaggressive. Parents are, of course, not the only transmitters of social-behavior patterns; a child who grows up in an area in which he is surrounded by crime and violence may adopt the prevailing sub-cultural standards even if his parents are nonviolent and law-abiding.[4] In our "blackboard jungles" children are both provided with ample opportunities to observe successful violence and rewarded for imitative aggressive behavior.

The advent of the motion picture and television permits the exposure of children to a range of models much wider than that which their immediate social environment can supply. Although some major studies of the influence of television on children's behavior do not support the view that the social influence of this medium of communication is generally deleterious,[5] there seems little doubt

[1] Value judgments are involved in the categorization of an act as aggressive. The concept of aggression is consequently not purely descriptive and thus has limited usefulness in guiding social-psychological research. However, a discussion of possible definitions is beyond the scope of this paper. The problems of defining quasi-objective social-psychological concepts are briefly discussed by Albert Bandura and Richard H. Walters, *Social Learning and Personality Development* (New York: Holt, Rinehart, and Winston, 1963), and by Richard H. Walters and Ross D. Parke, "Social Motivation, Dependency, and Susceptibility to Social Influence," *Advances in Experimental Social Psychology,* Vol. 1, ed. Leonard Berkowitz (New York: Academic Press, 1964), p. 231–76.

[2] For example: William McCord and Joan McCord, "The Effects of Parental Role Models on Criminality," *Journal of Social Issues* 14 (1958): 66–74; Albert Bandura and Richard H. Walters, *Adolescent Aggression* (New York: Ronald Press, 1959).

[3] Albert Bandura, "Relationship of Family Patterns to Child Behavior Disorders, Progress Report (1960)," U.S.P.H.S. Research Grant M-1734, Stanford University; Robert R. Sears, Eleanor E. Maccoby, and Harry Levin, *Patterns of Child-Rearing* (Evanston, Ill.: Row, Peterson, 1957).

[4] Clifford R. Shaw and Henry McKay, "Social Factors in Juvenile Delinquency," *Report on the Causes of Crime,* Vol. II (Washington, D.C.: U.S. Government Printing Office, 1931).

[5] Hilde T. Himmelweit, A. N. Oppenheim, and Pamela Vince, *Television and the Child: An Empirical Study of the Effect of Television on the Young* (New York: Oxford University Press, 1958); Wilbur Schramm, Jack Lyle, and Edwin B. Parker, *Television in the*

that, in some cases, seriously violent episodes might not have occurred if the agent or agents had not been exposed to aggressive movie or television models.

A series of laboratory studies by Bandura and his coworkers, in which children were exposed to real-life or film-mediated models, provide the strongest evidence in favor of the view that children should not be exposed to aggressive models if the goal of our society is to reduce violence. In the first of these studies,[6] nursery-school children participated in a "game" involving guessing which of two boxes contained a picture sticker. A female experimenter, the other participant, made functionless incidental responses while she took her turn in the game. For children in the experimental condition, the model's incidental responses included aggressive acts directed against dolls; for the control children, the model's behavior was entirely nonaggressive. In executing the discrimination task, aggressive behavior was exhibited by 90 percent of the children who had been exposed to the aggressive model. In contrast, not one of the control children displayed aggression.

A second study [7] indicated that the model need not be present for imitative aggression to occur. Two groups of nursery-school children spent ten minutes in a room where they could observe the behavior of an adult model. One group saw the model attack an inflated Bobo doll, both physically and verbally; the other group saw the model play with a thinker-toy set in a nonaggressive way. Following exposure to the model, the children were mildly frustrated and then taken to another room containing a variety of toys, some of which could be used as aggressive implements. A control group of children was given a similar experience without prior exposure to a model. Children who had been exposed to an aggressive model showed more imitative physical and verbal aggressive behavior than did children in the other two groups.

Bandura and his associates [8] next compared the influence of an aggressive model presented in person with that of aggressive models presented on film. Four conditions were employed: human adult model, filmed human adult model, filmed cartoon model (an adult dressed up as a cat), and no model. The procedure was otherwise essentially the same as in the study just described. All groups of children exposed to an aggressive model showed more aggression in the test situation than did the control group. The over-all findings, based on a variety of measures of specifically imitative and nonspecifically imitative aggression, indicated that exposure to human subjects portraying aggression in movies was the most effective method of eliciting and shaping aggressive behavior.

Lives of Our Children (Stanford, Calif.: Stanford University Press, 1961); J. T. Klapper, *The Effects of Mass Communication* (Glencoe, Ill.: Free Press, 1960).

[6] Albert Bandura and Aletha C. Huston, "Identification as a Process of Incidental Learning," *Journal of Abnormal and Social Psychology* 63 (1961): 311–18.

[7] Albert Bandura, Dorothea Ross, and Sheila A. Ross, "Transmission of Aggression through Imitation of Aggressive Models," *Journal of Abnormal and Social Psychology* 63 (1961): 575–82.

[8] Albert Bandura, Dorothea Ross, and Sheila A. Ross, "Imitation of Film-Mediated Models," *Journal of Abnormal and Social Psychology* 66 (1963): 3–11.

Two other studies indicate that observation of filmed aggression increases the probability that children will subsequently display aggressive behavior. In a study by Lövaas,[9] children in a day-care center were provided with the choice of depressing one of two levers, one of which operated a hitting doll, the other a ball in a cage. Half the children were shown an aggressive cartoon film, and the remainder a nonaggressive cartoon. Immediately after watching one of the films, the children were left with the two lever-operated toys for a four-minute period. Children who had seen the aggressive cartoon depressed the lever that operated the hitting doll more frequently than those who had watched the non-aggressive cartoon. Analogous findings are reported by Mussen and Rutherford,[10] who also used cartoon films, but assessed their effects by questioning children concerning their desire to "pop" an inflated balloon held by the experimenter.

The studies so far cited tested child subjects in a play setting and did not use a commercial film sequence typical of those that have been criticized for their possible effects on the viewer. Walters and Llewellyn Thomas [11] studied the effects of presenting the knife-fight scene from the movie *Rebel Without a Cause* to both adolescent boys and male and female adults. Both before and after viewing the movie, the subjects were given the task of inflicting electric shock on a confederate of the experimenter, who was supposedly another subject. In comparison to a control group, who saw a movie sequence depicting adolescents engaged in constructive art-work, the subjects who saw the knife-fight scene exhibited an increased tendency to give more intense shocks in the post-test session.

One recent study [12] examined the influence of both aggressive peer and aggressive adult models, male and female, on the behavior of children in a play situation. The children were tested immediately after seeing the filmed models and again six months later. Children in all four experimental groups, defined in terms of the age and sex of the model, showed more imitative aggression than children who saw no model but were slightly frustrated before being taken into the playroom. The male peer model elicited the most imitative aggression from both male and female subjects. After six months, however, the amount of imitative aggression markedly decreased in all four experimental groups; only exposure to the male adult seemed to have had any lasting effect, and even this was of borderline significance.

The series of studies reported above lend considerable support to the belief

---

[9] O. Ivar Lövaas, "Effect of Exposure to Symbolic Aggression on Aggressive Behavior," *Child Development* 32 (1961): 37–44.

[10] Paul H. Mussen and Eldred Rutherford, "Effects of Aggressive Cartoons on Children's Aggressive Play," *Journal of Abnormal and Social Psychology* 62 (1961): 461–64.

[11] Richard H. Walters and Edward Llewellyn Thomas, "Enhancement of Punitiveness by Visual and Audiovisual Displays," *Canadian Journal of Psychology* 16 (1963): 244–55; Richard H. Walters, Edward Llewellyn Thomas, and C. William Acker, "Enhancement of Punitive Behavior by Audiovisual Displays," *Science* 136 (1962): 872–73.

[12] David J. Hicks, "Imitation and Retention of Film-Mediated Aggressive Peer and Adult Models," *Journal of Personality and Social Psychology* 2 (1965): 97–100.

that the observation of violence in real life or on film or television can have harmful social consequences. However, it must be remembered that the subjects in the studies were tested in situations in which aggressive behavior was permitted, instigated, or even demanded, and that, with one exception that suggested that modeling effects may be transient, the tests were conducted almost immediately after the subjects had been exposed to the models. In real life, one is rarely provided with an opportunity or with instigation to express aggression immediately after exposure to a film or television sequence depicting violent aggression. Moreover, most acts of aggression incur consequences, both in fiction and in real-life situations; in most movies and television shows, for example, the villain is in some way punished. Studies of the effects of observing rewarding and punishing consequences dispensed to an aggressor are therefore of considerable interest.

Effects of Observing Rewards and Punishments Delivered to an Aggressive Model

Bandura, Ross, and Ross [13] assigned nursery-school children to one of four conditions: aggressive model rewarded; aggressive model punished; no exposure to a model; model expressive, but nonaggressive. Under the first two conditions, the children were shown a film depicting an adult male employing a great deal of physical and verbal aggression to secure the possessions of a second male adult. Under the model-rewarded condition, the aggressor was successful and was shown enjoying the fruits of his victory; under the model-punished condition, the aggressor was severely punished by the intended victim. In a subsequent testing situation, children who witnessed the aggressive model rewarded showed more verbal and physical aggression imitative of the model than did children who saw the model punished or children in the control groups. Aggressive responses that were not precisely imitative were also more frequent among children under the model-rewarded condition than among children under the model-punished and the no-film conditions.

Failure to reproduce a punished model's behavior in a subsequent test situation does not, however, indicate that learning through observation has not taken place. Bandura [14] exposed nursery-school children to one of three conditions: model rewarded for aggressive behavior, model punished for aggressive behavior, and model neither rewarded nor punished for such behavior. After exposure to one of these conditions, each child was observed during a ten-minute free-play situation. During this period, children under the model-rewarded and the no-consequence conditions displayed significantly more imitative aggression than children who saw the model punished. Immediately after the observation period, the children were provided with incentives to reproduce the model's aggressive

[13] Albert Bandura, Dorothea Ross, and Sheila A. Ross, "Vicarious Reinforcement and Imitation," *Journal of Abnormal and Social Psychology* 66 (1963): 3–11.

[14] Albert Bandura, "Influence of Models' Reinforcement Contingencies on the Acquisition of Imitative Responses," *Journal of Personality and Social Psychology* 1 (1965): 589–95.

responses. The introduction of these incentives eliminated differences among the three groups of subjects.

Evidence in support of the above findings has been provided by Walters and his associates [15] in studies of resistance to deviation. Generally speaking, these studies indicate that a model who is rewarded or is not punished for breaking a prohibition is likely to be imitated by children who witness the deviation, whereas imitative prohibition-breaking is unlikely to occur if the model is punished for his behavior. However, if the prohibition is subsequently removed, children who have seen the model punished can reproduce the model's deviant responses almost as precisely as children who have seen the model rewarded or escape without punishment.

Observed consequences to a model probably serve as cues indicating that a particular kind of behavior is permissible or nonpermissible in a given social context. Seeing a model rewarded leads the observer to anticipate that he, too, will be rewarded if he acts similarly to the model; if the model's behavior is deviant, according to prevailing social standards, but nevertheless goes unpunished, the observer anticipates that he, too, under similar circumstances may behave in a deviant manner. On the other hand, the observation of a punished deviant model provides a cue to the observer that he, too, is likely to be punished should he follow the model's example.

The importance of anticipated censure for aggression as an inhibitory mechanism has been demonstrated by Lefcourt and his associates,[16] who used the same dependent measures as Walters and Llewellyn Thomas together with the *Rebel Without a Cause* excerpt as an aggression-eliciting stimulus. For half the subjects, all of whom were college students, the experimenter's confederate expressed disapproval of the aggressive behavior of the adolescents while the film was being shown; for the remaining subjects, the confederate expressed approval of, and interest in, the aggressive sequence. Subjects under the former condition showed little change in the average level of shock that they administered to the experimenters' confederate, whereas a significant increase in shock intensity occurred among the subjects who heard the confederate condone and approve the aggression depicted in the film. This experimental manipulation may be an analogue of the home situation in which a child observes his father's excitement and involvement in a boxing or wrestling event while the participants inflict pain on one another.

Anticipation of censure or approval may also account for the finding of

---

[15] Richard H. Walters, Marion Leat, and Louis Mezei, "Inhibition and Disinhibition of Responses through Empathetic Learning." *Canadian Journal of Psychology* 17 (1963): 235–43; Richard H. Walters and Ross D. Parke, "Influence of Response Consequences to a Social Model on Resistance to Deviation" *Journal of Experimental Child Psychology* 1 (1964): 269–80; Richard H. Walters, Ross D. Parke, and Valerie A. Cane, "Timing of Punishing and the Observation of Consequences to Others as Determinants of Response Inhibition," *Journal of Experimental Child Psychology* 2 (1965): 10–30.

[16] Herbert M. Lefcourt, Keith E. Barnes, Ross D. Parke, and Fred S. Schwartz, "Anticipated Social Censure and Aggression-Conflict as Mediators of Response to Aggression Induction," *Journal of Social Psychology* 70 (1966): 251–63.

Berkowitz and his collaborators [17] that filmed violence is less likely to elicit aggressive reactions from recently frustrated observers for whom the violence is presented as unjustified than from those for whom it is presented as justified on account of the fact that the victim is a villain. Justifying filmed violence may provide the observer with a cue that aggression that is expressed against a frustrating agent is likely to be condoned and therefore unlikely to incur punishment. Thus, justification may function in the same way as the observation of reward of, or the omission of punishment for, behavior that ordinarily incurs social disapproval.

An evaluation of the possible influence of film and television productions that depict violence is complicated by the fact that the "hero" often engages in socially sanctioned aggression in order to overcome the violent and aggressive villain. In other words, in such productions aggression by some individuals is socially sanctioned and rewarded. While it is true that the hero's violence is usually depicted as counteraggression, these productions reflect an "eye for an eye, tooth for a tooth" philosophy, one danger of which is the perpetuation of violence. Moreover, in most cases the hero ultimately secures unconditional rewards for his counteraggression; consequently, there is an increased likelihood that his aggressive behavior will be imitated. Finally, as Berkowitz's [18] research indicates, the observer who witnesses "justifiable" aggression is inclined to behave violently toward someone who has recently angered him. Since experimental studies have consistently shown that immediately or shortly after exposure to a rewarded model, observers are very likely to imitate his behavior, the "violent-hero" drama may have a very strong potentiality for eliciting violent acts if the observer is already frustrated and has no other readily available means of securing his goals. Thus, the value systems that may be transmitted by such dramas, the models of behavior they present, and their apparent effectiveness as cues for eliciting violence may, in combination, render them a potential social danger.

Laboratory studies thus indicate that the presentation of violent models in real life or in fantasy productions may both provide observers with opportunities to learn new ways of expressing aggression and also provide cues that aggression can be socially acceptable. On the other hand, the pairing of punishment with the socially unacceptable acts of a model undoubtedly has a deterrent effect on the observer. Humanitarians who deny the deterrent effects of the punitive treatment of delinquents and criminals may be commended for their kindheartedness, but not for their objective appraisal of scientific evidence.

Effect of Rewarding Aggression

Walters and his coworkers conducted a series of studies in which children were rewarded with marbles for hitting a specially constructed Bobo clown which permitted the frequency and intensity of punches to be automatically recorded. Evi-

[17] Leonard Berkowitz and Edna Rawlings, "Effects of Film Violence on Inhibitions against Subsequent Aggression," *Journal of Abnormal and Social Psychology* 66 (1963): 405–12; Leonard Berkowitz, Ronald Corwin, and Mark Hieronimus, "Film Violence and Subsequent Aggressive Tendencies," *Public Opinion Quarterly* 27 (1962): 217–29.

[18] Berkowitz et al., "Film Violence and Subsequent Aggressive Tendencies."

dence was first secured that children who have been intermittently rewarded for hitting continue to hit, when rewards are discontinued, for a longer period of time than do children who have been continuously rewarded.[19] Since, in real-life situations, rewards for aggression are inevitably intermittent, conditions are present that facilitate the establishment of habits that are highly resistant to extinction.

In another study,[20] seven-year-old children were assigned to one of four experimental conditions. Under one condition the children were continuously rewarded for hitting the clown with at least moderate intensity during the training session; under a second condition rewards were only intermittently given. A third group of children played with the clown without receiving any rewards, while the fourth group was given no experience with the doll. Under the first three conditions, each child played with the doll in two sessions on different days and was tested on a third day; the remaining children participated only in the testing session.

In advance of the study, each child subject had been randomly paired with another child in his grade who served as a competitor during the testing session. Each subject and his competitor were required to participate in three physical-contact games, and the frequency with which the subject made aggressive responses, both during the games and during a free-play session, was recorded by observers. The intermittently rewarded children made significantly more aggressive responses than those under the other three conditions.

This finding appeared to support the high-magnitude theory of aggression,[21] which states that intense responses are more likely to be regarded as aggressive than are topologically similar responses of lower intensity. It seemed probable that intermittently rewarded subjects had increased the intensity of their punches while reward was delayed and were thus rewarded for relatively intense hits. The reinforced habit of responding intensely to the doll then generalized to the interpersonal situation.

A direct test of the high-magnitude theory followed.[22] In the first part of this study some children were rewarded only when they hit the doll intensely, whereas the remaining children were rewarded only for weak hits. Again, each subject was matched with an untrained competitor in physical-contact games. As anticipated, children who were rewarded for high-intensity responses to the doll were more physically aggressive during physical-contact games than were children who had been rewarded for responding weakly.

The high-magnitude theory leads to the prediction that training a child to respond intensely, though nonaggressively, may result in his responding intensely in other situations, including those in which an intense response would be regarded

---

[19] Philip A. Cowan and Richard H. Walters, "Studies of Reinforcement of Aggression," Part I: "Effects of Scheduling," *Child Development* 34 (1963): 543–52.

[20] Richard H. Walters and Murray Brown, "Studies of Reinforcement of Aggression," Part III: "Transfer of Responses to an Interpersonal Situation," *Child Development* 34 (1963): 563–72.

[21] Albert Bandura and Richard H. Walters, *Social Learning and Personality Development* (New York: Holt, Rinehart, and Winston, 1963).

[22] Richard H. Walters and Murray Brown, "A Test of the High-Magnitude Theory of Aggression," *Journal of Experimental Child Psychology* 1 (1964): 376–87.

as an aggressive act. Consequently, in the second part of this study, one group of children was rewarded for depressing a lever with considerable force in order to propel a ball to the top of a cage, while the remaining children were rewarded when they depressed the lever gently. The test for generalization effects, which was the same as in the first part of the study, supported the prediction. Children trained to respond forcefully in the ball-and-cage situation made a reliably greater number of responses that were classified by observers as aggressive than did children who had been trained to depress the lever weakly.

The studies of Walters and Brown indicate that children who are intermittently rewarded for aggressive behavior in play situations in which the target is an inanimate object are likely to behave aggressively in social interactions in which aggressive acts can cause harm and pain to other persons. A father who trains his son to hit a punch-bag and who praises the child when he hits the bag hard is thus providing training that increases the probability of the child's acting aggressively toward other children. Moreover, it seems probable that any treatment of a child that requires him to respond forcefully to gain rewards is liable to establish an habitual mode of responding that in many situations will be manifested in the form of aggressive behavior directed toward other persons.

Inhibition of Aggression

Psychologists have conducted very few experimental studies of the effects of punishment on human social behavior. It has indeed been customary for psychologists to regard punishment as a relatively ineffective means of discipline on account of its potentially undesirable side effects and of the assumed transience of its effect as a suppressor of undesirable behavior. A change in the climate of opinion is now in evidence,[23] but there has been no recent study of the effects of punishing aggression. On the other hand, evidence is mounting that punishment may, under some circumstances, be a very effective means of preventing a child from breaking a prohibition, with its degree of effectiveness depending on such factors as its nature, intensity, timing, and consistency, and on the relationship between the agent and recipient of punishment.[24]

Nevertheless, when a parent or other socialization agent frequently employs physical or other aggressive forms of punishment as a means of suppressing children's aggressive behavior, he is in danger of defeating his own purpose, since he is serving as an aggressive model.[25] The most likely outcome is that the

---

[23] Russell M. Church, "The Varied Effects of Punishment on Behavior," *Psychological Review* 70 (1963): 369–402; O. Hobart Mowrer, *Learning Theory and Behavior* (New York: John Wiley & Sons, 1960); O. Hobart Mowrer, *Learning Theory and the Symbolic Processes* (New York: John Wiley & Sons, 1960); Richard L. Solomon, "Punishment," *American Psychologist* 19 (1964): 239–53.

[24] Justin Aronfreed, "Conscience and Conduct: A Natural History of the Internalization Process," *Character Development,* ed. M. Hoffman (New York: Russell Sage Foundation, in press); Bandura and Walters, *Social Learning;* Ross D. Parke and Richard H. Walters, "Some Factors Determining the Efficacy of Punishment for Inducing Response Inhibition," to be published.

[25] Bandura and Walters, *Social Learning.*

child will avoid expressing aggression in the presence of his punisher but will behave aggressively in other situations, for example, when interacting with his peers. Much will depend, however, on the context in which the punishment occurs and especially on the relationship between the disciplinary agent and the child.

One very effective means of inhibiting socially undesirable behavior is to train children to make prosocial responses that are incompatible with aggression, either by exposing them to nonaggressive models or by rewarding them for socially approved behavior. Years ago, Chittenden [26] trained highly aggressive children to make nonaggressive responses to frustration by having them observe a series of "plays" in which dolls exhibited both nonaggressive and aggressive responses in problem situations that generated conflict. The consequences of the alternative aggressive and nonaggressive solutions were discussed with the children after each play in the series. As a consequence of this training, the children subsequently exhibited more co-operative and fewer aggressive responses in interactions with their peers.

In another early study, Davitz [27] praised and approved five groups of four children for making aggressive responses in competitive physical-contact games. Another five groups were praised for constructive and co-operative behavior. After several training sessions, the groups of children were severely frustrated. Films were taken of the groups' free-play behavior before training and again immediately after frustration. Children who had been trained to behave aggressively showed an increase in aggression in the second free-play session, whereas the equally frustrated children who had received training in co-operative behavior showed a decrease in aggression from the first to the second free-play session and an increase in co-operative responses.

Brown and Elliot [28] recently applied techniques derived from social-learning theory to the modification of children's aggressive behavior in a nursery-school setting. Teachers were instructed to ignore aggressive behavior and to reward co-operative and peaceful behavior by means of attention and praise. Observations of the children's behavior before and after each of two two-week treatment periods indicated that the procedure was capable of producing significant decreases in both physical and verbal aggression.

Controlled experimental studies thus provide considerable evidence that inhibition of aggression can be effectively developed through the strengthening of prosocial responses that are incompatible with aggression. The effects of punishing aggression, in the absence of planned reward for incompatible responses, have yet to be satisfactorily determined. It can be safely stated, however, that both direct punishment and the observation of punishment to others can have at least

---

[26] Gertrude E. Chittenden, "An Experimental Study in Measuring and Modifying Assertive Behavior in Children," *Monographs of the Society for Research in Child Development,* Vol. 7 (1942), No. 1 (Serial No. 31).

[27] Joel R. Davitz, "The Effects of Previous Training on Postfrustrative Behavior," *Journal of Abnormal and Social Psychology* 47 (1952): 309–15.

[28] Paul Brown and Rogers Elliot, "Control of Aggression in a Nursery-School Class," *Journal of Experimental Child Psychology* 2 (1965): 103–07.

a temporary suppressing effect and can thus provide an opportunity for alternative prosocial responses to be strengthened through reward.

Moreover, studies both of consequences to social models and of punishment training support the view that anticipation of punishment for deviant acts is a potent source of self-control. There is, indeed, some evidence that the level of aggression of some persons may increase, even in the absence of anger, rewards, or the example set by a model, if no untoward social consequences of their previous aggression are apparent.[29] It is probably only the continual expectation that the potential recipients or other members of society will retaliate that prevents many individuals from more freely expressing aggression.

The Choice of a Target for Aggression

An individual who has been attacked, thwarted, insulted, or blocked from attaining a goal is likely to direct aggression against the person he considers responsible for his condition unless external circumstances or internal restraints prevent him from doing so. Often, however, such circumstances or restraints exist. The agent may fear counteraggression, either direct or through some agent other than the target of his aggression; the source of his problem may be an impersonal or unidentifiable agency that cannot be directly attacked; it may be a physical or psychological deficit, or an event in his past history that is no longer under his control; he may fear to lose valued rewards as a result of his aggression; or he may respond emotionally to the direct expression of aggression because such behavior violates standards he has adopted. Under such circumstances, the agent may select a target for aggression who is not directly, or not all, responsible for his condition.

The dominant view in psychological theory has been that target choice is a joint function of the strength of the instigation to display aggression and the strength of the inhibition against directing aggression toward the source of frustration. It has been assumed that both the instigatory and the inhibitory tendencies generalize, the strength of the generalized responses being a positive function of the degree of similarity between the agent of frustration and possible object of aggression. If the assumption is made that the strength of the generalized inhibitory response decreases more rapidly than that of the generalized excitatory response, the conclusion is reached that at some point on the assumed dissimilarity continuum aggression will be manifested.[30]

This conceptualization is untenable for a number of reasons.[31] In particular, it ignores the influence of prior social-learning experiences that predispose the agent

---

[29] Walters and Llewellyn Thomas, "Enchantment of Punitiveness."

[30] Neal E. Miller, "Theory and Experiment Relating Psychoanalytic Displacement to Stimulus-Response Generalization," *Journal of Abnormal and Social Psychology* 43 (1948): 155–78; John W. L. Whiting and Irvin L. Child, *Child-Training and Personality* (New Haven: Yale University Press, 1953).

[31] Albert Bandura and Richard H. Walters, "Aggression," *Child Psychology: The Sixty-Second Yearbook of the National Society for the Study of Aggression,* Part 1 (Chicago: National Society for the Study of Education, 1963), pp. 364–415.

to direct his aggression toward one class of person rather than another. For example, Southern white children are provided with frequent examples of aggression toward colored people; they see such aggression rewarded, and are rewarded in turn when they emulate the adults in their society. Consequently, when they are prevented from expressing aggression toward a source of frustration, they are especially likely to "displace" the aggression toward the relatively defenseless minority group. Nevertheless, there is no reason to suppose that most aggression that is directed toward minority groups is, in fact, displaced; rather, it reflects the outcome of training deliberately aimed at teaching children to respond to such groups in an aggressive manner.

The external and cognitive cues that facilitate the learning of aggression directed toward minority groups are relatively easy to identify. The cues involved are much less easily identifiable when the target is a member of the agent's own subcultural group. Berkowitz [32] has tested the hypothesis that a potential target of aggression is capable of evoking aggressive responses only to the extent that it is associated with previous aggression instigators. His experimental procedure consists of introducing male college subjects to a peer, a confederate of the experimenter, who is to judge the subjects' performance on a task. For some subjects, the evaluation takes the form of the delivery of seven electric shocks (an unfavorable judgment), a condition that angers the subjects. The subject and the confederate then witness together either a prizefight scene or an exciting film without aggressive content. Subsequently, the subjects are given an opportunity to administer shocks to the confederate as a judgment of the adequacy of the latter's performance. The degree of association between the confederate and the agent or recipient of aggression in the film is varied by introducing the confederate to the subject by different fictitious names, related in varying degrees to the names given to the movie characters. The more closely the confederate is associated with the *victim* of aggression, the more likely is he to be the target of aggression.

This finding again suggests that anticipations of reward or punishment are crucial factors in determining the agent's selection of a target for aggression. The victim is the person in the film who is rendered incapable of retaliation and of punishing the aggressor for continued attacks. Generalizing Berkowitz's finding, one might say that a person who is associated with defenselessness is most likely to be attacked by others. The available evidence from studies of rewards and punishments received by aggressive models, Berkowitz's studies of the cue values of available targets of aggression, and his studies of justifiable versus non-justifiable aggression seem to lead to a similar conclusion: aggression is most likely to be expressed when punishment is not anticipated. Moreover, if displacement occurs, the target selected will most likely be one who cannot easily retaliate and against whom aggression can be displayed with the minimum of social censure.

---

[32] Leonard Berkowitz, "Some Aspects of Observed Aggression," *Journal of Personality and Social Psychology* 2 (1965): 359–69; Leonard Berkowitz and Russell G. Geen, "Film Violence and the Cue Properties of Available Targets," *Journal of Personality and Social Psychology* 3 (1966): 525–30.

A Comment on Catharsis

In the psychological literature, catharsis has been used in the Aristotelian sense to refer to the reduction of the anger of spectators through their vicarious participation in the aggressive behavior of others and also in the psychoanalytic sense to refer to the liberation of aggressive findings through their expression in fantasy, play, or real-life situations.

The outcome of studies of the influence of aggressive film-mediated models on the behavior of children lend no support whatsoever to the Aristotelian type of catharsis hypothesis.[33] Similarly, studies in which children have been encouraged to participate in aggressive play have not supported the hypothesis that participation has a cathartic effect.[34] While studies with adults have brought less consistent results, those that have demonstrated reduction of aggression among subjects who have observed filmed aggression or have been permitted to express aggression following frustration do not necessarily provide support for the catharsis hypothesis. In practically every case, the aggression reduction can be explained without assuming that catharsis has occurred.[35] The highly consistent evidence from studies of aggressive models by Bandura, Berkowitz, Walters, and others suggests that the catharsis doctrine is not merely mistaken, but that its promulgation can lead to the defense of mass-media content that has socially harmful effects.

The Frustration-Aggression Hypothesis

The influential frustration-aggression hypothesis [36] presented aggression as the naturally dominant response to frustration, so that nonaggressive responses to frustration were likely to occur only in situations in which aggressive responses previously had been punished or had brought no reward. This hypothesis has been severely criticized by Buss and by Bandura and Walters and has been defended, with some qualifications, by Berkowitz.[37]

Berkowitz holds that frustration arouses anger and so predisposes a person to respond in an aggressive manner, but that aggression will not occur unless appropriate stimuli are present. In contrast, Bandura and Walters have argued that

---

[33] Bandura and Walters, "Aggression."

[34] Douglas T. Kenney, "An Experimental Test of the Catharsis Theory of Aggression," Unpublished doctoral dissertation, University of Washington, 1952; Seymour Feshbach, "The Catharsis Hypothesis and Some Consequences of Interaction with Aggressive and Neutral Play Objects," *Journal of Personality* 24 (1956): 449–62.

[35] Leonard Berkowitz, "Aggressive Cues in Aggressive Behavior and Hostility Catharsis," *Psychological Review* 71 (1964): 104–22.

[36] John Dollard, Leonard W. Doob, Neal E. Miller, O. Hobart Mowrer, and Robert R. Sears, *Frustration and Aggression* (New Haven: Yale University Press, 1939).

[37] Albert Bandura and Richard H. Walters, *Social Learning and Personality Development* (New York: Holt, Rinehart, and Winston, 1963); Leonard Berkowitz, *Aggression: A Social Psychological Analysis* (New York: McGraw-Hill, 1962); Arnold H. Buss, *The Psychology of Aggression* (New York: John Wiley & Sons, 1961).

frustration (defined as delay of reward) has only a general energizing effect and that the behavior manifested by the frustrated person will depend on the relative dominance of the habits that are elicited by internal and external cues. These theories are, nevertheless, essentially in agreement in their emphasis on the importance of social-stimulus variables in determining whether or not aggression will occur on a particular occasion.

At the same time, the theories differ in their answer to the question: "Is aggression an innate, unlearned response to frustration?" Berkowitz [38] has marshaled considerable evidence that, at least in the case of some subhuman species, aggressive responses can be released by appropriate cues even if the organism has neither observed aggressive behavior by another member of its species nor previously been rewarded for aggression in the presence of these cues. Nevertheless, there are species-specific forms of behavior, and Berkowitz has not proved his case as far as humans are concerned. While it is possible that the emotional behavior exhibited by human infants when frustration occurs may be an unlearned rage response,[39] it seems much more likely that this behavior is an undifferentiated reaction to stress, which, when intense, is interpreted by adults as an instance of rage. Moreover, specific aggressive response patterns probably do not occur at the human level until some social learning has taken place. With the rapidly increasing research on infant behavior, data should soon be available that will bear on the question of the innateness of the frustration-anger or frustration-aggression association. At the present time, the disagreement represents more a conflict of faiths than a conflict based on facts.

---

[38] Berkowitz, *Aggression.*
[39] Sears, Maccoby, and Levin, *Patterns of Child Rearing.*

29

Isolation, Powerlessness, and Violence: A Study of Attitudes and Participation in the Watts Riot

H. EDWARD RANSFORD

It is a common observation that not all people are equally likely to participate in acts of violence. In light of differential participation, one approach to illuminating the causes of violence is to compare participants and non-participants on theoretically relevant characteristics. This is the approach taken by Ransford in the following selection.

Drawing upon some of the theoretical ideas of Durkheim and Marx, Ransford focused on three major variables to account for differential participation in the Watts riot of 1965: isolation, powerlessness, and dissatisfaction. He reasoned that racial isolation should be most important for determining participation in violence (a) when individuals feel powerless to determine their destiny under existing circumstances and (b) when individuals are highly dissatisfied with their racial treatment. These expectations were tested by means of a sample survey conducted in the Los Angeles area shortly after the Watts riot. In general, findings were consistent with Ransford's contention that blacks who are more disengaged from society, both in subjective and structural respects, are more likely to view violence as justified and to engage in violence than are those who are more highly integrated into society.

When Ransford analyzed his data by level of education, he found that powerlessness and dissatisfaction are predictors of violence only among the lower educated. His interpretation of this finding is essentially utilitarian. He suggests that the highly educated blacks may be unwilling to risk their positions by attacking the existing social structure, irrespective of their feelings of powerlessness or dissatisfaction.

Ransford's finding regarding education and participation in racial violence seems to offer further support for the contention that mass education for blacks is the solution to urban racial violence, but this is doubtless too

H. Edward Ransford, "Isolation, Powerlessness, and Violence: A Study of Attitudes and Participation in the Watts Riot," *American Journal of Sociology* 73 (1968): 581–91.

simplistic a solution. It assumes, for example, that with the mass education of blacks all other aspects of society will remain essentially as they are now. This is untenable, of course. You might wish to speculate about the consequences of different social policies in light of Ransford's research findings.

Since the summer of 1965, it is no longer possible to describe the Negroes' drive for new rights as a completely non-violent protest. Urban ghettos have burst at the seams. Angry shouts from the most frustrated and deprived segments of the Negro community now demand that we recognize violence as an important facet of the Negro revolution.

In attempts to understand the increase in violence, much has been said about unemployment, police brutality, poor schools, and inadequate housing as co-tributing factors.[1] However, there are few sociological studies concerning the characteristics of the participants or potential participants in racial violence.[2] Little can be said about which minority individuals are likely to view violence as a justifiable means of correcting racial injustices. It is the purpose of this paper to identify such individuals—specifically, to identify those Negroes who were willing to use violence as a method during a period shortly after the Watts riot.

A Theoretical Perspective

Studies dealing with political extremism and radical protest have often described the participants in such action as being isolated or weakly tied to the institutions of the community.[3] Kerr and Siegel demonstrated this relationship with their finding that wildcat strikes are more common among isolated occupational groups, such as mining, maritime, and lumbering.[4] These isolated groups are believed to

[1] See, e.g., "Violence in the City—an End or a Beginning?" (report of the Governor's Commission on the Los Angeles Riots, December 2, 1965 [commonly known as the "McCone Commission Report"]).

[2] One of the very few studies of the potential participants in race violence was conducted by Kenneth B. Clark, shortly after the Harlem riot of 1943 (see Clark, "Group Violence: A Preliminary Study of the Attitudinal Pattern of Its Acceptance and Rejection: A Study of the 1943 Harlem Riot," *Journal of Social Psychology* 29 [1944]: 319–37; see also Alfred McClung Lee and Norman D. Humphrey, *Race Riot* [New York: Dryden Press, 1943], pp. 80–87).

[3] See, e.g., William Kornhauser, *The Politics of Mass Society* (Glencoe, Ill.: Free Press, 1959), pp. 183–223; Seymour Martin Lipset, *Political Man: The Social Bases of Politics* (New York: Doubleday, 1960), pp. 94–130; and Clark Kerr and Abraham Siegel, "The Interindustry Propensity to Strike—an International Comparison," in Arthur Kornhauser, Robert Dubin, Arthur M. Ross, eds., *Industrial Conflict* (New York: McGraw-Hill, 1954), pp. 189–212.

[4] Kerr and Siegel, "Interindustry."

have a weak commitment to public pressures and the democratic norms of the community. Thus, when grievances are felt intensely and the bonds to the institutions of the community are weak, there is likely to be an explosion of discontent (the strike) rather than use of negotiation or other normative channels of expression.

More recently, mass society theory has articulated this relationship between isolation and extremism.[5] The mass society approach sees current structural processes—such as the decline in kinship, the increase in mobility, and the rise of huge bureaucracies—as detaching many individuals from sources of control, meaning, and personal satisfaction. Those who are most isolated from centers of power are believed to be more vulnerable to authoritarian outlooks and more available for volatile mass movements. Indeed, Kornhauser instructs us that the whole political stability of a society is somewhat dependent upon its citizens being tied meaningfully to the institutions of the community.[6] He suggests that participation in secondary organizations—such as unions and business groups—serves to mediate between the individual and the nation, tying the individual to the democratic norms of the society.

The relationship between structural isolation and extremism is further accentuated by the personal alienation of the individual. Isolated people are far more likely than non-isolated people to feel cut off from the larger society and to feel an inability to control events in the society.[7] This subjective alienation may heighten the individual's readiness to engage in extreme behavior. For example, Horton and Thompson find that perceived powerlessness is related to protest voting.[8] Those with feelings of political powerlessness were more likely to be dissatisfied with their position in society and to hold resentful attitudes toward community leaders. The study suggests that the discontent of the powerless group was converted to action through the vote—a vote of "no" on a local bond issue being a form of negativism in which the individual strikes out at community powers. This interpretation of alienation as a force for protest is consistent with the original Marxian view of the concept in which alienation leads to a radical attack upon the existing social structure.[9]

In summary, there are two related approaches commonly used to explain participation in extreme political behavior. The first deals with the degree to which

---

[5] Kornhauser, *Industrial Conflict;* and Leon Bramson, *The Political Context of Sociology* (Princeton, N.J.: Princeton University Press, 1961), p. 72.

[6] Kornhauser, *Industrial Conflict.*

[7] E.g., Neal and Seeman found that isolated workers (non-participants in unions) were more likely to feel powerless to effect outcomes in the society than the participants in unions (Arthur G. Neal and Melvin Seeman, "Organizations and Powerlessness: A Test of the Mediation Hypothesis," *American Sociological Review* 29 [1964]: 216–26).

[8] John E. Horton and Wayne E. Thompson, "Powerlessness and Political Negativism: A Study of Defeated Local Referendums," *American Journal of Sociology* 67 (1962): 485–93. For another report on the same study, see Wayne E. Thompson and John E. Horton, "Political Alienation as a Force in Political Action," *Social Forces* 38 (1960): 190–95.

[9] Erich Fromm, "Alienation under Capitalism," in Eric and Mary Josephson, eds., *Man Alone* (New York: Dell Publishing Co., 1962), pp. 56–73.

the individual is structurally isolated or tied to community institutions. The second approach deals with the individual's awareness and evaluation of his isolated condition—for example, his feeling of a lack of control over critical matters or his feeling of discontent due to a marginal position in society. Following this orientation, this research employs the concepts of racial isolation, perceived powerlessness, and racial dissatisfaction as theoretical tools for explaining the participation of Negroes in violence.

Study Design and Hypotheses

In the following discussion, the three independent variables of this study (isolation, powerlessness, and dissatisfaction) are discussed separately and jointly, as predictors of violence participation.

Racial Isolation

Ralph Ellison has referred to the Negro in this country as the "invisible man." [10] Although this is a descriptive characterization, sociological studies have attempted to conceptualize more precisely the isolation of the American Negro. For example, those studying attitudes of prejudice often view racial isolation as a lack of free and easy contact on an intimate and equal status basis.[11] Though the interracial contact may be frequent, it often involves such wide status differentials that it does not facilitate candid communication, nor is it likely to give the minority person a feeling that he has some stake in the system. In this paper, intimate white contact is viewed as a mediating set of relationships that binds the ethnic individual to majority-group values—essentially conservative values that favor working through democratic channels rather than violently attacking the social system. Accordingly, it is reasoned that Negroes who are more racially isolated (by low degrees of intimate contact with whites) will have fewer channels of communication to air their grievances and will feel little commitment to the leaders and institutions of the community. This group, which is blocked from meaningful white communication, should be more willing to use violent protest than the groups with greater involvement in white society.

Powerlessness and Racial Dissatisfaction

In contrast to structural isolation, powerlessness and racial dissatisfaction are the subjective components of our theoretical scheme. A feeling of powerlessness

---

[10] Ralph Ellison, *Invisible Man* (New York: Random House, 1952).

[11] Many studies have brought forth the finding that equal status contact between majority and minority members is associated with tolerance and favorable attitudes. For the most recent evidence of the equal status proposition, see Robin Williams, *Strangers Next Door* (Englewood Cliffs, N.J.: Prentice-Hall, Inc., 1964). For an earlier study, see Morton Deutsch and Mary E. Collins, *Interracial Housing* (Minneapolis: University of Minnesota Press, 1951).

is one form of alienation. It is defined in this research as a low expectancy of control over events.[12] This attitude is seen as an appropriate variable for Negroes living in segregated ghettos; that is, groups which are blocked from full participation in the society are more likely to feel powerless in that society. Powerlessness is also a variable that seems to have a logical relationship to violent protest. Briefly, it is reasoned that Negroes who feel powerless to change their position or to control crucial decisions that affect them will be more willing to use violent means to get their rights than those who feel some control or efficacy within the social system. For the Negro facing extreme discrimination barriers, an attitude of powerlessness is simply a comment on the society, namely, a belief that all channels for social redress are closed.

Our second attitude measure, racial dissatisfaction, is defined as the degree to which the individual feels that he is being treated badly because of his race. It is a kind of racial alienation in the sense that the individual perceives his position in society to be illegitimate, due to racial discrimination. The Watts violence represented an extreme expression of frustration and discontent. We would expect those highly dissatisfied with their treatment as Negroes to be the participants in such violence. Thus, the "highs" in racial dissatisfaction should be more willing to use violence than the "lows" in this attitude. In comparing our two forms of subjective alienation (powerlessness and racial dissatisfaction), it is important to note that, although we expect some correlation between the two attitudes (a certain amount of resentment and dissatisfaction should accompany the feeling of powerlessness), we propose to show that they make an independent contribution to violence.

Unification of Predictive Variables

We believe that the fullest understanding of violence can be brought to bear by use of a social-psychological design in which the structural variable (racial isolation) is joined with the subjective attitudes of the individual (powerlessness and dissatisfaction).

In this design, we attempt to specify the conditions under which isolation has its strongest effect upon violence. It is reasoned that racial isolation should be most important for determining participation in violence (*a*) when individuals feel powerless to shape their destiny under existing conditions or (*b*) when individuals are highly dissatisfied with their racial treatment. Each of the attitudes is seen as a connecting bridge of logic between racial isolation and violence.

For the first case (that of powerlessness), we are stating that a weak attachment to the majority group and its norms should lead to a radical break from law and order when individuals perceive they cannot effect events important to them; that is, they cannot change their racial position through activity within institutional channels. Violence, in this instance, becomes an alternative pathway

[12] This definition of subjective powerlessness is taken from the conceptualization proposed by Melvin Seeman, "On the Meaning of Alienation," *American Sociological Review* 24 (1959): 783–91.

of expression and gain. Conversely, racial isolation should have much less effect upon violence when persons feel some control in the system.

For the second case (racial dissatisfaction), we believe isolation should have a far greater effect upon violence when dissatisfaction over racial treatment is intense. Isolation from the society then becomes critical to violence in the sense that the dissatisfied person feels little commitment to the legal order and is more likely to use extreme methods as an outlet for his grievances. Statistically speaking, we expect an interaction effect between isolation and powerlessness, and between isolation and dissatisfaction, in the prediction of violence.[13]

Methods

Our hypotheses call for measures of intimate white contact, perceived powerlessness, and perceived racial dissatisfaction as independent variables, and willingness to use violence as a dependent variable. The measurement of these variables, and also the sampling techniques, are discussed at this time.

Social Contact

The type of social contact to be measured had to be of an intimate and equal status nature, a kind of contact that would facilitate easy communication between the races. First, each Negro respondent was asked if he had current contact with white people in a series of situations: on the job, in his neighborhood, in organizations to which he belongs, and in other situations (such as shopping). After this general survey of white contacts, the respondent was asked, "Have you ever done anything social with these white people, like going to the movies together or visiting in each other's homes?"[14] The responses formed a simple dichotomous variable: "high" contact scores for those who had done something social (61 percent of the sample) and "low" contact scores for those who had had little or no social contact (39 percent).[15]

Powerlessness

Following the conceptualization of Melvin Seeman, powerlessness is defined as a low expectancy of control over events.[16] Twelve forced-choice items were

---

[13] In contrast to the mass society perspective, in which structural isolation is viewed as a cause of subjective alienation, we are viewing the two as imperfectly correlated. For example, many Negroes with contact (non-isolates) may still feel powerless due to racial discrimination barriers. We are thus stressing the partial independence of objective and subjective alienation and feel it necessary to consider both variables for the best prediction of violence.

[14] This question was taken from Robin Williams, *Strangers,* p. 185.

[15] As a further indication that this measure was tapping a more intimate form of interracial contact, it can be noted that 88 percent of those reporting social contact with whites claimed at least one "good friend" ("to whom you can say what you really think") or "close friend" ("to whom you can talk over confidential matters"). Only 10 percent of those lacking social contact claimed such friendships with white people.

[16] Seeman, "Meaning of Alienation."

used to tap this attitude.[17] The majority of items dealt with expectations of control over the political system. The following is an example:

> ________The world is run by the few people in power, and there is not much the little guy can do about it.
>
> ________The average citizen can have an influence on government decisions.

After testing the scale items for reliability,[18] the distribution of scores was dichotomized at the median.

Racial Dissatisfaction

The attitude of racial dissatisfaction is defined as the degree to which the individual feels he is being treated badly because of his race. A five-item scale was developed to measure this attitude. The questions ask the Negro respondent to compare his treatment (in such areas as housing, work, and general treatment in the community) with various reference groups, such as the southern Negro or the white. Each of the five questions allows a reply on one of three levels: no dissatisfaction, mild dissatisfaction, and intense dissatisfaction. Typical of the items is the following: "If you compare your opportunities and the treatment you get from whites in Los Angeles with Negroes living in the South, would you say you are much better off________a little better off________or treated about the same as the southern Negro________?" After a reliability check of the items, replies to the dissatisfaction measure were dichotomized into high and low groups.[19] The cut was made conceptually, rather than at the median, yielding 99 "highs" and 213 "lows" in dissatisfaction.[20]

Violence Willingness

The dependent variable of the study is willingness to use violence. Violence is defined in the context of the Watts riot as the willingness to use direct aggression against the groups that are believed to be discriminating, such as the police and white merchants. The question used to capture this outlook is, "Would you be willing to use violence to get Negro rights?" With data gathered so shortly after the Watts violence, it was felt that the question would be clearly understood by

---

[17] The powerlessness scale was developed by Shephard Liverant, Julian B. Rotter, and Melvin Seeman (see Julian B. Rotter, "Generalized Expectancies for Internal vs. External Control of Reinforcements," *Psychological Monographs* 80 [Whole No. 609, 1966]: 1–28).

[18] Using the Kuder-Richardson test for reliability, a coefficient of .77 was obtained for the twelve items.

[19] Kuder-Richardson coefficient of .84.

[20] With a cut at the median, a good many people ($N = 59$) who were mildly dissatisfied on all five items would have been placed in the "high" category. It was decided that a more accurate description of the "high" category would require the person to express maximum dissatisfaction on at least one of the five items and mild dissatisfaction on the other four.

respondents.[21] At the time of data collection, buildings were still smoldering; violence in the form of looting, burning, and destruction was not a remote possibility, but a tangible reality. The violence-prone group numbered eighty-three.

A second measure of violence asked the person if he had ever used violent methods to get Negro rights.[22] Only sixteen respondents of the 312 reported (or admitted) that they had participated in actual violence. As a result of this very small number the item is used as an indicator of trends but is not employed as a basic dependent variable of the study.

Sample

The sample was composed of three hundred twelve Negro males who were heads of the household and between the ages of eighteen and sixty-five. The subjects responded to an interview schedule administered by Negro interviewers. They were chosen by random methods and were interviewed in their own homes or apartments. Both employed and unemployed respondents were included in the sample, although the former were emphasized in the sampling procedure (269 employed in contrast to 43 unemployed). The sample was drawn from three major areas of Los Angeles: a relatively middle-class and integrated area (known as the "Crenshaw" district) and the predominantly lower-class and highly segregated communities of "South Central" and "Watts." The sample could be classified as "disproportional stratified" because the proportion of subjects drawn from each of the three areas does not correspond to the actual distribution of Negroes in Los Angeles. For example, it was decided that an approximate fifty-fifty split between middle- and lower-class respondents would be desirable for later analysis. This meant, however, that Crenshaw (middle-class) Negroes were considerably overrepresented, since their characteristics are not typical of the Los Angeles Negro community as a whole, and the majority of Los Angeles Negroes do not reside in this, or any similar, area.

Results

We have predicted a greater willingness to use violent methods for three groups: the isolated, the powerless, and the dissatisfied. The data presented in Table 1 confirm these expectations. For all three cases, the percentage differences are statistically significant at better than the .001 level.

The empirical evidence supports our contention that Negroes who are more

[21] As an indication that the question was interpreted in the context of participation in violence of the Watts variety, it can be noted that our question was correlated with approval of the Watts riot ($\phi = .62$).

[22] The question, "Have you ever participated in violent action for Negro rights?" was purposely worded in general terms to avoid accusing the respondent of illegal behavior during the Watts violence. However, racial violence in the United States was somewhat rare at that time, so it is likely that most of the sixteen respondents were referring to participation in the Watts violence.

TABLE 1

PERCENTAGE WILLING TO USE VIOLENCE, BY SOCIAL CONTACT, POWERLESSNESS AND RACIAL DISSATISFACTION

Variables	*Not willing* (%)	*Willing* (%)	*Total* (%)
Social contact:[a]			
High	83	17	100 ($N = 192$)
Low	56	44	100 ($N = 110$)
Powerlessness:[b]			
High	59	41	100 ($N = 145$)
Low	84	16	100 ($N = 160$)
Racial dissatisfaction:[c]			
High	52	48	100 ($N = 98$)
Low	83	17	100 ($N = 212$)

[a] $\chi^2 = 24.93, P < .001$.
[b] $\chi^2 = 22.59, P < .001$.
[c] $\chi^2 = 30.88, P < .001$.
NOTE.—In this table and the tables that follow, there are often less than 312 cases due to missing data for one or more variables.

disengaged from the society, in the structural (isolation) and subjective (powerlessness and racial dissatisfaction) senses, are more likely to view violence as necessary for racial justice than those more firmly tied to the society.

It is one thing to establish a relationship based on action willingness and quite another thing to study actual behavior. Unfortunately, only sixteen of the 312 respondents (5 percent) admitted participation in violent action for Negro rights. This small number did, however, provide some basis for testing our hypotheses. Of the sixteen who participated in violent action, eleven were isolates while only five had social contact. More impressive is the fact that fifteen of the sixteen "violents" scored high in powerlessness, and thirteen of the sixteen felt high degrees of dissatisfaction. Even with a small number, these are definite relationships, encouraging an interpretation that those who are willing to use violence and those who reported actual violent behavior display the same tendency toward powerlessness, racial dissatisfaction, and isolation.

The next task is to explore the interrelationships among our predictive variables. For example, we have argued that powerlessness has a specific meaning to violence (a low expectancy of changing conditions within the institutional framework) that should be more than a generalized disaffection; that is, we expected our measures of powerlessness and racial dissatisfaction to have somewhat unique effects upon violence.

The data indicated an interaction effect (interaction $\chi^2 = 7.85$; $P < .01$) [23]

[23] The χ^2 interaction test is somewhat analogous to the interaction test in the analysis of variance. A total χ^2 is first computed from the two partial tables in which all three variables are operating. Second, χ^2 values are obtained by cross-tabulating each possible pair of variables (e.g., $\chi^2 AB$, $\chi^2 AC$, and $\chi^2 BC$). These three separate χ^2 values are then

between the two attitudes. The feeling of powerlessness is a more relevant determiner of violence for the highly dissatisfied or angry Negro. Similarly, racial dissatisfaction is far more important to violence for those who feel powerless. In sum, the data suggest that the powerless Negro is likely to use violence when his feelings of powerlessness are accompanied by intense dissatisfaction with his position. It can be noted, however, that, even among those who were relatively satisfied with racial conditions, powerlessness had some effect upon violence (a 13 percent difference, $\chi^2 = 5.41$; $P = .02$). Presumably, a low expectancy of exerting control has a somewhat unique effect upon violence.

As a second way of noting an interrelationship between our predictive variables, we turn to the more crucial test of the isolation-extremism perspective in which the effect of racial isolation upon violence is controlled by powerlessness and dissatisfaction.[24] It will be recalled that we expected the isolated people (with a lower commitment to democratic norms and organized channels) to be more violence-prone when these isolated inidividuals perceive they cannot shape their destiny within the institutional framework (high powerlessness) or when they perceive differential treatment as Negroes and, as a result, are dissatisfied. It is under these subjective states of mind that a weak attachment to the majority group would seem to be most important to extremism. Table 2, addressed to these predictions, shows our hypotheses to be strongly supported in both cases.

TABLE 2

Percentage Willing to Use Violence, by Social Contact Controlling for Powerlessness and Racial Dissatisfaction

	Percentage willing to use violence			
	Low powerlessness (%)	*High powerlessness* (%)	*Low dissatisfaction* (%)	*High dissatisfaction* (%)
Low contact	23 ($N = 31$)	53 ($N = 78$)	23 ($N = 47$)	59 ($N = 63$)
High contact	13 ($N = 123$)	26 ($N = 66$)	15 ($N = 158$)	26 ($N = 34$)
χ^2	$P < .20$	$P < .01$	$P < .20$	$P < .01$

Note.—The interaction χ^2 between powerlessness and contacts: $P < .05$. The interaction χ^2 between dissatisfaction and contact: $P < .01$.

Among the powerless and the dissatisfied, racial isolation has a strong effect upon violence commitment. Conversely, the data show that isolation is much less

summed and subtracted from the total χ^2. The residual, or what is left after subtraction, is the interaction χ^2. It can be viewed as the joint or special effect that comes when predictive variables are operating simultaneously. For a further description of this measure, see Phillip H. DuBois and David Gold, "Some Requirements and Suggestions for Quantitative Methods in Behavioral Science Research," in Norman F. Washburne, ed., *Decisions, Values and Groups* (New York: Pergamon Press, 1962), II, 42–65.

[24] The independent variables are moderately intercorrelated. For isolation and powerlessness, the ϕ correlation is .36, $P < .001$; for isolation and dissatisfaction, the ϕ is .40, $P < .001$; for powerlessness and dissatisfaction, the ϕ is .33, $P < .001$.

relevant to violence for those with feelings of control in the system and for the more satisfied (in both cases, significant only at the .20 level).[25]

The fact that isolation (as a cause of violence) produces such a small percentage difference for the less alienated subjects call for a further word of discussion. Apparently, isolation is not only a stronger predictor of violence for the people who feel powerless and dissatisfied, but is *only* a clear and significant determiner of violence for these subjectively alienated persons. For the relatively satisfied and control-oriented groups, the fact of being isolated is not very important in determining violence. This would suggest that a weak normative bond to the majority group (isolation) is not in itself sufficient to explain the participation of the oppressed minority person in violence and that it is the interaction between isolation and feelings of powerlessness (or racial dissatisfaction) that is crucial for predicting violence.

A final attempt at unification involves the cumulative effect of all three of our predictive variables upon violence. Since it was noted that each of the three predictive variables has some effect upon violence (either independently or for specific subgroups), it seemed logical that the combined effect of the three would produce a high violence propensity. Conceptually, a combination of these variables could be seen as ideal types of the alienated and non-alienated Negro. Accordingly, Table 3 arranges the data into these ideal-type combinations.

TABLE 3

PERCENTAGE WILLING TO USE VIOLENCE, BY THE COMBINED EFFECT OF SOCIAL CONTACT, POWERLESSNESS, AND RACIAL DISSATISFACTION

	Not willing (%)	*Willing* (%)	*Total* (%)
Ideal-type alienated (low contact, high powerlessness, and high dissatisfaction)	35	65	100 (*N* = 51)
Middles in alienation	76	24	100 (*N* = 147)
Ideal-type non-alienated (high contact, low powerlessness, and low dissatisfaction)	88	12	100 (*N* = 107)

NOTE.—$\chi^2 = 49.37$; $P < .001$ (2 d.f.).

The group at the top of the table represents the one most detached from society—individuals who are isolated and high in attitudes of powerlessness and dissatisfaction. The group at the bottom of the table is the most involved in the society; these people have intimate white contact, feelings of control, and greater satisfaction with racial conditions. The middle group is made up of those with different combinations of high and low detachment. Note the dramatic difference in willingness to use violence between the "ideal-type" alienated group

[25] The .05 level is considered significant in this analysis.

(65 percent willing) and the group most bound to society (only 12 percent willing). The "middles" in alienation display a score in violence between these extremes.

Spuriousness

It is possible that the relationship between our predictive variables and violence is due to an intercorrelation with other relevant variables. For example, social class should be related both to violence and to our isolation-alienation measures. In addition, we could expect a greater propensity toward violence in geographical areas where an extreme breakdown of legal controls occurred, such as the South Central and Watts areas (in contrast to the Crenshaw area, where no rioting took place). In such segregated ghettos, violence may have been defined by the inhabitants as a legitimate expression, given their intolerable living conditions, a group definition that could override any effects of isolation or alienation upon violence. In short, it seems essential to control our isolation-alienation variables by an index of social class and by ghetto area.[26]

Because of the rather small violent group, it is necessary to examine our predictive variables separately in this analysis of controls. Table 4 presents the original relationship between each of the independent variables and violence, controlled by two areas of residence: the South Central–Watts area, at the heart of the curfew zone (where violence occurred), and the Crenshaw area, on the periphery (or outside) of the curfew zone (where violent action was rare). In addition, Table 4 includes a control for education, as a measure of social class.[27]

When the ghetto residence of the respondent is held constant, it appears that our independent variables are important in their own right. Education (social class), however, proved to be a more powerful control variable. Among the college educated, only isolation persists as a predictor of violence; powerlessness and racial dissatisfaction virtually drop out. Yet each variable has a very strong effect upon violence among the high school (lower-class) group. In other words, we do not have an instance of spuriousness, where predictive variables are explained away in both partials, but another set of interaction effects—attitudes of powerlessness and dissatisfaction are predictors of violence only among lower-class respondents. These results may be interpreted in several ways. Persons higher in the class structure may have a considerable amount to lose, in terms of occupational prestige and acceptance in white society, by endorsing extreme methods. The college educated (middle class) may be unwilling to risk their position,

---

[26] Age was also considered as a control variable but was dropped when it was discovered that age was not correlated with violence or the independent variables. The *r*'s ranged from .04 to .09.

[27] For this sample, education was believed to be superior to other indexes of class. It is an index that is freer (than either occupation or income) from the societal restrictions and discrimination that Negroes face. Also, it was discovered that Negro occupations in the more deprived ghetto areas were not comparable to the same occupations listed in standardized scales, such as the North-Hatt or Bogue scales.

TABLE 4

PERCENTAGE WILLING TO USE VIOLENCE BY CONTACT, POWERLESSNESS, AND RACIAL DISSATISFACTION, CONTROLLING FOR TWO GEOGRAPHICAL AREAS AND EDUCATION

Independent variables	NEIGHBORHOOD		EDUCATION	
	South Central–Watts	*Crenshaw*	*Low (high school or less)*	*High (some college)*
Low contact	53** ($N = 62$)	33** ($N = 45$)	52** ($N = 77$)	24* ($N = 33$)
High contact	27 ($N = 83$)	10 ($N = 109$)	26 ($N = 86$)	10 ($N = 105$)
Low powerlessness	22** ($N = 73$)	11* ($N = 88$)	19** ($N = 67$)	14 ($N = 93$)
High powerlessness	55 ($N = 77$)	25 ($N = 68$)	51 ($N = 100$)	18 ($N = 45$)
Low dissatisfaction	26** ($N = 81$)	12** ($N = 130$)	22** ($N = 96$)	12 ($N = 114$)
High dissatisfaction	53 ($N = 68$)	39 ($N = 28$)	59 ($N = 73$)	17 ($N = 24$)

* $P < .05$. ** $P < .01$.

NOTE.—Interaction χ^2 between contact and neighborhood: P is not significant. Interaction χ^2 between powerlessness and neighborhood: $P < .02$. Interaction χ^2 between dissatisfaction and neighborhood: P is not significant. Interaction χ^2 between contact and education: P is not significant. Interaction χ^2 between powerlessness and education: $P < .02$. Interaction χ^2 between dissatisfaction and education: $.05 < P < .10$.

regardless of feelings of powerlessness and dissatisfaction. These results may further indicate that middle-class norms favoring diplomacy and the use of democratic channels (as opposed to direct aggression) are overriding any tendency toward violence.[28] An extension of this interpretation is that middle-class Negroes may be activists, but non-violent activists, in the civil rights movement. Thus, class norms may be contouring resentment into more organized forms of protest.

Conclusions

In an attempt to locate the Negro participant in violence, we find that isolated Negroes and Negroes with intense feelings of powerlessness and dissatisfaction are more prone to violent action than those who are less alienated. In addition, isolation has its strongest effect upon violence when individuals feel powerless to control events in the society or when racial dissatisfaction is intensely felt. For those with higher expectations of control or with greater satisfaction regarding racial treatment, isolation has a much smaller and non-significant effect (though in the predicted direction) upon violence. That is, a weak tie with the majority group, per se, appeared insufficient to explain wide-scale participation in extreme action. This study indicates that it is the interaction between a weak bond and a feeling of powerlessness (or dissatisfaction) that is crucial to violent participation.

Viewed another way, the combined or tandem effect of all three predictive variables produces an important profile of the most violence-prone individuals. Negroes who are isolated, who feel powerless, and who voice a strong disaffection because of discrimination appear to be an extremely volatile group, with 65 percent of this stratum willing to use violence (as contrasted to only 12 percent of the "combined lows" in alienation).

Ghetto area and education were introduced as controls. Each independent variable (taken separately) retained some significant effect upon violence in two geographical areas (dealing with proximity to the Watts violence) and among the less educated respondents. Powerlessness and dissatisfaction, however, had no effect upon violence among the college educated. Several interpretations of this finding were explored.

Applying our findings to the context of the Negro revolt of the last fifteen years, we note an important distinction between the non-violent civil rights activists and the violence-prone group introduced in this study. Suggestive (but non-conclusive) evidence indicates that the participants in organized civil rights protests are more likely to be middle class in origin, to hold considerable optimism for equal rights, and to have greater communication with the majority—this represents a group with "rising expectations" for full equality.[29] In contrast, this

[28] For a discussion of class norms, see Lipset, *Political Man.*

[29] See Ruth Searles and J. Allen Williams, Jr., "Negro College Students' Participation in Sit-ins," *Social Forces* 40 (1962): 215–20; H. Edward Ransford, *Negro Participation in Civil Rights Activity and Violence* (unpublished Ph.D. dissertation, University of California, Los Angeles, 1966); and Pearl M. Gore and Julian B. Rotter, "A Personality Correlate of Social Action," *Journal of Personality* 37 (1963): 58–64.

study located a very different population—one whose members are intensely dissatisfied, feel powerless to change their position, and have minimum commitment to the larger society. These Negroes have lost faith in the leaders and institutions of the community and presumably have little hope for improvement through organized protest. For them, violence is a means of communicating with white society; anger can be expressed, control exerted—if only for a brief period.

Aggression, Hostility, and Conflict:

Putting It into Perspective

Human aggression is a matter of great social concern and a fact of life for many in contemporary society. Crimes of violence are so commonplace in our urban areas that all but the most daring vacate their streets in the evening. Colleges and universities, long known for their quiet seclusion from the harsh realities of ordinary living, have in recent years become blood-bathed and ash-strewn battlegrounds. And urban riots have gained the regularity of the seasons, anticipated by almost everyone with the onset of summer.

In this milieu of violence, social psychologists have increasingly turned their attention to the following questions. First, what are the bases of human aggression and violence? Second, what implications does our present knowledge have for social policy?

One can easily identify three major foci in the social psychologists' search for the bases of human aggression: (a) the link between frustration and aggression; (b) aggressive models and other aggression-linked cues; and (c) interpersonal relations and participation in violence. One of the oldest and most widely accepted explanations is frustration-aggression theory. The theory postulates that frustration is a necessary and sufficient condition for aggression. By frustration is meant the blocking of ongoing goal-directed behavior. The blocking of such activity produces an emotional reaction, anger, which in turn heightens the probability of hostile behavior. Of course, whether overt hostile behavior occurs, depends upon a number of situational factors, such as the availability of a suitable target. This general line of reasoning has provided the theoretical base for literally hundreds of studies, both laboratory and field, since its original systematic presentation by Dollard and his associates at Yale more than three decades ago. Berkowitz reviews and evaluates this theory as a source of insight into urban violence in one of the papers reprinted in this section. While the original statement of the theory has been considerably refined, the evidence to date lends it substantial support. However, it is still but a partial theory. The theory is not sufficient to account for non-aggressive responses to frustration, nor is it capable of accounting for the selection of targets for aggression.

The second major focus that research into the sources of aggression has taken is on aggressive models and aggression-linked social cues. The particular questions which have received attention include the following. Does the observation of violence in a movie or on TV influence the subsequent behavior of viewers toward violence, or does it serve a catharsis function, thereby reducing the likelihood that viewers will aggress against others? Does playing with toy guns or other aggression-linked objects influence children toward aggressive behavior? Does watching contact sports, such as football or soccer, have any behavioral consequences for fans? If so, what are they? Walters reviews much of the research in this vein in a paper reprinted in this section, and Hoyt's research report focuses specifically upon the significance of media violence for subsequent viewer behavior. The combined evidence suggests that under specifiable conditions, the observation of violence and/or the mere presence of aggression-linked cues heightens the probability of interpersonal hostility. This evidence is contrary to the predictions of Lorenz's theory of aggression as endogenously motivated. (See Berkowitz's paper in this section for a review and critique.)

Still another major emphasis in studies of aggression is on the interpersonal relations of participants versus non-participants in acts of violence. Key theoretical variables include social isolation, personal and political efficacy, dissatisfaction, etc. It is hypothesized that these variables account for the frequent observation that a large segment of society can be frustrated in their attempts to realize some basic goal, but not all respond to this frustration with acts of aggression. As was pointed out earlier, one of the limitations of frustration-aggression theory is that it is incapable of accounting for differential participation in violence. But the focus on interpersonal relations does not account for, in any systematic way, differential tendencies toward aggression through time among persons of similar interpersonal networks. Thus, this focus too provides but a partial explanation. Ransford's research report concerning the Watts riot of 1965 is in this research tradition.

While we did not differentiate them as major foci, studies in socialization and in conformity and compliance processes have also given considerable insight into aggression. One of the basic characteristics of socialization is the formation and/or modification of beliefs and behaviors to meet the expectations of others. Much of the intergroup hostility in our society simply represents behavioral responses to internalized norms. Many whites act with hostility toward blacks because they have learned that that is an appropriate way to act toward them. The reciprocal also holds. The laboratory evidence reported by Milgram (see Chapter II) indicates the extent to which people will knowingly harm another simply to conform to the instructions of an experimenter. In fact, subjects were induced to administer sufficient electrical shock to what they thought was another subject to have been fatal. Such data are frightening in that they indicate with what ease aggression against selected others could be institutionalized.

As we indicated earlier, contemporary social psychologists have been interested in more than simply elucidating the causes of aggression. They have devoted explicit efforts to the exploration of the policy implications of current theory and research. Two of the readings reprinted in this section reflect this concern—

the reviews by Walters and Berkowitz. Proceeding on the premise that human aggression is undesirable, both Walters and Berkowitz outline courses of action with regard to such matters as child discipline, the sale of toy weapons, gun control legislation, capital punishment, media violence, methods of riot control, etc. While the theoretical bases for planning in some of these areas are equivocal, one is impressed with the amount of knowledge which we do have but do not act upon. Surely any really successful program to eliminate violence must be based on a theoretical synthesis of the numerous partial explanations of violence presently available.

Suggestions for Further Reading

Leonard Berkowitz, *Aggression: A Social Psychological Analysis.* New York: McGraw-Hill, 1962. This book builds on the classic work of Dollard et al. (cited below) but is not limited by it. The emphasis is on the aggressive actions of individuals in interpersonal settings.

Leonard Berkowitz, *Roots of Aggression: A Re-Examination of the Frustration-Aggression Hypothesis.* New York: Atherton Press, 1969. A work representing the continuing refinement of the frustration-aggression model.

Arnold H. Buss, *The Psychology of Aggression.* New York: John Wiley, 1961. Discusses in some detail the psychoanalytical model of aggression and aggression as psychopathological behavior.

John Dollard et al., *Frustration and Aggression.* New Haven, Connecticut: Yale University Press, 1939. The classic presentation of the frustration-aggression hypothesis.

Harry Kaufmann, *Aggression and Altruism.* New York: Holt, Rinehart and Winston, 1970. This brief volume provides a critical examination of some of the major contending theories of aggression and proposes an alternative model which encompasses both aggressive and altruistic behavior.

Konrad Lorenz, *On Aggression.* New York: Harcourt, Brace & World, 1966. A currently popular, alternative explanation for human aggression with significant policy implications.

Muzafer Sherif et al., *Intergroup Conflict and Cooperation: The Robber's Cave Experiment.* Norman, Oklahoma: University Book Exchange, 1961. The report of an ingenious field experiment designed to test a series of theoretical ideas about the origins and resolution of conflict between groups.

CHAPTER VIII

Socialization

30 M. J. Chombart de Lauwe, *Child Representation in Contemporary French Urban Society* · 401

31 E. Paul Torrance, *Achieving Socialization Without Sacrificing Creativity* · 416

32 Robert A. Scott, *The Socialization of the Blind in Personal Interaction* · 423

33 James H. Bryan, *Appenticeships in Prostitution* · 432

34 Walter M. Gerson, *Mass Media Socialization Behavior: Negro-White Differences* · 446

Putting It into Perspective · 461
Suggestions for Further Reading · 463

30

Child Representation in Contemporary French Urban Society

M. J. CHOMBART de LAUWE

All of us have observed children imitating someone else. Such behavior is frequently a source of amusement or consternation to adults, depending upon who or what is being imitated. But the imitation of others also is a significant process for child socialization. While some conscious effort is devoted to the socialization of the child by parents, teachers, clergymen, etc., the ways the child learns to react to social situations are influenced significantly by his identification with and imitation of models he encounters in the course of day-to-day activity.

In the following selection, Chombart de Lauwe emphasizes the influence of one category of models for the socialization of children—symbolic models. By symbolic models is meant the representations of the child that are encountered in advertisements, newspaper stories, pictures, children's books, sermons, and conversations. The emphasis on symbolic models is not intended to distract from the importance of "real others" as models, but rather, is intended to elaborate the role of imitation of models in socialization.

The influence of symbolic models on child socialization is two-fold. First, models have a direct influence on the child's conception of the kind of person he is expected to be. Second, parents and other socializing agents also confront symbolic models of the "ideal child," and these models influence their behavior toward children.

The author spends some time discussing the consequences of the frequent contradictions among the symbolic models encountered in society. On the one hand, the multiplicity of models is a source of conflict for the child. After all, how can the child be the innocent cherub described in bedtime stories and the dauntless hero depicted in his comic books? On the other

M. J. Chombart de Lauwe, "Child Representation in Contemporary French Urban Society," *Enfance* 15 (January–February 1962): 53–67.

hand, Chombart de Lauwe suggests that the diversity of models contributes to the child's adaptability to diverse circumstances.

The implications of this research are numerous, and the fact that the data used in the report come from French society contributes to its interest.

In every society individuals play certain roles, according to rules which vary with the value-systems of their culture and the resulting social structures. So that individuals may be able to conform to the roles expected of them, each society provides them with models, presented either in a direct, normative way, or in a more diffuse, indirect manner. As the individual participates in several social groups—work, family, sports club, trade union, political party, etc.—and as the demands made upon him by these groups are not always the same, he has to change his model constantly. Conflicts can arise between the different models: thus, for example, the role of militant supporter of a cause and the role of family man concerned for his children are not always compatible.

This continual re-adaptation is sometimes difficult for an adult personality, and for the child, whose personality is in the process of formation, it can be a source of conflicts. On the one hand, society has a spontaneous image of the child; on the other hand, it wants to impart to the child an ideal image of his own self on which, it hopes, he may model himself.

Many of the aspirations of a society are expressed through its models of the child, which it aims to turn into a certain type of adult. However, within a society the models are not the same for various social conditions. Thus in a Western-type hierarchical society like our own in France, the models vary according to the different social classes. Each class, in fact, tries to produce a type of man whose role is not necessarily the same as it is in society as a whole, and whose attributes vary not only with the role he is fulfilling, but also with changing living conditions and cultural trends.

When studying problems related to the maladjusted child,[1] we noticed that these children express their difficulties differently under varying social conditions. Although all the symptoms were present qualitatively in each type of environment, in the working-class environment the percentage of children who reacted violently was significantly higher than in well-to-do environments, while tendencies to repression and withdrawal varied inversely. Among those who have studied these two milieux it is well known that for the working class the externalization of feelings is more spontaneous, while in the middle class more

[1] M. J. Chombart de Lauwe, *Psychopathologie sociale de l'enfant inadapté* (Paris: C.N.R.S., 1959).

importance is attached to reserve. The children were expressing their problems in terms of behavior which was characteristic of their social environment.

Models also change in the course of history. The roles and behavior patterns of children as they appear in children's books of the nineteenth century, at the outbreak of the 1914 war, and today are not the same. As a result of the rapid changes undergone by our society, old and more recent models exist side by side and are an additional source of difficulty for the child who, brought up according to one value system, encounters others as he reaches adolescence, then adulthood; or the child who is torn between different models at a given moment.

Models also change in the course of the child's development. Many authors have noted that the child identifies at first with father or mother according to sex. In certain roles and types of behavior the child imitates the parent who is at that time serving as a model. Then the child very quickly becomes conscious of his own role, contrasts himself with the adult and constructs himself according to a child model which he guesses at tentatively through rewards and punishments. This picture, built up from what the child must and must not do, and the way he must do it, is the expression of a model of the role and behavior of the child as seen by his family.

As the child grows and as his socialization is no longer mediated solely through his parents, but directly, through contact with his area of residence, his school, and peer groups, he will encounter and seek out other models. As a result of the evolution of the family, whose exclusive influence is limited to an ever-decreasing period of the child's life, extra-familial socialization begins at an ever earlier stage.[2]

The analyses and observations contained in this article are based on research which is being carried out at present. This research has two principal directions: first, a study of the evolution of models and representations in a given society, as a function of events, changing living conditions and cultural trends; secondly, an attempt to shed light on the influences which affect a child in the course of socialization, after the imitative phase of the very young child and the phase of identification with the parents. The work of several psychologists, especially Wallon [3] and Piaget,[4] as well as interpretations by psychoanalysts,[5] have led to an understanding of these mechanisms, and more generally those of socialization. We are asking ourselves the opposite question: how does society, taken as a whole or considering each of its groups individually, present its models, what are they, and how does it wish to shape the child?

---

[2] On this subject see P. H. and M. J. Chombart de Lauwe, "L'évolution des besoins et la conception dynamique de la famille," *Revue française de sociologie* 1 (1960).

[3] H. Wallon, "Psychologie et éducation de l'enfance," *Enfance,* special edition, collection of articles and lectures, nos. 3–4, May–October 1959. Also *Les Origines du Caractère chez l'Enfant,* 2nd edn. (Paris, P.U.F.).

[4] J. Piaget, "Pensée égocentrique et pensée sociocentrique," in *Cahiers internationaux de sociologie,* vol. 10, year 6–1961.

[5] D. Lagache, "La personnalité et les relations avec autrui," *Bulletin de Psychologie,* 8 (1955).

To answer these questions, we have evolved a method which relies on various techniques. Model analysis is carried out by examining various documents with the aid of systematic questionnaires. On the one hand we examine publications specifically for the child: papers and novels, readers, moral guides, the lives and characters of famous children, and children's films; and on the other hand, the corresponding adult-directed documents. Ethnographic observations, as well as interviews with parents and educators, will give insight into the extent to which models are accepted and transformed. At the same time, the observation of major changes in educational trends may explain the transformation of models up to a point.

In this first study, we consider the analysis of models which influence the way a child's personality is built up. We also raise the problem of conflicts which may result when the child is caught between multiple and sometimes divergent models.

Models Offered to the Child

The models offered by society are presented in a direct, more or less normative way, or unconsciously and more indirectly. We shall attempt to ascertain where and how these models are presented in an urban environment. (Our current research is not concerned with the rural environment.) Although there is widespread distribution of the same images everywhere by mass media, the images provided by a village street and a city street are not identical, and the types of "ideal child" desired by the parents in the two environments doubtless also differ.

Models Presented Unintentionally

As soon as he leaves the house, the child encounters new models automatically emitted by our culture. First, there are the pictures: wall posters, papers displayed on kiosks, advertisements in shop windows. There are also the dummies in the clothes stores, whose pose and build express a certain mode of existence which is just as much a question of fashion as their clothes. Besides these images, he will hear the lyrical comments of neighbors and shopkeepers on some aspect of his own appearance or manner. In the streets where he lives (especially in working-class areas), in the park, and on visits to his parents' friends, he will soon have learnt the stereotypes of the sweet little child, the *enfant bien mignon et gentil.*

The child is not impervious to all these impressions of the outside world. Thus he "learns" his society, and forms himself, for better or for worse, according to its style. Even a pin-up girl posing on a music hall poster, or a gangster toting his Colt, may become engraved on his memory when he has passed it four times a day for a month, on his way to and from school, even if he pays it no particular attention or seems to have forgotten it. Moreover, he encounters the same characters again in the papers bought by his parents and left lying around, which he views with an indifferent or attentive eye. These characters, almost always adults, often appear to him as heroes he would like to emulate: artists, sportsmen, scholars—or gangsters. Although they are not child figures, the little boy or girl may imitate the attitude or behavior model they provide.

Figures of model children are to be found in similar situations, but are far less frequently met with than criminal figures. . . . An example of this is the case of an 8-year-old boy who, with courage and initiative, saved his father who had fallen in front of his tractor and was about to be run over: the boy managed to put the tractor into reverse. The papers gave up little space to this account; but spectacular crimes often make the headlines. Children who display heroism are less honored by the national press than the characters I have mentioned. Kidnapped children, on the other hand, get a lot of publicity—which is doubtless necessary if they are to be saved, but terrorizes children in certain neighborhoods,[6] and stimulates the imagination of unbalanced persons.

All these images and comments picked up here and there eventually paint for the child a portrait of an "ideal child" which will serve as his model. But there is not just one portrait; even if it were possible to compose an average "identikit" picture of its different aspects, each child would probably perceive several of these, and would either make his own personal synthesis, or would hesitate according to the situation in which he found himself. This multiplicity of models is seen more clearly when we observe the ways in which they are presented directly and intentionally to the child.

Models Presented Directly

There are various persons and groups concerned either to amuse or educate the child. In doing so, they show him children or adolescents playing certain roles, and behaving in certain ways which are presented as either bad or good.

Where and by Whom Are These Models Presented? The parents are the first to present the behavior of children they approve of: it may be a child from the same family who corresponds most closely to their ideals, the child of friends, or a little neighbor, who is always held up as an example. Sometimes the model put forward by one of the parents is him- or herself as a child, unconsciously idealized by the passage of time or the need to impress. Grandparents, cousins, etc., reinforce or sometimes contradict these models.

We shall later investigate, with the help of research done with parents, the question of which are the models most typical of different social environments and particular family situations. We shall also investigate the models presented by the school, in certain readers and in history books (the way famous men are described is very representative here). Additional examples will be taken from religious instruction. In its present phase, the research is directed above all to the presentation of models transmitted by the mass media. Many papers and comics

---

[6] In this connection, we have noted the conversation of children on their way back from school going past the newspaper stalls. The story of the little boy who saved his father went unnoticed.

of a varying standard are designed specifically for children; editors also produce for them various collections of novels, adventure stories, and so on. Lastly, there are special children's programs on television, and special films for children. Some of the characters in films and books, and on television, are the same: little "Rusty" is a television hero and also features in a monthly magazine; the same is true of the adult figures "Aigle Noir" (Black Eagle), "Tarzan," "Ivanhoe," and the children who are sometimes their companions.

Various authors have made good assessments of the situation in children's literature, and others ensure that analytical bibliographies of the various publications for children are available through specialized reviews. Certain authors have observed the behavior of the child with his comic, others have investigated the commercial mechanisms, and still others have written on the principal themes encountered. We do not intend to make a fresh study of these subjects, but rather, basing ourselves on the information contributed by this former research work, to analyze the models which may leave their impression on the child. The characters presented are intended to amuse and educate. In papers and magazines run by movements the educative purpose is always underlying, while in the commercial press the amusement takes precedence; but although certain commercial publications also purport to be educative, others do not put forward this point of view. Some of this last category are actually known by psychologists and educators to specialize in violence, racism, or mere vulgarity. The French Commission for Control over publications intended for the young [7] palliates the worst, but teachers and psychologists of various schools of thought [8] are unanimous in condemning the harmfulness of certain publications.

Although frequently the object of criticism, this press subsists, is read by the young, and is nonetheless an expression of our society. It justifies itself in its own eyes and those of the censors by the fact that the end pursued by the hero is in itself moral; but the child is admiring a man who will sometimes use the most barbaric means to attain his ends. There may be just as much identification with this character in violent behavior, as in the role of righter of wrongs. Although the child may give vent to his aggression in copying these heroes and arrogating to himself their strength which he lacks, we must not forget either the influence exerted by the image on a personality in the process of formation seeking for models to copy. The energy, courage, and zest for action which the child needs find very valuable expression in other papers.

The models in children's papers and children's books represent adults, adolescents, or children. Although we are interested principally in child models, we cannot pass by without comment the adult models which often, for the young child, embody an ideal view of the man or woman of the time. Besides, certain

---

[7] This "Commission de Contrôle sur les publications destinées à la jeunesse" has been in existence since a law of 16th July 1949 concerning publications for the young (modified in December 1958 and January 1959), and exercises control over child literature in France.

[8] Let us name for instance E. Gerin, of the Bonne Presse (Catholic), and R. Dubois, of Francs et Franches Camarades.

children prefer to identify with "grown-ups," or adolescents older than themselves.[9]

The Adult Image The adults that figure most frequently in contemporary child literature are: artists, sportsmen, royalty, soldiers, sailors, airmen and explorers, scholars, doctors, "Indians" of various types (wise or cruel), policemen, sheriffs, detectives, bandits, gangsters, etc. These figures of men and women are either real or credible. They are situated in the present or in the past. If the latter, they may either be famous people held up as an example, or imaginary heroes. There are also other mythical beings who arouse the admiration of children. They are of all degrees, from the slightly idealized knight to the "superman," whose powers far exceed those of the human race. The positive qualities which they most often possess are courage and initiative, characteristics which are often attributed also to child and adolescent heroes. We should also describe certain stereotypes, such as the naïve absent-mindedness of the professor, the ancient wisdom of the Indian, and so on. But our aim is limited to distinguishing some traits of these adult characters which are similar to those of the juvenile heroes with whom we are more particularly concerned here.

Much has been said generally about the adult characters presented in children's papers. Characters selected from real life pose problems in that often they show only one very specific aspect of the adult in our society. As for the made-up characters, they may correspond to the child's need for fantasy, but the dream world is a little too full of guns and punch-ups.[10]

Child Models Children copy, perhaps even more directly, models close to their own age which are presented to them, although the mechanism of identification is not simple.[11] The younger characters in children's books and papers are, as were the adult heroes, of various types: children of real appearance living in normal, everyday conditions, children whose appearance is still real but who are involved in extraordinary adventures (this is a very common type), and mythical children like "Superboy." Some characters are intermediate between these two last types. In this line there exist any number of little princes, ballet dancers, and young detectives. We may also include certain famous children from former times (for example, young saints and martyrs in religious magazines), or episodes from the childhood of famous men and women.

The qualities which typify most of these young heroes [12] are still courage,

---

[9] As several investigations have shown: the one by A. Brauner, in *Nos livres d'enfants ont menti,* ed. Sabri, 1951 by U.N.A.F.: "Résultat des travaux d'enquête de la Commission de l'U.N.A.F. sur la presse juvénile," in *Réalité familiale* No. 9, 1958; by the Centre de Recherches et d'Information pédagogique de la Bonne Presse—see the account given in F. Gerin, *Tout sur la presse enfantine* (Paris: Bonne Presse, 1958).

[10] Several magazines, especially those run by movements, are blameless in this respect.

[11] The type of identification involved here is obviously not the identification of object relations but rather the identification with models and roles. On this see D. LaGache, "La Personnalité."

[12] In the main, we are analyzing those characters in comics and magazines who are the heroes of regular serial features. Each magazine usually has one or more fairly characteristic examples of these.

initiative, and the ability to adapt to all manner of situations. Setting aside the tales written for very young children, few of them are seen at play. Some lead adult lives. Often, when the child lives with his family, the action of the story is hidden from his parents. The young hero wants to act alone. The absence of a family environment is no longer an occasion of grief for the child, as was so often the case in the nineteenth century, but gives him the independence he needs.

When they create these models, writers doubtless know that children will like them, but "the characters obey certain patterns of norms which can become behavior models" [13] and can become norms for the groups to whom they are presented. Unfortunately, these models are in the present instance sometimes incompatible, on the one hand with the models of the "ideal child" given to the adult by society, and on the other hand with the image of the roles that the child should fulfil with relation to the adult, as they are seen by parents and educators.

Representation of the Child Offered by Society to the Adult

Society offers various pictures of the child to adults, who absorb them, transforming them more or less, according to their needs and personal experience. Thus, through direct or indirect influences, they eventually form an idea of what the state of childhood is, and what the behavior of a model child should be.

Where Do Adults Encounter These Models?

The adult also perceives images of the child: pictures seen in the street, on advertisements and in shop windows, stereotypes heard in conversation with shopkeepers, and so on. Young mothers in particular receive a regular initiation from the more experienced mothers, in a city square or in the waiting-rooms of the clinics where they regularly take their babies. These images presented by everyday life are common to parent and child, while others are the province of adults only. Indeed the adult in his newspapers, novels, and films sees children with certain types of attitudes and behavior. Various French novelists have recounted their childhood memories in realistic or imaginative terms. Others have created characters which are famous today—for instance, Gavroche, le Petit Chose, Poil de Carotte, Trott, le Petit Prince—right up to the recent appearance of Zazie, and a very long list of others. Each of these young characters is a particular type of child.

In the cinema, child types have been memorably embodied by Jackie Coogan and Shirley Temple, and in the appearance since the last World War of the child of "The Bicycle Thieves" and other well-known films.

---

[13] P. Fouilhe, *Journaux d'enfant, journaux pour rire* (Paris: Centre d'activités pédagogiques, 1955).

Child victims, problem children, children misunderstood or whose reactions, different from our own, we try to understand—each type would require lengthy analysis. But each has his own way of experiencing a particular situation—dramatic, comic, or banal—which constitutes an explanation of the nature of the child.

Besides these literary and screen figures, some magazines do their best to provide objective information about the child. Women's magazines often feature series on child psychology and education. Moreover certain parents go even further, and with the help of publications and meetings of societies like "l'Ecole des parents" (the school for parents) try to acquire as much advanced information on education and child psychology as they can.

Some Models

From the wide variety of child representation prevalent in our society we have singled out some of the typical models that adults may have. The child is sometimes a poetic subject; a little, innocent figure of dreams, representing in a way our lost paradise. In these cases childhood corresponds for the individual to the mythical Golden Age of humanity. For others, the child is the "little one" of the species, touching and amusing; a tiny, appealing creature full of charm, with beautiful golden curls, dimples, pink or blue baby clothes—or with his turned-up nose, freckles, and jeans. Sometimes he is credited with a naïve and crude, even unmerciful child's-eye view of the "grown up" world.

Others see the child from a rather more sociological viewpoint, as the being on whom the future of society depends. Totalitarian states have made use of this vision of the child. From the same angle, many people consider the child as a future adult who will be able to restore the family fortunes, or at the least provide the opportunity for social advancement. Some people go even further: for them the child is "the transformer," no longer the symbol of the lost paradise, but the one who may perhaps be able to construct this paradise; the explorer in space, the discoverer of a cure for cancer. Certain people see the child also as the future adult to be educated, and have a more pessimistic attitude. For them, the nature of the child is essentially bad and has to be reformed. This attitude was frequently met with in the late nineteenth and early twentieth century in certain Catholic environments. We have found examples of it in manuals addressed to parents, counseling severity and even the use of corporal punishment. This vision of the child has not entirely disappeared today. From a viewpoint similar to the last, some adults regard the child as a source of worry and trouble. In this case a well-developed parental instinct or particular devotion is necessary to give them the courage to devote themselves to parenthood.

To others again the child appears as an object of material use, a source of profit to the parents who, by producing additional children entitling them to allowances, acquire household equipment. It seems very probable that this attitude exists only in a lower-class environment, but it is often expressed in the work of certain novelists (as Christiane Rochefort's *Les petits Enfants du Siècle*), or by opponents of social welfare.

Beside all these images of the child—the useful object; the nuisance or source of worries; the future adult, the hope either of humanity or of the family group; the repository of dreams or narcissistic transposition of an idealized picture of oneself as a child—there is also a school of thought which makes every effort to give an objective vision of the child. As we have indicated above, various magazines have articles which give psychological explanations and advice on the teaching of children. New information spreads, to a certain extent, to the public, modifying some of the prevalent images of the child. This information is extremely useful, but imperfect assimilation of some of its aspects can be dangerous. On the one hand, new awareness of needs in their children which they cannot fulfil may cause parents much distress; on the other hand, some over-anxious parents will tend to consider their child as "not to be frustrated," and in doing so will deprive him of the authority which is indispensable to him. It should also be said that some parents systematically try to make their child adopt models of behavior corresponding to a level of psycho-physiological or social maturity other than his own, in some cases by keeping him as long as possible at the stage of the sweet little child, dependent on his family, when the child is trying to assert himself and establish greater independence; in others, by constantly trying to make him appear in advance of the average for his age.

These various representations of the child, these trends of thought and adult attitudes, will lead to the formulation by parents and educators of certain models of the "ideal child" which will influence educative behavior patterns. The parents especially evoke these ideal types more or less consciously, and compare their own children with them, pleased when they find traits similar to the ideal, and sad or angry when the children do not correspond to the desired norms. The child suffers when he feels that he does not correspond to the wishes of his mother and father, but he enters into conflict with them if the ideal on which he himself wishes to model himself differs radically from the one proposed to him by his parents. Such conflicts are typical of adolescence, but are already present from childhood, though less clearly apparent or perhaps less externalized. Psychiatrists know how difficult it is to bring parents to view their child objectively, yet lovingly and without disillusionment, and to bring the child to a recognition of his own abilities, without discouragement or evasion. Our realization of the difficulties created for the child by the multiplicity of models may result in understanding of another source of maladjustment. More simply, it will serve to throw light on one of the ways in which the personality is socialized and built up through successive influences and choices.

Some Consequences of the Child's Encounter with These Models

The prevalent representations of the "ideal child" have repercussions on educative behavior. Sometimes a model is presented directly to the child and its qualities praised. Sometimes the child is oriented by approving certain aspects of his behavior and criticizing others. Some people proceed by reasoning, comparison, and encouragement, others use the game of rewards and punishments. But as we have seen, the child is subjected to the influence of many models—those given him by his parents and other adults he frequents, by the teachers whose charge he is in, by group leaders; those he encounters in the street, in his comics, and in the peer groups he participates in. . . . Confronted with this variety, how will he select and integrate his models, and how will he react to their multiplicity?

The Process of Identification and Integration of Models

To identify with the model is to think of oneself as, and wish oneself to be, identical with it; and to achieve this involves feeling as the model does, adopting the same types of behavior, and even the same attributes. Identification can be fairly indirect and confined to an imitation of some of the hero's behavior—but it can also take the form of conscious copying. In this last case, the child either feels affinity with the hero or, on the contrary, uses the hero's qualities to compensate for what he lacks. He may either copy certain forms of the hero's behavior and try to acquire some of his character traits; or he may take over the hero's role more generally, either in a largely imaginary way or in a more real sense, in a modified form. On reaching adolescence he will normally abandon the roles which society required him to enact as a child, and at the same time identification with certain characters in play or for compensation will cease. Socialization demands these successive adaptations. But it is by no means certain that some of the previous identifications will not have left a fairly deep imprint on his personality. The model for the role may be abandoned, while the behavior model persists in a fairly general form, or remains inscribed in specific attitudes of the young man or woman.

The child's choice of models depends on his personality and his level of physiological and social development. The analysis of the reasons for this choice is not the object of this research, any more than the analysis of the psychological mechanisms which impel the child to imitate and seek models in the course of his socialization. Our work is essentially concerned with the analysis of the models which society offers the child, but as our observation and systematic examination of papers, magazines, novels, educational advice manuals, etc., progresses, we find it impossible to ignore the repercussions of these models on the child.

The Consequences of the Multiplicity of Models: Conflicts

The multiplicity and great variety of models is a potential source of difficulty for the child, above all when these represent divergent or even contradictory value systems. The child may experience hesitation or even anxiety, not only when confronted with the personal choice which he is called upon to make, but also because the demands made upon him by parents, educators, or friends do not always tally. Is it not this uneasiness which, in some children, takes the form of instability and inattentiveness which today are two of the behavior deficiencies for which children are most often upbraided? Specialists rightly put down the increase in these symptoms to (among other factors) the accelerated rhythm of city life in our civilization. Another cause is doubtless the wide range of images, and more especially the wide variety of aims, ambitions and modes of existence.

Let us take examples of this disagreement of models at one point in the life of the child. Confronted with the image of naïve and fragile innocence which certain adults have of him, how should a child behave who is also an avid reader of comics in which the young heroes are full of courage, energy, and independence? Some will very astutely use this image to attract the adult's sympathy and favor. Others will revolt against this vision which underlines too heavily a weakness they do not want to admit to, and will turn back to the images supplied by their comics, of self-assured and independent child figures who, free from family constraint, embark upon extraordinary adventures. These children may tend either to relive these adventures in their imagination, or attempt to realize them apart from everyday life, especially if they share their admiration for these heroes with a group of friends.

We have met with many cases of this kind in neuropsychiatric consultations with children. Specialists in juvenile delinquency are also all too familiar with this question. Inversely, parents who present to their child a model which is too rigidly moral and overloaded too soon with responsibilities, can produce the same result. Many other instances could be quoted of the child's refusal to adopt the requirements of society. These problems have sometimes been laid at the door of the juvenile press; but the press merely provides the pretext for escapism. Imagination and makebelieve are not intrinsically harmful; indeed some, with whom we do not entirely agree, have seen them as the child's domain *par excellence.* But why should the child need to escape the reality of his day-to-day existence otherwise than in straightforward play, if not because of a lack of basic adjustment between this reality and himself?

To the contradictions listed above, we must add those introduced by the school environment. The teacher has more to do than he can cope with under present conditions and, in some cases, is no longer able to see the child as an individual in his social context, but sees him as someone who has to acquire a compulsory body of knowledge, often rather far removed from the day-to-day discoveries made by the child in his urban environment. Is it surprising that he displays little attention or interest in class, when he is subjected to so many other stimulating influences?

Not only are there differences between the models presented to the child by the different groups of society at any given stage in his development, but there are also clashes between the models presented to him at the different phases of his development. The roles which the boy or girl has to play will change, sometimes abruptly, as he or she develops socially and psycho-physiologically. These successive re-adaptations give rise to progress or to conflicts. An abrupt change of model as a function of age sometimes reveals a definite break between the roles expected of different age-groups, or can be a symptom of the evolution of certain social structures. Here is an example:

While analyzing, in the course of the last two years, papers and magazines for girls which were judged harmless by the specialists analyzing them (magazines run by movements, and various commercial publications), we found that the main girl characters have the following qualities: courage, initiative, strength of purpose, independence, devotion, and generosity. Sometimes a boy character accompanies them, displaying the same qualities in a more spectacular way and acting as their protector. But very often the two are on a equal footing, and sometimes the boy is even the weaker of the two, being the younger. The fragile little girl, victim of circumstances or of wicked persons, who appeared so often in the last century, is very rarely met with. The gentle, passive model, submissive and obedient, is less and less frequent. The traditional so-called "feminine" quality which is found in these heroines is devotion, but this is also frequently displayed by the boys. Both boy and girl characters live through the same adventures, tracking down the villains and protecting the victims. The girl herself is a pioneer on the trail to the West, simultaneously braving Indians and looking after her little brothers; or she is pursuing a bandit to vindicate her father's honor. There are also dancers who produce a ballet single-handed, to save the ballet school, despite obstacles and hostile men, from financial ruin.

How do girls, after steeping themselves in heroism and becoming more or less identified with these characters full of initiative, pass on to the sentimental reading which is so often proposed to them later? Above all, how are they going to adapt to the role of woman in the home, which society will expect of them when they are married, and which they often see their mother still enacting? It is true that now—as recent research has shown—girls often identify with heroes of the opposite sex, while boys virtually always identify with male characters. As the girl grows up she will (as will the boy) grow away from these dreams of adventure and these models for roles, but may she not retain the character models?

One feature in one of these magazines attempts to show some sort of transition. A teenage girl, robust and courageous, is competing with a boy-cousin of the same age. On an underwater fishing expedition the boy, who has less stamina, narrowly escapes drowning, is saved by his cousin, but loses his quarry and his equipment. The girl, when she sees his humiliation, gets him to believe that it was she who lost everything and panicked. At this point she makes a ". . . marvellous discovery: it is right and good that boys should be stronger, even if it is not strictly true . . . and . . . she had the delicious sensation of becoming a 'little woman.' " How will girls of 13 or 14, who are fairly wholehearted, accept this development based on a lie, albeit a generous one? Probably not very readily. This example is an illustration of conflicting models: the one society still often wants for the woman, and the one which is more attractive to girls, and of which editors are not unaware. This conflict encountered by girls in adolescence is more than the sign of a transference from one role to another according to age, it denotes the evolution of social structures concerning the woman.[14] We could give other examples of conflicting models. As they are so varied, we have tried to evolve a typology. This is at the tentative stage and has not reached its final form, for this research is very recent, and in view of the scope of the field of observation which presents itself, it will last several years.

Firstly, there can be divergence between the mother's and father's conception of the "ideal child," arising out of their different social environments or their own personal experience. Within the family, the concepts held by grandparents and other adults are not without influence.

There can also be divergence between the model experienced within the family, and the one more frequently found within the socio-professional or residential environment to which the family belongs. This disagreement may result from the fact that the family comes from a different environment or has personal problems. In these cases the child either adapts to the model presented at home and feels out of place with his friends, or else opposes his parents; unless he modifies his behavior according to whether he is with one or the other. But when he invites his friends home, he will not know how to behave.

The divergence between the models presented to society in adult and children's literature is enormous. Naturally, the publications are aimed at different age-groups, but beyond the stories and adventures which are supposedly adapted to the appropriate age-group, the models and images eventually make an impression. The image, a more or less direct expression of a society, eventually becomes a model for the same society.

The ideal model, which exists on the same plane as principles, can be too far removed from the actual situation, either because of the living conditions and cultural environment, or because of the intellectual and emotional capacity of the child and his level of development.

The models presented at school do not always correspond to the family models. On the one hand the image of the child's role in his family, as it is presented at school, has not always been re-thought-out in terms of the new living conditions (in new towns, for instance) or in terms of the changes in the parents' roles (as when the mother is working). On the other hand, the model schoolchild does not necessarily have the same role as does the model child as seen by the parents.

The models which exist within youth movements remain to be defined, and still more work has to be done on models created by the children themselves within their spontaneous groups. To resume the possible conflicts: the child may be torn between the models presented by his parents, by the school, by child literature, films, and television, and by spontaneous and organized peer groups in which he participates.

[14] A variety of research has been conducted by the Group of Social Ethnology on the image of the woman in society, on an international level: see "Images de la femme dans la société," special number of the *Revue des sciences sociales de l'UNESCO,* January 1962, and for France, in different socio-professional environments (see *Image de la femme dans la société perçue par des hommes et des femmes de différents milieux sociaux* (Paris: C.N.R.S., 1962).

Positive Gains from the Variety of Models

This multiplicity and variety of models does not, from the point of view of child psychology any more than sociology, present disadvantages only. For the child himself, such a situation offers a wide range of choices and opens up new perspectives. The variety of roles which he is called upon to fulfil gives him a large repertoire [15] which, when it is well integrated, is conducive to adaptability. As he develops, the readjustment of roles can also be a source of progress. The child, in this urban society, will very quickly escape from the single family model. A hundred years ago on the other hand, children of the aristocracy and upper middle classes had a tutor or governess to teach them at home. They read books which had been written by adults from the same environment, representing the same social framework and expressing the same value-systems; in this way they indeed received a consistent education, but also gained only a very limited vision of society and its value-systems. The mobility and variety of today bring with them the counterpart of the danger of instability, hesitancy and anxiety for some children, but the child, rarely contained within a single system, will doubtless have less tendency to burst the bounds of a too narrow social framework which he finds oppressive. In any case, he needs to be helped to discard certain models, and find others which are not always within his reach.

From the point of view of sociology rather than of child psychology, this state of affairs is, in fact, a sign of the rejection of some social structures, and the emergence of new forms, as yet incompletely defined, which are superimposed on the old. The aspect of disintegration is immediately striking, and is emphasized by certain specialists, particularly those who are concerned with maladjusted children, and see the negative results of the changes. This, however, is not the only aspect. The maladjustment of some may sometimes serve to accelerate the evolution of society, just as for the child periods of maladjustment often result in progress when they can be overcome.

One is impressed by the theoretical and applied work being done on the child, who occupies a more and more prominent place in society as a whole. In this direction the efforts of psychologists, educators, sociologists, doctors, and town planners, to understand the child and adapt social structures to his needs, are a sign which allows us to hope for a real advance, even though this work is only conducted by a very small number of specialists. On the other hand, certain models presented over and over again in children's books, for instance, express personality traits which one would like to see becoming widespread among the younger generation. If we are to reform and transform, criticism does not suffice; it may be necessary to catch and hold all the elements of progress which can be detected in a society as a whole, and in the various social environments which make it up.

---

[15] See A. M. Spenle, "La notion du rôle chez l'enfant," in *Cahiers Internationaux de sociologie,* Vol. 14, 1953.

31

Achieving Socialization Without Sacrificing Creativity

E. PAUL TORRANCE

In many respects socialization is a process of human homogenization. Indeed, one of the clues that a person is socialized is that he is inconspicuous when in the presence of others. That is, a socialized person can predict the behaviors of others in a situation and will himself behave in that situation in a predictable way. Of course, some variability is to be anticipated, and tolerated. But the thrust of much of socialization is learning to behave appropriately—like others.

If the foregoing characterization has any validity, then one might ask if socialization is not antithetical to creativity. In the selection which follows, Torrance argues that if socialization does typically stultify creativity, such need not be the case. In fact, he reviews a number of studies conducted with pre-school to college age subjects which indicate that many of the procedures which facilitate socialization also facilitate creativity. Torrance reports, for example, that subjects working in dyadic situations exhibited a greater production of ideas, worked longer at tasks, and tackled more difficult tasks than did control subjects working alone, i.e., were more creative. Both the dyadic interaction (as opposed to solo activity) and the creativity outcomes are consistent with basic socialization principles and goals.

The reader might find it profitable to evaluate each of Torrance's suggestions for creative development in terms of its consistency or inconsistency with what is known about child and adult socialization.

E. Paul Torrance, "Achieving Socialization Without Sacrificing Creativity," *The Journal of Creative Behavior* 4 (1970): 183–89. We print with permission from the Creative Education Foundation, from *The Journal of Creative Behavior,* Volume IV, 1970.

Poets, artists, parents, teachers, and child psychologists frequently have noted that many children begin sacrificing their creativity along with socialization training.

Generally, this decrement in curiosity and creative functioning has been perceived as a natural and quite desirable consequence of socialization. Even those who have been disturbed by it and see it as the result of man-made changes rather than purely genetic ones have conceded that when the child enters school he *must* be drawn into group activities and be impelled by its rules and regulations, thus surrendering his creativity (Pulsifer, 1963).

During my first three years at the University of Georgia, I had the opportunity to evaluate creative development resulting from the application of the Creative-Aesthetic approach to preprimary education. During the second and third years I had unprecedented opportunities to experiment with materials and procedures to improve the quality of both the socialization and creative skills within this program. From the results obtained at the end of the first year, it was obvious that five-year-old children participating in the Creative-Aesthetic preprimary program attained unusual heights in originality of thinking. They showed enormous growth on pre- and post-tests of creativity, both verbal and nonverbal. They excelled their controls on every measure of originality we had devised and also on those developed by Starkweather (1965). Their mean originality score at the end of the school year was 1.1 standard deviations above the mean of our fifth-grade norm group, actually a rather superior group by national standards (Torrance, 1966). However, on the measure of elaboration, which requires considerable intellectual discipline, their performance placed them a full standard deviation below our fifth-grade norms. There was also some indication that their socialization skills did not equal those of children in the traditional kindergarten program. Furthermore, children in the Structured-Cognitive preprimary model achieved a higher degree of elaboration (Torrance, 1968).

During the next two years, I began experimenting with materials and procedures that I hoped would increase socialization skills and ability to elaborate without causing a reduction in originality. By the third year, many of these materials and procedures had been tested experimentally and had been incorporated into the curriculum of the two classes of five-year-olds enrolled in the Creative-Aesthetic approach to preprimary educational stimulation. At least a part of the success attained thereby is reflected in the data presented in Table 1 (Torrance, 1969a), which shows the mean T-scores (based on fifth-grade norms) on figural fluency, flexibility, originality, and elaboration on the *Torrance Tests of Creative Thinking Ability* (1966). The originality scores at the end of the second and third years were at about the same high level as at the end of the first year. Fluency and flexibility also were at about the same level as in the first year. Elaboration, however, was about 1.36 standard deviations above that attained at the end of the first year. Similarly, studies of group functioning on creative tasks

TABLE 1

MEAN STANDARD SCORES AND STANDARD DEVIATIONS ON FIGURAL FORM OF TORRANCE TESTS OF CREATIVE THINKING OF FIVE-YEAR-OLDS AFTER ONE YEAR OF CREATIVE-AESTHETIC EDUCATIONAL STIMULATION FOR EACH OF THREE YEARS.

	1966–67 (*N* = 24)		*1967–68* (*N* = 44)		*1968–69* (*N* = 48)	
Variable	*Means*	*St. dev.*	*Means*	*St. dev.*	*Means*	*St. dev.*
Fluency	34.9	5.8	38.4	6.5	35.0	6.1
Flexibility	37.9	5.8	37.6	8.1	38.4	6.5
Originality	61.6	17.3	58.7	16.8	56.4	17.6
Elaboration	39.7	7.2	40.8	5.8	53.3	10.7

showed a higher level of organizing and cooperating behavior than was found during the second year. (No objective studies of group functioning were made during the first year.)

The major emphasis of my developmental work to refine certain aspects of the Creative-Aesthetic model (Fortson, 1969) has been focused on experimentation with factors influencing interaction processes. The pervasive objective has been to facilitate simultaneously the socialization and creative processes. We have been able to test rather carefully through experimental studies some of our hypotheses and I shall limit this paper to these studies. By this I do not mean to devalue such developments as the "Just Imagine Exercises" that set in motion creative currents that reverberate for days, the "Leadership Training Program," "Magic Net Creative Dramatics and Problem Solving," "Magic Story Teller Puppetry," the use of puppets in developing question asking skills, and the like. Through subjective and phenomenological ways I "know" that these procedures are effective in achieving the dual aim of encouraging both socialization and creativity, and this evidence has been discussed elsewhere (Torrance, 1970a; Torrance and Myers, 1970).

Dyadic Interaction

One series of studies has investigated the role of dyadic interaction in facilitating creativity. In the first study (Torrance, 1970b) I examined simultaneously five-year-old children and college students, investigating the simple hypothesis that dyadic interaction will facilitate the production of original ideas among individuals. Twenty college students (juniors) were administered four tasks from the *Torrance Tests of Creative Thinking* under standard conditions; twenty others randomly assigned to dyads from the same population were tested under the same conditions except that they were encouraged to hitchhike on one another's ideas but forbidden to repeat an idea produced by the other. Similarly, twenty-four five-year-olds were tested alone and twenty-two of their randomly selected classmates were tested in dyads. The results of both experiments indicate that dyadic interaction facilitated originality of thinking, but the differences are stronger for the college students than for the five-year-old children.

From these two simple experiments, two additional hypotheses cried for investigation. In both experiments, there were indications that the subjects enjoyed the experience more abundantly in the dyads than in the single performances and that they were willing to stick to the task longer.

One of my students, Robert D. Towell (1970), investigated the persistence hypothesis with five-year-old disadvantaged children, using my "What Can It Be" test (Torrance, 1970c). At the same time he replicated the initial study with very clear cut results. The mean number of ideas produced by each member of the dyad was about twice the number produced by children working individually under standard testing conditions. The mean originality score in dyads was also about twice that attained under standard conditions. Persistence, as measured by length of time, was also significantly greater in dyads than under standard conditions.

I have not investigated the degree of enjoyment variable among five-year-olds, but I have verified it with college students. The evidence through subjective and phenomenological ways of knowing is so strong that I doubt that I shall bother to investigate it by more objective means.

Dyads and Willingness to Try the Difficult

Creative people have to be willing to attempt the difficult, and children too, in order to learn and to grow, must be willing to tackle difficult tasks. To facilitate learning and growth, teachers should be able to create the social or peer conditions conducive to attempting tasks of appropriate difficulty. For another experiment (Torrance, 1969b), we hypothesized that five-year-old children would be more willing to attempt difficult tasks when placed in pairs than when alone or before their entire class. The task used in this study was a target game in which the children attempted to throw bean bags into a basket from distances that make the task either easy or difficult, depending upon the choice of the child. In Condition A, the children played the game in pairs; in Condition B, alone; and in Condition C, before the entire class. There were twenty-two children each in Conditions A and B and forty-four in Condition C. The results clearly supported the hypothesis and further suggested that children are least willing to attempt the difficult when performing before the entire class.

Group Size and Questioning Performance

The ability to support curiosity by skill in asking questions is also important both in socialization and creativity. John Dewey (1953), for example, formulated the stages through which curiosity develops or is lost. The initial stage of curiosity is marked by an expression of an abundant organic energy. A physiological uneasiness results in the child's "getting into everything." As socialization gets underway, a second stage of curiosity emerges. This stage is characterized by the abundance of "why" questions. These questions are not demands for scientific explanations but represent a simple eagerness to know more about the mysterious world. The third stage emerges when curiosity rises above the organic and social level and becomes intellectual. According to Dewey, unless there is a transition to an intellectual plane, curiosity degenerates or evaporates and is lost forever. On the basis of these observations, several experiments have been concerned with facilitating this transformation process.

The purpose of the first of these studies (Torrance, 1970d) was to examine the effects of group size on the question asking behavior of eight classes of five-year-old children engaged in programs of preprimary educational stimulation.

In the test task, groups were asked to produce as many questions as they could in a ten-minute period concerning Mother Goose prints. It was required that the questions be about things that could not be ascertained by looking at the picture. Groups of twenty-four, twelve, six and four were studied.

Group size had significant effects on number of different questions asked, number of discrepant event questions, and number of repeated questions. Production was significantly higher in the small groups, although in most respects four-child groups seemed to have little or no advantage over six-child groups.

In spite of the limitations of the study imposed by the sampling and design, the results support arguments for exploring the possible advantages of small-group instruction over individual instruction in developing certain intellectual skills such as question asking.

The Role of Task and Group Structure

Many early-childhood educators argue that any imposed structure discourages creativity, while others argue for its necessity. In one of our experiments an attempt was made to improve the small-group behavior of five-year-old children by increasing the task structure. The children were asked first to draw dream castles, then to decide which group member's castle they wanted to construct, and finally to build a castle. In the second experiment, an attempt was made to improve this type of behavior among five-year-olds through increasing the group structure by designating one member as leader. In the first experiment, there were twelve six-person groups in each condition; in the second experiment, there were six six-person groups in each condition. In the first experiment, the task structure achieved by the experimental manipulation resulted in an increase in planning and cooperating behavior and a decrease in verbal and physical aggressiveness. The second experimental manipulation tended to increase the planning behavior but decreased the verbal aggressiveness and physical aggression.

Manipulation of Objects and Question Asking

As the socialization process moves along, children find that increasingly they are forbidden to touch and to manipulate objects. In some of my earlier studies

(Torrance, 1963), I had found that degree of manipulation of the toys used in the product improvement test was highly related to the number of ideas produced and to the originality of those ideas. This suggested the hypothesis that the provision of opportunities to manipulate stimulus objects would facilitate question asking among five-year-old children. The forty-eight subjects were randomly assigned within classrooms to eight six-person groups. The manipulation and non-manipulation conditions were presented in an alternate form design in the two classrooms. The stimulus objects were a plastic bee which made a buzzing sound when twirled and a toy musical instrument which made a variety of sounds when manipulated. In one class the bee was used in the manipulation condition and in the other the musical instrument was manipulated. The manipulation condition compared with the non-manipulation condition produced a larger number of questions and a larger number of hypothesis-stating questions and questions about puzzling phenomena. The results suggest that previous findings concerning the facilitating effects of manipulation in the production of inventive ideas can be generalized to question asking skills.

Conclusion

I offer these experiments only as examples of possible ways through which we can explore the issues involved in facilitating simultaneously both socialization and creativity, test and refine hypotheses for achieving these dual purposes, and feed the results into the development and refinement of the Creative-Aesthetic model of educational stimulation. Much more experimentation of this nature is needed.

REFERENCES

Andrews, E. G. 1930. The development of imagination in the preschool child. *University of Iowa Studies in Character.*

Dewey, J. 1933. *How we think.* Boston: D. C. Heath.

Fortson, L. R. 1969. A creative-aesthetic approach to readiness and beginning reading and mathematics in the kindergarten. Doctoral dissertation, University of Georgia.

Montgomery, M. 1965. *Stones from the rubble.* Memphis, Tenn.: Argus Books.

Pulsifer, S. N. 1963. *Children are poets.* Cambridge, Mass.: Dresser, Chapman & Grimes.

Starkweather, E. K. 1965. An originality test for preschool children. Stillwater, Okla.: Oklahoma State University. (Mimeographed)

Torrance, E. P. 1962. *Guiding creative talent.* Englewood Cliffs, N.J.: Prentice-Hall.

———. 1963. *Education and the creative potential.* Minneapolis: University of Minnesota Press.

———. 1966. *The Torrance tests of creative thinking: norms-technical manual (Research Edition).* Princeton, N.J.: Personnel Press, 1966.

———. 1968. Must pre-primary educational stimulation be incompatible with creative development? In F. E. Williams Ed., *Creativity at home and in school.* St. Paul, Minn.: Macalester Creativity Project, Macalester College.

———. 1969a. *A three-year study of the influence of a creative-aesthetic approach to school readiness and beginning reading and arithmetic on creative development.* Athens, Ga.: Research and Development Center in Educational Stimulation, University of Georgia.

———. 1969. Peer influences on preschool children's willingness to try difficult tasks. *Journal of Psychology* 72: 189–94.

———. 1970a. *Encouraging creativity in the classroom.* Dubuque, Iowa: Wm. C. Brown.

———. 1970b. Influence of dyadic interaction on creative functioning. *Psychological Reports* 26: 391–94.

———. 1970c. Administration and scoring guide for "What can it be?" test. Athens, Ga.: Georgia Studies of Creative Behavior, 1970c. (Mimeographed)

———. 1970d. Group size and question performance of pre-primary children. *Journal of Psychology* 74: 71–75.

———, and R. E. Myers. 1970e. *Creative learning and teaching.* New York: Dodd, Mead & Co.

Towell, R. D. 1970. Influence of dyadic interaction on creative task performance. Unpublished research paper, University of Georgia, 1970.

32

The Socialization of the Blind in Personal Interaction

ROBERT A. SCOTT

In his book *The Making of Blind Men,* Robert A. Scott develops the thesis that blindness "is a social role that people who have serious difficulty seeing or who cannot see at all must learn to play." In other terms, it is argued that the attitudes, behaviors, and personal qualities that are generally assumed to be produced by the physical condition of blindness are rather the results of ordinary socialization processes.

The following excerpt from that book emphasizes the nature and consequences of interaction between the person who has difficulty seeing and those who can see. Scott identifies two aspects of such social encounters through which the blind are socialized. First, those who can see enter into an interaction situation with a variety of preconceptions about blindness. That is, the normal confronts a blind person with a set of notions and expectations which he acquired through his own socialization. The preconceptions help shape the normal's behavior toward the blind, and, in turn, increase the likelihood that he will elicit "blind" responses from the person who can't see. The reactions of the sighted during the interaction constitutes the second crucial aspect of the encounter through which the blind are socialized.

While the data on which Scott's conceptual analysis is based are admittedly limited (and not obvious in the excerpt), the analysis should suggest to the reader a number of researchable propositions. The dynamics of the socialization of the blind which is outlined should be equally applicable to many categories of people in our society, e.g., policemen, prostitutes, doctors, the insane, etc.

Robert A. Scott, "The Socialization of the Blind in Personal Interaction," in *The Making of Blind Men.* New York: Russell Sage, 1969, pp. 20–37, with editorial abridgment.

One of the ways in which a person who has difficulty seeing learns how to be a blind man is by interacting with those who see. When normals come face-to-face with someone who cannot see, their preconceptions about, and reactions to, blindness are expressed as expectations of how the blind man ought to behave. The blind man is poignantly reminded of the social identity imputed to him by others. All blind men respond to this identity in some way, even if only to dispute it; for those who internalize it, this putative social identity becomes a personal identity in fact.

There are two principal mechanisms of personal encounters through which the blind are socialized. The first relates to preconceptions about blindness that people who can see bring to encounters with blind men, the second to the reactions of the sighted during the encounter. . . .

Preconceptions about Blindness

The preconceptions that the sighted bring to situations of interaction with the blind are of two sorts. On the one hand, there are stereotypic beliefs about blindness and the blind that they have acquired through the ordinary processes of socialization in our culture; and, on the other, there is the fact that blindness is a stigmatizing condition. Each factor makes its special contribution to the social identity that is reserved for blind men. . . .

Stereotypic Beliefs about Blindness

Among the general beliefs that laymen have about the blind are notions of helplessness, docility, dependency, melancholia, aestheticism, and serious-mindedness. While few laymen accept all these beliefs, most of them do adhere to at least a few of them. These misconceptions are brought by them to situations of interaction with the blind and are expressed as expectations of the behavior and attitudes of the blind person. Because of them, deep and stubborn "grooves and channels" are created into which all the blind man's actions and feelings are pressed. Their existence makes it extremely difficult for meaningful communication and unstrained relationships to occur between the seeing and the blind.

The effects such beliefs have upon blind people when they interact with sighted people have been succinctly described by Gowman:

> An individual taking up the role of blind man is conceptually relocated along the margins of the dominant social structure and a peripheral social role is assigned to him. His rights and obligations are redefined in a manner which is believed to mesh with the character of the disability. The newly blinded person is reevaluated in all his aspects, and the evaluative scale shifts from the measurement of specific individual qualities or capabilities to the assessment of the global condition of blindness. What distinguishes the blind role from other types of roles is its all pervasive character. Blindness is not an attribute to be put on or cast off as the situation demands, but a constant characteristic which

> affects the quality of each of the individual's relationships in occupational, recreational, and other contexts. When evaluation is thus expanded to cover an individual's entire personality structure, a stereotype is operative. The blind may be assigned a social role which so transforms them that they emerge as a labeled segment of society. Social interaction becomes stunted and artificial under the impress of the stereotype.[1]

It is impossible for blind men to ignore these beliefs; they have no choice but to respond to them. These responses vary, but in a highly patterned way. Some blind people come to concur in the verdict that has been reached by those who see. They adopt as a part of their self-concept the qualities of character, the feelings, and the behavior patterns that others insist they must have. Docility, helplessness, melancholia, dependency, pathos, gratitude, a concern for the spiritual and the aesthetic, all become a genuine part of the blind man's personal identity. Such blind men might be termed "true believers"; they have become what others with whom they interact assume they must become because they are blind.

Not all blind people are true believers; there are many who explicitly, indeed insistently, reject the imputations made of them by others. They thereby manage to insulate a part of the self-concept from the assaults made on it by normals. The personal identity of such a person is not that of a blind man, but of a basically normal person who cannot see. For the blind man who responds in this way, there remains the problem that most people who see do not share the view he has reached about himself. Some blind men respond simply by complying with the expectations of the sighted, in a conscious and deliberate way. They adopt an external facade that is consistent with the normals' assumptions about them, but they are aware that it is a facade, and they are ready to drop it whenever occasions permit them to do so. Ordinarily, the reason for acquiescence is expedience; in fact, every blind man, whether he accepts or rejects the social identity imputed to him, will be found to acquiesce at least some of the time. . . .

Another way that blind men cope with discrepancies between putative and personal identity is to resist and negate the imputations of others at every turn. By so doing, personal integrity is preserved, but the cost is very high. It requires an enormous commitment and expenditure of energy to resist these forces, and the blind man who does so inevitably alienates himself from other people. Even those who follow this road successfully are left with a certain bitterness and frustration that is the inevitable residue of any attempt to break the stubborn molds into which the blind man's every action is pressed.

. . . . .

Blindness as Stigma

Blindness is a stigma, carrying with it a series of moral imputations about character and personality. The stereotypical beliefs I have discussed lead normal

---

[1] Alan G. Gowman, *The War Blind in American Social Structure* (New York: American Foundation for the Blind, 1957), p. 46.

people to feel that the blind are different; the fact that blindness is a stigma leads them to regard blind men as their physical, psychological, moral, and emotional inferiors. Blindness is therefore a trait that discredits a man by spoiling both his identity and his respectability.

When a person with a stigma encounters a normal person, barriers are created between them.[2] These barriers, though symbolic, are often impenetrable. They produce a kind of "moving away," much like the action of two magnetized particles of metal whose similar poles have been matched. These avoidance reactions are often induced by a fear that direct contact with a blind person may be contaminating, or that the stigmatized person will somehow inflict physical or psychic damage. Such reactions and fears are completely emotional and irrational in character.

The effects of these reactions on a blind man are profound. Even though he thinks of himself as a normal person, he recognizes that most others do not really accept him, nor are they willing or ready to deal with him on an equal footing. Moreover, as Goffman has observed, "the standards he has incorporated from the wider society equip him to be intimately alive to what others see as his failure, inevitably causing him, if only for moments, to agree that he does indeed fall short of what he really ought to be.[3] As a result, he may feel shame because he knows he possesses a defiling attribute. It is when the blind person finds himself in the company of the sighted that these self-derogating feelings are aroused. "The central feature of the stigmatized individual's situation in life," writes Goffman, "is a question of what is often, if vaguely, called 'acceptance.' Those who have dealings with him fail to accord him the respect and regard which the uncontaminated aspects of his social identity have led them to anticipate extending and have led him to anticipate receiving; he echoes this denial by finding that some of his own attributes warrant it." [4]

The stigma of blindness makes problematic the integrity of the blind man as an acceptable human being. Because those who see impute inferiority, the blind man cannot ignore this and is forced to defend himself. If, as sometimes occurs, the blind man shares the values of the sighted, the process becomes even more insidious; for when this is the case, a man's personal identity is open to attack from within as well as from without.

The Situation of Interaction

Preconceptions about blindness are not the only elements of personal encounters that determine a blind man's socialization experiences; certain features of the

---

[2] Fred Davis, "Deviance Disavowal: The Management of Strained Interaction by the Visibly Handicapped," in Howard S. Becker, ed., *The Other Side* (New York: Free Press, 1964), pp. 119–38, and Robert Kleck, Ono Hiroshi, and Albert H. Hastorf, "The Effects of Physical Deviance upon Face-to-Face Interaction," *Human Relations* 19 (1966): 425–36.

[3] Erving Goffman, *Stigma: Notes on the Management of Spoiled Identity* (Englewood Cliffs, N.J.: Prentice-Hall, 1963), p. 7.

[4] Ibid., pp. 8–9.

actual encounter play an important role as well. First of all, the norms governing ordinary personal interaction cannot, as a rule, be applied when one of the actors is unable to see. Furthermore, blind people, because they cannot see, must rely for assistance upon the seeing with whom they interact. As a result, many of the interactions that involve the sighted and blind men become relationships of social dependency. Each of these factors is intimately related to the kind of self-concept the blind man develops, and, because of them, this group of people is made even more homogeneous.

Blindness and the Conduct of Personal Relationships

Vision plays an extremely important role in the face-to-face encounters of everyday life. The initial impressions we have of people are acquired largely through vision, and the success of our subsequent relationships with them depends to a considerable extent on our ability to see. It is when one of the actors is blind that we recognize how central a part vision plays in our relationships with other people.

Establishing an Identity One of the things we do upon meeting someone for the first time is to impute to him a familiar social identity. We label him elderly, handsome, debonair, cultured, timid, or whatever. From the identity we have imputed to him, we anticipate what his tastes and interests will be, the kinds of attitudes he will have, and how he is likely to behave. We search for clues to help us to classify the person as a type of individual, and we then apply norms of conduct associated with "his type" in order to guide us in our subsequent interaction with him. Unless we can do this quickly and accurately, we are at a loss as to how to proceed, and experience the situation as embarrassing and stressful.

What people wear, how they look, the way they stand, and the gestures they use are important clues in helping us to reach some decision about the type of person we have encountered. Indeed, most of the initial impressions we form of persons are based on clues that must be seen to be detected. For this reason, initial encounters between the seeing and the blind are set awry; since one actor is blind, each is deprived of significant information about the other.

The blind person will be at a loss to know precisely with whom he is dealing, and what kind of behavior to expect from him. He will be slow to piece together the information he needs correctly to infer the person's social identity. This produces an ambiguity and uneasiness that can become so intense that the relationship never develops.

The inability to gather accurate information on which to form impressions is not a problem only for the blind person; it leads to uneasiness on the part of the sighted individual as well. He is uncertain that the image he tries to project will be received, or, if received, accurately interpreted. He will realize immediately that his general appearance is no longer useful for conveying information about himself. His uneasiness intensifies if he does not know which nonvisual clues the blind man is using to "size him up." Is it the tone of voice or the content of words? Does his tone of voice convey something about himself that he is unaware of or wishes to conceal? He does not know how to convey to the blind man an impression equivalent to the one conveyed through sight. When visual clues to a person's social identity are missing, a difficult and awkward situation is created for both the blind man, who does not develop a complete impression, and the sighted man, who is unsure of the impression he has made.

Conversely, there is the process of social identification of the blind person by the sighted individual. In addition to the stigmatizing quality of blindness, blind people may be insensitive to the role of visual factors in projecting accurate impressions, or they may not know how to create the kind of impression they want to. In this regard, the blind person is dependent upon others. They select his clothes and advise him on his posture. To some extent, then, his appearance is dependent on the tastes of his helpers. Clearly, ambiguities and uncertainties surround the identity of the blind man as well as that of those who see.

Norms Governing Personal Interaction These ambiguities and uncertainties will sometimes cause the encounter to terminate prematurely. If not, initial uncertainties are carried into the next stage of the relationship, for it is on the basis of initial impressions that we know what to expect of others, and how we should behave toward them. The rules that are applied to an individual on the basis of our identification of him, and the rules that he in turn applies to us, lend structure and substance to the relationship. Since a person's blindness tends to overwhelm those with whom he interacts, it is the blindness more than anything else that identifies him. Blindness is a comparatively rare event in any population, so that only a few sighted individuals ever interact with a blind man in any sustained way. What most of us know about blindness comes from the mass media, religious and other writings, common sense, hearsay, or from occasional contacts with a salesman of products made by the blind, or the solicitor from the local blindness agency. When we encounter a blind man, the rules we apply to him are extremely vague; they tell us what to expect in only the most tentative way. Our lack of direct experience makes the situation more uncertain. This normative ambiguity, indeed normlessness, applies as much to the blind person's understanding of the sighted individual's behavior as it applies to the sighted individual's understanding of how to behave with a blind person. In this sense, the difficulty lies with the relationship and not with the individual partners to it.

. . . . .

Communication Problems Vision plays an enormously important role in personal communication. When we speak to someone, it is customary for us to maintain eye contact. This is learned from the earliest age, so that by about the time a child begins school, this very important lesson has been learned. To turn away or focus on a distant object when addressing another person can be attributed to rudeness, shyness, or guilt. Frequently, the lack of visual contact is one of the factors responsible for the statement, "We simply could not communicate." Eye contact signifies honesty, directness, attentiveness, respect, and a variety of other virtues that are the important ingredients of successful human communication.

The important role of vision in personal interaction has many implications for the blind. The blind person is often able to follow a conversation more closely by turning his ear to the speaker. He may therefore develop the disconcerting habit of turning his head slightly away from the speaker's face. The speaker reacts as he would to a sighted individual turning away—he is not sure the listener is attentive.

But the problem is more complicated than this. In addition to the fact that the blind person may incline his head this way or that to maximize sound, the appearance of his eyes may be disconcerting. When blindness is due to accident, the face and eyes may be disfigured. Sometimes the eyes bulge or are set at peculiar angles; in other cases, they may be opaque or gray. When a person is losing vision, he may also lose the ability to control the eye muscles, so that the eyes constantly flutter and roll about in their sockets. These deformities present major difficulties in communication, because eye contact may be not only disturbing but repulsive to the observer.

Blindness prevents the blind person from getting visual feedback for his own body gestures. This may result in the inadvertent development of gestures and bodily movements that are disruptive of communication. A person who cannot observe his own expressions or others' reactions to them becomes insensitive to the importance of facial and bodily gestures in communication. The blind man often appears to be smiling the smile of a simpleton, or gesturing in a way that makes him appear retarded or mentally deranged. Once again, his unusual facial and body gestures are interpreted as they would be if he could see. This is especially a problem among the congenitally blind, who, out of a need for stimulation, develop peculiar body movements called "blindisms." They probe at the face, tilt the body and roll it, move up and down and back and forth, and often have ticks and twitches of the face. If the sighted person interprets these gestures as being responsive to what he has said, further misunderstandings in communication arise. Conversely, the gesture as a mechanism of communication by the sighted person is also eliminated, which limits the range of expressions he can use. These problems with communication serve to heighten the already difficult misunderstandings that have been created by normative ambiguity.

These three problems of establishing the desired personal identity in the mind of the other actor, of uncertainty as to how to interact with a blind man, and of miscommunication all work together to produce that peculiar blend of annoyance, frustration, ambiguity, anger, tension, and irritation that describes human interaction that is spoiled. The important point is that the source of this unhappy outcome is not to be found so much in the erroneous beliefs that the seeing hold about blindness, although such beliefs clearly are not entirely innocent; rather, it lies in what might be called "the mechanics" of interpersonal conduct. In this sense, the problem lies more with the relationship itself than with the erroneous conceptions held by those who are parties to it.

All of this has two important effects on the blind man's self-concept. First, he is once again reminded that he is different from most people and that the satisfying personal relationships that are commonplace to them are, for the most part, denied to him. Second, because so many of his relationships with other people are spoiled, he is denied the kind of honest and direct feedback that is so essential for maintaining clear and realistic conceptions about the kind of person he is.[5] Often the blind man gets no feedback at all, and when he does it is usually badly distorted. As a result, the blind man can easily acquire either an unduly negative or an unreasonably positive conception of his own abilities.

Even though many of the problems that characterize encounters between sighted and blind men arise from the mechanics of interpersonal conduct, it does not always follow that blind men explain these problems to themselves in this way. On the contrary, many of them apparently assume that a normal person's behavior is caused by his beliefs. Thus, when a sighted person behaves assertively toward a blind man so as to eliminate uncertainty, the blind man infers that the other's actions are caused by a belief that blindness makes him helpless. It is for this reason, I think, that blind people have placed so much stock in the notion of an elaborate, rigid stereotype of the blind.

Blindness and Social Dependency

. . . . .

A number of basic problems in personal associations between the blind and the sighted are clarified by viewing them from the perspective of social exchange theory. A person's evaluation of the potential social attractiveness of another will be radically affected if the person evaluated cannot see. Most sighted people will assume that they will have to offer more services to the blind man than the blind man will be able to offer them. Moreover, since blind persons require assistance in getting about in their environment, they will be automatically put into the sighted person's debt. This implies that persons cannot realistically expect to receive payment in kind for favors rendered. That this is recognized in our culture is evident from the fact that most encounters involving the blind and the sighted are defined as charitable. In charitable relationships, the donor person is expected to give generously to the one who is stigmatized, and not to expect to receive anything in return. Actually, this commonly held belief is only partly true, since the charitable person is repaid in part by the fact that his giving is usually public and therefore results in social approval and in part by receiving gratitude. But social approval and gratitude are not in themselves sufficient to sustain relationships. Reciprocity, to be genuine, must involve both socially valued compliance and the capacity to perform socially valued favors.

The blind person is, therefore, by virtue of his dependency, the subordinate in a power relationship. As a rule, none of the alternatives available to subordinates

[5] Stephen A. Richardson, "The Effects of Physical Disability on the Socialization of a Child," in David A. Goslin, ed., *Handbook of Socialization Theory and Research* (Chicago: Rand McNally & Company, 1969).

in power relationships are open to him. He cannot forego the service required, since performing important activities of daily life depends on the cooperation of sighted persons. It is unlikely that he will turn elsewhere, partly because he cannot always do that on his own and partly because his situation will be unlikely to change greatly if he does. Finally, he cannot very well rely on force to have favors done for him. He is, therefore, backed into a position of compliance.

Persons who are in positions of power must weigh the cost of granting a service to someone against the potential value of his compliance. Because of his marginal status, a blind man's compliance is only of limited worth to those who seek to gain powerful positions in the mainstream of society. Furthermore, the value of a blind person's compliance may be offset by the investment of time and effort required to render the service. For these reasons, many sighted people avoid encounters with the blind because they anticipate that the compliance of a blind person will be of little value to them. Once again, such avoidance is not achieved without feeling guilt. These guilt feelings become apparent whenever the blind and the sighted are thrust into one another's company.

These factors have several consequences for the blind person's socialization experiences in personal relationships. For one thing, since blindness is a social debit, it follows that blind persons will find it difficult to develop enduring associations with sighted persons who are otherwise their intellectual, psychological, and social equals. The fact that many blind people are not treated as "normal" in this respect is the motive behind a common reaction pattern in the blind. Some blind people disavow their blindness entirely by learning how to perform activities that are normally reserved for people who can see. These include such activities as skiing, golfing, driving automobiles, or doing elaborate repairs on the house. While such activities can be performed by certain blind people, competence in them is attained at the cost of a tremendous personal effort.

Even more fundamental than this, however, are the demoralizing and humiliating effects upon the self of continuously being treated charitably. The blind person comes to feel that he is not completely accepted as a mature, responsible person. As a second-class citizen, he must deal with the eroding sense of inadequacy that inevitably accompanies that status. Incidentally, it is important to note that this problem does not stem from the preconceptions others have about blindness; it is an effect of introducing the factor of blindness into the equation which describes the mechanics of interpersonal conduct.

There is one condition under which a blind person is able to escape this dilemma—the possession of a valued quality, trait, or attribute that he can use to compensate for his blindness. It is no accident that the blind persons who become most completely integrated into the larger society possess wealth, fame, or exceptional talent. These people can exchange prestige or money for the favors they must accept in order to function in daily life. They are unusual. A majority of blind people are elderly and poor, two traits that also have very low potential attractiveness to others.

33

Apprenticeships in Prostitution

JAMES H. BRYAN

Socialization is not a process that terminates with a person's youth. In a rapidly changing world, adults too must change and must be socialized into a variety of new roles. While the child may be socialized to one day anticipate being a husband or wife, parent, member of some occupational group, etc., upon actual entry into such new statuses, extensive efforts may be devoted to teaching him the expectations attached to those statuses. The prospective bride and groom may attend a premarital counseling group, expectant parents may enroll in classes on infant care, and of course, new employees regularly undergo an "orientation session" before actually assuming their job responsibilities.

The following selection focuses on the socialization of novices into one of the oldest occupations known to man—prostitution. Socialization into this occupation is particularly interesting for two reasons. First, it is unlikely that most prostitutes were socialized as children to anticipate entering this occupation. Second, this occupation is socially defined as deviant. While the technical skills required of the prostitute may not be great, the interpersonal skills required to deal effectively with clients, the police, pimps, and other girls in the profession are quite numerous and crucial for occupational success.

Bryan describes the novice's entry into the occupation as an apprenticeship relation, similar in many respects to the apprenticeship system in skilled occupations of the past. Based on data secured from 33 prostitutes from the Los Angeles area, he suggests that while some information is transmitted through explicit tutoring by another prostitute or a pimp, the girls learn the trade primarily through imitation. While the reader will find the content of the prostitute's socialization interesting, the significance of Bryan's presentation lies in his identification of structural and interpersonal factors which facilitate the transmission of information about the

James H. Bryan, "Apprenticeships in Prostitution," *Social Problems* 12 (1965): 287–97.

profession to initiates and which produce the desired internalization of attitudes, values, etc. among prostitutes.

While theoretical conceptions of deviant behavior range from role strain to psychoanalytic theory, orientations to the study of the prostitute have shown considerable homogeneity. Twentieth century theorizing concerning this occupational group has employed, almost exclusively, a Freudian psychiatric model. The prostitute has thus been variously described as masochistic, of infantile mentality, unable to form mature interpersonal relationships, regressed, emotionally dangerous to males and as normal as the average women.[1] The call girl, the specific focus of this paper, has been accused of being anxious, possessing a confused self-image, excessively dependent, demonstrating gender-role confusion, aggressive, lacking internal controls and masochistic.[2]

The exclusive use of psychoanalytic models in attempting to predict behavior, and the consequent neglect of situational and cognitive processes, has been steadily lessening in the field of psychology. Their inadequacy as models for understanding deviancy has been specifically explicated by Becker, and implied by London.[3] The new look in the conceptualization and study of deviant behavior has focused on the interpersonal processes which help define the deviant role, the surroundings in which the role is learned, and limits upon the enactment of the role. As Hooker has indicated regarding the study of homosexuals, one must not only consider the personality structure of the participants, but also the structure of their community and the pathways and routes into the learning and enactment of the behavior.[4] Such "training periods" have been alluded to by

---

[1] H. Benjamin "Prostitution Reassessed," *International Journal of Sexology* 26 (1951): 154–60; H. Benjamin & A. Ellis, "An Objective Examination of Prostitution," *International Journal of Sexology* 29 (1955): 100–05; E. Glover, "The Abnormality of Prostitution." In A. M. Krich, ed., *Women* (New York: Dell Publishing Company, Inc., 1953); M. H. Hollander, "Prostitution, The Body, and Human Relatedness" *International Journal of Psychoanalysis* 42 (1961): 404–13; M. Karpf, "Effects of Prostitution on Marital Sex Adjustment," *International Journal of Sexology* 29 (1953): 149–54; J. F. Oliven, *Sexual Hygiene and Pathology* (Philadelphia: J. B. Lippincott Co., 1955); W. J. Robinson, *The Oldest Profession in The World* (New York: Eugenics Publishing Co., 1929).

[2] H. Greenwald, *The Call Girl* (New York: Ballantine Books, 1960).

[3] H. S. Becker, *Outsiders: Studies in the Sociology of Deviance* (New York: Free Press, 1963). Also see *The Other Side,* H. S. Becker, ed. (New York: Free Press, 1964). P. London, *The Modes and Morals of Psychotherapy* (New York: Holt, Rinehart and Winston, 1964). For recent trends in personality theory, see N. Sanford, "Personality: Its Place in Psychology," and D. R. Miller, "The Study of Social Relationships: Situation, Identity, and Social Internation." Both papers are pesented in S. Koch, ed., *Psychology: A Study of a Science,* Vol. 5 (New York: McGraw-Hill Book Co., Inc. 1963).

[4] Evelyn Hooker, "The Homosexual Community." *Proceedings of the XIV International Congress of Applied Psychology,* 1961, pp. 40–59. See also A. Reiss, "The Social Integration of Queers and Peers." *Social Problems* 9 (1961): 102–20.

Maurer in his study of the con man, and by Sutherland in his report on professional thieves. More recently, Lindesmith and Becker have conceptualized the development of drug use as a series of learning sequences necessary for the development of steady use.[5]

This paper provides some detailed, albeit preliminary, information concerning induction and training in a particular type of deviant career: prostitution, at the call girl level. It describes the order of events, and their surrounding structure, which future call girls experience in entering their occupation.

The respondents in this study were 33 prostitutes, all currently or previously working in the Los Angeles area. They ranged in age from 18 to 32, most being in their mid-twenties. None of the interviewees were obtained through official law enforcement agencies, but seven were found within the context of a neuropsychiatric hospital. The remaining respondents were gathered primarily through individual referrals from previous participants in the study. There were no obvious differences between the "psychiatric sample" and the other interviewees on the data to be reported.

All subjects in the sample were call girls. That is, they typically obtained their clients by individual referrals, primarily by telephone, and enacted the sexual contract in their own or their clients' place of residence or employment. They did not initiate contact with their customers in bars, streets, or houses of prostitution, although they might meet their customers at any number of locations by prearrangement. The minimum fee charged per sexual encounter was $20.00. As an adjunct to the call girl interviews, three pimps and two "call boys" were interviewed as well.[6]

Approximately two thirds of the sample were what are sometimes known as "outlaw broads"; that is, they were not under the supervision of a pimp when interviewed. There is evidence that the majority of pimps who were aware of the study prohibited the girls under their direction from participating in it. It should be noted that many members of the sample belonged to one or another clique; their individually expressed opinions may not be independent.

The interviews strongly suggest that there are marked idiosyncrasies from one geographical area to another in such practices as fee-splitting, involvement with peripheral occupations (e.g., cabbies), and so forth. For example, there appears to be little direct involvement of peripheral occupations with call girl activities in the Los Angeles area, while it has been estimated that up to 10 percent of the population of Las Vegas is directly involved in activities of prostitutes.[7] What

[5] D. W. Maurer, *The Big Con* (New York: Signet Books, 1940). H. S. Becker, *Outsiders;* E. H. Sutherland, *The Professional Thief* (Chicago: University of Chicago Press, 1937). A. R. Lindesmith, *Opiate Addiction* (Evanston: Principia Press, 1955).

[6] This definition departs somewhat from that offered by Clinard. He defines the call girl as one dependent upon an organization for recruiting patrons and one who typically works in lower-class hotels. The present sample is best described by Clinard's category high-class independent professional prostitute. M. D. Clinard, *Sociology of Deviant Behavior* (New York: Rinehart & Co., 1957).

[7] E. Reid and O. Demaris, *The Green Felt Jungle* (New York: Pocket Books, Inc., 1963).

may be typical for a call girl in the Los Angeles area is not necessarily typical for a girl in New York, Chicago, Las Vegas, or Miami.

Since the professional literature (e.g., Greenwald; Pomeroy) concerning this occupation and its participants is so limited in quantity, and is not concerned with training per se, the present data may have some utility for the social sciences.[8]

All but two interviews were tape recorded. All respondents had prior knowledge that the interview would be tape recorded. The interviewing was, for the most part, done at the girls' place of work and/or residence. Occasional interviews were conducted in the investigator's office, and one in a public park. Interviews were semi-structured and employed open-ended questions. One part of the interview concerned the apprenticeship period or "turning out" process.

The Entrance

> I had been thinking about it [becoming a call girl] before a lot. . . . Thinking about wanting to do it, but I had no connections. Had I not had a connection, I probably wouldn't have started working. . . . I thought about starting out. . . . Once I tried it [without a contact]. . . . I met this guy at a bar and I tried to make him pay me, but the thing is, you can't do it that way because they are romantically interested in you, and they don't think that it is on that kind of basis. You can't all of a sudden come up and want money for it, you have to be known beforehand. . . . I think that is what holds a lot of girls back who might work. I think I might have started a year sooner had I had a connection. You seem to make one contact or another . . . if it's another girl or a pimp or just someone who will set you up and get you a client. . . . You can't just, say, get an apartment and get a phone in and everything and say, "Well, I'm gonna start business," because you gotta get clients from somewhere. There has to be a contact.

Immediately prior to entrance into the occupation, all but one girl had personal contact with someone professionally involved in call girl activities (pimps or other call girls). The one exception had contact with a customer of call girls. While various occupational groups (e.g., photographers) seem to be peripherally involved, often unwittingly, with the call girl, there was no report of individuals involved in such occupations being contacts for new recruits. The novice's initial contact is someone at the level at which she will eventually enter the occupation: not a street-walker, but a call girl; not a pimp who manages girls out of a house of prostitution, but a pimp who manages call girls.

Approximately half of the girls reported that their initial contact for entrance into the profession was another "working girl." The nature of these relationships is quite variable. In some cases, the girls have been long standing friends. Other initial contacts involved sexual relationships between a Lesbian and the novice. Most, however, had known each other less than a year, and did not appear to have a very close relationship, either in the sense of time spent together or of

---

[8] Greenwald, *Call Girl;* W. Pomeroy, *Some Aspects of Prostitution,* unpublished paper.

biographical information exchanged. The relationship may begin with the aspiring call girl soliciting the contact. That is, if a professional is known to others as a call girl, she will be sought out and approached by females who are strangers: [9]

> I haven't ever gone out and looked for one. All of these have fell right into my hands. . . . They turned themselfs out. . . . They come to me for help.

Whatever their relationship, whenever the professional agrees to aid the beginner, she also, it appears, implicitly assumes responsibility for training her. This is evidenced by the fact that only one such female contact referred the aspirant to another girl for any type of help. Data are not available as to the reason for this unusual referral.

If the original contact was not another call girl but a pimp, a much different relationship is developed and the career follows a somewhat different course. The relationship between pimp and girl is typically one of lovers, not friends:

> . . . because I love him very much. Obviously, I'm doing this mostly for him. . . . I'd do anything for him. I'm not just saying I will, I am. . . . [After discussing his affair with another woman] I just decided that I knew what he was when I decided to do this for him and I decided I had two choices—either accept it or not, and I accepted it, and I have no excuse.

Occasionally, however, a strictly business relationship will be formed:

> Right now I am buying properties, and as soon as I can afford it, I am buying stocks. . . . It is strictly a business deal. This man and I are friends, our relationship ends there. He handles all the money, he is making all the investments and I trust him. We have a legal document drawn up which states that half the investments are mine, half of them his, so I am protected.

Whether the relationship is love or business, the pimp solicits the new girl.[10] It is usually agreed that the male will have an important managerial role in the course of the girl's career, and that both will enjoy the gains from the girl's activities for an indefinite period:

> Actually a pimp has to have complete control or else its like trouble with him. Because if a pimp doesn't, if she is not madly in love with him or something in some way, a pimp won't keep a girl.

Once the girl agrees to function as a call girl, the male, like his female counterpart, undertakes the training of the girl, or refers the girl to another call girl for training. Either course seems equally probable. Referrals, when employed, are typically to friends and, in some cases, wives or ex-wives.

Although the data are limited, it appears that the pimp retains his dominance

---

[9] A point also made in the autobiographical account of a retired call girl. Virginia McManus, *Not For Love* (New York: Dell Publishing Co., 1960), p. 160.

[10] Two of the pimps denied that this was very often so and maintained that the girls will solicit them. The degree to which they are solicited seems to depend upon the nature and extent of their reputations. It is difficult to judge the accuracy of these reports as there appears to be a strong taboo against admitting to such solicitation.

over the trainee even when the latter is being trained by a call girl. The girl trainer remains deferential to the pimp's wishes regarding the novice.

Apprenticeship

Once a contact is acquired and the decision to become a call girl made, the recruit moves to the next stage in the career sequence: the apprenticeship period. The structure of the apprenticeship will be described, followed by a description of the content most frequently communicated during this period.

The apprenticeship is typically served under the direction of another call girl, but may occasionally be supervised by a pimp. Twenty-four girls in the sample initially worked under the supervision of other girls. The classroom is, like the future place of work, an apartment. The apprentice typically serves in the trainer's apartment, either temporarily residing with the trainer or commuting there almost daily. The novice rarely serves her apprenticeship in such places as a house of prostitution, motel, or on the street. It is also infrequent that the girl is transported out of her own city to serve an apprenticeship. Although the data are not extensive, the number of girls being trained simultaneously by a particular trainer has rarely been reported to be greater than three. Girls sometimes report spending up to eight months in training, but the average stay seems to be two or three months. The trainer controls all referrals and appointments, novices seemingly not having much control over the type of sexual contract made or the circumstances surrounding the enactment of the contract.

The structure of training under the direction of a pimp seems similar, though information is more limited. The girls are trained in an apartment in the city they intend to work and for a short period of time. There is some evidence that the pimp and the novice often do not share the same apartment as might the novice and the girl trainer. There appear to be two reasons for the separation of pimp and girl. First, it is not uncommonly thought that cues which suggest the presence of other men displease the girl's customers:

> Well, I would never let them know that I had a lover, which is something that you never ever let a john know, because this makes them very reticent to give you money, because they think that you are going to go and spend it with your lover, which is what usually happens.

(Interestingly, the work of Winick suggests that such prejudices may not actually be held by many customers.)[11] Secondly, the legal repercussions are much greater, of course, for the pimp who lives with his girl than for two girls rooming together. As one pimp of 19 years experience puts it:

> It is because of the law. There is a law that is called the illegal cohabitation that they rarely use unless the man becomes big in stature. If he is a big man in the hustling world, the law then employs any means at their command. . . .

---

[11] C. Winick, "Prostitutes' Clients' Perception of the Prostitute and Themselves," *International Journal of Social Psychiatry* 8 (1961–62): 289–97.

Because of the convenience in separation of housing, it is quite likely that the pimp is less directly involved with the day-to-day training of the girls than the call girl trainer.

The content of the training period seems to consist of two broad, interrelated dimensions, one philosophical, the other interpersonal. The former refers to the imparting of a value structure, the latter to "do's" and "don'ts" of relating to customers and secondarily, to other "working girls" and pimps. The latter teaching is perhaps best described by the concept of a short range perspective. That is, most of the "do's" and "don'ts" pertain to ideas and actions that the call girl uses in problematic situations.[12] Not all girls absorb these teachings, and those who do incorporate them in varying degrees.

Insofar as a value structure is transmitted it is that of maximizing gains while minimizing effort, even if this requires transgressions of either a legal or moral nature. Frequently, it is postulated that people, particularly men, are corrupt or easily corruptible, that all social relationships are but a reflection of a "con," and that prostitution is simply a more honest or at least no more dishonest act than the everyday behavior of "squares." Furthermore, not only are "johns" basically exploitative, but they are easily exploited; hence they are, in some respects, stupid. As explained by a pimp:

> . . . [in the hustling world] the trick or the john is known as a fool . . . this is not the truth. . . . He [the younger pimp] would teach his woman that a trick was a fool.

Since the male is corrupt, or honest only because he lacks the opportunity to be corrupt, then it is only appropriate that he be exploited as he exploits.

> Girls first start making their "scores"—say one guy keeps them for a while or maybe she gets, you know, three or four grand out of him, say a car or a coat. These are your scores. . . .

The general assumption that man is corrupt is empirically confirmed when the married male betrays his wife, when the moralist, secular or religious, betrays his publicly stated values, or when the "john" "stiffs" (cheats) the girl. An example of the latter is described by a girl as she reflects upon her disillusionment during her training period.

> It is pretty rough when you are starting out. You get stiffed a lot of times. . . . Oh sure. They'll take advantage of you anytime they can. And I'm a trusting soul, I really am. I'll believe anybody till they prove different. I've made a lot of mistakes that way. You get to the point, well, Christ, what the heck can I believe in people, they tell me one thing and here's what they do to me.

Values such as fairness with other working girls, or fidelity to a pimp, may occasionally be taught. To quote a pimp:

> So when you ask me if I teach a kind of basic philosophy, I would say that you could say that. Because you try to teach them in an amoral way that there

---

[12] H. S. Becker, Blanche Geer, and E. C. Hughes, A. L. Strauss, *Boys In White* (Chicago: University of Chicago Press, 1961).

is a right and wrong way as pertains to this game . . . and then you teach them that when working with other girls to try to treat the other girl fairly because a woman's worst enemy in the street [used in both a literal and figurative sense] is the other woman and only by treating the other women decently can she expect to get along. . . . Therefore the basic philosophy I guess would consist of a form of honesty, a form of sincerity and complete fidelity to her man [pimp].

It should be noted, however, that behavior based on enlightened self-interest with concomitant exploitation is not limited to customer relationships. Interviewees frequently mentioned a pervasive feeling of distrust between trainer and trainee, and such incidents as thefts or betrayal of confidences are occasionally reported and chronically guarded against.

Even though there may be considerable pressure upon the girl to accept this value structure, many of them (perhaps the majority of the sample) reject it.

People have told me that I wasn't turned out, but turned loose instead. . . . Someone who is turned out is turned out to believe in a certain code of behavior, and this involves having a pimp, for one thing. It also involves never experiencing anything but hatred or revulsion for "tricks" for another thing. It involves always getting the money in front [before the sexual act] and a million little things that are very strictly adhered to by those in the "in group," which I am not. . . . Never being nice or pleasant to a trick unless you are doing it for the money, getting more money. [How did you learn that?] It was explained to me over a period of about six months. I learned that you were doing it to make money for yourself so that you could have nice things and security. . . . [Who would teach you this?] [The trainer] would teach me this.[13]

It seems reasonable to assume that the value structure serves, in general, to create in-group solidarity and to alienate the girl from "square" society, and that this structure serves the political advantage of the trainer and the economic gains of the trainee more than it allays the personal anxieties of either. In fact, failure to adopt these values at the outset does not appear to be correlated with much personal distress.[14] As one girl describes her education experiences:

Some moral code. We're taught, as a culture . . . it's there and after awhile you live, breathe, and eat it. Now, what makes you go completely against everything that's inside you, everything that you have been taught, and the whole society, to do things like this?

Good empirical evidence, however, concerning the functions and effectiveness of this value structure with regard to subjective comfort is lacking.

A series of deductions derived from the premises indicated above serve to pro-

[13] The statements made by prostitutes to previous investigators and mental helpers may have been parroting this particular value structure and perhaps have misled previous investigators into making the assumption that "all whores hate men." While space prohibits a complete presentation of the data, neither our questionnaire nor interview data suggest that this is a predominant attitude among call girls.

[14] There is, from the present study, little support for the hypothesis of Reckless concerning the association of experience trauma and guilt with abruptness of entry into the occupation. W. C. Reckless, *The Crime Problem* (New York: Appleton-Century-Crofts, Inc., 1950).

vide, in part, the "rules" of interpersonal contact with the customer. Each customer is to be seen as a "mark," and "pitches" are to be made.

> [Did you have a standard pitch?] It's sort of amusing. I used to listen to my girl friend [trainer]. She was the greatest at this telephone type of situation. She would call up and cry and say that people had come to her door. . . . She'd cry and she'd complain and she'd say "I have a bad check at the liquor store, and they sent the police over," and really . . . a girl has a story she tells the man. . . . Anything, you know, so he'll help her out. Either it's the rent or she needs a car, or doctor's bills, or any number of things.

Any unnecessary interaction with the customer is typically frowned upon, and the trainee will receive exhortations to be quick about her business. One girl in her fourth week of work explains:

> [What are some of the other don'ts that you have learned about?] Don't take so much time. . . . The idea is to get rid of them as quickly as possible.

Other content taught concerns specific information about specific customers.

> . . . she would go around the bar and say, now look at that man over there, he's this way and that way, and this is what he would like and these are what his problems are. . . .

> . . . she would teach me what the men wanted and how much to get, what to say when I got there . . . just a line to hand them.

Training may also include proprieties concerning consuming alcohol and drugs, when and how to obtain the fee, how to converse with the customers and, occasionally, physical and sexual hygiene. As a girl trainer explains:

> First of all, impress cleanliness. Because, on the whole, the majority of girls, I would say, I don't believe there are any cleaner women walking the streets, because they've got to be aware of any type of body odor. . . . You teach them to French [fellatio] and how to talk to men.

> [Do they [pimps] teach you during the turning out period how to make a telephone call?] Oh, usually, yes. They don't teach you, they just tell you how to do it and you do it with your good common sense, but if you have trouble, they tell you more about it.

Interestingly, the specific act of telephoning a client is often distressing to the novice and is of importance in her training. Unfortunately for the girl, it is an act she must perform with regularity as she does considerable soliciting.[15] One suspects that such behavior is embarrassing for her because it is an unaccustomed role for her to play—she has so recently come from a culture where young women do *not* telephone men for dates. Inappropriate sex-role behavior seems to produce greater personal distress than does appropriate sex-role behavior even when it is morally reprehensible.

> Well, it is rather difficult to get on the telephone, when you've never worked before, and talk to a man about a subject like that, and it is very new to you.

---

[15] The topic of solicitation will be dealt with in a forthcoming paper.

What is omitted from the training should be noted as well. There seems to be little instruction concerning sexual techniques as such, even though the previous sexual experience of the trainee may have been quite limited. What instruction there is typically revolves around the practice of fellatio. There seems to be some encouragement not to experience sexual orgasms with the client, though this may be quite variable with the trainer.

> . . . and sometimes, I don't know if it's a set rule or maybe it's an unspoken rule, you don't enjoy your dates.

> Yes, he did [teach attitudes]. He taught me to be cold. . . .

It should be stressed that, if the girls originally accepted such instructions and values, many of them, at least at the time of interviewing, verbalized a rejection of these values and reported behavior which departed considerably from the interpersonal rules stipulated as "correct" by their trainers. Some experience orgasms with the customer, some show considerable affect toward "johns," others remain drunk or "high" throughout the contact.[16] While there seems to be general agreement as to what the rules of interpersonal conduct are, there appears to be considerable variation in the adoption of such rules.

A variety of methods are employed to communicate the content described above. The trainer may arrange to eavesdrop on the interactions of girl and client and then discuss the interaction with her. One trainer, for example, listened through a closed door to the interaction of a new girl with a customer, then immediately after he left, discussed, in a rather heated way, methods by which his exit may have been facilitated. A pimp relates:

> The best way to do this [teaching conversation] is, in the beginning, when the phone rings, for instance . . . is to listen to what she says and then check and see how big a trick he is and then correct her from there.

> . . . with everyone of them [trainees] I would make it a point to see two guys to see how they [the girls] operate.

In one case a girl reported that her pimp left a written list of rules pertaining to relating to "johns." Direct teaching, however, seems to be uncommon. The bulk of whatever learning takes place seems to take place through observation.

> It's hard to tell you, because we learn through observations.

> But I watched her and listened to what her bit was on the telephone.

To summarize, the structure of the apprenticeship period seems quite standard. The novice receives her training either from a pimp or from another more experienced call girl, more often the latter. She serves her initial two to eight months of work under the trainer's supervision and often serves this period in the trainer's apartment. The trainer assumes responsibility for arranging contacts and negotiating the type and place of the sexual encounter.

---

[16] In the unpublished paper referred to above, Pomeroy has indicated that, of 31 call girls interviewed, only 23 percent reported never experiencing orgasms with customers.

The content of the training pertains both to a general philosophical stance and to some specifics (usually not sexual) of interpersonal behavior with customers and colleagues. The philosophy is one of exploiting the exploiters (customers) by whatever means necessary and defining the colleagues of the call girl as being intelligent, self-interested and, in certain important respects, basically honest individuals. The interpersonal techniques addressed during the learning period consist primarily of "pitches," telephone conversations, personal and occasionally sexual hygiene, prohibitions against alcohol and dope while with a "john," how and when to obtain the fee, and specifics concerning the sexual habits of particular customers. Specific sexual techniques are very rarely taught. The current sample included a considerable number of girls who, although capable of articulating this value structure, were not particularly inclined to adopt it.

Contacts and Contracts

While the imparting of ideologies and proprieties to the prospective call girl is emphasized during the apprenticeship period, it appears that the primary function of the apprenticeship, at least for the trainee, is building a clientele. Since this latter function limits the degree of occupational socialization, the process of developing the clientele and the arrangements made between trainer and trainee will be discussed.

Lists ("books") with the names and telephone number of customers are available for purchase from other call girls or pimps, but such books are often considered unreliable. While it is also true that an occasional pimp will refer customers to girls, this does not appear to be a frequent practice. The most frequent method of obtaining such names seems to be through contacts developed during the apprenticeship. The trainer refers customers to the apprentice and oversees the latter in terms of her responsibility and adequacy in dealing with the customer. For referring the customer, the trainer receives forty to fifty percent of the total price agreed upon in the contract negotiated by the trainer and customer.[17] The trainer and trainee further agree, most often explicitly, on the apprentice's "right" to obtain and to use, on further occasions, information necessary for arranging another sexual contract with the "john" without the obligation of further "kick-back" to the trainer. That is, if she can obtain the name and telephone number of the customer, she can negotiate another contract without fee-splitting. During this period, then, the girl is not only introduced to other working colleagues (pimps and girls alike) but also develops a clientele.

---

[17] The fee-splitting arrangement is quite common at all levels of career activity. For example, cooperative activity between two girls is often required for a particular type of sexual contract. In these cases, the girl who has contracted with the customer will contact a colleague, usually a friend, and will obtain 40–50 percent of the latter's earnings. There is suggestive evidence that fee-splitting activities vary according to geographical areas and that Los Angeles is unique for both its fee-splitting patterns and the rigidity of its fee-splitting structure.

There are two obvious advantages for a call girl in assuming the trainer role. First, since there seems to be an abundant demand for new girls, and since certain service requirements demand more than one girl, even the well established call girl chronically confronts the necessity for making referrals. It is then reasonable to assume that the extra profit derived from the fee-splitting activities, together with the added conveniences of having a girl "on call," allows the trainer to profit considerably from this arrangement. Secondly, contacts with customers are reputedly extremely difficult to maintain if services are not rendered on demand. Thus, the adoption of the trainer role enables the girl to maintain contacts with "fickle" customers under circumstances where she may wish a respite from the sexual encounter without terminating the contacts necessary for re-entry into the call girl role. It is also possible that the financial gains may conceivably be much greater for most trainers than for most call girls, but this is a moot point.

A final aspect of the apprenticeship period that should be noted is the novice's income. It is possible for the novice, under the supervision of a competent and efficient trainer, to earn a great deal of money, or at least to get a favorable glimpse of the great financial possibilities of the occupation and, in effect, be heavily rewarded for her decision to enter it. Even though the novice may be inexperienced in both the sexual and interpersonal techniques of prostitution, her novelty on the market gives her an immediate advantage over her more experienced competitors. It seems quite likely that the new girl, irrespective of her particular physical or mental qualities, has considerable drawing power because she provides new sexual experience to the customer. Early success and financial reward may well provide considerable incentive to continue in the occupation.

A final word is needed regarding the position of the pimp vis-à-vis the call girl during the apprenticeship period. While some pimps assume the responsibility for training the girl personally, as indicated above, as many send the novice to another girl. The most apparent reason for such referral is that it facilitates the development of the "book." Purposes of training appear to be secondary for two reasons: (1) The pimp often lacks direct contact with the customers, so he personally cannot aid directly in the development of the girl's clientele; (2) when the pimp withdraws his girl from the training context, it is rarely because she has obtained adequate knowledge of the profession. This is not to say that all pimps are totally unconcerned with the type of knowledge being imparted to the girl. Rather, the primary concern of the pimp is the girl's developing a clientele, not learning the techniques of sex or conversation.

The apprenticeship period usually ends abruptly, not smoothly. Its termination may be but a reflection of interpersonal difficulties between trainer and trainee, novice and pimp, or between two novices. Occasionally termination of training is brought about through the novice's discovery and subsequent theft of the trainer's "book." Quite frequently, the termination is due to the novice's developing a sufficient trade or other business opportunities. The point is, however, that no respondent has reported that the final disruption of the apprenticeship was the result of the completion of adequate training. While disruptions of this relationship may be due to personal or impersonal events, termination is not directly due to the development of sufficient skills.

Discussion and Summary

On the basis of interviews with 33 call girls in the Los Angeles area, information was obtained about entrance into the call girl occupation and the initial training period or apprenticeship therein.

The novice call girl is acclimated to her new job primarily by being thoroughly immersed in the call girl subculture, where she learns the trade through imitation as much as through explicit tutoring. The outstanding concern at this stage is the development of a sizable and lucrative clientele. The specific skills and values which are acquired during this period are rather simple and quickly learned.

In spite of the girl's protests and their extensive folklore, the art of prostitution, at least at this level, seems to be technically a low-level skill. That is, it seems to be an occupation which requires little formal knowledge or practice for its successful pursuit and appears best categorized as an unskilled job. Evidence for this point comes from two separate sources. First, there seems to be little technical training during this period, and the training seems of little importance to the career progress. Length or type of training does not appear correlated with success (i.e., money earned, lack of subjective distress, minimum fee per "trick," etc.). Secondly, the termination of the apprenticeship period is often brought about for reasons unrelated to training. It seems that the need for an apprenticeship period is created more by the secrecy surrounding the rendering or the utilization of the call girl service than by the complexity of the role. In fact, it is reasonable to assume that the complexity of the job confronting a street-walker may be considerably greater than that confronting a call girl. The tasks of avoiding the police, sampling among strangers for potential customers, and arrangements for the completion of the sexual contract not only require different skills on the part of the street-walker, but are performances requiring a higher degree of professional "know-how" than is generally required of the call girl.[18]

As a pimp who manages both call girls and "high class" street-walkers explains:

> The girl that goes out into the street is the sharper of the two, because she is capable of handling herself in the street, getting around the law, picking out the trick that is not absolutely psycho . . . and capable of getting along in the street. . . . The street-walker, as you term her, is really a prima donna of the prostitutes . . . her field is unlimited, she goes to all of the top places so she meets the top people. . . .

[18] Needless to say, however, all of the sample of call girls who were asked for status hierarchies of prostitution felt that the street-walker had both less status and a less complex job. It *may* well be that the verbal exchange required of the call girl requires greater knowledge than that required of a street-walker, but the nonverbal skills required of the street-walker may be considerably greater than those of the call girl.

The fact that the enactment of the call girl role requires little training, and the introduction of the girl to clients and colleagues alike is rather rapid, gives little time or incentive for adequate occupational socialization. It is perhaps for this reason rather than, for example, reasons related to personality factors, that occupational instability is great and cultural homogeneity small.

In closing, while it appears that there is a rather well defined apprenticeship period in the career of the call girl, it seems that it is the secrecy rather than the complexity of the occupation which generates such a period. While there is good evidence that initial contacts, primarily with other "working girls," are necessary for entrance into this career, there seems no reason, at this point, to assume that the primary intent of the participants in training is anything but the development of an adequate clientele.

34

Mass Media Socialization Behavior: Negro-White Differences

WALTER M. GERSON

Few would dispute the assertion that the mass media influence human behavior. In fact, most would concur that the mass media have taken a place alongside the family, peer groups, and the schools as major socializing agents in society. Until recently, however, the extent and nature of the influence of mass media on beliefs, attitudes, and behavior were matters of mere speculation, lacking any systematic research evidence.

One of the recent attempts to specify how the mass media shape conceptualizations of appropriate behavior is the following selection by Gerson. The paper is a comparative analysis of the uses of the mass media as an agency of socialization in premarital cross-sex behavior among black versus white adolescents. Two socialization functions of the mass media are distinguished—reinforcement and norm-acquiring. As a reinforcement agency, the mass media simply provide support for the person to *try out* ideas he already has about premarital cross-sex behavior. As a norm-acquiring agency, the mass media are the source of the person's ideas.

Gerson reports that blacks and whites differ significantly in the uses they make of the mass media as a socializing agent in this behavior area. In general, greater use was made of the mass media as a socializing agent by blacks. Among both blacks and whites, the mass media served a norm-acquiring function more frequently than a reinforcement function. A number of plausible explanations for the black-white differences are presented and evaluated.

Walter M. Gerson, "Mass Media Socialization Behavior: Negro-White Differences," *Social Forces* 45 (1966): 40–50.

There has been relatively litle systematic research of the common assumption that the mass media constitute a significant agency of socialization. Considerable research has been directed toward the functions and effects of mass communication, but most of these inquiries relate only indirectly to socialization.[1] Researchers and theorists agree that the significance of mass media exposure is not generally found in the media-person experience alone, but in the link between media exposure and interpersonal environment. The dominant approach to recent mass communications research has been referred to by several names—"functional," [2] "situational," [3] "phenomenistic," [4] and "uses and gratifications." [5] The mass media are viewed as one factor working along with several others in the total milieu of the audience. Direct effects are not emphasized but rather the key question is: How do persons with different statuses and in different social structures use the media and what are the resulting gratifications and consequences? Respondents are seen not as discrete individuals, but rather as persons functioning within particular social contexts.[6]

Some lines of research have indicated that there are several functions of the mass media and that people "use" the media in numerous ways.[7] Socialization, then, is only one of several possible consequences of media exposure. Some of the ways in which the media are used, such as entertainment, may or may not have a relationship to the socialization of individuals. Concern should be directed toward concepts and data bearing on the social structures the media penetrate. Wilensky suggests that millions of persons in America "have no place to anchor an opinion, no vital culture through which to filter the media impact." [8] He says

[1] Two books that systematically elaborate upon the functions and effects of mass communications are Joseph T. Klapper, *The Effects of Mass Communication* (Glencoe, Illinois: The Free Press, 1960), and Elihu Katz and Paul F. Lazarsfeld, *Personal Influence* (Glencoe, Illinois: The Free Press, 1955). Two comprehensive studies of the uses of one medium, television, by children are Hilde T. Himmelweit, A. N. Opuenheim, and Pamela Vince, *Television and the Child* (London: Oxford University Press, 1958), and Wilbur Schramm, Jack Lyle, and Edwin B. Parker, *Television in the Lives of Our Children* (Stanford, California: Stanford University Press, 1961).

[2] Charles R. Wright, "Functional Analysis and Mass Communication," *Public Opinion Quarterly* 24 (Winter 1960): 605–20.

[3] Eliot Freidson, "The Relationship of the Social Situation of Contact to the Media in Mass Communication," *Public Opinion Quarterly* 17 (Summer 1953): 230–38.

[4] Klapper, *Effects;* and Joseph T. Klapper, "What We Know About the Effects of Mass Communication: The Brink of Hope," *Public Opinion Quarterly* 21 (Winter 1957–1958): 453–74.

[5] Elihu Katz, "Mass Communication Research and the Study of Popular Culture," *Studies in Public Communication* 3 (Summer 1959): 1–6.

[6] See John W. Riley, Jr. and Matilda White Riley, "Mass Communication and the Social System," in Robert Merton, Leonard Broom, and Leonard S. Cottrell, Jr., eds., *Sociology Today* (New York: Basic Books, 1959), pp. 537–78.

[7] Two good summaries of functions of the mass media are in Charles R. Wright, *Mass Communication: A Sociological Perspective* (New York: Random House, 1959), and in George Lundberg, Clarence Schrag, and Otto Larsen, *Sociology* (rev. ed.; New York: Harper & Row, 1963), pp. 254–58.

[8] Harold L. Wilensky, "Social Structure, Popular Culture, and Mass Behavior: Some Research Implications," *Studies in Public Communication* 5 (Summer 1961): 15–22, quote from p. 17. In a more recent paper, Wilensky elaborates upon and tests some of the

that "where local cultures offer no stable guide to good and bad . . . the media may reach the person directly and carry heavy weight." [9]

However, it is not sufficient merely to state that the media are important in the socialization of young persons. It is necessary to specify *how* persons use the media in their socialization. Some previous research suggests that the media can function as an agency of socialization in at least two ways: (1) by reinforcing existing values and attitudes, and (2) by serving as a source of norms and values which offer solutions to personal problems. Persons who are high in either or in both types of behavior can be called media socializees. This paper is an analysis of some conditions of media socialization.[10] Certain social structural contexts are more likely to produce media socialization behavior.

One indicator of social context which has been widely used in sociological investigations is racial or ethnic status. Race and ethnic status have been used as an analytical variable in a wide variety of studies by sociologists. It would seem, then, that an individual's racial status would be an important starting point in explaining his mass media behavior. However, relatively little systematic research has been conducted on the influence of ethnic status on media behavior and, except for sporadic references, practically no systematic mass media research has utilized the race variable. Very little is known about the functions of media for Negroes, for example.[11] Negroes are seldom included in the samples of mass communication studies.

---

ideas he put forth in the above article. See Harold L. Wilensky, "Mass Society and Mass Culture: Interdependence or Independence?", *American Sociological Review* 29 (April 1964): 173–97.

[9] Wilensky, "Social Structure," p. 16.

[10] Combining the two behaviors, media reinforcement and media norm-acquiring, into a general category called media socialization does have the consequence of virtually erasing pertinent *specific* data. In the present paper, space does not allow the *separate* consideration of the reinforcement and norm-acquiring behaviors. This analysis will be presented in a companion paper, in which it will be shown that, contrary to the main body of literature on the sociology of mass communication, our data suggest that more adolescents use the media as a normative agency than as a reinforcement agency.

[11] Frazier's *Black Bourgeoisie* is an example of a work where various references are made about Negroes' uses of the mass media. Such statements are seldom substantiated by systematic empirical research. See E. Franklin Frazier, *Black Bourgeoisie* (Glencoe, Illinois: The Free Press, 1957). A more recent article that touches upon the subject of the use of the mass media by Negro youth is Joseph S. Himes, "Negro Teen-Age Culture," *Annals* 338 (November 1961): 91–101. A recent psychological study by Lott and Lott reported a comparison between 116 Negro and 185 white adolescents in Kentucky with respect to television viewing and movie attendance. However, the study included only two items on mass media behavior, and those items measured only the amount of exposure. Albert J. Lott and Bernice E. Lott, *Negro and White Youth: A Psychological Study in a Border-State Community* (New York: Holt, Rinehart & Winston, 1963). One study which yields some information on the uses of the mass media by the members of an urban American ethnic group is Gans' comprehensive investigation of the Italian-American residents of the West End neighborhood of Boston. Gans found that West Enders tend to use the mass media primarily to reinforce their own values, rather than to acquire new ones. They felt that media are part of the "outside world" and hence, the media cannot be "trusted." The West Enders were suspicious of the media as an outside institution, and they interpreted the materials so as to protect themselves from the outside world. Whether or not other ethnic or racial groups interpret the media similarly is a problem for further research. Herbert Gans, *The Urban Villagers: Group and Class in the Life of Italian-Americans* (New York: The Free Press, 1962), esp. pp. 181–96.

The present paper is an attempt to fill gaps in the research literature of the fields of socialization, race relations, and mass communications. The paper is a comparative analysis of differences between Negro and white adolescents in their uses of the mass media as an agency of socialization.[12] The study is an exploratory one, and attempts are made to interpret the data in terms of the social contexts of the respondents.

For the purposes of the present study, the area of behavior in which socialization occurs will be somewhat narrowly defined, so as to make for more accurate empirical measurement. Accordingly, an agency of socialization is here defined as a mechanism, social structure, or person through which individuals learn to be motivationally and technically adequate in the performance of *certain* roles. For *certain* roles, such as in premarital cross-sex behavior, local social structures may not provide stable guides. The mass media are more likely to be used as a socializing agency in these particular behavioral areas. It seems reasonable to assume that under conditions such as these, the media may play an important part in the socialization process. The present paper analyzes only data relative to the premarital cross-sex socialization of Negro and white adolescents.

Research Procedures

The primary data-gathering instrument used in the study was a pretested questionnaire, calling for anonymous response, with most items precoded for IBM analysis. Since certain items required different wording for each sex, separate forms for boys and girls were used. The questionnaire was administered to 638 adolescent boys and girls in four communities in the San Francisco Bay region. Data were obtained in two kinds of settings: in schools and in the adolescents' homes. When unreliable responses were excluded, 623 respondents remained in the population for study. The final study population included 272 white persons (43.6 percent of the sample), and 351 Negroes (56.2 percent). The average age of the respondents was 15.2 years. Most respondents were from 13 to 17 years old; only 18 persons were age 12 or less and 28 were age 18 or more. Forty-nine percent (N = 306) were boys.

Each of the two socializing functions of the mass media—reinforcement and norm-acquiring—treated in the present study is measured by a single empirical indicator on the questionnaire. Since the study centers on socialization in premarital cross-sex behavior, the empirical measures pertain specifically to that type of behavior. The following item is the empirical indicator of the respondent's perceived use of the mass media as a reinforcing agent:

---

[12] Two studies of adolescents' media behavior are relative to the present investigation, even though neither paper deals with Negro adolescents. See Raymond Forer, "The Impact of a Radio Program on Adolescents," *Public Opinion Quarterly* 19 (Summer 1955): 184–94, and Charles H. Brown, "Self-Portrait: The Teen-Type Magazine," *Annals* 338 (November 1961): 13–21. The teen-type magazine is a phenomenon which originated since 1955. Magazines such as *Seventeen* are not classified in the category; *Seventeen* might possibly be seriously enjoyed by many adults. But the teen-type magazines are written purely for teenagers (and for preteen youngsters). Brown says that this type of magazine is "for all intents and purposes, practically written by teenagers themselves" (p. 14). Some typical titles are: *Teen Time, Dig,* and *Modern Teen.*

> Do you ever *try out* ideas you already have about dating and things like that by watching to see if that really happens in TV, movies, books, or magazines?
> ___(1) I do this all the time
> ___(2) Very often
> ___(3) I do this sometimes
> ___(4) Once in a while
> ___(5) I never do this

It is recognized that respondents may not be conscious of the mechanism of reinforcement. In fact, it may well be that persons are not conscious of most reinforcing behavior. The instrument measures only the admitted reinforcing behavior of the respondent. The following question was used to measure the respondent's perceived use of the mass media as a norm-acquiring agent: [13]

> Do you ever *get* any ideas or advice about dating and things like that from magazines or books or movies or TV or newspapers?
> ___(1) I get most of my ideas about dating, etc., from these sources
> ___(2) I get many ideas this way
> ___(3) I get some ideas this way
> ___(4) I get a few ideas this way
> ___(5) I never get any ideas about dating, etc., from these sources

Answers to each of the questions were dichotomized. Thus, respondents were divided into those who were "high" and those who were "low" in each of the behaviors. On each item, respondents who checked answers 1, 2, or 3 are high, and those who checked 4 and 5 are low.

Findings: Types of Media Socialization Behavior

Table 1 clearly shows that more Negro than white adolescents in the sample used the media for each of the two socialization behaviors.[14] Slightly over

---

[13] The norm-acquiring question poses the methodological problem of social desirability in response, which may be a particularly acute problem when inquiring into dating or other cross-sex behavior for adolescents. In American society, it is sometimes socially undesirable for a person to publicly admit that he "has" to seek advice about getting along with the opposite sex. Success in cross-sex relations is highly valued in the society, and it appears that dating success is an important pathway to popularity among adolescent peer cultures. Interviews of junior and high school students by the investigator have revealed reluctance, particularly among boys, to verbally admit using the mass media to acquire ideas about dating. The boys appear to feel that a fellow who does not "naturally" know about dating and other sex roles is some kind of a failure. So, in all likelihood, the social desirability factor will skew the distribution of answers to the norm-acquiring question toward the last two alternatives, i.e., "I get a few ideas this way" and "I never get any ideas . . . from these sources." However, as a counter to this influence, great effort was taken to emphasize anonymity to the respondents. Nevertheless, it must be made explicit that the empirical item measures the norm-acquiring behavior that *is admitted* by the respondents.

[14] Previous research investigations have suggested a tendency of Negroes and lower-class persons in general to give what they perceive as the most socially desirable answer to questionnaire items and interview questions. In other words, there may be a tendency for Negroes and lower-class persons to continually agree with the investigator from the "outside" (white or middle-class) world, or to further manipulate the investigator by telling him what they think he wants them to say. In the present study, there is, then, the possibility that the higher scores of Negro adolescents on the dependent variable might, in part,

TABLE 1

FREQUENCIES AND PERCENTAGES OF NEGROES AND WHITES WHO ARE HIGH IN MEDIA REINFORCEMENT AND HIGH IN MEDIA NORM-ACQUIRING BEHAVIORS

	ADOLESCENTS HIGH IN MM REINFORCEMENT		ADOLESCENTS HIGH IN MM NORM-ACQUIRING	
	N	*Percent*	*N*	*Percent*
Whites (N = 272)	81 of 272	29.8	99 of 272	36.4
Negroes (N = 351)	138 of 351	39.4	165 of 351	47.1
Total Sample	219 of 623	35.2	264 of 623	42.4

one-third (35.2 percent) of the total sample reported using the media relatively frequently for purposes of reinforcing attitudes and values they already possessed. About two-fifths (39.4 percent) of the Negro adolescents were high in media reinforcement behavior compared to 29.8 percent of the white respondents. As for norm-acquiring behavior, over two-fifths (42.4 percent) of the respondents reported often using the mass media in acquiring norms, values and ideas in cross-sex behavior. Almost half of the Negroes (47.1 percent) were high in media norm-acquiring compared to 36.4 percent of the white adolescents.

The dichotomies for the reinforcement and norm-acquiring items were cross-classified to form a typology consisting of four types of mass media socializees. The resulting four logical types are: (1) mass media high socializee (high in both media reinforcement and media norm-acquiring), (2) mass media reinforcement (high in reinforcement but low in norm-acquiring), (3) mass media norm-acquirer (high in norm-acquiring but low in reinforcement), and (4) mass media non-socializee (low in both media behaviors). Table 2 shows the proportions of white and Negro adolscents in each type. Proportionately, more Negroes

TABLE 2

TYPOLOGY OF MASS MEDIA SOCIALIZEES

	NEGRO-WHITE DIFFERENCES			
	WHITES		NEGROES	
Type of mass media socializee	*N*	*Percent*	*N*	*Percent*
MM High Socializee	37	13.6	76	21.6
MM Reinforcee	44	16.2	65	18.5
MM Norm-Acquirer	64	23.5	91	25.9
MM Non-Socializee	127	46.7	119	34.0
	272	100.0	351	100.0

be a function of their tendency to choose earlier alternatives (showing positive response) in answering questions concerning their uses of media. However a comparison was made of white and Negro responses to various other items in the questionnaire. The comparison suggested that the above "agreeable" tendency probably did not operate to any degree in the present study, although no statistical test of significance was used in the comparison.

than whites are found within three of the four types of mass media socializees. For example, 21.6 percent of the Negroes were media high socializees compared to 13.6 percent of the whites. Logically, more whites (46.7 percent) than Negroes (34.0 percent) are found within the media non-socializee type.

For the remainder of this paper, types 1, 2, and 3 will generally be treated collectively as mass media socializees. Therefore, a media socializee is one who is high in either media reinforcement or in media norm-acquiring *or* who is high in both behaviors. Defined in this way, about three-fifths (60.4 percent) of the study population of 623 adolescents used the media as an agency of socialization in cross-sex behavior. Again, we find definite differences between Negro and white respondents. Almost two-thirds (66.0 percent) of the Negroes were media socializees compared to 53.3 percent of the white teenagers.

Analysis and Interpretation: Controlling for Other Factors

It appears that regardless of how the data are grouped, the findings are consistently in the same direction. More Negroes than whites use the media in their cross-sex socialization behavior. However, so far the entire Negro subsample has been compared to the entire white subsample; no controls have been used in the analysis. It is quite possible that the apparent relationship between racial status and media socialization is a spurious one. In the following section, some variables felt to be significant will be individually held constant in order to further analyze the data. Some attempts will be made to interpret the findings. At times, the discussion may extend beyond the empirical data; such interpretative statements should be seen as hypotheses for future research. The data are taken from Table 3, a summary table which shows the percent of the adolescents within each of the Negro and white subsamples who are media socializees when certain variables are held constant. It can be seen that the general relationship remains essentially unchanged. Each subgroup of Negroes contains proportionately more media socializees than does the corresponding subgroup of white persons.

Age: Age was held constant by dichotomizing the respondents into younger (15 or less) and older (16 and over) subgroups. Overall, age within the limited range studied here, does not appear to significantly change Negro-white differences in media behavior. However, further analysis differentiated between media reinforcement and media norm-acquiring. These data suggest that among white adolescents, media reinforcement increases with age. About a fourth (26.1 percent) of the younger whites and one-third of the older white persons used the media as a reinforcement agency. On the other hand, among Negroes the primary change seems to be increased media norm-acquiring. The percentages of younger and older Negroes who used the media as a normative source are, respectively, 36.3 percent and 46.7 percent.

These differences by age among the racial subgroups might be partially explained by the factor of residential segregation. Most of the data on Negro respondents were obtained in a neighborhood in which almost all the residents were Negroes. Throughout the grade school years, the Negro youngster in the

TABLE 3

WHITE AND NEGRO ADOLESCENTS WHO ARE MASS MEDIA SOCIALIZEES: BY AGE, SEX, LEVEL OF DEVELOPMENT IN CROSS-SEX BEHAVIOR, SOCIOECONOMIC STATUS AND INTEGRATION IN PEER CULTURE

	WHITES		NEGROES	
	N	*Percent*	*N*	*Percent*
Total Samples (No controls)	145 of 272	53.3	232 of 351	66.0
Controlling for:				
Age				
16 and over	79 of 146	54.1	93 of 150	62.0
15 or less	66 of 126	52.4	139 of 201	69.2
Sex				
Boys	66 of 136	48.5	119 of 170	70.0
Girls	79 of 134	59.0	113 of 181	62.4
Level of Development in Cross-sex Behavior				
Non-dating	44 of 103	42.7	93 of 135	68.9
Competitive dating	62 of 112	55.4	67 of 119	56.3
Noncompetitive dating	39 of 57	68.4	72 of 97	74.2
Socioeconomic Status				
Middleclass	79 of 159	49.7	77 of 121	63.6
Workingclass	66 of 113	58.4	155 of 230	67.4
Integration in Peer Culture				
Integrated	99 of 178	55.6	128 of 216	59.3
Non-integrated	46 of 94	48.9	104 of 135	77.0

neighborhood attends schools which contain very large proportions of Negroes. Almost all of the social behavior of the child takes place in the rather limited area. Almost all of his contacts are with other Negroes. When the Negro adolescent goes to high school he enters into an overall situation in which he may not be very well prepared. He may suddenly be thrust into a situation with more white persons and other different kinds of individuals. He may be faced with numerous new problems in social relationships, among which is the problem of cross-sex behavior in a racial mixed atmosphere. A convenient normative source to help him make new adjustments in a dominantly white world may be the white-oriented mass media.

White adolescents, on the other hand, have had the advantage of growing up in the white world. They have had the opportunities to develop certain attitudes and learn norms and skills which better prepare them for the cross-sex behavior problems to come. As they grow older, they increasingly use the media to reinforce their attitudes.

Sex: The data suggest that media socializees are more likely to be girls in the white sample and boys in the Negro sample. Almost three-fifths (59.0 percent) of the white girls were media socializees compared to 48.5 percent of the white boys. Among the Negro adolescents, 70.0 percent of the boys and 62.4 percent of the girls engaged in media socialization. Sex, then, appears to be a useful explanatory variable. The differences between Negroes and whites in their media behavior is partially due to the response differences between Negro and white boys. Still, the overall general relationship remains the same. Each subgroup of Negroes still contains more media socializees than any subgroup of whites.

Level of Development in Cross-sex Behavior: Adolescents' level of development in cross-sex behavior appears to be a condition which significantly affects their media behavior. Among white adolescents, the data suggest that media socialization increases with the degree of involvement in heterosexual relations. About two-fifths (42.7 percent) of those who are not dating are media socializees. Over half (55.5 percent) of those persons dating two or more people (competitive daters) and over two-thirds (68.1 percent) of those participating in noncompetitive relationships (dating only one person steadily) are media socializees. Additional analysis indicates that much of the increase by cross-sex stage among whites lies in their use of the media as a reinforcing agent. Few (13.6 percent) of the non-dating persons participate in media reinforcement; they tend to use the media more for norm-acquiring (34 percent are high in norm-acquiring). Slightly more (19.4 percent) of the competitive daters use the media for reinforcement; at this stage norm-acquiring is still more prevalent. For those steadily dating only one person, though, the primary media use appears to be reinforcement. Almost half (47.1 percent) of the noncompetitive daters use the media to reinforce their attitudes.

Among the Negroes, the least amount of media socialization behavior occurs among those who are participating in competitive dating relationships. Media socialization is most likely to occur among those who are not dating at all or among those who are going steady or engaged. Of the non-daters, 68.9 percent are media socializees, while almost three-fourths (74.2 percent) of the noncompetitive daters use the media in their cross-sex socialization. The media reinforcement and norm-acquiring behaviors of Negro teenagers do not appear to change too much with the entrance into another level of boy-girl relations. At each cross-sex stage, several adolescents engage in each of the two media behaviors. Media norm-acquiring is especially prevalent among the Negroes who are not dating. Over half (54.0 percent) of the non-daters use the media as a normative source.

The difference between Negroes and whites when cross-sex stage is held constant might be explained by normative differences between the two subcultures. Whether or not whites and Negroes have different norms in premarital cross-sex relations cannot be established from the present data.[15] Sociologists have, how-

[15] Reiss' recent analysis of data obtained from both students and adults indicates that Negroes are generally more inclined to accept premarital permissiveness than are whites. See Ira L. Reiss, "Premarital Sexual Permissiveness Among Negroes and Whites," *American Sociological Review* 29 (October 1964): 688–98. His study is not strictly comparable to the present investigation, however, since all of the Negroes in his student sample (he also had an adult sample) were from the state of Virginia and attended segregated schools whereas all of the Negroes in the present study resided in the San Francisco Bay area of California and attended nonsegregated schools.

ever, frequently found that differential sex norms operate on different socio-economic levels, and data are available on the socio-economic status composition of each subgroup of respondents. Almost two-thirds of the Negro respondents (65.6 percent) were working-class individuals while almost three-fifths of the white adolescents (58.5 percent) were middle-class persons.

Some of the most pressing problems in heterosexual relationships for white persons may not appear until the adolescent is in a noncompetitive, steady dating situation which involves constant interaction with only one member of the opposite sex. The problem of erotic behavior—"How far should I go"—may, in such a case, become an increasing problem. The adolescent may require more reinforcement support in his behavior than he needed previously. The middle-class or conservative working-class white parents may not be of much assistance to the individual. At this stage, the informal system of the school appears to be a significant agency for socialization. The adolescent who is not integrated in the informal school system is especially in need of an alternative socialization source. Whereas during his non-dating or competitive dating days, the white adolescent did not have much reason to use the media as an agency of reinforcement, he now needs an alternative source for reinforcement behavior. The noncompetitive dater who is not integrated in the school may be in a bind. In order to establish order in his life, he may turn to the mass media for socialization assistance.

Within the working-class Negro subculture, the media constitute a significant agency in the cross-sex socialization of youngsters before they ever start dating. Their parents, many of whom had migrated to the Bay region from the South, did not have a background of "dating" of the same type which their sons and daughters were experiencing. The working-class Negro parents, then, may not be defined as adequate role models by their children. With the onset of adolescence, the Negro children often find that their parents are indeed the "older generation" from a decidedly different cultural background. Particularly for the non-integrated Negro adolescents, the media constitute an agency of socialization which represents the contemporary white-dominated American culture in which premarital cross-sex relations occur.

Socioeconomic Status: [16] In general, among both white and Negro adolescents, working-class persons tend to use the media as a socializing agency more than do middle-class individuals. This variable, when held constant, does not appear to significantly alter the basic differences in media behavior between the two racial subsamples.

---

[16] The index of socioeconomic status used in this study is based on two criteria of stratification—the occupation and education of the head of the adolescent's family. Usually, the father was the head of the family. In several cases where there was no father in the home (or no other man who took his place) and the mother was the chief source of income, the occupation and education of the mother was used to establish the socioeconomic status of the family. The index is similar to the one explained by Schramm, Lyle, and Parker, *Television,* pp. 105–106.

Integration in Peer Culture: [17] Holding constant the degree of integration in a peer culture was expected to help to specify some of the conditions under which the media operate to socialize adolescents. It would seem that the adolescent who is integrated in the peer culture would have less need to use the media for socialization. Although controlling this variable does not reverse the Negro-white differences, the data for the white subgroup are not in the expected direction. Among the whites, those who are integrated in a peer culture are more likely to be media socializees. Among the Negroes, the non-peer-integrated individuals are the most likely to be media socializees.

These findings suggest that peer culture serves different functions for white and Negro adolescents. The assumption could be made, although the present study offers no definite data, that the white adolescents studied tended to interact primarily with other whites in their primary-type relationships and that most primary relations of the Negro respondents were with other Negroes. If this is the case, the various peer cultures, to a large degree, constitute *racial* subcultures, in which all or almost all the members are of the same race. It may be that Negro adolescent subcultures perform different functions in cross-sex behavior than do white adolescent subcultures.

It may be that some white peer cultures tend to offer *support* for the use of certain mass media for socialization purposes. Within the white peer groups, certain media materials relating to cross-sex behavior may constitute an important topic of conversation. Many media materials, including some of the teen-oriented variety, are probably defined as legitimate pursuits within most white adolescent peer cultures. The discussion of these materials may constitute a positive sanction for the adolescent who is "in" the group. The sanction may result in media exposure on the part of peer-integrated persons. Although media socialization may not be the admitted *aim* of this exposure, a certain degree of media socialization is likely to be a latent function of the sanctioned media exposure.

Participants in Negro peer cultures may not discuss media materials as frequently as do the white adolescents, since, on the whole, mass media content is not oriented to Negro audiences. Except for a few specialized publications or productions, few media materials are oriented toward Negro adolescents. Instead

[17] Doubtless there are many different kinds of adolescent peer cultures. Description of the characteristics of the different cultural traits or differentiation of the behavior patterns distinctive to each subculture would have required much more depth of data than the present study could obtain. This study, then, does not distinguish between different peer cultures. Rather, degree of integration in a peer culture was felt to be the variable most significant to this study. A Likert-type scale composed of four items was constructed to measure the respondent's degree of integration in a peer culture. The index emphasizes integration in a social system, rather than the characteristics of the system itself. The index can be seen as an indicator of the peer-context of the respondent. Following are the four questions in the index: (1) "Suppose the circle below represented the activities that go on with kids your age around here. How far out from the center of things are *you?*" (2) "How many *close* friends do you have (including both boys and girls)?" (3) "Do you talk over your personal problems with your friends?" (4) "In general, during the school year, how often do you have dates?" The total scores were dichotomized into integrated and non-integrated categories.

of indirectly encouraging media socialization behavior, most Negro peer cultures may *negatively* sanction exposure to a great deal of materials. Peer-integrated Negro teenagers may not have the support of the peer culture in their media socialization behavior. If so, their media socializing behavior is likely to be kept separate from, and possibly secret from, their peers. From this line of reasoning, it is hardly surprising that the Negroes who are *not* integrated in a peer culture are more likely to use the media as an agency of socialization.

Discussion

The central overall finding of the present study was that Negro adolescents reported very different mass media behavior than did white adolescents. The differences between the two populations were especially prevalent in media socialization behavior. It was found that under almost every condition considered in the analysis, more Negro than white adolescents used the media as an agency of socialization. A basic questions is *why* do whites and Negroes apparently use the media in different ways? The differences possibly might be accounted for by the nature of the study population of the present investigation. Since that data were not obtained from some kind of a random sample, it is possible that the findings may be unique to the 623 persons studied. Other samples might not produce such significant Negro-white differences. It is quite likely, however, that investigation of successive samples over time would produce findings somewhat similar to the present data.

"Race" does not in itself *explain* differential behavior. Race is merely a socially visible variable about which data have been gathered. A person's racial status is often an indicator of a great many other factors, most of which unfortunately have not been measured in the present study. These *other* factors are what are important to a discussion of "causal" factors.

The different media-consuming patterns of Negroes and whites are especially significant when media *content* is considered. Is there anything in the content of mass communications materials themselves that may be generating the Negro exposure to the media? Content analysis has indicated that Negroes and members of other minority groups generally receive unfavorable symbolic treatment in the presentation by the media to the broader society. It would be useful to know how Negroes are being treated in contemporary media content. There is reason to expect that Negroes are receiving considerably more favorable treatment in media materials today than they did one or two decades ago. Still, it is not likely that the media itself could fully explain the high degree of Negro media socialization behavior. Except for a few specialized publications it would seem that the media in general are oriented primarily to white audiences. Overall, the media probably emphasize behaving in the way which is socially acceptable in the predominantly white broader society. The data of the present study suggest, then, that many Negro adolescents are using the mass media to learn how to behave like whites (i.e., behave in a socially acceptable way).

What factors might account for Negroes' learning how to behave like whites? One probable explanatory factor lies in the consideration of a Negro subcommunity, a partially bounded subsystem within the large community system. Various mechanisms operate to maintain the subcommunity. Mechanisms of maintenance of such a subsystem can be seen as functioning at three levels, each of which has implications for the interpretation of the data of this study.

The first set of boundary-maintaining mechanisms operates at the level of intergroup relations, i.e., Negro-white interactions. In general, Negroes are both ecologically and socially segregated from whites. Negroes are isolated from effective role models in the white community. They may have difficulty in obtaining access to the kinds of information which are needed to develop a satisfactory adjustment to the community setting. When the Negro adolescent goes to high school, he may be entering an overall community situation for which he has not been very well prepared by the socializing agents of his subcommunity. His social interactions may not provide satisfactory adjustment mechanisms, since most of his primary-group interactions are with other Negroes. The mass media may represent an agency of the broader community from which the Negro adolescents can learn to behave in ways acceptable in the white community. The media constitute an alternative structure through which symbolic anticipatory socialization can occur.

A second kind of boundary-maintaining mechanism can be found in the self-conceptions of Negro children. In certain respects, Negro children probably reflect self-concepts (identities) which can be differentiated from those of white persons. The self-concept can be seen as both an effect and as a causal factor. Negroes' self-concepts develop, in part, from the historical background of race relations in our society. Such history affects the attitudes and behavior of whites toward Negroes, and consequently, is reflected in the resulting self-concepts of Negroes. The self-concept is a causal factor in that it has implications for Negroes' actions, for their effective relations with others, both Negro and white, and for their aspirations and views of themselves and their lives. Often, a self-fulfilling prophecy is set in motion in that self-conceptions function as effective boundaries to interpersonal relations, thereby making for increased use of the mass media for socialization purposes.

In contemporary American society, many Negro adolescents are (presently or potentially) marginal persons. These marginal individuals may, in varying degrees, experience self-hate. As such, there may be pressures to be as "white" as possible in their behavior. Unless these Negroes have developed primary relationships with white significant others, they might be expected to be strong media socializees. It would be useful to compare the media behavior of Negroes with *close* white friends to that of those who do not have white friends. It would seem that those without white friendships would be more apt to be high in media socialization.

The final set of boundary-maintaining mechanisms, closely related to the other two types of factors, constitute subcultural differences. There are various differences of attitudes, value, and belief between whites and Negroes, perhaps even when social class is controlled. The subculture within the Negro subcommunity, as reflected by the parents, may not sufficiently enable Negro adolescents to adjust within their expanding social structural contexts. The parents and other socializing agencies within the Negro subcommunities may not be equipped to advise and direct youngsters as the adolescents increasingly broaden the scope of their interactions (through high school) to the white-dominated broader community. The media represent an alternative socializing agency.

A factor which may account for some of the boundaries between Negro subcommunities in northern and western cities and the broader community systems is spatial mobility. Many of the Negroes in such cities have, within the past one or two generations, migrated from the South. One consequence of the continued in-migration of southern Negroes into the non-southern cities is the continued existence of segregated Negro subsystems and the resulting subcultures.

Given such a bounded social subsystem, a history of recent migration from a very different region (the South), and an increasing aspiration to accommodate to the larger society, it is not surprising that Negro adolescents report a high degree of utilizing the mass media as an agency of socialization. There are social pressures to strive toward success, to reap the accepted rewards of the society. There are, particularly for young Negroes in northern and western cities, motivations to "behave like whites" and/or in a socially acceptable way.

The present investigation did not obtain data on the overall community context of the respondents. Actually, respondents resided in four separate communities. Most of the Negro respondents lived in an East Bay city of 71,895. The lack of descriptive data on the broader community itself posed problems for the interpretation of the data signifying Negro-white differences in media socializing behavior. Interpretations have to extend beyond the data collected. Further research might benefit by initially adapting a community-subcommunity framework so that some of the above-stated propositions could be tested. Media socialization behavior should be seen in light of the broader community social structure.

Related to community data are data on geographic mobility. The present data suggest that mobility increases media socializing for Negro adolescents, but not for whites. Further research might attempt to determine *why* more of the highly mobile or recently mobile *whites* did not use the media for socializing purposes. Significant information would be data on *where* they moved from. It may be that mobile whites tend to move from other areas or neighborhoods similar to their present ones. The adolescents and peer cultures and cross-sex behavior patterns of the various areas may be quite similar. The persons may tend to adjust to the socially approved behavior patterns relatively easily. Many *Negroes,* on the other hand, probably experience significant changes in their environments. They may have relatively large adjustments to make. To make these adjustments in the white world, they may be forced into using the media for socialization purposes.

The findings of the present study would lead to the expectation that certain other populations in particular structural situations might demonstrate a high amount of media socialization behavior. If the interpretation of Negro media socialization could be generalized to other population groups in somewhat similar social structural situations, the findings would have more impact on the mainstream of sociology. For example, it might be expected that vertical-mobility-oriented people, immigrants into metropolitan areas, and white adolescents who are not socially integrated might also use the media as a significant agency of socialization.

Socialization:

Putting It into Perspective

By socialization the social psychologist means the interaction process whereby the person's beliefs and behaviors are formed and/or modified to conform to the expectations of others in his social environment. Thus, socialization is essentially a social learning process. Its significance resides in the fact that man must learn to view himself and his environment in certain ways and develop a number of behavioral skills before he can engage in meaningful social intercourse. That is, he must learn beliefs and behaviors that will allow him to coordinate his own behavior with that of others, and thereby become a participant in ongoing social activity. Since the others with whom a person's beliefs and behaviors must be coordinated change with movement through the various stages of the life cycle, and since society itself undergoes almost constant change, a continual modification, or updating, of his beliefs and behaviors are necessitated.

While any attempt to characterize contemporary research in socialization within a few brief paragraphs must of necessity involve considerable simplification and reference to only major foci, such an effort should give the reader a better idea about how the readings reprinted in this volume "fit" into the larger area of inquiry. With this general objective in mind, three foci of current work are distinguished: socialization as process; socializing agents and other social stimuli involved in socialization; and specific socialization outcomes.

Social psychologists have concentrated most of their attention on the interpersonal processes of belief and behavior formation. Since the formation of beliefs and behavior patterns are particularly important and somewhat dramatic during childhood, research in this vein has typically been conducted with children. Within this general focus, of course, a variety of specific research questions have been posed. For example, a question that has stimulated considerable theorizing and research among the more sociologically oriented is: How does one come to form particular beliefs about himself? Answers to this query are sought in an analysis of the form and content of the person's interpersonal relations. Scott's study of the socialization of the blind, reprinted in this section, reflects this orientation. Another specific form that interest in belief formation has taken is the study of the moral development of children. This problem has been most frequently addressed by social psychologists strongly influenced by developmental psychology. While insofar as these researches are social psychological they focus on interpersonal processes, great emphasis is placed on cognitive and maturational factors. Still other social psychologists have focused on belief and behavior formation as merely special instances of learning and have applied general learning theory to an analysis of these processes.

Returning to our original definition of socialization, we find that it encompasses not only the formation of beliefs and behavior patterns but their modification as well. In contrast to the study of formative processes, research in belief and behavior modification has tended to concentrate on adult populations. Some of the most intriguing research in this area has been conducted with institutionalized populations, such as inmates, mental patients, and prisoners of war. In addition, occupational groups are frequently the focus of attention. But whether we talk about the rehabilitation of prisoners, the curing of mental illness, the indoctrination of prisoners of war, or the training of new employees, a major emphasis is the modification of selected beliefs and/or behaviors. Bryan's analysis of the initiation into prostitution which appears as a reading in this section is essentially concerned with this issue. In addition, Schein's article, "Interpersonal Communication, Group Solidarity, and Social Influence," reprinted in Chapter IV of this volume, can be interpreted as a study of the process of belief and behavior modification among prisoners of war. While both these studies are strongly sociological in emphasis, the same diversity of theories has been applied to the processes of belief and behavior modification that has been used to explain formative processes. There is a growing literature, for example, concerning the use of general learning principles in the treatment of mental patients and the rehabilitation programs of prisoners.

The second major focus in current socialization research which we identified earlier is on socializing agents and other social stimuli in the socialization process, particularly models. The simple assumption in these inquiries is that certain characteristics of the stimuli involved may exert significant influences on the process of socialization itself or on its outcomes. In accord with this line of reasoning, numerous studies have been conducted to determine the consequences of different personality characteristics, interpersonal behavior patterns, and disciplinary techniques of parents for the beliefs that the child develops about himself and others and the social skills that he acquires. The dynamics by which these different characteristics exert their influence are quite diverse. For instance, the personality characteristics of the parent influence the extent to which the child identifies with him, which, in turn, affects the child's response to the content of his interaction with that parent. On the other hand, the impact of disciplinary techniques has been interpreted in terms of the learning consequences of different patterns and modes of reinforcement.

The research report by Chombart de Lauwe which appears in this chapter is clearly within this research focus. In that report he identifies symbolic models as significant social stimuli for child socialization, and he explores some of the consequences of the frequent contradictions among these models. The particular process through which symbolic models have a direct impact is imitation. Of course, they have indirect effects on the child through belief and behavior modifications they produce in his parents and other socializing agents.

The final major research focus can be described as a concern with specific belief and behavior consequences of the socialization experience. In many instances, studies of this type are *ex post facto* analyses. That is, the researcher identifies some group on the basis of behavioral or belief peculiarities and attempts to account for these peculiarities by analyzing a reconstruction of particular segments of the subjects' socialization experiences—generally those of early childhood. Such studies are frequently Freudian in their orientation, with explanations cast in terms of psychosexual development. On the other hand, studies of this type may be strongly sociological, with explanations for belief or behavioral differences sought in the structure or content of the subjects' interpersonal relationships.

Another interest in socialization consequences is reflected by a growing body of research in deviance concerning the belief and behavior consequences of labeling someone as a deviant. Even when the explicit focus is on the processes by which labels come to be applied, the implicit assumption is that the resulting label has consequences for both the one labeled and those with whom he interacts. While labeling theory is not generally treated as a socialization theory, it certainly meets the criteria set out in our definition. It is an attempt to account for the formation and/or modification of both beliefs and behaviors.

While the foregoing characterization has been sketchy, it reflects something of the variety of interests among socialization researchers, and the *Suggestions for Further Reading* will provide the reader with an entree into more detailed study.

Suggestions for Further Reading

Justin Aronfreed, *Conduct and Conscience: The Socialization of Internalized Control Over Behavior.* New York: Academic Press, 1968. This book examines the origins of internalized control over behavior (conscience) from the perspective of child socialization. The new student will find this a very demanding book, but it is clearly one of the most significant books on socialization published in the last decade.

John A. Clausen, editor, *Socialization and Society.* Boston: Little, Brown and Company, 1968. A collection of eight essays whose unifying theme is the effects of social structure upon the socialization process.

K. Danziger, editor, *Readings in Child Socialization.* New York: Pergamon Press, 1970. This collection of papers touches upon a number of child socialization topics. The reader will find these selections focusing on other societies of particular interest. Danziger's "Introduction" is also very good.

Richard Dawson and Kenneth Prewitt, *Political Socialization.* Boston: Little-

Brown, 1969. A brief essay which attempts to organize existing knowledge about man's socialization as a political creature.

Erving Goffman, *Asylums: Essays on the Social Situation of Mental Patients and Other Inmates.* New York: Anchor, 1961. Emphasizes the mechanisms used in socializing selected inmate populations into a new life within the confines of a total institution.

David A. Goslin, editor, *Handbook of Socialization Theory and Research.* Chicago: Rand-McNally, 1969. One of the most exhaustive collections of essays on socialization available. The undergraduate and professional researcher alike will find it a useful reference.

Ronald A. Hoppe, G. Alexander Milton, and Edward C. Simmel, editors, *Early Experiences and the Processes of Socialization.* New York: Academic Press, 1970. Examines a variety of approaches to the study of socialization, including the biological. The editors provide a worthwhile service in exploring differences and similarities in the work from the different perspectives.

George H. Mead, *Mind, Self, and Society.* Chicago: University of Chicago Press, 1934. A work of historical interest and continued influence in theory and research on development of self.

CHAPTER IX

Collective Behavior

35 Carl J. Couch, *Collective Behavior: An Examination of Some Stereotypes* · 467

36 Maurice Pinard, Jerome Kirk, and Donald von Eschen, *Processes of Recruitment in the Sit-In Movement* · 481

37 Alan C. Kerckhoff, Kurt W. Back, and Norman Miller, *Sociometric Patterns in Hysterical Contagion* · 495

Putting It into Perspective · 508
Suggestions for Further Reading · 511

35

Collective Behavior: An Examination of Some Stereotypes

CARL J. COUCH

Sociologists have traditionally focused their attention on cultural patterns, behavior which corresponds to fairly well recognized norms and roles. Consequently, they have tended to view crowd behavior and other collective behavior phenomena as qualitatively different from institutionalized patterns. Building on the foundation provided by the early speculative work of Gustav LeBon, current conceptualizations of the acting crowd emphasize the bizarre, irrational, and even pathological nature of crowd behavior.

In this selection, Carl Couch examines some currently held assumptions about the distinctiveness of crowd behavior, and attempts to show that their validity is open to question. He argues that the emphasis on established cultural patterns rather than on the processes by which cultural elements are created, modified, and initially adopted has led sociologists to explain crowd behavior in terms of individual psychological characteristics such as suggestibility, irrationality, and lack of self-control.

While crowd behavior is more dramatic than that which occurs in most other interactional contexts, the author contends that the acting crowd is indeed "typical" when viewed as a social system human beings adopt to take action toward or change some other social system.

Carl J. Couch, "Collective Behavior: An Examination of Some Stereotypes," *Social Problems* 15 (1968): 310–22.

After years of relative neglect there has been a recent resurgence of interest in collective behavior. However, with the exception of Smelser's work [1] there has been almost no effort to apply a general theory to collective behavior, nor have there been many empirical studies testing propositions about human conduct in collective behavior situations.[2] One common theme presented in many of the discussions of collective behavior holds that collective behavior is a form of deviant behavior.

This state of affairs is partly the consequence of the continuing influence of LeBon's characterization of collective behavior (crowd behavior).[3] LeBon viewed collective behavior as a different order of behavior than that manifested in other human associations [4] and as a pathological form of behavior.

Several have taken issue with LeBon's characterization of the crowd [5] but nearly all who have attempted to present a "theory" of crowd behavior have incorporated many of the ideas of LeBon. Almost without exception, contemporary statements explicitly state or imply that crowd behavior is pathological or, at best, a more primitive form of conduct than non-crowd behavior.

LeBon's central thesis was this: "The conclusion to be drawn from what precedes is, that the crowd is always intellectually inferior to the isolated individual, but that, from the point of view of feelings and of the acts these feelings provoke, the crowd may, according to circumstances, be better or worse than the individual." [6]

Fifty years after LeBon's classical statement, Blumer (who has been widely used as an authoritative source) suggested:

---

[1] Neil J. Smelser, *Theory of Collective Behavior* (New York: Free Press, 1963).

[2] Exceptions include Alan C. Kerchoff, Kurt W. Back, and Norman Miller, "Sociometric Patterns in Hysterical Contagion," *Sociometry* 28 (March 1965): 2–15; and Robert E. Forman, "Resignation as a Collective Behavior Response," *American Journal of Sociology* 69 (November 1963): 385–90. An earlier exception is Seymour M. Lipset, *Agrarian Socialism* (Berkeley: University of California Press, 1950). His report of a rural protest movement contains little, if any, support for some of the more generally accepted propositions on the character of participants in protest collectivities. Perhaps this accounts for the lack of attention given to it by those concerned with collective behavior.

[3] Gustav LeBon, *The Crowd* (New York: Viking, 1960).

[4] Ralph H. Turner, "Collective Behavior," in Robert E. L. Faris, ed., *Handbook of Modern Sociology* (Chicago: Rand McNally, 1964), p. 384, questions this view: "It is altogether possible that the search will ultimately undermine all of the traditional dynamic distinctions between collective behavior and organizational behavior and suggest that no special set of principles is required to deal with this subject matter." The framework offered by Turner is one of the few that does not imply that collective behavior is pathological behavior.

[5] Robert K. Merton, "The Ambivalences of LeBon's *The Crowd*," introduction to the Compass Books Edition of Gustav LeBon, *The Crowd* (New York: Viking, 1960), pp. v–xxxix.

[6] LeBon, *The Crowd*, p. 32, states, "Moreover, by the mere fact that he forms part of an organized crowd, a man descends several rungs in the ladder of civilization." And on p. 43, "It is not necessary that a crowd should be numerous for the faculty of seeing what is taking place before its eyes to be destroyed and for the real facts to be replaced by hallucinations unrelated to them."

> Instead of acting, then, on the basis of established rule, it (the acting crowd) acts on the basis of aroused impulse. Just as it is, in this sense, a noncultural group, so likewise it is a non-moral group. In the light of this fact it is not difficult to understand that crowd actions may be strange, forbidding, and at times atrocious. Not having a body of definitions or rules to guide its behavior and, instead, acting on the basis of impulse, the crowd is fickle, suggestible, and irresponsible.[7]

Nor did Smelser differ greatly from LeBon when he observed:

> We can suggest already, however, why collective behavior displays some of the crudeness, excess and eccentricity that it does. By short-circuiting from high-level to low-level components of social action, collective episodes by-pass many of the specifications, contingencies, and controls that are required to make the generalized components operative. This gives collective behavior its clumsy or primitive character.[8]

None of the theorists of collective behavior have accepted LeBon's formulation of crowd behavior without qualification. Some have given attention to "mechanisms" of crowd behavior in attempts to explain its behavior. Brown presented a rather comprehensive review of mechanisms to account for crowd behavior;[9] others, particularly Turner and Killian,[10] have centered on the interaction within the crowd; many have focused on the social conditions giving rise to crowds.[11]

Relatively little attention has been given to the structure (relationships between self and others) or interaction patterns within crowds. Many discussions of crowd behavior have followed LeBon's lead and directed attention to delineating the "nature" of the behavior of members of crowds. Often the delineation focuses attention on either the primitive and/or pathological nature of the behavior. As a consequence, the significance of social relationships has been slighted.

This essay does not try to delineate the social relationships and processes distinctive of the acting crowd.[12] Rather it examines some widespread beliefs about

[7] Herbert Blumer, "Collective Behavior," in A. M. Lee, *New Outline of the Principles of Sociology* (New York: Barnes and Noble, 1946), p. 180. In a more recent statement Blumer has modied his position. Herbert Blumer, "Collective Behavior," in Joseph B. Gittler, ed., *Review of Sociology* (New York: Wiley, 1957), p. 131. "Latent with strong destructive and constructive potentialities the crowd is an important collectivity, particularly in societies undergoing transformation."

[8] Smelser, *Collective Behavior,* p. 72. Smelser's acceptance of LeBon's framework is indicated, p. 80, by the statement, "We hope to give more precise theoretical meaning to the insights of LeBon and others who have attempted to fathom the mysteries of these kinds of beliefs."

[9] Roger W. Brown, "Mass Phenomena," in Gardner Lindzey, ed., *Handbook of Social Psychology,* II (Cambridge: Addison-Wesley, 1954), pp. 833–76.

[10] Ralph H. Turner and Lewis M. Killian, *Collective Behavior* (Englewood Cliffs, New Jersey: Prentice-Hall, 1957), esp. chapter 6.

[11] Smelser, *Collective Behavior;* Rudolph Heberle, *Social Movements: An Introduction to Political Sociology* (New York: Appleton-Century-Crofts, 1951); and Stanley Lieberson and Arnold R. Silverman, "The Precipitants and Underlying Conditions of Race Riots," *American Sociological Review* 30 (December 1965): 887–98.

[12] The terms crowd and acting crowd will be used interchangeably; however, the acting crowd is only one type of crowd—the one most significant to the collective behavior process. Attention is directed specifically to the acting crowd but most of the propositions analyzed and offered are relevant to other forms of protesting collectivities.

the nature of crowd behavior. In short, it examines some stereotypes held by sociologists and others about the acting crowd. Hopefully, this examination will stimulate the re-analysis of the crowd as a social system.

Suggestibility

It is generally agreed that crowds are highly suggestible.[13] But if crowds are as suggestible as some critics claim, they would pose no problem for authorities; all that would be necessary to disperse a crowd would be to suggest they break up and go for a cold swim. In fact, one of the distinctive features of a crowd is its lack of receptivity to suggestions offered by outside authorities. Members of institutionalized social systems regularly follow the directive of others. Workmen commonly follow the instructions of foremen. Very few label workmen as suggestible because they follow instructions of accepted authorities.

In his laboratory study of the acting crowd, Swanson states, "They (members of acting crowds) are faced with an urgent problem for which they have no solution. This being true, they grasp at such ideas as are available as a guide for their behavior." [14] He found that laboratory groups composed of members who had not previously worked together and with no previous experience with the task gave more attention to outside suggestions than those who had worked together previously and had experience with the task. This finding is not of special relevance to the acting crowd; rather it demonstrates that in problematic situations persons are receptive to suggestions.

Acting crowds probably confront problematic situations more frequently than other social systems. In these situations suggestions are commonly offered, one or more of which may be accepted. The behavior within a crowd is no different from the behavior in other social systems when they confront unanticipated situations—except in institutionalized systems, those who formulate the plans of action are vested with the authority to do so by the institutional structure.

Most members of an acting crowd have strong feelings about some object; any suggestions (directions) calling for behavior that is defined as incompatible with their desires are likely to be rejected. Directions that come from within the crowd which are perceived as facilitating their aims may be adopted.

---

[13] Smelser, *Collecive Behavior,* pp. 152–53; G. E. Swanson, "A Preliminary Laboratory of the Acting Crowd," *American Sociological Review* 18 (October 1953): 528–29; Kurt Lang and Gladys Engel Lang, *Collective Dynamics* (New York: Crowell, 1961), pp. 221–25; Ralph H. Turner and Lewis M. Killian, *Colelctive Behavior* (Englewood Cliffs, N.J.: Prentice-Hall, 1957), p. 84. Most of the above note that suggestion is not a mechanism restricted to crowd situations but indicate it is of special importance in the crowd or other collective behavior situations. Turner and Killian, p. 84, state, "It (heightened suggestibility) amounts to a tendency to respond uncritically to suggestions that are consistent with the mood, imagery, and conception of appropriate action that have developed and assumed a normative character." Lang and Lang, p. 221, note, "The existence of a 'normal' suggestibility adds to the difficulty of explaining suggestibility in its contagious form." Smelser, p. 153, writes, "It should be stressed, however, that as an explanatory concept in collective behavior, suggestion should be limited to its appropriate place in the value-added process." Blumer, *New Outline,* p. 181, assigns suggestibility a more limited role than others. "It should be noted, however, that this suggestibility exists only along the line of the aroused impulses; suggestions made contrary to them are ignored."

[14] Swanson, "Laboratory," p. 528.

Destructiveness

The destructiveness of crowds is legendary.[15] Conflict engenders destruction; crowds do destroy property and human lives; participants in race riots do kill each other. But destructiveness is not restricted to crowds.

Crowds acting against the established authority system as part of a general movement to modify the authority structure have generally been as gentle as a loving mother when compared with the established authority. The outstanding current example is the civil rights movement in the United States. Nor is this case unique.

In the Gordon Riots of 1780, the demonstration took a heavy toll on property and freed inmates of prisons (a destructive act?) but there is no evidence that they killed anyone. However, 285 rioters were killed during the riots and another 25 were hanged afterwards.[16] Another extreme case was the Rebellion riots during the French Revolution when the rioters killed no one, but several hundred of them were killed by representatives (police and military) of the established authorities.[17] In most, if not all, cases of crowds attempting to overthrow the authorities and to establish a less authoritarian political system the number of people killed or maimed by crowds is smaller than the number killed or maimed by those suppressing the crowd.[18]

Lang and Lang in a description of riots provide an illustration that violence is not a one-way affair. In the Shanghai riot, "The police responded [to bricks and stones being thrown at them] by arresting several 'agitators' in the crowd, whom they pulled, one by one, into the station, beating them as they were being dragged." [19] In the same account they state, "The crowd was finally dispersed by machine-gun fire followed by a police charge, with bayonets and clubs, against the crowd." [20] It was only after this that ". . . the crowd began its rampage of Shanghai." [21]

Riots between ethnic groups are often marked by extensive destruction of life. Negro-white riots in the United States, religious riots in India, and other similar outbursts often have resulted in the death of many participants. Almost invariably a larger number of the minority are killed than are representatives of the domi-

[15] While this theme is not always explicitly developed, the way material is presented usually emphasizes the "destructive" nature of the crowd. See Lang and Lang, *Dynamics,* pp. 125–35; Smelser, *Collective Behavior,* Chapter 8; Brown, "Mass Phenomena," p. 846, clearly imputes destructive behavior to crowds by stating, "There may be lawless individuals whose brutal behavior in the mob is not completely discontinuous with their private lives." An exception is George Rudé, *The Crowd in History, 1730–1848* (New York: Wiley, 1964), p. 255, "Destruction of property, then, is a constant feature of the preindustrial crowd; but not the destruction of human lives. . . ."

[16] Rudé, *Crowd in History,* p. 59.

[17] Ibid., p. 256.

[18] This generalization appears to hold for mutinies also. See T. H. McGuffie, *Stories of Famous Mutinies* (London: Arthur Barker, 1966).

[19] Lang and Lang, *Dynamics,* p. 128.

[20] Ibid., p. 129.

[21] Ibid., p. 129. For a more recent and detailed account of reciprocal violence see: Fred C. Shapiro and James W. Sullivan, *Race Riots New York 1964* (New York: Crowell, 1964), esp. pp. 50, 57, 60–61, 83, 130, and 141.

nant group; [22] this is, in part, because the dominant group is most likely to have greater access to instruments of destruction. Some of the differential probably is a function of fear of reprisals by the minority group.

Lynch crowds of the United States have often been used to illustrate the lack of respect for human life by a crowd. However, a substantial number of Negroes have been killed by law enforcement agencies—from deputy sheriffs to the court system. Probably far more Negroes have been killed in the Southern part of the United States by the constituted authorities than by lynch mobs.

LeBon and others dealt extensively with the reign of terror of the French revolutions.[23] After the revolutionaries were in power a large number of the opposition were killed. An extreme case was the killing of over 1,000 people in September of 1792. The bulk of the victims were first given a "trial" and then executed. In more recent times, after the Cuba revolution, several of the opposition were killed. While these situations are often used to illustrate the results of a so-called crowd, the overlooked fact is that the action was taken by the authority of the day.[24] Whether the new authorities destroy more lives than the old is difficult to answer. But the significant factor is that most of the killing is accomplished by *the established authority,* not by the crowd. This suggests that it is something about the social relationships inherent in authority that is responsible for the widespread destruction of life—not the social system of crowds nor the personalities of members of the crowd.

The destruction of leaders of the opposition after a successful revolution is usually well publicized. The killing of revolutionaries by the entrenched authority receives much less publicity, often because the revolutionaries killed are less well known, other times because it is conducted secretly.

In the entire history of mankind, crowds have been responsible for only a very small percentage of the lives taken by fellow humans. In fact, it appears that systems with a highly authoritarian structure are more given to killing humans and are far more effective at it. Armies are the ultimate instance of an authoritarian social system and they are the social system par excellence for the destruction of human life.

Irrationality

Most students of the crowd have commented, in one form or another, on the irrationality of crowds.[25] The concepts of rationality and irrationality have limited

---

[22] Chicago Commission on Race Relations, *The Negro in Chicago* (Chicago: University of Chicago, 1922).

[23] LeBon, *Crowd,* pp. 160–165.

[24] Rudé, *Crowd in History.*

[25] Brown, "Mass Phenomena," p. 846, "There are, of course, mobs lacking any clear leadership that are nevertheless homogeneously irrational." Lang and Lang, *Dynamics,* p. 32, "There is an incontestable bit of truth in this contention that people in groups are often less rational than individuals on their own." Smelser, *Collective Behavior,* Chapter 5. Smelser does not employ the concepts rational and irrational. However in this discussion of belief systems he employs the concept "hysterical beliefs" in much the same manner others have used irrationality.

applicability for a sociological analysis.[26] The concepts are an attempt to characterize the nature of ideas or beliefs: they direct attention away from social processes. However, if we tentatively accept the definition of rational action as that action which represents the most effective means for achieving some goal, then acting crowds are frequently highly rational endeavors.

The potential lyncher, the striker in a plant without a union, and the student wishing to change rules governing students know that their chance of success as individuals are almost nil. They would be highly irrational if they attempted to achieve the desired results as individuals. At the same time, those enforcing the rules want to deal with dissatisfied personnel through established channels. Those wishing to strike out against the system know that numbers are a critical element to any chance of success.

Another basis of the charge of irrationality of crowds is the demands of crowds. As Katz noted, the member of parliament who defends the prevailing economic system is behaving on the basis of delusions as much as the members of the crowd crying for liberty and equality.[27] Coordinated human endeavor demands at least tacit acceptance of shared beliefs. The crowd is attempting to produce a situation where people organize their behavior on the basis of a different set of norms than those currently extant. Many economists well versed in traditional economics of the time knew that the programs proposed by the labor unions during the 1930s could not work. Similarly, most of the noted scholars of political systems knew that the programs voiced by the crowds of the French Revolution were unrealistic and irrational.

Rational thought is that which is supported by the established institutions of the day; irrational thought is that which is not supported by the current institutions. Irrational thought of today often forms the social institutions of tomorrow.

Emotionality

Compatible with the charge of irrationality is the one of emotionality. Crowd behavior usually does occur within a context of strong emotions. This does not distinguish crowd behavior from many other instances of human behavior. A sequence of interaction between a husband and wife or employer and employee can also be highly charged with emotion.

A crowd situation elicits a high level of emotion from both the participants and those they are acting against. The wrath of the factory owner confronted for the first time by a crowd of defiant workers is something to behold. School administrators confronted by demonstrating students and Southern white offcialdom confronted by civil rights demonstrators are seldom placid.

There is strong feeling among members of crowds because many are behaving

---

[26] Daniel Katz, "The Psychology of the Crowd." In J. P. Guilford, ed., *Fields of Psychology* (New York: D. Van Nostrand, 1940), p. 160; and Turner and Killian, *Behavior*, pp. 16–17, both indicate that the concept rationality is of little utility.

[27] Katz, "Psychology of the Crowd," p. 180.

to acquire rights they feel are justifiably theirs.[28] Those they are acting against usually feel that the crowd is making demands or taking liberties that they have no right to.

Another set of factors assures a high level of emotion—most members of an acting crowd know they are running high risks. The shooting of demonstrators is not unknown; unsuccessful demonstrations often result in some of the participants losing statuses that are important to them; organizers of unsuccessful strikes often lose their jobs; demonstrating students are often expelled.

Emotion among those in opposition to the crowd is also assured for their status is threatened. If the crowd is successful, this will result in restricting the rights of the opposition. When demonstrating strikers are successful the owner loses his rights to hire and fire at his own discretion and to set work and wage levels. People seldom easily relinquish rights they have exercised for some time, especially when they are supported by established institutions. Many have commented on the "righteous" nature of beliefs of crowds. In most instances, there is probably a greater degree of righteousness on the part of those opposing the crowd.

Mental Disturbances

Several have noted a similarity between the beliefs of crowd members and some forms of mental illness. One of the more extreme statements is Martin's. "Probably the most telling point of likeness between the crowd-mind and the psychoneurosis—paranoia especially—is the 'delusion' of persecution." [29] The farmer who was receiving fifteen cents a bushel for his corn in the early 1930s and joined the Farmer's Holiday Association knew that he had more than that invested in it and he thought something was wrong. He may have felt persecuted but to call it a delusion hardly illuminates the situation. The miner working 56 hours a week and unable to provide a doctor for his family often felt that things were against him and that someone somewhere was responsible for it. When he got into a crowd he often gave voice to these ideas.

In a way there is some similarity between the thought processes of crowd members and some forms of mental illness. The error in views such as Martin's is that mental illness is usually conceptualized as being a function of shortcomings of the individual, and it has been these so-called individual shortcomings of the

[28] Alvin W. Gouldner, *Wildcat Strike* (Yellow Springs, Ohio: Antioch Press, 1954), pp. 18–26.

[29] Everett D. Martin, *The Behavior of Crowds* (New York: Norton, 1920), p. 92. Elsewhere, p. 6, he states, "A crowd is a device for indulging ourselves in a kind of temporary insanity by all going crazy together." Lang and Lang, *Dynamics,* p. 32. "This view that the 'crowd' brings pathological elements to the fore is more than an ideological assumption. It has driven home with some force the observation that large unities often act irrationally and under the impact of emotion." Smelser, *Collective Behavior,* by his excessive use of phrases like hysterical beliefs, wish fulfillment beliefs, hallucinations, short-circuiting process and craze adopts a stance highly compatible with those who "explain" crowd behavior as a form of mental disturbance.

same nature that have been designated as the causal factors of crowd participation.

Lemert offered an analysis of paranoia based on relationships between the person classified as suffering from paranoia and others. "The paranoid relationship includes reciprocating behaviors with attached emotions and meanings which, to be fully understood, must be described cubistically from at least two of its perspectives." [30] Once the actor, who becomes classified as paranoid, develops a feeling that others are opposed to him he tends to behave in a manner that causes others to systematically exclude him from their interaction patterns. The exclusion furthers the actor's definition of the situation that others are "ganging up" on him.

In a highly parallel manner, some of the participants of a crowd or protest movement have attempted to correct undesirable situations prior to the formation of crowds. Such action usually elicits negative evaluations and sometimes repressive acts. The person then feels the authority figure is persecuting him and this will strengthen his conviction that the opposition is against him. Reciprocally, his actions will elicit a still more negative evaluation and more repressive action.

The result is a decrease in the sharing of points of view and a decrease in meaningful communication. Open conflict becomes the only mode left for a resolution of the situation, each side having only negative evaluations of the other.

Lower-Class Participation

Of all of the ideas current about crowds the one that is probably most strongly entrenched holds that crowds tend to be composed of the lower echelons of society. Examination of the evidence lends little support for this idea. Members of the crowd are not composed of those in positions of power, authority, or policy formation. Usually a crowd is acting against current social relationships formulated by policymakers and enforced by authorities, so policymakers and authorities seldom participate in acting crowds. However, those protesting are seldom if ever representatives of social categories with the lowest prestige and fewest rights. The farmers who formed picket lines to prevent sale of produce during the withholding action of the National Farmers' Organization in 1964 were not the poorest farmers, nor were they farm laborers.[31] Rudé, in an analysis of several crowds in England and France, supplies evidence that members of the crowds were not those with the lowest prestige and fewest privileges. He asks the question, "If, then, slum dwellers and criminal elements were not the main shock troops of the pre-industrial crowd or the mainstay of riot and revolution, who

---

[30] Edwin M. Lemert, "Paranoia and the Dynamics of Exclusion," *Sociometry* 25 (March 1962): 6.

[31] Carl J. Couch, "Interaction and Protest," paper presented at 1967 National Meetings of American Sociological Association (Mimeograph); Lipset, *Agrarian Socialism,* observed that the active participants of a movement tended to be those with some prior leadership status.

were?" [32] The answer he supplies is that they were of "the lower orders" as compared to the aristocracy, but those with an occupation and often from skilled occupations.

College administrators and other authorities often write off demonstrators as being ne'er-do-wells. The participants in student demonstrations are very likely to be some of the outstanding students.[33] It is not the uneducated, uninformed Negro who organizes or participates in demonstrations. Nor are those who organize a crowd for throwing bricks at the home of Negroes who have just moved into a previously all-white suburb, the riff-raff. Nor are the organizers of a lynching mob the down-and-outers. Those of the very lowest prestige do not command sufficient respect to organize others; nor do they usually have the skill and know-how to organize others.

An accepted axiom of human behavior is that dissatisfaction is an essential ingredient of any collective endeavor to strike out against established social institutions. There is a large body of evidence that level of satisfaction is directly associated with position in the prestige hierarchy and with privileges and rights.[34] From this it would follow that those with the fewest rights and least prestige would be most likely to participate in crowd behavior.

The paradox can be explained by taking cognizance of the fact that crowd behavior is an instance of coordinated social behavior. Those of the lowest status are the ones least likely to have stable role relationships with a number of others similar to themselves. Middle and upper-class people are much more likely to have stable relationships with others similar to themselves than the unemployed are with others who are unemployed. The lack of consistent and widespread stable associations with others similar to themselves prevents the lowest categories from developing consensus on the cause of dissatisfaction, on the solution to the situation, and on plans for coordinated action. A low status does not carry with it any features that make its occupants more satisfied with the established order. The crucial factor in explaining their lack of action is the absence of an opportunity to coordinate their behavior. Kerr and Siegel found those workers in industries where there is ample opportunity to interact with fellow workers have a higher rate of striking than do those who are isolated from each other.[35] Miners have one of the highest rates whereas farm laborers have the lowest rate. The failure of those of the very lowest status to participate in crowds cannot be accounted for by a lower level of dissatisfaction among those of very low status but by the lack of an opportunity to coordinate their behavior.

---

[32] George Rudé, *Crowd in History,* p. 204.

[33] Robert H. Somers, "The Mainsprings of the Rebellion: A Survey of Berkeley Students in November, 1964," in Seymour M. Lipset and Sheldon S. Wolin, eds., *The Berkeley Student Revolt* (New York: Doubleday, 1965), p. 544.

[34] Alex Inkeles, "Industrial Man: The Relation of Status to Experience, Perception, and Value," *American Journal of Sociology* 66 (July 1960): 1–31.

[35] Clark Kerr and Abraham Siegel, "The Interindustry Propensity to Strike—an International Comparison," in Arthur Kornhauser et al., *Industrial Conflict* (New York: McGraw-Hill, 1954), p. 190.

The formation of crowds composed largely of middle-class members—e.g., suburban home owners demonstrating against the purchase of a home by a Negro—is similar to that of other crowds. Such crowds also are opposing the policies formulated by authorities. They are a reaction to members of subordinate categories gaining access to the authority structure.

Spontaneity

Many commentators have assumed that crowds develop when a number of unconnected individuals suddenly and simultaneously strike out against some grievous condition or imagined wrong.[36] The formation of crowds and other protesting collectivities depends upon a plurality having common dissatisfying experiences. To share these common dissatisfactions and formulate a line of action, those with common dissatisfactions must engage in some planning.

In most cases, the crowd will act against those in authority and hide as much of the planning from authorities as possible. The first knowledge authorities and other outsiders have of the event is when the crowd is formed. They assume that as they were not aware of any prior activity, none had occurred.

Some observers have noted the presence of interaction among participants prior to the formation of a crowd, usually under the rubric of rumor. Allport and Postman state, "No riot ever occurs without rumors to incite, accompany and intensify the violence." [37] Certainly not all prior interaction (rumors) incite or intensify violence. Some of it is planning for the purpose of preventing or minimizing violence. The organizer who goes from person to person prior to the formation of the crowd pleading for no violence and instructing members on how to behave when the crowd is formed is not unknown. The advocating of violence by crowd participants is not unknown, but this does not distinguish them from generals of the army, governors or other authorities.

Nor does the planning of the crowd activity distinguish most crowds from institutionalized social systems. Prior to any act on the part of a large social system some members of the system plan the activities of others, e.g., school administrators planning a new building program, or a police department organizing a new push on delinquency, plan before the system acts. The crowd is distinctive in this dimension only by the fact that those planning the affair are not expected by tradition to plan the activities of collectivities.

In one account provided by Raper, an effort was made on three continuous nights to round up enough people to conduct a lynching, certainly evidence the crowd did not spring up without prior planning.[38] Rudé offers considerable in-

[36] Herbert Blumer, *New Outline,* p. 180. This proposition is implicitly accepted by those who advance a "convergence theory" interpretation of collective behavior. See Turner, "Collective Behavior," for a critique of this approach.

[37] Gordon W. Allport and Leo Postman, *The Psychology of Rumor* (New York: Henry Holt, 1947), p. 191.

[38] Arthur F. Raper, *The Tragedy of Lynching* (Chapel Hill: University of North Carolina, 1933), p. 226.

direct evidence that most crowds are preceded by extensive planning ahead of the actual formation of the crowd.[39] Quite in contrast to the idea of spontaneous formation, there is probably more time spent in the planning of crowd action than in the planning for action by more established social units of comparable size.

Creativeness

In contrast to the idea that crowds operate on a primitive intellectual level, others have developed the proposition that crowds are creative. The crowd is not a particularly inventive social system. A crowd does involve people relating themselves to each other in a fashion different from that of routine relationships. However, the ideas used to organize their behavior are seldom developed (invented) during the interaction within the crowd. The plans of action used to organize their behavior nearly always have a history that predates the formation of the crowd. The peasants' hatred and their plans to burn the manor were current long before the formation of the crowd. The desire for the opportunity to vote and the idea of confrontation of the white authority were current among many Negroes, and a topic of discussion, long before the crowds were formed.

The crowd is not more emergent than other forms of interaction. It involves a number of people organizing themselves to participate in non-traditional behavior. But many of the ideas used to organize their behavior are developed outside the crowd situation. The ideas of equality and liberty were current long before any crowd was formed to force their implementation.

Most innovations are developed in social situations that are vastly different from a crowd. The formation of new ideas results from people being reflective. Members of a crowd are not highly reflective. They have a narrow focus of attention. They do not stand back and wonder about how something can be done in a different fashion than ever done before. This activity most commonly occurs in small groups or by persons in relative isolation. Neither the ideas germane to democracy nor knowledge of how to produce more food nor any similar set of ideas were formulated within the context of a crowd.

Joint action by members of a crowd often forces the adoption of new norms but is seldom the original formulator of new norms.

Lack of Self-Control

Because people in a crowd behave differently within an acting crowd than in other situations is no reason to assume a loss of self-control.[40] The crowd partici-

[39] Rudé, *Crowd in History.*

[40] Blumer, *New Outline,* p. 180, "Such an individual (typical member of a crowd) loses ordinary critical understanding and self-control as he enters into rapport with other crowd members and becomes infused by the collective excitement which dominates them." Lang and Lang, *Dynamics,* p. 143, take an ambivalent position, "The extent to which individuals actually lose a clear awareness of what they are doing cannot be determined with any degree of finality."

pant often behaves without the concern for others that he normally takes into account in organizing his behavior. When the disenchanted worker hurls obscene words at management in a crowd, this is hardly evidence of lack of self-control. It is evidence that he is organizing his behavior by incorporating management into his acts in a different fashion than usual. Within the prior social system the worker incorporated the wishes and directions of management into his action. In the acting crowd, he is not organizing his behavior by incorporating the desires of management into his action.

Instead of a lack of self-control, it would be more accurate to characterize crowds as exhibiting a lack of control by others, particularly others who are in control within the institutional situations. "Normal social control is effective largely because the individual is known and identified and held responsible for his actions." [41] A crowd is formed to modify this condition.

Anti-Social Behavior

Nearly all discussions of the crowd assume that the members of a crowd become dehumanized—more specifically that they are anti-social. Quite the contrary is the case. The acting crowd is an instance of social conduct. The human organism becomes and remains a human being by engaging in a joint coordinated endeavor with other humans, by taking the role of others, or by a fusion of self and others. The social act requires that a plural of humans integrate or incorporate within their activity the acts of others; i.e., social behavior is behavior that incorporates the activity of others. Clearly, some members of a crowd identify with each other and they incorporate the acts of other members into their own activity.

In only a very limited sense is the behavior of the acting crowd anti- or nonsocial. As members of an institutionalized social system, humans incorporate into their acts the acts of the authorities of the system; a driver of an automobile incorporates the anticipated acts of the highway patrolman and other drivers into his own behavior; the student incorporates the anticipated acts of the school principal, teachers, and other students; and the "good" Southern Negro incorporates the on-going and anticipated acts of the white men. What members of the crowd do not do that has resulted in crowd activity being regarded as anti-social or dehumanized is this: they do not incorporate the norms carried and sanctioned by the authorities into their behavior. The demonstrating Negro takes policemen into account and guides his behavior accordingly, but not in terms of the norms the policeman is attempting to enforce. Such behavior may stamp him as anti-authority, but hardly as anti-social.

Conclusion

Sociologists have emphasized "cultural" factors in their analysis of behavior, and deemphasized the interaction among people. The tendency has been to exam-

[41] Turner, "Collective Behavior," p. 386.

ine how cultural factors influence or direct human behavior at the expense of questions of how cultural elements are created, modified, and adopted in interaction. Consequently, they find it hard to account for behavior that does not follow the "cultural patterns."

Discussions of crowd behavior often observe that cultural factors no longer provide the basis for the observed conduct. In the search for factors to account for crowd behavior many sociologists have employed concepts that suggest an explanation can be formulated by noting the traits and characteristics of the behavior. However, many of the ascriptions of these traits to crowd behavior are not empirically valid. Furthermore, the concepts commonly employed have restricted utility for a sociological analysis of crowds. Instead of directing attention to social processes and social relationships, concepts such as suggestibility, emotionality, and rationality suggest the explanation of crowds is to be made in terms of characteristics of the individual members.

The patterning of behavior by culture is much less marked than current sociological thought implies. Study of societies, particularly complex ones, leads one to conclude that numerous groups and collectivities are continually attempting to change their social structure. This should lead to the conclusion that many members of a society are dissatisfied with certain features of their daily life. These dissatisfactions arise in associations with other humans. Those dissatisfied often attempt to take action to modify the form of the associations that have led to dissatisfaction. In order to accomplish the task it often is necessary to develop new social systems or to modify the old one. The formation of crowds is but one of several lines of activity that may be taken to modify dissatisfying situations.

Crowd behavior is distinctive, but to emphasize the "abnormal" dimensions of crowd behavior appears to be fruitless. A more promising line of attack is one that conceptualizes the acting crowd as a social system that is distinctive in some ways from other social systems. It is a social system human beings adopt to take action with reference to other systems. As such, it is no more and no less pathological or bizarre than other systems they have developed.

36

Processes of Recruitment in the Sit-In Movement

MAURICE PINARD · JEROME KIRK
DONALD von ESCHEN

It is generally assumed that social movements arise in response to some "strain" in the social system. That is, they represent collective action undertaken because some segment of the population is economically deprived, politically oppressed, or otherwise faced with problems in living which result from structural arrangements. A further assumption often made is that there is a direct relationship between the amount of "strain" experienced by individuals and their tendency to participate in social movements.

As Pinard, Kirk, and von Eschen point out in the following selection, participation in social movements can involve at least two distinct sorts of behavior. First, participation may refer to how active a person is in a movement. On the other hand, participation may refer to the act of joining a movement.

Where the amount of activity is involved, Pinard et al. argue that it makes sense to predict that people experiencing greater strain will be more active once they have joined a movement. However, they argue further that the relationship between strain and initial recruitment is not quite so simple. They hypothesize that in the incipient stages of a movement recruitment of the most deprived people will be relatively unlikely. It is only after a movement has gained some initial successes and has effectively disseminated a radical ideology that a significant proportion of recruits will come from the ranks of the most deprived.

The data which Pinard et al. use to test these hypotheses come from a survey done during the early years of the civil rights movement when sit-ins and "freedom rides" were still novel strategies.

Maurice Pinard, Jerome Kirk, and Donald von Eschen, "Processes of Recruitment in the Sit-In Movement," *Public Opinion Quarterly* 33 (1969): 355–69.

The purpose of this paper is to examine the role of strain in the growth of social movements. Though it is generally taken for granted that behind any episode of collective behavior lie some form of strains, little is known about the processes through which these strains affect the recruitment of people into a social movement.

Strains and Social Movement Participation

Since the argument of this paper contains some paradoxes, let us present it briefly at the beginning. Our central argument is that contrary to frequent assumptions, one should not necessarily expect a monotonically positive relationship between strains [1] and the various modalities of participation in a social movement. Students in this field have usually failed to make appropriate distinctions between these modalities. As will be seen below, it seems important to distinguish between *recruitment to* (or *attraction to*) a social movement, and *intensity of activity* in that social movement once it has been joined. On the basis of these distinctions, the following propositions are offered.

On the one hand, we hypothesize a positive relationship between amount of strain and *intensity of activity* in a social movement. Most of the literature on collective behavior—though, as noted, it fails to make the distinction we are introducing—is consonant with the suggestion that the most deprived will always tend to be the most active participants in a social movement, once they have joined it. The only directly relevant finding, however, is reported by Lipset, who found that poor farmers, once aroused, became stronger supporters of the socialist C.C.F. party than well-to-do farmers.[2]

On the other hand, as we have suggested elsewhere,[3] only certain types of strain bear a direct linear relationship to *attraction* to a social movement. The most important strains of this type probably consist of *changes* for the worse in one's condition. But long-endured strains, which are relatively *stable* and *permanent*—poverty being probably the best example—present a handicap for the early recruitment of participants. The most deprived, in this latter sense, are *not* generally the early recruits of social movements. For instance, one's probability of joining a social movement may increase when, during a recession, one's economic hardships keep piling up, but this probability does not generally increase

[1] The concept of strain is borrowed from Smelser, who devotes a full chapter to its elaboration in his *Theory of Collective Behavior* (New York: Free Press, 1963), ch. 3. We use this concept as the most satisfactory generic term to refer to any impairment in people's life conditions. Though in Smelser's typology, the concept of deprivation refers to only one subtype of strains—in particular the loss of social rewards (wealth, power, prestige, esteem)—the two concepts of strain and deprivation are used here interchangeably, since most of our indicators of strain are of this latter type.

[2] S. M. Lipset, *Agrarian Socialism* (Berkeley and Los Angeles: University of California Press, 1950), p. 167.

[3] Maurice Pinard, *The Rise of a Third Party: The Social Credit Party in Quebec in the 1962 Federal Election* (Englewood Cliffs: Prentice-Hall, 1971; and Pinard, "Poverty and Political Movements," *Social Problems* 15 (Fall 1967): 250–63.

with one's degree of (stable) poverty. Again, most of the literature on the effects of social unrest, deprivation, frustration, etc. is consistent with the idea that *increasing* deprivations are directly related to recruitment to a social movement: the appearance of social movements is indeed generally explained by such conditions of strain, and one could cite an endless list of movements following, for instance, economic or political reverses. We shall not in fact try to test this last proposition again here.[4] At the same time, many observers have noted that the poor—the permanently deprived—do not spur revolts; the reader is referred to a summary of the literature and to empirical data presented elsewhere.[5] Rarely, however, have these various propositions been brought together, and hard data presented to test them within the context of the same movement.

Moreover, we know little about the mechanisms that initially inhibit the recruitment of those permanently deprived. It is suggested here that such steady strains render unlikely the presence of the sophisticated "generalized beliefs" that are essential for translating grievances into political action. Only at later stages, when these beliefs have developed because of the early successes of the movement, do the most deprived become candidates for recruitment.[6]

These hypotheses can be tested with data collected from participants in a sit-in demonstration. On December 16, 1961, some 500 to 600 members of CORE and other civil rights organizations staged a demonstration at eating places along U. S. Route 40 between Baltimore and Wilmington. We distributed questionnaires to the participants at the Baltimore central meeting place, and the questionnaires were filled out by 386 of them (i.e. by about 60 to 80 percent of the demonstrators).[7]

Strains and Activity in the Movement

Participation in a social movement is generally first a response to strains that the movement tries to correct. In this sense, racial strains must certainly have

[4] See, for instance, Smelser, *Collective Behavior,* pp. 267 ff.; Maurice Pinard, *The Rise of a Third Party,* ch. 6.

[5] Pinard, "Poverty and Political Movements," pp. 250–56.

[6] This is akin to Lipset's idea that because of "the lack of a rich, complex frame of reference," low-status people will always choose the least complex form of politics. Wherever the Communist party is small, he observed, it tends to be supported by the better-off segments of the working class, while where it is strong, as in France and Italy, for instance, the contrary is true; see his *Political Man* (Garden City: Doubleday, 1960), pp. 122 ff.

[7] For a brief history of the sit-ins and freedom rides in the United States, see Donald R. Matthews and James W. Prothro, *Negroes and the New Southern Politics* (New York: Harcourt, 1966), pp. 407 ff. The authors date the beginning of the sit-ins to February 1960, in Greensboro, North Carolina, though they report other sporadic instances in 1958 and 1959. In Maryland, the first activities of the sit-in movement take place in early 1960. The "Route 40 Freedom Ride," at which we distributed our questionnaires, was organized after African diplomats complained that they were refused service at eating places along the main artery from Washington to New York. The reason some participants did not fill out the questionnaire is that they either did not arrive at the Baltimore terminal or, more often, were organized in groups leaving for a demonstration before they could complete it. While the sample is not random, so that confidence or significance methods cannot be applied, we have been unable to discern any source of systematic non-response bias and we feel satisfied that these data present an undistorted picture of the group.

been an important determinant of activity in the sit-in movement.[8] But participation can also be a response to strains less clearly related to the goals of that movement; for example, it may represent a partial displacement of protest against targets more easily accessible than those which are the immediate source of one's tensions.[9]

In this instance, racial strains were not the only ones to find their expression among participants; socioeconomic deprivations were also involved.[10] If we take as our indicator of participation in the movement the amount of *activity* the participants engaged in since joining the movement, we find that the lower one's socioeconomic status (the higher one's deprivation), the more active one has been in the movement (Table 1, first panel); notice moreover that this is true for both Negro and white participants independently.[11]

Similarly, an experience of downward intergenerational occupational mobility can obviously be taken as an indicator of at least status, if not economic, deprivation. Again the data indicate that among non-students, both Negro and white participants who had experienced downward mobility had been more active than the others (Table 1, second panel). Finally, since it has been argued that status inconsistency is a source of stress,[12] we should find the same type of relationship with this indicator. This is once more borne out by the data (Table 1, third

---

[8] Though Matthews and Prothro do not carry out a separate analysis of recruitment to and activity in the sit-in movement, their data clearly indicate that dissatisfaction with race relations was monotonically related to participation in the sit-in movement; see ibid., pp. 419–24.

[9] According to Smelser (*Collective Behavior,* pp. 48–49), "any kind of strain may be a determinant of any kind of collective behavior," and the same kinds of strain lay behind a vast array of religious and political movements. See also, from a psychological perspective, John Dollard et al., *Frustration and Aggression* (New Haven: Yale University Press, 1939); Neal E. Miller, "The Frustration-Aggression Hypothesis," in M. H. Marx, *Psychological Theory* (New York: Macmillan, 1951).

[10] Most studies have indicated that lower-status people tend to have more complaints about their conditions, to be more dissatisfied, and to be less happy than others. See for instance Geneviève Knupfer, "Portrait of the Underdog," in R. Bendix and S. M. Lipset, eds., *Class, Status, and Power* (New York: Free Press, 1953), pp. 255–63; Alex Inkeles, "Industrial Man: The Relation of Status to Experience, Perception, and Value," *American Journal of Sociology* 66 (1960): 1–31; Norman M. Bradburn and David Caplovitz, *Reports on Happiness: A Pilot Study of Behavior Related to Mental Health* (Chicago: Aldine, 1965), ch. 2. One study which is partly in exception is that of W. G. Runciman, *Relative Deprivation and Social Justice* (Berkeley and Los Angeles: University of California Press, 1966), ch. 10. This study, moreover, along with others cited in Hyman and Singer, indicates that low socioeconomic status is not necessarily accompanied by perceived deprivation unless certain kinds of comparisons are made. See Herbert H. Hyman and Eleanor Singer, eds., *Readings in Reference Group Theory and Research* (New York: Free Press, 1968), pp. 166–221.

[11] In the case of white participants, the relationship suggests the "displacement" hypothesis, if we assume that segregation does not account for the strains they suffered. A slightly different interpretation of these relations is that feelings of unjust treatment lead one to help others in similar conditions and/or to desire to change a system in which one has no vested interests.

[12] See, for instance, Gerhard E. Lenski, *Power and Privilege* (New York: McGraw-Hill, 1966), pp. 86–88. Lenski suggests that status inconsistency can lead people to support liberal and radical movements.

TABLE 1

THE MOST DEPRIVED WERE THE MOST ACTIVE PARTICIPANTS

	PERCENT MORE ACTIVE [a]					
	Negroes		*Whites*		*Both*	
Status measures	*Percent*	*N*	*Percent*	*N*	*Percent*	*N*
Socioeconomic Status[b] (all R's)						
High	32	(28)	49	(76)	44	(104)
Medium	44	(63)	59	(108)	54	(171)
Low	67	(27)	83	(18)	73	(45)
Social Mobility[c] (non-students only)						
Upward	42	(12)	61	(23)	54	(35)
Stable	46	(11)	67	(12)	56	(23)
Downward	100	(2)	80	(15)	82	(17)
Status Consistency[d] (non-students only)						
Consistent	35	(23)	64	(14)	46	(37)
Inconsistent I	88	(8)	64	(25)	70	(33)
Inconsistent II	67	(12)	100	(15)	85	(27)

[a] Percent who reported having been out on demonstrations 3 times or more, in answer to the question: "How many times have you been out on demonstrations before today?"

[b] Socioeconomic status: determined by North-Hatt scores for occupations given in response to the question: "What job are you training for in school?" (students), or "What is your job?" (non-students). A high status corresponds to a score of 85 or above; a low status, to a score of 71 or below. (Notice that many low-status participants had at most a lower-middle-class occupational level, i.e. below, approximately, the status of an undertaker, a grade school teacher, or a reporter). The relationships remain the same for Negro students and non-students, and for white students and non-students.

[c] Social mobility: comparison, for non-students, of their socioeconomic score with that of their father ("What is your father's main occupation?"). The scores were broken into four classes (less than 72; 72–74; 75–84; 85 or more).

[d] Status consistency: based on a comparison of socioeconomic scores (see above) and educational levels. The educational levels used were: high—finished college or more; medium—some college; low—finished high school or less. The "inconsistent I" group comprises participants with a combination of high and medium statuses; group II, participants with medium-low or high-low status combinations.

panel). Those whose status was inconsistent were generally more active than those enjoying a consistent status.[13] Other data from the study (not presented here) also reveal that those whose income was lower than that of their friends, or who expected a discrepancy between their occupational expectations and their aspira-

[13] We are aware of the problems involved in measuring the effects of status inconsistency; see, for instance, the papers by Martin D. Hyman, "Determining the Effects of Status Inconsistency," *Public Opinion Quarterly* 30 (1966): 120–29, and H. M. Blalock, "Comment: Status Inconsistency and the Identification Problem," Ibid., pp. 130–32. But even if we hold constant status to obviate these difficulties, our results remain: among the consistent subgroup, 44, 50, and 44 percent of the high, medium, and low status participants were more active ($N = 16$, 12, and 9 respectively); this is much lower than the 70 and 85 percent of the two inconsistent subgroups (see Table 1; they are differentiated on the basis of their status components).

tions (the latter being higher), or who were unhappy in their jobs tended to be more active participants than the others. In short, the data so far convincingly demonstrate the existence of a direct linear relationship between *strains* and *intensity of activity* in the sit-in demonstrations.

Yet, and this is paradoxical, though deprivations led to active participation, the movement we studied was still a predominantly white and upper-middle-class movement. As indicated above, the denial to American Negroes of so many of the privileges enjoyed by whites should be a significant source of strain prompting Negroes to participate in this movement. And indeed, while Negroes formed only 8.6 percent of the population in the census regions from which the participants were recruited (New England, Middle Atlantic, East North Central, and South Atlantic), they constituted 36.4 percent of our sample, that is, a proportion more than four times what one would have expected on the basis of chance alone. Nevertheless, one may still wonder why this overrepresentation was not much larger, indeed why Negroes were not at least a majority in a movement devoted to the redress of Negro grievances.

Similarly, few of the movement's recruits came from the most deprived segments of the population. Although we found in Table 1 that those of a *relatively* [14] lower socioeconomic status were more active, it is nevertheless true that few participants were from the working classes proper. If we shift for a moment from a measure of relative position on the North-Hatt status scale to the more traditional census categories, we find that the vast majority of the participants (89 percent; $N = 311$) were either training for, or engaged in, jobs which are usually conesidered to be of an upper-middle-class status, that is, professionals or managerial jobs; only a very small minority (4 percent) were workers. The high proportion coming from the upper middle-class held pretty well in all subgroups of the sample: the corresponding figures were, for Negro non-students, 60 percent, for Negro students, 92 percent, for white non-students, 81 percent, and for white students, 100 percent. At the other extreme, the proportions from the working classes (skilled workers and below) in each of these four groups were respectively, 21, 2, 2, and 0 percent ($N = 43$, 75, 62, and 131). In short, while deprivations led to active involvement, Negroes were still a minority in the movement, and the most deprived Negro and white strata of the population were strongly underrepresented. How can we account for these apparently contradictory observations?

Strains and Attraction to the Movement

To answer this question, we must turn to the role of relatively permanent strains as a determinant of attraction to an incipient movement. If our argument about the role of this type of strain is correct, it should show up in the data. When

---

[14] Notice that with the North-Hatt measure used before, we classified as of low socioeconomic status people who were from the lower-middleclass or below, see note to Table 1.

considering as the dependent variable the *length of participation* in the movement, rather than the amount of activity engaged in since joining it, we should observe that those suffering from relatively stable deprivations, though the most active, were not the early recruits of the movement.

The reader should note first that the three indicators of deprivation we have used so far are all indicators of relatively stable, permanent deprivations: people's position in terms of socioeconomic status, or intergenerational mobility, or status consistency does not generally represent a sudden change in their share of society's rewards. If we turn again to these independent variables, we find first, assuming similar patterns of attrition,[15] that those of a relatively lower socioeconomic status tended to have been relatively late joiners, even though we found them to have been *the most active of all*. This is true for the sample as a whole, as well as for Negro students and non-students, and white non-students (Table 2A). Similarly, among non-students, those who had been downwardly mobile, or whose status was inconsistent (with some low components—group II), albeit the most active participants, as seen in Table 1, are now found to have been the latest joiners of the movement (Table 2B). And, though the number of cases becomes very small, the over-all pattern seems to hold for Negroes and whites separately. Thus, while those most deprived were the most active participants, *once they had joined*, they were nevertheless relatively late joiners.

TABLE 2A

THE MOST DEPRIVED, IN TERMS OF SOCIOECONOMIC STATUS, WERE AMONG THE LATEST RECRUITS

(Percent Early Joiners.[a])

	SOCIOECONOMIC STATUS[b]					
	High		*Medium*		*Low*	
	Percent	*N*	*Percent*	*N*	*Percent*	*N*
Negro Non-students	43	(7)	44	(18)	18	(17)
Negro Students	35	(20)	40	(42)	30	(10)
White Non-students	40	(5)	42	(40)	33	(18)
White Students	22	(65)	26	(61)	—	(0)
Total Sample	27	(97)	36	(161)	27	(45)

[a] Percent who joined the movement one year or more ago.
[b] Socioeconomic status: as in Table 1.

In short, while the relationship between steady deprivation and activity is positive and linear, the relationship between these deprivations and length of participation is curvilinear: the early joiners of this incipient movement tended to be people who were only moderately deprived. Neither the least deprived nor the

[15] A different, and more costly, kind of data would yield a more definitive demonstration of this point. In the absence of longitudinal data, it is impossible to discriminate conclusively between the effects of differential recruitment and the artifact of differential retention.

TABLE 2B

THE MOST DEPRIVED, IN TERMS OF SOCIAL MOBILITY AND STATUS CONSISTENCY, WERE AMONG THE LATEST RECRUITS

	PERCENT EARLY JOINERS [a]					
	Negroes		*Whites*		*Both*	
Status measures	*Percent*	*N*	*Percent*	*N*	*Percent*	*N*
Social Mobility[b] (non-students only)						
Upward	25	(12)	41	(22)	35	(34)
Stable	50	(10)	33	(12)	41	(22)
Downward	0	(2)	29	(14)	25	(16)
Status Consistency[b] (non-students only)						
Consistent	39	(21)	36	(14)	37	(35)
Inconsistent I	62	(8)	44	(25)	48	(33)
Inconsistent II	8	(12)	40	(15)	26	(27)

[a] As in Table 2A.
[b] As in Table 1.

most deprived tended to be early recruits.[16] Among the first, the presence of strains as a condition was lacking—and notice that they were not very active, once they had joined; among the second, though strains were present, something else was lacking: the ability to translate their grievances in political terms.

This process in part accounts for the fact that Negroes were a minority even in "their" movement and for the fact that the movement was so clearly a middle-class movement. The recruitment process just described meant that the bulk of the Negro population did not form the recruiting base of the movement, at least in its early stages. Hence, the movement had to rely on the relatively small Negro middle class and on that part of the white middle class which, as we shall see, was largely marginal.

Political Translation of Grievances

But what is it that prevents those affected by permanent deprivations from being the early participants of a new movement? As suggested before, it may be that

[16] Matthews and Prothro also found that Negro students from lower social classes were less likely to participate in the sit-in movement than others. They did not find, however, a lower rate of participation among the higher classes (i.e., their relationships do not appear to be curvilinear); this may be due to the use of less refined categories of status. See *Negroes,* pp. 418–19. It is interesting to note, however, that in their adult Negro sample, they found that the relationship between political participation and satisfaction with the community's race relations was curvilinear: both those who evaluated these relations as of the very best or as of the very worst kind were less likely to participate than those between these extremes; ibid., pp. 288–92.

they do not possess the ability to translate their grievances in political terms; there are presumably many facets to this factor, but we will examine only two.[17]

Ideology. First, to engage in any social movement, one must develop, as suggested before, a "generalized belief" that not only identifies the sources of one's strains but envisages an effective cure through some sort of specific program.[18] A particularly sophisticated generalized belief is necessary to compensate for the inherent weakness of a new movement.[19] The inability of those under permanent strains to develop such a sophisticated belief would be one of the reasons for their slow recruitment in the early phases of a movement.

A radical ideology, as a set of articulated beliefs together with moral commitment to a cause and a deep conviction that historical forces are on one's side, represents such a sophisticated belief. An indication of how important this element was in the early phases of the movement we are studying is afforded by the marginals of the data: only 7 percent of the participants said they would vote Republican in a presidential election, and while 56 percent mentioned the Democrats, no less than 37 percent answered Socialist or Independent (18 and 19 percent respectively; $N = 322$).[20] More strikingly, about 4 out of every 10 participants (42 percent) had political preferences to the *left* of their mother's political preferences ($N = 286$).[21] This hardly compares with the general population.[22]

[17] For other aspects of this factor, see Pinard, "Poverty and Political Movements," pp. 256–62.

[18] Smelser, *Collective Behavior,* ch. 5.

[19] Moreover, the more complex the forms of participation—demonstrating is more complex than voting—the stronger and the more sophisticated the belief must be. This certainly accounts in part for the fact that the early voters of new political movements often have a lower status than the early supporters of this movement, though in both cases the most deprived are not the early joiners; compare with the data presented in Pinard, "Poverty and Political Movements."

[20] The question asked was: "If you were to register in the presidential election, how would you vote?" (This was followed by "How would your parents [father, mother] vote," the data from which are used below.) The independent subgroup (61) includes 18 "others." In the present data, Independent empirically fits best not between Democrat and Republican, but between Socialist and Democrat, since people placing themselves in this category considered both major parties too conservative. It may be necessary to point out that when we refer to Socialists as ideologues, we do not mean totalitarian revolutionary socialists. Those who called themselves "socialists" were libertarian in their beliefs.

[21] Among the 42 percent classified as "left of mother," about half (20 percent) were Socialists (including five cases of Socialist sons of Socialist mothers); the others were either Independents (13 percent) or Democrats (9 percent) ($N = 286$). We assume here that any adopted preference to the left of one's parents' party preference is indicative of at least a moderately radical ideology, and that the Socialist sons of Socialist mothers similarly fit our nominal concept of "ideologue." And indeed we find that among those classified as left of mother, 39 percent of the Socialists and 34 percent of the others were early joiners, while the comparable proportion is 28 percent among those who were not to the left of their mother ($N = 56$, 65, and 165 respectively).

[22] The party identification of most people resembles that of their parents and, it seems, primarily that of their mother; see, for instance, Robert E. Lane and David O. Sears, *Public Opinion* (Englewood Cliffs: Prentice-Hall, 1964), pp. 20–21; Eleanor E. Maccoby, Richard E. Matthews, and Alton S. Morton, "Youth and Political Change," in Heinz Eulau, et. al., *Political Behavior* (New York: Free Press, 1956), p. 301. In general, the proportion of

The crucial role of ideology is particularly revealed by the strength of the relationship it bears to activity within the movement. While 26 percent of the Republicans and 47 percent of the Democrats had been among the more active participants, 62 percent of the Independents and 76 percent of the Socialists had been so ($N = 23$, 180, 60, and 59 respectively). Moreover, the data indicate that in the early phases of the movement at least, ideology was not just an intervening psychological process between deprivations and participation, since it exerted a strong effect of its own, as shown in Table 3. Indeed, ideology is almost as strong a predictor of activity as deprivation.[23]

TABLE 3

IDEOLOGY AND DEPRIVATIONS ARE INDEPENDENTLY RELATED TO ACTIVITY

	PERCENT MORE ACTIVE[a]					
	Democratic or Republican		*Independent*		*Socialist*	
Socioeconomic status	*Percent*	*N*	*Percent*	*N*	*Percent*	*N*
High	42	(55)	33	(12)	69	(16)
Medium	45	(91)	67	(33)	80	(25)
Low	67	(27)	86	(7)	100	(5)

[a] As in Table I. *N*s are reduced because of nonresponse.

That the lack of a sophisticated generalized belief was one of the factors preventing the most deprived from being early joiners is indicated in Table 4. When ideology is introduced as a control variable in the relationship between socioeconomic status and length of participation, the data suggest that, when *low-status participants were also ideologues,* far from being late joiners, *they tended to be the earliest joiners.*

Political alienation. Apart from a radical ideology, which represents the positive side of a strong generalized belief, there is a closely related cluster of factors, such as resignation, withdrawal, hopelessness, and retreatist alienation, which belongs to the negative side of the belief—the loss of faith in present arrangements and the potentialities of action. These could also help to account for the

young voters shifting their party preference seems to be about one out of four, and the proportion of them shifting left, less than 15 percent. This is suggested on the basis of data recomputed from Bernard R. Berelson, Paul F. Lazarsfeld, and William N. McPhee, *Voting* (Chicago: University of Chicago Press, 1954), pp. 88–89; also Herbert H. Hyman, *Political Socialization* (New York: Free Press, 1959), pp. 74 ff., and the other two sources cited above.

[23] The average effect of socioeconomic status (i.e., the average percentage difference) is .36, while the average effect of party preferences (ideology) is .27. [This follows James A. Coleman, *Introduction to Mathematical Sociology* (New York: Free Press, 1964), ch. 6.] These findings contrast with those reported by Surace and Seeman, who found ideology, as measured by a version of McClosky's liberal-conservative scale, to be "a weak interpreter of personal engagement in the civil rights movement." See Samuel J. Surace and M. Seeman, "Some Correlates of Civil Rights Activism," *Social Forces* 46 (1967): 204.

TABLE 4

IDEOLOGY PERMITS A LOWER-STATUS PERSON TO JOIN EARLY

	PERCENT EARLY JOINERS[a]			
	Left of mother[b] *(ideologues)*		*Not left of mother (non-ideologues)*	
Socioeconomic status	*Percent*	N	*Percent*	N
High	29	(28)	29	(49)
Medium	38	(61)	34	(71)
Low	43	(14)	18	(22)

[a] As in Table 2A. *N*s are reduced because of nonresponse.

[b] Based on a comparison of respondent's and his mother's party preference; see footnote 21.

early resistance of the most deprived to the appeals of a new movement; such attitudes would grow out of long-endured deprivations and would lead to a wait-and-see attitude until the new movement has proved itself. One measure of such feelings of hopelessness is political alienation, the belief that routine political action can yield no results. That political alienation is more common among low-status people is revealed both by our data and by many other studies.

Alienation did not seem to bear any clear-cut set of relationships to participation as measured by either of our two indicators.[24] But this is partly because strains are not the only source of alienation. A radical ideology, as a fully developed generalized belief, can itself be an important factor leading one to lose faith in present political arrangements. Indeed, ideology and deprivation seem to be alternative sources of political alienation (Table 5). But while alienation rooted in deprivation leads to retreatism,[25] one might expect that alienation rooted in

TABLE 5

THE TWO SOURCES OF POLITICAL ALIENATION

	PERCENT POLITICALLY ALIENATED[a]			
	Left of mother (ideologues)		*Not left of mother (non-ideologues)*	
Socioeconomic status	*Percent*	N	*Percent*	N
High	78	(25)	45	(47)
Medium	56	(59)	52	(66)
Low	64	(14)	77	(17)

[a] Percent agreeing with the statement: "Most politicans are corrupt." *N*s are reduced because of nonresponse.

[24] Surace and Seeman also report no zero-order relationship between generalized powerlessness and civil rights activism; see "Correlates," pp. 204–05.

[25] See, for instance, the literature cited in William Erbe, "Social Involvement and Political Activity: A Replication and Elaboration," *American Sociological Review* 29 (1964): 198–215. Erbe reports, however, that there is doubt whether alienation exerts any effect independently of socioeconomic status and organizational involvement.

ideology will produce rebellious tendencies,[26] for in this case it is associated with a belief that radical political action can yield results.

That these two variants of alienation can be identified and that they lead to opposite responses is suggested by the results presented in Table 6. Though we use only a one-item indicator of political alienation and though the number of cases is very small in some cells, it seems that among non-ideologues, alienation *prevents* one from being an early joiner, while, on the contrary, among ideologues, alienation *increases* one's probability of being an early joiner.[27]

TABLE 6
THE OPPOSITE RESPONSES PRODUCED BY TWO VARIANTS OF ALIENATION

	PERCENT EARLY JOINERS[a]							
	IDEOLOGUES				NON-IDEOLOGUES			
Socioeconomic	*Alienated*		*Not alienated*		*Alienated*		*Not alienated*	
status	*Percent*	*N*	*Percent*	*N*	*Percent*	*N*	*Percent*	*N*
Total Sample	39	(71)	30	(43)	28	(79)	30	(70)
High	28	(18)	29	(7)	20	(20)	31	(26)
Medium	39	(33)	32	(25)	31	(32)	36	(31)
Low	44	(9)	40	(5)	15	(13)	33	(6)

[a] As in Table 2A. *N*s are reduced because of nonresponse.

It is important to notice, moreover, that among ideologues, whether alienated or not, the previous curvilinear relationship between deprivation (social status) and length of participation disappears again, as in Table 5. Alienation, when rooted in ideology, is neither a restraining factor in general, nor among the low-status group in particular. On the other hand, among non-ideologues, the curvilinear relationship becomes particularly strong for the alienated subgroup, while it almost disappears for their nonalienated counterparts. Retreatist alienation, therefore, seems really part of the cluster of factors that retard the low-status group in its participation.[28] Obviously, the small number of cases in many cells of Table 6 prevents us from holding the findings above as firm conclusions, but we think they are suggestive enough to warrant consideration.

Summary and Implications

Our analysis revealed that various forms of strain, whether directly related to the civil rights movement or not, accounted in part for the degree of activity of mem-

[26] Erbe has called attention to these two variants of alienation, without, however, indicating their respective sources. See ibid., p. 206.

[27] Here, an almost identical set of relationships emerges when activity in the movement rather than length of participation is considered. All these factors—low status, ideology, and rebellious alienation—explain no less than 56 percent of the variation in activity.

[28] This strongly challenges the claims of mass society theorists that the isolated and the alienated are the prime recruits of mass movements. For other qualifications of this theory, see Maurice Pinard, "Mass Society and Political Movements: A New Formulation," *American Journal of Sociology* 73 (1968): 682–90; also Pinard, *The Rise of a Third Party*, chs. 10–12.

bers already recruited into the movement. Yet we found that Negroes were not even a majority in the movement we studied, and that the most deprived segments of the population were practically absent from its ranks. The key to these paradoxes seems to be that those most deprived, though having greater motives to participate and being in fact the most active, once involved, tend to be late joiners.

A complex of factors probably accounts for this inability of the steadily deprived to translate their grievances into political terms. We have suggested that the lack of a sophisticated generalized belief, indexed here by a radical ideology, and alienation, more specifically alienation rooted in deprivations, were two of the factors involved. The possession of a radical ideology, in particular, was shown to be a crucial factor in the early phases of the movement, a factor almost as important as deprivation. Moreover, ideology wiped out the negative portion of the relationship between early joining and social status, while retreatist alienation reinforced it. The lack of a sophisticated belief and the presence of retreatist alienation therefore both contributed to the processes uncovered here.

These findings have important implications, both for understanding the failure of the civil rights movement of the early 1960s to exhibit a strong Negro working-class base, and for the strategies such movements must use to maximize their numerical strength in the long run.[29]

Some writers have argued that civil rights leaders were tactically incorrect in attacking status rather than welfare goals; that had the movement stressed job and housing opportunities rather than public accommodations and voting, massive recruitment would have resulted. Our data suggest there are serious problems with this argument. If a sense of efficacy is important, not only would the movement have failed to recruit a larger base, it would have precluded the emergence of whatever level of mass mobilization (in the form of riots) now exists. By stressing welfare goals, it would have directed itself to a population which is very difficult to recruit, while failing at the same time to attract middle-class elements, thus missing *both* the moderately and the severely deprived. Furthermore, because welfare goals are harder to obtain—whites resist more in this area and the locus of power is more diffuse—the efforts of the movement would probably have resulted in failure, creating an image of weakness and thus further inhibiting recruitment. The concentration on status goals may thus have been tactically sound. It permitted the movement to give an image of strength, necessary for long-run recruitment.

That the movement was having this impact is suggested, although not proved, by some of our data. Its successes clearly created a feeling of optimism about political action. The participants, interviewed after substantial gains had already been made, indicated that their assessment of the possibilities of action had changed greatly. Fully 79 percent of the Negro participants reported that, since they had joined the movement, their expectations of desegregation had in-

[29] Additional implications of our findings on recruitment are discussed in Donald von Eschen, Jerome Kirk, and Maurice Pinard, "The Conditions of Direct Action in a Democratic Society," *Western Political Quarterly* 22 (1969): 309–25.

creased.[30] That this creation of an image of strength was important in recruiting working-class people is suggested by the successes the movement subsequently had in recruiting working-class participants in demonstrations on Maryland's Eastern Shore.

Thus, it may be functional at times for movements to select as initial targets goals that are only dimly related to the core problems faced by the deprived population, if in this way they develop faith in the movement's power to change things and thus maximize long-run recruitment.

[30] Only 19 percent said their expectations had remained about the same and, more strikingly, only 1 percent said they had decreased ($N = 139$); the changes were smaller among whites: the comparable proportions are, respectively, 57, 40, and 4 percent ($N = 239$).

37

Sociometric Patterns in Hysterical Contagion

ALAN C. KERCKHOFF · KURT W. BACK
NORMAN MILLER

The phenomenon of hypsterical contagion may be approached from a number of perspectives. Plausible explanations of contagion current in social psychology focus on such diverse factors as the personal characteristics of the individuals involved, the degree of "strain" experienced, and the role of "precipitating incidents." The following selection by Kerckhoff, Back, and Miller deals with yet another sort of explanation, one which points up the relevance of social relationships for hysterical contagion.

The authors present three presumably contradictory hypotheses concerning the relevance of sociometric patterns: (1) "that those who are linked together in a network of social relationships should be more likely to be affected, (2) that those who are isolated from others are more likely to be affected, and (3) that a person's position in a network of social relations is irrelevant to hysterical contagion."

Through a thorough and insightful analysis of sociometric data, the authors attempt to show that all three hypotheses can be supported, but at different times during the spread of hysterical symptoms. Their data indicate that isolates are more likely to be affected at the beginning of an "epidemic." Following the initial incidence of relatively few cases, symptoms spread rapidly among people who are integrated in a social network. Finally, as the number of people affected becomes large, a sort of "crowd reaction" occurs where contagion proceeds apparently independent of sociometric channels.

Alan C. Kerckhoff, Kurt W. Back, and Norman Miller, "Sociometric Patterns in Hysterical Contagion," *Sociometry* 28 (1965): 2–15.

We propose to offer an analysis of hysterical contagion in which the basic problem is to define the degree to which there is a sociometric pattern related to the spread of the hysterical symptoms. The central question will be: What relevance does an individual's position in a network of social relations have for predicting whether he will or will not exhibit the hysterical symptoms in question?

To raise this question is not to deny that other factors may *also* be important in a complete analysis of a case of hysterical contagion. Most of the literature on contagion would, in fact, lead one to minimize the importance of lasting social relationships as a significant factor in the spread of hysterical symptoms. More emphasis is given in such literature to a degree of strain experienced by the population in which the symptoms become contagious and to the personal characteristics of the individuals affected. Smelser, for instance, indicates that: "Some form of strain must be present if an episode of collective behavior is to occur," and he includes the spread of hysterical symptoms under the general rubric of collective behavior.[1] Similarly, the Langs note that it is necessary to find "areas of chronic stress which account for the failure of organized expectations to control a situation." [2] Personal characteristics of participants are also seen as important by the Langs. Although acknowledging the importance of the *relationship* between the characteristics of the person and the characteristics of the situation, they note that much of the literature in this area of inquiry points to the differential susceptibility to suggestion and contagion by different kinds of personalities.[3]

Our concern is not to dispute the importance of these situational and personality factors but to raise the further question of the relevance of social relations as channels of transmission of, or hindrance to, the hysterical pattern involved. It is undoubtedly true that, even in the situation we will investigate, these situational and personality factors played an important role. It will not be possible, however, within the limits of this report to take all such variables into account, and our attention will be directed solely to the question of whether or not patterns of social relations are relevant to an understanding of hysterical contagion.

The importance and complexity of this issue are enhanced by the fact that there is little literature that is directly relevant to the problem, and conflicting expectations may be derived from the several bodies of literature that are indirectly relevant. In order to simplify the discussion of these conflicting expectations, we will first describe the particular case of hysterical contagion analyzed in this study, and we will then indicate what basis there would be for each different expectation.

The incident under study occurred in a southern clothing manufacturing plant

---

[1] Neil J. Smelser, *Theory of Collective Behavior* (New York: The Free Press, 1963), p. 48.

[2] Kurt Lang and Gladys Engel Lang, *Collective Dynamics* (New York: Thomas Y. Crowell Company, 1961), p. 16.

[3] Ibid., Chap. 10.

in which raw fibers are spun, dyed, and woven, and the finished cloth is cut, sewn, boxed and shipped to wholesale and retail outlets. Within about one week in the summer of 1962, sixty-two persons suffered what purported to be insect bites, and received some kind of medical attention. Although some of these persons exhibited only very minor symptoms, most of them either fainted or complained of severe pain, nausea or feelings of disorientation. Almost all of the victims were women; almost all were white; almost all worked on the first shift; and the great majority were physically located within one functional area of the plant. A physician and an entomologist from the Communicable Disease Center in Atlanta visited the plant but could find no toxic element capable of causing these symptoms, although they searched for both insects and other possible causes, such as chemical elements in the dyes and the air conditioning system. The only reasonable conclusion seemed to be that this was a phenomenon that was "almost exclusively psychogenic in nature."

Since this was evidently a case of hysterical contagion, and given the fact that it occurred in a situation in which the members of the population had had an opportunity to develop patterns of social relations with each other, our basic question is whether these relations were in any way significant in the spread of the symptoms within the population.[4] There appear to be bases for three different expectations: that those who are linked together in a network of social relations should be more likely to be affected; that those who are outside the network of social relations should be more likely to be affected; and that the pattern of social relations should be irrelevant to the spread of the hysterical symptoms. We will refer to these under the following three headings: "Group Influence," "Social Isolation," and "Crowd Response." The basis for each of the expectations will be considered first, after which we will examine the data in hand in light of these three expectations.

Group Influence. There is a considerable body of literature which can be used to generate the prediction that the contagion should follow channels of interpersonal ties. This prediction undoubtedly has great appeal for sociologists, given the discipline's emphasis on social structure. The many studies of the adoption of innovations, especially those of farming innovations, indicate that social relations among adopters are often found, and that once informal leaders adopt a new

[4] We do not consider here the presumably prior question of why there should have been contagion with respect to insect bite fears at this time and in this place but no such contagion in other times and places. Briefly, our position on this question is that models of hysterical behavior occur frequently in any social situation, but they are generally either ignored or defined as the behavior of a deviant person and thus not worthy of concern. When they are attended to, we would expect that two other conditions are present: (1) There is a state of tension in the situation, and (2) the behavior is relevant to the situation being experienced by others as well as the person providing the model. There is evidence of a state of tension in the plant being studied. The women had worked a great deal of overtime, production pressures were great, the plant was not well-organized, and there was the prospect that a layoff would follow the peak season. Since insects of some kind or other are found in all such plants, the behavior was relevant to the situation in which the women experienced this tension.

practice, it is likely to be adopted by others.[5] Even more closely analogous to the present case is the study by Coleman, Katz and Menzel[6] of the diffusion of the use of a new drug among physicians. In that study it was found that the adoption of the drug followed sociometric channels, and that members of social cliques were likely to adopt the drug at about the same time. There is a body of experimental literature which might also lead to the expectation that sociometric channels would facilitate diffusion. The classical experiments of Sherif and Asch, and the numerous experimental variations and theoretical interpretations of them, all indicate that both perception and behavior can be made to conform to group definitions when the other members of the group define the situation consistently.[7]

There is thus considerable basis for expecting that interpersonal relations will be highly relevant to dissemination of a new pattern of behavior in a population. However, one may well question whether the literature just cited is, in fact, germane to our interests. The studies of the adoption of innovations deal with the spread of a behavior pattern which is positively related to a central value in the population studied. Farmers certainly value abundant crops and high quality produce, and the studies of innovation in farming deal with the adoption of practices which are supposed to serve these ends. The doctors studied by Coleman et al. value effective drugs as aids in their professional duties; and the drug whose adoption was studied was, in fact, an effective drug. On the other hand, it could hardly be argued that the behavior pattern whose spread we are studying was valuable in the same sense. However it was viewed, one must acknowledge that it was dysfunctional in the specific situation in which it was observed. Not only did the hysteria disrupt the operations of the plant and thus lead to losses for the company, it also led to lost work time for the affected persons and thus reduced their income for the period in question, not to mention the emotional costs involved. It may well be that the dissemination of *any* behavior pattern within a population follows the same channels, but the differences in the kinds of behavior studied in the earlier investigations and that found in the present situation makes such an assumption at least questionable.

The experimental studies noted above, although they often deal with bizarre and dysfunctional behavior (such as misperceiving the relative length of two

---

[5] See Herbert F. Lionberger, "Some Characteristics of Farm Operators Sought as Sources of Farm Information in a Missouri Community," *Rural Sociology* 18 (December 1953): 327–38. H. G. Barnett, although offering bases for several possible reactions to the "group influence" expectation, also gives support to this expectation in *Innovation: The Basis of Cultural Change* (New York: McGraw-Hill, 1953), pp. 323ff.

[6] James Coleman, Elihu Katz and Herbert Menzel, "The Diffusion of an Innovation among Physicians," *Sociometry,* 20 (December, 1957): 253–70.

[7] See Solomon E. Asch, "Studies of Independence and Conformity," *Psychological Monographs* 70 (1956): 9; Muzafer Sherif, "A Study of Some Social Factors in Perception," *Archives of Psychology* 27 (July 1935): 187. Also relevant are such discussions as that of Festinger which make the point that when beliefs cannot easily be tested by checking observable evidence, or even through logical processes, we often gain confidence in our beliefs through the knowledge that they are shared by others; cf., Leon Festinger, "Informal Social Communication," *Psychological Review* 57 (September 1950): 271–82.

lines), also provide some reason to doubt the "group influence" expectation in the present situation. These experiments indicate that *if* there is *consistent* behavior on the part of the members of the group, the naive subject will tend to adopt that behavior as his own, even though it might ordinarily be rejected by him. They also indicate that if there is *not* consistent behavior by the group members, the naive subject is much less likely to adopt the unusual behavior. In the plant we studied, the majority of the workers never exhibited the hysterical symptoms. Thus, there were always social reference points for those who might have tended to resist the contagion. Also, since the behavior in question was not only dysfunctional but also rather bizarre, it seems unlikely that we could assume that any social grouping had developed a facilitative "norm" regarding such behavior in advance of the initiation of the contagion. It is much more likely that most people in the plant would have defined the behavior as at least "unusual" and "undesirable." If a facilitative norm functioned at all, it must have evolved during the period of the contagion, and this would certainly take time and would probably have had to occur in the face of some social resistance. Finally, and perhaps most importantly, the relevance of this body of experimental literature might also be questioned because it is based on *ad hoc* groups in which prior social relations had not been formed, whereas the central focus of our inquiry is the importance of such previously established social relations.

Social Isolation. Given the fact that only a minority exhibited the hysterical symptoms, it seems likely that the average worker in the factory would have some significant social contacts with persons who did not exhibit hysterical symptoms and who rejected the seriousness of the threat. This would not be true, however, for the person who was a social isolate. The isolate would not have access to such social reference points. Although isolates might vary in the degree to which they would be personally susceptible to the effects of contagion, as a category they would seem to be more likely to be susceptible than would those who are socially integrated.

The converse of this can also be argued. At least since the work of McDougall, it has been noted that the structure of groups tends to inhibit the spread of contagion among its members.[8] If this is so, socially integrated women would be *less* likely to be susceptible. The same expectation would be reasonable if we interpret the hysterical behavior as an attention-getting device, isolates being seen as more in need of such social response than those with prior social ties. Finally, it has been noted by many students of collective behavior that the outcast, the person with little investment in the social system, is more likely to take part in all forms of collective behavior. This kind of person has been defined either in terms of his social position or his personal degree of "social adequacy," but in both cases the point is made that a lack of full integration into the network of social relations increases the tendency for a person to become a participant in collective

[8] William McDougall, *The Group Mind* (New York: G. P. Putnam's Sons, 1920), pp. 68–70.

behavior.[9] For all these reasons, then, we might expect isolates to exhibit the hysterical symptoms more frequently than those who are socially integrated.

Crowd Response. A third expectation is also possible from the literature on collective behavior, namely, that social relationships would have no relevance to the spread of the contagion. There is a common belief with respect to crowd behavior, substantiated by participants' reports, that contagion is often effective for persons who are not at all related to others in the crowd and who are not particularly concerned with the issue central to the crowd action.[10] The "magic" of contagion has been described and analyzed by many, but our knowledge remains less than adequate. Yet, it is very easy to find references to the unstructured nature of contagion, especially hysterical contagion, within a population. Perhaps this passage from the Langs' book says it as well as any: [11]

> The kind of identification that occurs in hysteria, Freud maintains, "may arise with every new perception of a common quality shared with some other person who is not an object of the sexual instinct. The more important this common quality is, the more successful may this partial identification become, and it may thus represent the beginning of a new tie." *The identification does not presuppose any prior emotional or sympathetic relationship; it results directly from the definition of the situation of those exhibiting the behavior as analogous to one's own.*

If this is the case, we might expect that the simple fact that all of those affected by the hysteria in the plant were fellow-workers, and the great majority of them were women, would be enough basis for the kind of identification just referred to. There would thus be no reason to expect that previously established social relations would be at all relevant to the spread of the symptoms.

We thus have three theoretical positions, each based on literature that is presumably relevant, and each calling for a different kind of relationship between sociometric position and the probability of being affected by the spread of hysterical contagion. Each is plausible in its own way, but seemingly all three cannot be correct. In fact, no two could seem to be correct. Yet it is our contention that all three *are* correct, within certain limits which we will attempt to define. We will make reference to the data of our study of the insect bite epidemic to help make our point; and though the data are not sufficient basis to demonstrate its adequacy, they justify its serious consideration.

Sample and Method

Because of the apprehensions on the part of management about what effect a series of interviews in the plant might have, it was not possible for us to begin

[9] See, for example, Ralph H. Turner and Lewis M. Killian, *Collective Behavior* (Englewood Cliffs, N.J.: Prentice-Hall, Inc., 1957), p. 110ff., and Lang and Lang, *Dynamics,* Chapter 10.

[10] An interesting example of this kind of contagion is presented in Turner and Killian, *Collective Behavior,* pp. 106–10.

[11] Lang and Lang, *Dynamics,* p. 227.

our formal research activities until two months after the incident. Throughout the investigation, however, we received cooperation from management, and we encountered little resistance from the employees.

In order to make the task feasible within the limits of our resources, we interviewed only women and only those who worked on the first shift. Within this population, we drew a systematic 25 percent sample, and then added all those women who had been affected by "the bug" who had not been drawn in the sample. We thus had both a sample of the first-shift women and the entire population of first-shift women who had been affected by "the bug." The total number of subjects was 185, of whom 58 were "affected" cases and 127 were "controls." All of these women were interviewed, the vast majority in the plant,[12] by two women interviewers who were employees of the National Opinion Research Center and who lived in the vicinity.

The present report is based largely on a question which asked the respondent to name her three best friends in the plant. In addition to the data from that question and our knowledge of which women were affected and which were controls, we also had a record of the date on which each affected case had been "bitten." We will thus be examining the relationship between sociometric position, the affected versus control distinction, and the date affected. Because the vast majority of the cases occurred on two successive days, we will simply divide the cases into those occurring on "Day One" (the first big day), "Day Two" (the second big day), and those which occurred "Before" and "After" these two days. The fifty-eight affected cases were distributed through time as follows: ten "Before," twenty-four on "Day One," twenty on "Day Two," and four "After."

We have noted that it is possible to generate three different hypotheses about the sociometric positions of the affected women. The first (based on a "group influence" argument) calls for a pattern of sociometric ties among the affected women which sets them off from the controls. The second (based on a "social isolation" argument) calls for a greater proportion of the affected women than the controls to be isolates. The third (based on a "crowd response" argument) calls for no relation between sociometric position and being affected by the contagion.

If we simply ask which of the three predictions comes closest to the mark, and if we base our evaluation on the overall differences between affected cases and controls (without considering the date a woman was affected), the prediction based on the "group influence" argument seems to be the best. (See "Total Sample" columns of Table 1.) First, there are no more isolates within the affected category than among the controls. In fact, there is a slightly higher proportion of isolates among the controls. Also, the affected women are chosen as

[12] Sixteen of the affected women were not interviewed in the plant. They had either terminated their employment there, or were on vacation or on leave or were ill at the time of the interviews. All of these were interviewed at their homes. Because of the expense involved, when a control subject was not available for interview in the plant, a substitution was made. The person interviewed in her place was the next one on the payroll list, this list having been used as the original definition of the population to be sampled.

friends somewhat more often on the average than are the controls.[13] Thus, there is certainly no general tendency for the affected women to be socially ostracized, and there may even be a limited positive relationship between sociometric position and being affected.

More important, we find that the links between affected women and *other* affected women are more common than between controls and affected women. A higher proportion of the choices *made* by affecteds go to other affecteds than do choices made by controls go to affecteds. A greater proportion of choices *received* by affecteds come from other affecteds than do the choices received by controls. Affecteds are twice as likely to be chosen solely by other affecteds, and controls are twice as likely to be chosen solely by other controls. Finally, of the mutual choices participated in by affecteds, three-fifths are with other affecteds. Similarly, of the mutual choices participated in by controls, two-thirds are with other controls. We find, therefore, that the affected women are not only generally integrated into a social network, but they are linked *together* much more closely than they are to women who were not affected. This is presumably evidence that the contagion followed sociometric channels.

There was one other matter that we thought should be taken into consideration before accepting this general picture, however. The vast majority of the women employed in the plant worked in one huge, open room in which the cutting, sewing, pressing, inspecting and packing operations were carried out. It was in this room that most of the affected cases had occurred. Our sample, however, also included women who were located elsewhere in the plant and who had less contact with and were visually separated from the women in this large room. Since the affected cases were not evenly distributed spatially throughout the plant, there was some concern on our part that we not err in the direction of over-estimating the differences between affected cases and controls due to the expected tendency of the women to choose as friends those who were spatially near them.

To test the relevance of such a spatial factor, we computed all of the indexes again using only those subjects who worked in this one large room where most of the affected cases occurred. These data are presented in the "Restricted Sample" columns of Table 1. They provide little evidence that the results are biased by the spatial distribution of our cases. Some of the indexes for the restricted sample

[13] There is considerable difficulty in interpreting such comparisons, however, since the affected cases are a population, and the controls are a sample. It might be argued, for instance, that this difference in the two groups would increase the probability that affecteds would be chosen since all of their potential "significant others" were asked to name their friends, whereas only a sample of the controls' potential friends were interviewed. Such an argument, however, assumes that there *is* a pattern of social relations among affecteds and/or among the controls, and to assume that there is such a pattern begs the central question of the study. But since, as is noted later, there does seem to be a pattern of relations among the affecteds, the merit of the argument cannot be fully denied. The fact that one group is a sample and the other a population also makes tests of significance rather meaningless. Since this is seen as an exploratory analysis, however, such tests might in any event be inappropriate.

TABLE 1

SOCIOMETRIC STATUS OF AFFECTED CASES AND CONTROLS

Characteristic	TOTAL SAMPLE *Affected*	TOTAL SAMPLE *Control*	RESTRICTED SAMPLE *Affected*	RESTRICTED SAMPLE *Control*
Proportion of cases which are isolates	.28 (58)	.33 (127)	.23 (47)	.30 (88)
Average number of times chosen	1.43	1.12	1.43	1.16
Proportion of choices directed toward affecteds*	.27 (167)	.09 (363)	.27 (140)	.10 (257)
Proportion of choices directed toward controls*	.25 (167)	.28 (363)	.22 (140)	.27 (257)
Proportion of choices received from affecteds	.57 (83)	.26 (142)	.58 (67)	.27 (102)
Proportion of choices received from controls	.43 (83)	.74 (142)	.42 (67)	.73 (102)
Proportion chosen by affecteds only	.31 (58)	.13 (127)	.34 (47)	.15 (88)
Proportion chosen by controls only	.21 (58)	.43 (127)	.26 (47)	.44 (88)
Proportion of mutual choices with affecteds	.59 (46)	.30 (64)	.64 (39)	.28 (50)
Proportion of mutual choices with controls	.41 (46)	.70 (64)	.36 (39)	.72 (50)

NOTE: The "Restricted Sample" is made up of those women from our total sample who were located in the one large room in which most of the affected cases were located. This analysis was carried out to insure that the differences between affecteds and controls were not simply a function of the spatial distribution of the affected cases.
The N on which each proportion is based is noted in parentheses. The total number of cases in each major category was: Affected, 58; Control, 127; Restricted Sample Affected, 47; Restricted Sample Control, 88. The asterisk indicates proportions which do not total to 1.00 because choices could be made of non-affected persons not in the sample.

are even more clearly in support of the "group influence" expectation than are those of the total sample. Thus, the use of the total sample and the conclusions based on it appear to be justified.

We can offer further insight, however, if we analyze the affected category according to the period in which the women were affected. It will be recalled that there are four periods: "Before" the two big days, "Day One," "Day Two," and "After" the two big days. Since there were only four cases in the "After" period, we will not refer to that period in most of what follows. Looking at the distribution of cases in the "Before" category, the first ones to exhibit the symptoms, we note that 50 percent of them are isolates. (See Table 2.) By contrast, no more than one-fourth of the cases occurring in any of the other periods are isolates. Thus, although isolates are found during all periods, they are most heavily concentrated at the beginning of the epidemic. This fact is also reflected

TABLE 2

SOCIOMETRIC STATUS OF AFFECTED CASES BY TIME AFFECTED

Characteristic	*"Before"*	*"Day One"*	*"Day Two"*
Proportion of cases which are isolates	.50 (10)	.21 (24)	.25 (20)
Average number of times chosen	1.00	1.67	1.35
Proportion of choices directed toward affecteds*	.27 (30)	.31 (70)	.25 (57)
Proportion of choices directed toward controls*	.23 (30)	.29 (70)	.21 (57)
Proportion of choices received from affecteds	.40 (10)	.58 (40)	.63 (27)
Proportion of choices received from controls	.60 (10)	.43 (40)	.37 (27)
Proportion chosen by affecteds only	.10 (10)	.29 (24)	.45 (20)
Proportion chosen by controls only	.20 (10)	.21 (24)	.15 (20)
Proportion of mutual choices with affecteds	.50 (4)	.61 (23)	.63 (16)
Proportion of mutual choices with controls	.50 (4)	.39 (23)	.38 (16)

NOTE: The N on which each proportion is based is noted in parentheses. The total number of cases in each time period was: "Before," 10; "Day One," 24; "Day Two," 20.
The asterisk indicates proportions which do not total to 1.00 because choices may be made of non-affected persons not in the sample.

in the differences in the average number of times the women in the three periods were chosen as friends, this number being much lower in the "Before" period than in any of the others.

We also find that through the three major periods, the later a woman is affected, the more likely she is to be chosen by other affected women and to be chosen *exclusively* by other affected women. Correspondingly, there is a *decreasing* tendency for affected women to be chosen only by controls. That is, there is an increasing tendency for the affected cases to be sociometrically linked exclusively with other affected cases and a decreasing tendency for them to be linked exclusively with controls. We find the same pattern of increase of the proportion of mutual choices within the affected category. This would seem to indicate an increasing tendency for the contagion to localize within one social network (or series of networks) to the exclusion of other networks.

We have thus far, then, seen that there is a concentration of isolates during the initial phase of the epidemic followed by an increasing tendency for the later cases to be linked together sociometrically. Thus, the pattern in the early phase is in keeping with the "social isolation" expectation, and the pattern in the major portion of the epidemic is in keeping with the "group influence" expectation. These findings would seem to indicate that the "crowd response" expectation is without support in these data. We are not certain that such a negative conclusion should be reached, however.

Although there are only four cases in the "After" phase, they present a rather different picture than the data in the earlier phases. One of these cases is an isolate, which continues the one-fourth proportion of "Day Two." These four women are chosen 1.50 times each on the average, which is comparable to "Day One" and "Day Two" women. On the other hand, only eighteen percent of their choices are directed toward other affecteds, and only half of their choices come from other affecteds. Only one is chosen solely by other affecteds, and two are chosen solely by controls. Of the mutual choices participated in by these women, two out of three are with controls. Thus, in every one of the indexes considered there is evidence of a spread of the epidemic to persons who have more links *outside* the affected category. If we assume that this is a meaningful rather than a chance ordering of a very small number of cases, two interpretations are possible. First, we might argue that what is occurring is simply the entry of the contagion into another sociometric network, and that since the spread is curtailed by the end of the entire epidemic, there are not enough cases to demonstrate this. On the other hand, it might be argued that what is happening is that a more random distribution of cases is occurring, that the spread of the epidemic has moved out of sociometric channels and is becoming more general. This would be another way of saying that it has become a "crowd response."

Discussion

We interpret these findings as being at least consistent with the following theoretical position. An epidemic such as this begins when one or more persons, due to idiosyncratic characteristics outside our present area of concern, exhibit symptoms which serve as a model for at least a limited number of others in the same situation. Since the symptoms and their explanation are somewhat unusual, those most likely to follow this lead are persons less well integrated into a set of social relationships which, for most of those present, provide a referential base for defining the model as irrelevant or objectionable. As a number of other persons follow the lead, however, it is increasingly likely that some persons who are socially integrated will be affected. (Perhaps these will be persons of somewhat unusual psychological make-up, or ones who are in a particularly anxiety-producing situation.) Through some such channel, the contagion enters social networks and is disseminated with increasing rapidity in what can be termed a "chain reaction." The acceleration is undoubtedly in part a function of the fact that, as more cases appear, the behavior becomes increasingly legitimized—increasingly accepted according to an evolving generalized belief in the group involved.[14] The rapidity of legitimation *within* such networks is greater than

[14] See Smelser, *Collective Behavior,* especially Chapter V, for a discussion of the importance of generalized beliefs in collective behavior. As Smelser puts it: "Present in all collective behavior is some kind of belief that prepares the participants for action." (p. 79) The position we are taking here is simply that such a belief was necessary in the situation we studied before a woman could become an affected case. Otherwise, even if she should be bitten by an insect, she would not define that bite as a serious threat to her physical well-being.

outside them, and "outsiders" are thus slower to respond. However, as larger and larger numbers of persons exhibit the behavior, the sheer size of the affected category makes the credibility of the phenomenon greater. We thus find that ultimately "everyone" believes in "the bug" (or whatever the belief is that justifies the behavior), and cases begin to occur throughout the population. It thus becomes a "crowd response."

We argue, then, that isolates are instrumental in providing the initial few cases and providing a credible model for one or more particularly vulnerable persons who are socially integrated. The behavior of such "insiders" is more influential vis-à-vis their friends and increases the likelihood of contagion within sociometric networks. Since such contagion accelerates due to increasingly greater legitimation within the group, it soon forms a phenonemon of such proportions that its credibility can no longer be easily denied by anyone in the population. Cases then begin to occur more frequently in scattered, unrelated segments of the population. The end of the epidemic comes when some additional factor enters the situation (in this case experts who denied the legitimacy of the behavior and exterminators whose sprays "killed the bugs") and/or when the behavior becomes seriously dysfunctional for the participants. We have thus attempted to bring about a synthesis of three different theoretical positions within the framework of the longitudinal analysis of an epidemic of hysterical symptoms and to indicate the contribution each makes to a fuller view of the phenomenon.[15]

In conclusion, it may be worthwhile to compare this study and our interpretation of the data with the study of doctors' adoption of a new drug referred to earlier.[16] The similarity of the two is striking, but there are important differences. Both the present study and the drug study point up the importance of a network of social relations for the dissemination of a new behavioral pattern. However, our data more clearly indicate a lag in the rate of adoption of the behavior pattern by persons integrated in the social network. In both studies there is an "S-shaped" accelerated curve of adoptions in the case of the socially integrated subjects, indicating a kind of "snowball" effect. Perhaps more noteworthy, however, is the fact that in our study the original rate of adoption by isolates is higher than for those who are socially integrated, whereas in the drug study the integrated doctors adopt the drug at a higher rate throughout the period studied.

We interpret this difference as being due to the *kind* of behavior involved. The doctor, whether socially isolated or integrated, presumably is highly receptive to the adoption of new practices which promote medical values. However, if we accept the general proposition that the leaders in any group are better informed and more fully reflect the group's norms and values, the difference between the

[15] It may be noted that some of our data are in keeping with this interpretation, although it is not possible to present a complete analysis here. For instance, although both affecteds and controls expressed a belief in the existence of a toxic insect, those controls who had sociometric links with affecteds (chose or were chosen by them) expressed this belief more often than those without such links. This adds support to the idea that the belief was disseminated through sociometric channels.

[16] Coleman, Katz and Menzel, "Diffusion."

integrated and isolated doctor is seen as a difference in the rapidity with which they will act in accordance with those norms and values when the occasion arises.[17] In the case of the hysterical behavior, however, there is no question about the normative preference for or legitimation of such behavior. There is no normatively based readiness to respond. Rather, we would argue, what occurs in such cases is the evolution of a generalized belief that is not previously held, in this case a belief that there *is* an insect, that it *is* dangerous, and that it *can* and *does* cause serious symptoms. Our data indicate that this belief, and the behavior based on it, develop among isolates at a steady rate, but among those who are socially integrated the rate is slow at first and accelerates rapidly in the later phases. In fact, the rate of acceleration and the ultimate level of acceptance is highest in the most fully integrated segment of the population.

Presumably, then, in our case the social network acted as both a resistor and a conductor, at different points during the epidemic. Thus, although there are important similarities between the present study and the earlier one, the content of the pattern being disseminated must also be taken into account. In this study, since the behavior involved was not normatively approved, the social network was both resistant and facilitative. The transition from resistance to facilitation was a function, we believe, of the evolution within the social network of a new definition of the situation, and the time required to develop this new definition is reflected in the lag of the rate of hysterical behavior among highly integrated women behind that of the isolates in the first phase of the epidemic.

Except in very special populations, behavior as unusual as that represented by the hysterical reaction found in the clothing plant would not originally be adopted by highly integrated persons. On the other hand, unless it were ultimately adopted by such persons, the contagion would not reach epidemic proportions. Thus, in cases of such unusual "innovations" as discussed here, we see isolates as crucial in the initial stages, and channels of interpersonal relations as important agencies of rapid dissemination in the pattern of behavior, until, finally, the number of cases is so great as to bring about a "crowd reaction" in which prior social relations are irrelevant.

---

[17] The position taken here is consistent with that taken by Menzel in another discussion of the drug adoption data in which he suggests ". . . that the locally well integrated physicians were early drug adopters because local integration itself afforded them a high flow of communication about the new drug; and that they were not deterred from adopting it by their adherence to the local norms because these norms, far from opposing the adoption of this innovation, actually favored it." Herbert Menzel, "Innovation, Integration, and Marginality: A Survey of Physicians," *American Sociological Review* 25 (October 1960): 707–08.

Collective Behavior:

Putting It into Perspective

Collective behavior refers to behavior which takes place outside institutionalized structures. Relative to other forms, collective behavior is more spontaneous, more emotional, less structured, and less dependent upon previously learned values and behavioral expectations. Under the heading of collective behavior, a social psychologist may study crowds and mobs, disasters, rumor, fads and fashions, social movements, and public opinion, to name just a few. Collective behavior tends to emerge in situations where norms are ambiguous or where there is dissatisfaction with the social order. It may be of brief duration, as in the case of panic in a burning theater, or may span several months or years, as in the case of a social movement.

Although most of his major notions have been discredited by contemporary researchers, the work of Gustav LeBon is usually cited as the first attempt at systematic analysis of collective behavior. In his highly speculative treatise, *The Crowd.* LeBon emphasized the irrationality, impulsiveness, and unpredictability of crowds. He argued that people in crowds tend to cede their power of critical judgment to the collective sentiments of the whole, the latter being a sort of mode or common denominator of the atavistic instincts of individual crowd members. As LeBon saw it, crowd members lose their sense of responsibility; their fear of punishment is replaced by a feeling of omnipotence; and they become suggestible to the most exaggerated and bizarre sentiments. He also noted that unfortunately the tendency toward exaggeration in crowds, more often than not, focuses action toward some malevolent end.

Contemporary analysts of crowd behavior no longer accept LeBon's "group mind" assumption, nor does research evidence support his notions of the inherent irrationality and unpredictability of crowd behavior. Even the most elementary form of collective behavior, panic, does not appear to follow the patterns described by LeBon. For example, while a crowd will flee as a body for an exit of a burning theater, the evidence from crisis and disaster research indicates that panic in emergencies is a momentary phenomenon. As soon as the threat of immediate danger is removed, people will revert back to familiar patterns of behavior, re-establish role-relationships, and attempt to cope with remaining problems in culturally defined ways.

Disaster research also indicates that the incidence of panic is much more rare than popular notions of emergencies would suggest. For example, there is usually a great deal of resistence to evacuation attempts by official agencies after such disasters as tornados and floods. Even during the heavy bombing of London in World War II, a large proportion of those evacuated returned to their homes, or homes of relatives, while the bombing continued. Rescue workers often arrive at the scene of a disaster to find residents already making progress toward housing displaced persons, administering first aid, repairing damage, and so forth. After some initial panic, people affected by a disaster seem to be quite concerned with the welfare of others, in making sure that relatives and friends are cared for, and in returning as quickly as possible to the normal daily round of activity.

LeBon was concerned with a type of crowd that has come to be known as an "acting crowd." In such a grouping the focus of attention falls on performing some collective action or pursuing some common goal. It is from examples of such crowds that most popular stereotypes of crowd behavior derive. However, all crowds are not the same—all are not hostile, aggressive, nor in a state of frenzy.

We participate in crowds almost daily without being swept up by some irresistible force toward monstrous behavior. Much more common than acting crowds are groupings referred to as "casual crowds," "conventionalized crowds," and "expressive crowds." "Casual crowds" are those which gather about a common focus of attention, such as an accident or store-window display. Emotions do not usually run high in such groupings, and there is little uniformity of action beyond the attending to a common object. The second type, the "conventionalized crowd," is exemplified by the crowd at a football game or a theatrical performance. In these latter groupings the uniformity of action and expression of emotion is culturally defined and quite predictable. Finally, the "expressive crowd" displays somewhat more spontaneity and emotionality than casual or conventionalized crowds. However, uniformity of physical movement and modes of expression serves mainly as a means of releasing individual tensions and as a display of common mood. Such groupings as rallies, revival meetings, and rock festivals are examples of expressive crowds.

Contemporary analysts, as represented by the selection by Carl Couch, have attempted to break away from "contagion" theories of collective behavior, and have attempted to cast collective behavior theory in terms of emergent norms, interpersonal relationships, or the social construction of reality. It is now recognized that a crowd is not a homogeneous "blob" with all members acting in unison. As their point of departure, modern theorists note the fact that there is fairly wide variation in the behavior of crowd members even in acting crowds. To be sure, individuals in crowds are under pressure to comply with situation-specific norms, but it is misleading to assume that they are inexorably drawn toward imitation by the mystical force of a "group mind." While people may conform in a crowd situation due to fear of reprisals or physical coercion, they are doubtless aware that such pressures are impinging upon them. Emotional contagion may facilitate compliance, but it alone cannot account for crowd behavior.

Consistent with the emergent-norm view of collective behavior, social psychologists have directed a good deal of attention toward rumor. Far from being a pastime restricted to gossips, rumors tend to emerge and be perpetuated in situations where there is a lack of information from official sources about some important and emotionally charged issue. Some theorists have pointed to the anxiety-reduction function of rumor, while others have emphasized the tendency of rumor to reinforce anxieties. But, most theorists agree that rumor represents a collective attempt to define or structure an ambiguous situation.

Studies of rumor indicate fairly consistently that rumors follow sociometric patterns as people tend to pass on the latest news to friends. Through the serial re-telling of a rumor, its content undergoes a good deal of transformation. This is not necessarily a result of willful distortion. Rather, selective perception and recall operate as each person in the rumor chain passes on what he has heard. The message become more concise (leveled) as presumably unimportant details are omitted. At the same time, certain other details may become the central foci of the message, a process referred to as sharpening. Also operating in the transmission of rumor is the process of assimilation, whereby the message is re-cast to make it consistent with existent values and expectations.

Perhaps the surest way to squelch a rumor is to provide "official" information through sources that are credible to the population involved. If official information is not forthcoming, chances are that a rumor will serve as its substitute. And, as often happens in collective behavior situations, people will act on the basis of the information they have at hand. It is important to bear in mind here that people may be acting on misinformation, but they are not necessarily behaving irrationally. On the basis of the information they possess, their behavior may, in fact, follow quite logically.

Within the range of collective behavior phenomena, social movements provide the social psychologist with some of his most significant opportunities to study the emergence of new social structures. Movements tend to arise when there is a strain in existing social structures. The dissatisfaction resulting from strain serves as a pre-condition for mobilizing action toward changing the status quo. In the early stages of a social movement participants are recruited on the basis of promise, i.e., the promise of better conditions in the immediate future. For a movement to sustain itself, however, it must assume some ideology, some rationale for action which goes beyond immediate goals. And, while initial adherents can be recruited and directed by a relatively small inner circle of leaders, a large-scale movement cannot be sustained without the establishment of a hierarchy of authority nor without specialists skilled in organizing, planning strategy, and propagandizing. Once a movement has reached this point, it is quite clear that it has become a fairly complex social system in its own right. Eventually, the movement may be accommodated or co-opted by the institutions it was originally organized to oppose. Those familiar with the history of the labor movement will no doubt be able to identify the various stages in the institutionalization of organized labor. Today, such mechanisms as collective bargaining, grievance procedures, and even a cabinet-level department of the Federal Government attest to the fact that organized labor is no longer a movement but a part of the establishment. It is perhaps difficult to envision some of our contemporary movements, e.g., the student movement, peace movement, or civil rights, reaching the degree of institutionalization which labor has experienced. Yet such processes are already operating.

What social psychologists study reflects to a large degree the condition of society and what gets defined as its important social problems. Over the past decade we have witnessed an apparent acceleration in social movements of various types as vilification of tradition has become the norm. Concurrently, fads, fashions and crazes seem to have become a more significant factor in our lives. We have seen skirts for men and pants for women, and hemlines which rise and fall with increasing frequency. The "in" colors and motifs in home furnishings have become as flamboyant as they are temporary, and we have been continuously forced to adopt the latest speech pattern, cliché, or "with-it" obscenity as if to demonstrate that we are oriented toward the "here and now," and hence are respectable.

While social psychologists have been concerned with fads and fashions for some time, we can predict that this form of collective behavior will occupy a much more important place as a strategic research site for exploring the intricacies of emerging norms.

The following *Suggestions for Further Reading* will give the interested student a preliminary foothold in the literature of collective behavior.

Suggestions for Further Reading

Gustav LeBon, *The Crowd.* London: Allen and Unwin, 1917. Primarily of historical interest, this work has served as the point of departure for much of the subsequent theory and research in collective behavior phenomena.

Stanley Milgrim and Hans Toch, "Collective Behavior," in G. Lindzey and E. Aronson, editors, *Handbook of Social Psychology.* Second Edition, Volume 4. Reading, Massachusetts: Addison-Wesley, 1969, pp. 507–610. A very thorough review of theory and research in two areas of collective behavior, vis., crowds and social movements. Includes a fine discussion of findings on the ecology and physical structure of crowds, and presents an evaluative summary of research methods used in studying crowd behavior.

Tomatsu Shibutani, *Improvised News: A Sociological Study of Rumor.* Indianapolis: Bobbs-Merrill, 1966. An intriguing exploration into the functions of rumor in collective behavior episodes and the factors which encourage or impede the spread of rumors.

Neil J. Smelzer, *Theory of Collective Behavior.* New York: Free Press, 1963. In this book, Smelzer has attempted to develop a comprehensive theory of collective behavior. While the theory has been criticized by a number of authors, the book provides a useful framework for analyzing what happens in a collective behavior episode.

Ralph H. Turner, "Collective Behavior," in R. E. L. Faris, editor, *Handbook of Modern Sociology.* Chicago: Rand McNally, 1964, pp. 382–425. An excellent brief overview of contemporary theories and empirical research in collective behavior. Focuses on crowds, rumor, and panic behavior.

CHAPTER X

Doing Social Psychology

38 Chris Argyris, *Some Unintended Consequences of Rigorous Research* · 515

39 J. David Martin, *Suspicion and the Experimental Confederate: A Study of Role and Credibility* · 533

40 Nicholas von Hoffman, *Sociological Snoopers* · 547

Irving Louis Horowitz and Lee Rainwater, *Journalistic Moralizers* · 547

Putting It into Perspective · 558

Suggestions for Further Reading · 559

38

Some Unintended Consequences of Rigorous Research

CHRIS ARGYRIS

Social scientists have long considered the rigorous experimental procedures of natural scientists as an ideal to be emulated in the study of human behavior. More recently, however, social scientists have begun to realize that the adherence to rigorous research designs and measurement procedures can result in unintended consequences which are actually self-defeating. It is becoming increasingly common for social scientists to devote their research energies to the effects of research itself on the responses of their subjects.

In the following selection, Chris Argyris attempts to summarize some of the findings reported on the problem of unintended consequences of research with human subjects and offers a frame of reference for further investigation of the problem. He contends that, in their observance of the tenets of good research design, the social scientist is placed in a manager-employee relationship vis-à-vis his subjects and his research assistants as well. Consequently, he argues, the application of theory developed for formal organizations can be fruitfully applied to, and yield a better understanding of, research situations.

Viewed as formal organizations, many of the unintended consequences of social science research are predictable and potentially controllable. For example, the adaptive strategies employed by subjects to "give the researcher what he is looking for," the subjects' hostility toward the researcher, and even the research assistant's tendency to conceal errors or to "fudge" data, all have parallels among lower-level employees in formal organizations and are quite well documented in this latter setting.

By extension of formal organization theory, Argyris sees the problem of unintended consequences in research settings as a lack of involvement

Chris Argyris, "Some Unintended Consequences of Rigorous Research," *Psychological Bulletin* 70 (1968): 185–97.

of subjects in the purposes and findings of the research. As a solution to this problem, he proposes a technique which has been found useful in getting lower-level employees personally involved in planned organizational change, namely, allowing subjects to participate in the formulation, design and execution of research.

Rigorousness is to a researcher what efficiency is to an executive: an ideal state that is always aspired to, never reached, and continually revered. Much literature exists regarding the best ways to approach both rigorousness and efficiency. In the case of efficiency, executives have traditionally assumed that when organizations are not efficient it is usually because the members have not been adhering to an efficient organizational strategy. One of the contributions of organizational behaviorists has been to study how executives and employees actually behave (not limit themselves to how they say they behave). One major result of these studies has been to show that a good deal of inefficiency may occur precisely when and because the members are following closely the most accepted strategies for efficiency.

Recently a new literature has been, and continues to be, developed by scholars studying the research situation (Friedman, 1967; Rosenthal, 1966). They too have not limited themselves to what researchers say they do in conducting research. They have studied research in terms of how it is actually carried out. As a result, they have reported dysfunctions and opened up important new questions.

An exploration of this literature from the viewpoint of an organizational theorist suggests that his field may be able to make a modest contribution in terms of a theoretical framework to organize the existing findings and suggest other possible conclusions that have yet to be documented systematically. This framework conceives of the researcher-subject relationship as a systemic one, be it temporary. By borrowing from the established literature on research methodology, we shall attempt to show that the properties of this temporary system are remarkably similar to the properties of formal organizations. Moreover, many of the dysfunctions reported between experimenter and subject are similar to the dysfunctions between management and employee.

The Underlying Assumptions about Rigorous Research

Let us begin by asking what are the underlying assumptions for conducting rigorous research. The first is that rigorousness is an ideal state which one can only approximate. The second assumption is that rigorousness is more closely approximated as the researcher is able to define unambiguously his problem and the relevant variables. Moreover, the more easily the variables can be observed and measured, the greater the reliability, the greater the probability for future public verifiability, the more rigorous will be the research. The third assumption is that the more control a researcher has over his variables, the more rigorous will be his research.

The Nature of the Relationship between Researcher and Subject

These assumptions provide the basis for elegant research designs. Like management principles, the designs are expected to work if subjects cooperate. It is precisely at the point when people are brought into the picture that the difficulties arise. Why is this so?

In order to answer this question let us examine the basic qualities of rigorous research. Most methodologists agree with Edwards (1954) that rigorous research tends to occur when:

1. The research is deliberately undertaken to satisfy the needs of the researcher and where the pace of activity is controlled by the researcher to give him maximum possible control over the subjects' behavior.

2. The setting is designed by the researcher to achieve his objectives and to minimize any of the subjects' desires from contaminating the experiment.

3. The researcher is responsible for making accurate observations, recording them, analyzing them, and eventually reporting them.

4. The researcher has the conditions so rigorously defined that he or others can replicate them.

5. The researcher can systematically vary the conditions and note the concomitant variation among the variables.

These conditions are remarkably similar to those top management defines when designing an organization. Top management (researcher) defines the worker's (subject's) role as rationally and clearly as possible (to minimize error) and as simply as possible (to minimize having to draw from a select population, thereby reducing the generalizability of the research findings); provides as little information as possible beyond the tasks (thereby minimizing the time perspective of the subject); and defines the inducements for participating (e.g., a requirement to pass a course, a plea for the creation of knowledge, or money). Indeed, if Edwards' description is valid, the rigorous research criteria would create a world for the subject in which his behavior is defined, controlled, evaluated, manipulated, and reported to a degree that is comparable to the behavior of workers in the most mechanized assembly-line conditions.

The Unintended Consequences of Rigorous Research Designs

If this similarity between conditions in organizations and those in research systems does exist, then the unintended consequences found in formal organizations should also be found, in varying degree, in the temporary systems created by research. These consequences have been discussed in detail elsewhere (Argyris, 1964). Briefly they are:

1. Physical withdrawal which results in absenteeism and turnover.

2. Psychological withdrawal while remaining physically in the research situation. Under these conditions the subject is willing to let the researcher manipulate his behavior, usually for a price. The studies that show subjects as all too willing to cooperate are, from this point of view, examples of subject withdrawal from involvement and not, as some researchers suggest, signs of subjects' high involvement. To give a researcher what he wants in such a way that the researcher does not realize that the subject is doing this (a skill long ago learned by employees and students) is a sign of nonresponsibility and of a lack of commitment to the effectiveness of the research.

3. Overt hostility toward the research. Openly fighting the research rarely occurs, probably because the subjects are "volunteers." If they are not volunteers, they may still feel pressured to participate. If so, they would probably not feel free to fight the researcher openly.

4. Covert hostility is a safer adaptive mechanism. It includes such behavior as knowingly giving incorrect answers, being a difficult subject, second-guessing the research design and trying to circumvent it in some fashion, producing the minimally accepted amount of behavior, coercing others to produce minimally, and disbelief and mistrust of the researcher.

5. Emphasis upon monetary rewards as the reason for participation.

6. Unionization of subjects.

Organizational theory would suggest that the exact degree to which any of these conditions would hold for a given subject would be, in turn, a function of:

1. The degree to which being dependent, manipulated, and controlled is "natural" in the lives of the subjects (e.g., research utilizing children or adults in highly authoritarian cultures may be more generalizable).

2. The length of time that the research takes and the degree of subject control it requires.

3. The motivations of the subjects (e.g., for the sake of science, to pass a course, to learn about self, for money).

4. The potency of the research (the involvement it requires of the subject).

5. The possible effect participation in research or its results could have on the subject's evaluation of his previous, and perception of his future, life.

6. The number of times the subject participates in other research.

7. The degree to which the research situation is similar to other situations in which the subject is immersed, about which he has strong feelings, few of which he can express. For example, in the case of students, the role in a lecture class is similar

to the role of a subject in a psychological experiment. (The teacher controls, has the long-range perspective, defines the tasks, etc.) To the extent that he is unable to express his frustration in relation to the class, he may find it appropriate, if indeed he does not feel himself inwardly compelled, to express these pent-up feelings during the research.

Some may question if these feelings would come out in such research situations because participating in an experiment, being interviewed, filling out a questionnaire tend to take a short time. This view may be questioned. Has not the reader watched how quickly people become involved in parlor games and noted how easy it is for them to surface competitive needs, power aspirations, and fears of failure? Indeed, is it not the fundamental assumption of the researcher than an experiment is genuinely involving? Is it not accepted that the data would hardly be generalizable if the subjects could be shown to be involved only peripherally because of the shortness of time? As Sales (1966), a proponent of experimentation pointed out, the

> "brevity" argument is not valid . . . the entire science of experimental social psychology rests upon the assumption that experimental periods are sufficiently lengthy for treatments to "take," an assumption which is supported in every significant finding obtained in the experimental laboratory [p. 28].

If experimental conditions "take" in short periods, then why should not the psychological conditions implicit in the researcher-subject relationship also "take"?

Illustration of the Existence of Adaptive Strategies

The next question is, to what extent are subjects beginning to adapt in ways suggested by the theoretical framework? Orne (1962), Mills (1962), and Rosenthal (1963) have presented evidence that subjects are willing to become dependent upon and submissive to the experimenter and, as Kiesler (1969) suggested, overcooperative with the researcher. Unfortunately, little systematic research exists beyond these studies. Some anecdotal evidence was collected by the writer at his own institution. The students have increasingly emphasized the importance of being paid for participating in research. This trend can be predicted by an organizational theory. The "market orientation" (so common among lower level employees in industry) is an inevitable consequence of being in a formal organization (Argyris, 1964).

Second-guessing and beating the researcher at his own game may also be becoming commonplace, especially in dissonance experiments. Many experiments have been reported where it was crucial to deceive the students. Naturally, in many cases the students were carefully debriefed (although to the writer's knowledge few, if any, researchers have provided evidence which was collected as rigorously for this assertion as were the data directly related to the goal of the experiment). One result that has occurred is that students now come to experiments expecting to be tricked. The initial romance and challenge of being subjects has left them and they are now beginning to behave like lower level employees in companies. Their big challenge is to guess the deception (beat the management). If one likes the experimenter, then he cooperates. If he does not, he may enjoy botching the works with such great skill that the experimenter is not aware of this behavior. This practice is frequent enough for Burdick (1957) to make it the subject matter of an entire chapter in his best seller, *The Ninth Wave*. He describes the hero who outguessed the experimenters and was eventually rejected by them. He also describes another subject who pleased the experimenters but who, it turned out, hated the experimenters deeply. In one major university a formal evaluation was made of the basic psychology course by nearly 600 undergraduates. They were given three topics from which they could choose one to evaluate thoroughly. The senior professor responsible for the course reported an overwhelming majority of the students focused on the requirement, in the course, that they had to participate as subjects. The students were very critical, mistrustful, and hostile to the requirement. In many cases they identified how they expressed their pent-up feelings by "beating the researcher" in such a way that he never found out (an activity frequently observed among frustrated employees).

These examples, incidentally, also serve to illustrate that students can generate strong feelings about experimentation in a very short time. They also raise the question, do we need systematic data showing that the briefing each subject received actually generated not only the correct cognitive maps but the proper psychological set upon which the experiment depends (Friedman, 1967)?

Another example of how students are beginning to react like employees is illustrated by a request received by the writer recently from a senior social psychologist at Yale. He had concluded that to identify an experiment openly and honestly would lead to a set of attitudes among students that would be harmful to the experiments. He wanted to know if a place could be found for him to conduct his experiment in an organizational setting. He assumed that people in an organizational setting are not so contaminated as students (especially along the dimension of expecting to be tricked). As we shall see, this assumption is not necssarily valid.

A graduate student was recently able to design an experiment with no deception and one in which he could honestly advertise (as he did) that the students might learn about themselves as a result of participating in the research. His experiment was a 10-hour T group. In the first four sessions at least 3 hours were spent by the members trying to deal with the students' deep beliefs that the ad was phony, that they were to be tricked, and that the researcher didn't really mean what he had said.

Recently, Kelman (1967) raised similar issues. He doubts that the subjects will remain naive. He quoted one subject as saying, "Psychologists always lie!" He also suggested, and this would be predicted by an organizational theory, that the subjects may come to resent the experimenter and throw a monkey wrench in the experiment.

Brock and Becker (1966) attempted to prove that deception may not have the harmful effects suggested by Kelman (1967). Their work is open to serious question. Nowhere do they provide evidence that the subjects were not dutifully playing the role of subject and doing everything asked of them. One could argue that they signed the petition, after being told they had just ruined the experimenter's mechanical box (which was contrived to blow up when a button was pressed), because they saw through the hoax and went along with the game. An explanation for those who refused to sign the petition could be that since they did not blow up the box they saw little reason to go along with the researchers. One would predict that the subjects might openly resist if they were given a rational opportunity to do so. This turned out to be the case. There was high resistance to the experimenter when it was possible to connect the massive debriefing with participation in the second experiment.

Two points require emphasis at this juncture. First, these adaptive strategies are predictable by organizational theory because the relationship between the researcher and the subject is similar to the one between the manager and the employee in formal organizations. Moreover, the adaptive strategies may well lead to internal psychological states, on the part of the subjects, that can significantly alter their perception of the research and their response to it. If this is the case, then the generalizability of the results may be seriously limited unless the researcher can show "rigorously" that he has been able to control the existence of subjects' adaptive strategies.

One way a research may respond to the problem of controlling these adaptive strategies is to obtain a large sample of subjects. He may assume that these kinds of behavior are "noise" that can be partialed out. If our theoretical view is valid, then any increase in the sample may simply tend to increase the difficulties, not decrease them. Moreover, as the "noise" increases it may eliminate any "real" effect that might be there. Another response may be to increase the controls over the subjects' behavior. According to this analysis, the problems would then be compounded.

In another illustration of dysfunctions, some enterprising students at two major universities have begun to think about starting a student organization that would be similar to Manpower or, if this were resisted by the university, similar to a union. Instead of secretaries, they would offer subjects. They believe that they can get students to cooperate because they would promise them more money, better debriefing, and more interest on the part of the researcher (e.g., more complete feedback). When this experience was reported to some psychologists their response was similar to the reactions of business men who have just been told for the first time that their employees were considering the creation of a union. There was some nervous laughter, a comment indicating surprise, then another comment to the effect that every organization has some troublemakers, and finally a prediction that such an activity would never succeed because "the students are too disjointed to unite."

To continue the comparison with business men, is there not a strong similarity of the attitudes held by the early lumber kings and those held presently by many researchers? The lumber kings consumed trees without worrying very much about the future supply. Researchers (field and experimental) seem to consume subjects without worrying very much about their future supply. For example, as was shown above, simple debriefing may not be enough. Students who serve as subjects talk about their experiences with other students; they may even magnify them as they are prone to do a fraternity initiation rite. The impact upon future subjects can be deadly and difficult to overcome.

An experience the writer had several years ago illustrates how much the formal, authoritarian, pyramidal relationships are endemic in many social science generalizations even though they are never made explicit.

A world-renowned learning theorist met with a group of executives. To his surprise, one of these, a senior corporate officer, had attempted to utilize the learning theorist's views in his workplace. For example, he wanted to see what would happen if he related to his subordinates in a more systematic way, that is, by following a carefully thought-through reinforcement schedule of rewards. He reported the following difficulties:

First, it was difficult to infer any guidelines or criteria as to what would be a valid schedule. Nevertheless, with the help of an advanced graduate student, one was developed. It was not too long before the executive found that he spent the majority of his time simply monitoring the schedules and giving the appropriate rewards according to schedule.

Although all subordinates seemed to respond favorably, there was an unexpected differential reaction. Many men, unlike the subjects in the experiment, reacted positively to their boss and to his rewards. They would say in effect, "Thank you, sir. I certainly appreciate your thoughtfulness." This genuine response tended to complicate matters for two reasons. First, being able to show gratitude toward a superior may in itself be gratifying. Second, such a warm response normally calls for an equally positive response from the recipient, such as "It's always a pleasure, Smith, to reward excellent behavior." In either case the subject is experiencing rewards that would not be in the reinforcement schedule.

The executive, although pleased with the "subject's" reaction, strove to minimize the pleasure so that the original reinforcement schedule would not be confounded. In doing this he found that he was creating a world where his subordinates had a relationship to him that was similar to the one rats (or children) have to an experimenter. This relationship was one in which the subordinate was dependent and had a short time perspective. The schedule, if it were to work, required a fundamentally authoritarian relationship!

To make matters worse, the "subjects" were constantly having their lives bombarded with meaningful rewards and penalties from other employees as well as from such administrative procedures as budgets. The executive began to realize that if these were to be systematically controlled, he would have to become a little Hitler, control the world of his subordinates completely, to the point that they would be isolated from the system in which they were embedded.

It is important to note that nowhere did the learning theorist state these conditions in his generalizations. For example, he had concluded that a specified reinforcement schedule seemed to lead to a specific level of learning. He failed to specify that this generalization held only if the subject was in a specified relationship to the one doing the rewarding and penalizing, namely, one that is similar to that of an experimenter with a rat. Thus, we see that the nature of person-to-person relationships and the nature of the research situation can serve as potent moderators of the variable relationships we often study. If this is the case, the generalizations from rigorous research studies of the types described above ought to "work" (in the sense that they account for substantial portions of the nonrandom variance) only in life situations which are analogous to the experimental situations in which the original data were collected. The analogous situations are those that contain authoritarian relationships and provide for social isolation of the participants. These generalizations ought not to hold up (and indeed ought not to be expected to hold up), however, in those cases where a controlling party and the object of control are engaged in a relationship which is of a qualitatively different type than that of the experimenter and subject in the experimental situation which gave rise to the data, and where the characteristics of the situation (i.e., of the task and social environment) are substantially different in the life situation than in the experimental situation.

Research in Field Settings

The problems discussed above also hold true for the researcher-subject relationship in field settings; indeed, in some cases the problems are compounded.

During the past several years, while conducting field research, the writer has interviewed 35 lower level employees and 30 upper level executives on the subject of how they heard about the research, how they felt coming to be interviewed or filling out the questionnaire, and how they felt while being interviewed or filling out a questionnaire.

The most consistent finding was the unanimity of responses. Apparently research conducted in organizations may create even deeper problems for subjects. Although the data are admittedly anecdotal, it seems appropriate to use them as suggestive of the problem. In doing so, it is important to keep in mind that in all the field studies from which these data were developed, the management at all levels had been briefed by the researcher in small groups with ample time for questions, and letters of explanation had gone to each employee from the president, as well as being displayed on all the bulletin boards.

Although the managers at the lower levels felt they understood the research program and were in favor of it, when it came to telling the employee such a seemingly simple thing as that he was scheduled to be interviewed the next day, many felt very uncomfortable in doing so. They did not feel they could honestly describe the research, nor did they feel they could answer employee anxieties, and more importantly, they reported, they did not want to try. This attitude is understandable because most managers tend to emphasize "getting the job done"; they rarely inquire about their interpersonal impact on the employees, nor about interpersonal problems (Argyris, 1962; 1965). Thus to discuss a research project that could arouse emotional responses would place the manager in an interpersonal situation that would be uncomfortable for him.

Instead of running the risk of engaging in possible difficult conversation with an employee, most managers reported (and employees confirmed) that they simply went up to the employee and notified him that he would be interviewed the next day at a particular time. Over 75 percent of the employees reported that their superiors either ordered them to go to be interviewed or said it in such way that they implied that they did not want any "noise." Thus, most employees felt they (the employees) knew very little about the research. Few reported open resentment (after all they were always being ordered to do something). Many reported feeling anxious.

The reasons for anxiety seemed to vary enormously. "Why did they pick me? Who picked me? Are they going to ask personal questions? Are they trying to get rid of me? Whose crazy idea was this? Will I be able to understand a professor or a researcher? Will the questions be too difficult? Will they ask me to write? How open should I be? Will it get anyone (including me) in trouble? What effect will this have on my wages earned for the day? What effect will my absence have upon others who are working and depend on me?" In some case the anxiety was compounded by informal employee kidding and discussion about the research. "Who goes to see the headshrinkers first?" "I hear they place a hot towel on your head and send electrical currents through you to make sure you don't lie." "They have a guy who can read your mind."

Few of these anxieties were openly stated and fewer were dealt with. Many employees, who came to be interviewed or to fill out the questionnaire with varying degrees of anxiety, attempted to cope with their feelings by becoming resigned ("They do things to me unilaterally all the time."), or by mild hostility and cautious withdrawal or noninvolvement.

The feelings of being controlled, or being pushed around, and of anxiety were reduced more quickly in the interview situation because the interviewer was able to answer many of their questions (without their having to raise them), helped them to feel that they did not have to participate, and encouraged them to alter the questions or the sequence in which they were asked, as well as to feel free to refuse to answer any questions. The negative feelings, reported the subjects, persisted over a longer period in the questionnaire situation. They reported that they felt more controlled, pushed around, and dealt with at a distance, while filling out the questionnaire. For example, many reported questions that arose in their minds but they hesitated to discuss them openly.

The reported feelings of being controlled, being dependent, and submissive to a researcher tended to decrease as one went up the hierarchy and with more participation people had in learning about the research and in deciding if permission was to be granted for its execution. Moreover, the fear of intellectual incompetence to participate was almost negligible. However, there were some anxieties about how open to be, how much risk to take, and how much to level with the interviewer. As in the case of the lower level employees, the (properly executed) questionnaire situation irritated a significantly higher proportion of the managers than did a (properly executed) interview. The executives reported that they resented the unilateral dependence that they experienced in filling out a questionnaire.

It seems that the research process, in a field setting, tends to place subjects in a situation *vis-à-vis* the researcher that is similar to the superior-subordinate relationship. This is not a neutral encounter for most people, especially for employees of organizations, and especially if the research is being conducted within the organization and during working time.

There is another impact that the research process tends to have upon people that has the effect of creating a double bind. Bennis (1966) has summarized the position of many scientists and philosophers of science that the underlying spirit of scientific research is the spirit of inquiry. It is the irresistible need to explore, the hypothetical spirit. The norm to be open, to experiment, is also crucial in the spirit of inquiry. Also there is a fundamental belief in the gratification derived from gaining knowledge for its own sake as well as the sharing of knowledge with all.

If we compare these conditions with those found in the living systems of organizations we find that the organizations tend to create the opposite conditions. For example, it has been shown that interpersonal openness, experimentation, and trust tend to be inhibited in organizations (Argyris, 1962). The same may be said for the concern for truth for its own sake. The sharing of knowledge is not a living value since that could lead to one's organizational survival being threatened. Thus, the subject is in a double bind. He is expected to be open, manifest a spirit of inquiry, and take risks when he is placed in a situation that has many of the repressive characteristics of formal organizations, which he has long ago learned to adapt to by not being open or taking risks.

The degree to which this double bind exists probably varies enormously with the living system of the organization, the personal and organizational security of the subjects, their intellectual competence, their position in the system as well as the research methods, research style, and the interpersonal skills of the researcher. However, the position being taken here is that these forces and binds should be taken into account by the researchers in designing, introducing, executing, analyzing, and feeding back the data to the subjects.

To complete the picture we should mention the relationship between the senior researcher and the junior members of a research team. After all, they too form a system in which superior-subordinate relationships exist. If our model is valid, we would expect that some of the adaptive mechanisms predicted above would be found in these relationships. Unfortunately, little systematic data exist on this subject. Recently, Roth (1966) presented some data that illustrate the writer's predictions. He presented evidence that the graduate students saw much of their work as being boring and tedious. In several cases the students adapted by withdrawing from work and by cheating. Observation time was cut, the number of observations reduced, and finally fake observations were submitted for full time periods. In other cases Roth suggests that guilt was reduced by becoming less able to hear what the people said and by reducing the richness of the observations on the (conscious) grounds that there was less going on. In still other cases, researchers who missed appointments or skipped questions, filled out their forms later by putting down what they thought the respondent should have answered. Of course, none of these informal behaviors was ever revealed to the senior researcher. As Roth correctly points out, the researchers acted pretty much like lower level employees in plants who perform repetitive tasks.

Recently, Rosenthal (1964) suggested another possibility which, if confirmed, is even more serious. He suggested that, in some cases, the junior investigator may be in such a dependency relationship to the senior investigator that he may, unknowingly, be more sensitized to instances that confirm his superior's views than to those that do not. These data raise serious questions about the standards usually accepted for checks on reliability and validity (i.e., the use of friends, colleagues, wives).

Before this discussion is ended, it may be helpful to note an important problem identified by research in organizations that social scientists may be faced with when conducting research in ongoing systems. The problem stems from the fact that in organizations, at the higher and lower levels, openness, concern for feelings, self-awareness, interpersonal experimentation, and trust tend to be suppressed. The reason for this, at the lower levels, is the technology which ties an employee to a highly molecularized and specialized job permitting little expression of self. At the upper levels, the technology decreases as a causal factor and the values executives hold about effective interpersonal relationships become dominant causal factors. In both cases therefore, organizational theory predicts, and to date the data support the prediction, that employees (lower and upper) will tend to be programmed to behave interpersonally more incompetently than competently, and to be unaware of this fact.

For example, in 35 different groups, with 370 participants, in 265 problem-solving and decision-making meetings, tackling issues ranging from investments, production, engineering, personnel, foreign policy, case discussions, new products, sales promotion, to physical science research discussions, it was found that the participants were unable to predict their interpersonal behavior accurately. Ninety-two percent predicted that the *most frequently* observed categories would be owning up, concern, trust, individuality, experimentation, helping others, and openness to feelings. The actual scores (in a sample of 10,150 units) showed that their prediction was accurate only in the case of owning up to ideas. The prediction was moderately accurate in the case of concern for ideas. Trust, experimentation, individuality, helping others, and the expression of positive or negative feelings—all the behaviors that they predicted would be frequent—were rarely observed. Conformity, a category which they predicted would be low in frequency, was the second most frequently observed category (Argyris, 1966). These data have been replicated with groups of students, clergy, nurses, teachers, and physical scientists. If these data continue to be replicated, then the researchers who are studying interpersonal relationships may have to include observational data of the subject's actual behavior because the interview or questionnaire data could be highly (but unknowingly) distorted.

To summarize up to this point: Organizational theory is an appropriate theory to use to understand the human system created by rigorous research designs. The theory predicts that the correct use of rigorous designs, in experimental or field settings, will tend to place subjects in situations that are similar to those organizations create for the lower level employees. Also predicted is that the research assistants may be placed in situations that are similar, at worst, to the low-skill and, at best, to the high-skill employees in organizations.

These conditions lead to unintended consequences. The subjects may adapt by becoming dependent. They may also fight the research by actively rejecting a positive contributive role or by covertly withdrawing this involvement and thereby provide minimally useful data. The subjects may also band together into an organization that may better represent their interest. Finally, an organized society may unintentionally program people who may be asked to be interpersonally incompetent and unaware of the fact.

Suggestions to Overcome the Problems

If the unintended consequences of rigorous research reside in the degree of control the researcher has over the subject and the subject's resultant dependence, submissiveness and short time perspective, then theoretically it would make sense to reduce the researcher's control over the subject. It would also follow from the theoretical framework that it would make sense to provide the subject with greater influence, with longer time perspective regarding, and greater internal involvement in, the research project.

It is understandable that researchers resist these action suggestions. They argue that all research could be ruined if subjects had greater influence.

These arguments are almost identical with the reactions of many executives when asked to consider giving greater influence to their employees in administration of the firm. However, after much research the executives have begun to learn that the situation is not as bleak as they pictured it would be. Thy have learned that workers do not demand nor desire complete control. They do not want to manage the entire plant. They wish greater influence, longer time perspective, and an opportunity for genuine participation at points and during time spans where it makes sense.

The same may be true of subjects. They would not tend to see the issue as one of complete versus no involvement. They would be willing to react reasonably if the researchers could show, by their behavior, that they assumed the subjects could be reasonable and are to be trusted.

Managers have developed from research an increasing number of guideposts regarding the conditions under which employee participation is helpful and harmful to the employee and to the organization. Unfortunately similar research is lacking in the area of conducting research. We have few data regarding when it is in the interests of the researcher and of the subject to invite the subject to participate in the design and execution of the research. It may be that, as a first step, much can be accomplished by having worker representative groups (in organizations) and student representative groups (in universities) to help in the design and execution of research as well as in the attraction and involvement of subjects in the research.

The most important fear expressed by researchers when considering subject influence is the fear of contamination of research. This is a legitimate fear. As we have seen, if subjects know what the research is about they may give the researcher what he wants. However, it should be noted in the studies where these results have been found they were *not* studies where the subject was to gain personally from participating (e.g., voting or marketing studies, Hyman, Cobb, Feldman, Hart, & Stember, 1954). One must be careful in generalizing from these studies to situations where the subject feels genuinely involved in the research.

There are further two points that may be worth considering about this position. Subjects *are* trying to please the researcher even when they are not told what the research is about. This means that much time and energy is being spent by the subject in second-guessing the researcher. If this is so, the researcher runs the risk of compounding the problem of unintended contamination.

The second point to be made about contamination is that it is inevitable. The issue therefore is *not* contamination versus no contamination. *The issue is under what conditions can the researcher have the greatest awareness of, and control over, the degree of contamination.*

Is it possible to create a psychological set on the part of the subject so that he is involved in giving as accurate replies as he can *and* in keeping the researcher informed as to when he (subject) is becoming defensive or could become defensive? Can the subject be helped to become as objective and verbal as he can about his subjectivity? Under what conditions can subjects be motivated to be so involved in the research that they strive to give valid data and warn the researcher when they (or others) may not be giving valid data?

Perhaps subjects will be motivated when they believe that it is in their interests to be so. Perhaps researchers may wish to consider designing research in such a way that the subject can gain from participating in the research (a gain that goes beyond simple feedback of results).

Motivating subjects by offering some possible help could make the situation more threatening rather than less threatening. For example, there are studies to show that people lie to their physicians when they describe their problems if they fear that there is something seriously wrong with them and they may be asked to undergo some stressful therapy like surgery. This is most certainly the case with employees who mistrust their management and would fear participation in research feedback and cooperating with management. In no case will valid research data be obtained where the subjects are fearful of the research or its consequences. If they are fearful, however, would it not be better to know this early in the relationship? Decisions could be made to drop the research or somehow account for the influence the fear would have upon the subjects' participation.

In field research, the biggest fear that we have discovered is that the research will not be relevant to their lives. They tend to see the researcher as a "long-hair" who wants to use them as guinea pigs and who, at most, promises a feedback session to give them the results and leaves them with the more difficult problem (for them) of what to do about their feelings. For example, the writer interviewed about 50 employees in a bank to test certain hypotheses. As an expression of gratitude he wrote a nontechnical report to the officers, who liked it so much that they provided the support to enlarge the study. In enlarging the number interviewed, 25 of the original sample were reinterviewed. The results showed that many of their answers were drastically different from their original answers to the same questions. When the subjects were confronted they replied as follows: During the first study they saw the writer as a researcher who wanted to use them as guinea pigs; during the second study the officers had described the research as helping them to make the bank a more effective system. "Now," they continued, "you could really make a difference in our lives, so we had to tell you the truth!"

In our experience the more subjects are involved directly (or through representatives) in planning and designing the research, the more we learn about the best ways to ask questions: the critical questions from the employees' views, the kinds of resistances each research method would generate, and the best way to gain genuine and long-range commitment to the research (Argyris, 1958). Moreover, subjects have told interviewers why they felt the interviewers were biasing their answers, so that they wondered if giving an answer during an interview might not bias an interviewer in his observations (which they expected since they had participated in the design of the research). Or, they have hesitated to tell the researcher certain information in the interview because they thought it might bias his observations. In reading protocols of interviews where feedback and help in exploring their problems is promised to subjects, one can find a great number of comments that indicate the subject is trying to be very careful not to distort his responses. For example, subjects have told the writer when they were not certain about an answer, or when they were biased, or how we should check their views with certain individuals.

Researchers are also concerned about telling subjects about the research lest such feedback influence them to change their behavior. In our experience this fear is more valid when the subject does *not* perceive the feedback of the results as relevant to his life or when he is asked to provide data that he perceives as inconsequential and nonrelevant. Also, the degree to which a subject can vary his response is much less if one is studying his behavior through observations rather than his reports of his behavior (either through interviews or questionnaires).

For example, telling the subjects the plan of a study did not alter their behavior. The subjects were unable to alter their behavior even when asked, told, cajoled, required to do so (Argyris, 1965). In one case 10 executives were observed for 3 months without telling them the variables that were being studied or the results. Their behavior showed no change during this period. Two men were then asked to alter their behavior in the direction that would make them more effective group members. They agreed to try and both were unable to do so. One man became so frustrated with himself that he wrote a large note to keep in front of himself with appropriate reminders (e.g., to listen more, to cut people off less, etc.). In the first 10 minutes of a meeting a topic was raised that certainly involved him and he returned immediately to his original style.

In another case feedback was given to a group of executives about their behavior. After the feedback session, they spent 3 hours deciding what behavior they wanted to change. Three of them committed themselves to work together to change their behavior. The researcher acknowledged their constructive intent but told them he doubted they could change their behavior. They became annoyed and insisted they could. Subsequent research showed that their behavior patterns never changed.

These observations should not be surprising to anyone who has to help people change behavior that is internalized, highly potent, and related to their feelings of intellectual and interpersonal competence, as well as to their career survival. Put in another way, the more researchers study such behavior, the less they may need to worry about such contamination.

Even if this were not the case, the researcher still has many ways to check as to whether involving the subject and offering help contaminate the research. For example, if the analysis is valid, predictions can be made as to how subordinates will respond on a superior's behavior (or vice versa), or how people will behave under particular conditions. If these predictions are not confirmed, then one can doubt the validity of the diagnosis.

It should be emphasized that we are not suggesting that we must swing from little subject influence and control to total subject influence and control. The major suggestion is that research needs to be conducted to learn more about the conditions where subject influence and control are possible and under what conditions more rigorous research (in the sense that the researcher has greater awareness and control over contamination) can be accomplished.

We may also have to reexamine the meaning of our present concepts of rigorousness and preciseness. They may imply a degree of precision about the nature of our universe which may not be the case. Is not the universe of human behavior more accurately characterized by redundancy and overdeterminedness? Human beings may design and build their interpersonal relationships the way engineers design and build bridges. The latter usually figure out precisely the stresses and strains and then triple their figures as a safety factor. Bridges are "over-built"; and behavior may be overdetermined. Human beings build their interpersonal relationships with the use of many imprecise and overlapping units. As Herbert

A. Simon has pointed out, people's problem-solving processes may be quite sloppy; they neither maximize nor optimize; they satisfice. However, he has also shown that these sloppier processes are subject to systematic understanding.

This view is similar to von Neumann's (1958) thesis that one of the crucial differences between the computer and the brain is the brain's capacity to be accurate with a lot of noise going on in its circuits. The brain can operate relatively accurately with a calculus that, for the computer, is relatively sloppy. Indeed, the computer would probably break down if it had to use the calculus characteristic of the brain. Perhaps what social science methodology needs to do is take on more of the characteristics of human problem solving. It would then enter a realm of overlapping, redundant concepts and thus be able to operate and predict in the world in which we live even though it is full of noise.

In closing, it may be worth noting that high validity and reliability scores with these concepts are best obtained with observers who manifest a relatively high degree of competence in the variables being studied. For example, in the development of a system of categories in organization and innovation, observers with relatively high degree of interpersonal openness and trust were able to devlop interobserver reliability scores with these variables ranging from 80 to 94 percent within 8 hours of scoring. Two of these observers were able within 2 hours to reproduce the score of 74 percent agreement after 1 year of not using the scoring system. However, two observers with relatively low capacity to be open and trusting were never able to reach a higher observer interreliability score than about 50 percent. The possession of the higher level of interpersonal competence made it possible for the first pair to see the interpersonal world more accurately and reliably. These findings are similar to Meehl's (1965) and Barron's (1965). They have suggested that the most reliable and valid raters of "creativity" were people who themselves were creative. Reliable and valid observation of interpersonal phenomena may also require a certain level of interpersonal competence. Research is needed to help us understand more precisely how social scientists can develop valid theories and rigorous operational measures in a universe which may be composed of overlapping and redundant parts; where interrelationships are so complex that concepts of steady state are needed to conceptualize them; where objective observations may be limited to researchers who already manifest a relatively high competence in the phenomena under study.

REFERENCES

Argyris, C. 1958. Creating effective relationships in organizations. *Human Organization* 17: 34–40.

———. 1962. *Interpersonal competence and organizational effectiveness.* Homewood, Ill.: Irwin.

———. 1964. *Integrating the individual and the organization.* New York: Wiley.

———. 1965. *Organization and innovation.* Homewood, Ill.: Irwin.

———. 1966. Interpersonal barriers to decision making. *Harvard Business Review* 44: 84–97.

———. 1967. Today's problems with tomorrow's organizations. *Journal of Management Studies* 4: 31–55.

———. 1970. *Intervention theory and method.* Reading, Mass.: Addison-Wesley.

Barron, F. 1965. Some studies of creativity at the Institute of Personality Assessment and Research. In H. A. Steiner, ed., *The creative organization.* Chicago: University of Chicago Press.

Bennis, W. 1966. *Changing organizations.* New York: McGraw-Hill.

Brock, C., & Becker, L. A. 1966. "Debriefing" and susceptibility to subsequent experimental manipulation. *Journal of Experimental Social Psychology* 2: 314–23.

Burdick, E. 1957. *The ninth wave.* New York: Dell.

Edwards, A. L. 1954. Experiments: Their planning and execution. In G. Lindzey, ed., *Handbook of social psychology.* Reading, Mass.: Addison-Wesley.

Friedman, N. 1967. *The social nature of psychological research.* New York: Basic Books.

Hyman, H. H., Cobb, W. J., Feldman, J. J., Hart, C. W., & Stember, C. M. 1954. *Interviewing in social research.* Chicago: University of Chicago Press.

Kelman, H. C. 1967. The problem of deception in social psychological experiments. *Psychological Bulletin* 67: 1–11.

Kiesler, C. 1969. Group pressure and conformity. In J. Mills, ed., *Advanced experimental social psychology.* New York: Macmillan.

Meehl, P. E. 1965. The creative individual: Why it is hard to identify him. In H. A. Steiner, ed., *The creative organization.* Chicago: University of Chicago Press.

Mills, T. M. 1962. A sleeper variable in small groups research: The experimenter. *Pacific Sociology Review* 5: 21–28.

Orne, M. T. 1962. On the social psychology of the psychology experiment; with particular reference to demand characteristics and their implications. *American Psychologist* 17: 776–83.

Rosenthal, R. 1963. On the social psychology of the psychological experiment: The experimenter's hypotheses as unintended determinants of experimental results. *American Scientist* 51: 268–83.

———. 1964. Experimenter outcome-orientation and the results of the psychological experiment. *Psychological Bulletin* 61: 405–12.

———. 1966. *Experimenter effects in behavioral research.* New York: Appleton-Century-Crofts.

Roth, J. A. 1966. Hired hand research. *American Sociologist* 1: 190–96.

Sales, S. M. 1966. Supervisory style and productivity: Review and theory. *Personnel Psychology* 19: 281–82.

von Neumann, J. 1958. *The computer and the brain.* New Haven: Yale University Press.

39

Suspicion and the Experimental Confederate: A Study of Role and Credibility

J. DAVID MARTIN

In small groups experiments, social psychologists often plant one or more of their own confederates among naïve subjects. This practice is followed for three main reasons. First, the use of confederates is a convenient method of manipulating a "treatment" variable. The confederate presents himself as just another subject and attempts to inject treatment stimuli according to some predetermined plan. The second reason for using a confederate is that it allows the experimenter to employ research designs that appear more "natural" to the subject in that he interacts with another human being rather than a mechanical contrivance. Finally, when stooges are used, subjects are exposed to a more uniform set of stimuli than would be the case if the independent variable were to be manipulated by matching subjects according to some pre-measured personality factor, social category, or other individual characteristic. Thus, the social psychologist is able to achieve better control over extraneous variables that would creep into his study if he were to use different, though carefully selected, naïve subjects to manipulate a treatment.

Presumably, the use of confederates can be successful only if the naïve subjects are indeed taken in by the deception. However, such deception is becoming more and more difficult to pull off. Certain populations, especially college students, are not quite as naïve as might be desired. The fact that experimenters use stooges and other forms of deception has become a matter of common knowledge.

There is reason to believe (mostly through speculation) that suspicious subjects behave differently from subjects who are completely duped by stooges. However, without something more than speculation to go on, the experimenter is poorly equipped to take corrective action. Exactly what form

J. David Martin, "Suspicion and the Experimental Confederate: A Study of Role and Credibility," *Sociometry* 33 (1970): 178–91.

behavioral differences take, and under what conditions they are likely to occur, are themselves important and researchable questions. The following selection by J. David Martin is a report of empirical research on some facets of the latter question.

Small group experiments often involve the manipulation of independent variables by means of a confederate of the experimenter (cf. Alvarez, 1968; Asch, 1953; Schachter, 1951; Sherif, 1958). This "stooge" plays the part of group member and attempts to inject stimuli on a predetermined basis. The assumption that he succeeds in his attempt has recently been questioned. A growing literature on demand characteristics and other spurious-effect factors in social-psychological research (see, e.g., Barber, 1961, 1965, 1966; Orne, 1962; Orne and Scheibe, 1964; Rosenberg, 1965; Sherman, 1967; Stricker, Messick and Jackson, 1967, 1969) has led to increased doubt about the apparent reality of many experimental situations. This caution logically entails a concern with the non-programmed effects of the confederate. Student subjects especially, who may have been made aware of the use of confederates in experimentation, must sometimes wonder if there might be a stooge in *their* experiment.

If a stooge's status as confederate is discovered, his success in injecting the desired stimuli would seem to be less likely. In a recent review of the literature, Stricker, Messick, and Jackson (1969) indicate that deceived subjects, including those deceived by confederates, behave quite differently from undeceived (or suspicious) subjects. They find a number of studies in which deceptions, including confederacy, indeed fail to deceive. The possibility of stooge detection exists, and it poses a potential threat to validity in studies involving confederates.

Important questions relating to stooge detection include: (1) *What conditions increase and decrease the suspiciousness of a stooge performance?* (2) *Are actual stooges more often suspected than naive subjects?* and (3) *Do some naive subjects detect stooges more readily than others?* Since the suspicious do behave differently from the unsuspecting, it is desirable to know, and where possible to correct, the conditions that enhance suspicion. Where stooges and naive subjects of similar social type (playing similar roles) are about equally suspicious, the results the stooge produces, while not free of the effect of suspicion, may approximate the results the stooge's "real" counterpart would have produced. If some kinds of spontaneous subjects detect confederates frequently, their elimination from stooge experiments may often be desirable.

Among the conditions especially likely to affect the suspiciousness of a stooge performance must be included the role performed. If this role is deviant, the non-deviants in the group may generalize from this to suspect the deviant of other kinds of deviance, including confederacy. Such generalization of deviance has been observed by the writer in other settings (Martin, 1968); and is consistent with the implications of Cohen's (1966) concept of "deviant characters" and with Merton's (1966) observation that people react negatively to all deviance because some deviance is disruptive. If being a confederate is deviant from the expectations held for "fellow subject," then it follows from the principle of generalization of deviance that:

Deviants, whether or not they are actually confederates, will be more frequently suspected to be confederates than will non-deviants. (Hypothesis 1)

Since deviance is more likely to receive reactions when it is conspicuous (Martin, 1968; Merton, 1966) it seems likely that:

Of two deviants, the more conspicuous will elicit more suspicion of confederacy. (Corollary 1a)

Deviance is usually defined to cover atypical or proscribed behavior; in a small group situation the person taking a minority position is typically the one who is called deviant (e.g., Schachter, 1951). Provided that this person makes his position clear by disagreeing overtly and repeatedly with other subjects, this definition indicates what I shall call *simple deviance.* Another kind of deviant behavior, which is harder to define concretely, also exists.

The "problem of keeping fresh" (Webb et al., 1966: 166) is a reflection of the fact that confederates are actors and there is always a danger of low-quality acting. Confederates can act out of character. Uninstructed subjects can behave in patterns which are internally inconsistent and appear to be "acting out of character." In either case, the failure of the presented self (both behavior and appearance) to exhibit internal consistency may be regarded as deviant. This kind of deviance I shall call *incongruity.* It should act to increase suspicion, as does simple deviance.

There is no clear basis for hypothesizing that confederates will be more frequently suspected than naive subjects, but this appears to the writer to be the general folklore of the discipline. It is intuitively plausible that subtle cues give away some confederates, though it is wholly possible that skilled confederates are as convincing as unskilled naive subjects. Given that Stricker, Messick, and Jackson (1969) have found substantial suspicion, it will be hypothesized that

Actual confederates will be more often designated as stooges than will non-confederates exhibiting similar levels of deviance. (Hypothesis 2)

The experimentally naive subject is usually preferred when available (see for example the advice of Stricker, Messick, and Jackson, 1969). The experienced subject may well be more suspicious; in addition, his experience may give him some skill in spotting accomplices. When the subject has *limited* experience, a further question is raised: Will he rely on experience, as people often do, and suspect the confederate in *this* study to be very much like confederates he has encountered in the past? Two partially contradictory hypotheses may be suggested—one dealing with the experience variable alone and one dealing with the nature of limited experience:

> *Subjects having limited previous experience with the use of confederates will tend to choose as stooges persons whose behavior resembles that of confederates they have previously encountered.* (Hypothesis 3a)
> *Subjects having previous experience with the use of stooges will be more likely to correctly identify confederates than will experimentally naive subjects.* (Hypothesis 3b)

To the extent that subjects in an experiment have previously encountered confederates who played the same roles being played by the stooges in the present experiments, the two hypotheses make the same prediction. To the extent that our subjects' past and present stooges play different roles, and their experience is limited, the hypotheses stand in contradiction. It is possible that Hypothesis 3b holds only for subjects of wide experience, who are aware that a stooge may play any of a number of roles.

Experiments Performed

The present investigation involves five experiments, each conducted in front of a classroom filled with undergraduate students like those typically used as subjects in small group experiments. While the design does not provide data from group members,[1] it does provide data from persons who have been attending closely to the group process, and who are reacting to a "live" group rather than to a filmed or video-taped performance (which might more plausibly be suspected of being staged). The design permits comparison of the proportion of subjects designating a deviant naive subject as stooge with the proportion so designative a deviant confederate. This is relatively difficult with studies of group members, as each naive deviant is only naive once. In the present study, one naive subject receives reactions from 35 to 55 subjects, as compared with three to six subjects in an experiment where the data-producing subjects are group members.

All experiments took place as follows: Subjects were informed that the experimenter wished to pre-test some interaction coding techniques; and that they were to spend a few minutes using the techniques, after which their comments about the techniques would be solicited. Coding instructions were read to the subjects. The demonstration group then entered and sat in a semi-circle facing the audience of subjects. The experimenter read a simple set of task instructions which speci-

---

[1] Data from pilot studies involving group members suggest that the same principles operate there as in this audience experiment series, but that the probability of designation may be lower for all conditions. Only a few subjects have yet been run.

fied a discussion of some social or campus issue, such as drugs, sexual standards, or restrictions placed on resident students. The group began interaction, and the subjects began coding.

After 20 minutes of interaction and coding, the discussion was ended and the subjects were given a questionnaire which asked them to: (1) Identify those members of the demonstration group, if any, whom they considered to be stooges. (2) Indicate what "gave away" these persons. (3) Indicate if they had been previously exposed to stooges, either in actual experiments, in reading, or in class, and to describe what was done by any stooges previously encountered. After finishing the questionnaire, subjects were debriefed and instructed not to discuss the experiment outside the class until the end of the term. They were also informed that subsequent experiments, if any were run, would not have the same group composition as theirs—which was true.

While it is true that the questionnaire introduced a demand characteristic for the reporting of relatively slight suspicion, it did not (except in Experiment 1) demand that suspicion be expressed; indeed, subjects were informed that some groups contained no stooges. Where the relative suspicion aroused by different kinds of subjects is of more interest than the absolute level of suspicion, as is the case here, such a limited demand characteristic is appropriate.

Experiment 1

In Experiment 1, all group members were stooges, who rehearsed for several hours before performing. Two played deviant roles (one conservative, one near-radical) two played modal roles, and one played a "moderator" role whose chief component was a low-key but consistent effort to get the others to agree. The experiment was replicated four times before "social problems" classes. (To minimize diffusion of the nature of the experiment, all replications were run within the space of a week.) While the "moderator" was the same person in all replications, the deviants and modes exchanged parts so that each of the four performers played a deviant part twice and a "mode" part twice. Subjects were informed by the questionnaire that a stooge was present in the group, and were asked to identify the stooge (and to give a second choice and a "least likely" choice if they were not sure of their primary designation). "What gave away the stooge" and past-experience questions were included, which were essentially identical to those used in Experiments 2 through 5.

As Table 1 indicates, the role of conspicuous deviant [2] received 55 percent of all designations as stooge and 19 percent of all second-choice designations. The inconspicuous deviant received 17 percent of all designations as stooge and 42 percent of the second-choice designations. The quiet conformers received, *to-*

[2] The most talkative subject was designated by the experimenter as conspicuous. Where a near tie for most talkative was present, two (or conceivably more) conspicuous subjects were defined to exist. In one group talking rates were sufficiently similar that no conspicuous subject was designated.

gether, 5 percent of the designations as stooge and 15 percent of the second-choice designations. Designation rates for conspicuous deviant (first choice) and inconspicuous deviant (second choice) were significantly higher than would be expected by chance; designation rates for quiet conformers were significantly lower than would be expected by chance. Designation rates for the "moderator" approximated what would be expected if designations had been made by chance.

TABLE 1
SUSPICION DATA: EXPERIMENT 1

	First-choice designations	*Second-choice designations*	*Least-likely designations*
Conspicuous deviant	52 (55%)*	14 (19%)	10 (14%)
Inconspicuous deviant	16 (17%)	31 (42%)*	5 (7%)
Moderator	22 (23%)	17 (23%)	6 (8%)
"Modal" (conformer)	5 (5%)**	11 (15%)**	53 (71%)*
Total	95 (100%)	73 (100%)	74 (100%)

* Significantly greater than would be expected if designations were made at random, $p < .01$.
** Significantly fewer than would be expected if designations were made at random, $p < .01$.
Significance tests were based on the cumulative binomial distribution. For the deviant and moderator roles, which had one role-player, $p_{null} = 20$; for the modal role, which had two role-players, $p_{null} = .40$.

Designation rates by role were nearly the same in all four replications of Experiment 1. All roles seemed to elicit the same suspicion levels, independent of player. (For details of the analysis see Martin, 1969.) Personality variables, at least among well-rehearsed stooges, seem to have relatively little influence in generating suspicion.

Experiment 2

In Experiment 2, all group members were naive subjects. The subject of discussion was sexual morality; the group focused on male homosexuality. As it happened, there were three relatively quiet subjects, two active subjects who took a permissive position (and who received more agreement than disagreement from the quiet subjects) and one active subject who took a very conservative position. The questionnaire used in Experiment 2 and all succeeding experiments asked subjects to rate each group member on a five-point "graphic scale" (Selltiz et al., 1959) whose end-points were "definitely was a stooge" (1) and "definitely was not a stooge" (5); and whose midpoint was "can't say" (3). "What gave away" and previous-experience items were essentially identical to those used in Experiment 1.

The consensus of audience opinion was that a stooge was present, facts to the

TABLE 2
SUSPICION DATA: EXPERIMENT 2

	DISTRIBUTION OF ANSWERS (N = 57; NO STOOGES PRESENT)							
Question	*1*	*2*	*3*	*4*	*5*	*Reply*	*Reply*	*Yes (1 & 2)*
Was a stooge present?	33	12	8	2	2	1	1	.79
Was (Incongruous) a stooge?	16	17	10	4	10	2	2	.58
Was (Conspicuous deviant) a stooge?	21	20	9	2	5	2	1	.72
Was (Modal) a stooge?	0	2	10	5	40	5	5	.04
Was (Modal) a stooge?	2	3	18	10	24	4	5	.09
Was (Modal) a stooge?	0	4	15	7	31	5	5	.07
Was (Conspicuous modal) a stooge?	2	5	20	6	24	4	5	.12

Note: Answer 1 = Definitely yes
3 = Can't say
5 = Definitely not

The following pairs of group members showed significantly different rates of stooge-designation (that is, of subjects answering the question "Was . . . a stooge?" with Answer 1 or Answer 2), $p < .05$:

Incongruous versus all Modals
Conspicuous deviant versus all Modals

The following group members were designated as stooge significantly more often than half the time, $p < .05$:

Conspicuous deviant

The following group members were designated as stooge significantly less often than two-fifths of the time:

All Modals

contrary.[3] Both the simple deviant and an incongruous subject were predominantly perceived to be stooges. (The incongruous subject's mention of a homosexual sibling was not consistent with his own dress and manner nor with his social situation in front of a classroom filled with strangers.[4]) All other subjects in the group were predominantly perceived not to be stooges.

The results of Experiments 1 and 2 are enough to suggest that role—either directly deviant or incongruous—is more important than status as a stooge in generating suspicion. Conclusive data on the question, however, must come from groups containing both confederate and naive subjects.

Experiment 3

In this experiment two confederates and two naive subjects comprised the group. While the confederates could not rehearse, they were given their roles

[3] It should be kept in mind that this consensus was stimulated to some extent by the experimental questionnaire, and probably exaggerates the "natural" level of suspicion in the subject pool.

[4] There is some question whether the act constitutes incongruity or simple deviance. The writer, and the subjects who mentioned it on their questionnaires, perceived it to be inconsistent and hence incongruous.

two weeks in advance and allowed time to prepare for their performances. The topic of discussion was college restrictions on personal liberty. One confederate was assigned the role of "swinger"; he favored, among other things, allowing

TABLE 3
SUSPICION DATA: EXPERIMENT 3

	DISTRIBUTION OF ANSWERS (N = 36)							
Question	*1*	*2*	*3*	*4*	*5*	*Median reply*	*Modal reply*	*Proportion yes (1 & 2)*
Was a stooge present?	21	10	4	0	1	1	1	.86
Was (Modal) a stooge?	1	7	12	4	12	3	3,5	.22
Was (Modal) a stooge?	3	6	16	2	9	3	3	.25
Was (Conspicuous deviant) a stooge?	19	10	5	0	2	1	1	.81
Was (Modal stooge) a stooge?	1	4	12	4	15	4	5	.14

Note: Answer 1 = Definitely yes
3 = Can't say
5 = Definitely not

The following pairs of group members showed significantly different rates of stooge-designation (that is, of subjects answering the question "Was. . . a stooge?" with Answer 1 or Answer 2), $p < .05$:

Conspicuous deviant versus Naive modal (two pairs)
Conspicuous deviant versus Modal stooge

The following group members were designated as stooge significantly more often than half the time, $p < .05$:

Conspicuous deviant

The following group members were designated as stooge significantly less often than two-fifths of the time, $p < .05$:

Modal stooge
Naive modal (Member #1 but not Member #2)

liquor in dormitory rooms and permitting persons of opposite sex to be roommates. The other (a female) was assigned to agree with the point of view dominant in the group and to interact at a moderate to low rate. (This assignment will be referred to as "conformer" or "modal.") The naive subjects were two married students of conventional moral persuasion.

The naive subjects proved to be conformers [5] who were less quiet than the conforming stooge. The distribution of responses to the question, "Is there a stooge in this group?" parallels that obtained in Experiment 2, suggesting that this suspicion may be relatively independent of actual stooge presence, at least in the audience situation.[6] The deviant stooge receives a predominant designation

[5] That is, they agreed with one another. The modal stooge then did as instructed and agreed with them. The deviant stooge thus was clearly deviant.

[6] This experiment was the only experiment run before a class other than "Social Problems"; it was run before a "Small Groups" class which had not been taught about confederates beyond mention of their existence at the time of the run.

as stooge; the quiet conforming stooge receives a predominant designation as non-stooge; and the naive subjects receive designation patterns whose median response is "can't say."

Experiment 4

In Experiment 4 the confederates used in Experiment 3 switched roles. The naive subjects were a co-ed of fairly liberal moral persuasion and a married male student of Bohemian appearance and moral views lying between conventional and slightly liberal, a self-inconsistency which was judged to be incongruous.

TABLE 4

SUSPICION DATA: EXPERIMENT 4

	DISTRIBUTION OF ANSWERS (N = 43)							
Question	*1*	*2*	*3*	*4*	*5*	*Median reply*	*Modal reply*	*Proportion yes (1 & 2)*
Was a stooge present?	28	6	6	1	2	1	1	.79
Was (Modal stooge) a stooge?	2	2	13	7	19	4	5	.09
Was (Mild deviant, naive) a stooge?	4	4	14	9	12	3	3	.19
Was (Deviant stooge) a stooge?	8	3	17	2	13	3	3	.24
Was (Very incongruous naive) a stooge?	25	7	4	2	5	1	1	.74

Note: Answer 1 = Definitely yes
3 = Can't say
5 = Definitely not

The following pairs of group members showed significantly different rates of stooge-designation (that is, of subjects answering the question "Was . . . a stooge?" with Answer 1 or Answer 2), $p < .05$:

Incongruous naive versus Modal stooge
Incongruous naive versus Mild deviant naive
Incongruous naive versus Deviant stooge
Deviant stooge versus Modal stooge (satisfies directional criterion only)

The following group members were designated as stooge significantly more often than half the time, $p < .05$:

Incongruous naive

The following group members were designated as stooge significantly less often than two-fifths of the time, $p < .05$:

Modal stooge
Mildly deviant stooge
Deviant stooge

The proportion of the audience subjects who felt that a stooge was present approximates the proportions observed in Experiments 2 and 3, further supporting the notion that suspicion may be independent of actual stooge presence. The incongruous male receives the highest proportion of stooge designations observed thus far; the deviant stooge and the other naive subject receive designations whose central tendency is "can't say." A majority of the subjects rated the modal stooge as "not a stooge." (The incongruous male dominated the discussion, with the result that the deviant stooge was less active than was the deviant stooge in Experiment 3. Also, since both naive subjects in Experiment 4 were more liberal than either naive subject in Experiment 3, the deviant stooge was less deviant by comparison.)

Experiment 5

One stooge was used in Experiment 5. He was assigned to dress in a manner inconsistent with his personal style and attitudes,[7] but was given no verbal programming. Among the three naive subjects in the group were one friend of his

TABLE 5
SUSPICION DATA: EXPERIMENT 5

	DISTRIBUTION OF ANSWERS (N = 51)							
Question	*1*	*2*	*3*	*4*	*5*	*Median reply*	*Modal reply*	*Proportion yes (1 & 2)*
Was a stooge present?	40	10	0	0	1	1	1	.98
Was (Conspicuous deviant, naive) a stooge?	30	14	1	2	4	1	1	.86
Was (Modal) a stooge?	0	1	12	6	32	5	5	.02
Was (Dress-incongruous stooge) a stooge?	15	13	15	3	5	2	1,3	.55
Was (Modal) a stooge?	5	3	17	10	16	4	3	.16

Note: Answer 1 = Definitely yes
3 = Can't say
5 = Definitely not

The following pairs of group members showed significantly different rates of stooge-designation (that is, of subjects answering the question "Was . . . a stooge?" with Answer 1 or Answer 2), $p < .05$:

Conspicuous deviant versus Modal (two pairs)
Dress-incongruous stooge versus Modal (two pairs)
Conspicuous deviant versus Dress-incongruous stooge

The following group members were designated as stooge significantly more often than half the time, $p < .05$:

Conspicuous deviant (naive subject)

The following group members were designated as stooge significantly less often than two-fifths of the time, $p < .05$:

Modal (both)

Note: When subjects were asked to say who they considered most likely to be a stooge, one choice only allowed, they chose as follows: Conspicuous deviant, 43; Incongruous stooge, 9; Both modal naive, 2 (one each).

---

[7] The young man is, in attitude and manner, something of a swinger. He wore a mohair sweater with wide stripes which, while not loud, is quite out of style by the standards of my undergraduate informants. His slacks "clashed" somewhat with the sweater. He looked a bit uncomfortable the first time he wore the outfit, further testifying to our success in producing moderate incongruity.

(who was warned that he might dress oddly, which the other two group members were not), and a person of strong moral convictions which proved to be clearly deviant from the views of the rest of the group.

A vast majority of the audience subjects felt that a stooge was present, but most of these designated the conspicuous naive deviant before the incongruous stooge. The stooge, it appears, was designated partly for incongruity, and at least as much because of his familiar manner with his friend (who receives a small amount of suspicion on account of this familiarity.)[8] When asked to designate a "most clearly confederate" subject, 43 of the 51 subjects chose the naive deviant and five the stooge.

Discussion

In all five experiments, a deviant is the person most suspected of confederate status. In four of the experiments, he or she is a simple deviant (that is, one who deviated from the central tendency of the group with respect to position on the discussion topic). In Experiment 4, incongruity between convincing Bohemian appearance and conventional moral views constitutes the deviance. In this Experiment 4, the incongruous deviant is more conspicuous than the simple deviant who is present, while in Experiment 2 and Experiment 5, where incongruous subjects also appear, the simple deviant is the more conspicuous. Among deviants, the more conspicuous are the more suspect. The data support Hypothesis 1 and the qualification concerning conspicuousness (Corollary 1a) which was made with it.

In Experiments 1 and 3, the most designated subject was an actual confederate, and a most-conspicuous deviant. In Experiments 2, 4, and 5, a naive subject was the most-conspicuous deviant, and in each experiment that naive subject was the most-designated stooge suspect. The two actual stooges received the lowest rate of suspicion of any most-suspected person (in Experiment 1, where the questionnaire may have influenced the result) and the second highest (in Experiment 3, the only experiment with only one deviant). The highest rate of suspicion was elicited by the naive deviant in Experiment 5, who was also the most conspicuous in terms of conversational dominance.

Ignoring Experiment I, there are 10 modal or nondeviant subjects, of whom 2 are stooges. The stooges rank 4th and 7th in suspicion rate; these ranks put them right in the middle of the distribution. Considering both conspicuous and modal stooges, the data do not support Hypothesis 2.

The data thus permit the inference that if a stooge receives the same reaction as would a naive subject exhibiting the proclivities he stimulates, that stooge will elicit varying amounts of suspicion depending on the role he plays. The deviant stooge who is not suspected may be more convincing than real life!

[8] A minority of those designating the stooge and about half of those designating the friend mentioned their familiarity as one thing that "gave them away."

(This conclusion is tentative pending replication with more subtle suspicion measurement, and should not be used to matter-of-factly dismiss moderate rates of suspicion.) On the other hand, slips of tongue and manner which throw the stooge out of character do indeed "give the show away," and seem likely to invalidate the experimental runs in which they occur.

Given Leik's (1965) finding that the dress and manner of a stooge affected judgments made of him by naive subjects, it is appropriate to ask if stooge personality could color these findings. For Experiments 2, 3, 4, and 5, where naive subjects were used and control was incomplete, it is difficult to ask the question experimentally. In Experiment 1, role rotation showed suspicion to fall upon the role rather than the incumbent, as did an analysis of reasons given for designating a given person as the stooge. The details of the analysis are given in Martin (1969).

Hypothesis 3 asserts that subjects having limited experimental experience will tend to select as stooge a person playing a role similar to the role played by a stooge of which they have heard. Subjects of wide experience, it was hypothesized, will be relatively skilled at stooge detection. Most of the subjects in this series of experiments had heard of few if any experiments involving stooges. Table 6 shows the relationship between the previous experience of these subjects and their designations.

This pattern holds up when only data from Experiment 1 are considered (Martin, 1969); it is not an artifact of the act of pooling data. As it happens, the designation pattern found among experienced subjects is essentially the same as that found for all subjects; the distribution of previous experience in these subjects was such as not to bias the overall results. Hypothesis 3b is not supported for all "experienced" subjects.

Too few highly experienced subjects were present, even in the one "Small Groups" class before which an experiment was run, to permit a test of Hypothesis 3b on highly experienced subjects alone.

Summary

When asked whether any member of a group they had just observed interacting might be a stooge, subjects showed a strong tendency to designate deviants as stooges, whether or not those deviants were in fact confederates. Relatively conspicuous deviants elicited relatively great suspicion. Actual stooge status (vs. naive-subject status) had little if any effect on suspicion. The data appear to warrant the conclusion that the role of the subject, rather than whether or not he in fact is a stooge, elicits suspicion.

Subjects who have heard of the use of stooges in research show some tendency, at least in these experiments, to designate as stooges those who act like the stooges of which they have heard. Experimenters should be cautious, as Stricker, Messick, and Jackson (1969) suggest, in using experienced subjects; however, if these subjects' previous experience will give them no clue about the confederate employed in one's current study, the use of subjects of limited experience may be acceptable.

The researcher concerned with suspicion of confederacy only as a source of data error is advised to "cast" his stooges carefully, to rehearse them well, and to use a debriefing interview on at least a "spot check" basis. Subjects who spontaneously express suspicion, or who express it in response to a question like "What did you think of the experiment?" may have to be discarded. Those who designate a deviant as stooge in response to a flat "Do you think there might have been a stooge in the group?" need not be—unless they are quite numerous, or designate a deviant stooge proportionately more often than they designate nonprogrammed deviants.

TABLE 6

BEHAVIOR OF STOOGE DESIGNATED BY BEHAVIOR OF PREVIOUS STOOGE ENCOUNTERS

	PREVIOUS STOOGE WAS	
Present stooge-designate is	*Deviant*	*Other*
Deviant/Incongruous	56 (92%)	35 (74%)
Modal/Conforming	5 (8%)	12 (26%)
Total	61 (100%)	47 (100%)

Chi-square, corrected by rounding expected values to the whole number nearer to the observed values, was computed to be 4.5, $.02 < p < .05$.

REFERENCES

Alvarez, Rodolfo. 1968. Informal reactions to deviant behavior. *American Sociological Review* 33 (December): 895–911.

Asch, Solomon E. 1953. Effects of group pressure upon the modification and distortion of judgments. Pp. 151–61 in Dorwin Cartwright and Alvin Zander, eds., *Group dynamics.* Evanston, Illinois: Row, Peterson.

Barber, Theodore X. 1961. Antisocial and criminal acts induced by "hypnosis." *Archives of General Psychiatry* 5 (September): 301–12.

———. 1965. Physiological effects of "hypnotic suggestions." *Psychological Bulletin* 63 (April): 201–22.

———. 1966. The effects of "hypnosis" and motivational suggestions on strength and endurance. *British Journal of Social and Clinical Psychology* 5: 42–50.

Cohen, Albert K. 1966. *Deviance and control.* Englewood Cliffs, New Jersey: Prentice-Hall.

Freeman, Linton C. 1965. *Elementary applied statistics.* New York: John Wiley and Sons.

Leik, Robert K. 1965. "Irrelevant" aspects of stooge behavior: implications for leadership studies and experimental methodology. *Sociometry* 28 (September): 259–71.

Martin, J. David. 1968. Reactions to deviant behavior in two settings. Paper read at the annual meetings of the Pacific Sociological Association, San Francisco (April).

———. 1969. Stooge role and stooge "detection." *Pacific Sociological Review* (Spring).

Merton, Robert K. 1957. *Social theory and social structure* (Revised and Enlarged Edition). Glencoe, Illinois: The Free Press.

———. 1966. Social problems and sociological theory. Epilogue in Robert K. Merton and Robert A. Nisbet, eds., *Contemporary social problems.* New York: Harcourt, Brace, and World.

Orne, Martin T. 1962. On the social psychology of the psychological experiment. *American Psychologist* 17: 776–83.

——— and Karl F. Scheibe. 1964. "The contribution of nondeprivation factors in the production of sensory deprivation effects." *Journal of Abnormal and Social Psychology* 68: 3–12.

Rosenberg, Milton J. 1965. When dissonance fails: on eliminating evaluation apprehension from attitude measurement. *Journal of Personality and Social Psychology* 1 (January): 28–42.

Schachter, Stanley. 1951. Deviation, rejection and communication. *Journal of Abnormal and Social Psychology* 46: 190–207.

Selltiz, Claire, Marie Jahoda, Morton Deutsch, and Stuart Cook. 1959. *Research methods in social relations* (Second Edition). New York: Holt-Dryden.

Sherif, Muzafer. 1958. Group influences upon the formation of norms and attitudes. Pp. 219–232 in Maccoby, Newcomb, and Hartley editors, *Readings in social psychology.* New York: Holt.

Sherman, Susan R. 1967. Demand characteristics in an experiment on attitude change. *Sociometry* 30 (September): 246–61.

Stricker, Lawrence J., Samuel Messick, and Douglas N. Jackson. 1967. Suspicion of deception: implications for conformity research. *Journal of Personality and Social Psychology* 5 (October): 379–89.

———. 1969. "Evaluating deception in psychological research." *Psychological Bulletin* 71 (May): 343–51.

Webb, Eugene, Donald Campbell, Richard Schwartz, and Lee Sechrest. 1966. *Unobtrusive measures.* Chicago: Rand McNally.

40

Sociological Snoopers

NICHOLAS von HOFFMAN

Journalistic Moralizers

IRVING LOUIS HOROWITZ · LEE RAINWATER

While the social scientist studies particular individuals and groups, his major aim in studying them is to generalize to some specified population. In the course of his research, however, he often acquires "guilty knowledge" about his subjects, i.e., information that could embarrass or even incriminate the subjects if it were made public. Although one of the first tenets the social scientist learns is to guarantee the anonymity of subjects regarding this "guilty knowledge," he may still confront the ethical dilemma of invading someone's privacy.

In certain types of research, scientific rigor may demand that information be obtained without a subject's knowledge or consent. In other cases, the social scientist may find it necessary to mislead subjects about what he is really looking for or how he will interpret what they say and do. To much of the lay public, who cherish privacy even as a God-given right, information gathering by social scientists is considered morally wrong.

The following dual selection deals with some of the more salient issues regarding privacy. In the first part by Nicholas von Hoffman, many of the popular arguments against privacy-violating research are stated. In the second part two sociologists, Irving Horowitz and Lee Rainwater, attempt to counter von Hoffman's arguments and to absolve social science research from the charge of violating privacy. This particular debate arose after a sociologist published the findings of his research on homosexuals—he posed as an insider to obtain observational data and later employed the ruse of a door-to-door survey in order to interview the homosexuals in their homes.

Nicholas von Hoffman, "Sociological Snoopers," *Trans-action* 7 (1970): 4–6. and Irving Louis Horowitz and Lee Rainwater, "Journalistic Moralizers," *Trans-action* 7 (1970): 5–7.

Sociological Snoopers

We're so preoccupied with defending our privacy against insurance investigators, dope sleuths, counterespionage men, divorce detectives and credit checkers, that we overlook the social scientists behind the hunting blinds who are also peeping into what we thought were our most private and secret lives. But they are there, studying us, taking notes, getting to know us, as indifferent as everybody else to the feeling that to be a complete human involves having an aspect of ourselves that's unknown.

If there was any doubt about there being somebody who wants to know about anything any other human being might be doing it is cancelled out in the latest issue of *Trans-action,* a popular but respected sociological monthly. The lead article, entitled "Impersonal Sex in Public Places," is a resumé of a study done about the nature and pattern of homosexual activities in men's rooms. Laud Humphreys, the author, is an Episcopal priest, a duly pee-aich-deed sociologist, holding the rank of assistant professor at Southern Illinois University. The article is taken from a forthcoming book called *Tearoom Trade: Impersonal Sex in Public Places* (Aldine Publishing Company, Chicago, March 1970).

Tearoom is the homosexual slang for men's rooms that are used for purposes other than those for which they were designed. However, if a straight male were to hang around a tearoom he wouldn't see anything out of the ordinary so that if you're going to find out what's happening you must give the impression that you're one of the gang.

"I had to become a participant observer of the furtive felonious acts," Humphreys writes in explaining his methodology, "Fortunately, the very fear or suspicion of tearoom participants produces a mechanism that makes such observation possible; a third man—generally one who obtains voyeuristic pleasure from his duties—serves as a lookout, moving back and forth from door to windows. Such a 'watchqueen,' as he is labeled in the homosexual argot, coughs when a police car stops nearby or when a stranger approaches. He nods affirmatively when he recognizes a man entering as being a 'regular.' Having been taught the watchqueen role by a cooperating respondent, I played that part faithfully while observing hundreds of acts of fellatio."

Most of the people Humphreys observed and took notes on had no idea what he was doing or that they, in disguised form, would be showing up in print at some time in the future. Of all the men he studied only a dozen were ever told what his real purpose was, yet as a sociologist he had to learn about the backgrounds and vital facts of the other tearoom visitors he'd seen. To do this Humphreys noted their license numbers and by tracing their cars learned their identities. He then allowed time to pass, disguised himself and visited these men under the color of doing a different, more innocuous door-to-door survey.

He describes what he did this way: "By passing as a deviant, I had observed their sexual behavior without disturbing it. Now I was faced with interviewing these men—often in the presence of their wives—without destroying them. . . . To overcome the danger of having a subject recognize me as a watchqueen, I changed my hair style, attire and automobile. At the risk of losing the more transient respondents, I waited a year between the sample gathering (in the tearoom) and the interviews, during which time I took notes on their homes and neighborhoods and acquired data on them from the city and county directories."

Humphreys said that he did everything possible to make sure the names of the men whose secrets he knew would never get out: "I kept only one copy of the master list of names and that was in a safe deposit box. I did all the transcribing of taped interviews myself and changed all identifying marks and signs. In one instance, I allowed myself to be arrested rather than let the police know what I was doing and the kind of information I had."

Even so, it remains true that he collected information that could be used for blackmail, extortion, and the worst kind of mischief without the knowledge of the people involved. *Trans-action* defends the ethics of Humphreys' methodology on the basis of purity of motive and the argument that he was doing it for a good cause, that is, getting needed, reliable information about a difficult and painful social problem.

Everybody who goes snooping around and spying on people can be said to have good motives. The people whom Sen. Sam Ervin is fighting, the ones who want to give the police the right to smash down your door without announcing who they are if they think you have pot in your house, believe they are well-motivated. They think they are preventing young people from destroying themselves. J. Edgar Hoover unquestionably believes he's protecting the country against subversion when he orders your telephone tapped. Those who may want to overthrow the government are just as well motivated by their lights. Since everybody can be said to be equally well motivated, it's impossible to form a judgment on what people do by assessing their intentions.

To this Laud Humphreys replies that his methods were less objectionable than getting his data by working through the police: "You do walk a really perilous tightrope in regard to ethical matters in studies like this, but, unless someone will walk it, the only source of information will be the police department, and that's dangerous for a society. The methods I used were the least intrusive possible. Oh, I could have hidden in the ceiling as the police do, but then I would have been an accomplice in what they were doing."

Humphreys believes that the police in many cities extort bribes from homosexuals they catch in tearooms. He also thinks that "what's more common is putting an investigation report on file. Often when they catch somebody, they don't arrest him but they get his name, address and employer. There's no defense against this and no way of knowing when the information will be used in the future. I agree there may be a dangerous precedent in studying deviant behavior this way but in some places vice squads use closed circuit TV to look into tearooms and in many cities they use decoys. To my mind *these* are the people who're the dangerous observers."

Some people may answer that by saying a study on such a topic constitutes deviant sociological behavior, a giving in to the discipline's sometimes peculiar taste for nosing around oddballs. But in the study of man anything men do should be permissible to observe and try to understand. Furthermore, Humphreys has evidence and arguments to show that, far from being a rare and nutty aberration, tearoom activity is quite common.

He cites a UCLA law review study showing that in a four-year period in Los Angeles 274 of a total of 493 men arrested for homosexual activities were picked up in tearooms. He has another study in Mansfield, Ohio, that rural fleshpot, saying that police operating with a camera behind a one-way mirror caught 65 men in the course of only two weeks. FBI national crime figures don't have a special category for tearoom arrests, but Humphreys has enough indicative evidence to allow him to say it's a big problem. Even if it weren't, so many parents are worried about their sons being approached by homosexuals that we believe it's a big problem.

Humphreys' study suggests that tearoom habitues stay clear of teen-agers. "I never saw an instance of a teen-ager being approached. The men in the tearoom are scared to death of teen-agers. When a teen-ager comes in the action breaks off and everybody gets out. You have to give a definite sign before you'll be approached (in his book he goes into detail) so they never approach anyone who hasn't done so. Anyway, there's no problem of recruiting teen-agers because teen-agers are too busy trying to join."

Incontestably such information is useful to parents, teen-agers themselves, to policemen, legislators and many others, but it was done by invading some people's privacy. This newspaper could probably learn a lot of things that the public has a right and need to know if its reporters were to use disguises and the gimmickry of modern, transistorized, domestic espionage, but there is a policy against it. No information is valuable enough to obtain by nipping away at personal liberty, and that is true no matter who's doing the gnawing, John Mitchell and the conservatives over at the Justice Department or Laud Humphreys and the liberals over at the Sociology Department.

Journalistic Moralizers

Columnist Nicholas von Hoffman's quarrel with Laud Humphreys' *Impersonal Sex in Public Places* starkly raises an issue that has grown almost imperceptibly over the last few years, and now threatens to create in the next decade a tame sociology to replace the fairly robust one that developed during the sixties. For most of their history, the disciplines of sociology and social psychology were considered a kind of joke, an oddball activity pursued by academic types who cultivated an arcane jargon that either concealed ivory tower views about human reality, or simply said things that everyone knew already.

Somehow, during the 1960s, that image began to shift quite dramatically. People suddenly began to look to sociologists and social psychologists for explanations of what was going on, of why the society was plagued with so many problems. Sociological jargon, perspectives and findings began to enter people's conversation and thinking in a way that no one would have imagined a few years before. All during the sixties enrollment in sociology classes in colleges and universities increased at an accelerating rate. What sociologists had to say about international relations, or race problems, or deviant behavior, or health care, or the crisis of the city became standard parts of the ways Americans explained themselves to themselves.

But as the sociological enterprise grew, there also grew up a reaction against it, especially among those who are also in the business of interpreting the society to itself. For, as sociologists know (even if they sometimes forget it), any statement, even of "fact," about a society is also a political assertion in that, whatever the motivation of the speaker, his views can have an impact on the political processes of the society. But there are other kinds of occupations that have traditionally had the right to make these kinds of statements. Foremost among them have been journalists, clergymen, politicians and intellectuals generally. When his perspectives and findings began to gain wider currency, the sociologist became willy-nilly a competitor in the effort to establish an interpretation of what we are all about. And so, these past few years, sociologists have been getting their lumps from those various groups.

With increasing stridency, traditional politicians have railed against university social scientists who exercise undue influence on the way public issues are defined. Right and left militants have sought to dry up their ability to influence public definitions through derision and systematic efforts to deny them access to sources of data. Beginning in the fifties, right wing groups launched successive campaigns against behavioral scientists, as both practitioners and teachers, culminating most recently in the John Birch Society campaign against sex education. All this has had a quiet influence on the research work of social scientists. Slowly but perceptibly over the last couple of years, and with no sign of abatement, sociologists and social psychologists are being told by a varied chorus that they talk too much, or if not too much, at least that too many of the things they say had better be left unsaid, or the saying of them ought to be left to the traditional spokesmen. What has proved particularly galling about the sociologist, as these other spokesmen view him, is his claim to the mantle of science. For all the tentativeness and roughness of sociological science, it makes at least that claim, and so represents a very powerful threat to the more traditional interpreters of reality.

Perhaps the closest competitors of all are journalists. The intertwinings of journalistic and sociological enterprise are complex indeed and have been from the early days of empirical American sociology. After all, Robert Park was a working journalist, and saw sociology simply as a better journalism because it got at the "big picture." Predictably, then, journalists often feel a deep ambivalence about empirical sociology. On the one hand, it represents a resource that can be quite useful in doing journalistic work. On the other hand, for the ambitious practitioner of personal journalism, there is always the threat to his authority, his potential punditry, by a group of fellow interpreters of the world who lay claim to science as the basis of what they say.

It is perhaps for this reason that von Hoffman so readily applies to sociologists a standard of investigative conduct that few journalists could measure up to, and why he is so unwilling to accept the relevance of the socially constructive purpose to which sociological activities are directed.

Sociologists have tended to assume that well-intentioned people fully accept the desirability of demystification of human life and culture. In the age of Aquarius, however, perhaps such a view will be recognized as naive.

"They are there, studying us, taking notes, getting to know us, as indifferent as everybody else to the feeling that to be a complete human involves having an aspect of ourselves that's unknown." Von Hoffman seems to mean this to be a statement about the right to privacy in a legal sense, but it really represents a denial of the ability of people to understand themselves and each other in an existential sense. This denial masks a fear, not that intimate details of our lives will be revealed to *others,* but rather that we may get to know *ourselves* better and have to confront what up to now we did not know about ourselves. Just as psychoanalysis was a scientific revolution as threatening to traditional conceptions as those of Galileo and Kepler had been, it may well be that the sociologist's budding ability to say something about the how's and why's of men's relationships to each other is deeply threatening not only to the established institutions in society, but also in a more personal way to all members of society.

Von Hoffman says he is talking about the invasion of privacy, but his celebration of the "aspect of ourselves that's unknown" shows a deeper worry about making rational and open what he conceives to be properly closed and dark in human reality. Von Hoffman concentrates his outrage on the methods Humphreys used to learn what he did, but we believe that at bottom he is not much different from other critics of behavioral science who make exactly the same points that von Hoffman makes with respect to research, even when it involves people who freely give their opinions, attitudes and autobiographical data to interviewers. This, too, is regarded as a threat because eventually it will remove some of the mystery from human life.

But von Hoffman recognizes that his most appealing charge has to do with privacy, and so he makes much of the fact that Humphreys collected information that could be used for "blackmail, extortion, and the worst kind of mischief without the knowledge of the people involved."

Here his double standard is most glaringly apparent. Journalists routinely, day in, day out, collect information that could be used for "blackmail, extortion, and the worst kind of mischief without the knowledge of the people involved." But von Hoffman knows that the purpose of their work is none of those things, and so long as their information is collected from public sources, I assume he wouldn't attack them. Yet he nowhere compares the things sociologists do with the things his fellow journalists do. Instead, he couples Humphreys' "snooping around," "spying on people" with similarly "well-motivated" invaders of privacy such as J. Edgar Hoover and John Mitchell.

To say the least, the comparison is invidious: the two kinds of enterprises are fundamentally different. No police group seeks to acquire information about people with any other goal than that of, in some way, prosecuting them. Policemen collect data, openly or under cover, in order to put someone in jail. Whatever it is, the sociological enterprise is not that. Sociologists are not interested in directly affecting the lives of the particular people they study. They are interested in those individuals only as representatives of some larger aggregate—in Humphreys' case, all participants in the tearoom action. Therefore, in almost all sociological research, the necessity to preserve the anonymity of the respondent is not an onerous one, because no purpose at all would be served by identifying the respondents.

In this respect, journalists are in fact much closer to policemen than sociologists are. Journalists often feel that their function is to point the finger at particular malefactors. Indeed their effort to acquire information about individuals is somewhat like that of the police, in the sense that both seek to affect importantly the lives of the particular individuals who are the object of their attention. Perhaps this kind of misconception of what the sociologist is about, and the total absence of any comment on the role of the journalist, leads von Hoffman to persistently misinterpret Humphreys' research as "invading some people's privacy." Yet everything Humphreys knew about the deviant behavior of the people he studied was acquired in a public context (indeed, on public land).

We believe in the work Humphreys has done, in its principled humaneness, in its courage to learn the truth and in the constructive contribution that it makes toward our understanding of all the issues, including the moral, raised by deviant behavior in our society. *Trans-action* has always been supportive of and open to the sort of enterprise he has so ably performed; we only wish there were more of it. Furthermore, a vigorous defense of Laud Humphreys' research (and that of others before and after him) is eminently possible and glaringly needed.

Sociologists uphold the right to know in a context of the surest protection for the integrity of the subject matter and the private rights of the people studied. Other groups in society may turn on different pivots: the right of law, the protection of individuals against invasion of privacy and so forth. But whoever is "right" in the abstract, there is a shared obligation for all parties to a controversy to step forth with fullness and fairness to present their cases before the interested public—and to permit that public to enter discussions which affect them so directly. Without this, a right higher than public disclosure or private self will be denied—the right to full public discourse.

Von Hoffman's points are: that in studying the sexual behavior of men in restrooms, Humphreys violated their rights to intimacy and privacy; that the homosexuals were and remain unaware of the true purpose of Humphreys' presence as a lookout; and that in the follow-up questionnaire the researcher further disguised himself and the true nature of his inquiry. For von Hoffman the point of principle is this: that although Humphreys' intent may have been above reproach and that in point of fact his purposes are antithetical to those of the police and other public officials, he nonetheless in his own way chipped away at the essential rights of individuals in conducting his investigations. Therefore, the ends, the goals, however noble and favorable to the plight of sexual deviants, do not justify the use of any means that further undermine personal liberties. Let us respond to these propositions as directly as possible.

Cops and Knowledge

First, the question of the invasion of privacy has several dimensions. We have already noted the public rather than the private nature of park restrooms. It further has to be appreciated that all participants in sexual activities in restrooms run the constant risk that they have among them people who have ulterior purposes. The vocabulary of motives is surely not limited or circumscribed by one man doing research but is as rich and as varied as the number of participants themselves. The fact that in this instance there was a scientific rather than a sexual or criminal "ulterior motive" does not necessarily make it more hideous or more subject to criticism, but perhaps less so.

Second, the question of disguising "the true nature" and purpose of this piece of research has to be put into some perspective. To begin with, let us assume that the research was worth doing in the first place. We know almost nothing about impersonal sex in public places, and the fact that we know so little has in no small way contributed to the fact that the cops feel that *they* know all that needs to be known about the matter. Who, then, is going to gather this countervailing knowledge? Von Hoffman implies that the research enterprise would be ethically pure if Humphreys were himself a full participant, like John Rechey. But to be able to conduct investigations of the type Humphreys performed requires a sociological imagination rare enough among his professional peers, much less homosexuals in public places. Moreover, to assume that the investigator must share all of his knowledge with those being investigated also assumes a common universe of discourse very rarely found in any kind of research, much less the kind involving sexual deviance. Furthermore, the conduct of Humphreys' follow-up inquiries had to be performed with tact and with skill precisely because he discovered that so many of the people in his survey were married men and family men. Indeed, one of the great merits of Humphreys' research is that it reveals clearly etched class, ethnic, political and occupational characteristics of sexual participants never before properly understood. Had he not conducted the follow-up interviews, we would once again be thrown back on simpleminded, psychological explanations that are truly more voyeuristic than analytic, or on the policeman's kind of knowledge. It is the sociological dimensions of sexuality in public places that make this a truly scientific breakthrough.

To take on the ethic of full disclosure at the point of follow-up interviews was impossible given the purposes of the research. If Humphreys had told his respondents that he knew they were tearoom participants, most of them would have cooperated. But in gaining their cooperation in this way he would have had to reveal that he knew of their behavior. This he could not responsibly do, because he could not control the potentially destructive impact of that knowledge. Folding the participants into a larger sample for a different survey allowed for the collection of the data without posing such a threat. And the purpose of the research was not, after all, destruction, as von Hoffman concedes. Therefore, the posture of Humphreys toward those interviewed must be viewed as humane and considerate.

But what von Hoffman is arguing is that this research ought not to have been done, that Humphreys should have laid aside his obligation to society as a sociologist and taken more seriously his obligation to society as a citizen. Von Hoffman maintains that the researcher's intentions—the pursuit of truth, the creation of countervailing knowledge, the demystification of shadowy areas of human experience—are immaterial. "Everybody who goes shopping around and spying on people can be said to have good motives," von Hoffman writes, going on to compare Humphreys' work with policemen armed with a "no-knock" statute.

This is offensive, but it is also stupid. We have called von Hoffman a moralizer, and his moralizing consists precisely in his imputing a moral equivalence to police action, under probably unconstitutional law, and the work of a scholar. Of course the road to hell is paved with good intentions, but good intentions sometimes lead to other places as well. The great achievement of Humphreys' research has been in laying bare the conditions of the tearoom trade, the social classes who engage in such activities and the appalling idiocy and brutality of society's (police) efforts to cope with the situation. Moreover, he has, relative to some of his professional colleagues, answered the question, Which side are you on? with uncharacteristic candor, while at the same time he has conducted himself in the best tradition of professional sociology.

The only interesting issue raised by von Hoffman is one that he cannot, being a moralizer, do justice to. It is whether the work one does is good, and whether the good it does outweighs the bad. "No information," he writes, "is valuable enough to obtain by nipping away at personal liberty. . . ." It remains to be proven that Humphreys did in fact nip away at anyone's liberty; so far we have only von Hoffman's assertion that he did and Humphreys' assurance that he did not. But no amount of self-righteous dogmatizing can still the uneasy and troublesome thought that what we have here is not a conflict between nasty snoopers and the right to privacy, but a conflict between two goods: the right to privacy and the right to know.

What is required is a distinction between the responsibilities of social scientists to seek and to obtain greater knowledge and the responsibilities of the legal system to seek and obtain maximum security for the private rights of private citizens. Nothing is more insidious or dangerous than the overprofessionalization of a trade. But for social scientists to play at being lawyers, at settling what the law is only now beginning to give attention to, is clearly not a sound way of solving the problems raised.

Liberal Contradictions

It is certainly not that sociologists should deliberately violate any laws of the land, only that they should leave to the courtrooms and to the legislatures just what interpretation of these laws governing the protection of private citizens is to be made. Would the refusal of a family to disclose information to the Census Bureau on the grounds of the right to privacy take precedence over the United States government's right to knowledge in order to make budgetary allocations and legislation concerning these people? The really tough moral problem is that the idea of an inviolable right of privacy may move counter to the belief that society is obligated to secure the other rights and welfare of its citizenry. Indeed one might say that this is a key contradiction in the contemporary position of the liberal: he wants to protect the rights of private citizens, but at the same time he wants to develop a welfare system that could hardly function without at least some knowledge about these citizens. Von Hoffman's strident defense of the right to privacy is laudable; we are all behind him. What is inexcusable in someone of his intelligence is that he will not see that the issues he raises pose a moral dilemma that cannot be resolved in the abstract, only in the particular case. He may think that Humphreys' research is the moral equivalent of John Mitchell's FBI. We don't, and we have tried to explain why.

Several other minor points in the von Hoffman article require at least brief recollection. First, *Trans-action* has made no statement until this time on the ethics of the kind of research conducted by Laud Humphreys. Indeed, our editorial statements have always emphasized the right to privacy of the researcher over and against the wishes of established authority. To say that *Trans-action* has defended this piece in terms of "priority of motive" is an error of fact. The intent of *Trans-action* is to present the best available social science research, and we believe Humphreys' work admirably fits that description.

Public Rights and Private Agony

Finally, von Hoffman's gratuitous linkage of the "conservatives over at the Justice Department" and the "liberals over at the sociology department" makes for a pleasant balance of syntax, but it makes no sense in real life terms. The political ideology of Laud Humphreys is first of all not an issue. At no point in the article or outside the article is the question of the political preference of the researcher raised.

We would suggest that von Hoffman is the real "liberal" in this argument, for it is he who is assuming the correctness of the classical liberal argument for the supremacy of the private person over and against the public commonweal. This assumption makes it appear that he is willing to suffer the consequences of the abuse of homosexuals by blackmailers, policemen or would-be participants, but that he is not willing to suffer the consequences of a research design or to try to change the situation by a factual understanding of the social sources of these problems.

Laud Humphreys has gone beyond the existing literature in sexual behavior and has proven once again, if indeed proof were ever needed, that ethnographic research is a powerful tool for social understanding and policymaking. And these are the criteria by which the research should finally be evaluated professionally. If the nonprofessional has other measurements of this type of research, let him present these objections in legal brief and do so explicitly. No such attempt to intimidate Humphreys for wrongdoing in any legal sense has been made, and none is forthcoming. The only indictment seems to be among those who are less concerned with the right to know than they are with the sublime desire to remain in ignorance. In other words, the issue is not liberalism vs. conservatism or privacy vs. publicity, but much more simply and to the point, the right of scientists to conduct their work as against the right of journalists to defend social mystery and private agony.

Doing Social Psychology:

Putting It into Perspective

Scientific knowledge is cumulative. It grows by bits and pieces, each scientist building on the work of others. This process does not proceed, however, through the uncritical acceptance of what others have done. Basic to any scientific enterprise is a "healthy skepticism" which treats all findings as tentative. Part of the scientist's skepticism is his self-consciousness about his methodology and about the ethical implications of his work. In this section, we have presented a small sampling of papers which represent expressions of this self-consciousness.

The scientist's self-consciousness is stimulated by debate. Within social psychology, psychologists challenge sociologists, and the latter challenge the former. People in other disciplines attempt to debunk the work of both psychologists and sociologists. Non-scientists add their criticisms, usually on some ethical issue. Finally, adherents of the various theoretical schools within social psychology level barbs at each other. For example, interactionists criticize learning theorists for their focus on molecular behavior, their adherence to "sterile" laboratory research, and for viewing man as merely a "complex rat." Learning theorists counter that interactionists are "soft," that they are too concerned with what goes on inside the "black box," and that their concepts are too vague and ill-defined to use in theory building. This inter-school debate serves a corrective function, since members of each school are forced to review their assumptions, their procedures, and the substantive significance of their findings.

The debate which engages social psychologists touches nearly every facet of the enterprise. And, the sampling of papers included in this chapter hardly span the range of important issues. These papers will serve their intended purpose, however, if they kindle a spark of "healthy skepticism" in the student of introductory social psychology, i.e., if they start him thinking about the problems involved in doing social psychology. We also hope that the introductory student will find these problems challenging and begin to think about their solutions.

Suggestions for Further Reading

David Bakan, *On Method: Toward a Reconstruction of Psychological Investigation.* San Francisco: Jossey-Bass, 1969. A collection of critical essays examining a variety of methodological issues relevant to social psychological research.

Phillip Hammond, *Sociologists at Work: Essays on the Craft of Social Research.* New York: Basic Books, 1964. Twelve different researchers contributed essays to this volume describing the day-to-day problems and events they each encountered in conducting a study of major sociological significance.

Larry T. Reynolds and Janice M. Reynolds, *The Sociology of Sociology.* New York: David McKay, 1970. A book of articles in which sociologists attempt to analyze and understand the social forces which shape sociological thought, define the research problems that are attended to, and determine the methodological tenets that are currently in vogue.

Robert Rosenthal, *Experimenter Effects in Behavioral Research.* New York: Appleton-Century-Crofts, 1966. The author presents an extensive review of studies in which the experimenter, rather than the subject, was under investigation. He also reports on his own program of research into the tendency for the experimenter's hypotheses or expectations to become self-fulfilling prophecies, and suggests corrective measures which can be taken to reduce "expectancy effect."

Robert Rosenthal and Ralph L. Rosnow, editors, *Artifact in Behavioral Research.* New York: Academic Press, 1969. A collection of articles which explore such problems as experimenter "expectancy effects," the dangers in using volunteer subjects, the subject's fear of evaluation, and the possible consequences of the subject's suspiciousness of the researcher's intent.

Eugene Webb, Donald Campbell, Richard Schwartz, and Lee Sechrest, *Unobtrusive Measures: Nonreactive Research in the Social Sciences.* Chicago: Rand McNally, 1966. The authors explore the problem of measuring social phenomena without affecting their structure or course. Numerous examples are offered as to how a researcher can use his ingenuity to obtain measures without changing that which is being measured.